FOR REFERENCE

NOT TO BE TAKEN FROM THIS ROOM

0084813

U.S. Higher Education

EDUCATION INFORMATION GUIDE SERIES

Series Editor: Francesco Cordasco, Professor of Education, Montclair State College, Upper Montclair, New Jersey

Also in this series:

BILINGUAL EDUCATION IN AMERICAN SCHOOLS—*Edited by Francesco Cordasco and George Bernstein*

HISTORY OF AMERICAN EDUCATION—*Edited by Francesco Cordasco, David N. Alloway, and Marjorie Scilken Friedman*

MEDICAL EDUCATION IN THE UNITED STATES—*Edited by Francesco Cordasco and David N. Alloway*

MUSIC EDUCATION—*Edited by Ernest E. Harris*

THE PHILOSOPHY OF EDUCATION—*Edited by Charles Albert Baatz*

THE PSYCHOLOGICAL FOUNDATIONS OF EDUCATION—*Edited by Charles Albert Baatz and Olga K. Baatz**

READING IN AMERICAN SCHOOLS—*Edited by Maria E. Schantz and Joseph F. Brunner*

SOCIOLOGY OF EDUCATION—*Edited by Francesco Cordasco and David N. Alloway*

WOMEN'S EDUCATION IN THE UNITED STATES—*Edited by Kay S. Wilkins*

*in preparation

The above series is part of the
GALE INFORMATION GUIDE LIBRARY

The Library consists of a number of separate series of guides covering major areas in the social sciences, humanities, and current affairs.

General Editor: Paul Wasserman, Professor and former Dean, School of Library and Information Services, University of Maryland

Managing Editor: Denise Allard Adzigian, Gale Research Company

U.S. Higher Education

A GUIDE TO INFORMATION SOURCES

Volume 9 in the Education Information Guide Series

Franklin Parker

Benedum Professor of Education
West Virginia University
Morgantown

Betty June Parker

West Virginia University
Morgantown

Gale Research Company
Book Tower, Detroit, Michigan 48226

188813

016. 378
P239

Library of Congress Cataloging in Publication Data

Parker, Franklin, 1921-
    U. S. higher education.

    (Education information guide series ; v. 9)
(Gale information guide library)
    Includes indexes.
    1. Education, Higher—United States—Informa-
tion services—United States. I. Parker, Betty
June, joint author. II. Title. III. Series.
LA227.3.P35   378.73   80-21959
ISBN 0-8103-1476-2

Copyright © 1980 by
Franklin Parker and Betty June Parker

No part of this book may be reproduced in any form without permission in
writing from the publisher, except by a reviewer who wishes to quote brief
passages or entries in connection with a review written for inclusion in a
magazine or newspaper. Manufactured in the United States of America.

To Ray Koppelman of
West Virginia University whose
encouragement made possible this book and
others of our works

VITAE

Franklin Parker has taught history and philosophy of education and comparative and international education at the University of Texas in Austin, the University of Oklahoma in Norman, and since 1968 has been Benedum Professor of Education at West Virginia University in Morgantown. He wrote GEORGE PEABODY, A BIOGRAPHY (Vanderbilt University Press, 1971); and three pamphlets for Phi Delta Kappa, international honor society in education: THE BATTLE OF THE BOOKS: KANAWHA COUNTY (1975); WHAT CAN WE LEARN FROM THE SCHOOLS OF CHINA? (1977); and BRITISH SCHOOLS AND OURS (1979).

Betty June Parker taught English in high school and in junior college and reading at the University of Texas in Austin. She was an adviser to the American Friends Service Committee, Southwest Region, and a League of Women Voters officer in two university communities. As a freelance bibliographer, she coedited with Franklin Parker EDUCATION IN PUERTO RICO (Inter American University Press, San Juan, Puerto Rico, 1978); and WOMEN'S EDUCATION--A WORLD VIEW: ANNOTATED BIBLIOGRAPHY, two volumes (Greenwood Press, 1979 and 1981).

The Parkers attended Berea College, near Lexington, Kentucky; the University of Illinois in Urbana-Champaign; and George Peabody College for Teachers, part of Vanderbilt University in Nashville, Tennessee. As a research and writing team, they have made four research trips to southern Africa, two to the People's Republic of China (1974, 1978), and a Middle East study trip to Israel, and sixteen visits to Britain for manuscript research and school visits. Since 1971, they have coedited a multivolume series on AMERICAN DISSERTATIONS ON FOREIGN EDUCATION; A BIBLIOGRAPHY WITH ABSTRACTS, in which volumes have appeared or are in progress on CANADA, INDIA, JAPAN, AFRICA, SCANDINAVIA, CHINA, KOREA, MEXICO, SOUTH AMERICA, CENTRAL AMERICA, PAKISTAN AND BANGLADESH, IRAN AND IRAQ, MIDDLE EAST, THAILAND, SOUTHEAST ASIA, and ISRAEL with anticipated world coverage.

CONTENTS

PREFACE

The alphabetical author arrangement seemed more useful to most readers since many books and reports annotated in U.S. HIGHER EDUCATION: A GUIDE TO INFORMATION SOURCES are on various levels, kinds, and topics in this rapidly growing field. The subject index is the key to locating specific topics in this omnibus work. Thus the reader interested in U.S. higher education finance or administration or history or counseling or nursing or medicine or women or any of its other multifaceted aspects can, by consulting the index, find appropriate books and reports, and many more sections and chapters within the books and reports.

What to include from the vast cornucopia of available materials? It was decided to include the most important nineteenth-century works and to approach comprehensive inclusion of twentieth-century works, particularly those published since World War II.

This work thus includes a panorama of annotated books and reports touching all aspects of U.S. higher education as public and private systems, a process, and an industry; and as a place of vocational, professional, and intellectual study and attainment. Entries explore U.S. higher education history, philosophy, administration, finance, governance, curriculum, student life, library and audiovisual services, and custodial concerns. Federal, state, and local relations, including urban involvement, are included. Recent innovations, and the needs of women, minorities, students, faculty, and staff dominate.

Gale Research Company showed bold foresight in considering the large manuscript in a time of economic stringency. Series editor Francesco Cordasco was indispensable for advice and encouragement and for finding ways to overcome difficulties. The book could not have been done without him, or a summer grant from West Virginia University Vice President for Graduate Studies, Ray Koppelman, or Doris Welch's intelligent summaries, or Lucy Bender's perceptive typing, or West Virginia University reference librarians' generous aid.

Higher Education in the United States found its most fertile ground. Nowhere else has it opened so wide a door of opportunity for so many of all creeds, colors, ages, and circumstances to develop talents, enrich lives, aid general welfare, and elevate the nation. It is hoped that U.S. HIGHER EDUCATION: A GUIDE TO INFORMATION SOURCES will help all seeking to understand better U.S. private, public, denominational, and secular junior colleges, community colleges, four-year colleges, universities, and multiversities.

ABBREVIATIONS

A.A.	Associate of Arts degree
AAHE	American Association for Higher Education
AAUP	American Association of University Professors
AAUW	American Association of University Women
ACE	American Council on Education
ACSA	Association of Collegiate Schools of Architecture
ACT	American College Testing Program
AIA	American Institute of Architects
AID	Agency for International Development
BBC	British Broadcasting Corporation
B. Litt.	Bachelor of Literature degree
CLEP	College Level Examination Program
CUNY	City University of New York
D.A.	Doctor of Arts degree
Ed. D.	Doctor of Education degree
EDUCOM	Educational Communications (Interuniversity Communications Council), a consortium of eighty-eight universities, Princeton, N.J.
EOPS	Extended Opportunity Programs and Services
ETV	Educational Television
G.E.D.	General Educational Development test
HEW	U.S. Department of Health, Education and Welfare
HPER	Health, Physical Education, and Recreation
LSAT	Law School Admission Test
M.A.	Master of Arts degree
MBO	Management by objectives
M.D.	Doctor of Medicine degree

Abbreviations

MIT	Massachusetts Institute of Technology
NAACP	National Association for the Advancement of Colored People
OCR	Office of Civil Rights
Ph. D.	Doctor of Philosophy degree
PSI	Personalized System of Instruction
ROTC	Reserve Officers Training Corps
SAT	Scholastic Aptitude Test
SDS	Students for a Democratic Society
SNCC	Student Nonviolent Coordinating Committee
TIAA-CREF	Teachers Insurance and Annuity Association--College Retirement Equities Fund
UCLA	University of California, Los Angeles
UNESCO	United Nations Educational, Scientific and Cultural Organization
USSR	Union of Soviet Socialist Republics

U.S. HIGHER EDUCATION

1   Abbott, Frank C. GOVERNMENT POLICY AND HIGHER EDUCATION:
    A STUDY OF THE REGENTS OF THE STATE OF NEW YORK, 1784-1949.
    Ithaca, N.Y.: Cornell University Press, 1958. 417 p.

    Broad history of the New York Board of Regents focuses on
    political forces which affect education policy. Details on
    circumstances which surrounded bringing all former state col-
    leges into the State University of New York system.

2   _____, ed. FACULTY-ADMINISTRATION RELATIONSHIPS. Washington,
    D.C.: American Council on Education, 1958. 90 p.

    Twenty-four conference spokesmen from the behavioral sciences,
    industrial organizations, labor relations, and public administra-
    tion discussed ways to alleviate specific tensions between higher
    education faculties and administrators.

3   Abramson, Joan. THE INVISIBLE WOMAN: DISCRIMINATION IN THE
    ACADEMIC PROFESSION. San Francisco: Jossey-Bass Publishers, 1975.
    248 p.

    Documented study of discrimination author experienced as an
    academic. She also describes discrimination against women
    outside higher education and recommends strategies for moving
    toward equality between the sexes in higher education.

4   Academy for Educational Development. Management Division. ADMIS-
    SIONS/RECRUITMENT: A STUDY OF COSTS AND PRACTICES IN IN-
    DEPENDENT HIGHER EDUCATION INSTITUTIONS. Washington, D.C.:
    1979. 145 p.

    Study on the costs of recruitment and admissions at twenty-one
    liberal arts institutions.

5   Adams, Frank C., and Stephens, Clarence W. COLLEGE AND UNIVER-
    SITY STUDENT WORK PROGRAMS: IMPLICATIONS AND IMPLEMENTA-
    TIONS. Carbondale: Southern Illinois University Press, 1970. 272 p.

    Comprehensive analysis of higher education student financial
    aid and work programs. Focuses on eighteen higher education
    work-study programs such as the largely campus program at
    Berea College, Kentucky, and the mainly off-campus coopera-
    tive program at Antioch College, Ohio. Also examines the
    research available on higher education work-study programs
    and their effect on the institutions, students, supervisors, and
    communities. Finds that this research has been insufficient.

6   Adams, Hazard. THE ACADEMIC TRIBES: A WRY VIEW OF THE AMERI-
    CAN UNIVERSITY--WITH A DASH OF BITTERS. New York: Liveright,
    1976. 144 p.

Humorous and sometimes wise look at higher education by a college English teacher and ex-dean who has an understandably strong bias toward liberal arts.

7   Adams, Henry. THE EDUCATION OF HENRY ADAMS: AN AUTOBIO-GRAPHY. Washington, D.C.: Privately printed, 1907. Reprint. Boston: Houghton Mifflin Co., 1918. 517 p.

Noted historian tells of the formal and informal education which influenced him: his boyhood in Boston, student years at Harvard College and in Berlin, experiences as secretary when his father was congressman and minister to England, as assistant professor of history at Harvard and editor of the NORTH AMERICAN REVIEW, his career as an author while living in Washington, D.C., his many travels, and his theory of history.

8   Adams, Walter. THE TEST. New York: Macmillan, 1971. 240 p.

Accounts of economist Walter Adams's nine months as Michigan State University's acting president during 1960s' student protest. Following the single-man rule of retiring president John Hannah, Adams chose a personal, pragmatic, optimistic leadership style which succeeded with militant students, white and black, and with concerned moderate students. Gives examples of relatively small incidents which, without careful attention, can disrupt a major university.

9   _____, ed. THE BRAIN DRAIN. New York: Macmillan, 1968. 273 p.

Historical account of talent migration from the time of ancient Egypt. Discusses difficulties of foreign students in U.S. institutions of higher education, reasons they fail to return home, and ways to encourage their return home. Shows the U.S. as principal brain-gain nation. Concludes with suggestions on how U.S. higher education can slow down the brain drain.

10 Adams, Walter, and Garraty, John A. IS THE WORLD OUR CAMPUS? East Lansing: Michigan State University Press, 1960. 180 p.

Critical survey of American universities' overseas programs, but limited to a few in Europe and particularly Turkey in 1957-58. Despite emphasizing difficulties, frustrations, and disappointments, the book is of value to administrators of such programs in discussing the need for cooperative planning between the U.S. university and the foreign university or program to be helped, qualifications for overseas personnel, importance of supervision, and the need for patience and perspective.

11 Adams, Walter H. THE PLACEMENT OF STUDENTS IN TEACHING POSI-

TIONS AS CARRIED ON BY HIGHER EDUCATIONAL INSTITUTIONS-- INCLUDING NORMAL SCHOOLS, TEACHERS COLLEGES, COLLEGES, AND UNIVERSITIES. Abilene, Tex.: Abilene Christian College, 1933. 120 p.

> Presents teacher job placement policies gathered from 585 teacher training institutions.

12   Adler, Mortimer J., et al. ON GENERAL AND LIBERAL EDUCATION: A SYMPOSIUM. Washington, D.C.: Association for General and Liberal Education, 1945. 127 p.

> Twenty-eight papers on how to restore general or liberal education to universities which have had to include more and more technical, vocational, and professional aspects of education.

13   Aiken, Henry David. PREDICAMENT OF THE UNIVERSITY. Bloomington: Indiana University Press, 1971. 404 p.

> Former Harvard and Brandeis philosophy professor, Aiken dislikes equally the multiversity service-station concept of Clark Kerr (p. 405) and the university conservatism of Sidney Hook (p. 356). He favors Kenneth Keniston's apologia for youthful dissent (p. 404) and feels that an unstructured confrontation can result in favorable catharsis and creative reformulation between students and faculty.

14   Alexander, Louis, et al. TEN DESIGNS: COMMUNITY COLLEGES. Houston, Tex.: Rice University, 1962. 100 p.

> Ten leading architects and fifty advanced architectural students planned ten hypothetical community colleges in different parts of the country.

15   Alexander, Thomas, et al. THE EDUCATION OF TEACHERS. Chicago: University of Chicago Press, 1935. 266 p.

> National Society of College Teachers of Education yearbook. Contributors criticize teacher admission, curriculum, demand, supply, and certification recommendations in six-volume National Survey of the Education of Teachers, released by the U.S. Office of Education.

16   Alford, Harold J. CONTINUING EDUCATION IN ACTION: RESIDENTIAL CENTERS FOR LIFELONG LEARNING. New York: John Wiley and Sons, 1968. 153 p.

> Evolution and experiences of ten university-based residential adult continuing education centers sponsored by the Kellogg Foundation. How-to-do-it handbook also intended for lay persons interested in lifelong learning.

17 Allen, Herman R. OPEN DOOR TO LEARNING: THE LAND-GRANT
    SYSTEM ENTERS ITS SECOND CENTURY. Urbana: University of Illinois
    Press, 1963. 193 p.

    A centennial synthesis of reports and speeches on the past,
    present, and future of land-grant colleges and universities,
    founded in 1862 to aid rural populations (when over half the
    U.S. was rural), but which need now to aid urban populations
    and developing nations. Part 1 of this combined history and
    philosophy of the land-grant colleges looks back on origins
    and growth; part 2 looks forward to the next century and
    urges strengthening the liberal arts, graduate work, research
    activities, and meeting other modern needs.

18 Allmendinger, David F., Jr. PAUPERS AND SCHOLARS: THE TRANS-
    FORMATION OF STUDENT LIFE IN NINETEENTH CENTURY NEW ENG-
    LAND. New York: St. Martin's Press, 1975. 160 p.

    Pioneer study of higher education in pre-Civil War New Eng-
    land struck down the myth that such colleges as Amherst, Bow-
    doin, Dartmouth, Harvard, and Yale were static and aristo-
    cratic. Because many students were poor, they did not live
    together in college-owned facilities where genteel pressures
    prevailed. Instead, working students often lived cheaply off
    campus, extended their course beyond the usual four years,
    and thus reduced the possibility for colleges to guide their
    behavior. Author culled statistics from college records and
    students' letters and diaries, all of which showed that in the
    early nineteenth century, students had great effect on the in-
    stitutions they attended.

19 Altman, Robert A. THE UPPER DIVISION COLLEGE. San Francisco:
    Jossey-Bass Publishers, 1970. 202 p.

    Examines bachelor degree-granting institutions offering the final
    years of college to those transferring from two-year junior col-
    leges or community colleges. Describes their history, problems,
    and significance in relation to current interest in restructuring
    higher education, particularly in states relying heavily on junior
    or community colleges.

20 Altman, Robert A., and Snyder, Patricia O., eds. THE MINORITY STU-
    DENT ON THE CAMPUS. Boulder, Colo.: Western Interstate Commission
    for Higher Education, 1970. 219 p.

    Papers describe ethnic course offerings, campus life of minority
    students, and personnel programs for minorities.

21 Ambrose, Stephen E. DUTY, HONOR, COUNTRY: A HISTORY OF
    WEST POINT. Baltimore, Md.: Johns Hopkins University Press, 1966.
    357 p.

West Point history from its beginning under President Thomas Jefferson to the present, including its leading administrators: Sylvanus Thayer, Dennis Hart Mahan, and Douglas MacArthur.

22　American Academy of Arts and Sciences. A FIRST REPORT: THE ASSEMBLY ON UNIVERSITY GOALS AND GOVERNANCE. Cambridge, Mass.: 1971. 51 p.

Report by president Martin Meyerson of the University of Pennsylvania and Stephen R. Graubard of Brown University lists eighty-five "theses" for improving higher education, including increased opportunities for the disadvantaged, broader opportunities for elder citizens, and more professional and graduate training for women.

23　American Association for Higher Education and National Education Association Task Force. FACULTY PARTICIPATION IN ACADEMIC GOVERNANCE. Washington, D.C.: 1967. 67 p.

Lack of academic decision making found to be the main source of faculty unrest, especially in public junior colleges and emerging four-year colleges. Recommends shared authority, academic senates authorized to settle faculty issues, and appeals procedure before resorting to teacher strikes.

24　American Association of Engineers. VOCATIONAL GUIDANCE IN ENGINEERING LINES. Easton, Pa.: Mack Printing Co., 1933. 520 p.

Describes professional courses to pursue in higher education for about forty special engineering fields, including aeronautical, ceramic, geological, hydraulic, municipal, reclamation, and other engineering specialties.

25　American College Public Relations Association. THE ADVANCEMENT OF UNDERSTANDING AND SUPPORT OF HIGHER EDUCATION: A CONFERENCE ON ORGANIZATIONAL PRINCIPLES AND PATTERNS OF COLLEGE AND UNIVERSITY RELATIONS. Washington, D.C.: 1958. 86 p.

Describes the need for unity of command and principles of staff organization in fund raising for higher education institutions.

26　American College Testing Program. COLLEGE STUDENT PROFILES: NORMS FOR THE ACT ASSESSMENT. Iowa City: 1966. 292 p.

Survey made during 1962–65 among 398 ACT colleges of such student characteristics as: ACT scores, high school grades, fields of study and vocational choices, vocational preferences and educational plans, goals, factors in college choice, type of residence, and nonacademic achievements.

27 _____. WOMEN IN SCIENCE AND TECHNOLOGY: CAREERS FOR TODAY AND TOMORROW. Iowa City: 1977. 16 p.

Encourages young women in high school and college to consider scientific or technical careers.

28 American Council on Education. GUIDE TO THE EVALUATION OF EDUCATIONAL EXPERIENCES IN THE ARMED SERVICES. 3 vols. Washington, D.C.: 1980.

Guide for postsecondary institutions in granting academic credit to ex-military personnel for courses taken in the armed services.

29 American Council on Education. Committee on Measurement and Evaluation. COLLEGE TESTING: A GUIDE TO PRACTICES AND PROGRAMS. Washington, D.C.: 1959. 190 p.

Intended for college administrators and faculty who have no training in standardized testing. Part 1, prepared by Educational Testing Service staff members, discusses the use of tests in college admissions, educational counseling, classroom instruction, course placement or accreditation, and institutional evaluation. Part 2 has descriptions of testing programs in seven colleges written by staff members of those colleges (including Chatham, Dartmouth, and San Francisco State College).

30 American Council on Education. Committee on Personnel Methods. MEASUREMENT AND GUIDANCE OF COLLEGE STUDENTS. Baltimore, Md.: Williams and Wilkins Co., 1933. 199 p.

Adopting the philosophy that educational and vocational guidance is part of the personnel function of a college dean's office, this book's main chapter headings are: "The Personnel Record Card," "Achievement Tests," "Personality Measurement," "Vocational Monographs," and "Factors in the Character Development of College Students."

31 American Home Economics Association. HOME ECONOMICS IN HIGHER EDUCATION. Washington, D.C.: 1949. 181 p.

After studying home economics instruction at selected colleges and universities, authors drew up a rating scale intended for use by any home economics department. Explains how criteria implicit in the rating scale could be adjusted to fit varying sizes and types of departments.

32 American Library Association and the Association of College and Reference Libraries. Committee on College and University Postwar Planning. COLLEGE AND UNIVERSITY LIBRARIES AND LIBRARIANSHIP. Chicago: American Library Association, 1946. 152 p.

Objective and informed review of management principles for college and university libraries, including library building trends and the preference for central stacks with broad subject reading rooms (as against departmental divisions).

33 Amory, Cleveland. WHO KILLED SOCIETY? New York: Harper and Row, 1960. 599 p.

Two impressionistic studies of the U.S. upper class in 1947 and 1960, describing the functions, characteristics and influence of private, upper class preparatory schools and private colleges and the clubs connected with them.

34 Anastasi, Anne, et al. THE VALIDATION OF A BIOGRAPHICAL IN-VENTORY AS A PREDICTOR OF COLLEGE SUCCESS. Research Monograph No. 1. New York: College Entrance Examination Board, 1960. 81 p.

Important study of nonintellectual criteria for college success found that a biographical inventory was a better predictor that a student would become the kind of person the college aimed to develop. Less reliable predictions resulted from achievement, personality, interest, and aptitude tests.

35 Anderson, Charles H., and Murray, John D., eds. THE PROFESSORS: WORK AND LIFE AMONG ACADEMICIANS. Cambridge, Mass.: Schenkman Publishing Co., 1971. 350 p.

Random rather than focused sociological articles about professors. Two of the several themes are publish or perish pressures, and their failure to take a more active role in social and political change. Among contributors to this book about "academic man as a social type" are Veblen, Jencks, Riesman, Barzun, and Nisbet.

36 Anderson, G. Lester, ed. EDUCATION FOR THE PROFESSIONS. Chicago: University of Chicago Press, 1962. 312 p.

An analysis of trends in professional education by such writers as John S. Brubacher, William W. Brickman, Earl J. McGrath, editor Anderson, and others. Besides emphasizing teaching, universities, and graduate education, chapters are on the medical, business, and engineering professions.

37 _____. LAND-GRANT UNIVERSITIES AND THEIR CONTINUING CHALLENGE. East Lansing: Michigan State University Press, 1976. 354 p.

The Morrill Act's purposes for land-grant institutions are reviewed; their failure to serve blacks, women, and urban areas is faced. Editor concludes that the fate of land-grant institutions will depend on their capacity to alter their goals and to respond to shifts in power and authority.

38   Anderson, Richard C., et al., eds. CURRENT RESEARCH ON INSTRUC-
      TION. Englewood Cliffs, N.J.: Prentice-Hall, 1969. 396 p.

      Somewhat technical papers addressed to educational psycholo-
      gists summarize recent research in instruction and learning.
      Discusses approaches to instructional research, objectives, and
      evaluation. Deals with specific techniques related to pro-
      grammed material, concept learning, and the organization and
      sequence of learning.

39   Anderson, Richard E. STRATEGIC POLICY CHANGES AT PRIVATE COL-
      LEGES. New York: Teachers College Press, Columbia University, 1977.
      97 p.

      Data from forty private colleges revealed: (1) the positive re-
      sult of changing from single sex to coeducation or of dropping
      religious ties was to attract more students; but (2) by aban-
      doning these special attributes colleges lost some educational
      effectiveness.

40   Andrews, F. Emerson. CORPORATE GIVING. New York: Russell Sage
      Foundation, 1952. 361 p.

      Chapter on higher education indicates that it received in 1950
      from a sample of 326 corporations only 16.7 percent of all cor-
      porate gifts. Describes foundations set up in recent years by
      individual corporations to aid their giving.

41   _____. PHILANTHROPIC GIVING. New York: Russell Sage Founda-
      tion, 1950. 318 p.

      Reports the total income for U.S. higher education for 1948
      was about $2.5 billion, 46 percent of which came from the
      three levels of government and 9 percent from philanthropy,
      half of this 9 percent from endowments or past philanthropy.

42   Anello, Michael, ed. GOALS FOR A CHANGING UNIVERSITY. Bos-
      ton: Boston College, 1975. 127 p.

      Conference papers on leadership in the university, liberal edu-
      cation, young people's changing values, role of governing
      boards, economic outlook for universities, and elitism and cul-
      ture and the university.

43   Angell, George W., et al. HANDBOOK OF FACULTY BARGAINING.
      San Francisco: Jossey-Bass Publishers, 1977. 593 p.

      Thirty-two authors explain processes used and problems involved
      in faculty collective bargaining. They recommend ways to
      handle each stage of the bargaining process.

44 Angell, James Rowland. AMERICAN EDUCATION: ADDRESSES AND ARTICLES. New Haven, Conn.: Yale University Press, 1937. 282 p.

Written during sixteen years as president of Yale on the aims of higher education, recruitment of outstanding students, research, finances, women's education, religion, athletics, housing, and the role of education in American society.

45 Angoff, William H., ed. THE COLLEGE BOARD ADMISSIONS TESTING PROGRAM: A TECHNICAL REPORT ON RESEARCH AND DEVELOPMENT ACTIVITIES RELATING TO THE SCHOLASTIC APTITUDE TEST AND ACHIEVEMENT TESTS. New York: College Entrance Examination Board, 1971. 181 p.

Technical aspects of probably the single most complex and massive educational testing program of recent years. Separate chapters on the history of the admissions testing program, the Scholastic Aptitude Test, the achievement tests, descriptive statistics of the program, and the predictive validity of the tests. Final chapter on test coaching, practice, fatigue, new item types, the English essay, and test bias.

46 Archer, Jerome W., ed. RESEARCH AND THE DEVELOPMENT OF ENGLISH PROGRAMS IN THE JUNIOR COLLEGE. Champaign, Ill.: National Council of Teachers of English, 1965. 134 p.

Papers discuss the relation of two-year colleges to high schools and to four-year colleges, the preparation of junior college English teachers, English courses for adults and community services, and research suggestions for junior college English.

47 Argyris, Chris, and Schon, Donald A. THEORY IN PRACTICE: INCREASING PROFESSIONAL EFFECTIVENESS. San Francisco: Jossey-Bass Publishers, 1974. 224 p.

Suggests ways professionals in such fields as law, city planning, medicine, education, and others can increase their effectiveness in their professional studies and on their jobs. Explains how professional schools can be reformed so that competent abilities are stressed and professional effectiveness increased.

48 Armstrong, W. Earl, et al. THE COLLEGE AND TEACHER EDUCATION. Washington, D.C.: American Council on Education, 1944. 312 p.

Report of a cooperative study of teacher education in participating colleges and universities stresses using an organic or integrated group approach to teacher education problems. Case studies are used to discuss such aspects as counseling, general education, major field, and professional education including student teaching.

49 Arnstein, George E. DESIGN FOR AN ACADEMIC MATCHING SERVICE. Washington, D.C.: Association for Higher Education, National Education Association, 1967. 72 p.

Report: (1) tells results of a feasibility study by the Association for Higher Education into a computer-based system to match professors and administrators with jobs, called MATCH (Manpower and Talent Clearing House); and (2) surveys existing placement services in higher education and existing computer-based systems in government and industry.

50 Ashby, Eric. ADAPTING UNIVERSITIES TO A TECHNOLOGICAL SOCIETY. San Francisco: Jossey-Bass Publishers, 1974. 158 p.

Calling for universities to adapt quickly to society's changing needs, Ashby examines such issues as the responsibilities of professors, the skills required of administrators, the influence of students, the problems posed by science and technology, and the vocational bent implicit in mass higher education.

51 _____. ANY PERSON, ANY STUDY: AN ESSAY ON HIGHER EDUCATION IN THE UNITED STATES. New York: McGraw-Hill Book Co., 1971. 110 p.

Essays describing, evaluating, and comparing American higher education with that in Britain and on the continent by the master of Clare College, Cambridge, and the vice chancellor of Cambridge. Author, who knows much about American higher education, lists among its weaknesses a high attrition rate (50 percent of U.S. college students fail to graduate compared to 13.3 percent of British college students), and an obsession with ranking the top ten, which results in solidifying a pecking order mentality. He lists U.S. higher education strengths as the innovative land-grant college idea, quality of research, and diversity of programs which are made possible by the absence of state exams, as in France and Germany. Although he sees U.S. professional schools as strong, he fears that they produce narrow specialists when generalists are needed.

52 Ashford, Mahlon, ed. TRENDS IN MEDICAL EDUCATION. New York: Commonwealth Fund, 1949. 320 p.

Papers by over fifty authorities in medical education mark the centennial in 1947 of the New York Academy of Medicine. They focus less on trends than on the weaknesses in medical education. They call for medical education to correlate basic science instruction closely with clinical teaching.

53 Ashworth, Kenneth H. SCHOLARS AND STATESMEN. San Francisco: Jossey-Bass Publishers, 1972. 160 p.

Essay on dangers inherent in the relationships between institutions of higher education and the federal government. Author, who has worked both sides of the scholar-statesman fence, criticizes government's restrictive, shortsighted view of higher education as a national resource. He believes universities should seek greater public understanding of the importance of academic freedom and the necessity for institutional autonomy and diversity. He gives practical guidelines for deciding which federal programs universities should undertake.

54 Associated Colleges of the St. Lawrence Valley. MANAGING INTER-INSTITUTIONAL CHANGE. Potsdam, N.Y.: 1975. 111 p.

Brings together knowledge about various administrative arrangements used in voluntary interinstitutional relationships among colleges and universities.

55 Astin, Alexander W. ACADEMIC GAMESMANSHIP: STUDENT-ORIENTED CHANGE IN HIGHER EDUCATION. New York: Praeger Publishers in cooperation with the Higher Education Research Institute, 1976. 224 p.

The American Council on Education provided nineteen colleges and universities with data on each institution's effect on its students. Purpose was to stimulate colleges and universities to change policies and programs in order to improve the educational environment for students. Insights include how institutional decisions are made, how committees operate, how data are used, and how and why faculty members resist change. Suggests practical ways planners, administrators, and faculty can use student data to work for change.

56 _____. THE COLLEGE ENVIRONMENT. Washington, D.C.: American Council on Education, 1968. 187 p.

Questionnaire data (1962) from 30,570 freshmen in 241 colleges and universities were on: administrative environment, classroom environment, college image, peer environment, physical environment, and student characteristics. Findings revealed: (1) the percentage of students who had checked out a book from the college library varied from 15 percent to 89 percent; and (2) the percentage who were well known to their instructors ranged from 22 percent to 100 percent. One major conclusion was that colleges which restrict student behavior and censor student publications also tend to be low in intellectualism.

57 _____. FOUR CRITICAL YEARS: EFFECTS OF COLLEGE ON BELIEFS, ATTITUDES, AND KNOWLEDGE. San Francisco: Jossey-Bass Publishers, 1977. 293 p.

Largest nationwide ten-year analysis of how college affects students. The eighty-four outcomes measured include student attitudes, self concepts, values, aspirations, behavior patterns, persistence, achievement, competence, career development, and satisfaction. Critical of explosive growth of public universities since 1945, author does not think that bigger is better. Students have not benefited from massive growth of public higher education and the decline of private institutions. Student achievement and involvement are favored in smaller institutions. He sees weakness in the coeducation trend, finding single-sex colleges more beneficial for both sexes. He is critical of the proliferation of public two-year community colleges, stating that they do not provide equal educational opportunity. He favors dormitories and deplores the expansion of commuting. He deplores grade inflation and believes undergraduate grade point average is still the best predictor of success.

58 _____. PREVENTING STUDENTS FROM DROPPING OUT. San Francisco: Jossey-Bass Publishers, 1975. 204 p.

Gives findings of a major longitudinal, multiinstitutional study of college dropouts and suggests policies likely to minimize dropouts, such as financial aid, employment, and residential arrangements. Provides information about student characteristics which predict dropping out. Shows how institutional characteristics relate to dropping out.

59 _____. WHO GOES WHERE TO COLLEGE? Chicago: Science Research Associates, 1965. 125 p.

Goal was to learn more about students at different institutions and to discover how successful institutions attracted students suited to their programs. Data from 127,212 freshmen in 248 colleges and universities assessed such institutional environmental factors as intellectualism, estheticism, socio-economic status, career orientation, and masculinity. Though not intended as a guide for picking a college, the book provides such information and also has implications for other research.

60 Astin, Alexander W., and Lee, Calvin B.T. THE INVISIBLE COLLEGES: A PROFILE OF SMALL, PRIVATE COLLEGES WITH LIMITED RESOURCES. New York: McGraw-Hill Book Co., 1972. 146 p.

Profiles the small and private colleges, their historical development, administrative structure, student characteristics, financial problems, and environmental features--places where it is hoped character can still be developed.

61 Astin, Alexander W., and Panos, Robert J. THE EDUCATIONAL AND VOCATIONAL DEVELOPMENT OF COLLEGE STUDENTS. Washington, D.C.: American Council on Education, 1969. 211 p.

Found that academic accomplishment and career choice depended more on the student's characteristics and plans when entering college than on his choice of an undergraduate institution.

62 Astin, Alexander W., et al. THE POWER OF PROTEST: A NATIONAL STUDY OF STUDENT AND FACULTY DISRUPTIONS WITH IMPLICATIONS FOR THE FUTURE. San Francisco: Jossey-Bass Publishers, 1975. 308 p.

Explored student unrest of the 1960s, based on American Council on Education-sponsored research. Activism seemed related to the stimulus of events rather than to drastic shifts in student attitudes. Protesters came largely from affluent, educated, irreligious, or Jewish backgrounds; and were mainly in the social sciences. Faculty were active protesters in one in ten episodes. When faculty were mediators (in four in ten incidents), police were less likely to be called in. Only 3 percent of faculty uncritically sided with protesters. Administrators were less favorable to dissent, which cast them in a negative light. Student activism was largely responsible for introducing ethnic studies and student involvement in governance, but did not change national political policies. Several case studies of particular institutions.

63 _____. A PROGRAM OF LONGITUDINAL RESEARCH ON THE HIGHER EDUCATIONAL SYSTEM. Washington, D.C.: Office of Research, American Council on Education, 1966. 42 p.

Tells of the American Council on Education data bank, which would hold detailed information about students, faculty, finances, curriculum, and administrative practices from a representative stratified sample of higher education institutions. The bank would provide data for ongoing research into American higher education.

64 Astin, Helen S. THE WOMAN DOCTORATE IN AMERICA: ORIGINS, CAREER, AND FAMILY. New York: Russell Sage Foundation, 1969. 196 p.

Findings in 1966 from 1,653 women who received doctorates during 1957 and 1958; about half were married (three-fourths of these had children), nine out of ten were working (eight out of ten full-time), and had worked steadily since receiving their doctorate. Most (three-fourths) worked in an academic institution, were associate or full professors, one-fifth had published books, and three-fourths had published articles. They averaged ten hours a week in child care, twenty hours a week doing home chores, and spent one and one-half hours daily in professional reading. Most had part-time cleaning women. Many reported discrimination in salary, promotion, and tenure; those most likely to complain were also the most committed and most successful women. Six autobiographical sketches were included. Recommends more child care facilities and tax deduction for child care. Acknowledging that the large sample were all successful doctoral graduates, author concluded that women students have higher attrition rates than male doctoral and medical students. Found little discrimination against women at the graduate or medical school level.

65   Atelsek, Frank J., and Gomberg, Irene L. FACULTY RESEARCH: LEVEL OF ACTIVITY AND CHOICE OF AREA. Washington, D.C.: American Council on Education, 1976. 32 p.

From graduate departments in the sciences and engineering, information was collected about faculty engaged in research, time spent on research, sources of support, and choice of research area.

66   Augenblick, John. ISSUES IN FINANCING COMMUNITY COLLEGES. Report No. F-78-4. Denver, Colo.: Education Finance Center, Education Commission of the States, 1978. 66 p.

Study of financing two-year colleges in California, Illinois, Mississippi, and New Jersey identified the problem of variation in property tax base and the less often acknowledged degree of willingness to spend on education. State funding had little effect on the effort to equalize educational expenditure.

67   Augustine, Grace M. SOME ASPECTS OF MANAGEMENT OF COLLEGE RESIDENCE HALLS FOR WOMEN. New York: F.S. Crofts and Co., 1935. 242 p.

Data from 389 colleges and universities were used to explore permanent staff, student workers, budgets, menu planning, per capita labor and food costs, and other problems in managing residence halls for women.

68   Averill, Lloyd J., and Jellema, William W., eds. COLLEGES AND COMMITMENTS. Philadelphia: Westminster Press, 1971. 236 p.

Essays discuss whether or not higher education institutions should give explicit attention to developing student values. They express hope that church-related liberal arts colleges will survive to impart strong values.

69   Axelrod, Joseph, et al. SEARCH FOR RELEVANCE: THE CAMPUS CRISIS. San Francisco: Jossey-Bass Publishers, 1969. 244 p.

Behind campus protests is the students' search for "relevance," defined here as understanding individuals rather than knowledge for jobs and careers. Student malaise and alienation arise because colleges do not help students find themselves, or broaden their horizons, or liberate them from dogma and prejudice.

The "relevance" the authors want is a total college environment enabling adolescents to become humane, understanding
persons. Four new college model curricular programs described
are intended to help produce mature graduates.

70   Aydelotte, Frank. BREAKING THE ACADEMIC LOCKSTEP. New York:
Harper and Brothers, 1944. 183 p.

To overcome the lowered standardization of instruction caused
by mass education, Swarthmore College's president advocates
the honors program he adopted from British universities for
selecting and guiding the best students toward superior, independent academic work during their last two college years.

71   Ayers, Archie R., and Russel, John H. INTERNAL STRUCTURE: OR-
GANIZATION AND ADMINISTRATION OF INSTITUTIONS OF HIGHER
EDUCATION. U.S. Department of Health, Education and Welfare, Bulletin 1962, No. 9. Washington, D.C.: Government Printing Office,
1962. 123 p.

Analysis of line-staff charts in 608 colleges and universities
provides data for this organizational design. Authors recommended that: (1) higher education institutions have a single
chief administrative officer responsible to a governing board;
(2) he/she should be the executive officer of that board; and
(3) he/she should delegate authority to four administrative officers serving in the academic, student services, business affairs, and institutional development areas.

72   Babbidge, Homer D., and Rosenzweig, Robert M. THE FEDERAL IN-
TEREST IN HIGHER EDUCATION. New York: McGraw-Hill Book Co.,
1962. 214 p.

History of federal interest in higher education; current involvement; the issues of church-state, racial and minority segregation, and federal control; and prescriptions and predictions.

73   Babbitt, Irving. LITERATURE AND THE AMERICAN COLLEGE. Boston:
Houghton Mifflin Co., 1908. 263 p.

Sees an all-important place for literature in American colleges
as the only way to preserve the true humanistic spirit in face
of romanticism and science.

74   Badger, Henry Glenn. JUNIOR COLLEGE ACCOUNTING MANUAL.
Washington, D.C.: American Council on Education, 1945. 128 p.

Guide for accounting officers on budgeting, costing, auditing,
forms, records, and reports. Helpful for administrators and for
preparing data for accrediting agencies and government agencies.

75   Badger, Henry Glenn, and Johnson, M. Clemens. STATISTICS OF HIGH-
     ER EDUCATION: 1955-56. FACULTY, STUDENTS, AND DEGREES.
     Washington, D.C.: Office of Education, 1958. 152 p.

     Biennial statistics of U.S. higher education faculty members
     classified by sex, position, type of institution, region, and
     state, with comparisons for earlier years. Notes that teaching,
     research, and administrative personnel rose 12.5 percent from
     1953-54 to 1955-56.

76   Baer, Betty L., and Federico, Ronald. EDUCATING THE BACCALAU-
     REATE SOCIAL WORKER: REPORT OF THE UNDERGRADUATE SOCIAL
     WORK CURRICULUM DEVELOPMENT PROJECT. Cambridge, Mass.: Bal-
     linger Publishing Co., 1978. 238 p.

     Identifies the knowledge and skills necessary for the beginning
     professional social worker and the curriculum content necessary
     to prepare them.

77   Bailey, Frederick George. MORALITY AND EXPEDIENCY: THE FOLK-
     LORE OF ACADEMIC POLITICS. Chicago: Aldine Publishing Co., 1977.
     230 p.

     Based on his experiences on the campus at La Jolla, Califor-
     nia, and the universities of London and Sussex, social anthro-
     pologist author writes about the practical adjustment which
     academics make to internal politics on their campuses in order
     to be free to solve problems of professional interest in the real
     world.

78   Bailey, Robert L. MINORITY ADMISSIONS. Lexington, Mass.: Lexing-
     ton Books, 1978. 213 p.

     Admission requirements for minorities to higher education: poli-
     cies, practices, predictions of academic success, testing, and
     relevance of race.

79   Bailey, Stephen K. EDUCATION INTEREST GROUPS IN THE NATION'S
     CAPITAL. Washington, D.C.: American Council on Education, 1975.
     87 p.

     Introductory guide to federal education politics by a distin-
     guished political scientist and vice-president of the American
     Council on Education; describes those who play consistently
     key roles in education policy, the mutually dependent relations
     between educators and lawmakers, and problems and conflicts
     facing education lobbyists.

80   Bailyn, Bernard. EDUCATION IN THE FORMING OF AMERICAN SO-
     CIETY. Chapel Hill: University of North Carolina Press, in conjunction
     with Institute of Early American History and Culture at Williamsburg,
     Virginia, 1960. 147 p.

Influenced American educational historians to go beyond school institutional history and to include the educational influence of family, media, and other environmental factors. Covers colonial education history and has a valuable comprehensive bibliographical essay.

81 Baird, Leonard L. THE EDUCATIONAL GOALS OF COLLEGE-BOUND YOUTH. Iowa City: American College Testing Program, 1967. 27 p.

Useful impressions of students' values and goals which they expressed while taking ACT tests, such as: to learn to enjoy life, to become a cultured person, to secure vocational or professional training, and others.

82 _____. THE GRADUATES: A REPORT ON THE PLANS AND CHARAC-TERISTICS OF COLLEGE SENIORS. Princeton, N.J.: Educational Testing Service, 1973. 210 p.

Survey of 21,000 college seniors, class of 1971, from diverse institutions. Sponsored by the Association of American Medical Colleges, the Graduate Record Examination Board, and the Law School Admission Council.

83 Baird, Leonard L., and Holland, John L. THE FLOW OF HIGH SCHOOL STUDENTS TO SCHOOLS, COLLEGES, AND JOBS. Iowa City: American College Testing Program, 1968. 19 p.

Examined academic and nonacademic ability in relation to college and vocational choices of 1966 high school seniors one year after graduation. Found variations in academic aptitudes, with students at four-year colleges having the highest ability. But the authors conclude that it is misleading to label those not going to a four-year college as less talented, since their choices represent a different use of a talent rather than a talent loss.

84 Baker, Carlos Heard. A FRIEND IN POWER. New York: Charles Scribner's Sons, 1958. 312 p.

Novel by the chairman of the English department at Princeton University about the search for and selection of a president of a large eastern university.

85 Baker, Curtis O. STUDENTS ENROLLED FOR ADVANCED DEGREES, FALL 1975, SUMMARY DATA. Washington, D.C.: Government Printing Office, 1977. 104 p.

Report from the National Center for Education Statistics on the number of students enrolled for advanced degrees in the fall of 1975 by field, sex, state, and full-time or part-time attendance.

86 Baker, Curtis O., and Wells, Agnes O. ASSOCIATES DEGREES AND OTHER FORMAL AWARDS BELOW THE BACCALAUREATE, 1974-75, SUMMARY DATA. Washington, D.C.: Government Printing Office, 1977. 44 p.

Report from the National Center for Education Statistics on the number of associate degrees and similar awards conferred in 1974-75.

87 _____. EARNED DEGREES CONFERRED, 1974-75, SUMMARY DATA. Washington, D.C.: Government Printing Office, 1977. 47 p.

Report from the National Center for Education Statistics on the number of higher education degrees awarded by U.S. colleges and universities from July 1974 through June 1975 by level of degree, type of institution, and sex of recipient.

88 Baker, Dorothy Dodds. TRIO. Boston: Houghton Mifflin Co., 1943. 234 p.

Novel about a brilliant woman professor, her attachment to a young female student, and the man the woman student wants to marry.

89 Baker, Liva. I'M RADCLIFFE! FLY ME! THE SEVEN SISTERS AND THE FAILURE OF WOMEN'S EDUCATION. New York: Macmillan Publishing Co., 1976. 246 p.

Polemical history of seven leading women's colleges: Barnard, Bryn Mawr, Mount Holyoke, Radcliffe, Smith, Vassar, and Wellesley. Charges the colleges as guilty of organizational timidity, academic imitation, and a failure to use the resources of women's higher education to advance the women's movement.

90 Bakke, E. Wight, and Bakke, Mary S. CAMPUS CHALLENGE: STUDENT ACTIVISM IN PERSPECTIVE. Hamden, Conn.: Archon Books, 1972. 573 p.

Less about college student activism in the United States than in examples drawn from India, Japan, Mexico, and Colombia. Study relates student activism more to political and social changes than to academic concerns.

91 Balderston, Frederick E. MANAGING TODAY'S UNIVERSITY. San Francisco: Jossey-Bass Publishers, 1974. 307 p.

Study of university management by a professor of business administration and former co-director of the Ford Foundation Program for Research in University Administration of the University of California. The work discusses the main features of university operations, their complexity and interconnections, with chapters devoted to values, economics of university management, institutional data systems, and current issues facing administrators.

92 Baldridge, J. Victor. POWER AND CONFLICT IN THE UNIVERSITY: RESEARCH IN THE SOCIOLOGY OF COMPLEX ORGANIZATIONS. New York: John Wiley and Sons, 1971. 238 p.

Case study of internal struggles surrounding several policy issues at New York University. Begins with a political model drawn from conflict theory, community power studies, and work on interest groups.

93 _____, ed. ACADEMIC GOVERNANCE: RESEARCH IN INSTITUTIONAL POLITICS AND DECISION MAKING. Berkeley, Calif.: McCutchan Publishers, 1971. 579 p.

Mainly theoretical articles exploring new directions in higher education administration, such as increased student involvement in decision making, reorganization of boards of trustees, and unionization. Included are statements from national higher education study commissions and college and university self-studies.

94 Baldridge, J. Victor, et al. POLICY MAKING AND EFFECTIVE LEADERSHIP: A NATIONAL STUDY OF ACADEMIC MANAGEMENT. San Francisco: Jossey-Bass Publishers, 1978. 290 p.

Survey of over five hundred educational institutions, ranging from small community colleges to public and private multiversities, about such areas as collective bargaining, campus bureaucracy, professional autonomy, faculty morale, presidential power, faculty work patterns, men and women's differing roles, and institutional organization. Final chapter outlines the historical development of U.S. higher education through 1970.

95 Barbash, Jack. UNIVERSITIES AND UNIONS IN WORKERS' EDUCATION. New York: Harper and Brothers, 1955. 206 p.

Study of a 1952 Fund for Adult Education experiment in workers' education at eight universities: Pennsylvania State, California at Los Angeles, Wisconsin, Chicago, Rutgers, Cornell, Roosevelt, and Illinois. Experimented in three areas of world affairs, community participation, and economic understanding. Results suggest the importance of planning programs with union representatives, need for more exploratory work, and the need for programs directly reaching rank-and-file membership.

96 Barber, Elsie Marion Oakes. TREMBLING YEARS. New York: Macmillan Co., 1949. 327 p.

Novel about a girl's battle in school and college to overcome the mental despair that followed an attack of crippling polio.

97   Barish, Norma N., ed. ENGINEERING ENROLLMENT IN THE UNITED STATES. New York: New York University Press, 1957. 226 p.

Engineering education enrollment trends suggest a critical shortage of engineers (1957) with high mathematical and scientific orientation and with analytic and creative design ability. General discussion is followed by eighteen chapters, each on an engineering specialty, representing the view of twenty-one contributors.

98   Barlow, William, and Shapiro, Peter. AN END TO SILENCE. New York: Pegasus, 1971. 330 p.

An anti-establishment interpretation of 1960s student unrest at San Francisco State College. The authors call the creation of the California system of higher education a plot and S.I. Hayakawa an intellectual lightweight.

99   Barnard, John. FROM EVANGELICALISM TO PROGRESSIVISM AT OBERLIN COLLEGE, 1866-1917. Columbus: Ohio State University Press, 1969. 171 p.

Transition of Oberlin College from a sectarian, evangelical institution to a nonsectarian liberal arts college with a social commitment; admitted women in 1833; blacks in 1835. Focus on student life and the effects of student pressure for better teaching in the physical and social sciences and in modern languages.

100   Barr, Stringfellow. PURELY ACADEMIC. New York: Simon and Schuster, 1958. 304 p.

Satirical college novel by the president of St. John's College and a founder of the Great Books program. The fictional college president spends his time raising funds, the students are lured by easy courses, and the faculty are involved in intrigues.

101   Barron's Educational Series. BARRON'S GUIDE TO THE TWO-YEAR COLLEGES. 6th ed. Vol. I: COLLEGE DESCRIPTIONS. Woodbury, N.Y.: 1978. 246 p.

Lists by state and describes two-year junior and community colleges, along with four-year colleges that have two-year programs. Volume II is titled OCCUPATIONAL PROGRAM SELECTOR (1979).

102   Barry, Coleman J. THE CATHOLIC UNIVERSITY OF AMERICA, 1903-1909:

THE RECTORSHIP OF DENIS J. O'CONNELL. Washington, D.C.: Catholic University of America Press, 1950. 298 p.

O'Connell's rectorship was distinguished by a nationwide finance drive and by his efforts to improve the academic prestige of Catholic University of America.

103 Barry, Toni, comp. THE PRESIDENTS. Washington, D.C.: American Association of Community and Junior Colleges, 1978. 127 p.

Biographical articles about the chief executive officers of almost nine hundred institutional members of the American Association of Community and Junior Colleges.

104 Bartlett, Willard W. EDUCATION FOR HUMANITY: THE STORY OF OTTERBEIN COLLEGE. Westerville, Ohio: Otterbein College, 1934. 285 p.

Otterbein College is a typical midwestern denominational liberal arts college. Major section gives the history of seven different phases of institutional activity and interest--such as student life and administration and control--and reflects the general problems of U.S. higher education.

105 Barzun, Jacques. THE AMERICAN UNIVERSITY: HOW IT RUNS, WHERE IT IS GOING. New York: Harper and Row, 1968. 319 p.

Scholarly (former literature professor) Columbia University provost and dean of faculties and author of the influential TEACHER IN AMERICA (below) characterizes recent upheavals in American higher education; reviews changing aims, organization, and stresses; and concludes with sixty-eight short provocative points in a final chapter on "The Choice Ahead."

106 _____. TEACHER IN AMERICA. Boston: Little, Brown and Co., 1945. 321 p.

Topics range from how to read and write, to intelligence tests, and faculty salaries. The author asserts teaching must be recognized as a dramatic art if it is to enlighten students' thinking and stir their imagination.

107 Baskin, Samuel, ed. HIGHER EDUCATION: SOME NEWER DEVELOPMENTS. New York: McGraw-Hill Book Co., 1965. 342 p.

Articles evaluating such innovations in four-year colleges as independent study, study abroad, use of new media and technology, off-campus experience, superior student programs, year-round use of facilities, community as a learning resource, improved college teaching, and others.

108 Bauer, Ronald C. CASES IN COLLEGE ADMINISTRATION. New York: Bureau of Publications, Teachers College, Columbia University, 1955. 213 p.

Applies the case method to the study of college administration. Author's goal is to increase students' problem-solving ability, to augment knowledge on a particular area or level of administration, to develop comprehension of principles, and to encourage or inculcate attitudes essential to successful administration.

109 Bayerl, Elizabeth. INTERDISCIPLINARY STUDIES IN THE HUMANITIES: A DIRECTORY. Metuchen, N.J.: Scarecrow Press, 1977. 1,102 p.

Describes interdisciplinary programs of study in the humanities at over 800 colleges and universities.

110 Beach, Arthur G. THE PIONEER COLLEGE: THE STORY OF MARIETTA. Marietta, Ohio: Marietta College, 1935. 325 p.

Centennial history of Marietta College, founded and influenced by New Englanders in a region where in 1787 Colonel Rufus Putnam led the first settlers. Nonsectarian but sternly Puritan. Marietta, despite meager resources, became a strong liberal arts college which did not admit women until well into the twentieth century.

111 Beach, Mark. A BIBLIOGRAPHIC GUIDE TO AMERICAN COLLEGES AND UNIVERSITIES: FROM COLONIAL TIMES TO THE PRESENT. Westport, Conn.: Greenwood Press, 1975. 314 p.

Nonannotated bibliography of 2,806 books, doctoral dissertations, master's theses, and significant journal articles on histories of U.S. higher education institutions, their famed administrators and professors, arranged by states, with subject index.

112 Beals, Ralph A. ASPECTS OF POST-COLLEGIATE EDUCATION. New York: American Association for Adult Education, 1935. 137 p.

This two-part continuation of Beals's ALUMNI AND ADULT EDUCATION (1929) has sections on liberal arts and the professions. The latter section contains separate chapters on such fields as medicine and engineering and the efforts by universities and professional societies to keep alumni abreast of developments in their professions.

113 Beals, Ralph L., and Humphrey, Norman D. NO FRONTIER TO LEARNING: THE MEXICAN STUDENT IN THE UNITED STATES. Minneapolis: University of Minnesota Press, 1957. 148 p.

Cultural anthropological study of Mexican students in the United States is limited by small sample size. Interviews of ten students at the University of California at Los Angeles were supplemented with material from fifty-two other Mexican students throughout the United States and twenty-six case histories of former students who had returned to Mexico. Analysis of Mexican culture was used to explain the data.

114 Bean, Donald E., and Ellsworth, Ralph E. MODULAR PLANNING FOR COLLEGE AND SMALL UNIVERSITY LIBRARIES. Iowa City: State University of Iowa, 1948. 41 p.

Workbook explains processes of planning small college libraries. It has many practical hints about such basic features as lighting, soundproofing, and color.

115 Beatty, Richmond Croom, ed. JOURNAL OF A SOUTHERN STUDENT, 1846-48, WITH LETTERS OF A LATER PERIOD. Nashville, Tenn.: Vanderbilt University Press, 1944. 105 p.

Journal kept by southern student Patterson at South Carolina College. As a successful lawyer, forty years later, he sends advice on higher education to his nephew.

116 Beaumont, Andre G., ed. HANDBOOK FOR RECRUITING AT THE TRADITIONALLY BLACK COLLEGES. Bethlehem, Pa.: College Placement Council, 1973. 95 p.

For graduate schools wanting to recruit students from historically black colleges, eighty-five such institutions supplied data on their academic majors and other information.

117 Beck, Hubert Park. MEN WHO CONTROL OUR UNIVERSITIES. New York: King's Crown Press, 1947. 229 p.

The economic and social composition of governing boards of thirty leading American universities.

118 Becker, Carl L. CORNELL UNIVERSITY: FOUNDERS AND THE FOUNDING. Ithaca, N.Y.: Cornell University Press, 1943. 240 p.

To mark the seventy-fifth anniversary of Cornell's opening, historian Becker's six essays are on such topics as American higher education before the founding of Cornell, the Morrill Act of 1862, Ezra Cornell, Andrew Dickson White, the incorporation of Cornell, and its opening in 1868. Also includes related documents.

119 Becker, Gary S. HUMAN CAPITAL: A THEORETICAL AND EMPIRICAL ANALYSIS, WITH SPECIAL REFERENCE TO EDUCATION. New York:

National Bureau of Economic Research, 1964. 187 p.

Empirical analysis of the effect on individual earnings, productivity, and the national economy gained from education and on-the-job training.

120 Becker, Howard S., ed. CAMPUS POWER STRUGGLE. Chicago: Aldine Publishing Co., 1970. 191 p.

Essays first published in TRANS-ACTION about student movements and campus unrest.

121 Becker, Howard S., et al. MAKING THE GRADE: THE ACADEMIC SIDE OF COLLEGE LIFE. New York: John Wiley and Sons, 1968. 150 p.

University of Kansas study during 1959-61 helps explain why university students behave as they do in situations emphasizing competitive grades. The authors offer evidence that campus life revolves around the "grade point average perspective."

122 Beckett, Frederick E. COLLEGE COMPOSITION: THE COURSE WHERE A STUDENT DOESN'T LEARN TO WRITE. Bruce, Miss.: Calcon Press, 1974. 175 p.

An analysis of eighty years of experiments and professional opinion about college composition courses, including technical and business writing.

123 Beecher, Henry K., and Altschule, Mark D. MEDICINE AT HARVARD: THE FIRST 300 YEARS. Hanover, N.H.: University Press of New England, 1977. 587 p.

A history of medical education at Harvard and its contribution to the teaching and practice of medicine.

124 Beezer, Robert H., and Hjelm, Howard F. FACTORS RELATED TO COLLEGE ATTENDANCE. Cooperative Research Monograph No. 8. Washington, D.C.: Government Printing Office, 1963. 42 p.

From statewide surveys in Arkansas, Indiana, and Wisconsin, the authors concluded: (1) lack of motivation is probably the greatest deterrent to college attendance for capable students; (2) other serious barriers are insufficient funds and negative parental attitudes, particularly toward college training for girls; (3) minority status and unequal opportunities deter college attendance; and (4) peer pressure is a possible tool for encouraging college attendance.

125 Beggs, David W. III, and Buffie, Edward G., eds. INDEPENDENT STUDY: BOLD NEW VENTURE. Bloomington: Indiana University Press, 1965. 236 p.

Presents methods and techniques appropriate for incorporating independent study into all school levels.

126 Begin, James P., et al. COMMUNITY COLLEGE COLLECTIVE BAR-GAINING IN NEW JERSEY. New Brunswick, N.J.: Institute of Management and Labor Relations, Rutgers University, 1977. 306 p.

A study of collective bargaining in the sixteen New Jersey public two-year colleges; compares the state's bargaining system with practices of other states.

127 Belcher, Jane C., and Jacobsen, Julia M. A PROCESS FOR THE DEVEL-OPMENT OF IDEAS. Washington, D.C.: Educraft, 1977. Unpaged.

A guide showing institutions or individuals how to develop a project idea and prepare a proposal that will likely secure financing from an appropriate foundation or government agency.

128 Belknap, Robert L., and Kuhns, Richard. TRADITION AND INNOVA-TION: GENERAL EDUCATION AND THE REINTEGRATION OF THE UNI-VERSITY: A COLUMBIA REPORT. Irvington, N.Y.: Columbia University Press, 1977. 130 p.

How Columbia University improved its general education program by various innovations, especially by "learning community" seminars involving teachers and students from both professional schools and arts and sciences. The innovations were aimed at reintegrating the undergraduate part of the modern "fractured" (i.e., overspecialized) university.

129 Bell, Daniel. THE REFORMING OF GENERAL EDUCATION: THE COLUMBIA COLLEGE EXPERIENCE IN ITS NATIONAL SETTING. New York: Columbia University Press, 1966. 320 p.

Landmark study of the general education curriculum at Columbia College begins with a review of general education models at Columbia, Harvard, and Chicago. The author discusses the challenge to higher education from: (1) the expansion of knowledge, (2) the exploding impact of federally funded university research, and (3) secondary school changes. Author's curriculum reforms for Columbia served to redefine general education widely.

130 Ben-David, Joseph. AMERICAN HIGHER EDUCATION: DIRECTIONS OLD AND NEW. New York: McGraw-Hill Book Co., 1972. 137 p.

Revealing analysis of American higher education by a sociology professor at Hebrew University, Jerusalem. Author praises the quality and comprehensiveness of U.S. higher education. He offers prescriptions for some of its major problems.

131 Bender, Louis W. FEDERAL REGULATION AND HIGHER EDUCATION.
Washington, D.C.: American Association for Higher Education, 1977.
79 p.

Considers how regulations for federal financial aid to higher
education may have adversely affected the autonomy of colleges and universities. Reviews government influence on American higher education since the founding of Harvard. Discusses
how regulations are written, cost to institutions of implementing
federal regulations, and strategies for reform.

132 Benet, Stephen Vincent. THE BEGINNING OF WISDOM. New York:
Henry Holt and Co., 1921. 359 p.

Novel about a youth at Yale (author was a Yale graduate)
and his later adventures.

133 Benezet, Louis T. GENERAL EDUCATION IN THE PROGRESSIVE COL-
LEGE. New York: Teachers College, Columbia University, 1943. 190 p.

Report on three progressive women's colleges which led the
way in the 1930s toward changes in higher education: Sarah
Lawrence, Bennington, and Bard.

134 Bengelsdorf, Winnie, et al. ETHNIC STUDIES IN HIGHER EDUCATION:
STATE OF THE ART AND BIBLIOGRAPHY. Washington, D.C.: American
Association of State Colleges and Universities, 1972. 260 p.

Has separate sections on Asian-American, black, Chicano, Indian, Puerto Rican, white ethnic, multiethnic, and cross-
cultural studies. Separate chapters are on multiethnic teacher
training, minority enrollment, and minority opportunities. Most
bibliographical entries are annotated.

135 Bennett, John W., et al. SEARCH OF IDENTITY: THE JAPANESE
OVERSEAS SCHOLAR IN AMERICA AND JAPAN. Minneapolis: University of Minnesota Press, 1958. 369 p.

Anthropological study of Japanese students on U.S. campuses.
Interprets Japanese modernization, Japanese-American cultural
interaction, and crosscultural education in general. Appendix
on the mutual contribution of the U.S. campus and the overseas student.

136 Bennett, Margaret Elaine. COLLEGE AND LIFE. New York: McGraw-
Hill Book Co., 1933. 456 p.

Bennett's two purposes are to assist in orienting students to college life and to give impetus to effective college counseling
and guidance programs.

137 Bennett, Robert L. CAREERS THROUGH COOPERATIVE WORK EXPERI-
ENCE. New York: John Wiley and Sons, 1977. 172 p.

Describes ways in which college students can define and pursue their career interests by combining work and study.

138 Bennett, Wendell C. AREA STUDIES IN AMERICAN UNIVERSITIES. New
York: Social Science Research Council, 1951. 82 p.

Appraises twenty-eight university training facilities, faculty
specialists, graduate students then in training, and graduate
students that could be trained in such geographical area
studies as Russia, the Far East, Southeast Asia, South Asia,
the Near East, Europe, Africa, and Latin America.

139 Bennis, Warren G. THE UNCONSCIOUS CONSPIRACY: WHY LEADERS
CAN'T LEAD. New York: American Management Association, 1976.
176 p.

Ten essays by the University of Cincinnati president about why
higher education presidents and other educational leaders get
bogged down by trivia and come to manage rather than to
lead and improve.

140 Benson, Charles S., ed. PERSPECTIVES ON THE ECONOMICS OF EDU-
CATION: READINGS IN SCHOOL FINANCE AND BUSINESS MANAGE-
MENT. Boston: Houghton Mifflin Co., 1963. 475 p.

Readings offer a broad perspective on the economics of higher
education: taxation, fiscal administration, economic structure
of public education, effective use of resources, and the economic returns from schooling.

141 Benson, Charles S., and Hodgkinson, Harold L. IMPLEMENTING THE
LEARNING SOCIETY: NEW STRATEGIES FOR FINANCING SOCIAL
OBJECTIVES. San Francisco: Jossey-Bass Publishers, 1974. 147 p.

Analysis of the university as an economic enterprise, showing
how manpower needs can be met, higher education financed,
and opportunities can be provided for all. Recommends charging
little or no tuition at public institutions and providing all students with maintenance grants.

142 Berdahl, Robert O., et al. STATEWIDE COORDINATION OF HIGHER
EDUCATION. Washington, D.C.: American Council on Education, 1971.
285 p.

Study on the relationship between state government and higher
education. Authors discuss the evolution of and indispensable
nature of statewide coordinating boards and agencies, their
membership and powers. State government's relationship to

private higher education is an emergent issue. Authors favor a specialized state coordinating board with a strong, independent staff.

143 Berdie, Ralph F., ed. COUNSELING AND THE COLLEGE PROGRAM. Minneapolis: University of Minnesota Press, 1954. 58 p.

Papers discuss research and evaluation for in-service training of counselors. Shows the pervasiveness of counseling theory and practice in pre-college clinics, admissions, residence halls, general education, and job placement.

144 Berdie, Ralph F., and Hood, Albert B. DECISIONS FOR TOMORROW: PLANS OF HIGH SCHOOL SENIORS AFTER GRADUATION. Minneapolis: University of Minnesota Press, 1965. 195 p.

Graduation plans of 46,000 Minnesota high school seniors in 1961 and a follow-up of their actual careers. Chapters on the relation of school, personal values and attitudes, and socioeconomic variables to college attendance.

145 Berdie, Ralph F., et al. AFTER HIGH SCHOOL. Minneapolis: University of Minnesota Press, 1954. 240 p.

Found a reasonably close relationship between stated plans of 1950 Minnesota high school seniors and their actual work or college placement a year later. Recommendations for salvaging talent lost to higher education include identifying and motivating talented students through more and better help from counselors and parents.

146 _____. WHO GOES TO COLLEGE? Minneapolis: University of Minnesota Press, 1962. 56 p.

Analyzed Minnesota's statewide testing program since 1928, covering all high school juniors, junior college students, and liberal arts college freshmen. Found similar average ability among college freshmen in 1938 and 1959 but differences in their average aptitude.

147 Bereday, George Z.F. UNIVERSITIES FOR ALL: INTERNATIONAL PERSPECTIVES ON MASS HIGHER EDUCATION. San Francisco: Jossey-Bass Publishers, 1973. 158 p.

Drawing on information from a new series of national surveys, the author compares higher education reform attempts in the United States with reforms in other North American countries, the Soviet Union, Japan, and Europe.

148 Bereday, George Z.F., and Lauwerys, Joseph A., eds. HIGHER EDU-CATION: THE YEARBOOK OF EDUCATION, 1959. Yonkers, N.Y.:

World Book Co., 1959. 526 p.

Some U.S. aspects among the thirty-four chapters on world
higher education include Isaac L. Kandel on American state
universities' attempts to combine respect for learning with
greater adaptability to contemporary needs; Robert Ulich's
comparison of European professors' high prestige with U.S. professors' lower prestige and the European undergraduate's academic independence with the American student's stricter curriculum regime; and John S. Brubacher's observation about
American students' keenness for narrow professional studies at
the expense of general subjects.

149 Berelson, Bernard. GRADUATE EDUCATION IN THE UNITED STATES.
New York: McGraw-Hill Book Co., 1960. 346 p.

History of graduate education beginning with Johns Hopkins
University, 1876; followed by major curriculum trends and
problems. Concludes that graduate education is basically
sound but can be improved by a few adaptive changes.

150 _____, ed. EDUCATION FOR LIBRARIANSHIP. Chicago: American
Library Association, 1949. 307 p.

A major examination of U.S. librarianship education and discussions from the 1948 library conference at the University of
Chicago, which followed a two-year comprehensive look at
the field. Papers are about professional education in general,
the historical development of library schools, and various aspects of librarianship training--including advanced study and
research.

151 Beresford-Howe, Constance. OF THIS DAY'S JOURNEY. New York:
Dodd, Mead and Co., 1947. 240 p.

Novel about a young woman college lecturer in English and
her unsuccessful love affair with the college president, who
has an invalid wife.

152 Berg, Ivar. EDUCATION AND JOBS: THE GREAT TRAINING ROBBERY.
New York: Praeger Publishers, 1970. 200 p.

Challenges the assumption that more education leads to better
job performance. Suggests that over-education is an important
cause of high turnover, low productivity, and worker dissatisfaction. Finds a negative relation between educational level
and work performance. Author wants increased demand for
labor.

153 Bergen, Dan, and Dureyea, E.D. LIBRARIES AND THE COLLEGE CLI-

MATE OF LEARNING. Syracuse, N.Y.: Syracuse University Press, 1966. 84 p.

Six essays suggesting practical contributions libraries and librarians can make to undergraduate learning needs.

154 Bergquist, William H., and Phillips, Steven R. A HANDBOOK FOR FACULTY DEVELOPMENT. Vol. 2. Cardiff, Calif.: Pacific Soundings Press, 1977. 313 p.

Theoretical and practical discussion of faculty motivation, leadership, course design, assessing faculty performance, and evaluation of faculty development programs.

155 Bergquist, William H., and Shoemaker, William, eds. A COMPREHENSIVE APPROACH TO INSTITUTIONAL DEVELOPMENT. San Francisco: Jossey-Bass Publishers, 1976. 109 p.

Describes a nine-step system-based approach to college and university planning. Gives examples of ways various institutions are applying new techniques.

156 Berkner, Lloyd Viel. THE SCIENTIFIC AGE: THE IMPACT OF SCIENCE ON SOCIETY. New Haven, Conn.: Yale University Press, 1964. 137 p.

Discusses need for better and broader education, particularly graduate education, in science and especially in the humanities, as necessary to maintain the present economic level.

157 Berkowitz, David S. INEQUALITY OF OPPORTUNITY IN HIGHER EDUCATION. A STUDY OF MINORITY GROUPS AND RELATED BARRIERS TO COLLEGE ADMISSION WITH SUPPLEMENTARY STUDIES BY E.F. FRAZIER AND R.D. LEIGH. Albany, N.Y.: Williams Press, 1948. 203 p.

Pioneer study which developed new techniques for data analysis documents the effects of discriminatory admission policies and practices in New York state colleges and universities.

158 Bernard, Jessie. ACADEMIC WOMEN. University Park: Pennsylvania State University Press, 1964. 331 p.

Examines sex differences in learning and academic career patterns, investigates the combination of career and family life, and explores supply and demand for highly trained women. Analyzes motivation and background of academic women; evaluates their academic contribution; and finds women doctorates superior to men in test intelligence, yet less productive in publications.

159 _____. WOMEN, WIVES, MOTHERS: VALUES AND OPTIONS. Chicago: Aldine Publishing Co., 1975. 286 p.

Sociologist says that because more women combine work and family, colleges and universities need to provide more career education and to increase the number of women on their faculties.

160 Berte, Neal R., ed. INDIVIDUALIZING EDUCATION THROUGH CONTRACT LEARNING. University: University of Alabama Press, 1975. 192 p.

Part 1 discusses such issues underlying student learning contracts as student advising and evaluation. Part 2 contains case studies of the contract approach as used in various institutions.

161 Berube, Maurice R. THE URBAN UNIVERSITY IN AMERICA. Westport, Conn.: Greenwood Press, 1978. 149 p.

States that the United States needs federal urban-grant universities modeled on the Morrill Act land-grant universities. Berube also discusses the history of urban universities, the implications of the Newman Reports on Higher Education, the Coleman Report on Equality of Educational Opportunity, and the rise and decline of black studies programs.

162 Bevis, Alma Darst Murray. DIETS AND RIOTS: AN INTERPRETATION OF THE HISTORY OF HARVARD UNIVERSITY. Boston: Marshall Jones Co., 1936. 127 p.

This lively scholarly history of Harvard's first three hundred years tells about food (often bad), other sidelights, and findings that, as early as 1640, those who chose the college president learned that "erudition is not the prime requisite."

163 Bidwell, Percy Wells. UNDERGRADUATE EDUCATION IN FOREIGN AFFAIRS. New York: King's Crown Press, 1962. 215 p.

Surveyed the teaching of undergraduate courses in foreign affairs at two hundred colleges and universities and recommended ways of making much-needed improvements in foreign affairs instruction.

164 Bigelow, Donald N., ed. THE LIBERAL ARTS AND TEACHER EDUCATION: A CONFRONTATION. Lincoln: University of Nebraska Press, 1971. 250 p.

The main thesis is that, by increasing the liberal arts component, teacher education programs will be improved and the teachers so prepared will then improve the quality of public school teaching.

165 Bildersee, Adele. STATE SCHOLARSHIP STUDENTS AT HUNTER COLLEGE OF THE CITY OF NEW YORK. New York: Teachers College, Columbia University, 1932. 138 p.

Subjects were equal numbers of New York state scholarship students and non-scholarship students at Hunter College. This study compared their college records and questionnaire responses, concluding that state scholarships were justified and that the stipend was inadequate for meeting college expenses.

166 Birenbaum, William M. OVERLIVE: POWER, POVERTY, AND THE UNIVERSITY. New York: Delacorte Press, 1968. 206 p.

Concerned for those who have been unjustly deprived of schooling and its benefits, author recommends salvaging higher education by allowing students to help one another.

167 Birmingham, Frederic A. THE IVY LEAGUE TODAY. New York: Thomas Y. Crowell Co., 1961. 257 p.

Former ESQUIRE editor presents common characteristics and individual personality, appeal, tradition, locale, academic strengths, weaknesses, and other characteristics of eight Ivy League universities: Brown, Columbia, Dartmouth, Harvard, Princeton, Yale, and the University of Pennsylvania.

168 Bisconti, Ann Stouffer. LOW INCOME STUDENTS IN COLLEGE AND CAREERS. Bethlehem, Pa.: CPC Foundation, 1978. 20 p.

Findings from a national survey showing progress made by low-income students who entered four-year institutions of higher education in 1961.

169 _____. WHO WILL SUCCEED? COLLEGE GRADUATES AS BUSINESS EXECUTIVES. Bethlehem, Pa.: CPC Foundation, 1978. 16 p.

Findings from the Utilization of Education survey made in 1974-75, showing which higher education graduates may become high-salaried business executives.

170 Bishop, Morris. A HISTORY OF CORNELL. Ithaca, N.Y.: Cornell University Press, 1962. 651 p.

University history with chapters on founder Ezra Cornell, President Andrew D. White, the early years, and reconstruction, 1881-85. Most of the book covers the period from 1890.

171 Bittner, Walton S., and Mallory, Hervey F. UNIVERSITY TEACHING BY MAIL: A SURVEY OF CORRESPONDENCE INSTRUCTION CONDUCTED BY AMERICAN UNIVERSITIES. New York: Macmillan Co., 1933. 355 p.

Origin, growth, value, and defense of university correspondence programs. Discusses courses, administrative policies and problems, standards, student characteristics and success. Also surveys correspondence instruction methods in biology, education, English, German, history, mathematics, mechanical drawing, psychology, and sociology.

172 Bixler, Julius Seelye. EDUCATION FOR ADVERSITY. Cambridge, Mass.: Harvard University Press, 1952. 34 p.

This 1951 Inglis Lecture by the president of Colby College is a moving essay on the uses of reason in an age of insecurity.

173 Bixler, Roy W., and Bixler, Genevieve K. ADMINISTRATION FOR NURSING EDUCATION IN A PERIOD OF TRANSITION. New York: G.P. Putnam's Sons, 1954. 483 p.

A well-organized analysis of nursing education administration: part 1, principles of democratic versus autocratic administration; part 2, functioning of administration, whether in a university, nursing school, or hospital; part 3, school operations and the philosophy underlying them; and part 4, a survey of regional, state, and national planning for nursing.

174 Bizzell, William Bennett. THE RELATIONS OF LEARNING. Norman: University of Oklahoma Press, 1934. 177 p.

Thirteen addresses, ten of them given to undergraduates at the beginning of each of Bizzell's first ten years as University of Oklahoma president.

175 Black, Hillel. THEY SHALL NOT PASS. New York: William Morrow and Co., 1963. 342 p.

Journalist's attack on overemphasis on standardized tests and the ineptness of many school people in utilizing such tests.

176 Blackwell, Thomas Edward. COLLEGE AND UNIVERSITY ADMINISTRATION. New York: Center for Applied Research in Education, 1966. 128 p.

Findings of a survey of administrative practices at both private and public institutions.

177 _____. COLLEGE LAW: A GUIDE FOR ADMINISTRATORS. Washington, D.C.: American Council on Education, 1961. 347 p.

Basic legal vocabulary is explained. Problems relating to employees, students, college property, research and publication, taxes, and handling of funds are explored and possible legal involvements identified. Includes many illustrative cases and citations of legal authority.

178 _____, ed. THE COLLEGE LAW DIGEST, 1935-1970. South Hackensack, N.J.: Fred B. Rothman and Co., 1974. 256 p.

Legal cases involving or concerning higher education are summarized.

179 Blackwood, James R. THE HOUSE ON COLLEGE AVENUE: THE COMPTONS AT WOOSTER, 1891-1913. Cambridge: MIT Press, 1968. 265 p.

Romanticized historical study of a famous American academic family, the Comptons. The children were brought up in a college community and in a home well supplied with books and ideas. Arthur Holly Compton (1872-1962) shared the 1927 Nobel Prize for physics; Karl Taylor Compton (1887-1954) was president of the Massachusetts Institute of Technology.

180 Blaesser, Willard W., et al. STUDENT PERSONNEL WORK IN THE POST-WAR COLLEGE. Washington, D.C.: American Council on Education, 1945. 95 p.

Envisions faculty members as part-time counselors, student personnel workers as part-time teachers, and a college community altered by the presence of mature postwar students. It provides a measure for evaluating local personnel programs and guidelines for revising them.

181 Blanshard, Frances. FRANK AYDELOTTE OF SWARTHMORE. Middletown, Conn.: Wesleyan University Press, 1970. 429 p.

Well-written biography whose author worked at Swarthmore for twenty years during Aydelotte's presidency. Aydelotte was an early Rhodes scholar who later helped choose a generation of recipients of that scholarship. At Swarthmore, he designed the honors program. A principal advisor to the Guggenheim Foundation; spent his last years as director of the Institute for Advanced Studies.

182 Blauch, Lloyd E., ed. EDUCATION FOR THE PROFESSIONS. Washington, D.C.: Government Printing Office, 1955. 317 p.

Specialists in thirty-four major professions and subdivisions of them wrote chapters on administrative, historical, and accreditation matters in their fields. Some discuss the supply and demand for teachers, their training, and ways of improving faculty quality.

183 Bledstein, Burton. THE CULTURE OF PROFESSIONALISM: THE MIDDLE CLASS AND THE DEVELOPMENT OF HIGHER EDUCATION IN AMERICA. New York: W.W. Norton and Co., 1976. 354 p.

Personalizes the rise of American universities in the lives of nine prominent university presidents, among them Charles W. Eliot of Harvard, Daniel C. Gilman of Johns Hopkins, Andrew D. White of Cornell, and James B. Angell of Michigan. Harshly critical of colonial colleges, Bledstein says that American universities are unique among Western higher education institutions and are seriously undervalued as a major force in shaping the United States as we know it today.

184 Blegen, Theodore C., et al. COUNSELING FOREIGN STUDENTS. Washington, D.C.: American Council on Education, 1950. 54 p.

Practical tips for those who work with foreign students.

185 Blessing, James H. GRADUATE EDUCATION: AN ANNOTATED BIBLIOGRAPHY. Washington, D.C.: Government Printing Office, 1961. 151 p.

A survey of 882 generally available studies on U.S. graduate education in the arts, sciences, and professions, mainly published between 1957 and 1960, but including many earlier works. Studies about a single field are excluded. Listings are classified: (1) history, nature, and purposes; (2) organization, administration, and support; (3) graduate programs; (4) the graduate student; (5) faculty; and (6) directories and bibliographies.

186 Blickensderfer, Joseph P. REPORT OF PROCEEDINGS OF THE CONFERENCE OF UNIVERSITY ADMINISTRATORS ON GENERAL AND LIBERAL EDUCATION. Norman: University of Oklahoma Press, 1944. 200 p.

Concerned primarily with liberal and general education, curriculum, and administration.

187 Blocker, Clyde E., ed. HUMANIZING STUDENT SERVICES. Sourcebook No. 8. San Francisco: Jossey-Bass Publishers, 1974. 111 p.

Examines problems in student personnel work and analyzes the struggle between professional student services staff and regular teaching faculty.

188 Blocker, Clyde E., et al. THE POLITICAL TERRAIN OF AMERICAN POSTSECONDARY EDUCATION. Fort Lauderdale, Fla.: Nova University Press, 1975. 223 p.

Higher education operates in a political environment, which the authors analyzed at these levels: (1) within the institution, (2) the community, (3) the state, (4) the federal government, and (5) nongovernmental organizations.

189 _____. THE TWO-YEAR COLLEGE: A SOCIAL SYNTHESIS. Englewood Cliffs, N.J.: Prentice-Hall, 1965. 298 p.

Discusses the relation between the two-year college and the community; and the internal organization of the two-year college, noting its unique characteristics. Chapters are on such topics as control and finance, students, faculty, administration, curriculum, instruction, and the future of two-year colleges.

190   Bloland, Harland G., and Bloland, Sue M. AMERICAN LEARNED SOCIETIES IN TRANSITION: THE IMPACT OF DISSENT AND RECESSION. New York: McGraw-Hill Book Co., 1974. 160 p.

An analysis of the effect of the 1960s campus unrest on learned societies, with case studies of the American Political Science Association, the Modern Language Association of America, and the American Physical Society.

191   Bloom, Benjamin S., and Peters, Frank R. THE USE OF ACADEMIC PREDICTION SCALES FOR COUNSELING AND SELECTING COLLEGE ENTRANTS. New York: Free Press of Glencoe, 1961. 145 p.

Authors claim that grades from different schools can be made valid for predicting college success by using their method, presented in this book, for compensating for inconsistencies in grading.

192   Bloom, Benjamin S., et al. HANDBOOK ON FORMATIVE AND SUMMATIVE EVALUATION OF STUDENT LEARNING. New York: McGraw-Hill Book Co., 1971. 923 p.

Reference work; a comprehensive analysis of evaluation techniques intended for use by students and teachers in teacher education. Section 1 is about general evaluation problems; section 2 examines evaluation in the major subject fields and levels of education. Emphasizes nontraditional methods of testing specific outcomes of education.

193   Bloomberg, Edward. STUDENT VIOLENCE. Washington, D.C.: Public Affairs Press, 1970. 91 p.

Conservative view of 1960s student unrest; author endorses police action and greater classroom rigor.

194   Blum, Richard H., et al. DRUGS. Vol. 1: SOCIETY AND DRUGS: SOCIAL AND CULTURAL OBSERVATIONS. Vol. 2: STUDENTS AND DRUGS: COLLEGE AND HIGH SCHOOL OBSERVATIONS. San Francisco: Jossey-Bass Publishers, 1969. 400 p., 399 p.

Volume 1 traces the history of various drugs, their use and abuse, and studies cross-cultural patterns of drug use and controls. Volume 2 presents results of interviews with students about their past and present use of psychoactive drugs. Authors conclude that those who took drugs differed little from those who did not take drugs.

195   Blum, Ronald, et al., eds. CONFERENCE ON COMPUTERS IN UNDER-GRADUATE SCIENCE EDUCATION--PHYSICS AND MATHEMATICS. New York: American Institute of Physics, 1971. 499 p.

Gives a wide variety of experiments and experiences in using computers in science education.

196   Blumer, Dennis Hull, ed. LEGAL ISSUES FOR POSTSECONDARY EDU-CATION, BRIEFING PAPERS I. Washington, D.C.: American Association of Community and Junior Colleges, 1975. 88 p.

Outline of basic legal issues confronting administrators in post-secondary education; gives an overview of higher education and the law, legal liabilities of faculty members, policies that govern personnel records, and First Amendment freedoms.

197   _____. LEGAL ISSUES FOR POSTSECONDARY EDUCATION, BRIEFING PAPERS II. Washington, D.C.: American Association of Community and Junior Colleges, 1976. 89 p.

Covers legal ramifications of various faculty and staff matters, campus security, copyright, grievance and arbitration proce-dures, and methods for dealing with federal regulatory agen-cies.

198   Boalt, Gunnar, and Lantz, Herman. UNIVERSITIES AND RESEARCH: OBSERVATIONS ON THE UNITED STATES AND SWEDEN. New York: John Wiley and Sons, 1970. 157 p.

Examines the part research and publications play in the modern university. Probes the conflict between research and good teaching. Mentions the feelings of those faculty who enter administrative roles. Provides details of a study comparing professors' values and their actual activities.

199   Boas, Louise Schutz. WOMAN'S EDUCATION BEGINS: THE RISE OF THE WOMEN'S COLLEGES. Norton, Mass.: Wheaton College Press, 1935. Reprint. New York: Arno Press, 1971. 295 p.

A general look at aims and curricula of early women's colleges, with detailed references to Wheaton Female Seminary, in whose centennial year it was published.

200   Bode, Boyd H., et al. MODERN EDUCATION AND HUMAN VALUES. Pittsburgh, Pa.: University of Pittsburgh Press, 1947. 165 p.

Lectures by such leading educators as Boyd Bode, Arthur H. Compton, Robert M. Hutchins, Ordway Tead, and Mark Van

Dusen, whose views often clash over such issues as great books and religion but who agree that education must transmit values.

201 Boley, Bruno A., ed. CROSSFIRE IN PROFESSIONAL EDUCATION: STUDENTS, THE PROFESSIONS, AND SOCIETY. Elmsford, N.Y.: Pergamon Press, 1977. 108 p.

Report of a conference on the role of the specialized professional in society and the goals of professional education in law, medicine, dentistry, education, engineering, and journalism.

202 Bond, Otto F. THE READING METHOD: AN EXPERIMENT IN COLLEGE FRENCH. Chicago: University of Chicago Press, 1953. 368 p.

A detailed history of thirty years of French teaching at the University of Chicago, where the famous "reading method" was developed which helped students learn to read French, not through translation, but by direct and immediate comprehension. Its dramatic success greatly influenced U.S. language teaching.

203 Bonithus, Robert H., et al. THE INDEPENDENT STUDY PROGRAM IN THE UNITED STATES: A REPORT ON AN UNDERGRADUATE INSTRUCTIONAL METHOD. New York: Columbia University Press, 1957. 260 p.

A detailed survey of undergraduate independent study programs. Gives opinions from faculty and student participants and provides how-to-do-it information.

204 Boroff, David. CAMPUS U.S.A.: PORTRAITS OF AMERICAN COLLEGES IN ACTION. New York: Harper and Brothers, 1961. 210 p.

Journalistic essays, mostly from popular magazines, which examine three kinds of colleges: those with a national clientele (Harvard, Wisconsin, Claremont, Swarthmore), those with a local flavor (Brooklyn, Parsons, Birmingham-Southern), and those "for ladies mostly" (Smith, Sarah Lawrence, and the University of Michigan).

205 Borrowman, Merle L. THE LIBERAL AND TECHNICAL IN TEACHER EDUCATION: A HISTORICAL SURVEY OF AMERICAN THOUGHT. New York: Teachers College, Columbia University, 1956. 247 p.

Examination of teacher education in four periods in U.S. history: the general forces influencing educational thought, the concept of general education, the relationship of general to professional education, and the liberal and technical functions within professional education.

206 Bowen, Howard R. THE FINANCE OF HIGHER EDUCATION. Berkeley,

Calif.: Carnegie Commission on the Future of Higher Education, 1968. 36 p.

Recommends innovative ways for both students and institutions to finance higher education. For students, the author advocates a national system of minimum grants (using means test) supplemented by a national system of long-term loans. For institutions, he favors allocating federal money to cover future increases in the cost of education. He proposes a yearly cost-of-education grant to institutions to be tied to the number of students enrolled.

207 _____. INVESTMENT IN LEARNING: THE INDIVIDUAL AND SOCIAL VALUE OF AMERICAN HIGHER EDUCATION. San Francisco: Jossey-Bass Publishers, 1977. 507 p.

Describes the effects of higher education on individuals and society in terms of learning, moral development, citizenship, economic productivity, family life, consumer behavior, leisure, and health.

208 _____, ed. EVALUATING INSTITUTIONS FOR ACCOUNTABILITY. NEW DIRECTIONS FOR INSTITUTIONAL RESEARCH. San Francisco: Jossey-Bass Publishers, 1974. 128 p.

Some important points made by contributors: (1) how outside evaluation can help institutions; (2) steps for organizing accountability systems; and (3) various methods of measuring educational outcomes and how to evaluate these methods.

209 Bowen, Howard R., and Douglass, Gordon K. EFFICIENCY IN LIBERAL EDUCATION. A STUDY OF COMPARATIVE INSTRUCTIONAL COSTS FOR DIFFERENT WAYS OF ORGANIZING TEACHING-LEARNING IN A LIBERAL ARTS COLLEGE. New York: McGraw-Hill Book Co., 1971. 151 p.

Economic models on how to reduce the high cost of liberal arts education.

210 Bowers, John Z., and Purcell, Elizabeth F., eds. NEW MEDICAL SCHOOLS AT HOME AND ABROAD. Port Washington, N.Y.: Independent Publishers Group, 1978. 552 p.

Conference reports from representatives of eleven U.S. and four foreign medical centers. Editors foresee a surfeit of doctors in developed countries.

211 Bowers, William. STUDENT DISHONESTY AND ITS CONTROL IN COLLEGE. New York: Bureau of Applied Social Research, Columbia University, 1965. 273 p.

Goals: to assess the extent and seriousness of student cheating,

identify its sources, and evaluate methods institutions use for
controlling it. Special focus on ways personal and social constraints prevent cheating.

212 Bowles, Frank. THE REFOUNDING OF THE COLLEGE BOARD, 1948-
1963: AN INFORMAL COMMENTARY AND SELECTED PAPERS. New
York: College Entrance Examination Board, 1967. 336 p.

Papers and speeches during Bowles's fifteen years as chief executive of the College Board reflect his concept of greater
access to higher education.

213 Bowles, Frank, and DeCosta, Frank A. BETWEEN TWO WORLDS: A
PROFILE OF NEGRO HIGHER EDUCATION. New York: McGraw-Hill
Book Co., 1971. 326 p.

History of black colleges, including descriptions of schools
which have large black enrollments. Problems of black colleges and detailed portraits of five of them plus Merritt College, a California community college with 35 percent black
enrollment. Recommendations for helping black students and
black higher education include attaching research and development centers to one or more colleges and giving federal
support for professional programs at black colleges.

214 Boyd, William M. II. DESEGREGATING AMERICA'S COLLEGES: A
NATIONWIDE SURVEY OF BLACK STUDENTS, 1972-73. New York:
Praeger Publishers, 1974. 110 p.

This first nationwide survey of blacks in predominantly white
colleges was of 979 black students in forty institutions. Most
black students went to college in their home area, felt that
their college really did not want blacks enrolled, and felt
discriminated against.

215 Brace, Gerald Warner. THE SPIRE. New York: W.W. Norton and Co.,
1952. 380 p.

Novel about a year in the life of a small New England college,
centered on a professor of English.

216 Brackett, Frank P. GRANITE AND SAGEBRUSH: REMINISCENCES OF
THE FIRST FIFTY YEARS OF POMONA COLLEGE. Los Angeles: Ward
Ritchie Press, 1944. 251 p.

First-hand account of the first fifty years of Pomona, a southern
California college on the New England pattern.

217 Branscomb, Harvie. TEACHING WITH BOOKS. Chicago: American
Library Association, 1940. 237 p.

Study of college libraries and their educational effectiveness. Interviews, local studies, visits to sixty college libraries, plus published literature provided data. Report, intended for college presidents, is valuable for libraries, higher education specialists, and college teachers.

218 Brantley, Russell. THE EDUCATION OF JONATHAN BEAM. New York: Macmillan Co., 1962. 186 p.

Novel by the director of communication at Wake Forest, a Southern Baptist college, about a rural youth who goes to a denominational college to become a preacher but is dismayed at the conflict he finds between fundamentalism and modernism.

219 Brawer, Florence B. NEW PERSPECTIVES ON PERSONALITY DEVELOPMENT IN COLLEGE STUDENTS. San Francisco: Jossey-Bass Publishers, 1973. 232 p.

Emphasizes the potential functioning level of students, recognizes individual differences, and considers students' emotional needs along with their learning abilities.

220 Breasted, James Henry. ORIENTAL INSTITUTE. Chicago: University of Chicago Press, 1933. 455 p.

A description of the Oriental Institute, University of Chicago, and the accomplishments in its scholarly pursuit of knowledge about the beginnings of Oriental history.

221 Breivik, Patricia Senn. OPEN ADMISSIONS AND THE ACADEMIC LIBRARY. Chicago: American Library Association, 1977. 131 p.

Citing the effects of open admission on the role of the college library, the author suggests that librarians and faculty members try harder to help students understand and use college library resources.

222 Breneman, David W., and Finn, Chester E., Jr., eds. PUBLIC POLICY AND PRIVATE HIGHER EDUCATION. Washington, D.C.: Brookings Institution, 1978. 468 p.

Alarmed at the uncertain future of private higher education, the editors want a national student marketplace created and price differences narrowed between public and private institutions. Private college presidents, despite financial problems, wonder whether conditions set for state and federal aid to their institutions would inevitably sap the colleges' independence. Topics include student aid, federal and state tax policies, politics of state aid, and state policy options.

223 Brewer, Waldo Lyle. FACTORS AFFECTING STUDENT ACHIEVEMENT AND CHANGE IN A PHYSICAL SCIENCE SURVEY COURSE. Contributions to Education No. 868. New York: Teachers College, Columbia University, 1943. 78 p.

Found in a one-semester study of physical science survey course at Queen's College that it duplicated much material covered in high school science course.

224 Brick, Michael. FORUM AND FOCUS FOR THE JUNIOR COLLEGE MOVEMENT. New York: Teachers College, Columbia University, 1963. 222 p.

A history of the American Association of Junior Colleges, 1920-62, and its relation to the junior college movement as a whole.

225 Brick, Michael, and McGrath, Earl J. INNOVATION IN LIBERAL ARTS COLLEGES. New York: Teachers College Press, 1969. 173 p.

A 1965-66 survey of such new practices at four-year colleges as interdisciplinary courses, honors programs, independent study, non-Western study, study abroad, use of television and teaching machines, language laboratories, new admissions policies, advanced placement, and others.

226 Brickman, William W., ed. EDUCATIONAL IMPERATIVES IN A CHANGING CULTURE: FIFTY-THIRD SCHOOLMEN'S WEEK PROCEEDINGS. Philadelphia: University of Pennsylvania Press, 1967. 232 p.

Half of the articles are concerned with postsecondary schooling, particularly interinstitutional cooperation.

227 Brickman, William W., and Lehrer, Stanley, eds. A CENTURY OF HIGHER EDUCATION: CLASSICAL CITADEL TO COLLEGIATE COLOSSUS. New York: Society for the Advancement of Education, 1962. 293 p.

Contributions covering 1862 to 1962 include legal developments, the state university, the liberal arts college, the land-grant college, the junior and community college, the church-related college, teacher education, graduate education, education of women and minorities, and international aspects of U.S. higher education.

228 Bridgman, Percy William. REFLECTIONS OF A PHYSICIST. New York: Philosophical Library, 1950. 392 p.

Nobel laureate physicist's twenty nontechnical essays on government and research and on the social and subjective nature of science.

229 Brigham, Carl C. EXAMINING FELLOWSHIP APPLICANTS. Princeton, N.J.: Princeton University Press, 1935. 58 p.

Critical analysis of the process used to select graduate students for Social Science Research Council fellowship grants.

230 _____. THE READING OF THE COMPREHENSIVE EXAMINATION IN ENGLISH. Princeton, N.J.: Princeton University Press, 1934. 48 p.

Analysis of errors made and recommendations for improving the reading by examiners of the English exams for the College Entrance Examination Board.

231 Brinton, Crane, ed. THE SOCIETY OF FELLOWS. Cambridge, Mass.: Society of Fellows of Harvard University, 1959. 268 p.

Papers illustrating the history of Harvard's Society of Fellows, with biographical sketches of the usually distinguished careers of these recipients of Harvard University fellowships.

232 Brody, Alexander. THE AMERICAN STATE AND HIGHER EDUCATION. Washington, D.C.: American Council on Education, 1935. 251 p.

Legal relations between the states, the federal government, and public institutions of higher education (author is lawyer and political scientist); legal aspect of founding charters, control by voters, and court decisions.

233 Bronson, Walter C. THE HISTORY OF BROWN UNIVERSITY, 1764-1914. Providence, R.I.: Brown University, 1941. Reprint. New York: Arno Press, 1975. 547 p.

Authoritative, well-written history of Brown University, from its founding as the College of Rhode Island to its development as a university.

234 Bronzan, Robert T. PUBLIC RELATIONS, PROMOTIONS, AND FUND RAISING FOR ATHLETIC AND PHYSICAL EDUCATION PROGRAMS. New York: John Wiley and Sons, 1977. 268 p.

How colleges and universities can generate financial and public support needed to maintain and improve competitive athletic and physical-education programs.

235 Brooks, Jean S., and Reich, David. THE PUBLIC LIBRARY IN NON-TRADITIONAL EDUCATION. Homewood, Ill.: ETC Publications, 1974. 244 p.

Using the Dallas, Texas, Public Library as an example, authors examine the role public libraries can play in aiding nontraditional college education.

236 Broome, Edwin Cornelius. A HISTORICAL AND CRITICAL DISCUSSION OF COLLEGE ADMISSION REQUIREMENTS. New York: Columbia University, 1903. Reprint. New York: College Entrance Examination Board, 1963. 157 p.

Reprint of an early work which stressed the relationship between college admissions and the public interest. Author urged college entrance examiners to uncover students' potential for independent thought rather than their ability to memorize facts.

237 Brough, Kenneth. SCHOLAR'S WORKSHOP: EVOLVING CONCEPTIONS OF LIBRARY SERVICE. Urbana: University of Illinois Press, 1953. 197 p.

Using Harvard, Columbia, Chicago, and Yale libraries as examples, author traces the evolution of many major higher education library problems.

238 Brouwer, Paul J. STUDENT PERSONNEL SERVICES IN GENERAL EDUCATION. Washington, D.C.: American Council on Education, 1949. 317 p.

Results of a survey of twenty-five colleges and universities on how to improve teaching and counseling of students in general education.

239 Brown, Charles H., and Bousfield, H.G. CIRCULATION WORK IN COLLEGE AND UNIVERSITY LIBRARIES. Chicago: American Library Association, 1933. 179 p.

General principles and specific routines to guide the library staff in aiding students to find and use college library materials.

240 Brown, Charles I., ed. REPORT CARD ON ENROLLMENT PROJECTIONS AND OTHER SELECTED PAPERS. Greenville, N.C.: Office of Institutional Research, East Carolina University, 1977. 59 p.

Conference papers on projecting enrollments for individual colleges and universities and for statewide and multicampus systems.

241 Brown, Clara M. EVALUATION AND INVESTIGATION IN HOME ECONOMICS. New York: F.S. Crofts and Co., 1941. 461 p.

Testing and other measurements of students plus research techniques and design for college teachers of home economics.

242 Brown, David G. THE MARKET FOR COLLEGE TEACHERS: AN ECONOMIC ANALYSIS OF CAREER PATTERNS AMONG SOUTHEASTERN SOCIAL SCIENTISTS. Chapel Hill: University of North Carolina Press, 1965. 301 p.

Author found a shortage of well-trained faculty in this survey of economists, historians, and sociologists at eighteen large southeastern universities (nine public, nine private).

243 _____. THE MOBILE PROFESSORS. Washington, D.C.: American Council on Education, 1967. 220 p.

Economic analysis of over thirteen thousand job-changing college teachers. Most place courses taught, teaching load, research facilities, and colleague competence ahead of salary. Contains twenty-five recommendations for improving the market mechanism.

244 Brown, Elmer Ellsworth. A FEW REMARKS. New York: New York University Press, 1933. 251 p.

Selections from Chancellor Brown's twenty-two years of reports and public addresses at New York University, written with wit about the problems of an urban university.

245 Brown, Francis J. EDUCATIONAL OPPORTUNITIES FOR VETERANS. Washington, D.C.: Public Affairs Press, 1946. 142 p.

Describes college and other training benefits for veterans under various federal public laws and state rehabilitation laws. Estimates that 19 percent of those in the armed forces will undertake full-time education, and that another 12 percent will study part-time. Discusses housing, summer sessions, types of training, adjustment, and other problems.

246 _____, ed. NATIONAL DEFENSE AND HIGHER EDUCATION. Washington, D.C.: American Council on Education, 1951. 121 p.

Conference papers on national defense and higher education about such topics as emergency manpower problems, education and present-day economics, education's place and responsiblity in civil defense, and veterans' education.

247 Brown, Francis J., and Sellin, Thorsten, eds. HIGHER EDUCATION UNDER STRESS. Philadelphia: American Academy of Political and Social Science, 1955. 210 p.

Conference papers on such higher education problems as: purposes of learning, academic freedom, finance, and others.

248 Brown, Frank, and Stent, Madelon D. MINORITIES IN U.S. INSTITUTIONS OF HIGHER EDUCATION. New York: Praeger Publishers, 1977. 200 p.

Comprehensive review of college enrollments and educational attainment of minorities. Lists major minority groups by institutional type and control, lower and upper division enrollment, minority enrollment in various disciplines and major professional schools, and socioeconomic characteristics of minority students.

249   Brown, J. Douglas. THE LIBERAL UNIVERSITY: AN INSTITUTIONAL ANALYSIS. New York: McGraw-Hill Book Co., 1969. 263 p.

Reflecting his elite institutional connection, the retired Princeton dean of the faculty provides a useful handbook to guide trustees, presidents, and deans.

250   Brown, James W., and Thornton, James W. COLLEGE TEACHING: A SYSTEMATIC APPROACH. 2d ed. New York: McGraw-Hill Book Co., 1971. 256 p.

Second edition of a popular text for graduate students preparing for college teaching: teaching methods (lecture, group discussion, others), use of audiovisual materials, and student evaluation.

251   Brown, John Nicholas. REPORT OF THE COMMITTEE ON THE VISUAL ARTS AT HARVARD UNIVERSITY. Cambridge, Mass.: Harvard University, 1956. 155 p.

Author chaired this committee, which reported on the Harvard art curriculum and made recommendations for improvements.

252   Brown, Kenneth Irving. A CAMPUS DECADE. Chicago: University of Chicago Press, 1940. 133 p.

Hiram College (Ohio) president describes the intensive study experiment during 1930 to 1940 when students concentrated on one course at a time. Interwoven is author's philosophy of education, his view on good teaching, and the joys of struggle at a private college.

253   Brown, Newell. AFTER COLLEGE . . . WHAT? A CAREER EXPLORATION HANDBOOK. New York: M.W. Lads, 1968. 246 p.

Describes eleven fallacies about career decisions, the effect of emotional and value attitudes on careers, and career classifications. Has information on career opportunities, qualifications, and likely salaries.

254   Brown, Robert D. STUDENT DEVELOPMENT IN TOMORROW'S HIGHER EDUCATION--A RETURN TO THE ACADEMY. Washington, D.C.: American Personnel and Guidance Association, 1972. 55 p.

Highly regarded summary and discussion of recommendations based on Carnegie, Hazen, and Newman evaluations of higher education; descriptions of optimum undergraduate learning en-

vironment and of special program innovations tried at pace-
setting campuses.

255 Brown, Robert L. COOPERATIVE EDUCATION. Washington, D.C.:
American Association of Junior Colleges, 1971. 32 p.

Guidelines for cooperative programs in occupational education
and for matching students with jobs. Suggests ways to coordinate junior, community, and other college programs with
employers' needs.

256 Brown, Rollo Walter. THE HILLIKEN. New York: Coward-McCann,
1935. 393 p.

This novel, sequel to two others, takes the hero as a student
through Harvard University and then as a teacher in a midwestern steel town.

257 _____. ON WRITING THE BIOGRAPHY OF A MODEST MAN. Cambridge, Mass.: Harvard University Press, 1935. 49 p.

Author describes his search for biographical data on Harvard
University Dean L.B.R. Briggs, and relates his remembrance
of Briggs's charm, personality, and ideas.

258 Brown, Sanborn C., and Clarke, Norman, eds. THE EDUCATION OF A
PHYSICIST: AN ACCOUNT OF THE INTERNATIONAL CONFERENCE
ON THE EDUCATION OF PROFESSIONAL PHYSICISTS. Cambridge:
MIT Press, 1966. 185 p.

Conference papers about ways physicists are educated, problems
of pure and applied research, role of small colleges, and problems at large universities.

259 Brown, Sanborn C., and Schwartz, Bryan B. SCIENTIFIC MANPOWER:
A DILEMMA FOR GRADUATE EDUCATION. Cambridge: MIT Press, 1971.
180 p.

Symposium on the supply, education, and utilization of doctorates in science and engineering. Urges the development
of more rapid and more sensitive indicators of changing trends,
conditions, and markets. Concerned by oversupply and under-
employment of scientists as of 1970.

260 Brown, William Adams. THE CASE FOR THEOLOGY IN THE UNIVER-
SITY. Chicago: University of Chicago Press, 1938. 124 p.

To Robert M. Hutchins' charge that the modern university is
adrift because it has no unifying theme, author replies that
the study of theology once was and should be reinstated to
its long-held position as the unifier of higher education, society, and civilization.

261 Brownell, Baker. THE COLLEGE AND THE COMMUNITY: A CRITICAL STUDY OF HIGHER EDUCATION. New York: Harper and Brothers, 1952. 248 p.

> Author sees hope for the improvement of higher education in a return to what he calls "the human condition"; for instance, a grassroots decentralization through adult education, community colleges, and group community centers so as to be in close touch with important human needs.

262 Brubacher, John S. BASES FOR POLICY IN HIGHER EDUCATION. New York: McGraw-Hill Book Co., 1965. 144 p.

> Brubacher treats historically and philosophically what he sees as the essential problem in higher education, a problem heightened by mounting enrollment: the extent higher education should be general or liberal and the extent it should be specialized and occupational.

263 _____. THE COURTS AND HIGHER EDUCATION. San Francisco: Jossey-Bass Publishers, 1971. 150 p.

> Himself a law school graduate, Brubacher covers major influential legal decisions affecting higher education, such as student dismissal, faculty and student rights, relevant constitutional questions, the state and private colleges and universities, union negotiations, and others.

264 _____. ON THE PHILOSOPHY OF HIGHER EDUCATION. San Francisco: Jossey-Bass Publishers, 1977. 143 p.

> On retirement after a distinguished career teaching the history and philosophy of education (mainly higher education) at Yale, the University of Michigan, and elsewhere, Brubacher discusses the diverse higher education theories of Veblen, Hutchins, Jaspers, and Kerr in relation to such issues as pure knowledge and objective research, social involvement and vocationalism, relevance of curriculum, and the ethics of scholarship.

265 Brubacher, John S., and Rudy, Willis Solomon. HIGHER EDUCATION IN TRANSITION: A HISTORY OF AMERICAN COLLEGES AND UNIVERSITIES, 1636-1976. 3d ed. New York: Harper and Row, 1976. 536 p.

> A recommended history of American higher education. Combined chronological and topical approach to individuals and movements. New material includes finance and growth in the 1950s and 1960s, arrested growth since the late 1960s, and inflation and recession effects in the 1970s. Excellent notes, bibliography, and index.

266 Bruce, Phillip Alexander. HISTORY OF THE UNIVERSITY OF VIRGINIA,

1819-1919. 5 vols. New York: Macmillan, 1920-22. 400 p., 305 p.,
403 p., 376 p., 477 p.

Divides the history of the University of Virginia into nine
periods with major emphasis on developments after 1842.

267   Brugger, Robert J. BEVERLEY TUCKER: HEART OVER HEAD IN THE
OLD SOUTH. Baltimore, Md.: Johns Hopkins University Press, 1978. 294 p.

Biography of a professor of law at the College of William and
Mary who was a secessionist during the antebellum period.

268   Brumbaugh, Aaron John. RESEARCH DESIGNED TO IMPROVE INSTITU-
TIONS OF HIGHER LEARNING. Washington, D.C.: American Council
on Education, 1960. 47 p.

Specifies the need for institutional research, points to areas
for study, ways it can be done, and its probable effects.

269   Brumbaugh, Aaron John, and Irwin, Mary, eds. AMERICAN UNIVER-
SITIES AND COLLEGES. 5th ed. Washington, D.C.: American Council
on Education, 1948. 1,054 p.

Guide to 820 accredited institutions, including their history,
enrollments, admission and degree requirements, and financial
data. Also contains general articles on U.S. higher education and information about veterans and foreign students. A
1973 edition was published by the American Council of Education (see entry 905).

270   Brush, Katharine Ingham. GLITTER. New York: A.L. Burt Co., 1926.
309 p.

Entertaining novel about college life.

271   Brustein, Robert. REVOLUTION AS THEATRE; NOTES ON THE NEW
RADICAL STYLE. New York: Liveright, 1971. 170 p.

Reflecting on student unrest at Yale University during the trial
of the Black Panthers, author is critical of radical student protesters and of adult sympathizers in and out of academe.

272   Bryson, Lyman, et al., eds. GOALS FOR AMERICAN EDUCATION.
New York: Harper and Brothers, 1950. 555 p.

Conference papers and participants' comments on such problems
as higher education and the unity of knowledge, function of
the university in a free society, and education as experiment.

273   Buchanan, James M., and Devletoglou, Nicos E. ACADEMIA IN AN-
ARCHY: AN ECONOMIC DIAGNOSIS. New York: Basic Books, 1970.
187 p.

In the context of student protests, iconoclastic authors view the chaos of higher education in economic terms: because students who consume higher education do not buy it, they become indifferent or even contemptuous; because faculty who produce it do not sell it, they maximize their own satisfactions and are exempt from normal market constraints; and because taxpayers who finance it do not control it, they are robbed and disenchanted. Authors believe that if boards of trustees reassert control, they can return higher education to a sound economy and better direction.

274 Buck, Solon F., ed. WILLIAM WATTS FOLWELL, THE AUTOBIOGRAPHY AND LETTERS OF A PIONEER OF CULTURE. Minneapolis: University of Minnesota Press, 1933. 287 p.

Autobiography and letters of W.W. Folwell (1833-1929), his Ohio upbringing, his year as a professor at Kenyon College, and his thirty-eight years as University of Minnesota's president, professor, and librarian.

275 Buckley, William F., Jr. GOD AND MAN AT YALE. Chicago: Regnery, 1951. Reprint. South Bend, Ind.: Gateway Editions, 1977. 280 p.

In 1951 at his alma mater's 250th anniversary, Yale graduate and since then conservative leader Buckley pointed out that Yale, morally founded and financially supported by Christians, has developed a curriculum, faculty, and attitude that turns out atheistic socialists. This 1977 edition contains author's reflective introduction.

276 Budig, Gene A. ACADEMIA AND THE STATEHOUSE: AN ESSAY ON THE RELATIONSHIP BETWEEN HIGHER EDUCATION AND STATE GOVERNMENT. Lincoln: University of Nebraska, 1970. 42 p.

West Virginia University President Budig, who had been administrative assistant to both the University of Nebraska's chancellor and Nebraska's governor, comments on financial, academic, and other concerns of state governors, legislators, and state university administrators.

277 _____, ed. PERCEPTIONS IN PUBLIC HIGHER EDUCATION. Lincoln: University of Nebraska Press, 1970. 163 p.

Ten University of Nebraska contributors' essays on duties and problems of the president, various deans, department heads, and professors, and the role of public relations, research and planning, and budget.

278 Budig, Gene A., and Rives, Stanley G. ACADEMIC QUICKSAND:

SOME TRENDS AND ISSUES IN HIGHER EDUCATION. Lincoln, Nebr.: Professional Educators Publications, 1973. 74 p.

Written for higher education administrators; what students, faculty, trustees, government, and the public expect from higher education institutions.

279 Bugliarello, George, and Simon, Harold A. TECHNOLOGY, THE UNI-VERSITY AND THE COMMUNITY: A STUDY OF THE REGIONAL ROLE OF ENGINEERING COLLEGES. Elmsford, N.Y.: Pergamon Press, 1975. 515 p.

Examines the engineering college as a source of manpower and of scientific and technical knowledge that might help solve the problems of states and local communities.

280 Bullock, Henry Morton. A HISTORY OF EMORY UNIVERSITY, 1836-1936. Nashville, Tenn.: Parthenon Press, 1936. 391 p.

Scholarly, objective, readable centennial history of denominational institution in the context of the history of higher education in the South.

281 Burgess, John William. REMINISCENCES OF AN AMERICAN SCHOLAR: THE BEGINNINGS OF AN AMERICAN SCHOLAR: THE BEGINNINGS OF COLUMBIA UNIVERSITY. New York: Columbia University Press, 1934. 430 p.

Author's autobiography (1844-1931) from his Tennessee youth to graduation from Amherst College, to his career at Columbia College which reached university status while he was professor, dean of the faculty of political science, and founder of the POLITICAL SCIENCE QUARTERLY.

282 Burkett, Jesse E., and Ruggiers, Paul G., eds. BACHELOR OF LIBERAL STUDIES: DEVELOPMENT OF A CURRICULUM AT THE UNIVERSITY OF OKLAHOMA. Brookline, Mass.: Center for the Study of Liberal Education for Adults at Boston University, 1965. 107 p.

Articles describing the development of the Bachelor of Liberal Studies degree at the University of Oklahoma, a highly publicized higher education program for working adults which combines independent study with several three-week seminars in residence. On the basis of entrance examinations, the curriculum is individually adjusted to each student's prior attainment.

283 Burnett, Collins W., ed. THE COMMUNITY JUNIOR COLLEGE: AN ANNOTATED BIBLIOGRAPHY WITH INTRODUCTIONS FOR SCHOOL COUNSELORS. Columbus: College of Education, Ohio State University, 1968. 122 p.

Bibliography covers history of the community and junior college, philosophy and objectives, functions, organization and administration, teaching-learning climate, student behavior and student personnel, trends and developments, and research and evaluation. Sections include introductory text, selected book references, and briefly annotated bibliography of journal articles.

284 Burns, Gerald P., ed. ADMINISTRATORS IN HIGHER EDUCATION: THEIR FUNCTIONS AND COORDINATION. New York: Harper and Brothers, 1962. 236 p.

Thirteen chapters by specialists on the history and philosophy of higher education and the role of the president, academic vice president, various deans, registrar, alumni secretary, and other administrators.

285 Burns, Martha A. NEW CAREERS IN HUMAN SERVICE: A CHALLENGE TO THE TWO-YEAR COLLEGE. University Park: Pennsylvania State University, 1971. 82 p.

Survey uncovered 1,006 programs (not critically analyzed) in twelve fields of human service in 176 two-year colleges.

286 Burrell, John Angus. A HISTORY OF ADULT EDUCATION AT COLUMBIA UNIVERSITY: UNIVERSITY EXTENSION AND THE SCHOOL OF GENERAL STUDIES. New York: Columbia University Press, 1954. 111 p.

Origin, development, and contributions of Columbia University's departments which have served and are serving adult needs, usually in afternoon, evening, special summer, and other sessions; the still surviving Institute of Arts and Sciences and the School of General Studies, and the defunct Home Study Department.

287 Burrin, Frank K. EDWARD CHARLES ELLIOTT, EDUCATOR. Lafayette, Ind.: Purdue University Studies, 1970. 187 p.

Biography of E.C. Elliott (1874-1960), his midwest schooling, his attendance at the University of Nebraska, his educational career in Colorado and as professor at the University of Wisconsin, and his presidencies at the University of Montana and Purdue University.

288 Burt, Forrest D., and King, Sylvia, eds. EQUIVALENCY TESTING: A MAJOR ISSUE FOR COLLEGE ENGLISH. Urbana, Ill.: National Council of Teachers of English, 1974. 52 p.

Conference discussion on placement, exemption, and credit in college English; the role of the English professor in equivalency programs; and the politics of equivalency testing.

289   Butler, Nicholas Murray. ACROSS THE BUSY YEARS. New York: Charles Scribner's Sons, 1939. 451 p.

Autobiography of influential educator (1862–1947) and his long association with Columbia University as student, professor, dean, and president; his elevation of professional schools of education by his founding and presidency of Teachers College, Columbia University; his influence in international education; and leading U.S. and world educators he knew.

290   Butterfield, William H. HOW TO USE LETTERS IN COLLEGE PUBLIC RELATIONS. New York: Harper and Brothers, 1944. 182 p.

Description and samples of public relations letters to alumni, parents, potential donors, students, and prospective students, and friends of institutions of higher education—by the chairman of the department of business communication, University of Oklahoma.

291   Buttrick, George Arthur. BIBLICAL THOUGHT AND THE SECULAR UNIVERSITY. Baton Rouge: Louisiana State University Press, 1960. 83 p.

Clergyman Buttrick insists that all religion courses at a secular university must be elective. Author's artful writing, religious conviction, and academic experience make the book acceptable to people of diverse religious and educational views.

292   Butts, R. Freeman. AMERICAN EDUCATION IN INTERNATIONAL DEVELOPMENT. John Dewey Society Lectureship Series, No. 6. New York: Harper and Row, 1963. Reprint. Freeport, N.Y.: Books for Libraries Press, 1970. 138 p.

Although focused on Africa, this discussion about relating education to people's needs is applicable to any country, including the United States. Special reference is made to the "Teachers for East Africa" program of Teachers College, Columbia University, to substantiate Butts's belief that teacher education is central to aiding developing countries.

293   _____. THE COLLEGE CHARTS ITS COURSE: HISTORICAL CONCEPTIONS AND CURRENT PROPOSALS. New York: McGraw-Hill Book Co., 1939. Reprint. New York: Arno Press, 1972. 464 p.

Well-documented historical study of conflicting ideas about liberal education and the continued effort to get away from fixed courses of study by incorporating the elective system. Included are sharp intellectual vignettes of higher education leaders from colonial times to the twentieth century.

294   Butz, Otto, ed. TO MAKE A DIFFERENCE: A STUDENT LOOK AT AMERICA. New York: Harper and Row, 1967. 174 p.

In this clear statement of students' thoughts and feelings in the middle 1960s, ten students (ages 22-28) at San Francisco State College wrote chapters which reflect their yearning for a society characterized by wholeness and integrity.

295 _____. THE UNSILENT GENERATION. New York: Rinehart, 1958. 189 p.

An impressionistic study of undergraduate life and culture in the 1950s.

296 Buxton, Claude E. COLLEGE TEACHING: A PSYCHOLOGIST'S VIEW. New York: Harcourt, Brace and World, 1956. 404 p.

Puts into psychological perspective such aspects of college teaching as instructional planning, teaching methods, evaluation, and counseling.

297 Buxton, Thomas H., and Prichard, Keith W., eds. EXCELLENCE IN UNIVERSITY TEACHING: NEW ESSAYS. Columbia: University of South Carolina Press, 1975. 291 p.

Attributes of excellent university teaching cited were enthusiasm, zest, love of subject; concern for student participation; and relevance of subject matter to life.

298 Byer, Herbert. TO THE VICTOR. Garden City, N.Y.: Doubleday, Doran and Co., 1936. 277 p.

A satirical, ironic novel about an American college football star whose fame fades fast and who later regrets not having made more of his college learning opportunities.

299 Byse, Clark, and Joughin, G. Louis. TENURE IN AMERICAN HIGHER EDUCATION. Ithaca, N.Y.: Cornell University Press, 1959. 212 p.

Report of faculty tenure procedures as practiced at eighty colleges. One of the several appendices gives procedural standards for faculty dismissal. No discussion of ways to assure that tenured faculty continue to grow and function at their peak.

300 Cady, Edwin H. THE BIG GAME: COLLEGE SPORTS AND AMERICAN LIFE. Knoxville: University of Tennessee Press, 1978. 254 p.

Calls college sports an American art form experienced by athletes, spectators, and home viewers. Reflecting their origin in religious festivals and in imitating war, college sports--more than professional sports--are a ritualized, dramatic, collective representation of the American dream. Using examples from literature, anthropology, psychology, and sociology, Cady explores the meaning and glorification by Americans of college sports.

301 Caffrey, John, ed. THE FUTURE ACADEMIC COMMUNITY--CONTIN-UITY AND CHANGE. Washington, D.C.: American Council on Education, 1969. 327 p.

Editor says all segments of the academic community must collaborate if change is to be constructive. Internationally known city planner Constantinos Doxiadis connected trends in urbanization with planning for universities.

302 Caffrey, John, and Isaacs, Herbert H. ESTIMATING THE IMPACT OF A COLLEGE OR UNIVERSITY ON THE LOCAL ECONOMY. Washington, D.C.: American Council on Education, 1971. 73 p.

Team of experts developed mathematical models and formulas for computing economic impact colleges and universities make on communities; for instance, the multiplier effect of their payrolls.

303 Caffrey, John, and Mosmann, Charles J. COMPUTERS ON CAMPUS. Washington, D.C.: American Council on Education, 1967. 221 p.

Computers as aids to administrators in decision making are discussed in their application to admissions, registration, scheduling, grade reporting, records, and other functions; to finance and business management; and to such academic services as research and instruction. Computers only amplify and implement decisions made by or approved by the college president.

304 Califano, Joseph A., Jr. THE STUDENT REVOLUTION: A GLOBAL CONFRONTATION. New York: W.W. Norton, 1970. 96 p.

Conservative critique based on U.S. and European campus visits. Author found common pattern of a small group of hardcore radical students with unclear objectives reflecting their crisis of belief. They created confrontation on issues, used instant communication to gain followers, and often succeeded when authorities overreacted.

305 California. Legislature. Joint Committee on Higher Education. THE CHALLENGE OF ACHIEVEMENT. Sacramento, Calif.: 1969. 158 p.

Study of California higher education results in some sweeping reorganization proposals, chief one being to create one board with responsibilities for all state-supported colleges and universities.

306 California. University. Berkeley. Academic Senate. EDUCATION AT BERKELEY: REPORT OF THE SELECT COMMITTEE ON EDUCATION.

Rev. ed. Berkeley and Los Angeles: University of California Press, 1968. 268 p.

More than a future corrective for Berkeley's 1960s campus unrest, the "Muscatine Report," named for its chairman, was a broad examination of higher education's unwieldy size and impersonality. Stressed better and more personalized teaching, curricular reforms to meet students' needs, and admissions policies to attract students fitted for Berkeley's research emphasis.

307 California. University. Los Angeles. Cooperative Institutional Research Program, Graduate School of Education. THE AMERICAN FRESHMAN: NATIONAL NORMS FOR FALL 1973. Los Angeles: 1976. 116 p.

Found among 186,406 freshmen entering 366 colleges and universities that: more (16.9 percent) women sought male-dominated careers in business, engineering, law, and medicine than had ten years before (5.9 percent); that black enrollment was at an all-time high of 9 percent; and that for the first time in seven years their high school grades were not higher than were students' grades the year before.

308 Calkins, Earnest Elmo. THEY BROKE THE PRAIRIE. New York: Charles Scribner's Sons, 1937. 451 p.

Founding, growth, and history of Knox College; is also a history of the religious pioneers of Galesburg, Illinois.

309 Callcott, George H. A HISTORY OF THE UNIVERSITY OF MARYLAND. Baltimore: Maryland Historical Society, 1966. 422 p.

Account of how independent proprietary schools of law, medicine, pharmacy, and agriculture, fed by an undergraduate college, merged into the University of Maryland, whose growth was largely aided by President Harry Clifton Byrd.

310 Calvert, Jack G., et al. GRADUATE SCHOOL IN THE SCIENCES: ENTRANCE, SURVIVAL, AND CAREERS. New York: Wiley-Interscience, 1972. 304 p.

On such topics as responsibilities of academic life, a spouse's role in one's graduate education, and protecting copyrights. Appendixes on salaries, fellowships, sources of research support, federally funded research, and related topics.

311 Calvert, Robert, Jr. EQUAL EMPLOYMENT OPPORTUNITY FOR MINORITY GROUP COLLEGE GRADUATES: LOCATING, RECRUITING, EMPLOYING. Garrett Park, Md.: Garrett Park Press, 1972. 248 p.

Information to aid in job placement for minority graduates

(blacks, Spanish-Americans, American Indians, Asian-Americans, and others). Lists black junior colleges, colleges, and universities; contains bibliography of books on employing minority group members.

312 Campbell, Alexander. THE TROUBLE WITH AMERICANS. New York: Praeger Publishers, 1971. 215 p.

British critic of American society sees no evidence that college education produces intellectual or value changes. He charges U.S. graduate education with being faddish.

313 Campbell, Jack K. COLONEL FRANCIS W. PARKER: THE CHILDREN'S CRUSADER. New York: Teachers College, Columbia University, 1967. 283 p.

Biography of progressive educator Francis Wayland Parker (1837-1902), who headed the Cook County Normal School in Chicago and was briefly associated with John Dewey at the then new University of Chicago education department.

314 Campbell, Oscar James, ed. THE TEACHING OF COLLEGE ENGLISH. New York: D. Appleton-Century Co., 1934. 164 p.

Recommendations from the National Council of Teachers of English on teaching English to undergraduate and graduate students.

315 Campbell, Thomas F. SASS: FIFTY YEARS OF SOCIAL WORK EDUCATION; A HISTORY OF THE SCHOOL OF APPLIED SOCIAL SCIENCES, CASE WESTERN RESERVE UNIVERSITY. Cleveland: Press of Case Western Reserve University, 1967. 131 p.

Traces the growing pains of social work education; its search for purpose, for professional identity, and for an adequate knowledge base.

316 Campbell, William Giles. A COMPARATIVE INVESTIGATION OF THE BEHAVIOR OF STUDENTS UNDER AN HONOR SYSTEM AND A PROCTOR SYSTEM IN THE SAME UNIVERSITY. Southern California Education Monographs, No. 6. Los Angeles: University of Southern California Press, 1935. 95 p.

History of the honor system in U.S. higher education; summarizes earlier studies of the system and compares honor and proctor systems at the University of Texas.

317 Canby, Henry Seidel. ALMA MATER: THE GOTHIC AGE OF THE AMERICAN COLLEGE. New York: Farrar and Rinehart, 1936. 259 p.

Well-known Yale English professor reminisces about his experiences as Yale student and faculty member. He describes New Haven, student life, his fellow students and colleagues, and Yale's role in shaping leaders "for the harsh competition of capitalism." Covers the years 1895 to 1914.

318 Cangemi, Joseph P. HIGHER EDUCATION AND THE DEVELOPMENT OF SELF-ACTUALIZING PERSONALITIES. New York: Philosophical Library, 1977. 96 p.

Development of a well-rounded person, rather than specialization, should be the goal of higher education.

319 Cantelon, John E. COLLEGE EDUCATION AND THE CAMPUS REVOLUTION. Philadelphia: Westminster Press, 1969. 143 p.

Author says that the real problem behind student unrest is that liberal arts college professors do not teach as well as they should.

320 Capen, Samuel P. THE MANAGEMENT OF UNIVERSITIES. Buffalo, N.Y.: Council of the University of Buffalo, 1952. 287 p.

University of Buffalo's Chancellor Capen's speeches and papers concerning teachers, trustees, administration, curriculum, and professional education.

321 Caplow, Theodore, and McGee, Reece J. THE ACADEMIC MARKETPLACE. New York: Basic Books, 1958. Reprint. Garden City, N.Y.: Anchor Books, 1965. 226 p.

Much referred-to and respected study of how academic appointments and promotions are made, based on information from ten major universities. Found that prestige, sponsorship (recommendations), reputation, past employer, and publications were significant factors in academic job selection.

322 Carbone, Peter F. THE SOCIAL AND EDUCATIONAL THOUGHT OF HAROLD RUGG. Durham, N.C.: Duke University Press, 1977. 225 p.

Rugg's career (1886-1960) as a Dartmouth-trained engineer, a civil engineering professor at the University of Illinois, education professor at Columbia University's Teachers College, social studies textbook writer, and leading social reconstructionist.

323 Carbone, Robert F. RESIDENT OR NONRESIDENT? TUITION CLASSIFICATION IN HIGHER EDUCATION IN THE STATES. Denver: Education Commission of the States, 1970. 58 p.

Studied higher education residency requirements and recommended more clearly defined requirements and standardized procedures.

324 Carey, James Charles. KANSAS STATE UNIVERSITY: THE QUEST FOR IDENTITY. Lawrence: Regents Press of Kansas, 1977. 333 p.

From its founding in 1858 as Bluemont Central College to the present, including founding of various departments. Updates Julius T. Willard's HISTORY OF THE KANSAS STATE COLLEGE OF AGRICULTURE AND APPLIED SCIENCE (1940).

325 Carl, Linda. THE ALUMNI COLLEGE MOVEMENT. Washington, D.C.: Council for Advancement and Support of Education, 1978. 63 p.

Origins, sponsors, students, curricula, and other facets of the growing movement of colleges and universities to attract their alumni back for summer and other programs.

326 Carlin, Edward Augustine, and Blackman, E.B., eds. CURRICULUM BUILDING IN GENERAL EDUCATION. Dubuque, Iowa: William C. Brown Co., 1960. 133 p.

Describes the reorganization of the general education program at Michigan State University into four basic courses: communication skills, natural sciences, social sciences, and humanities. Examines the evolution and philosophy of these course offerings.

327 Carling, Francis. "MOVE OVER": STUDENTS, POLITICS, RELIGION. New York: Sheed and Ward, 1969. 154 p.

Primarily concerned with religious aspects, the author discusses mid-1960s student activism from a radical Catholic viewpoint.

328 Carlisle, Robert D.B. MEDIA AND THE ADULT STUDENT: ONE MAN'S JOURNAL. Lincoln, Nebr.: Great Plains National Instructional Library, 1977. 211 p.

Describes the use of media and communication technology in teaching adult students.

329 Carlton, Wendy. 'IN OUR PROFESSIONAL OPINION . . .': THE PRIMACY OF CLINICAL JUDGMENT OVER MORAL CHOICE. Notre Dame, Ind.: University of Notre Dame Press, 1978. 207 p.

Sociologist finds ethical training of medical students nonexistent in the classroom, clinic, or hospital and calls for a change in training emphasis: ethical theory should be practiced as well as taught.

330 Carmichael, Oliver C. THE CHANGING ROLE OF HIGHER EDUCATION. New York: Macmillan Co., 1949. 102 p.

A noted educator examines changes occurring in higher education and resulting problems. He suggests evaluating the graduate in terms of social and individual effectiveness and says that "relevance" should be the theme in reshaping programs and policies.

331 _____. GRADUATE EDUCATION: A CRITIQUE AND A PROGRAM. New York: Harper and Brothers, 1961. 213 p.

Former president of the Carnegie Foundation finds graduate education inadequate and, in some cases, inappropriate. The authority of the graduate school, the time required to earn a degree, the kind of research being done, and the judgment of a candidate's worth are critical factors. Particular emphasis is on liberal arts, social sciences, and teacher training programs.

332 _____. NEW YORK ESTABLISHES A STATE UNIVERSITY: A CASE STUDY IN THE PROCESSES OF POLICY FORMATION. Nashville, Tenn.: Vanderbilt University Press, 1955. 414 p.

Brief history of the New York state education system from 1784 to 1946 is followed by an in-depth study of the establishment of the State University of New York as conceived by the Temporary Commission on the Need for a State University. The work of the commission is examined and documented through letters, magazine articles, memoranda, and editorials.

333 _____. UNIVERSITIES: COMMONWEALTH AND AMERICAN. A COMPARATIVE STUDY. New York: Harper and Brothers, 1959. 390 p.

Looks at various aspects of university education in the United States, United Kingdom, Australia, New Zealand, Canada, India, Pakistan, and South Africa. Examines the aims, organization, and financing of higher education, finding a trend toward the more comprehensive objectives of the American type of program.

334 Carnegie Commission on Higher Education. THE CAMPUS AND THE CITY: MAXIMIZING ASSETS AND REDUCING LIABILITIES. New York: McGraw-Hill Book Co., 1972. 205 p.

Ways urban colleges and universities can improve urban education and serve urban needs. The commission assumes that all students should have the option of a college education.

335 _____. THE CAPITOL AND THE CAMPUS: STATE RESPONSIBILITY FOR POSTSECONDARY EDUCATION. New York: McGraw-Hill Book Co., 1971. 160 p.

Policy statement encourages increased state support of higher education while allowing a large amount of institutional freedom. Strong state support is seen as a counterbalance to greater federal control.

336 _____ . A DIGEST OF REPORTS OF THE CARNEGIE COMMISSION ON HIGHER EDUCATION. New York: McGraw-Hill Book Co., 1974. 399 p.

Summaries of Commission reports with an index of recommendations make up this digest.

337 _____ . DISSENT AND DISRUPTION: PROPOSALS FOR CONSIDERA- TION BY THE CAMPUS. New York: McGraw-Hill Book Co., 1971. 320 p.

Guidelines for dealing with campus disruption and violence. Supports dissent as a reflection of fundamental problems of society but condemns disruption. Urges all institutions of higher education to adopt written procedures for dealing with the problems.

338 _____ . THE FOURTH REVOLUTION: INSTRUCTIONAL TECHNOLOGY IN HIGHER EDUCATION. New York: McGraw-Hill Book Co., 1972. 112 p.

Reviews experience with instructional technologies; summarizes capabilities and costs; and sets instructional goals for 1980, 1990, and 2000. Use of the new technology to best advantage requires faculty training. A multiple technique teaching approach is desirable.

339 _____ . FROM ISOLATION TO MAINSTREAM: PROBLEMS OF THE COLLEGES FOUNDED FOR NEGROES. New York: McGraw-Hill Book Co., 1971. 84 p.

Positive report on traditionally black colleges urges their continued emergence from isolation, competition for black and white students, and qualitative drive; also urges renewed private, state, and federal aid.

340 _____ . GOVERNANCE OF HIGHER EDUCATION: SIX PRIORITY PROBLEMS. New York: McGraw-Hill Book Co., 1973. 270 p.

Recommends more effective decision making by improving governing structures and processes. If the focus of governance is to manage conflict, more specific rules and more effective adjudication are required. Identifies the issues, outlines the perimeters, and proposes solutions to governance problems.

341 _____ . INSTITUTIONAL AID: FEDERAL SUPPORT TO COLLEGES

AND UNIVERSITIES. New York: McGraw-Hill Book Co., 1972. 304 p.

Federal assistance to higher education institutions should equalize opportunities for students to attend a variety of schools. Recommends institutional aid based on the number of needy students receiving certain forms of federal aid.

342 _____. LESS TIME, MORE OPTIONS: EDUCATION BEYOND THE HIGH SCHOOL. New York: McGraw-Hill Book Co., 1971. 40 p.

Modifications of the traditional four-year degree programs would help reduce the number of dropouts and give students more periods of career reassessment.

343 _____. THE MORE EFFECTIVE USE OF RESOURCES: AN IMPERATIVE FOR HIGHER EDUCATION. New York: McGraw-Hill Book Co., 1972. 224 p.

Suggestions for reducing the cost of higher education range from cuts in Ph.D. support to cost effective analysis of teaching methods.

344 _____. NEW STUDENTS AND NEW PLACES: POLICIES FOR FUTURE GROWTH OF AMERICAN HIGHER EDUCATION. New York: McGraw-Hill Book Co., 1971. 176 p.

Assuming a reduced rate of growth of higher education in the 1980s, author finds institutional capacities almost adequate. Some new institutions will be necessary to ensure that ninety percent of all Americans are within commuting distance of some type of higher education.

345 _____. THE OPEN-DOOR COLLEGES: POLICIES FOR COMMUNITY COLLEGES. New York: McGraw-Hill Book Co., 1970. 74 p.

A community college within walking or driving distance of most people in the United States is the goal for 1980. Estimates of the number of new institutions needed are broken down by states.

346 _____. QUALITY AND EQUALITY: NEW LEVELS OF FEDERAL RESPONSIBILITY FOR HIGHER EDUCATION. New York: McGraw-Hill Book Co., 1968. 64 p.

Supplement to the 1968 report revises the predicted levels of federal aid, with accompanying changes in emphasis.

347 _____. REFORM ON CAMPUS: CHANGING STUDENTS, CHANGING ACADEMIC PROGRAMS. New York: McGraw-Hill Book Co., 1972. 160 p.

Found that attempts at individualization, diversification, and relevance in U.S. higher education had failed. Suggested academic reforms are based on data gathered by 1969 Carnegie Commission Survey of Student and Faculty Opinion.

348 Carnegie Council on Policy Studies in Higher Education. A CLASSIFICA-TION OF INSTITUTIONS OF HIGHER EDUCATION. Rev. ed. Berkeley, Calif.: 1978. 127 p.

Persons engaged in research and analysis of colleges and universities will find this revised classification using 1976 data helpful.

349 _____. FACULTY BARGAINING IN PUBLIC HIGHER EDUCATION. San Francisco: Jossey-Bass Publishers, 1977. 191 p.

Examination of faculty collective bargaining and problems it raises.

350 _____. THE FEDERAL ROLE IN POSTSECONDARY EDUCATION: UN-FINISHED BUSINESS, 1975-1980. San Francisco: Jossey-Bass Publishers, 1975. 97 p.

Describes major current federal programs, their strengths, weaknesses, and recommendations for change. Federal role is seen as promoting equality of opportunity between states and students, and a general advancement of knowledge.

351 _____. LOW OR NO TUITION: THE FEASIBILITY OF A NATIONAL POLICY FOR THE FIRST TWO YEARS OF COLLEGE. San Francisco: Jossey-Bass Publishers, 1975. 88 p.

Looks at several alternative plans to cut tuition, their rationale, cost, and impact in various states, and their effect on increased accessibility to higher education.

352 _____. MAKING AFFIRMATIVE ACTION WORK IN HIGHER EDUCA-TION: AN ANALYSIS OF INSTITUTIONAL AND FEDERAL POLICIES WITH RECOMMENDATIONS. San Francisco: Jossey-Bass Publishers, 1975. 272 p.

Status of affirmative action to overcome discrimination on campuses; reviews federal involvement in affirmative action. Assesses weaknesses in federal affirmative action programs, calling them grossly inadequate. Twenty-seven recommendations for making affirmative action effective in higher education; a major premise is that institutions themselves--not the government--should take the initiative in ending discrimination.

353 _____. PROGRESS AND PROBLEMS IN MEDICAL AND DENTAL EDU-

CATION: FEDERAL SUPPORT VERSUS FEDERAL CONTROL. San Francisco: Jossey-Bass Publishers, 1976. 178 p.

Concluded after studying post-1970 developments in medical and dental education that too many new medical schools may be opening and that--because of unequal geographic distribution and facilities--undesirable federal interference in management might result.

354 _____. SELECTIVE ADMISSIONS IN HIGHER EDUCATION. San Francisco: Jossey-Bass Publishers, 1977. 256 p.

Overview of admission policies and procedures with emphasis on the strengths and weaknesses of testing.

355 _____. THE STATES AND PRIVATE HIGHER EDUCATION: PROBLEMS AND POLICIES IN A NEW ERA. San Francisco: Jossey-Bass Publishers, 1977. 206 p.

Comprehensive look at the present and future of state support of private higher education. Finds some public support necessary but would limit the type and amount.

356 Carnegie Foundation for the Advancement of Teaching. MISSIONS OF THE COLLEGE CURRICULUM: A CONTEMPORARY REVIEW WITH SUGGESTIONS. San Francisco: Jossey-Bass Publishers, 1977. 322 p.

Presents information about existing college curricula, major curricular issues, some suggested directions, and methods for obtaining desired curriculum change.

357 _____. MORE THAN SURVIVAL: PROSPECTS FOR HIGHER EDUCATION IN A PERIOD OF UNCERTAINTY. San Francisco: Jossey-Bass Publishers, 1975. 166 p.

Predicts enrollments to the year 2000, examines how changes caused by declining enrollment and financial support will affect different types of institutions, and recommends how institutions can make significant advances despite these changes.

358 _____. THE STATES AND HIGHER EDUCATION: A PROUD PAST AND A VITAL FUTURE. San Francisco: Jossey-Bass Publishers, 1976. 94 p.

Concludes that states and higher education function well together despite certain inadequacies, discusses such policy concerns as how to maintain dynamism without growth and how to preserve private colleges, and analyzes diversity in state higher education programs.

359 Carnoy, Martin, and Levin, Henry M., eds. THE LIMITS OF EDUCATIONAL REFORM. New York: David McKay, 1976. 290 p.

Essays argue that capitalism shapes our schools and colleges to perpetuate social, political, and economic inequalities. Proposals are for cooperative schooling under democratic socialism to extend the benefits of education to those now deprived.

360 Carrick, Gertrude. CONSIDER THE DAISIES. Philadelphia: J.B. Lippincott Co., 1941. 365 p.

Novel of student life at an Eastern woman's college, a thinly disguised Vassar.

361 Carron, Malcolm. THE CONTRACT COLLEGES OF CORNELL UNIVERSITY: A CO-OPERATIVE EDUCATIONAL ENTERPRISE. Ithaca, N.Y.: Cornell University Press, 1958. 188 p.

History of four state colleges at Cornell, a distinctive private corporation which became the nearest equivalent to an all-round land-grant college and state university before the 1948 founding of the State University of New York. Describes the State Veterinary College, College of Agriculture, College of Home Economics, and School of Industrial and Labor Relations, all founded between 1894 and 1944 amid controversy.

362 Cartter, Allan M. AN ASSESSMENT OF QUALITY IN GRADUATE EDUCATION. Washington, D.C.: American Council on Education, 1966. 131 p.

Compares graduate departments in twenty-nine academic disciplines in terms of rated quality of faculty and rated effectiveness of the graduate program. Designates highest ranked departments in each field.

363 _____. Ph.D.'S AND THE ACADEMIC LABOR MARKET. Prepared for the Carnegie Commission on Higher Education. New York: McGraw-Hill Book Co., 1976. 260 p.

This attempt to predict future demand for faculty members discusses the problems of such forecasting and the effects of the job market on different groups of faculty members as well as new doctoral graduates.

364 _____, ed. ASSURING ACADEMIC PROGRESS WITHOUT GROWTH. New Directions Quarterly Sourcebook No. 6. San Francisco: Jossey-Bass Publishers, 1975.

Creative management, called the key to academic progress in a time of no growth, can be implemented by such steps as planning for changing demographic trends, using numerical model studies to improve faculty quality, and coordinating faculty composition with job market trends.

365 _____. NEW APPROACHES TO STUDENT FINANCIAL AID: REPORT OF THE PANEL ON STUDENT FINANCIAL NEED ANALYSIS. New York: College Entrance Examination Board, 1971. 133 p.

Because insufficient aid has prevented students with greatest financial need from obtaining higher education, this report recommended giving enough aid to assure that neediest students have equal access to higher educational opportunity. Also recommended more student participation, increased study of financial needs of graduate students, and a national study of student and parent attitudes toward financial aid.

366 Cary, Harold Whiting. THE UNIVERSITY OF MASSACHUSETTS: A HISTORY OF ONE HUNDRED YEARS. Amherst: University of Massachusetts, 1962. 247 p.

Centennial history of one of the first land-grant colleges, by historian who taught there for thirty years.

367 Cary, Lucian. ONE LOVELY MORON. Garden City, N.Y.: Doubleday, Doran and Co., 1930. 293 p.

Novel about a psychology professor who wins the hand of the president's daughter.

368 _____. SECOND MEETING. Garden City, N.Y.: Doubleday, Doran and Co., 1938. 279 p.

Novel about a youthful president of a midwestern college and his marriage to a divorcee.

369 Cass, James, and Birnbaum, Max. COMPARATIVE GUIDE TO AMERICAN COLLEGES FOR STUDENTS, PARENTS, AND COUNSELORS. 8th ed. New York: Harper and Row, 1977. 1,017 p.

College addresses, type of control, enrollment, admissions requirements, academic environment, faculty, student body, costs, regulations for living arrangements, and other information.

370 _____. COMPARATIVE GUIDE TO JUNIOR AND TWO-YEAR COMMUNITY COLLEGES. New York: Harper and Row, 1972. 396 p.

Information on residential and nonresidential two-year colleges: address, enrollment, controlling agency, founding date, admissions requirements, academic environment, campus life, annual costs, and a list of four-year institutions conferring associate degrees.

371 Cassidy, Harold G. KNOWLEDGE, EXPERIENCE AND ACTION: AN ESSAY ON EDUCATION. New York: Teachers College Press, 1969. 205 p.

A call for restoring wholeness to the undergraduate curriculum by an opponent of narrow specialization. He believes students and faculty should actively oppose graduate school trends at the pre-baccalaureate level.

372 Cather, Willa Sibert. THE PROFESSOR'S HOUSE. New York: Alfred A. Knopf, 1925. 283 p.

Distinguished novel about a history professor in a Michigan state university whose book prize money goes into a new house desired by his wife. The architectural symbolism is depicted in his preference for the old house where he was creatively and happily involved.

373 Cazier, Stanford Orson. STUDENT DISCIPLINE SYSTEMS IN HIGHER EDUCATION. Higher Education Research Report No. 7. Washington, D.C.: American Association for Higher Education, 1973. 47 p.

Literature and commentary about the major events and developments since 1961 in student discipline.

374 Centra, John A. WOMEN, MEN, AND THE DOCTORATE. Princeton, N.J.: Educational Testing Service, 1974. 79 p.

Compares responses by men and women holding doctorates granted in 1950, 1960, and 1968 to a questionnaire about their jobs, activities, interests, income, marriage, family life, and views on women's rights.

375 _____, ed. RENEWING AND EVALUATING TEACHING. New Directions for Higher Education No. 17. San Francisco: Jossey-Bass Publishers, 1977. 110 p.

Uses research findings and experience at many higher education institutions to illustrate current techniques and desirable approaches toward evaluating and improving teaching quality.

376 Chalk, Ocania. BLACK COLLEGE SPORT. New York: Dodd, Mead and Co., 1976. 376 p.

Documented history of black athletes from the beginning of intercollegiate competition until 1941. Although some white colleges had black athletes, the most remarkable athletic accomplishments were at poorly funded primarily black institutions. Appendix on black participants in the Olympic Games.

377 Chalmers, Gordon Keith. THE REPUBLIC AND THE PERSON: A DISCUSSION OF NECESSITIES IN MODERN AMERICAN EDUCATION. Chicago: Henry Regnery Co., 1952. 270 p.

Author shares his experiences as a college teacher and administrator to advance his stance in favor of liberal education.

378 Chambers, Frederick. BLACK HIGHER EDUCATION IN THE UNITED STATES: A SELECTED BIBLIOGRAPHY ON NEGRO HIGHER EDUCATION AND HISTORICALLY BLACK COLLEGES AND UNIVERSITIES. Westport, Conn.: Greenwood Press, 1978. 268 p.

Includes theses, dissertations, journal articles, and books about the higher education of blacks since the Civil War.

379 Chambers, Merritt Madison. ABOVE HIGH SCHOOL. Danville, Ill.: Interstate Printers and Publishers, 1970. 61 p.

Presents major trends (especially methods of financing) which affect community colleges and their relations to state governments.

380 _____. THE CAMPUS AND THE PEOPLE: ORGANIZATION, SUPPORT AND CONTROL OF HIGHER EDUCATION IN THE UNITED STATES IN THE NINETEEN SIXTIES. Danville, Ill.: Interstate Printers and Publishers, 1960. 75 p.

Believing that everyone should be educated to the limit of his educational capacity, Chambers calls for greatly expanding junior colleges, stresses graduate education at universities, keeping tuition low, and generous funding of higher education by states and the federal government.

381 _____. THE COLLEGES AND THE COURTS: THE DEVELOPING LAW OF THE STUDENT AND THE COLLEGE. Danville, Ill.: Interstate Printers and Publishers, 1972. 316 p.

Study of over 300 state and federal court cases involving college students. Topics include torts against students, unreasonable searches and seizures, confidentiality, and freedom of speech and assembly. Chambers concludes that the trend is toward more enlightened concepts of the place of students in colleges.

382 _____. THE COLLEGES AND THE COURTS: FACULTY AND STAFF BEFORE THE BENCH. Danville, Ill.: Interstate Printers and Publishers, 1973. 260 p.

Examines court cases about such faculty-related issues as tenure, salaries, leaves of absence, promotion, and dismissal, and the responsibilities of administrators. Makes general interpretations despite differences in state laws.

383 _____. FINANCING HIGHER EDUCATION. Washington, D.C.: Center for Applied Research in Education, 1963. 117 p.

A readable general introduction to issues of higher education finance.

384 _____. HIGHER EDUCATION: WHO PAYS? WHO GAINS? Danville, Ill.: Interstate Printers and Publishers, 1968. 302 p.

Topics include capital improvements, annual operations, accounting and management, and the principal sources of income for public and private colleges and universities.

385 _____. HIGHER EDUCATION AND STATE GOVERNMENTS, 1970-1975. Danville, Ill.: Interstate Printers and Publishers, 1974. 290 p.

Sequel to HIGHER EDUCATION IN THE FIFTY STATES (below); presents financial information about higher education for the fiscal years 1971-74, including the amount of state tax funds appropriated for annual operating expenses of each institution of higher education, statistics of population and population growth, comparative rates of gain in state appropriations, and the state tax investment per citizen for higher education. Also comments on the degrees of state control of higher education.

386 _____. HIGHER EDUCATION IN THE FIFTY STATES. Danville, Ill.: Interstate Printers and Publishers, 1970. 452 p.

Vignettes of higher education in each of the fifty states; discusses governance and financial support and estimates success. Author is skeptical of tightly controlled systems of higher education.

387 _____. KEEP HIGHER EDUCATION MOVING. Danville, Ill.: Interstate Printers and Publishers, 1976. 348 p.

Reviews developments in higher education finance, explains implications of court decisions affecting the legal standing of students and faculty in higher education, and expresses the author's strong faith in the value of higher education.

388 _____. A RECORD OF PROGRESS: FOUR YEARS OF STATE TAX SUPPORT OF HIGHER EDUCATION, 1972-73 THROUGH 1975-76. Danville, Ill.: Interstate Printers and Publishers, 1976. 68 p.

One in a series of reports on how much money each state has appropriated during 1972 to 1976, for the operating expenses of institutions of higher education.

389 _____. VOLUNTARY STATEWIDE COORDINATION IN PUBLIC HIGHER EDUCATION. Ann Arbor: Office of Special Publications, University of Michigan, 1961. 83 p.

A proponent of voluntary coordination of higher education,

author says such coordination is practical because, as with local school boards, unanimous agreement is the usual outcome of fact finding and discussion. He believes university and college heads can work out among themselves arrangements necessary for voluntary coordination of higher education.

390 Champagne, Marion Mira Grosberg. THE CAULIFLOWER HEART. New York: Dial Press, 1944. 389 p.

Novel about students at Smith College during the 1930s.

391 Change Magazine. HOW TO SUCCEED AS A NEW TEACHER: A HANDBOOK FOR TEACHING ASSISTANTS. New Rochelle, N.Y.: 1978. 63 p.

Tips for the teaching assistant on teaching, evaluation, faculty and student relations, and administrative details.

392 _____. THE THIRD CENTURY: TWENTY-SIX PROMINENT AMERICANS SPECULATE ON THE EDUCATIONAL FUTURE. New Rochelle, N.Y.: 1977. 196 p.

Twenty-six higher education leaders describe the future importance of lifelong learning, predict increasing educational egalitarianism, and express some fear of growing federal influence.

393 Chauncey, Henry, and Dobbin, John E. TESTING: ITS PLACE IN EDUCATION TODAY. New York: Harper and Row, 1964. 123 p.

The purpose is to shape public attitudes about testing and to give a balanced overview of the development and use of tests, whether for teaching aids, selection and admission, or guidance.

394 Cheit, Earl Frank. THE NEW DEPRESSION IN HIGHER EDUCATION-- TWO YEARS LATER. A Report by the Carnegie Commission on Higher Education. New York: McGraw-Hill Book Co., 1973. 84 p.

Forty-one colleges reacted to their financial condition. Two years earlier they had been classified as "in financial difficulty," "headed for trouble," or "not in trouble." Author described each group's financial operation, analyzed the cost factors and income requirements for those institutions in financial trouble, and presented recommendations for necessary policy changes.

395 _____. THE USEFUL ARTS AND THE LIBERAL TRADITION. New York: McGraw-Hill Book Co., 1975. 166 p.

A plea for greater collaboration between liberal arts and such professional schools as agriculture, engineering, business administration, and forestry.

396 Cheydleur, Frederic D. CRITERIA OF EFFECTIVE TEACHING OF BASIC
FRENCH COURSES AT THE UNIVERSITY OF WISCONSIN. Madison:
Bureau of Guidance and Records, University of Wisconsin, 1945. 61 p.

> Results of twenty-seven years of teaching and testing in the
> University of Wisconsin's French department, using author's
> objective rating of teaching effectiveness. Conclusions are
> of general interest to college modern language teachers.

397 Cheyney, Edward Potts. HISTORY OF THE UNIVERSITY OF PENNSYL-
VANIA: 1740-1940. Philadelphia: University of Pennsylvania Press,
1940. Reprint. New York: Arno Press, 1977. 461 p.

> A bicentennial history of the University of Pennsylvania. Takes
> a broad view of American higher education (such aspects as
> the quest by early colleges for corporate neutrality, the im-
> pact of war on campuses, the expansion of academic services,
> and the problem of institutional growth).

398 Chicago. University. THE IDEA AND PRACTICE OF GENERAL EDUCA-
TION: AN ACCOUNT OF THE COLLEGE OF THE UNIVERSITY OF
CHICAGO. Chicago: University of Chicago Press, 1950. 333 p.

> How the undergraduate college of the University of Chicago
> freed itself from research and graduate-dominated education
> to pursue a program of general education under President Robert
> Maynard Hutchins. Essays on the philosophy of general educa-
> tion; the struggle to develop the program; the content and
> educational significance of the humanities, social sciences,
> natural sciences, mathematics, writing, and languages; and
> on teaching methods, student performance, and advising.

399 Chickering, Arthur W. COMMUTING VERSUS RESIDENT STUDENTS:
OVERCOMING EDUCATIONAL INEQUITIES OF LIVING OFF CAMPUS.
San Francisco: Jossey-Bass Publishers, 1974. 150 p.

> Evidence that commuting students do not learn as much, devel-
> op as fast, or last as long as residential college students.
> Suggests ways these differences can be overcome by some resi-
> dential requirement and new approaches to admissions, orien-
> tation, curriculum, and teaching.

400 _____. EDUCATION AND IDENTITY. San Francisco: Jossey-Bass
Publishers, 1969. 367 p.

> The theme in this award-winning book is that institutional
> operations should fit the needs and development of students.
> Has a realistic plan of action affecting the curriculum, teach-
> ing, living arrangements; and relationships with faculty, ad-
> ministration, and other students.

401 Childers, James Saxon. GOD SAVE THE DUKE. New York: D. Appleton and Co., 1933. 303 p.

> Novel about an Oxford graduate who becomes an English instructor at a southern U.S. university and eventually wins the respect of students.

402 Chorafas, Dimitrius N. THE KNOWLEDGE REVOLUTION: AN ANALYSIS OF THE INTERNATIONAL BRAIN MARKET. New York: McGraw-Hill Book Co., 1968. 142 p.

> Greater professional opportunities and financial reward primarily account for the brain drain of highly trained scientists and technologists from economically deprived European countries to the United States.

403 Christensen, Ernest Martin. ANNOTATED BIBLIOGRAPHY OF THE COLLEGE UNION. Ithaca, N.Y.: Cornell University, Association of College Unions--International, 1967. 268 p.

> Over 1,200 annotated articles and books published since 1950 about all phases of student union operations.

404 Christenson, Gordon A., ed. THE FUTURE OF THE UNIVERSITY: A REPORT TO THE PEOPLE. Norman: University of Oklahoma Press, 1969. 292 p.

> Moderate recommendations call for consulting students about university policy and other procedures.

405 Clapp, Margaret, ed. THE MODERN UNIVERSITY. Ithaca, N.Y.: Cornell University Press, 1950. 115 p.

> Historical essay tracing nineteenth-century influences on twentieth-century American university progress and problems.

406 Clapp, Verner W. THE FUTURE OF THE RESEARCH LIBRARY. Urbana: University of Illinois Press, 1964. 114 p.

> Author, thirty-three years a Library of Congress staff member, gave these Windsor Lectures in Librarianship in 1963 at the University of Illinois. Discusses the problems of research libraries, especially large general university libraries. Extensive appendix gives precise details about how to solve the problems discussed.

407 Clark, Burton R. THE DISTINCTIVE COLLEGE: ANTIOCH, REED, AND SWARTHMORE. Chicago: Aldine Publishing Co., 1970. 280 p.

> Case studies of Antioch, Reed, and Swarthmore as examples of distinctive colleges are examined, using data gathered before the mid-1960s. Cites factors that contribute to a college's

distinctiveness. The critical ingredient: a strong organizational saga or legend that captures the allegiance of staff and creates unifying coherence among students. A charismatic leader also characterized the first stage in forming the legend.

408 _____. THE OPEN DOOR COLLEGE: A CASE STUDY. Carnegie Series in American Education. New York: McGraw-Hill Book Co., 1960. 207 p.

Sociological examination of San Jose Junior College, California, administered by the local school district and oriented toward secondary education. The author's evaluation of the problems and potential of junior colleges makes this a landmark study. He concludes that the educational role of junior colleges is blurred by the many demands placed upon them.

409 Clark, Ellery Harding. DAUGHTERS OF EVE. Philadelphia: Dorrance and Co., 1924. 287 p.

Novel which reproduces the atmosphere of college student life in Boston and Cambridge. Author is a graduate of Harvard College.

410 Clark, Kenneth B., and Plotkin, Lawrence. THE NEGRO STUDENT AT INTEGRATED COLLEGES. New York: National Scholarship Service Fund for Negro Students, 1963. 59 p.

Detailed information about black students' lives and documentary evidence of their academic success on predominantly white campuses.

411 Clark, Thomas D. INDIANA UNIVERSITY: MIDWESTERN PIONEER. Vol. I: THE EARLY YEARS. Vol. II: IN MID-PASSAGE. Bloomington: Indiana University Press, 1970, 1973. 371 p., 429 p.

History of Indiana University. Volume one covers the 1820s to 1902; volume two ends with the self-study of 1938 and the installation of President Wells.

412 Clary, William W. THE CLAREMONT COLLEGES. A HISTORY OF THE DEVELOPMENT OF THE CLAREMONT GROUP PLAN. Claremont, Calif.: Claremont University Center, 1970. 314 p.

History of the unique cluster college idea at Claremont, California. Since the idea's inception by Pomona College in 1925, cooperation has increased among the individual schools which became Claremont University Center and Graduate School and the affiliated Claremont Colleges. Their cooperation was boosted by the 1965 Ford Foundation challenge grant; it required them to mount a cooperative fundraising campaign.

Author, who studied at Pomona, later served as a trustee and in other related roles.

413 Coffman, Lotus D. THE STATE UNIVERSITY: ITS WORK AND PROBLEMS. Minneapolis: University of Minnesota Press, 1934. 277 p.

Addresses given during the first twelve years of author's presidency at Minnesota; theme is that the state university is not only a company of scholars but is also an instrument for the advancement of democracy.

414 Cohen, Arthur A., ed. HUMANISTIC EDUCATION AND WESTERN CIVILIZATION: ESSAYS FOR ROBERT M. HUTCHINS. New York: Holt, Rinehart and Winston, 1964. 250 p.

Fifteen essays to honor the sixty-fifth birthday of Robert M. Hutchins. "Humanistic" is identified with moral education. Several contributors are pessimistic about prospects for general education courses, as is Champion Ward in his account of the failure of Chicago's three-year sequences in the humanities, social sciences, and natural sciences.

415 Cohen, Arthur M., and Brawer, Florence B. CONFRONTING IDENTITY: THE COMMUNITY COLLEGE INSTRUCTOR. Englewood Cliffs, N.J.: Prentice-Hall, 1972. 257 p.

Focuses on instructors at two-year colleges (a group neglected in higher education research). Authors assert that instructors hold the key to the identity of these institutions. Theme is that instructors need greater autonomy and responsibility for setting and policing standards.

416 _____. THE TWO-YEAR COLLEGE INSTRUCTOR TODAY. New York: Praeger Publishers, 1977. 190 p.

Two-year college instructors: their growing success, differences between those teaching part-time and full-time, their status, and possible strategies for advancing their career goals.

417 Cohen, Arthur M., et al. COLLEGE RESPONSES TO COMMUNITY DEMANDS: THE COMMUNITY COLLEGE IN CHALLENGING TIMES. San Francisco: Jossey-Bass Publishers, 1975. 190 p.

In discussing two-year college education, the authors look at such topics as growing state influence, collective bargaining, and affirmative action. They raise these questions: How active should the college be in the community? What are the measures for program success? What should be the relationship between the college and other community organizations? Final section deals with the two-year college faculty.

418 _____. A CONSTANT VARIABLE: NEW PERSPECTIVES ON THE COM-
MUNITY COLLEGE. San Francisco: Jossey-Bass Publishers, 1971. 238 p.

> Using the best evidence available in this collection of research
> stored in the ERIC Clearinghouse for Junior Colleges, Univer-
> sity of California at Los Angeles, the authors have examined
> many questions about two-year colleges.

419 Cohen, I. Bernard, and Watson, Fletcher G., eds. GENERAL EDUCA-
TION IN SCIENCE. Cambridge, Mass.: Harvard University Press, 1952.
217 p.

> Describes a general science program intended to inform non-
> scientists about elementary scientific techniques and concepts.

420 Cohen, Joseph W., ed. THE SUPERIOR STUDENT IN AMERICAN HIGH-
ER EDUCATION. Carnegie Series in American Education. New York:
McGraw-Hill Book Co., 1966. 299 p.

> The great variety of attempts of higher education to challenge
> all students to use all their intellectual capacity is presented
> here by author, who in 1930 helped develop the honors pro-
> gram, University of Colorado. Tells of the swing from depen-
> dence to independence, from course requirements to freedom
> of electives, and from added variety to reduction of numbers
> of courses. Major requirement for challenging superior stu-
> dents is a competent faculty and a well-equipped library.

421 Cohen, Michael D., and March, James G. LEADERSHIP AND AMBI-
GUITY: THE AMERICAN COLLEGE PRESIDENT. New York: McGraw-
Hill Book Co., 1974. 270 p.

> Surveyed practices at forty-two colleges and universities. Rec-
> ommended that functions of management decision making be
> reexamined, traditional views of planning be modified, methods
> of evaluation and procedures for social accountability be re-
> considered, and playfulness be accepted in social organizations.

422 Cohen, Morris R. A DREAMER'S JOURNEY: THE AUTOBIOGRAPHY OF
DR. MORRIS RAPHAEL COHEN. Boston: Beacon Press, 1949. 318 p.

> Autobiography conveys the intellectual atmosphere at New
> York's City College, where author (1880-1947) taught philos-
> ophy; his chapter on college teaching depicts the integrity
> which characterized his career.

423 Cohen, Robert D., and Jody, Ruth. FRESHMAN SEMINAR: A NEW
ORIENTATION. Boulder, Colo.: Westview Press, 1978. 142 p.

> Guidebook for a one-semester freshman orientation course
> developed and taught at Hunter College by the authors; in-

cludes curriculum design, teaching methods, and materials.
Presents questions and problems common to freshmen and suggests how to cope with them in the seminar.

424   Cole, Arthur C. A HUNDRED YEARS OF MOUNT HOLYOKE COL-
LEGE: THE EVOLUTION OF AN EDUCATIONAL IDEAL. New Haven,
Conn.: Yale University Press, 1940. 426 p.

Centennial history of Mount Holyoke recounts its founding in
1837. Includes biographical essays about founder Mary Lyon
(1797-1849) and later president Mary E. Woolley (1863-1947);
and relates Mount Holyoke developments to those at Amherst,
Barnard, Bryn Mawr, Dartmouth, Harvard, and other eastern
elite institutions. The atmosphere of student life is described,
and the influence of Mount Holyoke on midwestern and western
institutions is shown.

425   Cole, Charles C., Jr. ENCOURAGING SCIENTIFIC TALENT. New
York: College Entrance Examination Board, 1957. 259 p.

First national study to examine access to higher education.
Asked: How many talented young people, particularly those
gifted in science, do not go to college? How can more of
them be attracted to college? Recommended solutions were
to offer 100,000 new scholarships for the financially needy;
to improve teaching; increase federal, state, and local aid
to schools; and increase efforts to attract women to science.

426   Cole, Fred. INTERNATIONAL RELATIONS IN INSTITUTIONS OF HIGH-
ER EDUCATION IN THE SOUTH. Washington, D.C.: American Council
on Education, 1958. 169 p.

Study of the attitudes and practices in teaching about international relations in the South; found that only a few institutions offered programs to train specialists. Author suggested
ways to improve this situation.

427   Cole, Luella. THE BACKGROUND FOR COLLEGE TEACHING. New
York: Farrar and Rinehart, 1940. 616 p.

A comprehensive examination of problems faced by college
teachers.

428   Cole, Stewart G. LIBERAL EDUCATION IN A DEMOCRACY: A CHAR-
TER FOR THE AMERICAN COLLEGE. New York: Harper and Brothers,
1940. 309 p.

The search for a liberal college education in modern U.S.
democracy is crucial to overcome the lessened educational influence which once came from family, church, neighborhood,
region, and various other primary groups.

429 COLLEGE ADMISSIONS DATA SERVICE, 1979. 2 vols. Concord, Mass.: Orchard House, 1979.

> Detailed guide contains more information about each institution than do other well-known reference books used to help students, parents, and counselors through the maze of U.S. higher education institutions.

430 College Entrance Examination Board. THE CHALLENGE OF CURRICULAR CHANGE. New York: 1966. 181 p.

> Reflecting the 1955-65 curricular reforms, these papers by educators active in curricular change discuss strengths and weaknesses at the secondary and higher education levels.

431 _____. CHANGING PATTERNS FOR UNDERGRADUATE EDUCATION. New York: 1972. 45 p.

> Conference to consider how a Carnegie Commission recommendation for a three-year bachelor's degree program could be put into effect.

432 _____. COLLEGE ADMISSIONS POLICIES FOR THE 1970S. New York: 1968. 175 p.

> Papers by nationally known authorities on key issues of interest to a conference of eighty professional admissions officers.

433 _____. COLLEGE ENTRANCE GUIDE FOR AMERICAN STUDENTS OVERSEAS. New York: 1976. 95 p.

> Replaces GETTING INTO COLLEGE IN THE UNITED STATES; has concise information on financial aid, admissions requirements, how to establish residency requirements, and other helpful facts.

434 _____. THE COLLEGE HANDBOOK INDEX OF MAJORS. New York: 1977. 608 p.

> Lists over 350 major fields of study and shows state by state which colleges offer them and at what degree level.

435 _____. CRISIS IN STUDENT AID. Atlanta: Southern Regional Office, College Entrance Examination Board, 1970. 53 p.

> Conference papers with divergent views on ways states can bridge gap between higher education costs and students' financial resources.

436 _____. THE ECONOMICS OF HIGHER EDUCATION. New York: 1967. 89 p.

Conference papers on student financial aid, pricing problems, government role in financing, and alternative methods of educational financing.

437 _____. EFFECTS OF COACHING ON SCHOLASTIC APTITUDE TEST SCORES. New York: 1968. 28 p.

Concludes that coaching does not significantly improve Scholastic Aptitude Test scores, that changes are too small to affect admission.

438 _____. ENTERING HIGHER EDUCATION IN THE UNITED STATES: A GUIDE FOR STUDENTS FROM OTHER COUNTRIES. New York: 1977. 59 p.

Discusses problems foreign students encounter in entering U.S. colleges, including opportunities for study, steps in applying for admission, and where to register for Test of English as a Foreign Language.

439 _____. FINANCING EQUAL OPPORTUNITY IN HIGHER EDUCATION. New York: 1970. 44 p.

Conference of minority representatives urged federal lobbying by the National Association of Student Aid Administrators to achieve equal higher educational opportunity for minority and low income students.

440 _____. THE FOREIGN STUDENT IN THE UNITED STATES COMMUNITY AND JUNIOR COLLEGES. Princeton, N.J.: 1978. 96 p.

Estimates foreign student enrollment and lists policy guidelines for their admission and education.

441 _____. FROM HIGH SCHOOL TO COLLEGE: READINGS FOR COUNSELORS. New York: 1965. 86 p.

Readings for school counselors on advising students about the variety of higher education institutions, school-college transition, personality growth in college, and academic and non-academic factors in college success.

442 _____. INTERPRETIVE MANUAL FOR COUNSELORS, ADMINISTRATORS, AND FACULTY, 1969-1970. New York: 1969. 108 p.

Interpretive manual showing how students are placed in first college mathematics and English courses.

443 _____. MANUAL OF FRESHMAN CLASS PROFILES. Princeton, N.J.: 1961. Unpaged.

Statistical and other information on freshmen and the 128 colleges they attended; to aid counselors, teachers, and administrators.

444 _____. MIDDLE-INCOME STUDENTS: A NEW TARGET FOR FEDERAL AID? New York: 1978. 35 p.

Evaluates issues raised in spring 1978 congressional debate on financial aid to middle income college students.

445 _____. REPORT OF THE COMMISSION ON TESTS. 2 vols. New York: 1970. 118 p., 194 p.

Findings of a group of distinguished educators asked to assess operation of the College Board are contained in volume one, with suggested guidelines for the board's future development. A major suggestion was that the board devote more services to students and continue to serve institutions. Volume two contains papers about most issues on which the commission took a stand.

446 _____. RESEARCH IN HIGHER EDUCATION: GUIDE TO INSTITUTIONAL DECISIONS. New York: 1965. 66 p.

Papers about the nature and usefulness of research on higher education.

447 _____. THE SEARCH FOR TALENT. New York: 1960. 131 p.

Seventh Annual Admission Colloquium papers on such topics as identification of talented students, development of talent, and barriers to developing talent.

448 _____. STUDENT FINANCIAL AID AND NATIONAL PURPOSE. New York: 1962. 103 p.

Report on the first colloquium on financial aid; agreed that a comprehensive national student aid program was needed to remove all economic barriers to higher education.

449 _____. TESTS AND SERVICES: COLLEGE-LEVEL EXAMINATION PROGRAM. New York: 1970. 15 p.

How the College-Level Examination Program is used to award credit for knowledge acquired through self-study, industrial programs, military training, or other means.

450 College Entrance Examination Board. Colloquium on Barriers to Higher Education, Racine, Wisconsin, 1970. BARRIERS TO HIGHER EDUCATION. Princeton, N.J.: 1971. 151 p.

Questions of access to higher education, particularly among minorities and the poor, were explored at a 1970 conference. Topics include uses and abuses of standardized tests, test validity for the disadvantaged, new ways of evaluation for admission, and new programs appropriate to the disadvantaged student.

451 College of the City of New York. THE INAUGURATION OF HARRY NOBLE WRIGHT. New York: 1943. 54 p.

Addresses given at the inauguration of what is now City University of New York's sixth president, including those of its alumnus Justice Felix Frankfurter and of President Wright.

452 College Opportunities. FINANCIAL AID FOR UNDERGRADUATE STUDENTS 1970-71. Cincinnati, Ohio: 1970. 1,500 p.

Reference volume, conveniently arranged for use by students, parents, and counselors; has general information and detailed financial aid data on over 1,800 accredited institutions: scholarships and loans available; numbers, types, amounts, and restrictions of awards; general application procedures; and other facts.

453 College Student Personnel Institute. STUDENT HOUSING IN COLLEGES AND UNIVERSITIES: ABSTRACTS OF THE LITERATURE 1961-1966. Claremont, Calif.: 1966. 82 p.

Summaries of multidisciplinary literature on U.S. college housing.

454 Collins, Charles C. COLLEGE ORIENTATION: EDUCATION FOR RELEVANCE. Boston: Holbrook Press, 1969. 275 p.

Designed for small groups of beginning college students; has material on many educational issues, from alienation to values; useful for freshman orientation.

455 Collins, V. Lansing. PRINCETON PAST AND PRESENT. Princeton, N.J.: Princeton University Press, 1945. 154 p.

Guidebook and historical sketch of the university town, with photographs and maps.

456 Columbia University. A HISTORY OF COLUMBIA COLLEGE ON MORNINGSIDE. New York: Columbia University Press, 1954. 284 p.

History of Columbia College, part of Columbia University's bicentennial history series; begins with its move to Morningside Heights in 1897; has historical essays by Columbia faculty members: Irwin Edman, Lionel Trilling, Justus Buchler,

Charles W. Everett, Fon W. Boardman, Jack N. Arbolino, and Gene R. Hawes.

457 _____. A HISTORY OF THE FACULTY OF PHILOSOPHY, COLUMBIA UNIVERSITY. New York: Columbia University Press, 1957. 308 p.

Bicentennial history of Columbia University's graduate school (called "faculty of philosophy"). Includes histories, by separate contributors, of departments of English and comparative literature, philosophy, religion, general and comparative linguistics, Greek and Latin, Semitic languages, Romance languages, Slavic languages, Germanic languages, Chinese and Japanese, fine arts, archaeology, and music.

458 _____. THE RISE OF A UNIVERSITY. Vol. 1: THE LATER DAYS OF OLD COLUMBIA COLLEGE. FROM THE ANNUAL REPORTS OF FREDERICK A.P. BARNARD, PRESIDENT OF COLUMBIA COLLEGE, 1864-1889. Edited by William F. Russell. New York: 1937. 415 p. Vol 2: THE UNIVERSITY IN ACTION: FROM THE ANNUAL REPORTS, 1902-1935, OF NICHOLAS MURRAY BUTLER, PRESIDENT OF COLUMBIA UNIVERSITY. Edited by Edward C. Elliott. New York: 1937, 515 p.

Vol. 1: President Barnard's annual reports cover: (1) problems of college administration, (2) education of women, (3) development of professional education, (4) development of a university, and (5) free lectures. Vol. 2: President Butler's annual reports are on: (1) the university and society, (2) problems of American life and educational policy, (3) collegiate education, (4) postgraduate and professional education, (5) the faculty and problems of instruction, and (6) university administration.

459 Columbia University. American Assembly. GOALS FOR AMERICANS: THE REPORT OF THE PRESIDENT'S COMMISSION ON NATIONAL GOALS. Englewood Cliffs, N.J.: Prentice-Hall, 1960. 372 p.

The commission's goals for higher education were: (1) development of two-year colleges within commuting distance of most high school graduates, (2) doubling of graduate school capacity, and (3) emphasis on adult education and lifelong learning.

460 Colvard, Richard, and Bennett, A.M. PATTERNS OF CONCENTRATION IN LARGE FOUNDATIONS' GRANTS TO U.S. COLLEGES AND UNIVERSITIES. Iowa City: American College Testing Program, 1974. 30 p.

Analyzed most grants made for all purposes by 276 foundations in 1963, 1966, 1969, and 1970. Found that in each year at least 46 percent of the grants and 75 percent of the actual funds involved came from no more than twenty-five foundations.

461 Colvert, Clyde C. THE PUBLIC JUNIOR COLLEGE CURRICULUM: AN ANALYSIS. University: Louisiana State University Press, 1939. 177 p.

Analyzed catalogs of 195 of the 229 publicly controlled junior colleges reported to exist in 1937. Course offerings are summarized. One chapter deals with semiprofessional courses in twenty general fields; another chapter on curriculum trends quotes leaders in the junior college movement.

462 Commager, Henry Steele. THE AMERICAN MIND: AN INTERPRETATION OF AMERICAN THOUGHT AND CHARACTER SINCE THE 1880S. New Haven, Conn.: Yale University Press, 1950. 476 p.

Ideas of many university professors are placed alongside those of novelists, journalists, artists, and other intellectuals in this analysis of American thought between the 1880s and 1940s.

463 Commission on Academic Tenure in Higher Education. FACULTY TENURE: A REPORT AND RECOMMENDATIONS. San Francisco: Jossey-Bass Publishers, 1973. 276 p.

Ford Foundation-financed report about the history and future prospects of academic tenure, its legal dimensions, and faculty unionism. Extensive informative appendices.

464 Commission on Financing Higher Education. NATURE AND NEEDS OF HIGHER EDUCATION: THE REPORT OF THE COMMISSION ON FINANCING HIGHER EDUCATION. New York: Columbia University Press, 1952. 191 p.

Contains compact data about higher education's economic problems, discusses various sources of funding, and give hints about securing and spending funds. Warns liberal arts colleges against expansion; argues that higher education must have more money to meet national needs.

465 Commission on Medical Education. FINAL REPORT OF THE COMMISSION ON MEDICAL EDUCATION. New York: 1932. 560 p.

First such major report since the landmark monograph on medical education by Abraham Flexner in 1910. In 1925 this commission of seventeen educators, ten of whom had M.D. degrees, was named by the Association of Medical Colleges, to study medical education, general university education, and ways of adapting medical education to the shifting needs of society. Detailed data about findings and conclusions; extensive appendix.

466   Commission on Non-Traditional Study. DIVERSITY BY DESIGN. San
      Francisco: Jossey-Bass Publishers, 1973. 178 p.

      Comprehensive work about such programs as lifelong learning,
      external degrees, and college and community cooperation,
      with recommendations about awarding credit for nontraditional
      study programs, accrediting institutions that offer them, and
      other related concerns.

467   Committee for Economic Development. Research and Policy Committee.
      THE MANAGEMENT AND FINANCING OF COLLEGES: A STATEMENT
      ON NATIONAL POLICY. New York: 1973. 95 p.

      Report of a 200-member committee; higher education manage-
      ment and finance ideas dominate.

468   Committee on High School-College Relations of the Ohio College Associa-
      tion. TO COLLEGE IN OHIO. Rev. ed. Wooster, Ohio: 1944.
      167 p.

      Revision of 1939 edition provides information on member col-
      leges useful for counselors and prospective students.

469   Committee on Government and Higher Education. THE EFFICIENCY OF
      FREEDOM. Baltimore, Md.: Johns Hopkins University Press, 1959. 44 p.

      Report calls for state higher education institutions to have fis-
      cal autonomy. Thirty specific recommendations to institutions,
      state legislatures, and governors, two of which are that legis-
      latures should repeal statutes pertaining to fiscal controls of
      higher education which impede effective management of the
      institution by its governing board and officers, and that colleges
      and universities should not be required to use centralized state
      purchasing.

470   Committee on Television of the American Council on Education and the
      State University of Iowa. TEACHING BY CLOSED-CIRCUIT TELEVISION.
      Washington, D.C.: American Council on Education, 1956. 66 p.

      Reports on technical and other aspects of closed-circuit tele-
      vision teaching at the University of Iowa, Pennsylvania State
      University, New York University, and Stephens College.

471   Committee on the College and World Affairs. THE COLLEGE AND WORLD
      AFFAIRS. New York: 1964. 74 p.

      Recommendations to four-year colleges for a program to deepen
      and extend in undergraduate education the understanding of
      non-Western societies and cultures.

472   Committee on the College Student, Group for the Advancement of Psy-

chiatry. SEX AND THE COLLEGE STUDENT: A DEVELOPMENTAL PERSPECTIVE ON SEXUAL ISSUES ON THE CAMPUS. New York: Atheneum Publishers, 1966. 178 p.

After discussing the development and integration of sexuality in human personality, the committee relates most of the material to campus life: sexual issues on campus; college policy, campus regulations, and sexual conduct; and guidelines for college policy toward sexuality.

473 Committee on the Student in Higher Education. THE STUDENT IN HIGHER EDUCATION. New Haven, Conn.: Hazen Foundation, 1968. 66 p.

Calls for a reversal of the trend in higher education toward giantism and dehumanization; recommends using the freshman year primarily for orientation, expecting faculty commitment to the emotional development of students, and democratizing the rulemaking process on campus.

474 Community College Planning Center. COMMUNITY COLLEGES IN URBAN SETTINGS. Stanford, Calif.: Stanford University School of Education, 1964. 20 p.

Architectural, economic, educational, and sociological advice by planners who support locating new community colleges in inner-city depressed areas.

475 Conable, Charlotte Williams. WOMEN AT CORNELL: THE MYTH OF EQUAL EDUCATION. Ithaca, N.Y.: Cornell University Press, 1977. 211 p.

Chartered in 1865 to be coeducational; the first woman was admitted in 1870. Women were severely limited by dormitory space and steered away from academic and professional courses by sexist values. Turning point came with a 1969 conference at which Cornell women influenced the university to take a national lead in offering equal opportunity to women.

476 Conant, James Bryant. THE CITADEL OF LEARNING. New Haven, Conn.: Yale University Press, 1956. Reprint. Westport, Conn.: Greenwood Press, 1977. 79 p.

Discusses changes in American higher education, particularly in undergraduate history, language study, and geography instruction. These changes and others will result from East-West tensions and the West's belief in free inquiry. He foresees conflict between quality and quantity in American education as budget pressures increase.

477 _____. THE EDUCATION OF AMERICAN TEACHERS. Carnegie Series

in American Education. New York: McGraw-Hill Book Co., 1963. 275 p.

Important report of educator-statesman Conant's two-year intensive study of U.S. teacher education programs. He says that colleges and universities should preempt responsibility for training teachers, that teachers should be recruited from the top thirty percent of students, should receive a rigorous general education, and should learn teaching methods as part of a student teaching program rather than in methodology classes.

478   . SHAPING EDUCATIONAL POLICY. Carnegie Series in American Education. New York: McGraw-Hill Book Co., 1964. 139 p.

Plea for national standards and guidelines for education. Cites as ineffectual the leadership of such groups as professional organizations, regional accrediting associations, and state education systems in guiding policy decisions. Conant, believing an educated citizenry to be the vital resource of a free society, considers necessary a greatly increased financial expenditure, especially in higher education. This report led to the Education Commission of the States.

479   . THOMAS JEFFERSON AND THE DEVELOPMENT OF AMERICAN PUBLIC EDUCATION. Berkeley: University of California Press, 1962. 164 p.

Conant's Jefferson Memorial Lecture examined Jefferson's ideas about education. He cited the irony that Jefferson's proposal for free primary education, rejected by Virginia landowners, was accepted later by the urban society he distrusted. Not until our own time has the selective process Jefferson envisioned in higher education, loathed by egalitarian Americans, met some acceptance, primarily because of the international challenge in science and technology.

480 Conant, Ralph W. THE PROSPECT FOR REVOLUTION: A STUDY OF RIOTS, CIVIL DISOBEDIENCE, AND INSURRECTION IN CONTEMPORARY AMERICA. New York: Harper and Row, 1971. 290 p.

An in-depth examination of the 1960s student protests--civil disobedience against racial discrimination, followed by violence when Vietnam and other issues dissipated youthful faith in established society. The author foresees continuing unrest but is hopeful that, by being responsive, our social system can forestall a serious revolutionary threat.

481 Conference on Interinstitutional Cooperation, 2d, Corning, N.Y., 1969. INSTITUTIONAL COOPERATION IN HIGHER EDUCATION. Corning, N.Y.: College Center of the Finger Lakes, 1970. 126 p.

Self-study of the College Center of the Finger Lakes (New York state), which involves nine colleges in a consortium; reports that cooperation has been valuable and should be continued, but with changes to improve the style of governance.

482   Conger, Napoleon. SUMMARY: A STUDY OF THE CONTENT OF PRO-FESSIONAL COURSES IN EDUCATION IN INSTITUTIONS OF HIGHER LEARNING IN OKLAHOMA. Bulletin No. 33. Oklahoma City, Okla.: State Department of Public Instruction, 1933. 70 p.

Summarizes a two-thousand-page report which grew out of a desire to standardize titles and content of professional courses offered at Oklahoma teacher-training institutions. Included are a complete list of course titles, a list of textbooks with frequency of use, and recommendations on how to proceed further toward statewide reorganization of teacher education.

483   Connery, Robert H., ed. THE CORPORATION AND THE CAMPUS. New York: Praeger Publishers, 1970. 187 p.

Optimistic about cooperation between the business community and higher education institutions as a means toward mutual ends and toward meeting needs of blacks and other disadvantaged groups.

484   _____. TEACHING POLITICAL SCIENCE: A CHALLENGE TO HIGHER EDUCATION. Durham, N.C.: Duke University Press, 1965. 284 p.

Conference papers by middle-aged and older experienced professors who present their best thinking on the value and methods of teaching political science.

485   Connors, M. Austin, Jr., et al. GUIDE TO INTERINSTITUTIONAL ARRANGEMENTS: VOLUNTARY AND STATUTORY. Washington, D.C.: American Association for Higher Education, 1974. 51 p.

Contains listings, descriptions, and other relevant information on consortia and other cooperative arrangements among institutions of higher education.

486   Cook, Robert C., ed. PRESIDENTS OF AMERICAN COLLEGES AND UNIVERSITIES. 2d ed. Nashville, Tenn.: Who's Who in American Education, 1952. 244 p.

Data on training, experience, and professional activities of 1,433 presidents of accredited U.S. colleges, universities, teachers colleges, and two-year colleges.

487   _____. WHO'S WHO IN AMERICAN EDUCATION: AN ILLUSTRATED BIOGRAPHICAL DIRECTORY OF EMINENT LIVING EDUCATORS OF THE

UNITED STATES AND CANADA. 18th ed. Nashville, Tenn.: Who's Who in American Education, 1959. 1,272 p.

> Data on training, experience, and professional interests of several thousand educators, among them many university and college faculty members.

488 Coombs, Philip H. THE FOURTH DIMENSION OF FOREIGN POLICY: EDUCATIONAL AND CULTURAL AFFAIRS. New York: Harper and Row, for the Council on Foreign Relations, 1964. 158 p.

> Historical and evaluative study of U.S. higher education cultural exchanges, such as Fulbright and others; author was the first assistant secretary of state for educational and cultural affairs.

489 Coombs, Philip H., and Bigelow, Karl W. EDUCATION AND FOREIGN AID. Cambridge, Mass.: Harvard University Press, 1965. 76 p.

> Two lectures given at Harvard urge reappraisal of U.S. government and higher education overseas aid to serve better the needs of developing countries, especially African education needs as perceived by African educational leaders.

490 Coons, Arthur G. CRISES IN CALIFORNIA HIGHER EDUCATION. Los Angeles: Ward Ritchie Press, 1968. 256 p.

> Author, intimately involved in shaping California higher education, tells of its frictions, manipulations, and self-interests. He is critical of the state colleges with their drive to become little universities, and of the university for its neglect of undergraduates as it pursues esoteric research. He foresees the continuation of many academic problems but recognizes the urgency and moral pressure for equalizing educational opportunity.

491 _____ , et al. A MASTER PLAN FOR HIGHER EDUCATION IN CALIFORNIA, 1960-1975. Sacramento: California State Department of Education, 1960. 230 p.

> Prepared by the Master Plan Survey Team, this is California's third major post-1945 statewide survey of higher education. It created, with legislative sanction, a Board of Trustees of the State College System, which took state colleges out of the jurisdiction of the State Board of Education (the latter board continued to direct junior colleges). The plan also created an advisory body called the Coordinating Council for Higher Education and included many other recommendations.

492 Coons, Maggie, and Milner, Margaret, eds. CREATING AN ACCESSIBLE CAMPUS. Washington, D.C.: Association of Physical Plant Administrators of Universities and Colleges, 1978. 143 p.

Illustrated guide shows how colleges and universities can be made accessible to handicapped students, as required by the Rehabilitation Act of 1973.

493   Cooper, James M., et al. COMPETENCY BASED TEACHER EDUCATION. Berkeley, Calif.: McCutchan Publishers, 1973. 123 p.

Part 1 analyzes the competency-based approach to teacher education. Part 2 suggests ways to apply systems approaches to management, curriculum, and support as parts of an integrated teacher education program.

494   Cooper, Russell M., ed. THE TWO ENDS OF THE LOG: LEARNING AND TEACHING IN TODAY'S COLLEGE. Minneapolis: University of Minnesota Press, 1958. 317 p.

Report of an Association of Minnesota Colleges conference on college teaching, with faculty participants from almost all Minnesota higher education institutions, plus fourteen students. Speakers included Nevitt Sanford on contemporary undergraduates, Wilbert J. McKeachie on factors involved in learning, Harold Taylor on "The Teacher at His Best," and Ralph W. Tyler.

495   Cope, Robert, and Hannah, William. REVOLVING COLLEGE DOORS: THE CAUSES AND CONSEQUENCES OF DROPPING OUT, STOPPING OUT, AND TRANSFERRING. New York: Wiley-Interscience, 1975. 190 p.

Found that reasons for student withdrawal are poor choice of school and changed goals. Conversely, the best predictor of persistence in college is commitment to a goal. Dropout rates, especially among the talented, were lower than previously estimated. Useful comprehensive bibliography.

496   Copley, Frank O. THE AMERICAN HIGH SCHOOL AND THE TALENTED STUDENT. Ann Arbor: University of Michigan Press, 1961. 92 p.

Classics professor prefers enriched high school courses as alternative to early college admission for gifted secondary school students.

497   Coplin, William D., ed. TEACHING POLICY STUDIES: WHAT AND HOW. Lexington, Mass.: Lexington Books, 1978. 204 p.

Suggestions from twenty-four faculty members about curriculum content and teaching methods for policy studies.

498   Cordasco, Francesco. DANIEL COIT GILMAN AND THE PROTEAN PH.D.: THE SHAPING OF AMERICAN GRADUATE EDUCATION. Leiden, The Netherlands: E.J. Brill, Publisher, 1960. 160 p. Reprinted as THE

SHAPING OF AMERICAN GRADUATE EDUCATION; DANIEL COIT GIL-
MAN AND THE PROTEAN PH.D. Totowa, N.J.: Rowman and Littlefield, 1973. 163 p.

> Recounts Gilman's career as president of Johns Hopkins Uni-
> versity, 1875-1902, and his influence on the Ph.D. degree
> on American, not German, lines as first conceived at Yale
> and brought to fruition at Johns Hopkins. Includes checklist
> of 1878-1886 doctorates and theses, 1973 preface, and ex-
> panded bibliography.

499 Corey, Fay L. VALUES OF FUTURE TEACHERS: A STUDY OF ATTI-
TUDES TOWARD CONTEMPORARY ISSUES. New York: Teachers College, Columbia University, 1955. 146 p.

> Examined reactions of future teachers to such values as in-
> dividual worth, basic freedoms, integrity, responsibility for
> others, faith in God and man, democratic methods, and in-
> tellectual freedom.

500 Cornelius, Roberta D. HISTORY OF RANDOLPH-MACON WOMAN'S
COLLEGE. Chapel Hill: University of North Carolina Press, 1951.
428 p.

> Major credit goes to the founder, William Waugh Smith, whose
> imagination and enthusiasm gave life to Randolph-Macon Wom-
> an's College despite a storm of controversy, and to succeeding
> presidents who pursued Smith's dream.

501 Correa, Hector, ed. ANALYTICAL MODELS IN EDUCATIONAL PLAN-
NING AND ADMINISTRATION. New York: David McKay, 1975.
277 p.

> Shows the relevance of formal mathematical models to actual
> decision making. Of particular interest to higher education
> are Donald B. Johnson and Albert G. Holzman's "A Statisti-
> cal Decision-Theory Model of the College Admissions Process"
> and Karl A. Fox's "Practical Optimization Models for Univer-
> sity Departments."

502 Corrigan, Barbara. VOYAGE OF DISCOVERY. New York: Charles
Scribner's Sons, 1945. 302 p.

> Novel about a young woman's four years of sorority life and
> campus activities at a west coast university.

503 Corson, John J. THE GOVERNANCE OF COLLEGES AND UNIVERSITIES.
Rev. ed. Washington, D.C.: McKinsey and Co., 1975. 209 p.

> Compares and contrasts decision making in a university with
> that in business and government. Finds university decision

making unique because of the multiplicity of purposes and greater difficulty in evaluating the end product. Discusses the influence of governments on university governance, emphasizing such aspects as legislative pressures, administrative controls, and tax exemptions.

504 Cosper, Russell, and Griffin, E. Glenn, eds. TOWARD BETTER READING SKILL. New York: Appleton-Century-Crofts, 1953. 221 p.

Handbook to aid college students in improving comprehension and to develop flexible reading rates appropriate to the material being read.

505 Cottle, Thomas J. COLLEGE: REWARD AND BETRAYAL. Chicago: University of Chicago Press, 1977. 190 p.

Essays by sociologist and clinical psychologist about college women, failure in college, and problems of working class students. Case studies of Earlham College and Chicago's innovative Columbia College are based on personal observation and interviews. He considers the effect that changes in the American patriarchal family have had on higher education.

506 Coulter, Ellis Merton. COLLEGE LIFE IN THE OLD SOUTH. 2d ed. Athens: University of Georgia Press, 1951. 320 p.

The history of the University of Georgia, as an example of a typical antebellum southern college, is traced from its 1785 charter to the post-Civil War era.

507 Council for Financial Aid to Education. INTERFACE: GROWING INITIATIVES BY THE CORPORATION AND THE CAMPUS TOWARD GREATER UNDERSTANDING. New York: 1977. 67 p.

How business and higher education aid each other by endowed lectures and professorships, and student internships.

508 _____. SPECIAL PROGRAMS FOR MINORITIES AND WOMEN IN HIGHER EDUCATION. New York: 1978. 48 p.

A guide to college and university programs sponsored by corporations and other organizations to train women and minorities for careers.

509 Council of State Governments. HIGHER EDUCATION IN THE FORTY-EIGHT STATES: A REPORT TO THE GOVERNORS' CONFERENCE. Chicago: 1952. 317 p.

Brief history of major developments in higher education, public and private college programs, control, and governing boards; many statistical tables.

510 Council on Corporate/College Communications. BUSINESS PERSON-IN-RESIDENCE: A GUIDE FOR PLANNING AND OPERATING A COR-PORATE/COLLEGE PROJECT. Washington, D.C.: 1979. 31 p.

Trenton State College program for bringing business people to campus as adjunct faculty.

511 _____. FACULTY/MANAGEMENT FORUM: A GUIDE FOR PLANNING AND OPERATING A CORPORATE/COLLEGE PROJECT. Washington, D.C.: 1979. 19 p.

Outlines a program to help liberal arts faculty members and business people at the middle-management level resolve mutual problems.

512 Counelis, James Steve, ed. TO BE A PHOENIX. Bloomington, Ind.: Phi Delta Kappa, 1969. 104 p.

Essays on historical and emerging role of professors of education. At the turn of the century, theorists Cubberly, Thorndike, Judd, and Dewey added to the stature of this profession of essentially educational practitioners. Recent status has also been added by anthropologists, sociologists, and philosophers who focus on educational problems.

513 Covert, James T. A POINT OF PRIDE: THE UNIVERSITY OF PORT-LAND STORY. Portland, Oreg.: University of Portland Press, 1977. 328 p.

History of the university and the surrounding community.

514 Cowen, Philip A. OPPORTUNITIES FOR HIGHER EDUCATION IN NEW YORK STATE: PART I, DEGREE-GRANTING INSTITUTIONS AND JU-NIOR COLLEGES. Albany: University of the State of New York, 1944. 112 p.

Reports extensive research into New York state needs for education beyond secondary school and the capacity of existing institutions to meet them.

515 Cowley, William Harold. THE PERSONNEL BIBLIOGRAPHICAL INDEX. Columbus: Ohio State University Press, 1932. 433 p.

Lists and annotates over two-thousand books, pamphlets, monographs, and articles. The author also assigned ratings to indicate the relative importance of each entry.

516 Cowling, Donald J., and Davidson, Carter. COLLEGES FOR FREEDOM: A STUDY OF PURPOSES, PRACTICES AND NEEDS. New York: Harper and Brothers, 1947. 180 p.

By two college presidents; contains much about teaching loads, faculty committees, academic freedom, salary scale, admissions, alumni, relation of colleges to state universities, fundraising, and other subjects.

517   Coyne, John, and Hebert, Tom. THIS WAY OUT: A GUIDE TO AL-TERNATIVES TO TRADITIONAL COLLEGE EDUCATION IN THE UNITED STATES, EUROPE AND THE THIRD WORLD. New York: E.P. Dutton, 1972. 468 p.

Describes innovative, off-beat college programs in the United States and other countries. For students and counselors seeking alternatives to traditional college education.

518   Crabbs, Richard F., and Holmquist, Frank W. UNITED STATES HIGHER EDUCATION AND WORLD AFFAIRS. New York: Praeger Publishers, 1967. 160 p.

Classified, partially annotated bibliography of over nine-hundred books, articles, proceedings, reports, and government documents on different types of involvement of U.S. higher education with world affairs.

519   Craig, Hardin. WOODROW WILSON AT PRINCETON. Norman: University of Oklahoma Press, 1960. 175 p.

Wilson as student, professor, president, and educational reformer who introduced the preceptorial method of instruction at Princeton; by author who was student, instructor, and one of Wilson's original preceptors.

520   Cramer, Clarence H. CASE WESTERN RESERVE: A HISTORY OF THE UNIVERSITY, 1826-1976. Boston: Little, Brown and Co., 1976. 401 p.

Double history of Western Reserve University and Case Institute of Technology, which federated in 1967 to form Case Western Reserve University. Good on the nineteenth century and on relating the schools' histories to nearby communities.

521   Crane, Clarkson. THE WESTERN SHORE. New York: Harcourt, Brace and Co., 1925. 303 p.

Novel consists of character sketches of student life at a thinly disguised University of California at Berkeley.

522   Crane, Richard Teller. THE UTILITY OF AN ACADEMIC OR CLASSICAL EDUCATION FOR YOUNG MEN WHO HAVE TO EARN THEIR OWN LIVING AND WHO EXPECT TO PURSUE A COMMERCIAL LIFE. Chicago: Rand McNally, 1901. 70 p.

Concludes from replies from college presidents, students, and

businessmen, that college education is of little practical advantage in business.

523 Crane, Theodore Rawson, ed. THE COLLEGES AND THE PUBLIC, 1787–
1862. New York: Teachers College Press, 1963. 194 p.

Contains such important documents relating to the history of
U.S. higher education, 1787–1862, as Washington's letter
proposing a national university, Jefferson's ideas on higher
education in Virginia, and the 1862 Morrill Act.

524 Crawford, Albert B., and Burnham, Paul S. FORECASTING COLLEGE
ACHIEVEMENT: A SURVEY OF APTITUDE TESTS FOR HIGHER EDUCA-
TION. New Haven, Conn.: Yale University Press, 1946. 291 p.

Defines testing terms and presents an array of aptitude, achievement, general intelligence, traits, abilities, and other tests.

525 Crawford, Mary M. STUDENT FOLKWAYS AND SPENDING AT IN-
DIANA UNIVERSITY, 1940–41. New York: Columbia University Press,
1943. 271 p.

Analysis of 1,275 student budgets showed large expenses to
be rent, food, fees, and clothing. Examined social and economic factors for spending variations, and undergraduate motivation, ambitions, and standards of social behavior.

526 Creager, John A. THE AMERICAN GRADUATE STUDENT: A NORMA-
TIVE DESCRIPTION. Washington, D.C.: American Council on Education, 1971. 190 p.

Demographic and attitudinal characteristics of 33,000 graduate
students in 153 institutions.

527 _____. GOALS AND ACHIEVEMENTS OF THE ACE INTERNSHIP PRO-
GRAM IN ACADEMIC ADMINISTRATION. Washington, D.C.: American Council on Education, 1971. 46 p.

Along with EVALUATION AND SELECTION OF ACADEMIC
INTERNS 1967–1968 (1971), another ACE monograph, evaluates
an internship program for training young scholars in academic
administration. Compare the subsequent careers of interns with
those of rejected nominees.

528 Cremin, Lawrence A., et al. A HISTORY OF TEACHERS COLLEGE,
COLUMBIA UNIVERSITY. New York: Columbia University Press, 1954.
289 p.

Origins, growth, reorganization in the late 1920s and subsequent expansion, communist infiltration in the 1930s, and subsequent changes. Cremin is currently president of Teachers
College, Columbia University.

529 Crenshaw, Joseph W. STUDENT ADMINISTRATION OF ACTIVITY FUNDS. New York: Teachers College, Columbia University, 1954. 92 p.

> Case study of Pratt Institute (New York) student government's handling of its financial expenditure during 1946 to 1953. The theme is that student participation in student finance committee is educationally beneficial.

530 Cronbach, Lee J., and Gleser, Goldine C. PSYCHOLOGICAL TESTS AND PERSONNEL DECISIONS. Urbana: University of Illinois Press, 1965. 347 p.

> Recent and less technical than original 1957 edition in discussion of placing students on the basis of tests.

531 Cronkhite, Bernice Brown, ed. A HANDBOOK FOR COLLEGE TEACHERS: AN INFORMAL GUIDE. Cambridge, Mass.: Harvard University Press, 1950. 272 p.

> Lectures by Harvard and Radcliffe professors to aid novice college teachers.

532 Cross, Barbara M., ed. THE EDUCATED WOMAN IN AMERICA: SELECTED WRITINGS OF CATHARINE BEECHER, MARGARET FULLER, AND M. CAREY THOMAS. New York: Teachers College Press, 1965. 175 p.

> Besides many writings on undergraduate and graduate women, there is M. Carey Thomas's attack on Harvard's President Charles W. Eliot.

533 Cross, K. Patricia. ACCENT ON LEARNING: IMPROVING INSTRUCTION AND RESHAPING THE CURRICULUM. San Francisco: Jossey-Bass Publishers, 1976. 291 p.

> Suggesting that newer, lower ability students will increasingly enter higher education, author calls for higher education institutions to expand curriculum to serve vocational and other needs as well as narrow intellectual abilities.

534 _____. BEYOND THE OPEN DOOR: NEW STUDENTS TO HIGHER EDUCATION. San Francisco: Jossey-Bass Publishers, 1971. 200 p.

> Iconoclastic author believes that the next influx into higher education will be students of lower academic aptitude, achievement, and socioeconomic level and that colleges will need to be much more vocationally oriented to meet their needs.

535 _____. THE JUNIOR COLLEGE STUDENT: A RESEARCH DESCRIPTION. Princeton, N.J.: Educational Testing Service, 1968. 56 p.

> Characteristics of junior college students: academic, socio-

economic background, finance, self-concepts, interests, personality, reasons for attending college, reactions to college, choice of vocation, major field of study, and educational and occupational aspirations.

536   Cross, K. Patricia, et al. PLANNING NON-TRADITIONAL PROGRAMS: AN ANALYSIS OF THE ISSUES FOR POSTSECONDARY EDUCATION. San Francisco: Jossey-Bass Publishers, 1974. 263 p.

Surveys program needs of mainly adult and part-time nontraditional students; their characteristics, motivations, and interests.

537   Cross, Wilbur L. CONNECTICUT YANKEE: AN AUTOBIOGRAPHY. New Haven, Conn.: Yale University Press, 1943. 428 p.

Author's autobiography (1862-1948) as student, teacher, scholar, and dean at Yale University for over fifty years, after which he served as governor of Connecticut.

538   Cross, Wilbur L., and Florio, Carol. YOU ARE NEVER TOO OLD TO LEARN. New York: McGraw-Hill Book Co., 1978. 226 p.

Guide to older students' learning abilities, with anecdotes about older and retired students.

539   Crossland, Fred E. MINORITY ACCESS TO COLLEGE. New York: Schocken Books, 1971. 139 p.

Documents such higher education entrance barriers for minority students as admissions tests, race, motivation, and finance.

540   Crow, Mary Lynn. TEACHING ON TELEVISION. Arlington: University of Texas at Arlington Bookstore, 1977. 160 p.

Guidelines for higher education teaching by television; stages of production, learning theory applied to television, copyright, and visual and vocal presentation.

541   Cumberland, William Henry. THE HISTORY OF BUENA VISTA COLLEGE. Ames: Iowa State University Press, 1966. 233 p.

Intimate glimpses into persons and movements active in raising to college status this Iowa United Presbyterian institution.

542   Cuninggim, Merrimon. THE COLLEGE SEEKS RELIGION. New Haven, Conn.: Yale University Press, 1947. 319 p.

Proponent of religion on campus analyzes how secularization of higher education came about after the First World War, how the tendency has since reversed, and how college administrators seek constitutional ways to revive religious values on campus.

543 Cunningham, Charles E. TIMOTHY DWIGHT, 1752-1817: A BIOGRA-
PHY. New York: Macmillan Co., 1942. 403 p.

> Biography of Yale College student, tutor, and president (1795-
> 1817), whose grandson of the same name was also Yale's presi-
> dent (1886-99).

544 Cunningham, Donald H., and Estrin, Herman A., eds. THE TEACHING
OF TECHNICAL WRITING. Urbana, Ill.: National Council of Teachers
of English, 1975. 221 p.

> Articles about and examples of the importance of technical
> and scientific writing in two- and four-year colleges.

545 Cunningham, John T. UNIVERSITY IN THE FOREST: THE STORY OF
DREW UNIVERSITY. Florham Park, N.J.: Afton Publishing Co., 1972.
288 p.

> History from its opening in 1867 as Drew Theological Seminary.
> It added a liberal arts college in 1928 and became Drew Uni-
> versity. The graduate school opened in 1955. The 1969 char-
> ter dropped references to the seminary and ended the require-
> ment that all trustees be Methodists.

546 CURRENT CAMPUS ISSUES. Cambridge, Mass.: University Consultants,
1969.

> Essays prepared for the 1969 Institute on College and Univer-
> sity Administration on such topics as resource management,
> financial planning, and student demands for power.

547 Curti, Merle E., and Carstensen, Vernon R. THE UNIVERSITY OF WIS-
CONSIN: A HISTORY, 1848-1925. 2 vols. Madison: University of
Wisconsin Press, 1949. 739 p., 668 p.

> Centennial history by two distinguished intellectual historians
> who relate its development to social and intellectual move-
> ments in that region and in the country.

548 Curti, Merle E., and Nash, Roderick. PHILANTHROPY IN THE SHAPING
OF AMERICAN HIGHER EDUCATION. New Brunswick, N.J.: Rutgers
University Press, 1965. 340 p.

> Historical study from colonial times to the 1960s. Asserts that
> such gifts have often promoted innovation and reorientation in
> U.S. higher education. Many large late nineteenth century
> philanthropies enabled private institutions to set standards and
> become models for state higher education. Other philanthro-
> pists sometimes helped found small, weak colleges and some-
> times interfered with academic freedom. The authors conclude
> that effective philanthropists gave money for general purposes

and allowed educators to manage its use.

549 Cushman, Clarissa Fairchild. THE OTHER BROTHER. Boston: Little, Brown and Co., 1939. 307 p.

Novel about a sensitive, little understood youth at home and in college.

550 Cushman, Mantelle L. THE GOVERNANCE OF TEACHER EDUCATION. A Phi Delta Kappa Publication. Berkeley, Calif.: McCutchan Publishers, 1977. 296 p.

Comprehensive analysis of teacher education governance by the dean emeritus of the College of Education, University of North Dakota. On such topics as early recognition of faulty structure, influence on teacher education by funding agencies, the role of state agencies, and the politics of control.

551 Daigneault, George H. DECISION MAKING IN THE UNIVERSITY EVENING COLLEGE: THE ROLE OF THE RESIDENT DEPARTMENT CHAIRMAN. Chicago: Center for the Study of Liberal Education for Adults, 1963. 62 p.

Surveyed twelve colleges and universities to describe the administrative relationships between the evening college and other divisions of the institutions and to make recommendations.

552 Dalglish, Thomas Killin. PROTECTING HUMAN SUBJECTS IN SOCIAL AND BEHAVIORAL RESEARCH: ETHICS, LAW, AND THE DHEW RULES: A CRITIQUE. Berkeley: Center for Research in Management Sciences, University of California, 1977. 590 p.

Studied legal controls on the use of human subjects in social and behavioral science research. Found that the rules of the Department of Health, Education and Welfare and their impact on research at the University of California at Berkeley do not fully protect human subjects nor limit academic freedom as much as many researchers have claimed.

553 Dall, Caroline Wells Healey. THE COLLEGE, THE MARKET, AND THE COURT: OR WOMAN'S RELATION TO EDUCATION, LABOR, AND LAW. Concord, N.H.: Rumford Press, 1914. Reprint. New York: Arno Press, 1972. 511 p.

Lectures and articles by American-born women's rights advocate and author Caroline (Healy) Dall (1822-1912). Contains sections dealing with women's education and women as teachers; on women's rights under the law; and an appendix on various schools and colleges for women, medical education for women, women ministers, women's legal rights, suffrage, and civil rights.

554 Daniel, Walter Green. THE READING INTERESTS AND NEEDS OF NEGRO COLLEGE FRESHMEN REGARDING SOCIAL SCIENCE MATERIAL. Contributions to Education No. 862. New York: Teachers College, Columbia University, 1942. 128 p.

> Used reactions of Howard University freshmen as a guide to book selection. Found that students' tastes differed sharply from specialists' preferences.

555 Daniels, Arlene Kaplan, et al. ACADEMICS ON THE LINE: THE FACULTY STRIKE AT SAN FRANCISCO STATE. San Francisco: Jossey-Bass Publishers, 1970. 269 p.

> Papers by nineteen participants in the 1968–69 faculty strike at San Francisco State College which led to the presidency of S.I. Hayakawa. Some essays give penetrating insights into highly charged issues. Good appendices and index.

556 Daniere, Andre. HIGHER EDUCATION IN THE AMERICAN ECONOMY. Studies in Economics, 2. New York: Random House, 1964. 206 p.

> Identifies serious problems in the economics of higher education and proposes such solutions as a vast program of long-term low-interest loans. Discusses such questions as individual benefits versus social benefits.

557 Danton, J. Periam. EDUCATION FOR LIBRARIANSHIP: CRITICISMS, DILEMMAS, AND PROPOSALS. New York: School of Library Service, Columbia University, 1946. 35 p.

> Lists and examines major criticisms aimed at library schools and their programs. Proposes three levels of library training: the lowest would give technical and semiprofessional training in two-year colleges, the intermediate level would prepare professional librarians to do technical routines and some administration, and the highest level would prepare administrative specialists.

558 Darley, John G. PROMISE AND PERFORMANCE: A STUDY OF ABILITY AND ACHIEVEMENT IN HIGHER EDUCATION. Berkeley: Center for the Study of Higher Education, University of California, 1962. 191 p.

> Studied a national sample of students' ability levels at 200 higher education institutions, then did a more intensive analysis of students in Minnesota, Wisconsin, Texas, and Ohio. Found that: (1) too many able students do not enter higher education or drop out after enrolling; (2) too little effort is made to meet students' varying needs; (3) socio-economic factors too often determine the distribution of students in types of institutions; (4) superior students receive too little attention; and (5) U.S. higher education is not a national system with planned use of instructional resources.

559 Dave, Ravindra H., ed. FOUNDATIONS OF LIFELONG EDUCATION. Elmsford, N.Y.: Pergamon Press, 1976. 382 p.

Unesco Institute of Education commissioned these essays by five scholars from several countries about lifelong education.

560 David, Henry. MANPOWER POLICIES FOR A DEMOCRATIC SOCIETY: THE FINAL STATEMENT OF THE NATIONAL MANPOWER COUNCIL. New York: Columbia University Press, 1965. 121 p.

Report of Columbia University's National Manpower Council. Summarizes its conclusions and outlines serious manpower problems related to race, family, social class, mobility, and the role of work in society.

561 _____, ed. EDUCATION AND MANPOWER. New York: Columbia University Press, 1960. 326 p.

Columbia University's National Manpower Council selections on manpower, education, and national efficiency; secondary education; vocational guidance; and higher education.

562 David, Opal D., ed. THE EDUCATION OF WOMEN: SIGNS FOR THE FUTURE. Washington, D.C.: American Council on Education, 1959. 154 p.

American Council on Education conference papers present status and prospective research trends on the education of women. Excellent papers by Elizabeth Douvan, Nevitt Sanford, and David Tiedeman.

563 Davidson, Philip G., and Kuhlman, A.F., eds. THE DEVELOPMENT OF LIBRARY RESOURCES AND GRADUATE WORK IN THE COOPERATIVE UNIVERSITY CENTERS OF THE SOUTH. Nashville, Tenn.: Joint University Libraries, 1944. 81 p.

Conference report about four cooperative university centers in the southeastern United States (Georgia, Louisiana, North Carolina, and Tennessee) and their voluntary sharing of library and research resources. Urges institutions in these university centers to coordinate facilities, establish union catalogs, and avoid duplication.

564 Davis, James A. GREAT ASPIRATIONS: THE GRADUATE SCHOOL PLANS OF AMERICA'S COLLEGE SENIORS. Chicago: Aldine Publishing Co., 1964. 319 p.

Demographic information and future plans of 33,982 June 1961 graduates of 135 colleges and universities.

565 _____. UNDERGRADUATE CAREER DECISION. Chicago: Aldine Publishing Co., 1965. 307 p.

Focuses on changes in occupational preferences that occur during the undergraduate years. Concludes that such changes are minor and that most students finish college oriented to jobs they chose as freshmen.

566 _____, et al. STIPENDS AND SPOUSES: THE FINANCES OF AMERI-CAN ARTS AND SCIENCE GRADUATE STUDENTS. Chicago: University of Chicago Press, 1962. 294 p.

National Opinion Research Center study of three-thousand graduate students in twenty-five universities. Found a strong negative relationship between the amount of employment and course work completed; students in the social sciences and humanities have very low rates of support.

567 Davis, James R. GOING TO COLLEGE: THE STUDY OF STUDENTS AND THE STUDENT EXPERIENCE. Boulder, Colo.: Westview Press, 1977. 248 p.

To explore the undergraduate experience at an urban university, Davis depicts a composite typical student's college career and raises important issues.

568 _____. TEACHING STRATEGIES FOR THE COLLEGE CLASSROOM. Boulder, Colo.: Westview Press, 1976. 136 p.

Contends that effective college teaching depends on having clear goals and using an appropriate strategy to accomplish them. Focuses on four teaching strategies and learning theories underlying them: instructional systems (such as programmed instruction), lecturing, facilitating inquiry, and group processes. Excellent bibliographical essay.

569 Davis, Jerry S. STUDENT FINANCIAL AID NEEDS AND RESOURCES IN THE SREB STATES: A COMPARATIVE ANALYSIS. Atlanta: Southern Regional Education Board, 1974. 147 p.

Analyzes data from the southern states about the ability of students and their parents to pay for their higher education; presents information to help assess unmet needs of full-time students.

570 Davis, John W. LAND-GRANT COLLEGES FOR NEGROES. Institute: West Virginia State College, 1934. 73 p.

President of West Virginia State College tells the history of separate land-grant education for blacks, as provided by the Morrill Act of 1890. Almost all students at the seventeen black institutions in 1916 were enrolled at the elementary and secondary levels. By 1931-32 no elementary students were enrolled; secondary students constituted only one-third of the student body. But facilities were scant, and not one of the black land-grant colleges had an experiment station.

571 Davis, Richard Beale, ed. CORRESPONDENCE OF THOMAS JEFFERSON AND FRANCIS WALKER GILMER (1814-1826). Columbia: University of South Carolina Press, 1946. 163 p.

Letters between Jefferson and the young attorney who went to Britain to buy books and equipment and to recruit faculty for the University of Virginia. Prospective faculty members he met there were concerned about such contemporary matters as faculty participation in university governance.

572 Dearborn, Ned Harland. THE OSWEGO MOVEMENT IN AMERICAN EDUCATION. Contributions to Education No. 183. New York: Teachers College, Columbia University, 1925. Reprint. New York: Arno Press, 1969. 189 p.

Describes the founding of the Oswego State Normal and Training School and its operations, 1861-86, under Edward A. Sheldon, who led in spreading Pestalozzian methods of "object teaching."

573 DeCoster, David A., and Mable, Phyllis, eds. STUDENT DEVELOP-MENT AND EDUCATION IN COLLEGE RESIDENCE HALLS. Washing-ton, D.C.: American Personnel and Guidance Association, 1974. 278 p.

Topics include the philosophy of student personnel work, its implications for personal relationships within college residences, and the role of residence hall staff.

574 Deegan, William L., et al. JOINT PARTICIPATION AND DECISION MAKING. Berkeley: Center for Research and Development in Higher Education, University of California, 1970. 114 p.

Papers by Higher Education Center representatives analyzing faculty government and administration at Fresno State College. Favored shared responsibility in governance, which would re-duce the role of college and university presidents.

575 Deferrari, Roy J., ed. COLLEGE ORGANIZATION AND ADMINISTRA-TION. Washington, D.C.: Catholic University of America Press, 1947. 403 p.

Proceedings of the Workshop on College Organization and Ad-ministration conducted at the Catholic University of America in June 1946.

576 _____. THE CURRICULUM OF THE CATHOLIC COLLEGE. Washington, D.C.: Catholic University of America Press, 1952. 236 p.

Workshop proceedings which proposed a curriculum of concentration, instead of majors and minors, with upper division students doing extensive reading in their field and taking a coordinating seminar and a final comprehensive examination. Differing views in various papers reflect the divergence among Catholic educators.

577   _____. DISCIPLINE AND INTEGRATION IN THE CATHOLIC COLLEGE. Washington, D.C.: Catholic University of America Press, 1951. 197 p.

Lectures and reports suggesting ways to give unifying meaning to the experiences and training provided in Catholic colleges.

578   _____. GUIDANCE IN CATHOLIC COLLEGES AND UNIVERSITIES. Washington, D.C.: Catholic University of America Press, 1949. 303 p.

Workshop papers in 1948 on Catholic higher education, many of them devoted to Catholic doctrine; summaries of five seminars conducted during the workshop on fields of work for college students. Several papers on vocational guidance.

579   _____. INTEGRATION IN CATHOLIC COLLEGES AND UNIVERSITIES. Washington, D.C.: Catholic University of America Press, 1950. 416 p.

Workshop papers in 1949 on Catholic higher education; on philosophical and theological approach toward making a unified whole of Catholic college education.

580   _____. THE PROBLEMS OF ADMINISTRATION: THE AMERICAN COLLEGE. Washington, D.C.: Catholic University of America Press, 1956. 191 p.

Workshop findings as reported by participants, many of whom hold important administrative positions in Catholic colleges.

581   _____. SELF-EVALUATION AND ACCREDITATION IN HIGHER EDUCATION. Washington, D.C.: Catholic University of America Press, 1959. 362 p.

Report on the 1958 Catholic higher education workshop. Provides much information about the history and nature of institutional self-study and accreditation.

582   _____. THEOLOGY, PHILOSOPHY, AND HISTORY AS INTEGRATING DISCIPLINES IN THE CATHOLIC COLLEGE OF LIBERAL ARTS. Washington, D.C.: Catholic University of America Press, 1953. 336 p.

Workshop in 1953 on Catholic higher education emphasized theology as an integrative discipline. Chapters on the interrelationship between theology and such wide ranging fields as history, literature, sociology, and physical and biological science.

583 _____. VITAL PROBLEMS OF CATHOLIC EDUCATION IN THE UNITED STATES. Washington, D.C.: Catholic University of America, 1939. 231 p.

> Lectures by Catholic educators about all levels of Catholic schooling. Those about graduate schools and accrediting agencies, about non-Catholic philosophies, and about the Catholic contribution to the American college are of special interest to non-Catholic educators.

584 Deitrick, John E., and Berson, Robert C. MEDICAL SCHOOLS IN THE UNITED STATES AT MID-CENTURY. New York: McGraw-Hill Book Co., 1953. 380 p.

> Recommendations of the American Medical Association's Council on Medical Education and Hospitals: analyzes medical education cost and concludes that the expense is not extravagant; opposes orienting undergraduate basic science teaching to its immediate medical application; differentiates between the general goals of undergraduate education and later stages of training; and cautions medical schools against over-preoccupation with community service and public health projects.

585 DeLand, Edward C., ed. INFORMATION TECHNOLOGY IN HEALTH SCIENCE EDUCATION. New York: Plenum Publishing, 1979. 608 p.

> Analyzes several computer-based instructional systems in use at biomedical educational facilities.

586 Demerath, Nicholas J., et al. POWER, PRESIDENTS, AND PROFESSORS. New York: Basic Books, 1967. 275 p.

> Authors examine organization principles that can reduce conflict between college administrators and faculty. They present studies of the university presidency, academic departments, and administrative change at the University of North Carolina under two succeeding chancellors; and draw major conclusions about improving institutional management (the key is more faculty involvement).

587 Denison, Edward F. THE SOURCES OF ECONOMIC GROWTH IN THE UNITED STATES AND THE ALTERNATIVES BEFORE US. New York: Committee for Economic Development, 1962. 297 p.

> Classic study of U.S. economic growth. Attributes three-fifths of income differentials among males of the same age to their level of formal education.

588 Denison, John Hopkins. MARK HOPKINS, A BIOGRAPHY. New York: Charles Scribner's Sons, 1935. 327 p.

Written by his grandson, this biography of Mark Hopkins (1802-87) gives a rich account of New England in the early nineteenth century. Details of Hopkins' student days at Williams College--where he graduated (1824), later taught, and then served as president for thirty-six years--are a revealing picture of college life and higher education.

589 Dennis, Lawrence E., and Jacob, Renate M., eds. THE ARTS IN HIGHER EDUCATION. San Francisco: Jossey-Bass Publishers, 1968. 157 p.

Concerned with the imbalance between the arts and sciences in higher education, this book grew out of a project of the American Association for Higher Education, jointly financed by the National Endowment for the Arts. Calls for innovations in art education as sweeping as those begun in the late 1950s in secondary science education.

590 Dennis, Lawrence E., and Kauffman, Joseph F., eds. THE COLLEGE AND THE STUDENT: AN ASSESSMENT OF RELATIONSHIPS AND RESPONSIBILITIES IN UNDERGRADUATE EDUCATION, BY ADMINISTRATORS, FACULTY MEMBERS, AND PUBLIC OFFICIALS. Washington, D.C.: American Council on Education, 1966. 390 p.

Papers from the 1965 meeting of the American Council on Education devoted to the problems of college students; those about the curriculum are particularly useful.

591 Dennison, Charles P. FACULTY RIGHTS AND OBLIGATIONS IN EIGHT INDEPENDENT LIBERAL ARTS COLLEGES. New York: Bureau of Publications, Teachers College, Columbia University, 1955. 186 p.

The author, knowledgeable about faculty affairs in higher education, used sixteen principles--a sort of academic bill of rights dealing with such matters as promotion, tenure, and salaries--to judge faculty status in eight independent colleges in the Northeast.

592 Denver. University. THE UNIVERSITY OF DENVER CENTENNIAL SYMPOSIUM: THE RESPONSIBLE INDIVIDUAL AND A FREE SOCIETY IN AN EXPANDING UNIVERSE. Denver: 1965. 322 p.

Lectures by scholars from the sciences, the social sciences, and the humanities, including humanists Charles Frankel, Sir Zafrulla Kahn, and W. Averill Harriman; and scientists Fred Hoyle, Herbert H. Rose, and Theodore Puck.

593 Derbigny, Irving A. GENERAL EDUCATION IN THE NEGRO COLLEGE. Stanford, Calif.: Stanford University Press, 1947. 255 p.

Examined aims and patterns of general education programs in twenty black colleges of varying size and type, using catalogs

and other printed sources, firsthand observations, interviews
with faculty and administrators, and group conferences. Compared these programs with those at St. John's, Bennington,
Stephens, and the University of Chicago and gave many suggestions for improving general education in black colleges.

594 Dermer, Joseph. HOW TO RAISE FUNDS FROM FOUNDATIONS. New
York: Public Service Materials Center, 1979. 95 p.

Includes sections on types of grants, sources of information
about foundations, writing proposals, and interviews.

595 Deutsch, Steven E. INTERNATIONAL ASPECTS OF HIGHER EDUCATION
AND EXCHANGE. A COMMUNITY STUDY. Cleveland, Ohio: Western Reserve University, 1965. 182 p.

Report of five higher education institutions in the Cleveland,
Ohio, area. Data were gathered during a two-year period
from foreign students, host families, and American students
and faculty; and interviews were conducted with educational
administrators, labor and business leaders, and international
program staff.

596 _____. INTERNATIONAL EDUCATION AND EXCHANGE: A SOCIO-
LOGICAL ANALYSIS. Cleveland, Ohio: Case Western Reserve University, 1970. 207 p.

Reports attitudes of foreign students; their community hosts;
and American students, professors, and administrators on Cleveland campuses.

597 DeVane, William Clyde. THE AMERICAN UNIVERSITY IN THE TWEN-
TIETH CENTURY. Baton Rouge: Louisiana State University Press, 1957.
72 p.

Four lectures by the dean of Yale College about the scope
and function of contemporary institutions of higher education.

598 _____. HIGHER EDUCATION IN TWENTIETH-CENTURY AMERICA.
Cambridge, Mass.: Harvard University Press, 1965. 211 p.

A sophisticated examination of U.S. higher education trends
and their historical background.

599 DeVoto, Bernard Augustine. WE ACCEPT WITH PLEASURE. Boston:
Little, Brown and Co., 1934. 471 p.

Novel about a professor fired during World War I for his
pacifist views.

600 Dewey, John. THE EDUCATIONAL SITUATION. Chicago: University of Chicago Press, 1902. Reprint. New York: Arno Press, 1969. 104 p.

Dewey calls for articulating the content and purposes of elementary, secondary, and higher education. Also includes many details about the colonial college--its purposes, policies, and programs.

601 Dexter, Franklin Bowditch, ed. DOCUMENTARY HISTORY OF YALE UNIVERSITY, 1701-1745. New Haven, Conn.: Yale University Press, 1916. Reprint. New York: Arno Press, 1969. 382 p.

Legislative documents, trustee minutes, letters, and other source material about the history of Yale, 1701-45.

602 Dibden, Arthur James, ed. THE ACADEMIC DEANSHIP IN AMERICAN COLLEGES AND UNIVERSITIES. Carbondale: Southern Illinois University Press, 1968. 289 p.

Articles by nineteen distinguished educators and commentators (among them John J. Corson, Lewis B. Mayhew, Roy F. Nichols, W. Gordon Whaley, and Harlan Cleveland) about many aspects of the deanship.

603 Diehl, Carl. AMERICANS AND GERMAN SCHOLARSHIP, 1770-1870. Yale History Publications; Miscellany, No. 115. New Haven, Conn.: Yale University Press, 1978. 194 p.

Author estimates the number of American students studying in Germany between 1770-1870, where they came from, how they lived, and what their impact was on returning home. German historical scholarship was more influential on them than was German humanism.

604 Diekhoff, John S. DEMOCRACY'S COLLEGE: HIGHER EDUCATION IN THE LOCAL COMMUNITY. New York: Harper and Brothers, 1950. 208 p.

Recognizing that the masses have moved into higher education, the author calls for applying American mass production techniques to meet two-year college student needs. Routine tasks like testing and marking should be done by assistants so that instructors will be freed for more important teaching.

605 _____. THE DOMAIN OF THE FACULTY IN OUR EXPANDING COLLEGES. New York: Harper and Brothers, 1956. 204 p.

Well-informed director of institutional research poses probing questions about how U.S. higher education is to cope effectively with rapidly growing enrollments and also with rising demands for adult programs.

606 Diener, Thomas, ed. COLLEGE TEACHING AND TEACHERS: LEGAL IMPLICATIONS OF ACADEMIC AFFAIRS. University, Ala.: Institute of Higher Education Research and Services, 1974. 69 p.

Conference papers about women's rights in higher education, faculty collective bargaining, and the courts and academic affairs.

607 Dill, David D. CASE STUDIES IN UNIVERSITY GOVERNANCE. Washington, D.C.: National Association of State Universities and Land Grant Colleges, 1971. 192 p.

The rise of academic senates in response to the 1960s campus unrest is analyzed in the experiences of Columbia, Florida A and M, Minnesota, and New Hampshire. In their early stages academic senates were preoccupied with campus crises and with organizing themselves. If senatorial governance proves inadequate, author sees its place being taken by collective bargaining.

608 Dilley, Josiah S. HIGHER EDUCATION: PARTICIPANTS CONFRONTED. Dubuque, Iowa: William C. Brown, 1970. 123 p.

Gives a brief historical overview and describes higher education administration problems that might arise on a college campus.

609 DiMichael, Salvatore G. IMPROVING PERSONALITY AND STUDY SKILLS IN COLLEGE. Catholic Education Series, No. 3. Milwaukee, Wis.: Bruce Publishing Co., 1951. 304 p.

College orientation textbook relates the value of college attendance to students' life goals, lists characteristics of personal effectiveness, and suggests ways to improve study skills and critical thinking.

610 Dobbins, Charles G., ed. EXPANDING RESOURCES FOR COLLEGE TEACHING: A REPORT OF THE CONFERENCE ON COLLEGE TEACHING. Washington, D.C.: American Council on Education, 1956. 137 p.

Conference considered problems in college teaching, especially the faculty shortage. Suggested using more graduate assistants and secretaries for routine faculty tasks, increasing class size of able faculty (students prefer such teachers despite large numbers), recruiting outstanding graduate students to college teaching, and reducing faculty pressure to do research. Less conventional ideas were to end faculty ranking (a discouraging irritant to young instructors) and reduce the number of clock hours required for a class.

611 Dobbins, Charles G., and Lee, Calvin B.T., eds. WHOSE GOALS FOR

AMERICAN HIGHER EDUCATION? Washington, D.C.: American Council on Education, 1968. 241 p.

Essays, most of them written at the height of student unrest, define higher education's goals and shaping forces, and suggest new directions.

612 Dodds, Harold W., et al. THE ACADEMIC PRESIDENT--EDUCATOR OR CARETAKER? Carnegie Series in American Education. New York: McGraw-Hill Book Co., 1962. 294 p.

Meticulous exploration of the roles and leadership styles possible for a university president and of the problems of state university presidents because of politics.

613 Doermann, Humphrey. CROSSCURRENTS IN COLLEGE ADMISSIONS: INSTITUTIONAL RESPONSE TO STUDENT ABILITY AND FAMILY INCOME. New York: Teachers College Press, 1968. 180 p.

Sourcebook for private college admissions officers estimates, through 1975, potential college entrants by scholastic aptitude and by the ability of their families to pay college costs. Also considers admissions and financial problems facing black colleges.

614 _____. TOWARD EQUAL ACCESS. Princeton, N.J.: College Board Publications, 1978. 143 p.

Assessment of the projected downward trend in enrollments, and its meaning for postsecondary institutions, students, and taxpayers.

615 Doherty, Robert E. THE DEVELOPMENT OF PROFESSIONAL EDUCATION. Pittsburgh, Pa.: Carnegie Institute of Technology, 1950. 58 p.

Calls for broadening engineering education to include more humanities and social science courses and to encourage the development of humane personal and social values.

616 Doi, James I., ed. ASSESSING FACULTY EFFORT. New Directions in Institutional Research No. 2. San Francisco: Jossey-Bass Publishers, 1974. 106 p.

Explains ways of measuring faculty effort. Discusses comparative trend analyses of teaching loads, government concern about workloads, and workload clauses in bargaining contracts.

617 Donahue, Wilma T., et al., eds. THE MEASUREMENT OF STUDENT ADJUSTMENT AND ACHIEVEMENT. Ann Arbor: University of Michigan Press, 1949. 256 p.

Fifteen papers given at a University of Michigan conference about developments in measurement and guidance.

618   Donham, Walter Brett. EDUCATION FOR RESPONSIBLE LIVING. Cambridge, Mass.: Harvard University Press, 1944. 309 p.

Former dean of Harvard Business School criticizes U.S. higher education for failing to help people solve problems. With Robert M. Hutchins, he deplores departmentalization and specialization. But he disagrees with Hutchins's faith in great books and philosophy. Donham's ideal college curriculum would give students a broad, generalized outlook on life and prepare them to deal with human relations.

619   Donley, Marshall O., Jr. POWER TO THE TEACHER. Bloomington: Indiana University Press, 1976. 242 p.

History of U.S. teacher activism from the 1850s; examines reasons teachers organized, how teachers' unions evolved, and the future of faculty militancy and collective bargaining.

620   Donnelly, Walter A., et al., eds. THE UNIVERSITY OF MICHIGAN: AN ENCYCLOPEDIC SURVEY. 4 vols. Ann Arbor: University of Michigan Press, 1942-1958. 2,066 p.

Conceived during the University of Michigan's 1937 centennial celebration. Volume 1: history, administration, organization, services, and alumni information; volumes 2 and 3: descriptions of the various colleges and schools; volume 4: libraries, university publications, museums, buildings, student life, and athletics.

621   Donohue, John W. JESUIT EDUCATION: AN ESSAY ON THE FOUNDATIONS OF ITS IDEA. New York: Fordham University Press, 1963. 221 p.

Schooling as discussed in these principles of Jesuit education exists for the sake of students, is a tool for guiding them to salvation, and, ultimately, for the glory of God.

622   Donovan, George F., ed. COLLEGE AND UNIVERSITY INTERINSTITUTIONAL COOPERATION. Washington, D.C.: Catholic University of America Press, 1965. 158 p.

Workshop report which explored in detail some patterns, problems, and opportunities of cooperation among universities and colleges, both large and small.

623   _____. COLLEGE AND UNIVERSITY STUDENT PERSONNEL SERVICES. Washington, D.C.: Catholic University of America Press, 1962. 272 p.

Contains eighteen workshop papers about student personnel services.

624 Donovan, Herman Lee. KEEPING THE UNIVERSITY FREE AND GROW-
ING. Lexington: University of Kentucky Press, 1959. 162 p.

> University of Kentucky president for fifteen years, Donovan
> describes typical problems and emphasizes a fear that state
> universities will lose their autonomy. He pleads for freedom
> from politicians, many of them unaware that state institutions
> are financed not merely by taxes but by private funds.

625 Donovan, John D. THE ACADEMIC MAN IN THE CATHOLIC COLLEGE.
New York: Sheed and Ward, 1963. 238 p.

> Study of Catholic intellectual life by a survey of seventy
> percent of the total faculty in Catholic colleges and univer-
> sities, plus interviews from a smaller sample. Lists advantages
> and disadvantages of Catholic scholars and tells of restrictions
> on academic freedom in Roman Catholic higher education insti-
> tutions.

626 Douglas, Paul. TEACHING FOR SELF-EDUCATION AS A LIFE GOAL.
New York: Harper and Brothers, 1960. 153 p.

> A biographical memoir of William S. Learned, long-time (1913-
> 46) staff member at the Carnegie Foundation for the Advance-
> ment of Teaching, architect of the Graduate Record Examina-
> tion, and a major founder of Educational Testing Service. With
> IBM he developed the first automatic test scoring machine.
> His educational ideas were concerned mainly with ways to
> serve the superior student.

627 Douglass, Paul F. SIX UPON THE WORLD: TOWARD AN AMERICAN
CULTURE FOR AN INDUSTRIAL AGE. Boston: Little, Brown and Co.,
1954. 443 p.

> James Bryant Conant, one of six men described; underscores
> major educational ideas and policies he implemented during
> his presidency of Harvard University.

628 Dowd, Jerome. THE LIFE OF BRAXTON CRAVEN: BIOGRAPHICAL AP-
PROACH TO SOCIAL SCIENCE. Durham, N.C.: Duke University Press,
1939. 246 p.

> Craven (1822-82) taught in North Carolina (1841-82), and
> developed the South's first normal school at Trinity, which
> later became Trinity College. Author depicts central North
> Carolina life by telling of Craven's career.

629 Dowlin, Cornell M. THE UNIVERSITY OF PENNSYLVANIA TODAY.
Philadelphia: University of Pennsylvania Press, 1940. 209 p.

> Guidebook, a natural supplement to Cheyney's history of the

University of Pennsylvania, tells of the development of each department and of the university's then-current operations.

630 Downs, Robert B. AMERICAN LIBRARY RESOURCES: A BIBLIOGRAPHI-CAL GUIDE. Chicago: American Library Association, 1951. 428 p.

Significant bibliography, intended to promote cooperation among libraries, has 5,578 entries of printed library catalogs, union lists of books and serials, surveys of library holdings, selected library reports, and similar publications.

631 _____, ed. THE STATUS OF AMERICAN COLLEGE AND UNIVERSITY LIBRARIANS. Chicago: American Library Association, 1958. 180 p.

Contains sixteen articles about the efforts of professional libra-rians (most of them not head librarians) to attain appropriate academic status. Several writers describe plans that place librarians with administrators and faculties in a wide variety of possible arrangements.

632 Drake, Donald. MEDICAL SCHOOL: THE DRAMATIC TRUE STORY OF HOW FOUR YEARS TURNED A CLASS OF RAW STUDENTS INTO QUALI-FIED PHYSICIANS. New York: Rawson, Wade Publishers, 1978. 265 p.

By a medical reporter who observed the 1978 class during their four years at the University of Pennsylvania medical school; vignettes reveal their sexism, racism, and various moods.

633 Draper, Hal. BERKELEY: THE NEW STUDENT REVOLT. New York: Grove Press, 1965. 246 p.

Pro student articles on the 1964-65 University of California at Berkeley student riots by an adviser to the free speech move-ment. Introduction by rebel leader Mario Savio is a particu-larly good extended account of events.

634 Dresch, Stephen P. AN ECONOMIC PERSPECTIVE ON THE EVOLUTION OF GRADUATE EDUCATION. Washington, D.C.: National Academy of Sciences, 1974. 76 p.

Develops a theoretical economic model to explain the growth of graduate education since World War II. Shows the economic interplay of graduate education with research and undergraduate education. The same model is used to project alternative pat-terns for graduate education.

635 Dressel, Paul L. COLLEGE AND UNIVERSITY CURRICULUM. Berkeley, Calif.: McCutchan Publishers, 1968. 232 p.

Stresses that faculties need to decide what competencies the college curriculum should produce; tries to show how colleges can organize programs to achieve these competencies. Instead of a departmental major, recommends that a student study two different fields in depth and relate them to solving a selected current problem.

636 _____. HANDBOOK OF ACADEMIC EVALUATION: ASSESSING INSTITUTIONAL EFFECTIVENESS, STUDENT PROGRESS, AND PROFESSIONAL PERFORMANCE FOR DECISION MAKING IN HIGHER EDUCATION. San Francisco: Jossey-Bass Publishers, 1976. 518 p.

Covers the broad spectrum of evaluation which author sees as a complex, value-laden task with no easily workable methodology. Checklists pose controversial but insightful questions about goals, procedures used to strive for them, and their underlying value assumptions.

637 _____. LIBERAL EDUCATION AND JOURNALISM. New York: Teachers College, Columbia University, 1960. 102 p.

Brief but comprehensive picture of how journalism education developed and its relation to the liberal arts. Has suggestions for improving journalism education.

638 _____, ed. COMPREHENSIVE EXAMINATIONS IN A PROGRAM OF GENERAL EDUCATION. East Lansing: Michigan State College Press, 1950. 165 p.

Analyzes the distinctive achievement testing program in Michigan State's Basic College and describes its general education curriculum. The strengths and weaknesses of giving separate responsibilities to examiners and instructors are probed, as is the process of preparing examinations for the seven departments.

639 _____. EVALUATION IN THE BASIC COLLEGE AT MICHIGAN STATE UNIVERSITY. New York: Harper and Brothers, 1958. 248 p.

Using the word "evaluation" in its broadest sense, contributors discuss its relation to such matters as curriculum planning, student characteristics, and examination and grading practices.

640 _____. THE NEW COLLEGES: TOWARD AN APPRAISAL. Iowa City: American College Testing Program, 1971. 326 p.

Conference papers describe and criticize new experimental colleges. The editor discusses problems of evaluation, one of which is to convince faculty to go along with a rigorous evaluation program.

641 Dressel, Paul L., and DeLisle, Frances H. UNDERGRADUATE CURRI-

CULUM TRENDS. Washington, D.C.: American Council on Education, 1969. 83 p.

Comprehensive ten-year study (1957-67) of undergraduate curriculum in a representative sample of 322 institutions; found expansion of individualized programs such as work-study, study abroad, community service, and independent study. Among specific changes were reductions in English, literature, philosophy, and religion requirements and increases in foreign language and science requirements. Also reviews the historical background of curriculum development and of provisions for individualized instruction. Nine types of comprehensive programs, including traditional and experimental curriculums, are identified.

642 Dressel, Paul L., and Faricy, William H. RETURN TO RESPONSIBILITY: CONSTRAINTS ON AUTONOMY IN HIGHER EDUCATION. San Francisco: Jossey-Bass Publishers, 1972. 232 p.

Tells how universities can find a balance between excessive autonomy and needed controls, and how controls do and do not affect academic freedom. Recommends that universities define and clarify their roles, upgrade teaching, carry out long-range planning and budgeting, and develop management information systems.

643 Dressel, Paul L., and Mayhew, Lewis B. GENERAL EDUCATION: EXPLORATIONS IN EVALUATION. Washington, D.C.: American Council on Education, 1954. 302 p.

Landmark cooperative study at nineteen universities and colleges to determine the status and effectiveness of undergraduate general education programs. Concludes that the most important outcome of general education is critical thinking.

644 _____. HIGHER EDUCATION AS A FIELD OF STUDY: THE EMERGENCE OF A PROFESSION. San Francisco: Jossey-Bass Publishers, 1974. 214 p.

Describes the most desirable types of higher education studies; reviews higher education research--kind, amount, and impact; assesses strengths and weaknesses of existing programs; formulates principles for improving programs or starting new ones; and clarifies issues in creating new model programs.

645 Dressel, Paul L., and Pratt, Sally B. THE WORLD OF HIGHER EDUCATION: AN ANNOTATED GUIDE TO THE MAJOR LITERATURE. San Francisco: Jossey-Bass Publishers, 1971. 238 p.

Almost eight-hundred annotated research studies (books, articles, reports, unpublished dissertations, and government publications) are arranged in these categories: institutional research as a field of activity; governance, administration, management;

students; faculty and staff; curriculum and instruction; research methodology; related bibliographies and other research materials. Brief essays describe main features of higher education research.

646 Dressel, Paul L., and Schmid, John. AN EVALUATION OF THE TESTS OF GENERAL EDUCATIONAL DEVELOPMENT. Washington, D.C.: American Council on Education, 1951. 57 p.

Studied purposes, uses and effectiveness of GED tests. Found the tests reliable and an acceptable equivalent on many jobs requiring a high school diploma. Colleges, however, were less likely to accept the GED certificate.

647 Dressel, Paul L., and Thompson, Mary Magdala. A DEGREE FOR COLLEGE TEACHERS: THE DOCTOR OF ARTS. Berkeley, Calif.: Carnegie Council on Policy Studies in Higher Education, 1978. 70 p.

The authors, on the basis of 1975-76 visits to institutions having Doctor of Arts (D.A.) programs, examine alternatives to the D.A., compare it with the Ph.D., describe the many variations in D.A. programs, and conclude that the D.A. is an established feature of U.S. higher education.

648 _____. INDEPENDENT STUDY: A NEW INTERPRETATION OF CONCEPTS, PRACTICES, AND PROBLEMS. San Francisco: Jossey-Bass Publishers, 1973. 162 p.

Assesses current practices in independent study, including the six Ford Foundation-financed programs. Gives guidelines for setting up, improving, implementing, or evaluating such programs.

649 Dressel, Paul L., et al. THE CONFIDENCE CRISIS: AN ANALYSIS OF UNIVERSITY DEPARTMENTS. San Francisco: Jossey-Bass Publishers, 1970. 268 p.

Studied academic departments--considered the key unit in contemporary American universities--and found them to be complex bodies that vary little between academic disciplines. Departments which have high national standing had more informal administrative organization than did departments of less stature, and were less involved in local institutional matters.

650 _____. EVALUATION IN HIGHER EDUCATION. Boston: Houghton Mifflin Co., 1961. 480 p.

On the nature of the learning and evaluation processes; various aspects and problems of student evaluation, including the broad areas of the social sciences, natural sciences, humanities, and communications; and the evaluation of teachers and higher education institutions.

651 _____. INSTITUTIONAL RESEARCH IN THE UNIVERSITY: A HAND-
BOOK. San Francisco: Jossey-Bass Publishers, 1971. 347 p.

>Essays treat comprehensively the nature of institutional research
(particularly in large institutions)--what it is, what can be
achieved by it, how offices of institutional research can be
established, and current trends. Appendix lists depositories
of institutional research data.

652 Drew, David E. A PROFILE OF THE JEWISH FRESHMAN. ACE Research
Reports. Vol. V, no. 4. Washington, D.C.: American Council on
Education, 1970. 53 p.

>Mainly statistical information on Jewish men and women stu-
dents at different types of higher education institutions; shows
them to be upper middle class, liberal, verbally oriented,
and high academic achievers.

653 Drinan, Robert F., ed. THE RIGHT TO BE EDUCATED: STUDIES TO
COMMEMORATE THE TWENTIETH ANNIVERSARY OF THE ADOPTION
BY THE UNITED NATIONS OF THE UNIVERSAL DECLARATION OF
HUMAN RIGHTS, DEC. 10, 1948. Sponsored by the International Federa-
tion of Catholic Universities. Washington, D.C.: Corpus Books, 1968.
271 p.

>Catholic educators examine the philosophical foundations of
education as a human right and identify historical origins and
direction that all levels of Catholic education can take to
meet the needs of contemporary society and religion.

654 Drummond, Carl E. GOING RIGHT ON: INFORMATION AND AD-
VICE FOR MINORITY STUDENTS WHO WANT TO CONTINUE THEIR
EDUCATION AFTER HIGH SCHOOL. Princeton, N.J.: College En-
trance Examination Board, 1976. 48 p.

>Popular guide to postsecondary education; uses the author's
own experiences as a black, a student, and a higher education recruiter to answer many questions, ranging from how to
apply to what is a degree.

655 Duberman, Martin. BLACK MOUNTAIN: AN EXPLORATION IN COM-
MUNITY. New York: E.P. Dutton and Co., 1972. 527 p.

>Chronicle of experimental Black Mountain College, North
Carolina, which served (1933-56) as a counterculture center
for artists and such intellectuals as Buckminster Fuller and Paul
Goodman.

656 Dubin, Robert R., et al. THE MEDIUM MAY BE RELATED TO THE MES-
SAGE: COLLEGE INSTRUCTION BY TV. Eugene: Center for the Advanced Study of Educational Administration, University of Oregon, 1969.
114 p.

Review of research on educational television (ETV) in colleges and universities by proponents of its use who devote chapters to ETV and reactions to it by professors, students, and administrators.

657 Du Bois, Cora. FOREIGN STUDENTS AND HIGHER EDUCATION IN THE UNITED STATES. Studies in Universities and World Affairs. Washington, D.C.: American Council on Education, 1956. 221 p.

Guide for advisers and others on U.S. campuses who work professionally with foreign students on such matters as selection, orientation, placement, policies, and practices.

658 DuBois, Cornelius, and Murphy, Charles J.V. HARVARD 1926: THE LIFE AND OPINIONS OF A COLLEGE CLASS. Cambridge, Mass.: Harvard University Press, 1951. 98 p.

After twenty-five years, leaders of the 1926 Harvard class used professional pollsters to glean extensive details about their classmates.

659 Duffus, Robert Luther. DEMOCRACY ENTERS COLLEGE: A STUDY OF THE RISE AND DECLINE OF THE ACADEMIC LOCKSTEP. New York: Charles Scribner's Sons, 1936. 244 p.

Concerned with college admission. Shows the rise and decline of rigid entrance requirements and of the unit system of admission. Analyzes trends and experimentation in admission requirements at such colleges as Antioch, Bennington, Bard, Sarah Lawrence, and Stephens.

660 Duggan, Stephen, and Drury, Betty. THE RESCUE OF SCIENCE AND LEARNING. New York: Macmillan Co., 1948. 214 p.

About refugee scholars: their impact on American intellectual life, reactions to their experiences, and their evaluations of U.S. higher education (few felt free to be openly critical). Also contains opinions of college and university administrators about these refugee scholars, the work of the Emergency Committee in Aid of Displaced German Scholars formed in 1933 by author Duggan, and other philanthropic aid for them.

661 Dugger, Ronnie. OUR INVADED UNIVERSITIES: FORM, REFORM, AND NEW STARTS. New York: W.W. Norton and Co., 1974. 457 p.

A case study of the University of Texas at Austin by a journalist, himself an alumnus and well-known liberal spokesman, who asserts that universities are being taken over by the corporate and political establishment in order to repress dissenting professors. Conclusion contains criticism of professors and universities and recommendations for reforming higher education.

662 Duke, Daniel Linden. THE RETRANSFORMATION OF THE SCHOOL: THE EMERGENCE OF CONTEMPORARY ALTERNATIVE SCHOOLS IN THE UNITED STATES. Chicago: Nelson-Hall Publishers, 1978. 204 p.

> Has a chapter on the influence of universities, administrators, foundations, and government agencies on the growth of alternative schools.

663 Duley, John, ed. IMPLEMENTING FIELD EXPERIENCE EDUCATION. San Francisco: Jossey-Bass Publishers, 1974. 110 p.

> Field-based higher education--its potential and its problems-- is discussed by students, faculty, administrators, and off-campus agency supervisors.

664 Dulles, Foster Rhea. AMERICANS ABROAD: THE CENTURIES OF EURO-PEAN TRAVEL. Ann Arbor: University of Michigan Press, 1964. 202 p.

> European influence on American higher education is illustrated in this study of scholars and university presidents who studied there--most often in Germany--and brought back influential ideas. Includes James B. Angell, Charles W. Eliot, Andrew D. White, Daniel Coit Gilman, William Graham Sumner, and Herbert Baxter Adams.

665 Dumpson, James, et al. TOWARD EDUCATION FOR EFFECTIVE SOCIAL WELFARE ADMINISTRATIVE PRACTICE. New York: Council on Social Work Education, 1979. 48 p.

> Calls for including sound courses in social work administration in the curricula of schools of social work.

666 Dunbar, Willis F. THE MICHIGAN RECORD IN HIGHER EDUCATION. HISTORY OF EDUCATION IN MICHIGAN. Vol. IV. Detroit: Wayne State University Press, 1963. 463 p.

> A chronological account of all postsecondary educational insti-tutions in Michigan, where higher education has had sustained public support beginning when Michigan decided--on being admitted to statehood--to establish a public university.

667 Dunham, E. Alden. COLLEGES OF THE FORGOTTEN AMERICANS: A PROFILE OF STATE COLLEGES AND REGIONAL UNIVERSITIES. New York: McGraw-Hill Book Co., 1969. 206 p.

> Carnegie Commission on Higher Education study made on the basis of visits to state colleges and regional universities, most of them former teachers colleges. Cautions them not to strive for equal status with major state universities and recommends, instead, that state colleges and regional universities develop programs for a new teaching doctorate, the Doctor of Arts degree.

668   Durkin, Joseph T. GEORGETOWN UNIVERSITY: THE MIDDLE YEARS, 1840-1900. Washington, D.C.: Georgetown University Press, 1963. 333 p.

    Sequel to John M. Daley's GEORGETOWN UNIVERSITY: ORIGIN AND EARLY YEARS (1957). Major figures in this volume are Presidents James Ryder (opened medical school in 1851), Bernard Maguire (led in founding law school), and Patrick F. Healey (influenced the decision to make Georgetown a university).

669   Durso, Joseph, et al. THE SPORTS FACTORY: AN INVESTIGATION INTO COLLEGE SPORTS. New York: New York Times Book Co., Quadrangle, 1975. 207 p.

    Sports journalists examine college athletics and find them to be largely commercial ventures tangentially related to educational processes. This is cited as a decades-old problem as shown in the 1929 Carnegie Foundation Report, AMERICAN COLLEGE ATHLETICS.

670   Duryea, Edwin D., and Fisk, Robert S. COLLECTIVE BARGAINING, THE STATE UNIVERSITY AND THE STATE GOVERNMENT IN NEW YORK. Buffalo: Department of Higher Education, State University of New York, Buffalo, 1975. 51 p.

    Shows that collective bargaining by faculty and nonteaching professional staff at the State University of New York has had a substantial impact on relationships between the university and the state government.

671   Duryea, Edwin D., et al. FACULTY UNIONS AND COLLECTIVE BARGAINING. San Francisco: Jossey-Bass Publishers, 1973. 236 p.

    Comprehensive survey of faculty unions and collective bargaining in higher education, with details about such facets as union accomplishments, grievance procedures and personnel complaints, and the scope and variety of existing contracts.

672   Dussault, Gilles. A THEORY OF SUPERVISION IN TEACHER EDUCATION. New York: Teachers College Press, 1970. 275 p.

    Presents research findings and informed opinion about the supervision of student teachers and, using Carl Rogers's concepts, advances a theory of teaching by supervisors.

673   Dyer, John Percy. IVORY TOWERS IN THE MARKET PLACE: THE EVENING COLLEGE IN AMERICAN EDUCATION. Indianapolis: Bobbs-Merrill Co., 1956. 205 p.

    Examines problems of adult education in general; then sum-

marizes and evaluates the evening college. For the evening
school, recommends a liberal arts curriculum relevant to community needs and a specially selected staff primarily interested
in the evening school.

674 _____. TULANE: THE BIOGRAPHY OF A UNIVERSITY, 1834-1965.
New York: Harper and Row, 1966. 370 p.

Begun as undergraduate professional schools from 1834; chartered in 1882. Early growth and subsequent history provide
interesting view of higher education growth in this part of
the U.S. South.

675 Dyson, Walter. HOWARD UNIVERSITY: THE CAPSTONE OF NEGRO
EDUCATION. Washington, D.C.: Howard University, 1941. 553 p.

Howard University history professor marks the University's
seventy-fifth anniversary; tells of early confusion and anarchy
before the period of its growth and scholarly development,
1926-1940. Some issues which plagued its development were
possible denominational control, segregation versus racial and
social equality, and industrial versus classical education. W.
E.B. DuBois was not hired as classics professor; Booker T.
Washington became a trustee; both decisions caused dissension.

676 Dziuba, Victoria, and Meardy, William, eds. ENHANCING TRUSTEE
EFFECTIVENESS. San Francisco: Jossey-Bass Publishers, 1976. 109 p.

Community college trustees explain to other trustees their
various functions and suggest ways to influence programs.

677 Earnest, Ernest P. ACADEMIC PROCESSION: AN INFORMAL HISTORY
OF THE AMERICAN COLLEGE, 1636 TO 1953. Indianapolis: Bobbs-
Merrill, 1953. 368 p.

History of undergraduate liberal arts colleges and their relationships with American society. Students' academic pursuits
are shown in the context of their way of life.

678 Easterby, James H. A HISTORY OF THE COLLEGE OF CHARLESTON,
FOUNDED 1770. Charleston, S.C.: Trustees of the College of Charleston, 1935. 379 p.

College history through the 1920s, when women were admitted.
Shows impact of major events such as the Civil War, Reconstruction, and World War I on enrollments and the curriculum.
Appendices: charts and lists of trustees, faculty, students,
degree recipients; bibliography, and editorial notes.

679 Ebaugh, Franklin G., and Rymer, Charles A. PSYCHIATRY IN MEDICAL

EDUCATION. New York: Commonwealth Fund, 1942. 619 p.

Analysis of psychiatric instruction at undergraduate, graduate, and postgraduate levels in sixty-six U.S. medical schools and two in Canada. Done under auspices of the Division of Psychiatric Education of the National Commission for Mental Hygiene to gather information about administrative organization, faculty, curriculum, and teaching methods.

680   Ebel, Robert L. ESSENTIALS OF EDUCATIONAL MEASUREMENT. Englewood Cliffs, N.J.: Prentice-Hall, 1972. 622 p.

Textbook on testing in schools and colleges; a revision and extension of MEASURING EDUCATIONAL ACHIEVEMENT (1965). The six parts are on the history and philosophy of measurement, classroom test development, test scores, test analysis and evaluation, and published tests and testing programs.

681   _____. MEASURING EDUCATIONAL ACHIEVEMENT. Englewood Cliffs, N.J.: Prentice-Hall, 1965. 81 p.

For secondary and college teachers needing help in classroom testing. Describes uses and characteristics of essay and objective questions. How to write multiple choice items and to evaluate classroom tests.

682   Eble, Kenneth Eugene. THE ART OF ADMINISTRATION: A GUIDE FOR ACADEMIC ADMINISTRATORS. San Francisco: Jossey-Bass Publishers, 1978. 160 p.

Believing administration to be a subtle art, author examines administrative leadership, gives detailed recommendations for handling simple and complex administrative tasks, and makes concrete suggestions for working effectively with faculty, students, and staff.

683   _____. THE CRAFT OF TEACHING: A GUIDE TO MASTERING THE PROFESSOR'S ART. San Francisco: Jossey-Bass Publishers, 1976. 179 p.

English professor and former director of the American Association of University Professors' Project to Improve College Teaching believes good teaching is pleasurable and can be nurtured. Explores methods, teaching devices, and extends Gilbert Highet's teaching concepts.

684   _____. THE PROFANE COMEDY: AMERICAN HIGHER EDUCATION IN THE SIXTIES. New York: Macmillan Co., 1962. 234 p.

A humanist's witty, iconoclastic attack on mediocrity in higher education. Deplores organized athletics and other nonintel-

lectual features of campus life. Suggests giving domestic
Fulbright-type aid to lagging institutions as well as scrapping
grades and all academic bookkeeping.

685 _____. PROFESSORS AS TEACHERS. San Francisco: Jossey-Bass Publishers, 1972. 202 p.

Two-year study of college teaching deals with approaches to
teaching, evaluation, student inputs, and the effect of attitudes and personal qualities on good teaching. Recommends
improving teacher evaluation, increasing rewards for good
teaching, revitalizing teacher-training programs, dropping research as a major criterion for advancement, and creating a
more favorable teaching environment.

686 _____. THE RECOGNITION AND EVALUATION OF TEACHING. Salt
Lake City, Utah: Project to Improve College Teaching, 1970. 111 p.

Advocates student evaluation of college teachers. Found that
student evaluations are reasonably effective and that faculty
resistance to student evaluation is less widespread than expected.

687 Eckelberry, Rosco Huhn. THE HISTORY OF THE MUNICIPAL UNIVER-
SITY IN THE UNITED STATES. Office of Education Bulletin, 1932, no.
2. Washington, D.C.: Government Printing Office, 1932. 213 p.

Presents the history and development of eleven municipal universities; compares them, and concludes that they are important because they extend educational opportunity and also
help secularize education.

688 Eckert, Ruth E., and Keller, Robert J., eds. A UNIVERSITY LOOKS
AT ITS PROGRAM: THE REPORT OF THE UNIVERSITY OF MINNESOTA
BUREAU OF INSTITUTIONAL RESEARCH, 1942-1952. Minneapolis: Uni-
versity of Minnesota Press, 1954. 223 p.

Recounts the development of institutional research at the University of Minnesota, which pioneered in self-analysis. Many
of the studies done between 1942-52 are summarized and grouped
under general studies, studies of undergraduate and graduate
programs, and related staff activities. Includes a ten-year
study of curriculum development, faculty promotion policies
and practices, and enrollment trends.

689 Eddy, Edward Danforth, Jr. THE COLLEGE INFLUENCE ON STUDENT
CHARACTER. Washington, D.C.: American Council on Education, 1959.
186 p.

A view of education that links excellence of mind with values
based on conversations with students and faculty at twenty
selected colleges.

690   _____. COLLEGES FOR OUR LAND AND TIME: THE LAND-GRANT
IDEA IN AMERICAN EDUCATION. New York: Harper and Brothers,
1957. 328 p.

> History of the sixty-nine land-grant institutions from the early
> nineteenth-century free school movement, to the 1862 Morrill
> Act, to mid-twentieth century. The land-grant idea is viewed
> in its larger social, political, and economic setting. Negro
> land-grant colleges are treated separately.

691   Edgar, Day. IN PRINCETON TOWN. New York: Charles Scribner's
Sons, 1929. 351 p.

> Ten short stories about the same group of Princeton College
> men involved in proms, clubs, honors, and campus escapades.

692   Educational Policies Commission. MANPOWER AND EDUCATION.
Washington, D.C.: National Education Association and American Association of School Administrators, 1956. 128 p.

> Recommends six ways to solve the serious teacher shortage
> facing schools and colleges.

693   Educational Testing Service. THE THIRD CENTURY: POSTSECONDARY
PLANNING FOR THE NONTRADITIONAL LEARNER. Princeton, N.J.:
1977. 344 p.

> Findings about nontraditional postsecondary education in Iowa,
> how to identify nontraditional learners, their educational needs,
> and supporting services.

694   Education and World Affairs. THE PROFESSIONAL SCHOOL AND WORLD
AFFAIRS: A REPORT. Albuquerque: University of New Mexico Press,
1968. 408 p.

> About the involvement of U.S. higher education in world
> affairs and the international dimension of business administra-
> tion, public administration, agriculture, engineering, law,
> medicine, public health, education, and such other fields
> as research, teaching, technical assistance, and foreign stu-
> dent training. Concludes that these fields should have greater
> international involvement.

695   _____. THE UNIVERSITY LOOKS ABROAD: APPROACHES TO WORLD
AFFAIRS AT SIX AMERICAN UNIVERSITIES. New York: Walker and Co.,
1965. 300 p.

> After examining six universities (Cornell, Indiana, Michigan
> State, Tulane, Wisconsin, and Stanford), concluded that, des-
> pite differences, international education is a significant part
> of U.S. higher education. Michigan State stressed overseas
> contracts; Wisconsin allowed individual faculty members to

add the international dimension. Many universities have separate offices to coordinate international service. The report discusses foreign students, studies abroad, and area programs.

696 Education Commission of the States. STATE POSTSECONDARY EDUCATION INSTITUTIONAL AUTHROIZATION AND OVERSIGHT: A NATIONAL REPORT AND INSERVICE EDUCATION PROGRAM. Denver: 1979. 48 p.

Conference on the state's role in postsecondary institutional eligibility for federal funding.

697 EDUCOM. WE CAN IMPLEMENT COST-EFFECTIVE INFORMATION SYSTEMS NOW. Princeton, N.J.: 1977. 126 p.

Examines costs and benefits of using the computer in administrative decision making and planning and in managing academic libraries.

698 Edwards, Clifford H., et al. PLANNING, TEACHING, AND EVALUATING: A COMPETENCY APPROACH. Chicago: Nelson-Hall, 1977. 350 p.

Model for a competency-based teacher education program aims to help students develop the skills needed to become effective teachers; requires prospective teachers to demonstrate competency in the classroom before they receive teaching certification.

699 Eells, Walter Crosby. COLLEGE TEACHERS AND COLLEGE TEACHING: AN ANNOTATED BIBLIOGRAPHY. Atlanta: Southern Regional Education Board, 1957. 282 p. 1st supplement, 1959. 134 p.; 2d supplement, 1962. 192 p.; 3d supplement, by Litton, Maurice L., and Stickler, W. Hugh, 1967. 127 p.

Lists works on college teachers and teaching published since 1945, primarily in the United States. Main volume contains 2,665 entries arranged in ninety topical groups. Supplements have the same plan.

700 _____. SURVEYS OF AMERICAN HIGHER EDUCATION. New York: Carnegie Foundation for the Advancement of Teaching, 1937. 538 p.

Refers to almost three-hundred surveys of U.S. higher education dealing with staff (including student-faculty ratio, selection and appointment, sex, professional growth, tenure, salary, teaching load, and retirement) and with teaching methods (including independent study, lectures, evaluation, and forty special fields in the curriculum).

701 _____. WHY JUNIOR COLLEGE TERMINAL EDUCATION? Washington, D.C.: American Association of Junior Colleges, 1941. 365 p.

A general summary of terminal education based on personal observations and on questionnaire responses from administrators at some three-hundred two-year colleges. Comprehensive coverage includes history of junior college movement, curriculum enrollment, faculty qualifications, library needs, and methods of financing. Most important problem: developing terminal programs to meet student and community needs.

702 _____, ed. AMERICAN DISSERTATIONS ON FOREIGN EDUCATION. Washington, D.C.: Committee on International Relations, National Education Association, 1959. 300 p.

Lists 5,716 theses and dissertations in comparative education, classified by continent and country, many comparing foreign higher education with that in the United States.

703 _____. PRESENT STATUS OF JUNIOR COLLEGE TERMINAL EDUCATION. Washington, D.C.: American Association of Junior Colleges, 1941. 340 p.

Stresses the importance of terminal education and implications of social, economic, and educational changes for junior colleges. Summarizes opinions gathered from almost a thousand educators and business and professional men.

704 Eells, Walter Crosby, and Hollis, Ernest V. ADMINISTRATION OF HIGHER EDUCATION: AN ANNOTATED BIBLIOGRAPHY. Washington, D.C.: Government Printing Office, 1960. 410 p.

Lists and annotates 2,708 books, periodical articles, proceedings, and doctoral dissertations in thirteen major divisions about most phases of college and university administration.

705 _____. STUDENT FINANCIAL AID IN HIGHER EDUCATION: AN ANNOTATED BIBLIOGRAPHY. Washington, D.C.: Government Printing Office, 1961. 87 p.

Contains 451 entries about U.S. student financial aid, 95 percent of which appeared after 1955.

706 Ehrenreich, Barbara, and Ehrenreich, John. LONG MARCH, SHORT SPRING: THE STUDENT UPRISING AT HOME AND ABROAD. New York: Monthly Review Press, 1969. 189 p.

Student activism in England, France, Germany, Italy, and the United States, with a chapter on the 1968 Columbia University uprising. Analyzes and compares the aims, programs, and goals of student movements.

707 Ehrmann, Henry, et al. THE TEACHING OF THE SOCIAL SCIENCES IN THE UNITED STATES. New York: Columbia University Press, 1954. 150 p.

About teaching various social sciences, including anthropology, economics, law, political science, and sociology. Characteristics of social science teaching in U.S. higher education institutions are national inbreeding--with overwhelming emphasis on American culture--and preoccupation with statistics, measurement, and methodology.

708 Eichel, Lawrence E., et al. THE HARVARD STRIKE. Boston: Houghton Mifflin, 1970. 381 p.

Chronicles and interprets sympathetically the 1969 Harvard student strike, blaming the Vietnam war, ROTC, and Harvard's political involvement for activating students under SDS leadership. Underlying the unrest was the belief that Harvard was unresponsive to undergraduate needs.

709 Einstein, Bernice W. COLLEGE ENTRANCE GUIDE. New York: Grosset and Dunlap, 1964. 96 p.

How-to guide for high school counselors, students, and their parents. Has answers to twenty important questions about college admission and advice on how to proceed in the various stages of the admissions process.

710 Eisenberg, Gersun G. LEARNING VACATIONS: A GUIDE TO COLLEGE SEMINARS, CONFERENCE CENTERS, EDUCATIONAL TOURS. Baltimore, Md.: Eisenberg Educational Enterprise, 1977. 117 p.

Gives subject matter, dates, costs, and facilities for summer programs (particularly "alumni colleges") at about eighty colleges and other institutions in the United States (also several in Canada and Great Britain). Most are open to the public.

711 Eisenhart, Luther P. THE EDUCATIONAL PROCESS. Princeton, N.J.: Princeton University Press, 1945. 87 p.

Author, almost fifty years a college teacher and administrator, favors preceptorial conferences instead of faculty lectures, and a comprehensive exam and independent study culminating in a thesis in one's major field. Deplores the proliferation of the Ph.D., which he believes should be reserved for distinction in research.

712 Eisner, Richard, and Ferrin, Richard. DEVELOPMENTAL PROGRAMS IN MIDWESTERN COMMUNITY COLLEGES. New York: College Entrance Examination Board, 1971.

Report of a questionnaire survey made of midwestern community colleges' remedial course offerings.

713 Elam, Stanley M., and McLure, William P., eds. EDUCATIONAL RE-
QUIREMENTS FOR THE 1970S: AN INTERDISCIPLINARY APPROACH.
New York: Praeger Publishers, 1967. 266 p.

Conference report explores changes likely in educational requirements. Papers by experts in economics, political science,
sociology, science, education, and government planning.
Among specific problems examined are the interaction between
race relations and economic planning and between government
subsidies and government interference.

714 Elam, Stanley M., and Moskow, Michael H., eds. EMPLOYMENT RE-
LATIONS IN HIGHER EDUCATION. Bloomington, Ind.: Phi Delta Kappa,
1969. 215 p.

Papers on current problems in higher education governance discuss collective bargaining by the American Association of University Professors, National Education Association, and American Federation of Teachers. Other papers deplore such an
adversary style, favor instead shared responsibility, which re-
duces power held by central administration and assigns responsibility to faculty organizations.

715 Eliot, Charles William. EDUCATIONAL REFORM: ESSAYS AND AD-
DRESSES. New York: Century Co., 1898. Reprint. New York: Arno
Press, 1969. 418 p.

Essays and addresses by President Eliot (1834-1926) of Harvard,
who helped transform it from a small regional college to a
great university.

716 _____. A TURNING POINT IN HIGHER EDUCATION: THE INAUGU-
RAL ADDRESS OF CHARLES WILLIAM ELIOT AS PRESIDENT OF HARVARD
COLLEGE, OCTOBER 19, 1869. Introduction by Nathan M. Pusey.
Cambridge, Mass.: Harvard University Press, 1969. 30 p.

Reprint of Eliot's great address which presaged the birth of
U.S. higher education in its modern form, with introduction
by Harvard's 1969 president.

717 _____. UNIVERSITY ADMINISTRATION. Boston: Houghton, 1908.
266 p.

Six lectures at Northwestern University in 1908 about university trustees, alumni influence, faculty, the elective system,
methods of instruction, and social organization.

718 Elliott, Edward C., and Chambers, Merritt Madison. CHARTERS AND
BASIC LAWS OF SELECTED AMERICAN UNIVERSITIES AND COLLEGES.
New York: Carnegie Foundation for the Advancement of Teaching, 1934.
640 p.

> On the legal basis of U.S. higher education. Contains char-
> ters and certain basic laws of fifty-one representative U.S.
> colleges, universities, and technical schools.

719 Elliott, Edward C., et al. THE GOVERNMENT OF HIGHER EDUCATION.
New York: American Book Co., 1935. 289 p.

> Treats important aspects of college trustees' work in 554 ques-
> tions and answers. Includes the legal basis for the roles of
> trustees and their actual and ideal internal organization and
> methods of functioning.

720 Elliott, Orrin Leslie. STANFORD UNIVERSITY, THE FIRST TWENTY-
FIVE YEARS. Stanford, Calif.: Stanford University Press, 1937. 624 p.

> Account by Stanford's former registrar during its founding
> period, including a drop in funds, an earthquake, and a
> notorious academic freedom case.

721 Ellis, Constance Dimock, ed. THE MAGNIFICENT ENTERPRISE: CHRON-
ICLE OF VASSAR COLLEGE. Poughkeepsie, N.Y.: Vassar College, 1961.
138 p.

> Student letters, alumnae reports, newspaper commentary, and
> trustee minutes depict Vassar's history. Weaves in major his-
> torical events and Vassar's intellectual growth as a leading
> women's college. Program innovations include teaching Rus-
> sian from 1932 and having one of the country's first majors
> in child study.

722 Ellis, Elmer, ed. TOWARD BETTER TEACHING IN COLLEGE. Columbia:
Curators of the University of Missouri, 1954. 87 p.

> Thirteen papers about improving college teaching are on such
> topics as student motivation, lecturing techniques, grading,
> and teacher evaluation.

723 Ellis, John Tracy. THE FORMATIVE YEARS OF THE CATHOLIC UNIVER-
SITY OF AMERICA. Washington, D.C.: American Catholic History Association, 1946. 415 p.

> Documented history of the post-Civil War period and events
> which preceded the opening of Catholic University of America,
> 1889.

724 Ellis, Joseph, and Moore, Robert. SCHOOL FOR SOLDIERS: WEST

POINT AND THE PROFESSION OF ARMS. New York: Oxford University Press, 1974. 291 p.

Two former West Point professors who call for reform, analyze the Academy's academic policies, staffing, curriculum, teaching methods, and intellectual values. They question using a faculty of unevenly prepared army officers who are neither professional teachers nor scholars and call the honor system psychologically oppressive and a menace to the academic program.

725 Ellner, Carolyn Lipton, and Barnes, B.J. SCHOOLMAKING: AN ALTERNATIVE IN TEACHER EDUCATION. Lexington, Mass.: Lexington Books, 1977. 208 p.

Describes an alternative graduate teacher education program at Claremont Graduate School in 1970-72 and a follow-up study five years later of the fourteen students involved. The program consisted of an academic year of course work and nondirective seminars, a six-week summer mini-school in which students planned and conducted programs in the community, and a year of internship.

726 Ellsworth, Frank L., and Burns, Martha A. STUDENT ACTIVISM IN AMERICAN HIGHER EDUCATION. Washington, D.C.: American College Personnel Association, 1970. 64 p.

Introduction to student activism intended for higher education guidance personnel.

727 Ellsworth, Ralph E. THE ECONOMICS OF BOOK STORAGE IN COLLEGE AND UNIVERSITY LIBRARIES. Metuchen, N.J.: Scarecrow Press, 1969. 135 p.

Describes twelve methods for storing books in academic libraries and compares the cost and space efficiency of each. Reports results of experience and studies at Harvard, Yale, Princeton, Michigan, Chicago, Berkeley, and MIT. Conclusions: all compact storage systems save space; none of them saves money; and faculty members are generally opposed to storage programs.

728 Elsbree, Willard S. THE AMERICAN TEACHER: EVOLUTION OF A PROFESSION IN A DEMOCRACY. New York: American Book Co., 1939. 556 p.

Account of teaching from colonial days to the early years of nationhood and the later emergence of the professional teacher.

729 Ely, Richard T. GROUND UNDER OUR FEET: AN AUTOBIOGRAPHY. New York: Macmillan, 1938. 330 p.

Autobiography of a leading late nineteenth-century social

scientist (1854-1943), a founder of the American Economic Association, who opposed the laissez faire doctrine, supported the social gospel, and favored making economics study inductive and pragmatic. He taught at Johns Hopkins, Northwestern and the University of Wisconsin, where his 1890s dismissal trial was a cause célèbre among proponents of academic freedom.

730 Embling, Jack. A FRESH LOOK AT HIGHER EDUCATION: EUROPEAN IMPLICATIONS OF THE CARNEGIE COMMISSION REPORTS. New York: American Elsevier Publishing Co., 1974. 263 p.

Using Great Britain as a focal point, author considers the applicability of the Carnegie Commission's U.S. higher education proposals to European education.

731 Emery, James C., ed. CLOSING THE GAP BETWEEN TECHNOLOGY AND APPLICATION. Boulder, Colo.: Westview Press, 1978. 215 p.

Conference proceedings which analyzed computer technology in higher education from the perspectives of the technician, the administrator, and the user.

732 Endicott, Frank S. A COLLEGE STUDENT'S GUIDE TO CAREER PLANNING: WHAT COLLEGE STUDENTS NEED TO KNOW ABOUT CAREER PLANNING AND JOBS. Chicago: Rand McNally, 1967. 96 p.

Answers fifty questions on college students' career planning.

733 Engel, Monroe. THE VISIONS OF NICHOLAS SOLON. New York: Sagamore Press, 1959. 249 p.

Novel about the hero's premarital affair with a college faculty wife; the memory returns to haunt him.

734 Engineering Manpower Commission. ENGINEERING AND TECHNOLOGY ENROLLMENTS FALL 1973. New York: Engineers Joint Council, 1974. 155 p.

Designed for engineering manpower planners. Reports findings in an enrollment survey of 279 schools with engineering programs and 580 technical institutions about curricular groups, accrediting agencies, women, minorities, and foreign nationals.

735 _____, comp. SALARIES OF ENGINEERING TECHNICIANS AND TECHNOLOGISTS, 1977: A DETAILED INDUSTRY REPORT. New York: Engineers Joint Council, 1978. 112 p.

Reports the average 1977 salaries of graduates of two-year college-level programs in technology, nongraduates qualified to do the same kind of work on the basis of experience and education, and bachelor's degree graduates in technology.

736 Engleman, Lois E., and Eells, Walter Crosby. THE LITERATURE OF JUNIOR COLLEGE TERMINAL EDUCATION. Washington, D.C.: American Association of Junior Colleges, 1941. 322 p.

> Contains 1,438 annotated entries about such aspects of junior college terminal education as faculty, curriculum, and teaching methods.

737 English, Thomas Hopkins. EMORY UNIVERSITY, 1915–1965; A SEMI-CENTENNIAL HISTORY. Atlanta: Emory University, 1966. 120 p.

> Based on Henry M. Bullock's HISTORY OF EMORY UNIVERSITY 1836–1936 (1936) and other memoranda and documents. Has separate chapters on each decade, 1915–65, on each school and college, and on student affairs, religious life, athletics, public cultural activities, and the alumni association.

738 Ennis, Richard M., and Williamson, J. Peter. SPENDING POLICY FOR EDUCATIONAL ENDOWMENTS: A RESEARCH AND PUBLICATION PROJECT OF THE COMMON FUND. Naugatuck, Conn.: Money Market Reports, 1976. 93 p.

> Summarizes studies of endowment spending process done by the Common Fund, established by several New York investment counselors to help colleges and universities invest their endowments.

739 Epler, Stephen Edward. HONORARY DEGREES: A SURVEY OF THEIR USE AND ABUSE. Washington, D.C.: American Council on Public Affairs, 1943. 224 p.

> Reviews history of honorary degrees. Investigates practices in some two-hundred colleges and universities, seven of which were studied in detail (California, Columbia, Harvard, Nebraska, North Carolina, Smith, and Wisconsin). Also gathered and analyzed opinions about such degrees. Found discrimination based on sex, politics, and religions; absence of uniform standards; and poorly qualified selection committees. Recommends that such degrees be abandoned or that college faculties select candidates for such degrees and that accrediting agencies approve granting them.

740 Epstein, Cy. HOW TO KILL A COLLEGE. Los Angeles: Sherbourne Press, 1971. 201 p.

> Case study by a radical professor of student revolt at California State College, Fullerton, where the pattern common to other such revolts emerges: small group of protesters, police called to campus, and inept administrators.

741 Epstein, Leon D. GOVERNING THE UNIVERSITY. San Francisco: Jossey-Bass Publishers, 1974. 253 p.

By a political scientist who explores the complexities of public university governance and the diverse interests of the state, trustees, administrators, and faculty members. Suggests resolving clashes by setting up a pluralistic government that would reconcile conflicting interests.

742 ERIC Clearinghouse for Junior Colleges. THE HUMANITIES IN TWO-YEAR COLLEGES: WHAT AFFECTS THE PROGRAM? Los Angeles: University of California, 1979. 50 p.

Humanities programs from viewpoint of student needs, community forces, job market, and college transfer requirements.

743 Ericksen, Stanford C. MOTIVATION FOR LEARNING: A GUIDE FOR THE TEACHER OF THE YOUNG ADULT. Ann Arbor: University of Michigan Press, 1974. 259 p.

Ways college teachers can apply theory and research findings about learning, motivation, personality, and group dynamics.

744 Ericson, Edward E., Jr. RADICALS IN THE UNIVERSITY. Stanford, Calif.: Hoover Institution Publications, 1975. 281 p.

Uses a detailed case study of radicals in the Modern Language Association to illustrate the role radicals played in academic life during the 1960s and gives a general overview of other radical activities by academic groups.

745 Erlich, John, and Erlich, Susan, eds. STUDENT POWER: PARTICIPATION AND REVOLUTION. New York: Association Press, 1970. 254 p.

Student statements about the late 1960s protest movement. Editors believe the student movement against capitalism, racism, and militarism to be a necessary step toward freedom.

746 Erskine, John. BACHELOR--OF ARTS. Indianapolis: Bobbs-Merrill Co., 1933. 331 p.

Novel about four years at Columbia set against the 1930s Great Depression. Written by a well-known scholar who influenced the modern revival of the Great Books program in literature at Columbia University.

747 _____. MY LIFE AS A TEACHER. New York: J.B. Lippincott Co., 1948. 249 p.

Memories of teaching by an innovative teacher-writer-musician, with critical observations about college teaching and the Ph.D.

748 Eschenbacher, Herman F. THE UNIVERSITY OF RHODE ISLAND: A HISTORY OF LAND-GRANT EDUCATION IN RHODE ISLAND. New York: Appleton-Century-Crofts, 1967. 548 p.

Case study of U.S. land-grant education as exemplified by the University of Rhode Island (its name since 1951), incorporated in 1892 as Rhode Island College of Agriculture and Mechanical Arts. Examines rivalry with Brown University, tensions between practical-vocational education and liberal education, and continuing dependence of the college on state politics.

749 Essert, Paul L. CREATIVE LEADERSHIP OF ADULT EDUCATION. Englewood Cliffs, N.J.: Prentice-Hall, 1951. 333 p.

Discusses goals of creative leadership in adult education, criteria applicable to adult study for personal growth as well as community development, a guide for training creative leadership, and ways for adult education to improve the community.

750 Estrin, Herman A., and Sanderson, Arthur M., eds. FREEDOM AND CENSORSHIP OF THE COLLEGE PRESS. Dubuque, Iowa: William C. Brown Co., 1966. 310 p.

Explores policy differences toward student newspapers in state, private, and church-supported colleges. Agrees that a college or university newspaper cannot be compared with other newspapers.

751 Eszterhas, Joe, and Roberts, Michael D. THIRTEEN SECONDS: CONFRONTATION AT KENT STATE. New York: Dodd, Mead, 1970. 308 p.

Journalistic account of May 1970 events at Kent State University and the aftermath.

752 Eulau, Heinz, and Quinley, Harold. STATE OFFICIALS AND HIGHER EDUCATION: A SURVEY OF THE OPINIONS AND EXPECTATIONS OF POLICY MAKERS IN NINE STATES. New York: McGraw-Hill Book Co., 1970. 209 p.

Gathered attitudes, opinions, and information on higher education held by legislators in nine states. Found that legislators in responsible positions were aware of higher education, proud of their state's achievement in higher education, and willing to help find needed resources. Legislators not in important positions related to higher education knew less about it and their constituencies were less concerned about higher education.

753 Eurich, Alvin C. REFORMING AMERICAN EDUCATION: THE INNOVA-

TIVE APPROACH TO IMPROVING OUR SCHOOLS AND COLLEGES.
New York: Harper and Row, 1969. 269 p.

> To improve schooling, the executive director of the Ford Foun-
> dation for the Advancement of Education suggests: free out-
> standing teachers of routine tasks; put the best teachers on
> educational television; improve recruitment from liberal arts
> graduates by offering fifth-year teacher education; use team
> teaching, programmed learning, language labs, nongraded sys-
> tems, and new physics and math programs; and teach human-
> istic subjects to integrate the curriculum.

754 _____, ed. CAMPUS 1980: THE SHAPE OF THE FUTURE IN AMERICAN
HIGHER EDUCATION. New York: Delacorte Press, 1968. 327 p.

> Issues raised by such educators as John Gardner, Clark Kerr,
> David Riesman, Nevitt Sanford, and Logan Wilson include in-
> volving universities in solving urban and other social problems
> and fitting programs and teaching methods to student needs.

755 _____. GENERAL EDUCATION IN THE AMERICAN COLLEGE. National Society for the Study of Education 38th Yearbook, Part II. Chicago: University of Chicago Press, 1939. 382 p.

> Emphasizes relationships between college and community, aca-
> demic fields, and levels of education. Discusses fitting edu-
> cational objectives to student needs. Contributors include
> Karl W. Bigelow, Earl J. McGrath, Malcolm S. MacLean,
> Homer P. Rainey, John Dale Russell, and Henry M. Wriston.

756 Evans, D. Luther. ESSENTIALS OF LIBERAL EDUCATION. Boston: Ginn
and Co., 1942. 199 p.

> Tells undergraduates that a liberal education will provide basic
> knowledge and moral vision. Sections on self-discovery, self-
> discipline, self-development, and self-denial.

757 Evans, Franklin R. APPLICATIONS AND ADMISSIONS TO ABA AC-
CREDITED LAW SCHOOLS: AN ANALYSIS OF NATIONAL DATA FOR
THE CLASS ENTERING IN THE FALL OF 1976. Princeton, N.J.: Edu-
cational Testing Service, 1977. 108 p.

> Analyzes over 76,000 law school applicants. Presents accep-
> tance rates for applicants with each level of Law School Ad-
> mission Test score and separately for males, females, and sev-
> eral minority groups. Explores impact of a policy against
> using ethnic identity as a factor in admissions.

758 Evans, Richard I., and Leppmann, Peter K. RESISTANCE TO INNOVA-
TION IN HIGHER EDUCATION: A SOCIAL PSYCHOLOGICAL EXPLORA-

TION FOCUSED ON TELEVISION AND THE ESTABLISHMENT. San Francisco: Jossey-Bass Publishers, 1967. 198 p.

Findings on reactions to educational television are used to illustrate widespread resistance to innovation.

759   Evenden, Edward Samuel. NATIONAL SURVEY OF THE EDUCATION OF TEACHERS. SUMMARY AND INTERPRETATION. Vol. VI. U.S. Office of Education, Bulletin no. 10, 1933. Washington, D.C.: 1935. 253 p.

Clarifies problems, issues, and trends in teacher education. Proposes improvements and ways of solving problems.

760   Evenden, Edward Samuel, and Butts, R. Freeman, eds. COLUMBIA UNIVERSITY CO-OPERATIVE PROGRAM FOR THE PRE-SERVICE EDUCATION OF TEACHERS. New York: Teachers College, Columbia University, 1942. 120 p.

Experimental three-year program for elementary and secondary teachers at Barnard and Columbia Colleges and Teachers College used a seminar during the junior and senior years to replace such basic courses as educational psychology, education principles, and history of education. Two seminars during the fifth year (concluding in the M.A. degree) were in educational theory and in the student's teaching field.

761   Everett, Edward. ORATIONS AND SPEECHES ON VARIOUS OCCASIONS. 2d ed. 4 vols. Boston: C.C. Little and J. Brown, 1850–68. Reprint. New York: Arno Press, 1972.

Several speeches on education by famous statesman discuss benefits of university education, importance of scientific knowledge, women's education, teacher education, medical education, John Harvard and Harvard College, John Lowell and Lowell Institute, and state aid to higher education.

762   Ewen, Robert B. CHOOSING THE COLLEGE FOR YOU. New York: Franklin Watts, 1976. 60 p.

Tips for secondary students on how to find a suitable college and how to succeed in college.

763   Fackenthal, Frank Diehl. THE GREATER POWER. New York: Columbia University Press, 1949. 87 p.

Eighteen speeches on university affairs by Columbia University faculty member and administrator for almost thirty years (the last four years as president).

764   Falvey, Frances E. STUDENT PARTICIPATION IN COLLEGE ADMINISTRATION. New York: Teachers College, Columbia University, 1952. 206 p.

Used 1947–48 data to illustrate practices and trends in student participation in college administration. Stressed the educational value of such participation, still limited to a few campuses.

765 Farber, Evan Ira, and Walling, Ruth, eds. THE ACADEMIC LIBRARY: ESSAYS IN HONOR OF GUY R. LYLE. Metuchen, N.J.: Scarecrow Press, 1974. 171 p.

Twelve essays on college libraries by a library science educator; bibliography of his writings during his forty-year career in academic libraries.

766 Farmer, Martha L., ed. STUDENT PERSONNEL SERVICES FOR ADULTS IN HIGHER EDUCATION. Metuchen, N.J.: Scarecrow Press, 1967. 211 p.

About the needs of evening college students for personnel services.

767 Farnsworth, Dana L. MENTAL HEALTH IN COLLEGE AND UNIVERSITY. Cambridge, Mass.: Harvard University Press, 1957. 244 p.

The role of counselors and psychiatrists in an effective college mental health program. Says psychiatrists should treat the severely ill and should assist admissions officers in selecting most promising applicants, particularly for professional schools.

768 Farrand, Max, ed. BENJAMIN FRANKLIN'S MEMOIRS. Berkeley: University of California Press, 1949. 422 p.

Autobiography of the famous American, including his part in founding the Philadelphia Academy, which became the University of Pennsylvania. Contains texts of Franklin's original manuscript, French translations of it, and version edited by his grandson.

769 Farrell, James T. MY DAYS OF ANGER. New York: Vanguard Press, 1943. 403 p.

Novel, part of author's Danny O'Neill series, covers the years from 1924 to 1927 when Danny works in a gas station to finance his study at the University of Chicago, where he determined to become a writer.

770 Fashing, Joseph, and Deutsch, Steven E. ACADEMICS IN RETREAT: THE POLITICS OF EDUCATIONAL INNOVATION. Albuquerque: New Mexico University Press, 1971. 325 p.

Student problems and academic innovations at University of California at Berkeley and at Los Angeles, San Francisco

State, University of Oregon, Western Washington State College, and Stanford. Detailed study of experimental colleges; cluster concepts; racial and minority curricula; and student, faculty, and administrative interaction and conflict.

771 Fass, Paula S. THE DAMNED AND THE BEAUTIFUL: AMERICAN YOUTH IN THE 1920S. New York: Oxford University Press, 1977. 497 p.

Characterizes 1920s white middle class college rebels as essentially conservative, but more willing than adults to experiment and adjust to change.

772 Federated Council on Art Education. REPORT OF THE COMMITTEE ON ART INSTRUCTION IN COLLEGES AND UNIVERSITIES. New York: 1927. 69 p.

Questionnaire findings about college credit for high school art courses, art instructional problems, and art degree requirements.

773 Fein, Rashi, and Weber, Gerald I. FINANCING MEDICAL EDUCATION: AN ANALYSIS OF ALTERNATIVE POLICIES AND MECHANISMS. New York: McGraw-Hill Book Co., 1971. 279 p.

Evaluation of the fiscal administration of medical schools. Shows origin and present (1971) financial situation of medical education. Half of full-time medical faculty receive some federal support, 16.5 percent receive full federal support, and 63 percent of the cost of medical schooling comes from federal sources. Shows why many low-income students are financially barred from medical education and why medical school graduates move from "have not" states. Considers alternative methods of financing medical education. Advocates greater government support to students.

774 Feingold, S. Norman. SCHOLARSHIPS, FELLOWSHIPS AND LOANS. 5 vols. Boston: Bellman Publishing Co., 1949, 1951, 1955, 1962, 1972. 254 p., 312 p., 471 p., 368 p., 280 p.

Guide to financial aid (scholarships, loans, grants) available directly to graduate and undergraduate students. Indexed by vocations, organizations, and institutions granting aid.

775 _____, et al., eds. COLLEGE GUIDE FOR JEWISH YOUTH, 1978-1979. Washington, D.C.: B'nai B'rith Career and Counseling Services, 1978. 190 p.

Lists institutions in the United States and Canada having twenty-five or more Jewish students; also lists Jewish facilities, programs, and services.

776   Feinstein, Otto, et al. HIGHER EDUCATION IN THE UNITED STATES: ECONOMICS, PERSONALISM, QUALITY. Lexington, Mass.: D.C. Heath and Co., 1971. 197 p.

Critical of the credit-hour kind of measurement process through which college students attain graduation; seeks alternative ways to develop student personalities and achieve learning.

777   Felder, Dell, ed. COMPETENCY BASED TEACHER EDUCATION: PROFESSIONALIZING SOCIAL STUDIES TEACHING. Washington, D.C.: National Council for the Social Studies, 1978. 118 p.

Explores using competency-based teacher education to strengthen social studies teaching as a profession.

778   Feldman, Edmund Burke, ed. ART IN AMERICAN HIGHER INSTITUTIONS. Washington, D.C.: National Art Education Association, 1970. 112 p.

Eleven papers describing university art education.

779   Feldman, Kenneth A. RESEARCH STRATEGIES IN STUDYING COLLEGE IMPACT. Iowa City: American College Testing Program, 1970. 35 p.

Discussion of research strategies used in measuring the impact of college upon students.

780   Feldman, Kenneth A., and Newcomb, Theodore M. THE IMPACT OF COLLEGE ON STUDENTS. Vol. I: AN ANALYSIS OF FOUR DECADES OF RESEARCH. Vol. II: SUMMARY TABLES. San Francisco: Jossey-Bass Publishers, 1969. 474 p., 171 p.

Summarizes and evaluates nearly fifteen-hundred studies of the effect college experiences have on students. Topics included are types of colleges, residence patterns, faculty, and student culture.

781   Feldman, Saul D. ESCAPE FROM THE DOLL'S HOUSE: WOMEN IN GRADUATE AND PROFESSIONAL SCHOOL EDUCATION. New York: McGraw-Hill Book Co., 1974. 208 p.

Questionnaire data from undergraduates, graduate students, and faculty at all types of U.S. higher education institutions. Found that women resemble men in their own fields more than they resemble women in other fields. Did not prove why women perform less well than men in graduate school. Recommends ways to end sex bias in graduate education.

782   Feltner, Bill D., ed. COLLEGE ADMINISTRATION: CONCEPTS AND TECHNIQUES. Athens: Institute of Higher Education, University of Georgia, 1971. 51 p.

Papers dealing with needed reform in college administration advocate using some type of administrative team.

783 Felton, Gary S., and Biggs, Barbara E. UP FROM UNDERACHIEVE-MENT. Springfield, Ill.: Charles C Thomas, Publisher, 1977. 208 p.

About the problems of college underachievers, with specific methods of helping them.

784 Fenske, Robert H., and Scott, Craig S. THE CHANGING PROFILE OF COLLEGE STUDENTS. Washington, D.C.: American Association for Higher Education, 1974. 77 p.

Enrollment trends and profile of current college students, based upon research literature and analysis of a national sample of students, 1968-73.

785 Fenton, William Nelson. AREA STUDIES IN AMERICAN UNIVERSITIES. Washington, D.C.: American Council on Education, 1947. 92 p.

Examined multidisciplinary area and language studies begun during World War II at fifty-five universities and colleges to train enlisted men for work in specified countries. Findings are about personnel and administration, integration of disciplines, teaching methods, and prospects.

786 Ferrari, Michael R. PROFILES OF AMERICAN COLLEGE PRESIDENTS. East Lansing: Division of Research, Graduate School of Business Administration, Michigan State University, 1970. 175 p.

Profiles of lives, careers, and opinions of 760 university and college presidents. Studied their social origins, professional training, and career patterns. No major significant differences were found.

787 Ferre, Nels F.S. CHRISTIAN FAITH AND HIGHER EDUCATION. New York: Harper and Brothers, 1954. 251 p.

A theologian's discussion of religion's relation to higher education. Highly critical of narrowly sectarian colleges. Favors a curriculum emphasizing humanities, especially literature. Deplores heavy reliance on counseling; prefers that students handle their own problems.

788 Ferrin, Richard I. BARRIERS TO UNIVERSAL HIGHER EDUCATION. New York: College Entrance Examination Board, 1970. 54 p.

Identifies as barriers to attending college: financial, academic, motivational, and geographic problems. Discusses attempts to reduce these barriers.

789 _____. A DECADE OF CHANGE IN FREE-ACCESS HIGHER EDUCA-
TION. New York: College Entrance Examination Board, 1971. 75 p.

Used Warren W. Willingham's FREE-ACCESS HIGHER EDUCA-
TION (1968) and 1958 data. Compared changes in accessibility to low-cost, nonselective higher education nationally and
regionally. Important changes included new colleges, increased
cost and selectivity in existing colleges, college closings and
relocations, and increased urbanization. Largest net increase
was in suburbs of twenty-nine major U.S. cities. Greatest
regional increases were in the Northeast and South.

790 _____. DEVELOPMENTAL PROGRAMS IN MIDWESTERN COMMUNITY
COLLEGES. New York: College Entrance Examination Board, 1971.
50 p.

Examined sixteen programs for educationally disadvantaged students in midwestern community colleges. Found that one student in nine was involved in remedial courses, special academic skill services, and/or formal developmental programs.

791 _____. STUDENT BUDGETS AND AID AWARDED IN SOUTHWESTERN
COLLEGES. New York: College Entrance Examination Board, 1971.
40 p.

Compared 1970-71 student aid and expenses in Southwest colleges: aid met 16 percent of student expenses in private colleges, 10 percent in public four-year colleges, and 7.7 percent in public two-year colleges.

792 Ferrin, Richard I., and Arbeiter, Solomon. BRIDGING THE GAP: A
STUDY OF EDUCATION-TO-WORK LINKAGES. Princeton, N.J.: College Entrance Examination Board, 1976. 180 p. Supplement. 68 p.

Among recommendations to match skills derived from education
with skills needed for work: all secondary and postsecondary
institutions provide and require work experience of all students;
a statewide interagency task force responsible for manpower
supply and demand data; and National Institute of Education
support for competency-based teacher certification proposals.

793 Ferrin, Richard I., and Willingham, Warren W. PRACTICES OF SOUTH-
ERN INSTITUTIONS IN RECOGNIZING COLLEGE-LEVEL ACHIEVEMENT.
New York: College Entrance Examination Board, 1970. 42 p.

Found in a questionnaire survey of 141 southern colleges that
two-thirds gave course exemption in 1970 based on advanced
standing achievement tests. Only one freshman in nine received such exemption.

794 Fetters, William B. NATIONAL LONGITUDINAL STUDY OF THE HIGH

SCHOOL CLASS OF 1972. Washington, D.C.: Government Printing Office, 1976. 61 p.

Studied 1972 high school graduating class; their plans, values, attitudes, education, and work experiences. Made comparative profiles based on sex, academic background, ability, race, and other factors.

795 Feuer, Lewis S. THE CONFLICT OF GENERATIONS: THE CHARACTER AND SIGNIFICANCE OF STUDENT MOVEMENTS. New York: Basic Books, 1969. 543 p.

Worldwide historical survey of radical student movements shows that they are not unique to the present nor to the United States. Detailed study of the 1964-65 Berkeley protests. Concludes that youth's anger at elders causes such movements, which then provoke reactions from the right wing and threaten democracy.

796 Fichter, Joseph Henry. GRADUATES OF PREDOMINANTLY NEGRO COLLEGES--CLASS OF 1964. Washington, D.C.: U.S. Public Health, 1967. 262 p.

Study of 1964 black college graduates--their job aspirations, career decisions, and graduate school plans.

797 Fields, Ralph R. THE COMMUNITY COLLEGE MOVEMENT. New York: McGraw-Hill Book Co., 1962. 360 p.

Explains origins of community colleges in the junior college movement, community colleges' varied goals, and their need for a comprehensive curriculum. In-depth descriptions of four colleges in rural, urban, agricultural, and industrial communities.

798 Fife, Jonathan D. APPLYING THE GOALS OF STUDENT FINANCIAL AID. Washington, D.C.: American Association for Higher Education, 1976. 67 p.

Asks such questions about federal aid to students as: does the aid promote access to college and widen choice of college and does the aid help equalize educational opportunity?

799 Figueroa, Peter M.E., and Persaud, Ganga, eds. SOCIOLOGY OF EDUCATION: A CARIBBEAN READER. New York: Oxford University Press, 1977. 284 p.

Assesses teacher education and mobility among university graduates in the Caribbean area.

800 File, M. Jeanne. A CRITICAL ANALYSIS OF CURRENT CONCEPTS OF ART IN AMERICAN HIGHER EDUCATION. Washington, D.C.: Catholic University of America Press, 1958. 107 p.

About contemporary art education in higher education. Examines teaching concepts of Plato, Aquinas, and Kant.

801 Finch, Edith. CAREY THOMAS OF BRYN MAWR. New York: Harper and Brothers, 1947. 342 p.

Biography of Bryn Mawr's President Thomas (1857–1935). Depicts her early feminism; her drive for the Bryn Mawr presidency; conflicts with faculty, alumni, and directors; and her insistence that women were entitled to the same scholarly instruction as men.

802 Finch, James Kip. A HISTORY OF THE SCHOOL OF ENGINEERING, COLUMBIA UNIVERSITY. New York: Columbia University Press, 1954. 138 p.

History of the Columbia School of Engineering against a background of the history of engineering education from early Roman times. Shows that U.S. industrial and scientific development paralleled the growth of this engineering school.

803 Fincher, Cameron, et al. THE CLOSING SYSTEM OF ACADEMIC EMPLOYMENT. Atlanta: Southern Regional Education Board, 1978. 78 p.

Suggests institutional responses, nonacademic job opportunities, and statewide program reviews to deal with the projected surplus of Ph.D.'s in the South in the 1980s.

804 Fine, Benjamin. BARRON'S PROFILES OF AMERICAN COLLEGES. Woodbury, N.Y.: Barron's Educational Series, 1970. 882 p.

Student-oriented annual directory of all accredited, four-year colleges and universities. Institutional descriptions include statistics and general information describing each college's social and academic environments. Also groups colleges in seven categories on the basis of academic selectivity.

805 _____. COLLEGE PUBLICITY IN THE UNITED STATES. Contributions to Education No. 832. New York: Teachers College, Columbia University, 1941. 78 p.

Critical analysis of publicity in U.S. colleges and universities: its nature, history, objectives, organization, techniques, and social implications. Some conclusions and recommendations: separate sports publicity from general news, free publicity directors of teaching assignments, and establish closer relations with the press.

806 _____. DEMOCRATIC EDUCATION. New York: Thomas Y. Crowell Co., 1945. 251 p.

Surveys U.S. higher education history, describes the present
(1945) higher education situation, and concludes that state-
supported vocationally oriented higher education more nearly
meets people's needs.

807 _____. HOW TO BE ACCEPTED BY THE COLLEGE OF YOUR CHOICE.
Rev. ed. Great Neck, N.Y.: Channel Press, 1960. 291 p.

Informative sourcebook for college-bound students.

808 Fine, Carla. BARRON'S GUIDE TO FOREIGN MEDICAL SCHOOLS:
SELECTING THEM, SURVIVING THEM, AND SUCCESSFULLY PRACTIC-
ING IN THE UNITED STATES. Woodbury, N.Y.: Barron's Educational
Series, 1978. 188 p.

Lists admissions requirements, procedures, degree requirements,
and other facts needed by Americans wishing to attend a foreign medical school.

809 Fink, Ira Stephen. THE ECONOMIC IMPACT OF INSTITUTIONS OF
HIGHER EDUCATION ON LOCAL COMMUNITIES: AN ANNOTATED
BIBLIOGRAPHY. Berkeley: University of California, 1977. 99 p.

Annotates studies that explore the economic impact of universities on their surrounding communities.

810 Fink, Ira Stephen, and Cooke, Joan. MARRIED STUDENTS: A STUDY
OF DECREASING MARRIAGE RATES AND FAMILY SIZES AT THE UNI-
VERSITY OF CALIFORNIA. Berkeley: University of California, 1973.
63 p.

Shows a gradual decrease in the percentage of married students
and a sharp decrease in their family size.

811 Finkelstein, Martin. THE INCENTIVE-GRANT APPROACH IN HIGHER
EDUCATION: A 15-YEAR RECORD. Washington, D.C.: Postsecondary
Education Convening Authority, Institute for Educational Leadership, 1975.
56 p.

Describes incentive grants, their history, who uses them, how
they work, and how they have been reviewed and evaluated.

812 Finn, Chester E., Jr. SCHOLARS, DOLLARS, AND BUREAUCRATS.
Washington, D.C.: Brookings Institution, 1978. 238 p.

Examines the complex federal government–higher education relationship, reviews and suggests correctives to federal regulatory acts, and likes and wants continuance of Washington's
piecemeal approach, which author says has vitalized colleges
and universities. Discusses move to establish cabinet-level department of education.

813 First, Wesley, ed. UNIVERSITY ON THE HEIGHTS. Garden City, N.Y.: Doubleday, 1969. 199 p.

> Vignettes of famous Columbia University faculty by such alumni as Mark Van Doren, Lionel Trilling, Clifton Fadiman, John Berryman, and Paul Gallico.

814 Fishel, Andrew, and Pottker, Janice. NATIONAL POLITICS AND SEX DISCRIMINATION IN EDUCATION. Lexington, Mass.: Lexington Books, 1979. 159 p.

> Analyzes, through case studies, recent political and legal efforts to end sex discrimination in education including higher education.

815 Fisher, Dorothea Frances Canfield. THE BENT TWIG. New York: Henry Holt and Co., 1915. 497 p.

> Novel about the daughter of a midwest university professor and her career while attending the same university (reflecting author's experience--her father taught at the University of Kansas, was chancellor of the University of Nebraska, president of The Ohio State University, and librarian at Columbia University).

816 _____. ROUGH HEWN. New York: Harcourt, Brace and Co., 1922. 504 p.

> Novel about a young couple, the young man's college education, and their subsequent career.

817 Fisher, Margaret B., and Smith, Margaret Ruth. WRITING AS A PROFESSIONAL ACTIVITY. Washington, D.C.: National Association for Women Deans, Administrators and Counselors, 1977. 48 p.

> Guidelines for writing theses, dissertations, journal articles, monographs, anthologies, and books, and for collaborating with others.

818 Fisher, Vardis. NO VILLAIN NEED BE. Garden City, N.Y.: Doubleday, Doran and Co., 1936. 387 p.

> Fourth novel in author's series on a young man at college and graduate school, and subsequently as a professor-writer with pacifist leanings in World War I.

819 _____. ORPHANS IN GETHSEMANE. Denver: Alan Swallow, 1960. 987 p.

> Novel, part of a series, brings up to date the professor-writer hero's subsequent career.

820 _____. PASSIONS SPIN THE PLOT. Garden City, N.Y.: Doubleday, Doran and Co., 1934. 428 p.

Novel, part of a series, about the same young man at college in Salt Lake City, Utah.

821 _____. WE ARE BETRAYED. Garden City, N.Y.: Doubleday, Doran and Co., 1935. 369 p.

Novel, part of author's series, about the same hero doing graduate work at a university in Chicago.

822 Fisk, Robert S., and Duryea, Edwin D. ACADEMIC COLLECTIVE BAR-GAINING AND REGIONAL ACCREDITATION: AN OCCASIONAL PAPER. Washington, D.C.: Council on Postsecondary Accreditation, 1977. 34 p.

Study of effects of faculty unionism on the accreditation process.

823 Fitch, Albert Parker. NONE SO BLIND. New York: Macmillan Co., 1924. 366 p.

Novel in which a Harvard professor of French wins the hand of a coed over competition from a college student; the couple then go off to a midwestern university. Author, a Harvard graduate, taught theology at Amherst and Carleton Colleges.

824 Fitzgerald, Francis Scott Key. THIS SIDE OF PARADISE. New York: Charles Scribner's Sons, 1920. 305 p.

Novel which is said to epitomize youth of the 1920s, whose hero, like the author, attended Princeton.

825 Fitzgerald, Laurene E., et al. COLLEGE STUDENT PERSONNEL; READINGS AND BIBLIOGRAPHIES. Boston: Houghton Mifflin, 1970. 488 p.

Humanizing higher education should be the general goal of student personnel workers.

826 Fitzpatrick, Edward A. HOW TO EDUCATE HUMAN BEINGS. Milwaukee, Wis.: Bruce Publishing Co., 1950. 174 p.

Lectures on liberal education in honor of the centennial of Wisconsin's statehood and of various Milwaukee religious orders. One chapter on college teaching.

827 _____. McCARTHY OF WISCONSIN. New York: Columbia University Press, 1944. 316 p.

Biography of Charles McCarthy (1873-1921), pioneer in public administration who helped develop training for public service and such adult education programs as continuation schools and university extension.

828 Five College Long Range Planning Committee. FIVE COLLEGE COOPERA-
TION: DIRECTIONS FOR THE FUTURE. Amherst: University of Massachusetts Press, 1969. 228 p.

Examines planned cooperation of Amherst, Smith, Mount Holyoke, and Hampshire Colleges, and the University of Massachusetts. Recommends "academic complementarity," pointing out
financial and educational advantages, as well as student desire for coeducational facilities. Suggests a governance framework and joint fund raising.

829 Flannagan, Zoe. GREY TOWERS: A CAMPUS NOVEL. Chicago: Covici-
McGee Co., 1923. 286 p.

Novel about the return to a midwestern institution of a young
woman as English instructor, ambitious to raise the standard
of literacy, but who is disillusioned to find the intimate college she knew has become a huge impersonal university.

830 Flaugher, Ronald L., et al. CREDIT BY EXAMINATION FOR COLLEGE-
LEVEL STUDIES: AN ANNOTATED BIBLIOGRAPHY. New York: College Entrance Examination Board, 1967. 233 p.

Lists and annotates more than three-hundred articles and research studies on transfer students, credit by examination, and
sources of instruction open to unaffiliated students.

831 Fleming, John E., et al. THE CASE FOR AFFIRMATIVE ACTION FOR
BLACKS IN HIGHER EDUCATION. Washington, D.C.: Howard University Press, 1979. 416 p.

Assesses blacks' status on campuses before affirmative action,
discusses affirmative action legislation, and evaluates affirmative action programs in colleges and universities (with case
studies of a state university, a major research university, a
liberal arts college, and a community college). Concludes that
the legal foundations of affirmative action are sound.

832 _____. THE LENGTHENING SHADOW OF SLAVERY: A HISTORICAL
JUSTIFICATION FOR AFFIRMATIVE ACTION FOR BLACKS IN HIGHER
EDUCATION. Washington, D.C.: Howard University Press, 1976. 158 p.

Examines black education historically, citing key obstacles and
stepping stones.

833 Fleming, Margaret, ed. TEACHING THE EPIC. Urbana, Ill.: National
Council of Teachers of English, 1974. 114 p.

Analyzes content and critical background material of twenty-
four major epics. Includes projects; lists art, music, and
literature based on the epics.

834   Fleming, Thomas J. WEST POINT: THE MEN AND TIMES OF THE
UNITED STATES MILITARY ACADEMY. New York: William Morrow and
Co., 1969. 402 p.

History of West Point and its problems and accomplishments
since the Civil War.

835   Fleming, Walter L. LOUISIANA STATE UNIVERSITY 1860–1896. Baton
Rouge: Louisiana State University Press, 1936. 499 p.

History of the university plus background on Louisiana and its
education before the Civil War. Describes the effect of the
Civil War and the university's struggle to survive.

836   Fletcher, C. Scott, ed. EDUCATION FOR PUBLIC RESPONSIBILITY.
New York: W.W. Norton and Co., 1961. 192 p.

Fourteen essays about the private and public moral responsibi-
lities of the educator and the educated. Contributors include
Adlai Stevenson, Margaret Mead, Henry Kissinger, Henry
Wriston, and Henry Steele Commager.

837   Fletcher, Robert Samuel. A HISTORY OF OBERLIN COLLEGE FROM ITS
FOUNDATION THROUGH THE CIVIL WAR. 2 vols. in 1. Oberlin,
Ohio: Oberlin College, 1943. Reprint. New York: Arno Press, 1971.
1,004 p.

History of Oberlin reflects nineteenth-century religious zeal
and social reform, especially the drive to abolish slavery.
Oberlin was coeducational from the first. Its academic freedom gave expression to many new ideas.

838   Flexner, Abraham. THE AMERICAN COLLEGE: A CRITICISM. New
York: Century Publishing Co., 1908. Reprint. New York: Arno Press,
1969. 237 p.

Criticizes higher education for strict entrance requirements
which control secondary education, for too many electives,
and for overemphasizing graduate research. Recommends ways
to change. Based on a critical study of Harvard College the
year before, this book influenced President Henry S. Pritchett
of the newly founded Carnegie Foundation for the Advancement
of Teaching to commission Flexner's landmark study: MEDICAL
EDUCATION IN THE UNITED STATES AND CANADA (1910).

839   _____. AUTOBIOGRAPHY: A REVISION BROUGHT UP TO DATE OF

I REMEMBER. New York: Simon and Schuster, 1960. 363 p.

Flexner's revision of his autobiography, I REMEMBER (1940), before his death in 1959 at age 92. Flexner's study at the new Johns Hopkins University; his subsequent reports for the Carnegie Foundation for the Advancement of Teaching (especially on medical education); his work for the General Education Board; his advice to millionaires John D. Rockefeller, Andrew Carnegie, George Eastman, Julius Rosenwald, J.P. Morgan, and others when they were beginning their philanthropy; and especially his part in founding the Institute for Advanced Studies at Princeton, which secured Albert Einstein as its first professor—all show the vast impact of early twentieth-century philanthropy on higher education.

840 _____. DANIEL COIT GILMAN: CREATOR OF THE AMERICAN TYPE OF UNIVERSITY. New York: Harcourt, Brace, 1946. 173 p.

A brief biography of Gilman (1831-1908) and an examination of his influence as president of the University of California, the Carnegie Institute of Technology, and Johns Hopkins University, first U.S. graduate university. By combining teaching and research functions at Johns Hopkins, Gilman created a new type of university which became standard in the United States.

841 _____. THE FLEXNER REPORT ON MEDICAL EDUCATION IN THE UNITED STATES AND CANADA. New York: Carnegie Foundation for the Advancement of Teaching, 1910. Reprint. Bethesda, Md.: National Health Directory, 1979. 340 p.

Reprint of influential report on the early twentieth-century medical schools which revolutionized the teaching of medicine in America. Includes a history of medical education, a detailed description of each medical school, and a call for revolutionary changes in medical training.

842 _____. HENRY S. PRITCHETT. New York: Columbia University Press, 1943. 211 p.

Biography of Pritchett (1857-1939), who after an early career as an astronomer, headed the U.S. Coast and Geodetic Survey, became president of MIT and then for twenty-five years was president of the Carnegie Foundation for the Advancement of Teaching. Each of his annual reports at Carnegie was about a college activity or an aspect of professional education. The Foundation during his presidency published ten bulletins, including MEDICAL EDUCATION by Flexner (1910), LEGAL EDUCATION (1921 and 1928), and AMERICAN COLLEGE ATHLETICS (1929).

843 _____. A MODERN COLLEGE AND A MODERN SCHOOL. Garden City, N.Y.: Doubleday, 1923. 142 p.

> Urges a vocationally oriented college curriculum; fewer electives; more emphasis on science, industrial training, domestic arts, and modern languages; and the usual liberal arts courses.

844 _____. UNIVERSITIES: AMERICAN, ENGLISH AND GERMAN. New York: Oxford University Press, 1930. 381 p.

> Weighty criticism of American universities, alleging their intellectual standards to be far below those of English and German universities.

845 Flournoy, Don M., et al. THE NEW TEACHERS. San Francisco: Jossey-Bass Publishers, 1972. 206 p.

> First-person accounts of college teaching cite the importance of student ideas and participation.

846 Foerster, Norman. THE AMERICAN STATE UNIVERSITY: ITS RELATION TO DEMOCRACY. Chapel Hill: University of North Carolina Press, 1937. 300 p.

> Stimulating criticism of the loss of democratic principles of the American university. Author attacks the emphasis on the monetary value of degrees rather than the knowledge acquired.

847 _____. THE FUTURE OF THE LIBERAL COLLEGE. New York: D. Appleton-Century Co., 1938. Reprint. New York: Arno Press, 1969. 103 p.

> A humanist view of the liberal arts college; sharply critical of reforms offered by Charles W. Eliot and John Dewey. Recommends a curriculum based on great books and a new world view.

848 Foley, James A., and Foley, Robert K. THE COLLEGE SCENE: STUDENTS TELL IT LIKE IT IS. New York: Cowles Educational Books, 1969. 187 p.

> Cautions administrators against ignoring student views.

849 Foley, Louis. HOW WORDS FIT TOGETHER. Babson Park, Mass.: Babson Institute Press, 1958. 125 p.

> An English-usage handbook containing word histories and common sense directions to help college students edit their own work.

850 Folger, John K. THE SOUTH'S COMMITMENT TO HIGHER EDUCATION:

PROGRESS AND PROSPECTS. Atlanta: Southern Regional Education
Board, 1978. 27 p.

Shows that, during the last quarter century, accomplishments
in higher education in the South have come to equal those in
the rest of the country.

851 _____, ed. INCREASING THE PUBLIC ACCOUNTABILITY OF HIGHER
EDUCATION. San Francisco: Jossey-Bass Publishers, 1977. 99 p.

Suggests options for colleges and universities in response to demands for program review, performance audits, and performance
budgeting, with cases from six states.

852 Folger, John K., et al. HUMAN RESOURCES AND HIGHER EDUCATION:
STAFF REPORT OF THE COMMISSION ON HUMAN RESOURCES AND
ADVANCED EDUCATION. New York: Russell Sage Foundation, 1970.
475 p.

Report on the supply of and the demand and need for educated
manpower, especially in the professions. Discusses the market
for college graduates, factors which determine career choices,
employment of women, and manpower policies. Calls for con-
sistent federal support of higher education and for a permanent,
national body to review policies of human resources utilization.

853 Foote, Caleb, et al. THE CULTURE OF THE UNIVERSITY: GOVER-
NANCE AND EDUCATION. San Francisco: Jossey-Bass Publishers, 1968.
228 p.

Report on University of California, Berkeley, campus protests.
Majority found the 1966 Berkeley governance system unworkable.
Many recommendations for strengthening faculty and student
roles. Dissenting minority report disagrees with recommendations for revamping chancellor's and faculty's authority, for
providing student participation, and for regulating student conduct.

854 Ford, Guy Stanton. ON AND OFF THE CAMPUS. Minneapolis: University of Minnesota Press, 1938. 511 p.

Essays by a college dean, historian, and one-time president of
the American Historical Association on the function of history
in the schools, selection of college faculty, and aspects of
graduate study. An administrator's major role, author says,
is to choose good faculty and build a good library.

855 Ford, Nick Aaron. BLACK STUDIES: THREAT-OR-CHALLENGE. Port
Washington, N.Y.: Kennikat Press, 1973. 217 p.

Concluded after seeing black studies at over one hundred campuses that the concept of black studies is valid and viable.

856   Ford Foundation. ABOUT THE FORD FOUNDATION. New York: 1958. 39 p.

Booklet about the organization and activities of the Ford Foundation. Sections on faculty salaries, recruiting faculty, libraries and library methods, and training law, business, and economics professors.

857   Foresi, Joseph, Jr. ADMINISTRATIVE LEADERSHIP IN THE COMMUNITY COLLEGE. Hicksville, N.Y.: Exposition Press, 1974. 106 p.

Overview of administrative concepts and successful administrative techniques in the community college.

858   Forman, Sidney. WEST POINT: A HISTORY OF THE UNITED STATES MILITARY ACADEMY. New York: Columbia University Press, 1950. 255 p.

Partisan history of West Point by the archivist of the U.S. Military Academy.

859   Fortenbaugh, Samuel B., Jr. IN ORDER TO FORM A MORE PERFECT UNION: AN INQUIRY INTO THE ORIGINS OF A COLLEGE. Syracuse, N.Y.: Syracuse University Press, 1978. 130 p.

History of Union College, Schenectady, founded in 1795, the first college chartered by New York Regents.

860   Foshay, Arthur W., ed. THE PROFESSIONAL AS EDUCATOR. New York: Teachers College Press, 1970. 128 p.

Agreeing that society does not regard school teachers as professionals, six scholars (including Mario Fantini and Talcott Parsons) say a discipline of education is needed but disagree on its prospects.

861   Foster, Julian, and Long, Durward, eds. PROTEST! STUDENT ACTIVISM IN AMERICA. New York: William Morrow and Co., 1969. 596 p.

Scholarly readings on student activism since 1964 discuss research findings, case histories (at such universities as San Francisco State and Howard), ways campus power is being redistributed, and offers practical recommendations.

862   Foster, Margery Somers. "OUT OF SMALLE BEGINNINGS . . .": AN ECONOMIC HISTORY OF HARVARD COLLEGE IN THE PURITAN PERIOD (1636 TO 1712). Cambridge, Mass.: Belknap Press of Harvard University Press, 1962. 243 p.

Historical study of financial problems Harvard faced in its early years. One-third of Harvard's revenues were from government grants. Faculty salaries, dependent on tuition and Charlestown Ferry profits, were always precarious.

863 Foster, Robert C., and Wilson, Pauline Park. WOMEN AFTER COLLEGE. New York: Columbia University Press, 1942. 305 p.

Studied the adequacy of college educational experiences of one hundred women graduates. Individual biographical sketches substantiate the conclusion that colleges fail to prepare women to meet their problems.

864 Foundation Center. FOUNDATION GRANTS TO INDIVIDUALS. New York: 1977. 227 p.

Information on higher education grants available to individuals, including their number and size, application deadlines, eligibility requirements, and program objectives of the foundations.

865 Fowlkes, John Guy, ed. HIGHER EDUCATION FOR AMERICAN SOCIETY. Madison: University of Wisconsin Press, 1949. 420 p.

University of Wisconsin centennial papers on five aspects of higher education--appraising and planning, problems, goals, personal values, and effectiveness.

866 Foxley, Cecelia H. LOCATING, RECRUITING AND EMPLOYING WOMEN: AN EQUAL OPPORTUNITY APPROACH. Garrett Park, Md.: Garrett Park Press, 1976. 358 p.

Statistics and summaries of studies on women in the labor force, touching on their education, occupation, and salaries.

867 Frankel, Charles. EDUCATION AND THE BARRICADES. New York: W.W. Norton and Co., 1968. 90 p.

Essay supporting U.S. system of higher education despite student protests and university administration problems.

868 _____, ed. ISSUES IN UNIVERSITY EDUCATION: ESSAYS BY TEN AMERICAN SCHOLARS. New York: Harper and Brothers, 1959. 175 p.

Ten essays based on discussions by Fulbright scholars about American higher education in a world context. Robert B. Brode, John Hope Franklin, J. Robert Oppenheimer, and about 150 other American and five-hundred foreign scholars were contributors.

869 Frankfort, Roberta. COLLEGIATE WOMEN: DOMESTICITY AND CAREER

IN TURN-OF-THE-CENTURY AMERICA. New York: New York University Press, 1977. 121 p.

> Studied Bryn Mawr, which emphasized women's scholarship, and Wellesley, which acknowledged women's domesticity, and their alumnae's career patterns. Concluded that, after the first generation, women educated at these colleges did little to help women transcend domestic roles.

870 Fraser, Mowat G. THE COLLEGE OF THE FUTURE. New York: Columbia University Press, 1937. 529 p.

> Deals with fundamental issues and policies of the American college and educational and social trends. Also depicts an ideal college in operation.

871 Fraser, Stewart E., ed. THE EVILS OF A FOREIGN EDUCATION: OR BIRDSEYE NORTHROP ON EDUCATION ABROAD, 1873. Nashville: International Center, George Peabody College for Teachers, 1966. 78 p.

> In Fraser's introduction to this reprint of Birdseye Northrop, ON EDUCATION ABROAD (1873), he mentions the popularity of graduate study in Germany among mid-to-late nineteenth-century American students. Also comments on Americans studying in France and England.

872 Frede, Richard. ENTRY E. New York: Random House, 1958. 247 p.

> Novel about a college architectural student facing a moral dilemma.

873 Frederiksen, Norman, and Schrader, W.B. ADJUSTMENT TO COLLEGE. Princeton, N.J.: Educational Testing Service, 1951. 504 p.

> Statistical report comparing the adjustment of veterans and non-veterans to college. Differences were slight, but usually favored the veteran.

874 Freedman, Mervin B. THE COLLEGE EXPERIENCE. San Francisco: Jossey-Bass Publishers, 1967. 202 p.

> Using data from women at Vassar and other findings, author thinks most students are complacent but sees possibilities for much change during student years.

875 _____. THE STUDENT AND CAMPUS CLIMATES OF LEARNING. Washington, D.C.: Government Printing Office, 1967. 89 p.

> Recent American research literature on characteristics of students, personality and intellectual development during college, and influences exerted by society on learning and academic processes.

876 _____, ed. FACILITATING FACULTY DEVELOPMENT. San Francisco: Jossey-Bass Publishers, 1973. 122 p.

> Maintains that faculty members can become better teachers through greater self-awareness and broader perspective. Details strategies for faculty development.

877 Freedman, Mervin B., and Hatch, Winslow R. IMPACT OF COLLEGE. Washington, D.C.: Government Printing Office, 1960. 27 p.

> Surveys research, particularly at Vassar and other women's colleges, on the impact college has on student values, attitudes, and personalities.

878 Freedman, Morris. CHAOS IN OUR COLLEGES. New York: David McKay Co., 1963. 241 p.

> Professor's personal view of many debatable issues in higher education and suggested reforms.

879 Freedman, Ronald, et al. FUTURE SCHOOL AND COLLEGE ENROLLMENTS IN MICHIGAN, 1955 TO 1970. Ann Arbor, Mich.: J.W. Edwards, 1954. 65 p.

> Study of the quantitative and qualitative problems facing Michigan elementary, secondary, and higher education. Used census and other data to project Michigan population and enrollment trends. Predicted that Michigan college enrollment would double by 1970.

880 Freeman, Richard B. THE OVER-EDUCATED AMERICAN. New York: Academic Press, 1976. 218 p.

> Analyzes the possible declining economic value of a college education, and presents data on consequences of such over-education.

881 Freeman, Richard B., and Breneman, David W. FORECASTING THE PH.D. LABOR MARKET: PITFALLS FOR POLICY. Washington, D.C.: National Academy of Sciences, 1974. 50 p.

> Critical analysis of labor-market forecasting techniques for doctoral manpower; stresses limitations of existing procedures.

882 Freeman, Roger A. CRISIS IN COLLEGE FINANCE? TIME FOR NEW SOLUTIONS. Washington, D.C.: Institute for Social Science Research, 1965. 243 p.

> Reviews U.S. higher education problems of rising enrollments and growing financial needs. Explains and defends the sliding tax credit plan for adding new money for higher education.

883 Freeman, Stephen A. UNDERGRADUATE STUDY ABROAD, WITH AN ANALYSIS OF THE SITUATION. New York: Institute of International Education, 1964. 126 p.

Compilation of undergraduate study-abroad programs sponsored by U.S. colleges under their own name, and a critical evaluation of these programs.

884 French, John C. A HISTORY OF THE UNIVERSITY FOUNDED BY JOHNS HOPKINS. Baltimore, Md.: Johns Hopkins University Press, 1946. 492 p.

Tells of Johns Hopkins's founding bequest. Chapters on medical education, applied sciences, fine arts, and nursing. Appendix has official documents.

885 French, Peter. THE LONG REACH: A REPORT ON HARVARD TODAY. New York: Ives Washburn, 1962. 243 p.

Journalist's illustrated nontechnical view of life at Harvard.

886 French, Sidney J., ed. ACCENT ON TEACHING. New York: Harper and Row, 1954. 334 p.

Articles emphasize the contributions of psychology and sociology to undergraduate teaching. Basic survey courses replaced traditional liberal arts courses during 1930 to 1945. After 1945 the shift was either to courses that tried to meet student needs or that presented significant concepts from basic fields.

887 Fretwell, Elbert K., Jr. FOUNDING PUBLIC JUNIOR COLLEGES: LOCAL INITIATIVE IN SIX COMMUNITIES. New York: Bureau of Publications, Teachers College, Columbia University, 1954. 148 p.

Case studies of six public junior colleges revealed that similar factors influenced their founding (such as enrollment pressures and general citizen support). Describes interactions among those who help start junior colleges and draws conclusions about ways to establish junior colleges.

888 Friedan, Betty. THE FEMININE MYSTIQUE. New York: W.W. Norton, 1963. 384 p.

Discussion of role conflicts of the college-educated suburban housewife. Seeing higher education as the route to an appropriate vocation, author concludes that women (as well as men) need to establish their identity through creative work outside the home. Influenced women's rights movement of the 1960s and since.

889 Friedenberg, Edgar Z., and Roth, Julius A. SELF-PERCEPTION IN THE

UNIVERSITY: A STUDY OF SUCCESSFUL AND UNSUCCESSFUL GRADU-ATE STUDENTS. Chicago: University of Chicago Press, 1954. 102 p.

Studied attitudes toward their university of 244 graduate students, one-fourth of whom the faculty considered highly successful. Found that the remaining three-fourths less effective students had passive attitudes and perceived the university as a barrier.

890 Friedlander, Albert H., ed. NEVER TRUST A GOD OVER 30: NEW STYLES IN CAMPUS MINISTRY. New York: McGraw-Hill Book Co., 1967. 224 p.

Catholic, Protestant, and Jewish counselors contrast students of the 1950s and 1960s and say that campus ministers must understand modern issues to be effective with college students.

891 Friedman, Renee C. THE CONTINUING SAGA OF INSTITUTES AND CENTERS. University Park: Center for the Study of Higher Education, Pennsylvania State University, 1977. 41 p.

Discusses recent changes in research institutes and centers affiliated with universities.

892 Froomkin, Joseph. NEEDED: A NEW FEDERAL POLICY FOR HIGHER EDUCATION. Washington, D.C.: Institute for Educational Leadership, George Washington University, 1978. 82 p.

In preparation for 1980, when the U.S. Higher Education Act must be renewed, discusses such problems as declining enrollments and rising costs. Concludes that without major new financing, many faculty jobs will be lost and institutions closed. Urges federal support for more part-time and older students.

893 Fuess, Claude M. THE COLLEGE BOARD: ITS FIRST FIFTY YEARS. New York: Columbia University Press, 1950. 222 p.

History of the College Board from its founding by Nicholas Murray Butler in 1900 until 1950 and its merger with other agencies to form the Educational Testing Service. Important account of the testing movement.

894 _____. INDEPENDENT SCHOOLMASTER. Boston: Little, Brown and Co., 1952. 371 p.

Autobiography of former Phillips Academy headmaster, educated at Amherst and Columbia, who was associated with such agencies as the College Entrance Examination Board and who believes teaching is not a science but an art.

895 Fuller, C. Dale. TRAINING OF SPECIALISTS IN INTERNATIONAL RE-

LATIONS. Washington, D.C.: American Council on Education, 1957. 136 p.

Report on international affairs programs. Surveyed catalogs of 184 institutions, studied thirty-eight institutions with substantial programs, gathered data from 152 graduates in international affairs and fifty-six institutions which employ such specialists. Cites programs' strengths and weaknesses. Suggests improvements.

896 Fuller, Edmund, ed. SCHOOLS AND SCHOLARSHIP--THE CHRISTIAN IDEA OF EDUCATION: PART II. New Haven, Conn.: Yale University Press, 1962. 345 p.

Kent Seminar lectures (1960) by George N. Shuster, Edward Teller, and other scholars who believe good teaching is an expression of Christian ideals.

897 Fuller, Henry Blake. BERTRAM COPE'S YEAR. Chicago: R.F. Seymour, 1919. 314 p.

Novel about a graduate student at a midwestern university, supposedly the University of Chicago, preparing to teach at a New England college.

898 Fuller, R. Buckminster. EDUCATION AUTOMATION: FREEING THE SCHOLAR TO RETURN TO HIS STUDIES. Carbondale: Southern Illinois University Press, 1962. 88 p.

Suggestions on improving the physical and educational environment of higher education facilities. Some autobiographical anecdotes of the architectural iconoclast-inventor of the geodesic dome.

899 Fund for the Advancement of Education. BETTER UTILIZATION OF COLLEGE TEACHING RESOURCES. A SUMMARY REPORT. New York: 1963. 63 p.

Concluded from studying the internal economies of U.S. colleges and universities that they should use modern technology to overcome teaching shortages.

900 _____. THEY WENT TO COLLEGE EARLY. New York: 1957. 117 p.

Over thirteen hundred sixteen-year-olds admitted to college after completing only the tenth or eleventh grade adjusted as well socially and academically as did the average eighteen-year-old freshman.

901 Funkenstein, Daniel H., and Wilkie, George H. STUDENT MENTAL HEALTH: AN ANNOTATED BIBLIOGRAPHY 1936-1955. Geneva,

Switzerland: World Federation for Mental Health, 1956. 297 p.

Partially annotated bibliography of 1,803 books and articles about the mental health of college students.

902 Furniss, Edgar S. THE GRADUATE SCHOOL OF YALE: A BRIEF HIS-
TORY. New Haven, Conn.: Graduate School, Yale University, 1965.
181 p.

History of the oldest U.S. graduate school by its former head,
who espouses an arts and science graduate school and cites
ingredients necessary for its success.

903 _____, ed. HIGHER EDUCATION FOR EVERYBODY? ISSUES AND
IMPLICATIONS. Washington, D.C.: American Council on Education,
1971. 284 p.

Papers by Daniel P. Moynihan and others about universal higher
education, new structures needed to replace the outdated emphasis on full-time undergraduate study, reorientation to serve
new student clienteles, and financial arrangements to assure
equal educational opportunity.

904 Furniss, Warren Todd, and Graham, Patricia Albjerg, eds. WOMEN IN
HIGHER EDUCATION. Washington, D.C.: American Council on Education, 1974. 336 p.

Papers on equal rights for women in higher education. Editors
hope to establish ideological base for changed practices on
women's higher education. Contains sections on women in
higher education, the woman student, the woman professional
in higher education, academic programs, and affirmative action.

905 Furniss, Warren Todd, et al., eds. AMERICAN UNIVERSITIES AND COL-
LEGES. 11th ed. Washington, D.C.: American Council on Education,
1973. 1,879 p.

Authoritative information on accredited U.S. senior colleges
and universities. Revised every four years since 1928. Part
1 outlines evolution of higher education, structure of higher
education, undergraduate education, graduate and professional
education, the federal government and education, and the
foreign student in the United States. Part 2 lists accredited
colleges and universities for various professions. Part 3, arranged by states, gives essential facts about each college and
university. Valuable appendices.

906 Fussler, Herman H.,ed. THE FUNCTION OF THE LIBRARY IN THE MOD-
ERN COLLEGE: PAPERS PRESENTED BEFORE THE NINETEENTH ANNUAL
CONFERENCE OF THE GRADUATE LIBRARY SCHOOL OF THE UNIVER-

SITY OF CHICAGO, JUNE 14-18, 1954. Chicago: University of Chicago Press, 1954. 117 p.

Essays on such topics as the nature of a good college book collection, audiovisual departments in libraries, the ambiguous position of a librarian, and recruiting practices.

907 Gaddy, Dale. THE SCOPE OF ORGANIZED STUDENT PROTEST IN JUNIOR COLLEGES. Washington, D.C.: American Association of Junior Colleges, 1970. 26 p.

Respondents from six hundred two-year colleges surveyed showed that two-fifths had experienced student protests, most of them large public ones with a small minority of radical students. Gives geographical location, protest control procedures, issues involved, and faculty participation. Reform recommendations include administrative accessibility, student and faculty governance participation, attention to such off-campus issues as the draft, and responsiveness to curriculum and financial needs of minorities.

908 Gaff, Jerry G. TOWARD FACULTY RENEWAL: ADVANCES IN FACULTY, INSTRUCTIONAL, AND ORGANIZATIONAL DEVELOPMENT. San Francisco: Jossey-Bass Publishers, 1975. 244 p.

Focuses on three approaches to instructional improvement: faculty enrichment, course redesign, and institutional reorganization.

909 _____, et al. THE CLUSTER COLLEGE. San Francisco: Jossey-Bass Publishers, 1970. 249 p.

Progress report on "cluster colleges"; i.e., nearby cooperating semiautonomous colleges, each often part of a multiversity, which share facilities and services that focus on undergraduate needs, and pool resources. This reform movement is evaluated going back to the mid-1950s. Looks at the five undergraduate Claremont colleges in California, the six institutions making up Atlanta University Center in Georgia, and those at the University of California at Santa Cruz and San Diego.

910 Gage, Nathaniel Lees. THE SCIENTIFIC BASIS OF THE ART OF TEACHING. New York: Teachers College Press, 1978. 122 p.

Three lectures about research into teaching and student achievement.

911 _____, ed. HANDBOOK OF RESEARCH ON TEACHING; A PROJECT OF THE AMERICAN EDUCATIONAL RESEARCH ASSOCIATION. Chicago: Rand McNally, 1963. 1,218 p.

About research into teaching several subjects at all levels, including higher education.

912 Galambos, Eva C. LAW, MEDICINE, VETERINARY MEDICINE: ISSUES IN SUPPLY AND DEMAND. Atlanta: Southern Regional Education Board, 1978. 54 p.

Found an uneven geographical distribution of legal, medical, and veterinary services despite a potential oversupply of these professions in the South.

913 Gale, Barry, and Gale, Linda. THE NATIONAL CAREER DIRECTORY: AN OCCUPATIONAL INFORMATION HANDBOOK. New York: Arco Publishing Co., 1978. 240 p.

Provides sources of education information needed for more than two thousand careers, ranging from abstractor to zoologist.

914 Gallagher, Buell Gordon. AMERICAN CASTE AND THE NEGRO COLLEGE. New York: Columbia University Press, 1938. 463 p.

Former CUNY and Talladega College president examines in sociological and psychological context the dilemmas in educating blacks at segregated colleges as preparation for life in the American mainstream.

915 _____. CAMPUS IN CRISIS. New York: Harper and Row, 1974. 288 p.

Chapters on research into civil rights and the 1960s student revolts reflect author's experience as college administrator, president (CUNY), and educational activist. He sees campus crisis as part of general social unrest and advocates a return to teaching values.

916 _____, ed. COLLEGE AND THE BLACK STUDENT: NAACP TRACT FOR THE TIMES. New York: National Association for the Advancement of Colored People, Committee on Campus Trouble, 1971. 56 p.

Reviews the evolution of black education and the 1960s campus unrest; provides a checklist to guide perplexed administrators in correcting problems arising from black students on white campuses.

917 Gallagher, Phillip J., and Demos, George D., eds. THE COUNSELING CENTER IN HIGHER EDUCATION. Springfield, Ill.: Charles C Thomas, Publisher, 1970. 399 p.

About counseling centers and their relationship to students, faculty, and administration. Reviews innovative programs at various California colleges and ways they tried to counteract the depersonalization of mass education.

918 Galloway, Sylvia W., and Fisher, Charles F., eds. A GUIDE TO PRO-
FESSIONAL DEVELOPMENT OPPORTUNITIES FOR COLLEGE AND UNI-
VERSITY ADMINISTRATORS, 1978: SEMINARS, WORKSHOPS, CON-
FERENCES, INSTITUTES, AND INTERNSHIPS. Washington, D.C.: Ameri-
can Council on Education, 1978. 169 p.

   Describes short-term professional development programs in such
   areas as personnel, student services, public relations, financial planning, and budgeting.

919 Gannon, Robert I. THE POOR OLD LIBERAL ARTS: A PERSONAL MEM-
OIR OF A LIFETIME IN EDUCATION. New York: Farrar, Straus and
Cudahy, 1961. 207 p.

   Jesuit Father Gannon reminisces about his student days at
   Georgetown and Cambridge Universities and his career as a
   teacher and president at Fordham University. Traces liberal
   arts education from its beginning to the present, and speculates on its future.

920 Ganss, George E. SAINT IGNATIUS' IDEA OF A JESUIT UNIVERSITY:
A STUDY IN THE HISTORY OF CATHOLIC EDUCATION. Milwaukee,
Wis.: Marquette University Press, 1954. 368 p.

   As background to the thirty-seven U.S. Jesuit colleges and
   universities (1954), this survey of four hundred years of Jesuit
   higher education reflects the influence on Ignatius of his ten
   years' orderly progression of studies at the University of Paris.
   Contains a translation of education "Principles" from part 4
   of Ignatius's CONSTITUTIONS (c. 1550). Concludes that
   Jesuit education has been successful because of its adaptability.

921 Garbarino, Joseph William, and Aussieker, Bill. FACULTY BARGAINING:
CHANGE AND CONFLICT. New York: McGraw-Hill Book Co., 1975.
278 p.

   Report on collective bargaining in higher education. Main
   thesis is that the faculty union, as differentiated from traditional faculty representation in governance, is a response to
   dramatic late 1960s changes in higher education.

922 Garber, Lee O., and Micken, Charles M. THE LAW AND THE TEACHER
IN PENNSYLVANIA: A HANDBOOK FOR TEACHERS, ADMINISTRATORS,
AND SCHOOL BOARD MEMBERS. 3d ed. Danville, Ill.: Interstate
Printers and Publishers, 1978. 202 p.

   About faculty collective bargaining, tenure rights and staff-
   reduction procedures, and retirement legislation.

923 Gardner, David P. THE CALIFORNIA OATH CONTROVERSY. Berkeley

and Los Angeles: University of California Press, 1967. 329 p.

Case study of the loyalty oath controversy between the faculty and the board of regents of the University of California
during the McCarthy era.

924 Gardner, Donfred H. THE EVALUATION OF HIGHER INSTITUTIONS,
NUMBER V: STUDENT PERSONNEL SERVICE. Chicago: University of
Chicago Press, 1936. 235 p.

Evaluates student personnel services at fifty-seven higher education institutions: admissions, orientation, record-keeping,
counseling (personal, vocational), extracurricular activities,
financial aid, health, and placement.

925 Garfin, Molly, ed. COLLECTIVE BARGAINING IN HIGHER EDUCA-
TION: BIBLIOGRAPHY NO. 6. New York: National Center for the
Study of Collective Bargaining in Higher Education, Baruch College,
CUNY, 1978. 110 p.

A bibliography of 1977 publications about faculty and staff
collective bargaining at public and private colleges and universities.

926 _____. COLLECTIVE BARGAINING IN HIGHER EDUCATION: FIFTH
ANNUAL BIBLIOGRAPHY. New York: National Center for the Study
of Collective Bargaining in Higher Education, Baruch College, CUNY,
1977. 158 p.

Survey of recent publications about the unionization of academic and nonacademic personnel in public and private higher
education institutions.

927 Garms, Walter I. FINANCING COMMUNITY COLLEGES. New York:
Teachers College Press, 1977. 120 p.

Argues that community colleges provide some educational benefits not given by other institutions, and attempts to justify
economic support of community colleges by state governments.
Evaluates some possible methods of financing both community
and private junior colleges.

928 _____, et al. SCHOOL FINANCE: THE ECONOMICS AND POLITICS
OF PUBLIC EDUCATION. Englewood Cliffs, N.J.: Prentice-Hall, 1978.
464 p.

Comprehensive report on raising and spending funds for public
schools and higher education.

929 Garraty, John A., and Adams, Walter. FROM MAIN STREET TO THE

LEFT BANK: STUDENTS AND SCHOLARS ABROAD. East Lansing: Michigan State University Press, 1959. 216 p.

Used interview data to evaluate higher education programs for Americans in Europe and suggested improvements.

930 Garrison, Roger H. THE ADVENTURE OF LEARNING IN COLLEGE: AN UNDERGRADUATE GUIDE TO PRODUCTIVE STUDY. New York: Harper and Brothers, 1959. 270 p.

Intended to help college freshmen see higher education as an active process.

931 Gartner, Alan. THE PREPARATION OF HUMAN SERVICE PROFESSION-ALS. New York: Human Sciences Press, 1976. 272 p.

Compares the professional education of doctors, lawyers, social workers, and teachers in the United States. Calls for a balance between academic study and clinical practice in their training.

932 Gates, Charles M. THE FIRST CENTURY AT THE UNIVERSITY OF WASHINGTON. Seattle: University of Washington Press, 1961. 252 p.

Centennial history: founded in 1861 as the Territorial University of Washington, it closed for lack of funds during 1865 to 1875; reopened, it gained financial support and endowment through lease of land; and political interference ended with a 1943 state law.

933 Gatewood, Willard B., Jr. PREACHERS, PEDAGOGUES, AND POLITI-CIANS: THE EVOLUTION CONTROVERSY IN NORTH CAROLINA, 1920-1927. Chapel Hill: University of North Carolina Press, 1966. 268 p.

Examines the struggle between proponents of biological evolution and scriptural literalism, with the North Carolina mountain and Piedmont areas as strongholds of fundamentalism, while the presidents of the leading Baptist college, Wake Forest, and the state university were defenders of evolution.

934 Gauss, Christian, ed. THE TEACHING OF RELIGION IN AMERICAN HIGHER EDUCATION. New York: Ronald Press Co., 1951. 158 p.

Five educators look at the historic role of American colleges and universities in teaching religion and urge its importance.

935 Gee, Helen Hofer, and Cowles, John T. THE APPRAISAL OF APPLI-CANTS TO MEDICAL SCHOOLS. Evanston, Ill.: Association of American Medical Colleges, 1957. 228 p.

Examines methods of appraising medical school applicants (emphasizes psychological factors). Summarizes current research on medical school admissions.

936 Gee, Helen Hofer, and Glaser, Robert J., eds. THE ECOLOGY OF THE MEDICAL STUDENT. Evanston, Ill.: Association of American Medical Colleges, 1958. 262 p.

Papers for the fifth teaching institute of the Association of Medical Colleges are about the students' attitudes, opinions, socioeconomic backgrounds, and relationships with faculty and patients. Theme is to find ways to make medical education effective.

937 Gee, Wilson. SOCIAL SCIENCE RESEARCH ORGANIZATION IN AMERICAN UNIVERSITIES AND COLLEGES. New York: D. Appleton-Century Co., 1934. 275 p.

Handbook for college administrators. Presents findings from questionnaires and case studies about college and university social science research, 1932-33.

938 Gegenheimer, Albert Frank. WILLIAM SMITH: EDUCATOR AND CHURCHMAN, 1727-1803. Philadelphia: University of Pennsylvania Press, 1943. 233 p.

Biography of the colorful Scotsman (1727-1803), first provost of what later became the University of Pennsylvania. The general education curriculum he started was long a model for American colleges. He was an effective administrator, fundraiser, and teacher.

939 Geiger, Louis G. HIGHER EDUCATION IN A MATURING DEMOCRACY. Lincoln: University of Nebraska Press, 1963. 92 p.

Points to German technical high schools of agriculture and mechanics as models for land-grant colleges. Cites contributions and deficiencies of land-grant colleges. Criticizes their neglect of liberal education, their failure to develop students' civic interests, their preoccupation with political sources of funding, and their costly duplication of programs available in nearby states.

940 Gellhorn, Walter, and Greenawalt, R. Kent. THE SECTARIAN COLLEGE AND THE PUBLIC PURSE: FORDHAM--A CASE STUDY. Dobbs Ferry, N.Y.: Oceana Publications, 1970. 212 p.

Two law professors commissioned by Fordham University looked into sectarian education finance and into federal and state laws affecting government funding of sectarian higher education.

941   Genova, William J. MUTUAL BENEFIT EVALUATION OF FACULTY AND ADMINISTRATORS IN HIGHER EDUCATION. Cambridge, Mass.: Ballinger Publishing Co., 1976. 222 p.

     A guide for developing an evaluation program for faculty members and administrators.

942   Gershenfeld, Walter J., and Mortimer, Kenneth P. FACULTY COLLECTIVE BARGAINING IN PENNSYLVANIA: THE FIRST FIVE YEARS (1970-1975). Philadelphia: Center for Labor and Manpower Studies, Temple University, 1976. 337 p.

     Development of collective bargaining in Pennsylvania's public and private universities, colleges, and two-year institutions. Contrasts their experiences with such aspects of bargaining as negotiations, governance, and the involvement of interested groups such as the state board of education.

943   Gerth, Donald R., et al. AN INVISIBLE GIANT: THE CALIFORNIA STATE COLLEGES. San Francisco: Jossey-Bass Publishers, 1971. 239 p.

     Essays on successes, failures, and problems of the California State University system. Emphasizes structure and governance.

944   Gessner, Robert. YOUTH IS THE TIME. New York: Charles Scribner's Sons, 1945. 269 p.

     Novel about a Boston-born Harvard graduate who, while lecturing in a New York City college, finds the students a complete surprise.

945   Gideonse, Harry D. THE HIGHER LEARNING IN A DEMOCRACY: A REPLY TO PRESIDENT HUTCHINS' CRITIQUE OF THE AMERICAN UNIVERSITY. New York: Farrar and Rinehart, 1937. 34 p.

     Refutes the claim that higher education fails to educate and calls the apparent chaos the very essence of a democratic society.

946   Giele, Janet Zollinger. WOMEN AND THE FUTURE: CHANGING SEX ROLES IN MODERN AMERICA. New York: Free Press, 1978. 386 p.

     "Education for the Future" chapter reviews women's educational inequalities, mainly in higher education, and recent gains. Summarizes important studies in women's rights movement and women's rising contributions.

947   Gies, Joseph. A MATTER OF MORALS. New York: Harper and Brothers, 1951. 245 p.

     Novel about several persons who unsuccessfully defy authorities

at a midwestern university in a struggle over academic freedom.

948   Gifford, James F., Jr., ed. UNDERGRADUATE MEDICAL EDUCATION
AND THE ELECTIVE SYSTEM: EXPERIENCE WITH THE DUKE CURRICULUM,
1966-75. Durham, N.C.: Duke University Press, 1978. 243 p.

Examines Duke University's experiences with a new medical
education curriculum which introduced the students to more
and earlier clinical experience. Various Duke medical faculty
members and administrators explain the effects of the new
curriculum on their own specialties.

949   Gilbert, Amy M. ACUNY: THE ASSOCIATED COLLEGES OF UPPER
NEW YORK. Ithaca, N.Y.: Cornell University Press, 1950. 524 p.

History of the private corporation which the New York State
Board of Regents chartered in 1946 to provide the freshman and
sophomore years for veterans and others seeking higher education. Operating in converted military bases and other make-
shift facilities, these centers prepared the way for establishing
the State University of New York.

950   Gilbert, Benjamin Franklin. PIONEERS FOR ONE HUNDRED YEARS:
SAN JOSE STATE COLLEGE, 1857-1957. San Jose, Calif.: San Jose
State College, 1957. 244 p.

Centennial history since its beginning as a San Francisco evening
normal school. Emphasizes leading administrators and their
problems. Appendix describes contemporary departments and
lists achievements of various college divisions.

951   Gilbert, Dorothy Lloyd. GUILFORD: A QUAKER COLLEGE. Guilford,
N.C.: Guilford College, 1937. 359 p.

History of Guilford College, begun in 1888, where Quakers
had fifty years earlier founded a coeducational secondary
boarding school. Guilford pioneered in orientation courses
and other curricular innovations in the South.

952   Gildersleeve, Virginia C. MANY A GOOD CRUSADE. New York: Macmillan Co., 1954. 434 p.

Autobiography of a leading woman educator (1877-1965) who,
at Barnard College, led in opening Columbia University's professional schools to women.

953   Gillers, Stephen, ed. LOOKING AT LAW SCHOOL: A STUDENT
GUIDE FROM THE SOCIETY OF AMERICAN LAW TEACHERS. New York:
Taplinger Publishing Co., 1977. 234 p.

A guide for prospective law school students describing curricula, teaching methods, and careers.

954 Gilli, Angelo C., Sr. MODERN ORGANIZATIONS OF VOCATIONAL EDUCATION. University Park: Pennsylvania State University Press, 1977. 302 p.

Describes vocational education in high schools, colleges, and industrial and government training programs. Reviews such recent developments as on-the-job specialized training. Presents an ideal model for vocational education and forecasts its development.

955 Gilman, Daniel Coit. THE LAUNCHING OF A UNIVERSITY AND OTHER PAPERS: A SHEAF OF REMEMBRANCES. New York: Dodd, Mead and Co., 1906. 386 p.

Articles and speeches of the first president of Johns Hopkins University about a wide range of educational topics.

956 _____. UNIVERSITY PROBLEMS IN THE UNITED STATES. New York: Century Co., 1898. Reprint. New York: Arno Press, 1971. 319 p.

First president of Johns Hopkins University reflects on the nature and purpose of the American university.

957 Ginzberg, Eli. HUMAN RESOURCES: THE WEALTH OF A NATION. New York: Simon and Schuster, 1958. 153 p.

Interesting account of the early development of the concept of human resources by the director of studies for Columbia University's National Manpower Council, which did much post-World War II research into utilizing human potential.

958 Ginzberg, Eli, and Herma, John L. TALENT AND PERFORMANCE. New York: Columbia University Press, 1964. 265 p.

Studied the careers of several hundred talented male Columbia graduate fellows. Found that their personality and social reality, and the interaction between these two factors, determined their career performance. Recommended ways to conserve and develop talent among the gifted, especially by guidance within educational institutions.

959 Ginzberg, Eli, and Yohalem, Alice M. EDUCATED AMERICAN WOMEN: SELF-PORTRAITS. New York: Columbia University Press, 1966. 198 p.

Portraits of twenty-six women selected from among more than three hundred studied in Ginzberg's LIFE STYLES OF EDUCATED WOMEN (1966) reveal the complexity inherent in the lives of highly educated women.

960   Ginzberg, Eli, et al. LIFE STYLES OF EDUCATED WOMEN. New York: Columbia University Press, 1966. 224 p.

> Studied the careers of over three hundred talented female graduates. Paralleled similar research into talented males, reported in Ginzberg's TALENT AND PERFORMANCE (1964). Almost all the women studied were satisfied with their lives. Authors recommended that the parents of talented girls be counseled about the many options open to their daughters. Urged careful guidance at school and college for talented young women.

961   _____. OCCUPATIONAL CHOICE. New York: Columbia University Press, 1951. 271 p.

> Studied determinants of occupational choice and found three decision-making periods roughly corresponding to childhood, adolescence, and early adulthood. Concluded that occupational choice is a developmental process that is largely a compromise and irreversible.

962   Gittinger, Roy. THE UNIVERSITY OF OKLAHOMA: 1892-1942. Norman: University of Oklahoma Press, 1942. 282 p.

> A chronological record of the University of Oklahoma's first fifty years. Extensive appendices list students, degrees conferred, faculty members, and members of the board of regents.

963   Giuliano, Vincent, et al. INTO THE INFORMATION AGE: A PERSPECTIVE FOR FEDERAL ACTION ON INFORMATION. Chicago: American Library Association, 1978. 134 p.

> Explains three methods of organizing scientific and technical information for social purposes.

964   Gladieux, Lawrence E., and Wolanin, Thomas R. CONGRESS AND THE COLLEGES: THE NATIONAL POLITICS OF HIGHER EDUCATION. Lexington, Mass.: Lexington Books, 1976. 288 p.

> A study of the enactment and implementation of the education amendments of 1972. Shows lobbying mistakes and chance events that altered the law and made it so complicated that few congressmen understood it. Also traces pre-1972 federal higher education legislation.

965   Glass, Bentley. SCIENCE AND LIBERAL EDUCATION. Baton Rouge: Louisiana State University Press, 1960. 115 p.

> Contains three 1958 Davis Washington Mitchell Lectures at Tulane University about genetics in the service of man, liberal education in a scientific age, and the influence of Darwinism on Western religious and philosophical views.

966 _____. THE TIMELY AND THE TIMELESS: THE INTERRELATIONSHIPS OF SCIENCE, EDUCATION, AND SOCIETY. New York: Basic Books, 1970. 100 p.

> Three essays about science as a socially responsible activity discuss the responsibility of scientists who are educators, the potential of science for producing a better world, and the stresses which have resulted from the expansion of knowledge and opportunity for higher education. Author foresees a slowing in support for science and lists limiting factors.

967 Glaze, Thomas Edward. BUSINESS ADMINISTRATION FOR COLLEGES AND UNIVERSITIES. Baton Rouge: Louisiana State University Press, 1962. 206 p.

> Such principles of management are applied to university business administration as planning, organization, operational policies, and financing. The author believes that management skills can overcome future problems of higher education.

968 Glazer, Nathan. REMEMBERING THE ANSWERS; ESSAYS ON THE AMERICAN STUDENT REVOLT. New York: Basic Books, 1970. 311 p.

> Essays, most written from 1964 to 1970, trace the author's shifting perception of the student protest movement. Clearly sympathetic in 1964, he eventually became highly critical. The final chapter attempts to analyze the change.

969 Gleazer, Edmund J., Jr. PROJECT FOCUS: A FORECAST STUDY OF COMMUNITY COLLEGES. New York: McGraw-Hill Book Co., 1973. 239 p.

> Study by the American Association of Community and Junior Colleges about changes occurring in U.S. two-year colleges: organization and governance, financial support, enrollment, curriculum, and community needs.

970 _____. THIS IS THE COMMUNITY COLLEGE. Boston: Houghton Mifflin Co., 1968. 151 p.

> The executive director of the American Association of Junior Colleges gives an overview of the past, present, and future impact of two-year colleges. He sees staffing and able administrative leadership as decisive factors. Calls for continuing open-door and low-tuition policies.

971 Gleazer, Edmund J., Jr., and Cooke, Jane Follett, eds. AMERICAN JUNIOR COLLEGES. Washington, D.C.: American Council on Education, 1971. 850 p.

> Standard reference directory to all recognized two-year colleges lists characteristics, statistical information, and offerings for each institution.

972 Gleazer, Edmund J., Jr., and Yarrington, Roger, eds. COORDINATING STATE SYSTEMS. San Francisco: Jossey-Bass Publishers, 1974. 126 p.

Shows how to achieve state coordination of community colleges and thereby reduce duplication of services.

973 Glenny, Lyman A. THE ANONYMOUS LEADERS OF HIGHER EDUCATION. Berkeley: Center for Research and Development in Higher Education, University of California, 1971. 96 p.

Unknown members of both campus and national bureaucracies have increasingly usurped traditional functions of higher education administration.

974 _____. AUTONOMY OF PUBLIC COLLEGES: THE CHALLENGE OF COORDINATION. New York: McGraw-Hill Book Co., 1959. 325 p.

Found in twelve selected states that statewide coordination of higher education took three forms: consolidation, compulsory coordination, or voluntary coordination. The greatest problem is to avoid destroying institutional initiative, flexibility, and diversity. Recommends that institutions improve their business administrative practices to avoid intrusion from economy-minded state agencies.

975 Glenny, Lyman A., and Kidder, James R. STATE TAX SUPPORT OF HIGHER EDUCATION: REVENUE APPROPRIATION TRENDS AND PATTERNS, 1963-1973. Denver: Education Commission of the States, 1974. 50 p.

An update and expansion of an earlier report, TRENDS IN STATE FUNDING IN HIGHER EDUCATION.

976 Glenny, Lyman A., et al. COORDINATING HIGHER EDUCATION FOR THE 70'S: MULTI-CAMPUS AND STATEWIDE GUIDELINES FOR PRACTICE. Berkeley: Center for Research and Development in Higher Education, University of California, 1971. 96 p.

After reviewing the coordinating practices of thirty-five state higher education systems, the authors favored the state coordinating board because it permits institutional autonomy and independence not possible with a state governing board.

977 _____. PRESIDENTS CONFRONT REALITY: FROM EDIFICE COMPLEX TO UNIVERSITY WITHOUT WALLS. San Francisco: Jossey-Bass Publishers, 1976. 261 p.

Report of a 1974 Carnegie Council on Policy Studies in Higher Education questionnaire investigation among over one thousand university presidents about enrollment, funding, curricula, and related topics. Statistical section is over half the book.

978   Godbold, Albea. THE CHURCH COLLEGE OF THE OLD SOUTH. Durham, N.C.: Duke University Press, 1944. 221 p.

History to 1860 of denominational colleges (Episcopal, Baptist, Presbyterian, and Methodist) in Virginia, North Carolina, South Carolina, and Georgia. Shows that in the South, as throughout the United States, religion was one of the most potent forces in stimulating higher education.

979   Godshalk, Fred I., et al. THE MEASUREMENT OF WRITING ABILITY. New York: College Entrance Examination Board, 1966. 84 p.

Research into the measurement of writing ability found that the College Board's English Composition Test is a valid indicator.

980   Godwin, Winfred, and Mann, Peter B., eds. HIGHER EDUCATION: MYTHS, REALITIES AND POSSIBILITIES. Atlanta: Southern Regional Education Board, 1972. 184 p.

Financing, time-shortening, nontraditional learning, and governmental relations are discussed in papers for a Southern Regional Education Board meeting. Among contributors are Ernest Boyer, Allan Cartter, Samuel Gould, and Lyman Glenny.

981   Goepp, Ada. SMALL POND. Philadelphia: Westminster Press, 1956. 204 p.

Novel about romantic and other rivalry between two young women on the English faculty at a Massachusetts women's college.

982   Goetsch, Helen Bertha. PARENTAL INCOME AND COLLEGE OPPORTUNITIES. Contributions to Education No. 795. New York: Teachers College, Columbia University, 1940. 157 p.

Studied higher educational opportunities of Milwaukee high school students. Concluded that a college education was an exceptional privilege available primarily to the wealthy. Recommended greatly increasing college scholarships.

983   Goheen, Robert F. THE HUMAN NATURE OF A UNIVERSITY. Edited by William McCleery. Princeton, N.J.: Princeton University Press, 1969. 116 p.

Excerpts from papers, speeches, and reports of Princeton's president stress the importance of the liberal tradition and the dynamism implicit in the tensions within modern universities.

984   Golann, Stuart, et al. THE BETHLEHEM DIARIES: STUDENT-MENTAL PATIENT ENCOUNTERS. San Francisco: Canfield Press, 1974. 229 p.

Contains year-long diaries of five women college students who visited assigned mental patients weekly, interviews about patients' reactions to students' visits, and patients' hospital charts. Intended as a supplementary textbook in behavioral disorders.

985 Goldberg, Maxwell H. DESIGN IN LIBERAL LEARNING. San Francisco: Jossey-Bass Publishers, 1971. 188 p.

Essay espousing classical liberal education values. Includes a proposed curriculum.

986 Goldhor, Herbert, ed. EDUCATION FOR LIBRARIANSHIP: THE DESIGN OF THE CURRICULUM OF LIBRARY SCHOOLS. Urbana: University of Illinois Graduate School of Library Science, 1971. 195 p.

Conference papers about library science curriculum reflect on relevant social and behavioral sciences, professional ethics, and applied experience in library education.

987 Goldman, Eric F. JOHN BACH McMASTER. Philadelphia: University of Pennsylvania Press, 1943. 194 p.

Biography of McMaster (1852-1932), called by some the founder of the modern school of U.S. historians. Taught college English, earned a civil engineering degree, and taught history at the University of Pennsylvania, 1883-1919. A prolific author, his eight-volume HISTORY OF THE PEOPLE OF THE UNITED STATES (1883-1913) was the first U.S. social history. Critical analysis of his career and writings.

988 Goldman, Freda H., ed. EDUCATIONAL IMPERATIVE: THE NEGRO IN THE CHANGING SOUTH. Chicago: Center for the Study of Liberal Education for Adults, 1963. 101 p.

Conference report on the role of Negro colleges and especially their adult education programs amid changes in the South. Examined forces for change and their impact on the southern Negro.

989 Goldsen, Rose K., et al. WHAT COLLEGE STUDENTS THINK. Princeton, N.J.: D. Van Nostrand Co., 1960. 240 p.

Sociological study of beliefs and attitudes of 4,800 college students toward their college education, choice of career, fraternity systems, sex relations, religion, and other college-related matters.

990 Goldstein, Gloria, ed. COLLEGE BOUND: DIRECTORY OF SPECIAL PROGRAMS AND FINANCIAL ASSISTANCE FOR BLACK AND OTHER MINORITY GROUP STUDENTS. White Plains, N.Y.: Urban League of Westchester, 1970. 140 p.

Information about many college programs for minority and disadvantaged students: financial assistance, admissions policies, and organizations that help such students.

991 Goldwin, Robert A., ed. TOWARD THE LIBERALLY EDUCATED EXECUTIVE. White Plains, N.Y.: Fund for Adult Education, 1957. 111 p.

A call for the liberal education of corporation executives to assure that corporations accomplish their role in America's economic and social life.

992 Gollattscheck, James F., et al. COLLEGE LEADERSHIP FOR COMMUNITY RENEWAL: BEYOND COMMUNITY-BASED EDUCATION. San Francisco: Jossey-Bass Publishers, 1976. 160 p.

Describes the "community renewal college"--one that serves the community by providing educational programs, courses, and activities to satisfy local residents, and that works with local businesses and groups to bring about social change. Says community colleges must become centers for community renewal.

993 Gollay, Elinor, and Bennett, Alwina. THE COLLEGE GUIDE FOR STUDENTS WITH DISABILITIES; A DETAILED DIRECTORY OF HIGHER EDUCATION SERVICES, PROGRAMS, AND FACILITIES ACCESSIBLE TO HANDICAPPED STUDENTS IN THE UNITED STATES. Cambridge, Mass.: Abt Publications, 1976. 545 p.

A directory of programs, facilities, and services of higher education institutions serving handicapped students. Has information about two-year and four-year colleges and universities: disabled student enrollments, numbers of buildings with accessible ramps and restrooms, special counseling programs, and such resources as Braille materials.

994 Gomberg, Irene L., and Atelsek, Frank J. NONTENURE-TRACK SCIENCE PERSONNEL: OPPORTUNITIES FOR INDEPENDENT RESEARCH. Washington, D.C.: Higher Education Panel, American Council on Education, 1978. 37 p.

Results of a survey to find out the number and characteristics of principal scientific investigators not on the tenure track who are conducting research at doctoral-level universities.

995 Good, Carter V. TEACHING IN COLLEGE AND UNIVERSITY: A SURVEY OF THE PROBLEMS AND LITERATURE IN HIGHER EDUCATION. Baltimore, Md.: Warwick and York, 1929. 557 p.

A comprehensive reference work with extensive partially annotated bibliographies on higher education objectives, curriculum, psychology of learning, and classroom methodology.

996 _____, ed. A GUIDE TO COLLEGES, UNIVERSITIES, AND PROFES-
SIONAL SCHOOLS IN THE UNITED STATES. Washington, D.C.: American Council on Education, 1945. 681 p.

> Reference information intended especially for World War II
> veterans on junior colleges, liberal arts colleges, teachers col-
> leges, and 1,594 professional schools.

997 Goodall, Leonard E., ed. STATE POLITICS AND HIGHER EDUCATION.
Dearborn, Mich.: LMG Associates, 1979. 317 p.

> Readings on the nature of participation by state-supported in-
> stitutions of higher education in state politics. Topics include
> the relations between leaders of universities and state govern-
> ment officials, university "lobbying," and the competition for
> state funds.

998 Goode, Delmer M. THESE BOOKS WERE STIMULATING: SEVENTY
BOOKS ON COLLEGE TEACHING. Corvallis: Oregon State College,
1955. 13 p.

> Annotated bibliography produced by a seminar on college
> teaching.

999 Goodlad, Sinclair, ed. EDUCATION AND SOCIAL ACTION: COM-
MUNITY SERVICE AND THE CURRICULUM IN HIGHER EDUCATION.
New York: Barnes and Noble, 1975. 203 p.

> Focuses on the educational benefits of linking direct practical
> experience to the curriculum and making universities and col-
> leges resource centers for the whole community.

1000 Goodman, Paul. THE COMMUNITY OF SCHOLARS. New York: Random
House, 1962. 175 p.

> Social critic Goodman says the community of scholars has given
> way to the community of administrators and the overorganiza-
> tion for which they are responsible. His proposed antidote is
> for cells of professors and students to break away to form small
> associations for teaching and learning.

1001 Goodrich, John Thomas. COTTON CAVALIER. New York: Farrar and
Rinehart, 1933. 346 p.

> Novel set in a small coeducational Presbyterian college in the
> South, where conflict arises between modern science and reli-
> gious fundamentalism and between modern love and southern
> chivalry.

1002 Goodspeed, Thomas Wakefield. A HISTORY OF THE UNIVERSITY OF
CHICAGO. Chicago: University of Chicago Press, 1916. 522 p.

Emphasizes the 1890 founding of the university; includes articles of agreement with the Baptist Theological Union.

1003 Gordon, Edmund W., and Wilkerson, Doxey A. COMPENSATORY EDUCATION FOR THE DISADVANTAGED. PROGRAMS AND PRACTICES: PRESCHOOL THROUGH COLLEGE. New York: College Entrance Examination Board, 1966. 299 p.

Nationwide guide to and critical evaluation of compensatory programs for disadvantaged students, from preschool through college. Includes information on teacher recruitment and training, curriculum innovation, and the role of parents and the community.

1004 Gordon, Linda W., and Schub, Judy H., eds. ON-CAMPUS/OFF-CAMPUS DEGREE PROGRAMS FOR PART-TIME STUDENTS. Washington, D.C.: National University Extension Association, 1977. 119 p.

Describes international, national, state, and local degree programs available for part-time students.

1005 Gore, Daniel, ed. FAREWELL TO ALEXANDRIA: SOLUTIONS TO SPACE, GROWTH, AND PERFORMANCE PROBLEMS OF LIBRARIES. Westport, Conn.: Greenwood Press, 1976. 184 p.

Associated Colleges of the Midwest conference papers on the growing pains of libraries and possible solutions.

1006 Gorovitz, Samuel, ed. FREEDOM AND ORDER IN THE UNIVERSITY. Cleveland, Ohio: Press of Western Reserve University, 1966. 218 p.

Essays (authors include Paul Goodman, Walter P. Metzger, and John R. Searle) discuss the conflict between individual freedom and the need for social order, with particular emphasis on problems arising out of this conflict within the university.

1007 Gossman, Charles S., et al. MIGRATION OF COLLEGE AND UNIVERSITY STUDENTS IN THE UNITED STATES. Seattle: University of Washington Press, 1968. 180 p.

Used 1963 data about student migration from over two thousand U.S. higher education institutions. Analyzed student migration trends, 1938-63, and found the rate relatively constant. Developed ways to predict migration; identified variables.

1008 Gould, Samuel B. TODAY'S ACADEMIC CONDITION. New York: McGraw-Hill Book Co., 1970. 101 p.

Former chancellor of the State University of New York says contemporary universities should be more deeply involved with community problems and the nation's social needs. He envisions development of a "communiversity."

1009 Gould, Samuel B., and Cross, K. Patricia, eds. EXPLORATIONS IN NONTRADITIONAL STUDY. San Francisco: Jossey-Bass Publishers, 1972. 137 p.

> Examines concepts basic to nontraditional study, identifies people who benefit from it, and describes the kinds of instruction, counseling, and recognition appropriate to those students. Tells of various credit and degree arrangements for nontraditional study in England (University of London, Open University) and in the United States.

1010 Gould, Samuel B., et al. THE ARTS AND EDUCATION: A NEW BEGINNING IN HIGHER EDUCATION. New York: Rockefeller Brothers Fund, 1968. 31 p.

> Papers about the arts presented at 1967 meetings sponsored by the Mary Reynolds Babcock Foundation, Rockefeller Brothers Fund, Twentieth Century Fund, and New York State Council on the Arts.

1011 Govan, Gilbert E., and Livingood, James W. THE UNIVERSITY OF CHATTANOOGA: SIXTY YEARS. Chattanooga, Tenn.: University of Chattanooga, 1947. 271 p.

> History of a southern liberal arts college founded by Methodists in 1872. First part is about the early organization, administration, and problems of interracial education. Second part identifies 1889-1904 as a period of consolidation with Grant Memorial University (located at Athens, Tennessee). Remaining sections deal with modern (1904-46) academic and social developments.

1012 Gowan, John C. AN ANNOTATED BIBLIOGRAPHY ON THE ACADEMICALLY TALENTED STUDENT. Washington, D.C.: National Education Association, 1961. 156 p.

> Annotated bibliography of post-1950 material about the academically talented at all educational levels. Excludes popular works and case studies.

1013 Graeffe, Arnold Didier. CREATIVE EDUCATION IN THE HUMANITIES. New York: Harper and Brothers, 1951. 199 p.

> A plea for an integrated approach to the teaching of the arts and philosophy in humanities courses, with the teacher acting as a catalyst. Includes course plans and suggests many practical teaching tools and methods.

1014 Grafton, Cornelius Warren. MY NAME IS CHRISTOPHER NAGEL. New York: Farrar and Rinehart, 1947. 357 p.

Novel about a man looking back twenty years to his college career as a basketball player and pre-med student.

1015 Graham, George A. EDUCATION FOR PUBLIC ADMINISTRATION: GRADUATE PREPARATION IN THE SOCIAL SCIENCES AT AMERICAN UNIVERSITIES. Chicago: Public Administration Service, 1941. 366 p.

Appraisal of public administration programs in U.S. universities. The importance of combining liberal and professional education is stressed and the potential job market is explored.

1016 Grandy, Jerilee, and Shea, Walter M. THE CLEP GENERAL EXAMINATIONS IN AMERICAN COLLEGES AND UNIVERSITIES. Princeton, N.J.: College Board Publications, 1976. 23 p.

Reports on the use of the College Level Examination Program tests at 535 colleges and universities.

1017 Grant, Arthur T., ed. THE STATE LEGISLATIVE PROCESS AND HIGHER EDUCATION. Tucson: Center for the Study of Higher Education, University of Arizona, 1979. 46 p.

Five conference papers on the relations between higher education and the state.

1018 Grant, Gerald, and Riesman, David. THE PERPETUAL DREAM: REFORM AND EXPERIMENT IN THE AMERICAN COLLEGE. Chicago: University of Chicago Press, 1978. 478 p.

Insightful survey of what two renowned, knowledgeable research professors learned from the 1965-75 decade of higher education experimentation, with historical background. Grant from Syracuse and Riesman from Harvard during seven years visited over four hundred campuses, interviewing three hundred professors and many more students. They urge restoring quality ("honors") without compromising open access, and such reforms as using best retired professors, making better use of teaching fellows, upgrading mid-career faculty, using peer learning situations, and calling for "more inventiveness, more imagination, more willingness to experiment and hence to fail, than is generally present."

1019 Grant, Gerald, et al. ON COMPETENCE: A CRITICAL ANALYSIS OF COMPETENCE-BASED REFORMS IN HIGHER EDUCATION. San Francisco: Jossey-Bass Publishers, 1979. 592 p.

Translating higher education course goals into measurable outcomes is this book's efficiency-productivity theme, an extension into higher education of recent competency-based public school and teacher education programs. Explores the national need for such proficiency; the impact on faculty, students, and

administration; and gives examples of competency-based liberal
arts programs.

1020 Grattan, C. Hartley, ed. AMERICAN IDEAS ABOUT ADULT EDUCA-
TION 1710-1951. New York: Teachers College Press, 1959. 140 p.

Documents illustrating American thinking about adult education.

1021 Graves, Ralph A. THANKS FOR THE RIDE. Philadelphia: J.B. Lippincott Co., 1949. 251 p.

Novel about a youth who tries but fails to keep his hometown
friends together as a group when they all go to college.

1022 Gray, James. THE UNIVERSITY OF MINNESOTA: 1851-1951. Minneapolis: University of Minnesota Press, 1951. 609 p.

Centennial history of the University of Minnesota as it evolved
through eight presidents: William Watts Folwell, Cyrus Northrop, George Edgar Vincent, and others.

1023 Gray, William S., ed. CURRENT ISSUES IN HIGHER EDUCATION.
Chicago: University of Chicago Press, 1937. 153 p.

Ninth volume of proceedings of the Institute for Administrative
Officers of Higher Institutions contains papers about such questions as the place of liberal arts and the pros and cons of electives.

1024 _____. NEEDED READJUSTMENTS IN HIGHER EDUCATION. Chicago:
University of Chicago Press, 1933. 283 p.

Papers at the 1933 Institute for Administrative Officers of
Higher Institutions reflected the Depression's effects, as seen
in such titles as "The Nature of the Emergency" and "Financial Readjustments in Typical Institutions."

1025 _____. PREPARATION AND IN-SERVICE TRAINING OF COLLEGE
TEACHERS. Chicago: University of Chicago Press, 1938. 230 p.

Papers for the 1938 Institute of Administrative Officers of
Higher Institutions, whose theme was the college teacher: the
ideal, selection, training, and recruitment.

1026 _____. PROVISION FOR THE INDIVIDUAL IN COLLEGE EDUCATION.
Chicago: University of Chicago Press, 1932. 262 p.

Papers given at the 1932 Institute for Administrative Officers
of Higher Institutions deal with selecting and advising students,
course offerings, and student services.

1027 Greeley, Andrew M. THE CHANGING CATHOLIC COLLEGE. Chicago: Aldine Publishing Co., 1968. 226 p.

> Studied thirty-six Catholic and six non-Catholic higher education institutions. Concluded that the difference between improvement or stagnation in a college or university rests in the competence and independence of its top administrators.

1028 _____. FROM BACKWATER TO MAINSTREAM: A PROFILE OF CATHOLIC HIGHER EDUCATION. New York: McGraw-Hill Book Co., 1969. 184 p.

> Brief historical sketch and contemporary overview show that Catholic higher education is not a monolith and is following the pattern typical of other colleges as they strive for the mainstream. Author considers Notre Dame the Catholic pacesetter and fund raising a pervasive problem.

1029 _____. RELIGION AND CAREER: A STUDY OF COLLEGE GRADUATES. New York: Sheed and Ward, 1963. 267 p.

> Acknowledging past Catholic intellectual lag, author used 1961 data to compare 33,000 Catholic and non-Catholic students from 135 colleges: percentages going to graduate school, grade achievement, socio-economic status, and professional goals. Concluded that Catholic students are achieving intellectual parity with non-Catholics.

1030 Green, Edwin L. A HISTORY OF THE UNIVERSITY OF SOUTH CAROLINA. Columbia, S.C.: State Co., 1916. 475 p.

> History of the University of South Carolina from its conception. Topics include the curriculum, trustees and faculty, student life, the library, and finances. Appendix of relevant documents.

1031 Greenberger, Martin, et al., eds. NETWORKS FOR RESEARCH AND EDUCATION: SHARING COMPUTER AND INFORMATION RESOURCES NATIONWIDE. Cambridge, Mass.: MIT Press, 1974. 418 p.

> Report of three 1972-73 seminars conducted by the Interuniversity Communications Council which found that institutions are abandoning self-sufficiency in order to share computer resources.

1032 Greene, Harry Washington. HOLDERS OF DOCTORATES AMONG AMERICAN NEGROES. Boston: Meador Publishing Co., 1946. 275 p.

> Studied 381 black Americans who as of 1943 held doctorates from fifty-seven U.S. universities and fourteen foreign ones: source of the degree, its quality, and the area of concentration. A directory lists occupation, research, and previous academic training of the black doctorates.

1033 Greene, Howard, and Minton, Robert. SCALING THE IVY WALL: GETTING INTO THE SELECTIVE COLLEGES. New York: Abelard-Schuman, 1975. 290 p.

> Explains the admissions process to prospective college students: the importance of grades, recommendations from the right persons, and extracurricular activities.

1034 Greene, Theodore Meyer. LIBERAL EDUCATION RECONSIDERED. Cambridge, Mass.: Harvard University Press, 1953. 46 p.

> Author, who wrote LIBERAL EDUCATION REEXAMINED: ITS ROLE IN A DEMOCRACY (1943), reinterprets liberal education as the basic purpose and direction of higher education. The ultimate goal is the development of the individual in society.

1035 Greene, Theodore P., ed. ESSAYS ON AMHERST'S HISTORY. Amherst, Mass.: Vista Trust, 1978. 452 p.

> Fifteen essays on the academic town of Amherst, Massachusetts, and the influences on it of its three institutions of higher education: Amherst College, the University of Massachusetts at Amherst, and Hampshire College.

1036 Grennan, Jacqueline. WHERE I AM GOING: EXCERPTS FROM THE SPEECHES OF JACQUELINE GRENNAN. New York: McGraw-Hill Book Co., 1968. 179 p.

> Woman president of a women's college relates her philosophy on higher education. She sees all education as a public trust, filled with value choices.

1037 Gribbons, Warren D., and Lohnes, Paul R. EMERGING CAREERS. New York: Teachers College Press, 1968. 202 p.

> A study of the career development of 111 youths during seven years, from the eighth grade through two years after high school. Includes statistical interpretation.

1038 Griffin, Clifford S. THE UNIVERSITY OF KANSAS: A HISTORY. Lawrence: University Press of Kansas, 1974. 808 p.

> Relates the inauspicious beginnings of the university in the 1860s, its growing pains, and continuing development.

1039 Griswold, A. Whitney. IN THE UNIVERSITY TRADITION. New Haven, Conn.: Yale University Press, 1957. 162 p.

> Yale University president, in speeches and articles, identifies and interprets the values of the university tradition.

1040 _____. LIBERAL EDUCATION AND THE DEMOCRATIC IDEAL. New Haven, Conn.: Yale University Press, 1959. 136 p.

> The importance to the individual of a liberal education is the theme of these speeches and essays by Yale University president.

1041 Gronlund, Norman Edward. MEASUREMENT AND EVALUATION IN TEACHING. New York: Macmillan Co., 1965. 420 p.

> Introductory principles and procedures in measuring the effectiveness of teaching, applied to higher education.

1042 Gropper, George L., and Fitzpatrick, Robert. WHO GOES TO GRADUATE SCHOOL? Pittsburgh, Pa.: American Institute for Research, 1959. 66 p.

> Some findings among 3,581 students in thirty graduate schools: (1) 49 percent went mainly for career purposes, 21 percent for educational purposes, and 14 percent because of other people's influence; (2) women went more for educational purposes and less for vocational purposes; (3) the higher the undergraduate grades, the weaker were career aims and the greater were educational aims; (4) more undergraduates who taught or did research part-time undertook graduate study; (5) more physics undergraduate majors and fewer engineering undergraduate majors did graduate work; and (6) 63 percent of graduate students had to work part-time or had to receive scholarship aid.

1043 Gross, Edward, and Grambsch, Paul V. CHANGES IN UNIVERSITY ORGANIZATION, 1964-1971. New York: McGraw-Hill Book Co., 1974. 257 p.

> Authors surveyed sixty-eight universities in 1964 and 1971 and found no change in these two goals of faculty and administrators: (1) to protect academic freedom, and (2) to develop and advance their careers.

1044 Gross, Michael J. THE HOW TO GO TO COLLEGE BOOK: HUNDREDS OF SPECIFIC TECHNIQUES TO MAKE COLLEGE EASIER. Thornwood, N.Y.: Caroline House Publishers, 1979. 166 p.

> Student's guide to coping with classes, studying, term papers, and exams.

1045 Gross, Ronald. A HANDBOOK FOR THE LIFELONG LEARNER. New York: Simon and Schuster, 1978. 190 p.

> Describes the value and rewards of self-education. Discusses the characteristics of adult learning and suggests a number of sources for learning, such as television, libraries, clubs and learning groups.

1046 Grote, Caroline. HOUSING AND LIVING CONDITIONS OF WOMEN STUDENTS. Contributions to Education No. 507. New York: Teachers College, Columbia University, 1932. 106 p.

Study of the effect living arrangements have on academic, health, and social achievement of women students living in and away from Western Illinois State Teachers College. Found that dormitory living provided better health opportunities, and that living at home in the same college town provided the best social experiences.

1047 Group for the Advancement of Psychiatry. Committee on the College Student. THE EDUCATED WOMAN: PROSPECTS AND PROBLEMS. New York: 1975. 257 p.

Chapters on the expectations of women in college, the feminine-masculine axis, college and after, psychotherapy, toward change, and recommendations.

1048 Gruber, Carol S. MARS AND MINERVA: WORLD WAR I AND THE USES OF THE HIGHER LEARNING IN AMERICA. Baton Rouge: Louisiana State University Press, 1976. 293 p.

Looks at higher education's climate of opinion before, during, and after World War I: a change from a concept of serving social welfare to one of service to the state, as academic freedom was submerged and the campuses militarized. Author says that the same academics who criticized German scholars' support of militarism in 1914 compromised their own social uplift roles when they wedded themselves to patriotic purposes in 1917-18.

1049 Gruenberg, Sidonie M., and Krech, Hilda Sidney. THE MANY LIVES OF MODERN WOMAN. Garden City, N.Y.: Doubleday and Co., 1952. 255 p.

What should constitute appropriate higher education for women? The authors explore the question against the backdrop of the kinds of roles expected of men and women.

1050 Grupe, Fritz H. MANAGING INTERINSTITUTIONAL CHANGE: CONSORTIA IN HIGHER EDUCATION. Potsdam, N.Y.: Associated Colleges of the St. Lawrence Valley, 1975. 111 p.

Practical information on managing higher education cooperative efforts by a consortium director who predicts the future growth of such interinstitutional arrangements.

1051 Guerard, Albert Joseph. THE HUNTED. New York: Alfred A. Knopf, 1944. 288 p.

Novel about crime and evil at a New England college.

1052 Guest, Mary Lapsley Caughey. THE PARABLE OF THE VIRGINS. New York: Richard R. Smith, 1931. 359 p.

Novel about life at a Vassar-like women's college.

1053 Gugman, Jessie P., ed. RECORDS AND RESEARCH PAMPHLETS. Tuskegee, Ala.: Tuskegee Institute, 1949-61. Various pagings. Reprinted as EIGHT NEGRO BIBLIOGRAPHIES. Millwood, N.Y.: Kraus Reprint Co., 1970.

These bibliographies about black problems and achievements include a selected list of references relating to the elementary, secondary, and higher education of blacks from 1949 to June 1955; and a selected list of references relating to the black teacher from 1949 to June 1955.

1054 Gunthorp, Charles Lawrence. A PRACTICAL GUIDE TO EFFICIENT STUDY: A DETAILED DESCRIPTION OF WHAT YOU CAN DO TO MAKE LEARNING EASIER. New York: Exposition Press, 1957. 118 p.

Guide for college students on how to study, write, and learn.

1055 Gurin, Patricia, and Epps, Edgar. BLACK CONSCIOUSNESS, IDENTITY AND ACHIEVEMENT: A STUDY OF STUDENTS IN HISTORICALLY BLACK COLLEGES. New York: John Wiley and Sons, 1975. 545 p.

An eight-year study of the family background, values, behavior, and impact of the civil rights and black power movements on black students at predominantly black colleges. Over one hundred pages of tables.

1056 Gustad, John W. THE CAREER DECISIONS OF COLLEGE TEACHERS. Atlanta: Southern Regional Education Board, 1960. 87 p.

A survey of college teachers, ex-college teachers, and graduate students in chemistry, English, and psychology: their life histories and motivations, job activities and values, conditions of work, career goals, and plans.

1057 Gustavson, Reuben G., et al. EDUCATION IN A FREE SOCIETY. Pittsburgh, Pa.: University of Pittsburgh Press, 1958. 47 p.

Three lectures on education's role in preserving freedom. Gustafson stressed combining science with the social sciences and humanities to foster sound values. Peter Viereck called for exploring man's inner dimensions through poetry, art, psychology, and religion. Paul Woodring advocated a new synthesis of liberal and professional studies.

1058 Gutwillig, Robert. AFTER LONG SILENCE. Boston: Little, Brown and Co., 1958. 350 p.

Novel about undergraduate life about the time of the Korean War.

1059 Haagan, C. Hess. VENTURING BEYOND THE CAMPUS: STUDENTS WHO LEAVE COLLEGE. Middletown, Conn.: Wesleyan University Press, 1977. 272 p.

Investigated the almost forty percent dropout rate in five private New England colleges and universities. Explored why students drop out, whether they return, what they do after dropping out, and their subsequent careers.

1060 Habecker, Eugene B. AFFIRMATIVE ACTION IN THE INDEPENDENT COLLEGE: A PRACTICAL PLANNING MODEL. Washington, D.C.: Council for the Advancement of Small Colleges, 1977. 174 p.

Outlines a plan for creating equal educational opportunity. Includes instructional worksheets on how to avoid "underutilization of women and minorities" and federal documents governing activities of the colleges.

1061 Haberman, Martin, and Stinnett, T.M. TEACHER EDUCATION AND THE NEW PROFESSION OF TEACHING. Berkeley, Calif.: McCutchan Publishers, 1973. 257 p.

Examines the evolution of teacher education and such major aspects and influences as student recruitment, programs offered, competency-based training, evaluation, governance, research, and accreditation. Concludes with trends in teacher education and effects of teacher militancy.

1062 Haddow, Anna. POLITICAL SCIENCE IN AMERICAN COLLEGES AND UNIVERSITIES, 1636-1900. New York: D. Appleton-Century Co., 1939. 308 p.

On the evolution of political science as a subject in higher education from colonial times. Those who developed it as a discipline included Woodrow Wilson at Princeton, A. Lawrence Lowell at Harvard, W.W. Folwell at Minnesota, and Edmund J. James at the Wharton School of the University of Pennsylvania. Professor William Anderson of the University of Minnesota added a concluding chaper on political science as a subject in the twentieth century.

1063 Hadley, Morris. ARTHUR TWINING HADLEY. New Haven, Conn.: Yale University Press, 1948. 282 p.

Biography of Arthur Hadley (1856-1930) by his son. An economist, as Yale's president (1899-1921) he helped it become a well-coordinated university with strong graduate and professional schools. Nationally he was a founder of the Interstate Commerce Commission, was chairman of the Carnegie Foundation for the Advancement of Teaching, and on many other important boards.

1064 Hage, Robert K. VERIFYING PARENTS' FINANCIAL INFORMATION: A GUIDE FOR FINANCIAL AID ADMINISTRATORS. Princeton, N.J.: College Board Publications, 1978. 33 p.

Describes how to verify reliability of parents' financial statements. Emphasizes the use of income tax returns: how to get them, analyze them, and what to do when discrepancies appear.

1065 Haggerty, Melvin E. THE EDUCATIONAL PROGRAM. Chicago: University of Chicago Press, 1937. 335 p.

North Central Association of Colleges and Secondary Schools' study on college accreditation. Chapters on the purposes of higher education, institutional individuality, the curriculum, instruction, and the improvement of instruction.

1066 _____. THE FACULTY. Chicago: University of Chicago Press, 1937. 218 p.

North Central Association of Colleges and Secondary Schools' study on accreditation. Focuses on faculty evaluation: their competence, organization, and conditions of service.

1067 Haines, John, and Penney, Sherry, eds. WOMEN AND MANAGEMENT IN HIGHER EDUCATION. Albany, N.Y.: Resource Center on Women in Higher Education, New York State Education Department, 1976. 136 p.

Examines the status of women in higher education. Has sections on attitudes toward women in education, women in management and psychology, and affirmative action.

1068 Hall, Everett, and Barger, Ben. EDUCATIONAL ATTAINMENT OF PARENTS AS RELATED TO STUDENTS' FEELINGS ABOUT SELF AND FAMILY. Gainesville: University of Florida, 1967. 20 p.

Survey of University of Florida undergraduates about vocational choice, accomplishment, parental relationship, and other personal feelings.

1069 Hall, G. Stanley. LIFE AND CONFESSIONS OF A PSYCHOLOGIST. New York: Appleton, 1923. Reprint. Ann Arbor, Mich.: Xerox University Microfilms, 1972. 622 p.

Autobiography of renowned psychologist Hall (1844–1924), who established the first formal psychological laboratory at Johns Hopkins University and for over thirty years headed Clark University as its first president (1889–1920).

1070 Hall, Laurence, et al. NEW COLLEGES FOR NEW STUDENTS. San Francisco: Jossey-Bass Publishers, 1974. 210 p.

Journalistic account of nontraditional colleges and innovative programs for minority groups, women, immigrants, and older people. Also has chapters on the institutions' teaching methods, their relations with government, and reasons for their success.

1071 Hall, Oakley. THE CORPUS OF JOE BAILEY. New York: Viking Press, 1953. 479 p.

Novel of a poor San Diego youth, his football and fraternity experience at the University of California at Berkeley, and his marriage and subsequent business career.

1072 Hallam, Kenneth J., ed. INNOVATIONS IN HIGHER EDUCATION. Baltimore: Towson State College, 1966. 131 p.

Papers about trends in higher education curriculum and instruction, teacher education, instructional media, and educational research.

1073 Hall-Quest, Alfred Lawrence. THE UNIVERSITY AFIELD. New York: Macmillan Co., 1926. 292 p.

About university extension programs for teaching adults: courses offered, teaching methods, teachers, students, finance, and problems.

1074 Halperin, Samuel. A UNIVERSITY IN THE WEB OF POLITICS. New York: Holt, Rinehart and Winston, 1960. 16 p.

Uses the first election of trustees for Wayne State University after it became a state institution to illustrate the effect of partisan politics on higher education.

1075 Halstead, D. Kent. HIGHER EDUCATION PRICES AND PRICE INDEXES. Washington, D.C.: Government Printing Office, 1976. 114 p.

Price indexes for these university expenditures: current operations, research and development, new construction, capital equipment, and student charges. Explains the uses and limitations of price indexes and the effects of inflation on real expenditures.

1076 _____. STATEWIDE PLANNING IN HIGHER EDUCATION. Washington, D.C.: Government Printing Office, 1974. 812 p.

Encyclopedic look at how states provide higher education. Discusses principal higher education issues states faced, 1949 to 1974, including access to higher education, student financial aid, library operations, finance, facilities planning, and space management.

1077 Ham, Roswell Gray, Jr. FISH FLYING THROUGH AIR. New York: G.P. Putnam's Sons, 1957. 311 p.

Novel tracing the lives of three boys through prep school and then Yale, from the 1930s to 1955.

1078 Hamelman, Paul W., ed. MANAGING THE UNIVERSITY: A SYSTEMS APPROACH. New York: Praeger Publishers, 1972. 139 p.

Papers by university business managers and other specialists about using systems analysis in higher education management. Provide data and help in planning for emerging social and political developments.

1079 Hamilton, Thomas H., and Blackman, Edward, eds. THE BASIC COLLEGE OF MICHIGAN STATE. East Lansing: Michigan State College Press, 1955. 127 p.

Examines the Basic College, a two-year general education core for all students: organizational framework, curriculum areas, student services, and evaluation procedures.

1080 Hammond, Edward H., and Shaffer, Robert H., eds. THE LEGAL FOUNDATIONS OF STUDENT PERSONNEL SERVICES IN HIGHER EDUCATION. Washington, D.C.: American Personnel and Guidance Association, 1978. 174 p.

Contains legal information to help student personnel professionals meet the growing number of situations in which students might use litigation.

1081 Hammond, Phillip E. THE CAMPUS CLERGYMAN. New York: Basic Books, 1966. 171 p.

A sociological study of campus clergymen, excluding Roman Catholics and Jews. Concerned primarily with problems about their campus role and why many soon leave.

1082 Hammond, William Gardiner. REMEMBRANCE OF AMHERST: AN UNDERGRADUATE'S DIARY (1846-48). New York: Columbia University Press, 1946. 307 p.

Diary of William Gardiner Hammond, who for two years (1846–48) recorded his daily experiences as an Amherst undergraduate. He gives glimpses of campus life, the classroom, study hours and playtime, discussions with teachers and friends, and other fascinating bits.

1083 Hammons, James O., ed. CHANGING INSTRUCTIONAL STRATEGIES. San Francisco: Jossey-Bass Publishers, 1977. 95 p.

Suggests most effective approaches to instruction in two-year colleges.

1084 Hanawalt, Leslie L. A PLACE OF LIGHT: THE HISTORY OF WAYNE STATE UNIVERSITY. Detroit: Wayne State University Press, 1968. 512 p.

History of each of the Detroit-run colleges and graduate and professional schools which joined in 1933 to become Wayne University. Tells of administrative, financial, and curricular affairs, and the 1956 shift to a state university.

1085 Handlin, Oscar, and Handlin, Mary F. THE AMERICAN COLLEGE AND AMERICAN CULTURE; SOCIALIZATION AS A FUNCTION OF HIGHER EDUCATION. New York: McGraw-Hill Book Co., 1970. 104 p.

Historical essay which illustrates that American colleges have changed because of larger social changes. Colonial colleges stressed the religion, discipline, and missionary spirit characteristic of the time. After 1870 higher education served an industrializing, urbanizing society.

1086 Hanfmann, Eugenia. EFFECTIVE THERAPY FOR COLLEGE STUDENTS: ALTERNATIVES TO TRADITIONAL COUNSELING. San Francisco: Jossey-Bass Publishers, 1978. 338 p.

Blueprint for a successful college counseling service. Advocates educational, not medical counseling. Tells how to keep costs down.

1087 _____, et al. PSYCHOLOGICAL COUNSELING IN A SMALL COLLEGE. Cambridge, Mass.: Schenkman Publishing Co., 1963. 131 p.

Based on author's eleven years at Brandeis University. Outlines problems involved in establishing a mental health service. Discusses the role and scope of psychological counseling.

1088 Hankin, Joseph N. NEGOTIATING A BETTER FUTURE: PLANNING AND ORGANIZING FOR COLLECTIVE NEGOTIATIONS IN COMMUNITY AND JUNIOR COLLEGES. Washington, D.C.: American Association of Community and Junior Colleges, 1978. 34 p.

Gives basic steps in preparing for collective bargaining in two-year colleges, a brief history of collective bargaining, and guidelines for successful bargaining. Summarizes relevant state legislation.

1089 Hanley, Edna Ruth. COLLEGE AND UNIVERSITY LIBRARY BUILDINGS. Chicago: American Library Association, 1939. 152 p.

The essentials of library planning, with cost and size data for forty-two college libraries including floor plans and photos. Bibliography on the physical aspects of 102 college libraries.

1090 Hansen, Allen Oscar. EARLY EDUCATIONAL LEADERSHIP IN THE OHIO VALLEY. Originally published as Monograph No. 5 of the JOURNAL OF EDUCATIONAL RESEARCH (1923). Reprint. New York: Arno Press, 1969. 120 p.

Historical study of the pre-Civil War role of the Western Library Institute and the College of Professional Teachers in the Ohio Valley.

1091 Hansen, James E. II. DEMOCRACY'S COLLEGE IN THE CENTENNIAL STATE: A HISTORY OF COLORADO STATE UNIVERSITY. Fort Collins: Colorado State University Bookstore, 1977. 494 p.

Illustrated history of the university since its founding in 1878 as Colorado Agricultural College. After two other name changes, it became in 1957 Colorado State University. Book's theme is the tension between teaching the practical and the liberal arts. Discusses curriculum, student life, faculty contributions, research, and extension services. Puts the institution into the context of Colorado politics and national and international events.

1092 Hansen, Janet S., and Gladieux, Lawrence E. MIDDLE-INCOME STUDENTS: A NEW TARGET FOR FEDERAL AID? New York: College Board Publications, 1978. 35 p.

An analysis of 1978 college student assistance legislation and an assessment of such alternatives as tuition tax credits.

1093 Hansen, L. Sunny, and Rapoza, Rita S., eds. CAREER DEVELOPMENT AND COUNSELING OF WOMEN. Springfield, Ill.: Charles C Thomas, Publisher, 1978. 642 p.

Of the thirty-seven readings by forty-seven contributors to this book on counseling women toward careers, several are specifically on and others touch upon higher education for women. The contributors, mainly women, are secondary school counselors and professors of psychology, sociology, and economics.

1094 Hansen, W. Lee, and Weisbrod, Burton E. BENEFITS, COST AND FI-
NANCE OF PUBLIC HIGHER EDUCATION. Chicago: Markham, 1969.
114 p.

> Economic analysis done in 1965 for the California state legis-
> lature about who should pay for higher education. Findings:
> (1) most graduates of tax-supported public institutions were
> from rather high-income groups; and (2) the state's contribu-
> tion to an individual's education is not likely to be recouped
> in taxes. Implies that tuition should be raised.

1095 Hansl, Eva B. TRENDS IN PART-TIME EMPLOYMENT OF COLLEGE
TRAINED WOMEN. New York: Woman's Press, 1949. 63 p.

> Examines the critical and growing social issue of the dilemma
> of the educated wife, mother, and worker. What kind of
> higher education best equips her to enter the job market at
> various times in her life? Argues that if education is to fit
> women's needs, they should be educated differently from men.

1096 Hanson, Gary R., and Cole, Nancy S., eds. THE VOCATIONAL IN-
TERESTS OF YOUNG ADULTS. Iowa City: American College Testing
Program, 1973. 132 p.

> Papers which interpret the world of work in terms of a college
> student's characteristics and vocational interests.

1097 Hanus, Paul H. ADVENTURING IN EDUCATION. Cambridge, Mass.:
Harvard University Press, 1937. 259 p.

> Author's autobiographical account of helping create Harvard's
> school of education, a task given him in 1891 by President
> Charles W. Eliot. Also tells of his considerable work for pub-
> lic education.

1098 Harbeson, Gladys E. CHOICE AND CHALLENGE FOR THE AMERICAN
WOMAN. Cambridge, Mass.: Schenkman Publishing Co., 1967. 185 p.

> Reviews the historical and cultural bases of feminine rights and
> opportunities for self-fulfillment. Examines the status of women
> in other parts of the world.

1099 Harcleroad, Fred F. EDUCATIONAL AUDITING AND ACCOUNTABILITY.
Washington, D.C.: Council on Postsecondary Accreditation, 1977. 34 p.

> Proposes that accrediting organizations use an evaluation and
> reporting system similar to one developed by the Securities and
> Exchange Commission for auditing business. Such a system
> would provide valid, reliable, and comparable information on
> educational institutions and programs.

1100 _____. INSTITUTIONAL EFFICIENCY IN STATE SYSTEMS OF PUBLIC HIGHER EDUCATION. Washington, D.C.: American Association of State Colleges and Universities, 1976. 43 p.

A study of effects state boards of higher education have on the effectiveness and efficiency of individual institutions.

1101 _____, ed. ISSUES OF THE SEVENTIES: THE FUTURE OF HIGHER EDUCATION. San Francisco: Jossey-Bass Publishers, 1970. 192 p.

Conference papers look back to the 1950s and 60s. Meredith Wilson is concerned about mixups in national and institutional priorities, Nevitt Sanford thinks there is a shortage of educational leaders, and David P. Campbell urges diversity on higher education.

1102 Hardee, Melvene Draheim. FACULTY ADVISING IN COLLEGES AND UNIVERSITIES. Washington, D.C.: American College Personnel Association, 1970. 36 p.

Summarizes a large body of information about advising; advocates motivating faculty members to become advisers to students.

1103 _____. THE FACULTY IN COLLEGE COUNSELING. New York: McGraw-Hill Book Co., 1959. 391 p.

Analysis of faculty counseling practices and in-service training for counseling.

1104 Hardesty, Cecil Donald. PROBLEMS AND PRACTICES IN HOUSING THE JUNIOR-COLLEGE PROGRAM IN CALIFORNIA. Los Angeles: University of Southern California Press, 1934. 153 p.

Examines space requirements for junior college classrooms, lockers, library, auditorium, and offices. At time of writing, most such colleges shared facilities with high schools.

1105 Harding, Thomas S. COLLEGE LITERARY SOCIETIES: THEIR CONTRIBUTION TO HIGHER EDUCATION IN THE UNITED STATES, 1815-1876. New York: Pageant Press, 1971. 537 p.

Historical study of literary societies, which were widespread at colleges in the North and South, 1815-40, and in the West later in the century. Such societies declined as college curricula became flexible enough to include their concerns; they disappeared with the spread of such extracurricular activities as athletics, music, and drama.

1106 Harkness, Charles A. CAREER COUNSELING: DREAMS AND REALITY. Springfield, Ill.: Charles C Thomas, Publisher, 1976. 311 p.

For career counselors and for students planning their careers. Describes effective career counseling programs and facilities. Chapters on testing, counseling women (especially about combining marriage and career), nontraditional careers, self-employment, and labor projects. Author tells of his experience as a career counselor and how his career developed.

1107 Harlacher, Ervin L. THE COMMUNITY DIMENSION OF THE COMMUNITY COLLEGE. Englewood Cliffs, N.J.: Prentice-Hall, 1969. 140 p.

Studied ways thirty-seven community colleges serve their communities with cultural activities, non-credit courses, and other programs. Surveyed trends and urged that two-year colleges become catalytic centers in their communities. Comprehensive bibliography and index.

1108 Harman, David, ed. EXPANDING RECURRENT AND NONFORMAL EDUCATION. San Francisco: Jossey-Bass Publishers, 1976. 112 p.

How to meet the needs of such nontraditional students as adults and part-time students.

1109 Harman, Linda, ed. STATUS OF WOMEN IN HIGHER EDUCATION: 1963-1972; A SELECTIVE BIBLIOGRAPHY. Ames: Iowa State University Library, 1972. 124 p.

Annotated bibliography of selected books, dissertations, and other materials on women faculty, students, administrators, and librarians. Appendix lists pertinent national laws and identifies institutions charged with sex bias.

1110 Harmon, Lindsey R. CENTURY OF DOCTORATES: DATA ANALYSES OF GROWTH AND CHANGE: U.S. PH.D.S--THEIR NUMBERS, ORIGINS, CHARACTERISTICS, AND THE INSTITUTIONS FROM WHICH THEY COME. Washington, D.C.: National Academy of Sciences, 1978. 173 p.

Among findings: after 1870 the number of doctorates rose by about seven percent annually; time lapse between earning baccalaureate and doctoral degrees is least in chemistry, greatest in education; postdoctoral study and interim job taking is rising, especially among women; and the number of doctoral-degree granting institutions rose from sixty-one in the early 1920s to 307 in 1974, with rapid post-World War II increases in the mountain states and the South.

1111 Harno, Albert J. LEGAL EDUCATION IN THE UNITED STATES. San Francisco: Bancroft-Whitney, 1953. 211 p.

Deals with such aspects of legal education as part-time attendance which give lower class and ethnic minorities' limited access to the legal profession.

1112 Haro, Carlos Manuel, ed. THE BAKKE DECISION: THE QUESTION OF CHICANO ACCESS TO HIGHER EDUCATION. Los Angeles: Chicano Studies Center Publications, 1977. 198 p.

Contains documents and other materials about California courts' handling of the Bakke case regarding medical school admission and its specific effects on Chicanos.

1113 Harper, Charles A. A CENTURY OF PUBLIC TEACHER EDUCATION: THE STORY OF THE STATE TEACHERS COLLEGES AS THEY EVOLVED FROM THE NORMAL SCHOOLS. Washington, D.C.: Birch-Mann for American Association of Teachers Colleges, 1939. Reprint. Westport, Conn.: Greenwood Press, 1970. 175 p.

History of public teacher education, which began in Massachusetts and spread westward. Discusses the contributions of normal schools and the transition to state teachers colleges in the twentieth century.

1114 _____. DEVELOPMENT OF THE TEACHERS COLLEGE IN THE UNITED STATES. Bloomington, Ill.: McKnight Publishing Co., 1935. 384 p.

History of Illinois State Normal University from 1850 to 1930. Also discusses founding and pattern of normal schools, Herbartian influences, and David Felmley's part in the teachers' college movement.

1115 Harper, William A., ed. 1970 JUNIOR COLLEGE DIRECTORY. Washington, D.C.: American Association of Junior Colleges, 1970. 112 p.

Tuition, enrollment, address, and other information are contained in this directory of two-year institutions of higher education.

1116 Harrington, Fred Harvey. THE FUTURE OF ADULT EDUCATION: NEW RESPONSIBILITIES OF COLLEGES AND UNIVERSITIES. San Francisco: Jossey-Bass Publishers, 1977. 238 p.

History, recent development, and the increasing importance of adult education. Discusses the education of ethnic, poor, and elderly groups. Makes recommendations on the organization, management, leadership, and funding of adult programs. Shows how higher education institutions are serving more adults with on-campus credit, non-credit, and external degree programs.

1117 Harrington, Thomas F. STUDENT PERSONNEL WORK IN URBAN COLLEGES. New York: Intext Publishing Group, 1974. 328 p.

Identifies needs of urban students and problems in providing student personnel services in urban universities. Author presented his own model for improving the effectiveness of student personnel workers. Has case studies and bibliography.

1118 Harris, Barbara J. BEYOND HER SPHERE: WOMEN AND THE PROFES-
SIONS IN AMERICAN HISTORY. Westport, Conn.: Greenwood Press,
1978. 212 p.

> Shows how and why pioneer women doctors, lawyers, ministers,
> and other professionals came from middle class women whose
> educational aspirations and abolitionist activities were frus-
> trated by the cult of domesticity. Final chapter on unprece-
> dented post-1965 movement of women into higher education
> and the professions and its enormous impact on U.S. society.

1119 Harris, Ben M. SUPERVISORY BEHAVIOR IN EDUCATION. 2d ed.
Englewood Cliffs, N.J.: Prentice-Hall, 1975. 438 p.

> Graduate-level textbook in educational administration. About
> functions, strategies, and practices for promoting instructional
> change in schools.

1120 Harris, James F., Jr. ETHICS AND ACADEMICS. Athens: University
of Georgia, 1968. 33 p.

> Philosophy professor contends that faculty members have a
> moral obligation to take public stands on social issues and on
> college admissions, faculty-administration relations, student
> rights, and other ethical questions in higher education.

1121 Harris, Janet, ed. STUDENTS IN REVOLT. New York: McGraw-Hill
Book Co., 1970. 176 p.

> Essays about U.S. and worldwide student protests, 1964-69,
> state that institutions have grown too rapidly, become too com-
> plex, and tried to serve too heterogeneous student bodies.

1122 Harris, Mark. WAKE UP, STUPID. New York: Alfred A. Knopf, 1959.
233 p.

> Novel about a professor of English and an aspiring playwright.

1123 Harris, Michael R. FIVE COUNTERREVOLUTIONISTS IN HIGHER EDU-
CATION: IRVING BABBITT, ALBERT JAY NOCK, ABRAHAM FLEXNER,
ROBERT MAYNARD HUTCHINS, ALEXANDER MEIKLEJOHN. Corvallis:
Oregon State University Press, 1970. 224 p.

> Analysis of the ideas of five leading conservative-reactionary
> intellectual critics of the utilitarian and egalitarian directions
> of twentieth-century American higher education: humanist
> Irving Babbitt, 1865-1933; editor Albert Jay Nock, 1870-1945;
> foundation official Abraham Flexner, 1866-1959; and university
> presidents Robert Maynard Hutchins, 1899-1977; and Alexander
> Meiklejohn, 1872-1964. Other academic reactionaries mentioned
> include Mortimer Adler, Stringfellow Barr, Scott Buchanan, and
> Mark Van Doren. Preliminary and concluding chapters provide

interesting background and current analysis of conflicts in the purpose of American higher education.

1124 Harris, Norman C. TECHNICAL EDUCATION IN THE JUNIOR COLLEGE/ NEW PROGRAMS FOR NEW JOBS. Washington, D.C.: American Association of Junior Colleges, 1964. 103 p.

Provides career education information for high school counselors, discusses problems of technical education in the junior college, and tells how to plan such a program.

1125 _____, ed. UPDATING OCCUPATIONAL EDUCATION. San Francisco: Jossey-Bass Publishers, 1973. 134 p.

Presents developments in occupational education in community colleges, federal policy changes affecting occupational programs, and methods of forecasting manpower needs.

1126 Harris, Norman C., and Grede, John F. CAREER EDUCATION IN COLLEGES: A GUIDE FOR PLANNING TWO- AND FOUR-YEAR OCCUPATIONAL PROGRAMS FOR SUCCESSFUL EMPLOYMENT. San Francisco: Jossey-Bass Publishers, 1977. 419 p.

Advocates of college-level career education offer a complete planning guide for orienting all postsecondary education toward jobs, particularly toward middle manpower occupations, in line with national manpower needs.

1127 Harris, Seymour E. THE ECONOMICS OF HARVARD. New York: McGraw-Hill Book Co., 1970. 519 p.

Traces financing of Harvard University from its inception. Shows Harvard's slow transition from regional to national stature, the uneven rise in tuition, faculty salaries, and overall costs; students' periodic revolts; and the long struggle against religious and government control.

1128 _____. HIGHER EDUCATION: RESOURCES AND FINANCE. New York: McGraw-Hill Book Co., 1962. 713 p.

Discusses sources of higher education funding: student tuition, government support, endowments, philanthropic giving. Author foresees the need for lowering costs by increasing class size, more independent work, using machine technology, and other means. Looks at the economic status of faculty members.

1129 _____. THE MARKET FOR COLLEGE GRADUATES. Cambridge, Mass.: Harvard University Press, 1949. 207 p.

Studies the relation of higher education to employment and the problems of supply and demand in certain professions. Part II has detailed statistical analysis to support findings.

1130 _____. MORE RESOURCES FOR EDUCATION. New York: Harper and Brothers, 1960. 86 p.

> Cites ways to reduce higher education costs. Favors paying for higher education with tuition and fees only so that most tax revenues can go to public schools.

1131 _____. A STATISTICAL PORTRAIT OF HIGHER EDUCATION: A REPORT FOR THE CARNEGIE COMMISSION ON HIGHER EDUCATION. New York: McGraw-Hill Book Co., 1972. 978 p.

> Emphasizes economic aspects; presents higher education problems relating to students, enrollment, faculty, income and expenditures, and productivity and structure. Has a seven hundred-table statistical digest. Data from many sources, most important of which is the U.S. Office of Education.

1132 Harris, Sherry S., ed. ACCREDITED INSTITUTIONS OF POSTSECONDARY EDUCATION: PROGRAMS/CANDIDATES, 1978-79. Washington, D.C.: American Council on Education for the Council on Postsecondary Accreditation, 1978. 367 p.

> Annual directory which includes complete listings and descriptions of accredited U.S. colleges and universities and a few abroad. Includes institutions with "Candidate for Accreditation" status. Institutional index.

1133 Harrison, Cynthia Ellen. WOMEN'S MOVEMENT MEDIA: A SOURCE GUIDE. New York: R.R. Bowker, 1975. 269 p.

> Describes about 550 organizations which supply books and other media information and services in the United States and Canada about women's concerns. Education section, pages 149-62, lists women's education associations and women's programs at colleges and universities.

1134 Harrison, George Bagshawl. PROFESSION OF ENGLISH. New York: Harcourt, Brace and World, 1962. 183 p.

> Autobiographical advice to graduate students contemplating becoming college English teachers by a distinguished professor of English literature.

1135 Harrison, Shelley A., and Stolurow, Lawrence M., eds. IMPROVING INSTRUCTIONAL PRODUCTIVITY IN HIGHER EDUCATION. Englewood Cliffs, N.J.: Educational Technology Publications, 1975. 272 p.

> Papers urge massive research in using technology-based systems to improve college instruction. Designing ways to evaluate teaching effectiveness and defining specific learning objectives should accompany the expanding use of education technology.

1136 Hartnett, Rodney T. ACCOUNTABILITY IN HIGHER EDUCATION: A CONSIDERATION OF SOME OF THE PROBLEMS OF ASSESSING COLLEGE IMPACTS. New York: College Entrance Examination Board, 1971. 21 p.

> Accountability requires that the efficiency and effectiveness of higher education institutions be measured. Before undertaking such measurement, an institution must clearly define its goals and functions.

1137 _____, et al. THE BRITISH OPEN UNIVERSITY IN THE UNITED STATES: ADAPTATION AND USE AT THREE UNIVERSITIES. Princeton, N.J.: Educational Testing Service, 1974. 34 p.

> A report on the first year of a pilot program modeled after the British Open University at the Universities of Maryland and Houston and at Rutgers University.

1138 Hartshorne, Hugh, and Froyd, Milton C. THEOLOGICAL EDUCATION IN THE NORTHERN BAPTIST CONVENTION. New York: Board of Education of the Northern Baptist Convention, 1945. 242 p.

> Surveyed Baptist clergymen and theological students about training in Northern Baptist schools of theology. Concluded that the largely liberal arts curriculum failed to meet clergymen's need for a professional program, especially for community-related activities.

1139 Hartwell, Henry, et al. THE PRESENT STATE OF VIRGINIA, AND THE COLLEGE. 1697. Reprint. Princeton, N.J.: Princeton University Press, 1940. 105 p.

> This important document, written by members of the "college faction" in the Virginia colonial government, was addressed to England's Board of Trade. Reflecting planters' desires for improved conditions, it may have hastened the opening in 1701 of the College of William and Mary, founded a decade earlier.

1140 Harvard College and the Graduate School of Education. THE TRAINING OF SECONDARY SCHOOL TEACHERS. Cambridge, Mass.: Harvard University Press, 1942. 173 p.

> Controversial issues in English teaching are a main focus of this report, which also decries dictatorial practices by schools and teachers and university dominance of secondary education.

1141 Harvard Committee. GENERAL EDUCATION IN A FREE SOCIETY: REPORT OF THE HARVARD COMMITTEE ON THE OBJECTIVES OF A GENERAL EDUCATION IN A FREE SOCIETY. Cambridge, Mass.: Harvard University Press, 1945. 267 p.

Influential report in U.S. higher education which marked Harvard's shift away from the elective system started by President Charles W. Eliot in 1869 and toward a curriculum combining liberal arts courses with courses to help each student prepare for a specialized vocation or profession.

1142 _____. THE GRADUATE STUDY OF EDUCATION: REPORT OF THE HARVARD COMMITTEE. Cambridge, Mass.: Harvard University Press, 1966. 125 p.

Report's purpose was to bring greater balance to the School of Education's graduate program (which concentrates on the doctorate) and to improve its offerings. The curricular emphasis should be on the academic disciplines and their application to education. Calls for a curriculum with six interdependent areas of concentration: teaching, guidance, administration, humanities, social sciences, and psychology.

1143 Harvard Student Agencies. MAKING IT: A GUIDE TO STUDENT FINANCES. Edited by Amy Edith Johnson. New York: E.P. Dutton and Co., 1973. 319 p.

Lists sources of scholarships, grants-in-aid, and loans. Prepared by students and for students. Gives tips on finding jobs and/or running one's own business while a student.

1144 Harvard University. PRELIMINARY REPORT ON THE STATUS OF WOMEN AT HARVARD. Cambridge, Mass.: Harvard University Press, 1970. 16 p.

A women's faculty group posed policy questions needing investigation. Cited such problems as the status of women faculty (none held associate or full professorships) and equal access to financial aid for women graduate students.

1145 Harvard University. University Commission to Advise on the Future of Psychology at Harvard. THE PLACE OF PSYCHOLOGY IN AN IDEAL UNIVERSITY: THE REPORT OF THE UNIVERSITY COMMISSION TO ADVISE ON THE FUTURE OF PSYCHOLOGY AT HARVARD. Cambridge, Mass.: Harvard University Press, 1947. 42 p.

Divergent views on clinical and applied psychology as a university discipline and as a profession; its research methodology; and its contributions to social sciences, education, medicine, and other fields.

1146 Harveson, Mae Elizabeth. CATHARINE ESTHER BEECHER: PIONEER EDUCATOR. Philadelphia: University of Pennsylvania Press, 1932. 295 p.

Biography of Beecher (1800-78), founder of Hartford, Conn., Female Seminary and Western Female Institute, Cincinnati,

Ohio. Describes her work for women's educational equality
and to provide more qualified women teachers.

1147 Harvey, James. REFORMING UNDERGRADUATE CURRICULUM: PROB-
LEMS AND PROPOSALS. Washington, D.C.: ERIC Clearinghouse on
Higher Education, 1971. 21 p.

Overview of several studies about reform of undergraduate curriculum.

1148 Harvey, L. James. ZERO BASE BUDGETING IN COLLEGES AND UNI-
VERSITIES. Washington, D.C.: McManis Associates, 1978. 51 p.

Explains how to use zero-base budgeting in colleges and universities along with older management systems.

1149 Harway, Michele, and Astin, Helen S. SEX DISCRIMINATION IN CA-
REER COUNSELING AND EDUCATION. New York: Praeger Publishers,
1977. 172 p.

About sex bias against women in career counseling and higher
education. Identifies sex-biased counseling materials. Offers
research findings about and alternatives to traditional counseling.

1150 Haskell, Thomas L. THE EMERGENCE OF PROFESSIONAL SOCIAL
SCIENCE: THE AMERICAN SOCIAL SCIENCE ASSOCIATION AND THE
NINETEENTH-CENTURY CRISIS OF AUTHORITY. Urbana: University of
Illinois Press, 1977. 276 p.

An intellectual historian's look at the late nineteenth-century
attempt to professionalize social science by founding in 1865
the American Social Science Association (ASSA). The ASSA
gradually declined as various disciplines formed their own
groups: American Historical Association (1884), American
Economic Association (1885), and American Political Science
Association (1903).

1151 Hassenger, Robert, ed. THE SHAPE OF CATHOLIC HIGHER EDUCATION.
Chicago: University of Chicago Press, 1967. 378 p.

Historical and analytical essays about Catholic higher education:
its striving for excellence, academic freedom, intra-Catholic
relations, women, and problems and trends.

1152 Hatch, Richard A., ed. AN EARLY VIEW OF THE LAND-GRANT COL-
LEGES: CONVENTION OF FRIENDS OF AGRICULTURAL EDUCATION
IN 1871. Urbana: University of Illinois Press, 1967. 147 p.

Historical study of the 1871 Convention of Friends of Agricultural Education and its part in the uniquely American land-

grant college idea. The convention created a group identity among the then-new land-grant institutions.

1153 _____. SOME FOUNDING PAPERS OF THE UNIVERSITY OF ILLINOIS. Urbana: University of Illinois Press, 1967. 139 p.

Historical papers concerning the University of Illinois, such as the text of the 1862 Morrill Act and of Illinois legislation pertinent to the university's founding.

1154 Hatch, Winslow R., and Richards, Alice L. APPROACH TO INDEPENDENT STUDY. Washington, D.C.: Government Printing Office, 1965. 73 p.

About specific independent study programs at various types of higher education institutions. Conclusions are that independent study develops intellectual independence and inquiry skills but that it is no more effective than traditional methods in producing content mastery.

1155 Hauser, Jane Zech, and Lazarsfeld, Paul F. THE ADMISSIONS OFFICER IN THE AMERICAN COLLEGE: AN OCCUPATION UNDER CHANGE. A REPORT FOR THE COLLEGE ENTRANCE EXAMINATION BOARD. New York: Bureau of Applied Social Research, Columbia University, 1964. Various paginations.

Surveyed admissions officers about the present and future status of admissions work. Found a trend toward specialization among higher education admissions officers. Many tables analyze the profession of admissions officer.

1156 Havemann, Ernest, and West, Patricia Salter. THEY WENT TO COLLEGE. New York: Harcourt Brace, 1952. 277 p.

Insight into late 1940s U.S. higher education is found in this analysis by Columbia University's Bureau of Applied Social Research of data TIME magazine collected on the meaning and purpose of a college education.

1157 Havice, Charles W., ed. CAMPUS VALUES: SOME CONSIDERATIONS FOR COLLEGIANS. New York: Charles Scribner's Sons, 1971. 175 p.

Papers intended to help college students form value systems. Topics include aims of college education, campus activism, drugs, religion, and sex.

1158 Havighurst, Robert James. AMERICAN HIGHER EDUCATION IN THE 1960'S. Kappa Delta Pi Lecture Series. Columbus: Ohio State University Press, 1960. 92 p.

Foresees a major crisis in higher education when supplies of college-trained persons exceed demand. Examines the resultant social stratification and status effects.

1159 Hawes, Gene R. HAWES COMPREHENSIVE GUIDE TO COLLEGES. New York: New American Library, 1978. 416 p.

Rates two- and four-year higher education institutions in the fifty states, District of Columbia, and Puerto Rico on: (1) social prestige, (2) social achievement, (3) faculty salaries, and (4) student expense (identifies "best buys").

1160 _____. EDUCATIONAL TESTING FOR THE MILLIONS. New York: McGraw-Hill Book Co., 1964. 290 p.

Explanation and defense of educational testing directed to parents and substantiated by research findings. Describes twenty-five most widely used tests. Extensive discussion of college admissions tests.

1161 _____. GETTING COLLEGE COURSE CREDITS BY EXAMINATION TO SAVE $$$. New York: McGraw-Hill Book Co., 1979. 180 p.

Guide to independently administered exams by which tuition-free degree credits can be earned at more than 2,100 colleges and universities, including the College Level Examination Program (CLEP), Defense Activity for Non-Traditional Education (DANTES), the Proficiency Examination Program of the American College Testing Program (PEP), the Advanced Placement Program of the College Board (AP), and others used by new external degree colleges.

1162 Hawes, Gene R., and Brownstone, David M. HOW TO GET THE MONEY TO PAY FOR COLLEGE. New York: David McKay, 1978. 176 p.

Describes financial aid available to college students (federal, state, and private programs) and how to apply for aid and get it. Provides application form samples and explains the information and supporting documents the forms require. Discusses long-range planning, including investments and forms of insurance parents could use for their children's education.

1163 Hawes, Gene R., and Novalis, Peter N. THE NEW AMERICAN GUIDE TO COLLEGES. New York: Columbia University Press, 1972. 640 p.

Location, tuition, degrees offered, academic requirements, and other pertinent information on all institutions of higher education in the country.

1164 Hawkes, Herbert E., et al. FIVE COLLEGE PLANS. New York: Columbia University Press, 1931. 115 p.

Lectures on new individualized educational programs at Columbia by Dean Hawkes, Harvard by Dean A. Chester Hanford, Swarthmore by President Frank Aydelotte, Wabash by President Louis B. Hopkins, and Chicago by Dean Chauncey S. Boucher.

1165 Hawkins, Hugh. BETWEEN HARVARD AND AMERICA: THE EDUCATIONAL LEADERSHIP OF CHARLES W. ELIOT. New York: Oxford University Press, 1972. 404 p.

Historical study of Eliot's forty-year presidency of Harvard and its transformation by administrative changes and academic reform into one of the nation's leading universities.

1166 _____. PIONEER: A HISTORY OF THE JOHNS HOPKINS UNIVERSITY, 1874-1889. Ithaca, N.Y.: Cornell University Press, 1960. 368 p.

Historical study of Johns Hopkins University, 1874-89: philanthropist Hopkins's founding gift; the trustees' decision to make it the nation's first graduate university and their selection of the first president, Daniel Coit Gilman (just returned from study in Germany); and its subsequent pioneering use of the laboratory, seminar, and scholarly journal.

1167 Hawkins, Thom. GROUP INQUIRY TECHNIQUES FOR TEACHING WRITING. Urbana, Ill.: ERIC Clearinghouse on Reading and Communication Skills, National Institute of Education, 1976. 41 p.

On using small group techniques in higher education to teach writing.

1168 Hayes, Harriet. PLANNING RESIDENCE HALLS. New York: Teachers College, Columbia University, 1932. 247 p.

Construction, planning, and operation of residence halls. Recommends procedures and ways to plan residence halls.

1169 Haynes, Leonard L. III, ed. A CRITICAL EXAMINATION OF THE ADAMS CASE: A SOURCE BOOK. Washington, D.C.: Institute for Services to Education, 1978. 416 p.

Traces the desegregation of public higher education from Adams v. Richardson (the 1970 NAACP suit against the Department of Health, Education and Welfare) and analyzes the effect of judicial processes on historically black public educational institutions.

1170 Edward W. Hazen Foundation and the Committee on Religion and Education, American Council on Education. COLLEGE READING AND RELIGION. New Haven, Conn.: Yale University Press, 1948. 348 p.

Scholars from many fields surveyed books used in basic courses at liberal arts colleges to judge their fairness toward religion. Found that while many ignored religion the trend was toward respectful treatment.

1171 Headley, Leal A., and Jarchow, Merrill E. CARLETON: THE FIRST CENTURY. Northfield, Minn.: Carleton College, 1966. 489 p.

Centennial history of Carleton shows its evolution into a distinguished liberal arts college. Curriculum and finance are presented chronologically.

1172 Heald, Henry T., et al. MEETING THE INCREASING DEMAND FOR HIGHER EDUCATION IN NEW YORK STATE. Albany, N.Y.: Board of Regents, State Education Department, 1960. 74 p.

To counteract the student outflow for higher education, New York Governor's study committee recommended charging tuition at municipal colleges, offering more scholarships statewide, subsidizing private institutions, and freeing higher education of bureaucratic intrusion.

1173 Healy, Charles C. CAREER COUNSELING IN THE COMMUNITY COLLEGE. Springfield, Ill.: Charles C Thomas, Publisher, 1974. 140 p.

Tells how to make and implement career plans and how to measure career development. Reviews pertinent research.

1174 Heath, Douglas H. GROWING UP IN COLLEGE: LIBERAL EDUCATION AND MATURITY. San Francisco: Jossey-Bass Publishers, 1968. 326 p.

Ten-year study of the maturing process among students and alumni of Haverford College. Presents a theoretical model of the maturing process. Suggests that specialization and "universitizing" liberal arts colleges weakens the maturing process in education.

1175 Heath, G. Louis. THE HOT CAMPUS: THE POLITICS THAT IMPEDE CHANGE IN THE TECHNOVERSITY. Metuchen, N.J.: Scarecrow Press, 1973. 360 p.

Essays about the 1960s student revolt cite American higher education as unresponsive and conservative.

1176 Heaton, C.P., ed. MANAGEMENT BY OBJECTIVES IN HIGHER EDUCATION: THEORY, CASES, AND IMPLEMENTATION. Durham, N.C.: National Laboratory for Higher Education, 1975. 110 p.

Examines five case histories of management by objectives. Conclusions are pessimistic because administrators do not independently develop objectives and faculty members distrust the management-by-objectives system.

1177 Heaton, Kenneth L., and Koopman, G. Robert. A COLLEGE CURRICU-
LUM BASED ON FUNCTIONAL NEEDS OF STUDENTS. Chicago: University of Chicago Press, 1936. 157 p.

> Two-year study of experimental teacher education curriculum
> at Central State College, Mount Pleasant, Michigan; striking
> features are its use of technical advances and consideration
> for student needs.

1178 Heaton, Kenneth L., et al. PROFESSIONAL EDUCATION FOR EXPERI-
ENCED TEACHERS. Chicago: University of Chicago Press, 1940. 142 p.

> Summer workshops (1936-40) for experienced teachers, an ex-
> panding program which by 1940 involved fourteen major U.S.
> universities in cooperation with the Progressive Education Asso-
> ciation. Workshop projects dealt with such areas as curricu-
> lum planning, educational philosophy, and adolescent psychol-
> ogy.

1179 Hebert, Tom, and Coyne, John. GETTING SKILLED. New York: E.P.
Dutton and Co., 1976. 262 p.

> A vocational education guide for students and counselors.
> Finds community colleges out of touch with job market; stresses
> trade schools.

1180 Hecht, Joy. WHERE TO LOOK: A SOURCEBOOK ON UNDERGRADU-
ATE INTERNSHIPS. Washington, D.C.: American Association for Higher
Education, 1977. 20 p.

> Describes twenty-two internship programs and lists other direc-
> tories to off-campus learning and work opportunities.

1181 Hedley, George. AURELIA HENRY REINHARDT: PORTRAIT OF A WHOLE
WOMAN. Oakland, Calif.: Mills College, 1961. 311 p.

> Biography of Mills College president and leader in the Ameri-
> can Association of University Women, Aurelia Henry Reinhardt
> (1877-1948).

1182 Heermann, Barry. COOPERATIVE EDUCATION IN COMMUNITY COL-
LEGES. San Francisco: Jossey-Bass Publishers, 1973. 219 p.

> Handbook on cooperative vocational education in community
> colleges which combines study with related work.

1183 _____, ed. CHANGING MANAGERIAL PERSPECTIVES. San Francisco:
Jossey-Bass Publishers, 1976. 110 p.

> Shows relation of student learning to higher education manage-
> ment and organization. Looks at innovative practices, manage-
> ment by objectives, and the cluster college concept.

1184 Hefferlin, J.B. Lon. DYNAMICS OF ACADEMIC REFORM. San Francisco: Jossey-Bass Publishers, 1969. 240 p.

Study of academic reform process. Looked at higher education characteristics that respond to and also resist change, using surveys and interviews at 110 representative institutions. Concluded that most reform originates outside the institution.

1185 Hefferlin, J.B. Lon, and Phillips, Ellis L., Jr. INFORMATION SERVICES FOR ACADEMIC ADMINISTRATION. San Francisco: Jossey-Bass Publishers, 1971. 160 p.

Guide for college administrators to vast range of information available within and between campuses, consulting services, and campus publications. Recommends ways to select information and share it.

1186 Hegener, Karen C., and Hunter, Joan, eds. GENERAL GUIDE TO THE SIX VOLUMES OF PETERSON'S ANNUAL GUIDES TO GRADUATE AND UNDERGRADUATE STUDY. Princeton, N.J.: Peterson's Guides, 1974. 25 p.

Index to Peterson's six volumes containing information on all courses, programs, and departments in graduate and undergraduate institutions.

1187 Heilbron, Louis H. THE COLLEGE AND UNIVERSITY TRUSTEE: A VIEW FROM THE BOARD ROOM. San Francisco: Jossey-Bass Publishers, 1973. 239 p.

By, for, and about higher education trustees: their powers and responsibilities, their relations with administrators, and suggestions for understanding their role.

1188 Heinlein, Albert C., ed. DECISION SCIENCES IN ACADEMIC ADMINISTRATION CONFERENCE. Kent, Ohio: Kent State University, 1973. 139 p.

Conference papers for higher education administrators on management information and decision systems, simulation models, and mathematical models.

1189 Heirich, Max. THE SPIRAL OF CONFLICT: BERKELEY, 1964. New York: Columbia University Press, 1970. 502 p.

Analyzes reasons for the 1964 University of California, Berkeley, student protest which sparked student unrest in the United States: administrative ineptitude (a campus president and university chancellor on the same campus with mixed lines of responsibility), rigid opposition to student politics in a student activity area, capricious discipline of a few students for common infractions, the role of chance, and the changing temper of American society.

1190 Heise, J. Arthur. THE BRASS FACTORIES: A FRANK APPRAISAL OF
WEST POINT, ANNAPOLIS, AND THE AIR FORCE ACADEMY. Washington, D.C.: Public Affairs Press, 1969. 190 p.

> Critical of the three service academies and such weaknesses as
> overcrowded curriculum, faculty inbreeding, hazing, and over-
> emphasis on athletics.

1191 Heiss, Ann M. CHALLENGES TO GRADUATE SCHOOLS. San Francisco:
Jossey-Bass Publishers for Center for Research and Development in Higher
Education, 1970. 328 p.

> Intensive examination of U.S. graduate education. Studied
> the Ph.D. at ten institutions. Made recommendations about
> basic Ph.D. requirements, preparation for college teaching,
> administration, and research.

1192 Heiss, Ann M., and David, Anne. GRADUATE AND PROFESSIONAL
EDUCATION. Berkeley: Center for Research and Development in Higher
Education, University of California, 1967. 126 p.

> Annotated bibliography about graduate and professional educa-
> tion in such fields as biological sciences, clinical psychology,
> library science, teaching, and the ministry.

1193 Heist, Paul, ed. THE CREATIVE COLLEGE STUDENT: AN UNMET
CHALLENGE. San Francisco: Jossey-Bass Publishers, 1968. 253 p.

> Found from 50 to 80 percent dropout rate among creative stu-
> dents in eight diverse institutions of higher learning. Agreed
> that colleges do not meet the needs of creative students who
> are characterized as independent, innovative, open to a wide
> range of experiences, love to play with ideas and concepts,
> and have broad cultural and intellectual interests. Proposed
> solutions are to develop personalized student-teacher relations,
> revise the grading system, encourage creative students in honors
> programs, and encourage independent thinking.

1194 Heist, Paul, and Warren, Jonathan R., eds. RESPONDING TO
CHANGING HUMAN RESOURCE NEEDS. San Francisco: Jossey-Bass
Publishers, 1975. 110 p.

> Examines problem of coordinating higher education with the
> working world. Explores such key issues in vocational educa-
> tion as adequacy of college training, appropriate vocational
> placement, and difficulty of arriving at human resource needs.

1195 Heller, Louis G. THE DEATH OF THE AMERICAN UNIVERSITY: WITH
SPECIAL REFERENCE TO THE COLLAPSE OF CITY COLLEGE OF NEW
YORK. New Rochelle, N.Y.: Arlington House, 1973. 213 p.

Reactions to 1960s campus disturbances at New York's City College by a language professor who believed the riots were a plot to undermine the educational system and thus the United States. He deplored declining academic standards at City College.

1196 Helliwell, Carolyn B., and Jung, Steven M. CONSUMER PROTECTION STRATEGIES: A LITERATURE REVIEW AND SYNTHESIS. Palo Alto, Calif.: American Institutes for Research in the Behavioral Sciences, 1976. 64 p.

Reviews research about consumer protection in postsecondary education.

1197 Helmantoler, Michael C., ed. THE MASS MEDIA COLLEGE CATALOG. Washington, D.C.: American Association of Community and Junior Colleges, 1978. 100 p.

Describes undergraduate courses available to the public in the video, audio, or print media.

1198 Henderson, Algo D. HIGHER EDUCATION IN TOMORROW'S WORLD: A SYMPOSIUM OF THE INTERNATIONAL CONFERENCE ON HIGHER EDUCATION COMMEMORATING THE SESQUICENTENNIAL OF THE UNIVERSITY OF MICHIGAN, APRIL 26-29, 1967. Ann Arbor: University of Michigan Press, 1968. 189 p.

Conference papers on such university topics as the relation of theory to practice, problems of food and poverty, and the need for basic general-liberal education. Contributors include Eric Ashby, Cambridge University; Kenneth E. Boulding, University of Michigan; Ingvar Svennilson, University of Stockholm; and Constantine Zurayk, American University of Beirut.

1199 _____. THE INNOVATIVE SPIRIT. San Francisco: Jossey-Bass Publishers, 1970. 308 p.

Antioch College's former dean and president prefers work-study, reform-oriented, problem-solving, nonivory tower higher education. He also prefers selecting presidents as leaders rather than managers, and faculty-student-administrator cooperation rather than businessmen-trustee governance.

1200 _____. POLICIES AND PRACTICES IN HIGHER EDUCATION. New York: Harper and Brothers, 1960. 338 p.

Broad view of higher education by an experienced administrator who wants to interweave vocational and general education, wants college teaching improved, and wants high-ability students to receive extra credit. He probes problems of mass education and higher education's strengths and weaknesses.

1201 _____. VITALIZING LIBERAL EDUCATION. New York: Harper and Brothers, 1944. 202 p.

> When it is most needed, the liberal arts college is threatened by uncertainty of purpose and low student motivation. Antioch College president's recommendations for improving liberal education include more understanding counselors, emphasizing fields of knowledge instead of college departments, and more practical teaching.

1202 Henderson, Algo D., and Gumas, Natalie B. ADMITTING BLACK STU-DENTS TO MEDICAL AND DENTAL SCHOOLS. Berkeley: Center for Research and Development in Higher Education, University of California, 1971. 102 p.

> Authors examine admissions practices and preprofessional factors which favor white middle class. Recommendations: (1) aid more blacks to gain admission, and (2) rearrange professional health curricula.

1203 Henderson, Algo D., and Hall, Dorothy. ANTIOCH COLLEGE: ITS DESIGN FOR LIBERAL EDUCATION. New York: Harper and Brothers, 1946. 280 p.

> The president and the college editor describe Antioch College's alternating academic study and cooperative job experience, explain its ideology as set forth by President Arthur E. Morgan in 1921, and describe its aims and purposes in relation to higher education in general.

1204 Henderson, Algo D., and Henderson, Jean Glidden. HIGHER EDUCA-TION IN AMERICA: PROBLEMS, PRIORITIES, AND PROSPECTS. San Francisco: Jossey-Bass Publishers, 1974. 282 p.

> Surveys problems resulting from rapid growth of higher education: new students, more programs, and less money.

1205 Henderson, Archibald. THE CAMPUS OF THE FIRST STATE UNIVERSITY. Chapel Hill: University of North Carolina Press, 1949. 412 p.

> Comprehensive account of the architecture, landscaping, grounds, and buildings of the University of North Carolina at Chapel Hill. For prospective planners and innovators.

1206 Henderson, Jean Glidden, and Henderson, Algo D. MS. GOES TO COL-LEGE. Carbondale: Southern Illinois University Press, 1975. 191 p.

> Handbook for college-age women on selecting a college, career guidance, and other pertinent topics.

1207 Henderson, Robert. WHETHER THERE BE KNOWLEDGE. Philadelphia: J.B. Lippincott Co., 1935. 343 p.

Novel about a student who becomes editor of the college newspaper.

1208 Hendricks, Luther V. JAMES HARVEY ROBINSON: TEACHER OF HIS-
TORY. New York: King's Crown Press, 1946. 124 p.

Career of a leader of the "new history," teachers who influenced him, the development of his famous Intellectual History
course at Columbia University, his part in founding the New
School for Social Research, his influence as a history textbook
writer, and his belief that history should be used for social
reform.

1209 Henry, David D. CHALLENGES PAST, CHALLENGES PRESENT: AN
ANALYSIS OF AMERICAN HIGHER EDUCATION SINCE 1930. San Francisco: Jossey-Bass Publishers, 1975. 173 p.

Former University of Illinois president and professor of higher
education briefly reviews the history of U.S. higher education
since 1636 and then considers post-1930 developments in finance, administration, political relationships, and public attitudes.

1210 _____. WHAT PRIORITY FOR EDUCATION? THE AMERICAN PEOPLE
MUST SOON DECIDE. Urbana: University of Illinois Press, 1961. 92 p.

University of Illinois president's addresses appealing for more
financial backing: (1) to raise educational standards in high
schools and colleges, (2) to overcome shortages of teachers
and teaching materials, and (3) to extend opportunities for
continuing education.

1211 Henry, Nelson B., ed. EDUCATION FOR THE GIFTED: THE FIFTY-
SEVENTH YEARBOOK OF THE NATIONAL SOCIETY FOR THE STUDY
OF EDUCATION. Part II. Chicago: University of Chicago Press, 1958.
420 p.

Deals with psychological aspects of programs for superior students from nursery school to university, discusses training
teachers for talented students and explaining programs to the
community, and evaluates such programs.

1212 _____. GENERAL EDUCATION. FIFTY-FIRST YEARBOOK OF THE
NATIONAL SOCIETY FOR THE STUDY OF EDUCATION. Part I. Chicago: University of Chicago Press, 1952. 377 p.

On issues, principles, and problems of general education.
Chapters on philosophy, psychology, curriculum and instruction,
planning, teacher education, and the purposes of education.

1213 _____. GRADUATE STUDY IN EDUCATION: FIFTIETH YEARBOOK, PART I, OF THE NATIONAL SOCIETY FOR THE STUDY OF EDUCATION. Chicago: University of Chicago Press, 1951. 369 p.

> About U.S. graduate instruction in education: its history, graduate programs, and underlying concepts.

1214 _____. THE PUBLIC JUNIOR COLLEGE. FIFTY-FIFTH YEARBOOK OF THE NATIONAL SOCIETY FOR THE STUDY OF EDUCATION. Chicago: University of Chicago Press, 1956. 347 p.

> Fifteen chapters by several authors on the junior college program.

1215 Herbst, Jurgen. THE GERMAN HISTORICAL SCHOOL IN AMERICAN SCHOLARSHIP: A STUDY IN THE TRANSFER OF CULTURE. Ithaca, N.Y.: Cornell University Press, 1965. 262 p.

> Rise and decline of the German historical school of social science in American higher education from 1876, when Johns Hopkins University was founded as the first U.S. graduate university based on German models, to 1914 and World War I. Describes the influence of those thousands of Americans who studied history, political science, economics, and sociology in Germany and brought back German and European scholarly methods and influence to dozens of American colleges and universities they staffed, departments they headed, and universities they administered. Chapters on German and American higher educational history in the nineteenth century; chapter on German-American twentieth-century issues. Focuses on these German-educated American scholars: Johns Hopkins University historian Herbert Baxter Adams, Columbia University political scientist John W. Burgess, University of Wisconsin economist Richard T. Ely, University of Chicago sociologist Albion Small, and Harvard University professor of social ethics Francis Greenwood Peabody.

1216 Herge, Henry C. THE COLLEGE TEACHER. New York: Center for Applied Research in Education, 1965. 118 p.

> Information about the college teaching profession for prospective faculty members; cites the shortage of qualified faculty, and looks at future trends.

1217 Herr, Edwin L., and Cramer, Stanley H. GUIDANCE OF THE COLLEGE BOUND: PROBLEMS, PRACTICES, PERSPECTIVES. New York: Appleton-Century-Crofts, 1968. 305 p.

> Intended to help guidance counselors ease students' transition from high school to four-year college. Contains sample admissions and financial forms. Appendix has a bibliography of

audiovisual materials and commercial, governmental, and professional guidance publications.

1218 Herrick, Robert. CHIMES. New York: Macmillan Co., 1926. 310 p.

Novel reflecting the author's own career: about a Harvard graduate who teaches English at a thinly disguised University of Chicago.

1219 Hersh, Charles M. COLLEGE SENIORS AND FEDERAL EMPLOYMENT: A REPORT OF A RESEARCH STUDY CONDUCTED BY THE AMERICAN UNIVERSITY FOR THE DIVISION OF PSYCHOLOGICAL SCIENCES, OFFICE OF NAVAL RESEARCH. Washington, D.C.: American University, 1953. 123 p.

Surveyed 660 college seniors in engineering, physical science, and social science at Oberlin, Johns Hopkins, Purdue, Syracuse, and West Virginia Universities on attitudes toward federal and industrial employment. Found that they tended to prefer industrial jobs but felt federal employment offered better security and benefits.

1220 Hesburgh, Theodore M. THE HESBURGH PAPERS: HIGHER VALUES IN HIGHER EDUCATION. Mission, Kans.: Andrews and McMeel, 1979. 206 p.

Concern about values is a main theme of eighteen speeches by the University of Notre Dame president. He defines the college president's role, tells how his thoughts have evolved about Catholic universities, Christian higher education, problems of U.S. higher education, and the late 1960s student unrest. Concludes that Catholic universities must lead in building student commitment to human dignity and human rights.

1221 _____, et al. PATTERNS FOR LIFELONG LEARNING. San Francisco: Jossey-Bass Publishers, 1973. 135 p.

Reports from leading educators on continuing education emphasize lifelong education; suggestions on leadership, structure, and courses.

1222 Heston, Francis Marion. A SURVEY OF COLLEGE SURVEYS. Lexington: University of Kentucky Press, 1934. 229 p.

Analysis of thirty of the hundreds of surveys taken between 1909 and 1934 on U.S. higher education. Recommendations for improving such surveys.

1223 Hewer, Vivian H., ed. NEW PERSPECTIVES IN COUNSELING. Minneapolis: University of Minnesota Press, 1955. 60 p.

Papers of University of Minnesota administrators on the selection and training of campus counselors. One paper said that in eleven years the University of Minnesota student body expanded 23.6 percent and counseling costs increased 303 percent.

1224 Heydinger, Richard B., and Norris, Donald M. COOPERATIVE COMPUTING: A PROCESS PERSPECTIVE ON PLANNING AND IMPLEMENTATION. EDUCOM Monograph Series, No. 1. Princeton, N.J.: EDUCOM, 1977. 153 p.

Presents studies of computer network systems in Illinois, Minnesota, and New Jersey, and tells how colleges and universities in the fifty states share and coordinate computer systems for instructional, research, and administrative purposes.

1225 Heywood, John. ASSESSMENT IN HIGHER EDUCATION. New York: John Wiley and Sons, 1977. 289 p.

University of Dublin professor compares assessment in British and U.S. higher education. Sections on marking examinations, assigning grades, and the teacher's role in evaluation.

1226 Hiestand, Dale L. CHANGING CAREERS AFTER THIRTY-FIVE; NEW HORIZONS THROUGH PROFESSIONAL AND GRADUATE STUDY. New York: Columbia University Press, 1971. 170 p.

Most who change careers after age thirty-five enter the humanities and education fields. Concluded that people change, not from dissatisfaction with their careers, but because they want a different direction in their lives.

1227 Higher Education Management Institute. MANAGEMENT DEVELOPMENT AND TRAINING PROGRAM FOR COLLEGES AND UNIVERSITIES. Coconut Grove, Fla.: 1979. 82 p.

Handbook for academic administrators interested in a comprehensive, campus-based, ongoing training program.

1228 Highet, Gilbert. THE ART OF TEACHING. New York: Alfred A. Knopf, 1950. 291 p.

Reflections of a classical scholar on attributes of good teachers, tasks for teachers, professional performance, great teachers of the past, and teaching in daily life.

1229 _____. THE IMMORTAL PROFESSION: THE JOYS OF TEACHING AND LEARNING. New York: Weybright and Talley, 1976. 223 p.

As in his respected THE ART OF TEACHING (1950), Highet's essays are again on great teaching, with inspirational chapters

on great teachers: Socrates, Plato, Aristotle, Jesus, and con-
temporaries, for example, Gilbert Murray.

1230 Hildebrand, Joel H. SCIENCE IN THE MAKING. New York: Columbia
University Press, 1957. 118 p.

Essays about author's course at the University of California designed to combine scientific principles with liberal education.
The first essay is about stages of problemsolving and the last
is on the role of science today.

1231 Hill, Carol Denny. WILD. New York: John Day Co., 1927. 246 p.

Novel about a Barnard College student and her adventures in
New York City.

1232 Hill, David Spence. CONTROL OF TAX-SUPPORTED HIGHER EDUCA-
TION IN THE UNITED STATES. New York: Carnegie Foundation for the
Advancement of Teaching, 1934. 385 p.

Studied whether tax-supported higher education serves society
better with decentralized or centralized state control. Findings
favored unified state control. Contains examples of such systems in different states and concludes that no one plan would
work in every state.

1233 Hill, David Spence, and Kelly, Fred J. ECONOMY IN HIGHER EDU-
CATION. New York: Carnegie Foundation for the Advancement of
Teaching, 1933. 127 p.

Discusses ways university and college administrators might cope
with decreasing financial support as it affects higher education
curriculum, research, and business administration.

1234 Hill, Robert Russell. THE RELATION OF TEACHER PREPARATION TO
PUPIL ACHIEVEMENT. Nashville: George Peabody College for Teachers,
1936. 34 p.

Found a positive but low relationship between pupil achievement on standardized tests and the number of education credit
hours teachers had earned.

1235 Hills, John R. PROFICIENCY TESTING: IMPLICATIONS FOR HIGHER
EDUCATION. Atlanta: Southern Regional Education Board, 1978. 30 p.

Examines the use of proficiency tests in southern schools and
colleges, including experimental programs, and discusses implications for higher education.

1236 Hirsch, Eric Donald, Jr. THE PHILOSOPHY OF COMPOSITION. Chicago: University of Chicago Press, 1978. 200 p.

University of Virginia English professor develops a deductive philosophy and subject matter content for freshman composition course. Says the goal is "relative readability" and gives several ways to write so that the reader's task is easier.

1237 Hislop, Codman. ELIPHALET NOTT. Middletown, Conn.: Wesleyan University Press, 1971. 680 p.

Nott (1773–1866), longtime charismatic president of Union College, was an innovative educational leader at Union and founder of the American Association for the Advancement of Education.

1238 History of Science Society. REPORT ON UNDERGRADUATE EDUCATION IN THE HISTORY OF SCIENCE. Ames, Iowa: 1977. 56 p.

Report on growth of courses dealing with the historical role of the scientist in society.

1239 Hobbs, Walter C., ed. GOVERNMENT REGULATION OF HIGHER EDUCATION. Cambridge, Mass.: Ballinger Publishing Co., 1978. 119 p.

Nine authors' essays about regulatory agencies' involvement in higher education and its likely effects. Most consider regulation necessary, but a lawyer for Johns Hopkins University believes it is unnecessary and unwise.

1240 Hochman, William R. THE COUNCIL ON CURRICULUM. New York: College Entrance Examination Board, 1968. 26 p.

Proposes forming a Council on Curriculum as an adjunct to the College Board. Identifies major issues relating to curriculum articulation from the eleventh grade to the college sophomore year.

1241 Hodenfield, G.K., and Stinnett, Timothy M. THE EDUCATION OF TEACHERS: CONFLICT AND CONSENSUS. Englewood Cliffs, N.J.: Prentice-Hall, 1961. 177 p.

Report on three teacher education conferences, 1958–60. Chapter on conflicts in teacher education and data on who prepares and certifies teachers.

1242 Hodgkinson, Harold L. HOW MUCH CHANGE FOR A DOLLAR? A LOOK AT TITLE III. Washington, D.C.: American Association for Higher Education, 1974. 53 p.

Presents a model of institutional development and applies it to case studies of institutions receiving aid authorized by Title III of the 1965 Higher Education Act.

1243 _____. INSTITUTIONS IN TRANSITION. Berkeley, Calif.: Carnegie Commission on Higher Education, 1970. 295 p.

> Found: (1) higher education institutions becoming increasingly alike, and (2) size as the most important factor in institutional growth and rate of change.

1244 Hodgkinson, Harold L., and Bloy, Myron B., Jr., eds. IDENTITY CRISIS IN HIGHER EDUCATION. San Francisco: Jossey-Bass Publishers, 1971. 212 p.

> Ten contributors on what higher education is supposed to be doing about the curriculum, students, black consciousness, and society.

1245 Hodgkinson, Harold L., and Meeth, L. Richard, eds. POWER AND AUTHORITY: TRANSFORMATION OF CAMPUS GOVERNANCE. San Francisco: Jossey-Bass Publishers, 1971. 215 p.

> Essays by Daniel Bell, Kingman Brewster, Rodney Hartnett, Earl McGrath, the editors, and others on campus governance, rise of faculty unions, increased administrative accountability, composition of boards of trustees, and the need for greater student participation in campus decision making (the last point received consensus).

1246 Hodinko, Bernard A., and Whitley, Sterling D. STUDENT PERSONNEL ADMINISTRATION: A CRITICAL INCIDENT APPROACH. Washington, D.C.: College Guidance Associates, 1971. 75 p.

> Supplementary textbook in student personnel administration gives vignettes of such typical problems as drug use and suicide threats, each with a brief bibliography.

1247 Hodnett, Edward. INDUSTRY-COLLEGE RELATIONS. New York: World Publishing Co., 1955. 158 p.

> About industry-sponsored scholarships and fellowships, work-study programs, and industry's role in higher education finance and planning.

1248 _____. WHICH COLLEGE FOR YOU? New York: Harper and Brothers, 1960. 122 p.

> Handbook for secondary school guidance counselors, to help students find the best college for their career ambitions, and to train guidance counselors.

1249 Hoffmann, Banesh. THE TYRANNY OF TESTING. New York: Crowell-Collier, 1962. 223 p.

Condemns standardized tests as intimidating to students. Deplores multiple choice items to the neglect of essay questions. Proposes reviewing and improving testing procedures.

1250 Hoffmann, Earl, ed. ANXIOUS DAYS; STUDENT TEACHERS REPORT THEIR EXPERIENCES. Danville, Ill.: Interstate Printers and Publishers, 1971. 183 p.

Summarizes actual problems student teachers experience. For teacher education classes.

1251 Hoffmann, Randall W., and Plutchik, Robert. SMALL-GROUP DISCUSSION IN ORIENTATION AND TEACHING. New York: G.P. Putnam's Sons, 1959. 168 p.

Describes course content and techniques for small-group discussion in liberal arts college freshman orientation classes.

1252 Hofstadter, Richard, and Hardy, C. DeWitt. THE DEVELOPMENT AND SCOPE OF HIGHER EDUCATION IN THE UNITED STATES. New York: Columbia University Press, 1952. 254 p.

Hofstadter summarizes the history of higher education. Hardy, on the staff of the Commission on Financing Higher Education, describes the contemporary academic scene, liberal and general education, and professional education.

1253 Hofstadter, Richard, and Metzger, Walter P. DEVELOPMENT OF ACADEMIC FREEDOM IN THE UNITED STATES. New York: Columbia University Press, 1955. 527 p.

Historical analysis of the academic freedom of U.S. higher education faculty, with background on religious, intellectual, and political issues involved.

1254 Hofstadter, Richard, and Smith, Wilson, eds. AMERICAN HIGHER EDUCATION: A DOCUMENTARY HISTORY. 2 vols. Chicago: University of Chicago Press, 1961. 474 p., 542 p.

Historical documents on U.S. higher education from Harvard's 1636 founding until 1947 and President Truman's Commission on Higher Education. Issues include: finances, general versus professional education, academic freedom, and the land-grant movement. Volume 1 to 1850; volume 2 to 1947.

1255 Hogarth, Charles P. CRISIS IN HIGHER EDUCATION. Washington, D.C.: Public Affairs Press, 1957. 60 p.

A college president outlines higher education administrative problems relating to finance, physical plant, faculty and staff, students, curriculum, and alumni. Stresses need for goals and long-range planning.

1256 Hoke, George Wilson. BLAZING NEW TRAILS. Rochester, N.Y.: Rochester Athenaeum and Mechanics Institute, 1937. 164 p.

> History of Rochester (New York) Athenaeum and Mechanics Institute, which pioneered in vocational education. It used work-study programs to train students for broad areas of industry rather than for specific jobs.

1257 Holbrook, Clyde A. RELIGION, A HUMANISTIC FIELD. Englewood Cliffs, N.J.: Prentice-Hall, 1963. 229 p.

> Discusses the need for religion in liberal arts programs, analyzes the purpose of religious instruction, and urges more financial backing to increase religion in the liberal arts program.

1258 Holcomb, Hope M., ed. REACHING OUT THROUGH COMMUNITY SERVICE. San Francisco: Jossey-Bass Publishers, 1976. 122 p.

> Tells how two-year colleges can serve the community with recreational programs, cultural activities, and adult education courses.

1259 Holland, John L., and Whitney, Douglas R. CHANGES IN VOCATIONAL PLANS OF COLLEGE STUDENTS: ORDERLY OR RANDOM? Iowa City: American College Testing Program, 1969. 31 p.

> Describes the use of Holland's classification scheme to predict career decisions on the basis of earlier career choices of college students.

1260 Holland, Rupert Sargent. THE COUNT AT HARVARD: BEING AN ACCOUNT OF THE ADVENTURES OF A YOUNG GENTLEMAN OF FASHION AT HARVARD UNIVERSITY. Boston: L.C. Page and Co., 1906. 320 p.

> Novel about a Harvard student involved in sporting activities, writing for the student newspaper, taking exams, and in other campus activities.

1261 Hollander, Patricia A. LEGAL HANDBOOK FOR EDUCATORS. Boulder, Colo.: Westview Press, 1978. 287 p.

> Explains laws, regulations, and court rulings affecting education. Identifies areas where legal action is most likely: admissions, employment, and collective bargaining; and possible solutions. Appendix analyzes relevant federal statutes.

1262 Holleb, Doris B. COLLEGES AND THE URBAN POOR: THE ROLE OF PUBLIC HIGHER EDUCATION IN COMMUNITY SERVICE. Lexington, Mass.: Lexington Books, 1972. 175 p.

A social planner looked for ways that colleges in Illinois urban areas might help overcome poverty in their communities.

1263 Hollinger, David A. MORRIS R. COHEN AND THE SCIENTIFIC IDEAL. Cambridge: MIT, 1975. 262 p.

Intellectual biography of famed philosophy professor who taught at City College of New York (1912-38) and also taught adults at the New School for Social Research. He influenced many students and made a lasting contribution by opposing antiliberal and antiintellectual thought.

1264 Hollinshead, Byron S. WHO SHOULD GO TO COLLEGE. New York: Columbia University Press, 1952. 190 p.

Comprehensive study by the College Board for the Commission on Financing Higher Education. Reflects the trend toward greater educational opportunity. Recommends scholarship aid to assure that the upper half of secondary school graduating classes go to four-year colleges and universities and that the other half attend two-year colleges.

1265 Hollis, Ernest Victor. PHILANTHROPIC FOUNDATIONS AND HIGHER EDUCATION. New York: Columbia University Press, 1938. 365 p.

Clarifies philanthropic foundations' motives and methods of giving to U.S. higher education and appraises their influence. Shows that the Carnegie and Rockefeller philanthropies, greatly interested in promoting higher education, set the pattern for other foundations.

1266 _____. TOWARD IMPROVING PH.D. PROGRAMS. Washington, D.C.: American Council on Education, 1945. 204 p.

Analysis of education and employment (1930-31 to 1939-40) of 22,509 Ph.D.s. Concluded that arts and sciences Ph.D. programs are overspecialized and inappropriate for the economic and social situations in which their graduates function. Recommended that all graduate students receive a "core of common experiences" and that graduate schools strive to operate as an integrated whole rather than as a collection of autonomous departments.

1267 Holmberg, Borje. DISTANCE EDUCATION: A SURVEY AND BIBLIOGRAPHY. New York: Nichols Publishing Co., 1977. 167 p.

Guide to upgrading higher education correspondence courses: how to organize them, how to communicate with students, and how to evaluate student progress.

1268 Holmes, Brian, et al. THE WORLD YEAR BOOK OF EDUCATION 1971/ 1972: HIGHER EDUCATION IN A CHANGING WORLD. London: Evans Brothers, 1971. 410 p.

> Surveys major world university changes. Two American professors and a German observer of university life describe the organizational and functional changes in U.S. universities in comparative, international, and historical perspective.

1269 Holmes, Dwight Oliver Wendell. THE EVOLUTION OF THE NEGRO COLLEGE. Contributions to Education No. 609. New York: Teachers College, Columbia University, 1934. Reprint. New York: AMS Press, 1972. 221 p.

> History, status, and trends of black higher education. Author calls for continued support of black colleges.

1270 Holsten, George H., Jr. BICENTENNIAL YEAR: THE STORY OF A RUTGERS CELEBRATION. New Brunswick, N.J.: Rutgers University Press, 1968. 294 p.

> Description of Rutgers scholastic year in honor of the Bicentennial. Includes the 1965 academic freedom case of professor Eugene D. Genovese.

1271 Holt, Rackham. GEORGE WASHINGTON CARVER. Garden City, N.Y.: Doubleday, Doran, and Co., 1943. 342 p.

> Black educator Carver's life (1861?-1943) and college career, including his outstanding accomplishments in plant hybridization and pathology and his improving of agriculture for the South at Tuskegee Institute.

1272 _____. MARY McLEOD BETHUNE: A BIOGRAPHY. Garden City, N.Y.: Doubleday, 1964. 306 p.

> Bethune (1875-1955), former black slave and leading educator, founded and was president of Bethune-Cookman College, Florida.

1273 Holt, W. Stull, ed. HISTORICAL SCHOLARSHIP IN THE UNITED STATES, 1876-1901: AS REVEALED IN THE CORRESPONDENCE OF HERBERT B. ADAMS. Baltimore, Md.: Johns Hopkins University Press, 1938. 314 p.

> Adams, at Johns Hopkins University (1876-1904), developed the seminar and began publishing the nation's first history and political science scholarly series. His students as professors helped establish history teaching and writing as a profession. He helped found in 1884 the American Historical Association. His correspondence about courses, textbooks, research, curriculum, and many other topics was with Henry Adams, George Bancroft, James Bryce, Frederick Jackson Turner, Woodrow Wilson, and others.

1274 Hood, Albert B. WHAT TYPE OF COLLEGE FOR WHAT TYPE OF STU-
DENT? Minneapolis: University of Minnesota Press, 1968. 84 p.

Study of Minnesota high school graduates and those who went
to Minnesota colleges focuses on evaluating their college
choice and academic achievement. Draws implications for
high school counselors, college student personnel workers,
and educational planners. Clarified problem of access to
higher education.

1275 Hook, Sidney. ACADEMIC FREEDOM AND ACADEMIC ANARCHY. New
York: Cowles Book Co., 1970. 269 p.

Conservative look at student disruption; declares that students
should have no role in higher education governance.

1276 _____. EDUCATION AND THE TAMING OF POWER. La Salle, Ill.:
Open Court Publishing Co., 1973. 295 p.

Essays attacking job-oriented curriculum at the expense of
liberal arts. Critical of educators Paul Goodman, Jonathan
Kozol, and Earl McGrath. Critical of Vietnam-era protesting
students and faculty activists.

1277 _____. EDUCATION FOR MODERN MAN. New York: Dial Press,
1946. 238 p.

A plea for more liberal education; criticizes the higher education ideas of such educators as Robert M. Hutchins, Fulton
J. Sheen, and Mortimer Adler.

1278 _____, ed. IN DEFENSE OF ACADEMIC FREEDOM. Indianapolis, Ind.:
Pegasus, 1971. 266 p.

Articles on 1960s student unrest. Hook and other conservative
contributors believe that faculty should make university decisions and that students should not embroil universities in politics.

1279 _____, et al., eds. THE IDEA OF A MODERN UNIVERSITY. New
York: Prometheus Books, 1974. 290 p.

Among contributors are Nathan Glazer, Sidney Hook, and S.
M. Lipset, who at a conference sponsored by the University
Centers for Rational Alternatives (founded to oppose student
unrest) expressed traditional views about university governance.

1280 _____. THE PHILOSOPHY OF THE CURRICULUM: THE NEED FOR
GENERAL EDUCATION. New York: Prometheus Books, 1975. 281 p.

Articles from liberal arts scholars on general education curriculum. Separate sections on humanities, physical sciences, biological sciences, and social sciences.

1281 _____. THE UNIVERSITY AND THE STATE: WHAT ROLE FOR GOVERNMENT IN HIGHER EDUCATION? New York: Prometheus Books, 1978. 296 p.

Contributors examine the relationships between American colleges and universities and their increasing services to and support from state and federal governments. Comparisons with European universities. Some contributors criticize government regulations, required reports, and monitored evaluations, and state that higher education's true functions are being distorted. Others favor continued and increased state and federal support, believe that excessive influence can be curbed, and assert that the relationship is mutually convenient.

1282 Hooker, Clifford P., ed. THE COURTS AND EDUCATION. THE SEVENTY-SEVENTH YEARBOOK, PART I, OF THE NATIONAL SOCIETY FOR THE STUDY OF EDUCATION. Chicago: University of Chicago Press, 1978. 350 p.

Chapters by educators and lawyers about the impact of court decisions on various levels of public and private education, including academic freedom.

1283 Hoole, Stanley W., ed. NORTH TEXAS REGIONAL UNION LIST OF SERIALS. Denton: North Texas State Teachers College, 1943. 532 p.

Serial holdings of six neighboring higher education libraries and the Dallas Public Library to facilitate planning for acquisitions and for sharing journals and newspapers.

1284 Hoopes, Robert, and Marshall, Hubert. THE UNDERGRADUATE IN THE UNIVERSITY. Stanford, Calif.: Stanford University, 1957. 130 p.

Faculty study on Stanford's undergraduate program and its impact on students.

1285 Hope, Arthur J. NOTRE DAME ONE HUNDRED YEARS. Notre Dame, Ind.: University of Notre Dame Press, 1943. 482 p.

Centennial history of Notre Dame, its presidents, memorable instructors, and colorful happenings.

1286 Hopkins, Bruce R. THE LAW OF TAX-EXEMPT ORGANIZATIONS. New York: John Wiley and Sons, 1979. 653 p.

Handbook on federal tax laws on income-tax exemptions for non-profit organizations, including educational and scientific organizations and foundations.

1287 Hopkins, David S.P., and Schroeder, Roger G., eds. APPLYING ANA-
LYTIC METHODS TO PLANNING AND MANAGEMENT. San Francisco:
Jossey-Bass Publishers, 1977. 117 p.

Research techniques, conceptual tools, and analytic models
effective in improving institutional planning and management.
Suggests ways to adapt them to particular institutions.

1288 Hoppe, William A., ed. POLICIES AND PRACTICES IN EVENING COL-
LEGES, 1969. Metuchen, N.J.: Scarecrow Press, 1969. 253 p.

Responses from 107 institutions offering evening classes on such
concerns as adult admissions policies, student expenses, and
faculty.

1289 Hormel, Olive Deane. CO-ED. New York: Charles Scribner's Sons,
1926. 345 p.

Novel about a young woman at a large midwestern state university in the early twentieth century concerned with games,
dates, and academic crises.

1290 Horn, Francis H. CHALLENGE AND PERSPECTIVE IN HIGHER EDUCA-
TION. Carbondale: Southern Illinois University Press, 1971. 224 p.

Calls for combining liberal arts and sciences with vocational
education, for strong college presidential leadership, and for
professors who will leave their ivory towers for everyday realities.

1291 _____, ed. CURRENT ISSUES IN HIGHER EDUCATION, 1953. Washington, D.C.: Association for Higher Education, National Education Association, 1953. 292 p.

Proceedings of 1953 National Conference on Higher Education.

1292 _____. GO FORTH, BE STRONG: ADVICE AND REFLECTIONS FROM
COMMENCEMENT SPEAKERS. Carbondale: Southern Illinois University
Press, 1978. 169 p.

Commencement speeches by Kingman Brewster, Robert Goheen,
Theodore Hesburgh, Clark Kerr, Nathan Pusey, and other prominent educators.

1293 Hornberger, Theodore. SCIENTIFIC THOUGHT IN THE AMERICAN COL-
LEGES, 1638-1800. Austin: University of Texas Press, 1945. 108 p.

Historical essay about science teaching in U.S. colleges tells
of early entrance requirements, teaching methods, and libraries;
says science was important in the curriculum by 1800.

1294 Hornby, David Brock. HIGHER EDUCATION ADMISSION LAW SERVICE. Princeton, N.J.: Educational Testing Service, 1973-- . Various pagings.

Comprehensive information on legal issues related to higher education admissions, in loose-leaf form for periodic updatings.

1295 Horner, Harlan H. DENTAL EDUCATION TODAY. Chicago: University of Chicago Press, 1947. 420 p.

Reviews history of U.S. dental education. Describes physical facilities, faculty organization, curriculum, and teaching methods. Examines strengths, weaknesses, and future trends.

1296 _____. THE LIFE AND WORK OF ANDREW SLOAN DRAPER. Urbana: University of Illinois Press, 1934. 291 p.

Draper (1848-1913), teacher, lawyer, judge, president of the University of Illinois (1894-1904), and first commissioner of education of New York State. Appendix: chronology and excerpts of speeches.

1297 Horowitz, Irving Louis, and Friedland, William H. THE KNOWLEDGE FACTORY: STUDENT POWER AND ACADEMIC POLITICS IN AMERICA. Chicago: Aldine Publishing Co., 1971. 354 p.

Global interpretation of post-1964 student unrest which disagrees with assertions that the Vietnam War and impersonal universities were causes. Asserts that the conflict was over differences in attitudes adults and students held toward the means of production.

1298 Horowitz, Milton J. EDUCATING TOMORROW'S DOCTORS. New York: Appleton-Century-Crofts, 1964. 264 p.

Report of controlled observation of twenty medical students' performance, self-image, growth, and other changes during four years when Western Reserve University Medical School made major shifts in curriculum and teaching methods.

1299 _____. RESEARCH IN PROFESSIONAL EDUCATION: THE EXAMPLE FROM MEDICAL EDUCATION, INCLUDING REFERENCE TO NURSING AND DENTAL EDUCATION. U.S. Office of Education: New Dimensions in Higher Education. Washington, D.C.: Government Printing Office, 1967. 77 p.

Reviews trends and developments in medical education, including curriculum development, student characteristics, career studies, and postgraduate and continuing education. Annotated bibliography.

1300 Horton, Lowell, and Horton, Phyllis, eds. TEACHER EDUCATION: TRENDS, ISSUES, INNOVATIONS. Danville, Ill.: Interstate Printers and Publishers, 1974. 366 p.

> Fifty-eight articles on teacher education which emphasize field experiences of prospective teachers.

1301 Hosford, Frances Juliette. FATHER SHIPHERD'S MAGNA CHARTA: A CENTURY OF COEDUCATION IN OBERLIN COLLEGE. Boston: Marshall Jones Co., 1938. 180 p.

> Centennial history of coeducation at Oberlin College, the first to admit both sexes, by a long-time woman professor there.

1302 Hoskins, Robert L. BLACK ADMINISTRATORS IN HIGHER EDUCATION: CONDITIONS AND PERCEPTIONS. New York: Praeger Publishers, 1978. 206 p.

> Study of 457 black administrators at sixty-six land-grant institutions. Found that many who were appointed in the turbulent 1960s feel uncomfortable now that social pressure has decreased. Predicts that fewer blacks will become administrators in white institutions because many capable blacks are not receiving tenure and because many prefer working in black institutions where they feel more welcome.

1303 Hosmer, LaRue Tone. ACADEMIC STRATEGY: THE DETERMINATION AND IMPLEMENTATION OF PURPOSE AT NEW GRADUATE SCHOOLS OF ADMINISTRATION. Ann Arbor: University of Michigan, 1978. 247 p.

> Recommends that faculty and administrators jointly define objectives of their institutions and policies necessary to reach those objectives. Uses case histories of three new management schools to illustrate this approach.

1304 Houle, Cyril O. THE DESIGN OF EDUCATION. San Francisco: Jossey-Bass Publishers, 1972. 323 p.

> Major analysis of the theory and mechanics of adult and continuing education written by one of the nation's first professors of adult education. Includes a systematic blueprint that can be tailored to any educational situation. Extensive bibliographic essay.

1305 _____. THE EXTERNAL DEGREE. San Francisco: Jossey-Bass Publishers, 1973. 214 p.

> Describes and assesses the best U.S. and European external degree programs; reviews their history and likely future. Presents statistical data substantiating the need for such programs.

1306 Houle, Cyril O., and Nelson, Charles A. THE UNIVERSITY, THE CITI-
ZEN, AND WORLD AFFAIRS. Washington, D.C.: American Council
on Education, 1956. 179 p.

> Carnegie Endowment for International Peace study says univer-
> sities should include instruction about world affairs in both
> degree and nondegree programs for adults. Analyzes the im-
> pact of public opinion and states principles which should guide
> universities in educating adults about world affairs.

1307 House, Robert B. THE LIGHT THAT SHINES. Chapel Hill: University
of North Carolina Press, 1964. 216 p.

> Recollections of his University of North Carolina student days
> (1912-16) by its chancellor emeritus.

1308 Houser, Lloyd J., and Schrader, Alvin M. THE SEARCH FOR A SCIEN-
TIFIC PROFESSION: LIBRARY SCIENCE EDUCATION IN THE U.S. AND
CANADA. Metuchen, N.J.: Scarecrow Press, 1978. 180 p.

> Stresses the need for a scientific or analytic approach to
> solving information problems in higher education libraries.

1309 Howard, Lawrence C. THE DEVELOPING COLLEGES PROGRAM: A
STUDY OF TITLE III, HIGHER EDUCATION ACT OF 1965. Washington,
D.C.: Government Printing Office, 1967. 180 p.

> On federal aid to economically deprived colleges (most of them
> black): the history of such aid, characteristics of schools re-
> ceiving it, and patterns of cooperation among developing col-
> leges and well-financed institutions. Recommends improvements.

1310 Howard, Lowry S. THE ROAD AHEAD. Yonkers, N.Y.: World Book
Co., 1941. 402 p.

> College freshman orientation textbook includes study rules,
> time budgeting instructions, reading guide, and tips on choosing
> a vocation.

1311 Howard, Suzanne. BUT WE WILL PERSIST: A COMPARATIVE RESEARCH
REPORT ON THE STATUS OF WOMEN IN ACADEME. Washington, D.C.:
American Association of University Women, 1978. 86 p.

> Compares the status of women administrators, faculty members,
> and students on campuses in 1970 and 1976.

1312 Howard University. Institute for the Study of Educational Policy. AFFIR-
MATIVE ACTION FOR BLACKS IN HIGHER EDUCATION: A REPORT.
Washington, D.C.: 1978. 96 p.

> Examines the effect of affirmative action strategies in employing
> blacks in higher education.

1313 _____ . EQUAL EDUCATIONAL OPPORTUNITY FOR BLACKS IN U.S. HIGHER EDUCATION: AN ASSESSMENT. Washington, D.C.: Howard University Press, 1976. 330 p.

> Report based on the Institute's extensive data about the status of blacks during 1973-74 in higher education and economic returns of education for blacks. Concludes that educational opportunity for blacks remains unequal.

1314 Howe, Helen Huntington. WE HAPPY FEW. New York: Simon and Schuster, 1946. 345 p.

> Novel of academic life among a small group of Harvard professors and their wives before and during World War II.

1315 Howells, Dorothy Elia. A CENTURY TO CELEBRATE: RADCLIFFE COLLEGE, 1879-1979. Cambridge, Mass.: Radcliffe College, 1978. 152 p.

> A pictorial centennial history of Radcliffe's approach to the higher education of women.

1316 Howes, Raymond F., ed. VISION AND PURPOSE IN HIGHER EDUCATION: TWENTY COLLEGE PRESIDENTS EXAMINE DEVELOPMENTS DURING THE PAST DECADE. Washington, D.C.: American Council on Education, 1962. 223 p.

> College presidents' addresses on many educational matters, including the perennial problem of finance.

1317 Hoxie, R. Gordon, et al. A HISTORY OF THE FACULTY OF POLITICAL SCIENCE, COLUMBIA UNIVERSITY. Bicentennial History of Columbia University. New York: Columbia University Press, 1955. 326 p.

> History of the first U.S. graduate political and social sciences faculty and Columbia's first graduate college. Hoxie examines its origins, achievements, and each department (treated in separate chapters). Gives insights into competition between graduate and undergraduate interest, relations with trustees and administrators, and rivalries between professional and nonprofessional schools.

1318 Hoyt, Donald P., and Munday, Leo A. YOUR COLLEGE FRESHMAN. 1968-69 ed. Iowa City: American College Testing Program, 1968. 249 p.

> A tool to help institutional researchers and administrators understand and use data provided by various ACT research services, described in detail.

1319 Hoyt, Janet. WINGS OF WAX. New York: J.H. Sears and Co., 1929. 358 p.

Novel about the failings of a midwestern university president, bent on reforms but incapable of carrying them out. Author was dean of women at a state university.

1320 Hoyt, John W. ADDRESS ON UNIVERSITY PROGRESS: DELIVERED BEFORE THE NATIONAL TEACHERS' ASSOCIATION AT TRENTON, N.J., AUGUST 20, 1869. New York: D. Appleton and Co., 1870. 80 p.

A post-Civil War critique of U.S. higher education reviews its history, calls it unsatisfactory, and says universities should be comprehensive institutions embracing high intellectual achievement and every profession.

1321 Hubbell, Leigh G. THE DEVELOPMENT OF UNIVERSITY DEPARTMENTS OF EDUCATION. Washington, D.C.: Catholic University Press, 1924. 125 p.

Traces the growth of university departments of education in Illinois, Indiana, Iowa, Ohio, Michigan, and Wisconsin; their relations with secondary schools, influence on accreditation, and research activities.

1322 Hudgins, Garven, and Phillips, Ione. PEOPLE'S COLLEGES IN TROUBLE. Washington, D.C.: National Association of State Universities and Land Grant Colleges, 1971. 29 p.

Questionnaire findings illustrate serious financial plight, remedies attempted, and need for more support of public higher education institutions.

1323 Hughes, Clarence R., et al., eds. COLLECTIVE NEGOTIATIONS IN HIGHER EDUCATION: A READER. Carlinville, Ill.: Blackburn College Press, 1973. 226 p.

Essays published between 1968 and 1973 on academic collective bargaining: its causes and consequences, administrators' roles, and likely effects on both faculty and students.

1324 Hughes, Everett C., et al. EDUCATION FOR THE PROFESSIONS OF MEDICINE, LAW, THEOLOGY, AND SOCIAL WELFARE. New York: McGraw-Hill Book Co., 1973. 273 p.

Surveys of medical, legal, theological, and social welfare professional education, especially in the 1960s.

1325 Hughes, John F., and Mills, Olive, eds. FORMULATING POLICY IN POST-SECONDARY EDUCATION: THE SEARCH FOR ALTERNATIVES. Washington, D.C.: American Council on Education, 1975. 338 p.

Student aid, nontraditional programs, and statewide higher education planning are among topics of papers given at the Council's 1974 meeting by such educators as K. Patricia Cross and Harold Hodgkinson.

1326 Hughes, Raymond M. A MANUAL FOR TRUSTEES OF COLLEGES AND UNIVERSITIES. 2d ed. Ames: Iowa State College Press, 1945. 172 p.

Handbook by Iowa State's president emeritus clarifying the role of higher education trustees.

1327 Huie, William Bradford. MUD ON THE STARS. New York: L.B. Fischer, 1942. 341 p.

Novel of an Alabamian as a college student, his later involvement in labor union and racial strife and in World War II.

1328 Hull, Helen Rose. THE ASKING PRICE. New York: Coward-McCann, 1930. 370 p.

Novel about a budding poet and professor whose money-conscious wife drives him to become head of a college English department.

1329 Hull, W. Frank IV. FOREIGN STUDENTS IN THE UNITED STATES OF AMERICA: COPING BEHAVIOR WITHIN THE EDUCATIONAL ENVIRON-MENT. New York: Praeger Publishers, 1978. 249 p.

Foreign students usually have good U.S. academic experience. But interaction with Americans is hampered by limited free time, language problems, and being regarded as "outsiders." Recommends taking practical steps to help them adapt to all aspects of their life here.

1330 Hull, W. Frank IV, and Yankovic, Donald C. ECONOMIC PRINCIPLES II: A GENERAL SURVEY COURSE WITHOUT LECTURES. Toledo, Ohio: Center for the Study of Higher Education, University of Toledo, 1971. 39 p.

Found that students in an experimental section of an economics class learned adequately without formal lectures.

1331 Hull, W. Frank IV, et al. THE AMERICAN UNDERGRADUATE, OFF-CAMPUS AND OVERSEAS: A STUDY OF THE EDUCATIONAL VALIDITY OF SUCH PROGRAMS. New York: Council on International Educational Exchange, 1977. 60 p.

Analyzes American undergraduates' assessments of the intellectual and personal rewards of living and studying abroad. Examines international educational exchange programs' effectiveness in promoting understanding and friendship among nations.

1332 HUMANISTIC VALUES FOR A FREE SOCIETY. Proceedings of the Third Regional Conference on the Humanities, Estes Park, Colorado, June 1946. Denver: University of Denver Press, 1947. 189 p.

About different types of U.S. general education courses and the status of the humanities abroad.

1333 Human Resources Research Organization. ACADEMIC COMPUTING DIRECTORY. Alexandria, Va.: 1978. 114 p.

Lists educational institutions where computers are used successfully for classroom teaching and individual learning. Includes descriptions of the computing system and persons to contact for additional information.

1334 Humphrey, David C. FROM KING'S COLLEGE TO COLUMBIA, 1746-1800. New York: Columbia University Press, 1976. 413 p.

Eighteenth-century origins and development. Emphasizes Columbia's involvement in the struggle between revolutionaries and loyalists during the Revolution.

1335 Humphrey, Richard A., ed. UNIVERSITIES AND DEVELOPMENT ASSISTANCE ABROAD. Washington, D.C.: American Council on Education, 1967. 196 p.

Evaluative and ideological aspects of using universities to serve U.S. foreign policy strategy via Agency for International Development (AID) programs in developing countries.

1336 Humphreys, J. Anthony, and Traxler, Arthur E. GUIDANCE SERVICES. Chicago: Science Research Associates, 1954. 438 p.

Concepts and procedures for counseling and guidance at all levels, including higher education.

1337 Hungate, Thad L. FINANCE IN EDUCATIONAL MANAGEMENT OF COLLEGES AND UNIVERSITIES. New York: Teachers College, Columbia University, 1954. 202 p.

Comptroller and educational administration professor at Teachers College, Columbia University, analyzes higher education financial practices, stressing management techniques and procedures.

1338 _____. FINANCING THE FUTURE OF HIGHER EDUCATION. New York: Teachers College, Columbia University, 1946. 310 p.

Trends in higher education finance. Says states should play a greater role in supplying higher education and that students' financial share should be reduced.

1339 _____. MANAGEMENT IN HIGHER EDUCATION. New York: Teachers College, Columbia University, 1964. 348 p.

> Analyzes four functions of higher education management: delegating, organizing, directing, and evaluating functions. Stresses the necessity of consensus in governance.

1340 Hunt, Everett Lee. THE REVOLT OF THE COLLEGE INTELLECTUAL. New York: Human Relations Aids, 1963. 172 p.

> Swarthmore professor and dean writes about the revolt among Swarthmore undergraduate intellectuals against rigid emphasis on intellectual supremacy. Shows history of the college and its educational policies that have fostered its tradition of excellence. Finds that the Swarthmore tradition has placed growth of character above disciplining the mind.

1341 Hunter, John O. VALUES AND THE FUTURE: MODELS OF COMMUNITY COLLEGE DEVELOPMENT. Sherman Oaks, Calif.: Banner Books International, 1978. 166 p.

> Dean of Niagara County (New York) Community College identifies and discusses such major issues facing community colleges as accountability, adaptive planning, collective bargaining, and general education.

1342 Hunter, Sam. A SURVEY, ANALYSIS AND PROPOSAL FOR ACTION FOR THE DEVELOPMENT OF THE VISUAL ARTS IN PUBLIC HIGHER EDUCATION IN MASSACHUSETTS. Boston: Massachusetts Advisory Council on Education, 1969. 177 p.

> Examines art education in Massachusetts colleges and universities in the framework of conditions prevailing in U.S. art education generally.

1343 Husband, Joseph Biegler. HIGH HURDLES. Boston: Houghton Mifflin Co., 1923. 232 p.

> Novel about a spoiled rich New England youth who wastes his time and fails at Harvard, loses his status and wealth, and finally works his way up painfully in business.

1344 Hutchins, Robert Maynard. THE CONFLICT IN EDUCATION IN A DEMOCRATIC SOCIETY. New York: Harper and Brothers, 1953. 112 p.

> Lectures which summarize twenty years of criticism of U.S. higher education, express disdain for John Dewey's theories about adjustment and social reform, and call for lifelong liberal education.

1345 _____. EDUCATION FOR FREEDOM. Baton Rouge: Louisiana State University Press, 1943. 108 p.

Speeches condemn American antiintellectualism and extol classical humanism and liberal education through great books.

1346 _____. THE HIGHER LEARNING IN AMERICA. New Haven, Conn.:
Yale University Press, 1936. 120 p.

Analyzes what he sees as confusion in American higher education, clarifies the causes, and recommends improvements in
keeping with his own classical humanism.

1347 _____. THE LEARNING SOCIETY. New York: Praeger Publishers,
1968. 142 p.

Expanding on themes in his THE HIGHER LEARNING IN
AMERICA (1936), Hutchins sees a liberal-theoretical education and lifelong learning (not vocationally oriented) as the
ideal for America's future.

1348 _____. NO FRIENDLY VOICE. Chicago: University of Chicago Press,
1936. Reprint. Westport, Conn.: Greenwood Press, 1968. 197 p.

Addresses by the president of the University of Chicago, mostly
on university education, dedicated to his father, William S.
Hutchins, Berea College president.

1349 _____. SOME OBSERVATIONS ON AMERICAN EDUCATION. Sir
George Watson Lectures. Cambridge, Engl.: Cambridge University Press,
1956. 112 p.

In lectures given at British universities about American education, Hutchins describes its weaknesses and asserts benefits of
liberal education.

1350 _____. UNIVERSITY OF UTOPIA. 2d ed. Chicago: University of
Chicago Press, 1964. 103 p.

To overcome hazards that industrialization, specialization, philosophical diversity, and social and political conformity pose
for U.S. higher education, Hutchins proposes a University of
Utopia along the lines he espoused as chancellor at the University of Chicago.

1351 Hyde, William D., Jr., ed. ISSUES IN POSTSECONDARY EDUCATION
FINANCE. Denver, Colo.: Education Commission of the States, 1978.
43 p.

Topics: fairness in public support for higher education, state
and local roles in financing community colleges, and the effect that tuition and financial aid have on student access and
choice of higher education institution.

1352 Hyman, Herbert H., and Wright, Charles R. EDUCATION'S LASTING INFLUENCE ON VALUES. Chicago: University of Chicago Press, 1979. 162 p.

Evaluated thirty-eight surveys of 45,000 whites aged twenty-five to seventy-two during 1950-75. Found that those more educated better supported such values as civil liberties for nonconformists, freedom of information, freedom from arbitrary restraints, wiretap protection, and equality of opportunities for minorities. These findings, together with correlation found between those having more education and their propensity to seek new knowledge (in authors' ENDURING EFFECTS OF EDUCATION, below), led to conclusion that formal education has been a strong force over a long period in molding character as well as intellect.

1353 Hyman, Herbert H., et al. THE ENDURING EFFECTS OF EDUCATION. Chicago: University of Chicago Press, 1975. 313 p.

Analysis of fifty opinion polls conducted among American adults, 1949-74, led authors to conclude that formal education has large, long-lasting effects on what people know and on their receptivity to further learning.

1354 Iffert, Robert E. RETENTION AND WITHDRAWAL OF COLLEGE STUDENTS. Washington, D.C.: Government Printing Office, 1957. 177 p.

Analysis of retention, transfer, and withdrawal of about 13,600 students who entered higher education in fall 1950.

1355 Iffert, Robert E., and Clarke, Betty S. COLLEGE APPLICANTS, ENTRANTS, DROPOUTS. Washington, D.C.: Government Printing Office, 1965. 88 p.

At twenty campuses, mostly east of the Mississippi, studied admissions-related problems: multiple applications, students admitted who never enroll, and sources for paying college expenses.

1356 Ikenberry, Stanley O., and Friedman, Renee C. BEYOND ACADEMIC DEPARTMENTS: THE STORY OF INSTITUTES AND CENTERS. San Francisco: Jossey-Bass Publishers, 1972. 144 p.

About the functions and conflicts of interest between special-purpose university institutes and traditional university departments. Recommendations for better governance procedures.

1357 Illich, Ivan, et al. DISABLING PROFESSIONS. Salem, N.H.: Marion Boyars, 1979. 127 p.

Questions the view that such professions as law, medicine, the ministry, education, and management are selflessly devoted to society's good.

1358 Imbs, Bravig. THE PROFESSOR'S WIFE. New York: Dial Press, 1928. 305 p.

> Novel thinly disguises author's year at Dartmouth College, where he roomed in a professor's house. Shows how college teaching can be affected by social competition among faculty.

1359 Indiana State Policy Commission on Post High School Education. AN INDIANA PATTERN FOR HIGHER EDUCATION. Indianapolis: 1968. 148 p.

> Recommendations of statewide Indiana higher education planning include coordinating Board of Regents, community college system, and the conversion of regional state university campuses into autonomous institutions.

1360 Ingham, Roy J., ed. INSTITUTIONAL BACKGROUNDS OF ADULT EDUCATION. DYNAMICS OF CHANGE IN THE MODERN UNIVERSITY. Brookline, Mass.: Center for the Study of Liberal Education for Adults at Boston University, 1966. 115 p.

> Papers about increasing the effectiveness of administrators in the adult education divisions of higher education.

1361 Ingham, Travis. YOUNG GENTLEMEN, RISE. New York: Farrar and Rinehart, 1935. 313 p.

> Novel about Yale undergraduate life during the 1920s.

1362 Ingraham, Mark H. MY PURPOSE HOLDS: REACTIONS AND EXPERIENCES IN RETIREMENT OF TIAA-CREF ANNUITANTS. New York: Educational Research Division, TIAA-CREF, 1974. 163 p.

> Approximately 1,500 TIAA-CREF annuitants responded about their age, health, housing, finances, activities, problems, retirement experiences, and advice for those soon to retire.

1363 Ingraham, Mark H., and King, Francis P. THE MIRROR OF BRASS: THE COMPENSATION AND WORKING CONDITIONS OF COLLEGE AND UNIVERSITY ADMINISTRATORS. Madison: University of Wisconsin Press, 1968. 336 p.

> Study of the salary, benefits, and working conditions of six thousand major U.S. higher education administrators.

1364 _____. THE OUTER FRINGE: FACULTY BENEFITS OTHER THAN ANNUITIES AND INSURANCE. Madison: University of Wisconsin Press, 1965. 304 p.

Study of faculty fringe benefits (library facilities, housing, parking, and secretarial help) at over 750 colleges and universities.

1365 Ingram, Anne. BELIEFS OF WOMEN FACULTY ABOUT DISCRIMINATION. College Park: Status of Women Committee, University of Maryland, 1973. 23 p.

University of Maryland's women faculty reported that their most critical problems were unequal pay for equal work and qualifications (64 percent), discrimination in promotions (61 percent), and unequal advancement opportunities (61 percent).

1366 Institute for Educational Leadership. FEDERALISM AT THE CROSSROADS: IMPROVING EDUCATIONAL POLICYMAKING. Washington, D.C.: 1977. 107 p.

On who makes and who ought to make educational policies; roles played by the federal and local governments, states, and public and private institutions of higher education.

1367 Institute for Local Self Government. COMMUNITY COLLEGE PROGRAMS FOR PUBLIC SERVICE OCCUPATIONS. Berkeley, Calif.: 1969. 160 p.

California-based study of community college vocational-technical programs; correlates curriculum guidelines with job specifications for various local governmental positions.

1368 Institute of International Education. THE COMMUNITY, TECHNICAL, AND JUNIOR COLLEGE IN THE UNITED STATES: A GUIDE FOR FOREIGN STUDENTS. New York: 1979. 92 p.

Lists over four hundred two-year colleges explicitly interested in accepting foreign students, with admissions requirements, housing information, fields of study offered, accreditation, the credit system, grading, and visa requirements. Practical guide on sponsorship; lists counseling services overseas.

1369 _____. U.S. COLLEGE-SPONSORED PROGRAMS ABROAD. New York: 1977. 140 p.

Provides information on courses, credits, enrollment requirements, and costs of study abroad programs, sponsored by accredited U.S. colleges and universities.

1370 Interuniversity Communications Council. POLICIES, STRATEGIES, AND PLANS FOR COMPUTING IN HIGHER EDUCATION. Princeton, N.J.: 1976. 113 p.

Role of the minicomputer in higher education; describes colleges' experiences with regional sharing of computer resources.

1371 Irving, Clifford. ON A DARKLING PLAIN. New York: G.P. Putnam's Sons, 1956. 320 p.

> Novel about three young men and their postcollege years, one of whom was influenced by a socialist friend at Cornell University.

1372 Jackson, Dorothy J., and Pitterle, Kenneth J. EDUCATIONAL RESEARCH INTERNSHIP FOR WOMEN AND MINORITY JUNIOR FACULTY: A FEASIBILITY STUDY. Philadelphia: Higher Education Resources Services, Mid-Atlantic, University of Pennsylvania, 1979. 71 p.

> Model internship program to aid women and minority faculty; includes training seminars and collaboration with senior faculty on a research paper.

1373 Jackson, Shirley. HANGSAMAN. New York: Farrar, Straus and Young, 1951. 280 p.

> Novel about a sensitive young woman student initiated into adult life at a progressive college. Author, wife of an English professor, shows the connection between the heroine's experiences and the college program.

1374 Jacob, Philip E. CHANGING VALUES IN COLLEGE: AN EXPLORATORY STUDY ON THE IMPACT OF COLLEGE TEACHING. New York: Harper and Brothers, 1957. 174 p.

> Found that changes in student values did not result primarily from the formal education process but from such influences as a sensitive teacher or value-laden personal experience.

1375 Jacobs, Paul, and Landau, Saul, eds. THE NEW RADICALS: A REPORT WITH DOCUMENTS. New York: Random House, 1966. 333 p.

> Origins and ideals of the New Left and roles played by various student groups. Documents include the Port Huron Statement and C. Wright Mills's "On the Left."

1376 Jacobson, Harvey K., ed. EVALUATING ADVANCEMENT PROGRAMS. San Francisco: Jossey-Bass Publishers, 1978. 117 p.

> Public relations defined as developing understanding and support from all constituencies to further university goals; model based on one at University of Michigan.

1377 Jacobson, Myrtle S. NIGHT AND DAY: THE INTERACTION BETWEEN THE ACADEMIC INSTITUTION AND ITS EVENING COLLEGE. Metuchen, N.J.: Scarecrow Press, 1970. 358 p.

> Looks at extension education and its effect on university governance, with Brooklyn College as one example.

1378 Jaffe, Abram J., and Adams, Walter. AMERICAN HIGHER EDUCATION IN TRANSITION. New York: Bureau of Applied Social Research, Columbia University, 1969. 239 p.

> Concluded that the spread of two-year colleges had lowered financial barriers to higher education and that students were unrealistic about the relation between education and careers.

1379 Jaffe, Abram J., et al. ETHNIC HIGHER EDUCATION: NEGRO COLLEGES IN THE 1960S. New York: Bureau of Applied Social Research, Columbia University, 1966. 42 p.

> Compares black students enrolled in sixty-eight predominantly black public and private two-year and four-year colleges with those enrolled in integrated but predominantly white colleges in the South and border states.

1380 _____. NEGRO HIGHER EDUCATION IN THE 1960S. New York: Praeger Publishers, 1968. 290 p.

> Compares white and black colleges mainly in the South. Concludes that black colleges are of questionable quality.

1381 Jaffe, Rona. CLASS REUNION. New York: Delacorte Press, 1979. 338 p.

> Novel traces the educational experiences of four women students from their freshman year at Radcliffe College in 1953 through their subsequent life experiences to their twentieth class reunion in 1977.

1382 James, Henry. CHARLES W. ELIOT: PRESIDENT OF HARVARD UNIVERSITY, 1869-1909. 2 vols. Boston: Houghton Mifflin Co., 1930. 382 p., 393 p.

> Volume 1: Eliot's use of electives and his campaign for standards in professional schools. Volume 2: source materials.

1383 Jameson, Sanford, ed. THE ADMISSION AND PLACEMENT OF STUDENTS FROM THE PACIFIC-ASIA AREA: A WORKSHOP REPORT. Washington, D.C.: National Association for Foreign Student Affairs, 1969. 93 p.

> Previews educational systems of ten Pacific-Asian countries. Has a selected bibliography and recommendations on the admission and placement of applicants in U.S. institutions.

1384 Jacques Cattell Press (comp.). LEADERS IN EDUCATION. 5th ed. New York: R.R. Bowker, 1974. 1,309 p.

> Lists biographical information on 17,000 foremost educators in

the United States and Canada, including heads of colleges and universities, officers on accreditation boards, leaders in private schools, officials of educational associations, and authors of important education books.

1385 Jarchow, Merrill E. PRIVATE LIBERAL ARTS COLLEGES IN MINNESOTA: THEIR HISTORY AND CONTRIBUTIONS. St. Paul: Minnesota Historical Society, 1973. 345 p.

History of each of Minnesota's sixteen private, accredited, four-year liberal arts colleges in three chronological periods since 1850, and their roles in the history of the state.

1386 Jarrell, Randall. PICTURES FROM AN INSTITUTION. New York: Alfred A. Knopf, 1954. 277 p.

Novel critically dissects a woman's progressive college; modeled on author's own teaching experiences at Kenyon and Sarah Lawrence Colleges and at the Woman's College of the University of North Carolina.

1387 Jellema, William W. FROM RED TO BLACK? THE FINANCIAL STATUS OF PRIVATE COLLEGES AND UNIVERSITIES. San Francisco: Jossey-Bass Publishers, 1973. 174 p.

Describes fiscal problems of 554 U.S. private four-year institutions, classified according to area, size, degrees granted, and affiliation.

1388 _____, ed. EFFICIENT COLLEGE MANAGEMENT. San Francisco: Jossey-Bass Publishers, 1972. 156 p.

Sourcebook about such higher education management matters as collective bargaining, budget planning, governance, and expenditures on students.

1389 _____. INSTITUTIONAL PRIORITIES AND MANAGEMENT OBJECTIVES. Washington, D.C.: Association of American Colleges, 1971. 150 p.

Informed advice about how liberal-arts colleges can avoid serious financial problems.

1390 Jencks, Christopher, and Riesman, David. THE ACADEMIC REVOLUTION. Garden City, N.Y.: Doubleday, 1968. 580 p.

Defines "academic revolution" as the rise to power of professors. Says meritocracy has partially triumphed. Concludes that: (1) a meritocracy may overvalue technical competence, and (2) U.S. higher education has affected only slightly the rate of social mobility or the degree of equality in American society.

1391 Jenny, Hans Heinrich. EARLY RETIREMENT, A NEW ISSUE IN HIGHER EDUCATION--THE FINANCIAL CONSEQUENCES. New York: Teachers Insurance and Annuity Association of America, 1974. 52 p.

> Discusses the economic impact of early retirement on educational institutions and their staff members.

1392 Jenny, Hans Heinrich, and Wynn, G. Richard. THE GOLDEN YEARS: A STUDY OF INCOME AND EXPENDITURE GROWTH AND DISTRIBUTION OF FORTY-EIGHT PRIVATE FOUR-YEAR LIBERAL ARTS COLLEGES, 1960-1968. Wooster, Ohio: College of Wooster, 1970. 217 p.

> About the enormous growth in liberal arts colleges during the 1960s and their likely financial difficulties.

1393 Jerome, Judson. CULTURE OUT OF ANARCHY: THE RECONSTRUCTION OF AMERICAN HIGHER LEARNING. New York: Herder and Herder, 1970. 330 p.

> Study of experimental colleges such as Bensalem and the Washington-Baltimore campus of Antioch College.

1394 Johnson, Alvin Saunders. PIONEER'S PROGRESS: AN AUTOBIOGRAPHY. New York: Viking, 1952. 413 p.

> Autobiography of the founder and first director of the New School for Social Research, an adult education center.

1395 _____. THE PROFESSOR AND THE PETTICOAT. New York: Dodd, Mead and Co., 1914. 402 p.

> Novel about a Harvard doctoral graduate who teaches philosophy at a Texas university.

1396 Johnson, Annabel. AS A SPECKLED BIRD. New York: Thomas Y. Crowell Co., 1957. 310 p.

> Novel about life in an academy of fine arts with conflicts among the president, a teacher, and a pupil.

1397 Johnson, Byron Lamar. GENERAL EDUCATION IN ACTION. Washington, D.C.: American Council on Education, 1952. 409 p.

> Findings of the California Study of General Education in the Junior Colleges. Suggestions for improvement are applicable nationwide.

1398 _____. ISLANDS OF INNOVATION EXPANDING: CHANGES IN THE COMMUNITY COLLEGE. Beverly Hills, Calif.: Glencoe Press, 1969. 352 p.

Found much innovation and imaginative teaching in 200 two-year colleges surveyed: work-study programs, programmed instruction, television teaching, simulation games, and independent study. Discussed aids and obstacles to innovation and made recommendations.

1399 _____, ed. WHAT ABOUT SURVEY COURSES? New York: Henry Holt and Co., 1937. 377 p.

Authors present divergent views on the policy and technique of survey courses for mainly college freshmen and sophomores, but agree that a competent teaching staff is the key to success.

1400 Johnson, Byron Lamar, and Lindstrom, Eloise. THE LIBRARIAN AND THE TEACHER IN GENERAL EDUCATION: A REPORT OF LIBRARY-INSTRUCTIONAL ACTIVITIES AT STEPHENS COLLEGE. Chicago: American Library Association, 1948. 69 p.

A report of library-instructional activities at Stephens College, Missouri; calls for improved relations between students and the library.

1401 Johnson, Burges. CAMPUS VERSUS CLASSROOM: A CANDID APPRAISAL OF THE AMERICAN COLLEGE. New York: Ives Washburn, 1946. 305 p.

English professor's anecdotes and observations about his higher education experiences at Amherst, Vassar, Syracuse, and Union College.

1402 _____. THE PROFESSOR AT BAY. New York: G.P. Putnam's Sons, 1937. 243 p.

A mixed serious and satirical view of the plight of the college professor and his various duties.

1403 Johnson, Carl L. PROFESSOR LONGFELLOW OF HARVARD. Eugene: University of Oregon Press, 1944. 112 p.

Focuses on poet Henry Wadsworth Longfellow's eighteen years at Harvard University as Smith Professor of Modern Languages and Belles Lettres.

1404 Johnson, Charles B., and Katzenmeyer, William G., eds. MANAGEMENT INFORMATION SYSTEMS IN HIGHER EDUCATION: THE STATE OF THE ART. Durham, N.C.: Duke University Press, 1969. 191 p.

Stresses the role of computers. Among topics: basic principles and procedures in developing management information systems, development of large-scale multiinstitutional systems, and possibilities of using modeling or simulation techniques in problem solving.

1405 Johnson, Eldon L. FROM RIOT TO REASON. Urbana: University of Illinois Press, 1971. 127 p.

> Reacting to Vietnam War era student unrest, University of Illinois vice president sees need for university reform, believes U.S. higher education has been good for society, and hopes that by strong presidential leadership and stress on teaching universities will continue to flourish.

1406 Johnson, Henry. THE OTHER SIDE OF MAIN STREET. New York: Columbia University Press, 1943. 263 p.

> Autobiography (1867-1953) of education professor at Columbia University Teachers College, where he helped to prepare history teachers. Relates his Minnesota upbringing, college years, teaching experiences, and memories of such colleagues as Deans John William Burgess of the Graduate School and James Earl Russell of Teachers College.

1407 Johnson, Jeffrey N. FACULTY DEVELOPMENT IN INDIVIDUALIZED EDUCATION PROJECT (1976-1978): FINAL REPORT. Minneapolis: University of Minnesota, 1979. 192 p.

> Results of a two-year project to improve faculty involvement in one-to-one undergraduate education.

1408 Johnson, Kent R., and Ruskin, Robert S. BEHAVIORAL INSTRUCTION: AN EVALUATIVE REVIEW. Washington, D.C.: American Psychological Association, 1978. 182 p.

> Explains behavioral systems such as the personalized system of instruction (PSI) and compares them with conventional teaching methods.

1409 Johnson, M. Clemens, and Ramsey, Leah W. FACULTY IN INSTITUTIONS OF HIGHER EDUCATION, NOVEMBER 1955. Washington, D.C.: U.S. Office of Education, 1957. 40 p.

> Statistical summaries and reports on 301,582 higher education faculty members.

1410 Johnson, Mark D., and Mortimer, Kenneth P. FACULTY BARGAINING AND THE POLITICS OF RETRENCHMENT IN THE PENNSYLVANIA STATE COLLEGES, 1971-1976. University Park: Center for the Study of Higher Education, Pennsylvania State University, 1978. 112 p.

> Chronology of the relationship between Pennsylvania's state government and state colleges on faculty bargaining, governance policies, and political aspects.

1411 Johnson, Nora. A STEP BEYOND INNOCENCE. Boston: Little, Brown and Co., 1961. 274 p.

Novel of a woman student at Smith College and her struggle
to choose between marriage and career achievement.

1412 Johnson, Owen MacMahon. STOVER AT YALE. New York: Frederick
A. Stokes Co., 1912. 386 p.

Influential novel by Yale graduate which criticizes Yale's curriculum as fossilized and its society as undemocratic; influenced
novelist Thomas Wolfe, who mentions it in LOOK HOMEWARD,
ANGEL (1929).

1413 Johnson, Roosevelt. BLACK AGENDA FOR CAREER EDUCATION. Columbus, Ohio: ECCA Publications, 1974.

Papers about career education for black Americans.

1414 _____, ed. BLACK SCHOLARS ON HIGHER EDUCATION IN THE 70'S.
Columbus, Ohio: ECCA Publications, 1974. 392 p.

Articles by black scholars on problems and issues facing higher
education for blacks: black studies, compensatory programs,
and the future role of black colleges.

1415 Johnson, Simon S. UPDATE ON EDUCATION: A DIGEST OF THE NA-
TIONAL ASSESSMENT OF EDUCATIONAL PROGRESS. Denver: Education Commission of the States, 1977. 147 p.

Reports on the educational achievement of students ages nine, thirteen, seventeen, and twenty-five to thirty-five in science, social
studies, music, literature, reading, writing, and citizenship.

1416 Johnson, Stanley. PROFESSOR. New York: Harcourt, Brace and Co.,
1925. 312 p.

Novel satirizing a philandering English professor at a Vermont
university.

1417 Johnson, William R. SCHOOLED LAWYERS: A STUDY IN THE CLASH
OF PROFESSIONAL CULTURES. New York: New York University Press,
1978. 215 p.

A study of legal education and the legal profession from the
decline of apprenticeships in the nineteenth century to the
rise of the law school in the twentieth century, illustrated by
the history of the profession in Wisconsin.

1418 Johnston, James M., ed. BEHAVIOR RESEARCH AND TECHNOLOGY IN
HIGHER EDUCATION. Springfield, Ill.: Charles C Thomas, Publisher,
1975. 517 p.

Papers by fifty-four persons at the First (1973) National Conference on Behavior Research and Technology in Higher Education are on personalized system of instruction (PSI).

1419 Johnston, Thomas R., and Hand, Helen. THE TRUSTEES AND THE OF-
FICERS OF PURDUE UNIVERSITY, 1865-1940. Lafayette, Ind.: Purdue
University, 1940. 428 p.

> Almost one hundred biographies and portraits of former Purdue
> trustees, treasurers, and presidents.

1420 Jonas, Steven. MEDICAL MYSTERY: THE TRAINING OF DOCTCRS IN
THE UNITED STATES. New York: W.W. Norton, 1979. 426 p.

> Says that medical education should emphasize health and pre-
> ventive medicine rather than disease and cures.

1421 Jones, Ann. UNCLE TOM'S CAMPUS. New York: Praeger Publishers,
1973. 225 p.

> English teacher's year's experience in a small southern black
> college. Says the power structure of the college and the town
> is the root of the problem.

1422 Jones, Barbara. BENNINGTON COLLEGE: THE DEVELOPMENT OF AN
EDUCATIONAL IDEA. New York: Harper and Brothers, 1946. 239 p.

> Describes the first fourteen years (1932-45) of this progressive
> women's college whose founders included William H. Kilpatrick:
> the school's education ideas, the development of the curriculum,
> community life, and nonresident work experience.

1423 Jones, Edward Safford. COMPREHENSIVE EXAMINATIONS IN AMERICAN
COLLEGES. New York: Macmillan Co., 1933. 436 p.

> Origin and philosophy of comprehensive examinations and their
> general use. The main concern is with using comprehensive
> exams to stimulate students to greater scholarly attainment.

1424 Jones, Emmett L., et al. MASTERY LEARNING: A STRATEGY FOR ACA-
DEMIC SUCCESS IN A COMMUNITY COLLEGE. Los Angeles: ERIC
Clearinghouse for Junior Colleges, University of California, 1976. 51 p.

> Describes attempts to adapt to the community college some of
> the ideas of "mastery learning"--a program in which attain-
> ment of previously specified goals constitutes mastery of a
> course.

1425 Jones, Faustine Childress. THE CHANGING MOOD IN AMERICA:
ERODING COMMITMENT? Washington, D.C.: Howard University Press,
1977. 314 p.

> Sees American commitment shifting away from the underprivi-
> leged and minorities. Examines the mood of the majority,
> blacks, the federal government, and the effects on educational
> policy.

1426 Jones, Howard Mumford. EDUCATION AND WORLD TRAGEDY. Cambridge, Mass.: Harvard University Press, 1946. 178 p.

> To avoid future wars, author wants U.S. higher education to teach about representative government, the USSR, the Orient, and personal relationships. He is also critical of the Great Books program and the Ph.D. requirement for college teaching.

1427 Jones, John Harding. THE CORRESPONDENCE EDUCATIONAL DIRECTORY: SECOND EDITION, 1979-80. Oxnard, Calif.: Racz Publishing Co., 1979. 176 p.

> Describes correspondence programs offered by accredited colleges and universities and trade, technical, and professional schools in the United States, England, Canada, and Australia.

1428 Jones, Phillip E., ed. HISTORICAL PERSPECTIVES ON THE DEVELOPMENT OF EQUAL OPPORTUNITY IN HIGHER EDUCATION. Iowa City: American College Testing Publications, 1978. 35 p.

> Six essays on historical efforts to provide higher educational opportunity for blacks.

1429 Jones, Rufus M. HAVERFORD COLLEGE: A HISTORY AND AN INTERPRETATION. New York: Macmillan Co., 1933. 244 p.

> Centennial history of Haverford College from its beginning in 1833; by a longtime Haverford philosophy professor.

1430 Jones, Thelma. SKINNY ANGEL. New York: McGraw-Hill Book Co., 1946. 334 p.

> Novel of a family involved with several small-town struggling midwestern and western colleges.

1431 Jones, Theodore Francis, ed. NEW YORK UNIVERSITY, 1832-1932. New York: New York University Press, 1933. 459 p.

> Centennial history describing the founding, separate schools and colleges, and administrative history under chief administrative officers Albert Gallatin, John W. Draper, Chancellor McCracken, and others.

1432 Jones, Thomas E., et al. LETTERS TO COLLEGE PRESIDENTS. Englewood Cliffs, N.J.: Prentice-Hall, 1964. 192 p.

> Three retired college presidents reflect higher education problems gathered from visits to over 250 institutions. Has advice for new presidents of small church-related colleges about a wide range of common problems.

1433 Jones, Thomas Firth. A PAIR OF LAWN SLEEVES: A BIOGRAPHY OF WILLIAM SMITH (1727-1803). Radnor, Pa.: Chilton Book Co., 1972. 210 p.

> Life of the first president of the University of Pennsylvania with references to educational ideas of Benjamin Franklin and Benjamin Rush.

1434 Jordan, David Starr. THE CARE AND CULTURE OF MEN: A SERIES OF ADDRESSES ON THE VALUE OF HIGHER EDUCATION. San Francisco: Whitaker and Ray Co., 1896. 267 p.

> Addresses by Stanford University president on the value of higher education, evolution of the college curriculum, the education of women, training physicians, law school and lawyers, science, and the new university.

1435 Judd, Charles Hubbard, and Parker, Samuel Chester. PROBLEMS INVOLVED IN STANDARDIZING STATE NORMAL SCHOOLS. Washington, D.C.: Government Printing Office, 1916. 141 p.

> Recommended that teacher education in normal schools become scientific, that students be taught to think, and that student teaching be central to teacher training.

1436 Judd, Cornelius D. THE SUMMER SCHOOL AS AN AGENCY FOR THE TRAINING OF TEACHERS IN THE UNITED STATES. Nashville, Tenn.: George Peabody College for Teachers, 1921. 88 p.

> History of summer schools for training teachers. Compares them to teacher education conducted during the regular school year. Lists their strengths and weaknesses and suggests improvements.

1437 Julian, Alfred C., et al., eds. OPEN DOORS/1977-78. REPORT ON INTERNATIONAL EDUCATIONAL EXCHANGE. New York: Institute of International Education, 1979. 110 p.

> Tabular material on the number, location, characteristics, and origin of foreign students in U.S. colleges and universities.

1438 Juster, Francis Thomas. EDUCATION, INCOME, AND HUMAN BEHAVIOR. New York: McGraw-Hill Book Co., 1975. 438 p.

> Carnegie Commission on Higher Education study shows that educational attainment produces higher earnings. Also, empirical findings on the relation between education and fertility, family size, and political attitudes.

1439 Justman, Joseph, and Mais, Walter H. COLLEGE TEACHING: ITS PRACTICE AND ITS POTENTIAL. New York: Harper and Brothers, 1956. 257 p.

On college teaching, goals and curriculum, teacher responsibility and professional growth, teaching methods, and instruction techniques.

1440 Kahn, Ely Jacques, Jr. HARVARD: THROUGH CHANGE AND THROUGH STORM. New York: W.W. Norton, 1969. 388 p.

Written at the time of the student protests, author describes admiringly his alma mater, its students, admission process, and government contribution.

1441 Kaludis, George, ed. STRATEGIES FOR BUDGETING. San Francisco: Jossey-Bass Publishers, 1973. 106 p.

Practical guide to improved higher education budget strategies. Sample procedures from Case Western Reserve and Brown University and data on formula budgeting.

1442 Kandel, Isaac Leon. WILLIAM CHANDLER BAGLEY: STALWART EDUCATOR. New York: Teachers College, Columbia University, 1961. 131 p.

Life and influence of Teachers College, Columbia University, professor Bagley (1874-1946), essentialist movement leader and a founder of Kappa Delta Pi education honor society, which commissioned this book.

1443 _____, ed. HIGHER EDUCATION IN ENGLISH-SPEAKING COUNTRIES. New York: Teachers College, Columbia University, 1943. 297 p.

Describes higher education in nine English-speaking countries including the United States. Articles on status of higher education, wartime difficulties and likely postwar needs.

1444 Kaplan, Martin, ed. THE MONDAY MORNING IMAGINATION: REPORT FROM THE BOYER WORKSHOP ON STATE UNIVERSITY SYSTEMS. New York: Praeger Publishers, 1977. 180 p.

Eight large state university administrators conclude that university systems can use their advantages of size, organization, and leadership to achieve diversity, stimulate experimentation, and assure greater accountability.

1445 Kaplan, Max. LEISURE: PERSPECTIVES ON EDUCATION AND POLICY. Washington, D.C.: National Education Association, 1978. 128 p.

Assessment of issues that underlie efforts to establish leisure studies; i.e., adult education.

1446 Kaplin, William A. THE LAW OF HIGHER EDUCATION: LEGAL IMPLICATIONS OF ADMINISTRATIVE DECISION MAKING. San Francisco: Jossey-Bass Publishers, 1979. 500 p.

Law for administrators and college officials. Covers relationships between officials and college staff, students, and the
community. Includes principles of law, future trends, and
advice for handling problems.

1447 Karabel, Jerome, and Halsey, A.H., eds. POWER AND IDEOLOGY IN
EDUCATION. New York: Oxford University Press, 1977. 670 p.

Contributors Daniel Bell, Samuel Bowles, Martin Trow, and
others discuss the role, content, and schools of thought on
educational research in higher education.

1448 Karagueuzian, Dikram. BLOW IT UP! THE BLACK STUDENT REVOLT
AT SAN FRANCISCO STATE COLLEGE AND THE EMERGENCE OF DR.
HAYAKAWA. Ipswich, Mass.: Gambit, 1971. 196 p.

San Francisco State's former student newspaper editor describes
major events in the institution's student revolt.

1449 Karwin, Thomas J. FLYING A LEARNING CENTER: DESIGN AND
COSTS OF AN OFF-CAMPUS SPACE FOR LEARNING. Berkeley, Calif.:
Carnegie Commission on Higher Education, 1973. 29 p.

Technical report on design and costs of physical facilities for
off-campus learning programs.

1450 Katsh, Abraham I. HEBREW IN AMERICAN HIGHER EDUCATION AND
AN ANALYSIS OF HEBREW INFLUENCE ON AMERICAN LIFE. New York:
New York University Bookstore, 1941. 182 p.

Hebrew and the Judaic tradition in America and its status in
American higher education.

1451 Katz, Joseph, ed. SERVICES FOR STUDENTS. San Francisco: Jossey-
Bass Publishers, 1973. 144 p.

Focuses on such services as housing, advising, and psychiatric
help. Emphasizes the humanizing and learning function of student services.

1452 Katz, Joseph, and Hartnett, Rodney T. SCHOLARS IN THE MAKING:
THE DEVELOPMENT OF GRADUATE AND PROFESSIONAL STUDENTS. Cambridge, Mass.: Ballinger Publishing Co., 1976. 288 p.

Historical overview of U.S. graduate education, student characteristics, admissions, learning environment, and reputations.
Chapters on women and minorities; and a 1930 to 1970s comparison of Harvard University and the University of California
at Berkeley.

1453 Katz, Joseph, et al. EDUCATIONAL AND OCCUPATIONAL ASPIRA-

TIONS OF ADULT WOMEN. Stanford, Calif.: Institute for the Study of Human Problems, Stanford University, 1970. 261 p.

Role conflicts of college educated women, their career choice, alumnae attitudes toward career and family life, and women's image in popular women's magazines.

1454 _____. NO TIME FOR YOUTH: GROWTH AND CONSTRAINT IN COLLEGE STUDENTS. San Francisco: Jossey-Bass Publishers, 1968. 463 p.

Study of 3,500 freshmen and interviews with two hundred of them during subsequent four years. Includes two detailed case studies; a section on differences in the way students learn, their motivations, and the interplay of choice and coercion in career decisions.

1455 Katz, Michael B. CLASS, BUREAUCRACY, AND SCHOOLS: THE ILLU-SION OF EDUCATIONAL CHANGE IN AMERICA. Exp. ed. New York: Praeger Publishers, 1975. 208 p.

Author believes that reform of public and higher education is not possible until bureaucracy is eliminated.

1456 Kaufman, Martin. AMERICAN MEDICAL EDUCATION: THE FORMATIVE YEARS, 1765-1910. Westport, Conn.: Greenwood Press, 1976. 208 p.

Analyzes forces that changed U.S. medical education, among them scientific discoveries, education for other professions, the American Medical Association, and the Association of American Medical Colleges.

1457 Kaufman, Myron S. REMEMBER ME TO GOD. Philadelphia: J.B. Lippincott Co., 1957. 640 p.

Novel about a sensitive Jewish Harvard undergraduate undergoing a religious crisis at home and at college.

1458 Kaufmann, William. ONE BOOK/FIVE WAYS: THE PUBLISHING PRO-CEDURES OF FIVE UNIVERSITY PRESSES. Edited by Association of American University Presses. Los Altos, Calif.: William Kaufmann, 1979. 337 p.

Compares publishing procedures when one manuscript was submitted to five presses.

1459 Kavanaugh, Robert. THE GRIM GENERATION. New York: Trident Press, 1970. 219 p.

Says college students are overprivileged but deadly serious about fighting social injustice. Favors elimination of in loco parentis service to youth and the return of effective teaching.

1460 Kaylor, Paul E., ed. THE EARLY COLLEGE IN THEORY AND PRAC-
TICE. Great Barrington, Mass.: Simon's Rock Early College, 1978.
94 p.

> Assesses Simon's Rock Early College's first decade. Compares
> the early-college concept, which combines the last two years
> of high school with the first two years of college, to early
> admissions options of other institutions.

1461 Kaysen, Carl. THE HIGHER LEARNING, THE UNIVERSITIES, AND THE
PUBLIC. Princeton, N.J.: Princeton University Press, 1969. 85 p.

> Economist appeals for federal funding of public and private
> higher education, particularly for science research.

1462 Keats, John. THE SHEEPSKIN PSYCHOSIS. Philadelphia: J.B. Lippincott Co., 1965. 190 p.

> Journalist indicts universities for not being more selective; sug-
> gests alternatives for youths with no sound educational reason
> for entering college, whose status-seeking parents push them
> into college.

1463 Keene, Roland, et al., eds. MONEY, MARBLES, OR CHALK: STUDENT
FINANCIAL SUPPORT IN HIGHER EDUCATION. Carbondale: Southern
Illinois University Press, 1975. 343 p.

> Essays on higher education student financial aid: its philosophy,
> history, development, programs, problems, administration, and
> professional careers in financial aid.

1464 Keeslar, Oreon. FINANCIAL AIDS FOR HIGHER EDUCATION: 76-77
CATALOG. Dubuque, Iowa: William C. Brown, 1976. 699 p.

> Guide to 3,400 higher education financial aid programs, ar-
> ranged in sixteen categories; for high school seniors, parents,
> and counselors.

1465 Keeton, Morris T. MODELS AND MAVERICKS; A PROFILE OF PRIVATE
LIBERAL ARTS COLLEGES. New York: McGraw-Hill Book Co., 1971.
191 p.

> Carnegie Commission reports that private liberal arts colleges
> should have higher academic aims but also enroll more students,
> a goal that is possible only with more tax support for students
> and more efficient management.

1466 Keeton, Morris T., and Tate, Pamela J., eds. LEARNING BY EXPER-
IENCE--WHAT, WHY, HOW. San Francisco: Jossey-Bass Publishers, 1978.
109 p.

Recent trends in giving academic credit for on- or off-campus experiences, the problem of maintaining quality, and ways to justify such credits to accrediting agencies.

1467 Keeton, Morris T., et al. EXPERIENTIAL LEARNING: RATIONALE, CHARACTERISTICS, AND ASSESSMENT. San Francisco: Jossey-Bass Publishers, 1976. 265 p.

Defines experiential learning (work-study-travel), and shows how it is currently being measured, assessed, and credited. Discusses factors to be considered in improving assessment practices.

1468 _____. SHARED AUTHORITY ON CAMPUS. Washington, D.C.: American Association for Higher Education, 1971. 166 p.

Based on an extensive study of campus governance. Concludes that campuses need a wider sharing of authority but does not dictate a precise governance pattern.

1469 Keezer, Dexter M., ed. FINANCING HIGHER EDUCATION, 1960-70. New York: McGraw-Hill Book Co., 1959. 304 p.

Papers on financing higher education during growth expected in the 1960s; discusses efficiency, students, government and private support, and research contracts.

1470 Kellams, Samuel E. EMERGING SOURCES OF STUDENT INFLUENCE. Washington, D.C.: American Association for Higher Education, 1976. 55 p.

Finds that college students express their concerns and exert influence through such established routes as student government and through separate student lobbies and interest groups. The latter seems most promising for expanding and legitimatizing student power.

1471 Kelley, Brooks Mather. YALE: A HISTORY. New Haven, Conn.: Yale University Press, 1974. 588 p.

Yale history, 1701-1963, divided into administrative periods. The theme is its emergence as a major university. Emphasizes that Yale's funds have always been from public as well as private sources.

1472 Kelley, Janet Agnes. COLLEGE LIFE AND THE MORES. New York: Teachers College, Columbia University, 1949. 308 p.

Used anthropological and sociological methods and language to study the college as a society with a distinctive culture.

1473 Kelley, Win, and Wilbur, Leslie. TEACHING IN THE COMMUNITY JUNIOR COLLEGE. New York: Appleton-Century-Crofts, 1970. 295 p.

>For prospective community college faculty: brief history, employment requirements, professional duties and functions, and advice on effective teaching practices.

1474 Kelly, Frederick James. TOWARD BETTER COLLEGE TEACHING. Washington, D.C.: Government Printing Office, 1950. 71 p.

>Methods and devices for improving undergraduate teaching include faculty evaluation by themselves, their students, and alumni; and at the graduate level, recruitment and apprentice teaching.

1475 _____. VOCATIONAL EDUCATION OF COLLEGE GRADE. Washington, D.C.: Government Printing Office, 1946. 126 p.

>Describes vocational education programs, their teaching staffs and instructional methods, in sixteen representative higher education institutions.

1476 _____, ed. IMPROVING COLLEGE INSTRUCTION. Washington, D.C.: American Council on Education, 1951. 195 p.

>On improving college teaching by such methods as setting course objectives and improving faculty performance.

1477 Kelly, Frederick James, and McNeely, John H. THE STATE AND HIGHER EDUCATION: PHASES OF THEIR RELATIONSHIP. New York: Carnegie Foundation for the Advancement of Teaching, 1933. 282 p.

>Examines need for statewide coordination of higher education to reduce duplication between private and public institutions. Cites differences in states' ability to support education. Gives examples of ways several states coordinate their higher education.

1478 Kelly, Robert Glynn. A LAMENT FOR BARNEY STONE. New York: Holt, Rinehart and Winston, 1961. 255 p.

>Novel about an English professor about to be appointed dean when a scandal threatens his career.

1479 Kelly, Robert Lincoln. THE AMERICAN COLLEGES AND THE SOCIAL ORDER. New York: Macmillan Co., 1940. 380 p.

>Historical study from colonial times to the 1930s. Chapters on academic freedom, finance, and relations between college and church and college and state.

1480 Kelman, Steven. PUSH COMES TO SHOVE: THE ESCALATION OF STU-DENT PROTEST. Boston: Houghton Mifflin Co., 1970. 287 p.

A Harvard student's diary of his first two years (1966–68) at Harvard and his analysis of the 1968 Harvard student strike.

1481 Kelsey, Roger R. AAHE BIBLIOGRAPHY ON HIGHER EDUCATION. Washington, D.C.: American Association for Higher Education, 1970. 60 p.

Includes 1,473 current books (excluding texts) on higher education, classified under sixteen headings.

1482 Kemeny, John G. RANDOM ESSAYS ON MATHEMATICS, EDUCATION AND COMPUTERS. Englewood Cliffs, N.J.: Prentice-Hall, 1964. 163 p.

Math and math-computer courses for college liberal arts students particularly, as well as for those in physics and engineering. Presents a Dartmouth College experimental math plan.

1483 Kemerer, Frank R., and Baldridge, J. Victor. UNIONS ON CAMPUS: A NATIONAL STUDY OF THE CONSEQUENCES OF FACULTY BAR-GAINING. San Francisco: Jossey-Bass Publishers, 1975. 248 p.

How collective bargaining affects higher education governance. Critical interpretation from presidents, other administrators, and faculty in 511 colleges and universities, unionized and non-unionized.

1484 Kemerer, Frank R., and Satryb, Ronald P., eds. FACING FINANCIAL EXIGENCY. Lexington, Mass.: Lexington Books, 1977. 137 p.

Articles on ways to cope with higher education finances by efficient management techniques and planning systems.

1485 Kempton, Kenneth Payson. SO DREAM ALL NIGHT. New York: G.P. Putnam's Sons, 1941. 296 p.

Novel about Harvard English instructor and his growing family trying to make ends meet during the 1920s and 1930s.

1486 Kendall, Elaine. PECULIAR INSTITUTIONS: AN INFORMAL HISTORY OF THE SEVEN SISTER COLLEGES. New York: G.P. Putnam's Sons, 1976. 272 p.

History of seven eastern women's colleges (1830s-1970s): founders, students' life and customs, and the varied nature of feminism over these years.

1487 Kendall, Katherine A. REFLECTIONS ON SOCIAL WORK EDUCATION,

1950–1978. New York: International Association of Schools of Social Work, 1978. 201 p.

Author's articles and speeches during many years in international social work education.

1488 Keniston, Kenneth. THE UNCOMMITTED: ALIENATED YOUTH IN AMERICAN SOCIETY. New York: Harcourt, Brace and World, 1965. 500 p.

Examines characteristics and origins of college student alienation. Concludes that alienation is a response to one's early development and to rapid social change and will end only when society changes and individuals develop a greater capacity for commitment and dedication.

1489 _____. YOUNG RADICALS: NOTES ON COMMITTED YOUTH. New York: Harcourt, Brace and World, 1968. 368 p.

Interviews with fourteen college student activists reveal social and historical forces which led to their political commitment.

1490 Kennedy, Gail, ed. EDUCATION AT AMHERST: THE NEW PROGRAM. New York: Harper and Brothers, 1955. 331 p.

Major curricular and other changes Amherst undertook in 1945 which stressed honors. Evaluates those changes in 1954, when 46 percent of the graduates received honors degrees.

1491 Kephart, William M., et al. LIBERAL EDUCATION AND BUSINESS. New York: Teachers College, Columbia University, 1963. 110 p.

Reviews the history of business education, curricula, and the attitudes of academic and business communities toward them. Concludes that business schools should not gear themselves only to the highest management levels.

1492 Kerr, Chester. A REPORT ON AMERICAN UNIVERSITY PRESSES. Washington, D.C.: American Council of Learned Societies, 1949. 302 p.

Survey of members of the Association of American University Presses found that their scholarly books and periodicals made a unique contribution to U.S. publishing.

1493 Kerr, Clark. THE URBAN-GRANT UNIVERSITY: A MODEL FOR THE FUTURE. New York: City University of New York, 1968. 15 p.

Suggests that cities of over 250,000 establish urban-grant universities, which would apply for federal grants. Federal government would grant land for such universities as part of urban renewal programs to help solve urban problems.

1494 _____. THE USES OF THE UNIVERSITY. Cambridge, Mass.: Harvard University Press, 1963. 140 p.

> Former University of California president introduced the term "multiversity" to describe the bigness and diversity of American higher education and the changes occurring because of expanding research and mass enrollment.

1495 Kerr, Clark, et al. TWELVE SYSTEMS OF HIGHER EDUCATION: SIX DECISIVE ISSUES. New York: Interbook, 1979. 208 p.

> Comparison of important issues facing higher education in a dozen countries, including France, Germany, Japan, and the United States.

1496 Kershaw, Joseph A. THE VERY SMALL COLLEGE. New York: Ford Foundation, 1976. 24 p.

> Examined three accredited small colleges to see if their small size has made them particularly vulnerable to financial pressures. Concluded that with additional capital and careful management they can survive.

1497 Kertesz, Stephen D., ed. THE TASK OF UNIVERSITIES IN A CHANGING WORLD. Notre Dame, Ind.: University of Notre Dame Press, 1971. 503 p.

> Papers on International higher education: impact of social change in the United States on various disciplines, student unrest in France in partial consequence of unsystematic student selection, and other developments.

1498 Kesselman, Judi R. STOPPING OUT. New York: M. Evans and Co., 1976. 219 p.

> A how-to guide for students wanting to interrupt their college years. Insists that such "stopping out" is a bad idea for most students and that those doing it should have a structured, well-planned experience.

1499 Kevles, Daniel J. THE PHYSICISTS: THE HISTORY OF A SCIENTIFIC COMMUNITY IN MODERN AMERICA. New York: Alfred A. Knopf, 1978. 489 p.

> Historical study of science teaching, especially physics teaching, 1865–1977. Focuses on interaction between professional physics leaders and the several elites who head private philanthropies, major universities, and branches of the federal government. Includes such dynamic physicist politicians as Robert A. Millikan and J. Robert Oppenheimer. Shows science's ties to the military and concedes that relations between democracy and physics, always difficult, are likely to remain so.

1500 Kidd, Charles V. AMERICAN UNIVERSITIES AND FEDERAL RESEARCH. Cambridge, Mass.: Harvard University Press, 1959. 272 p.

Author believes post–World War II federal support of research in American universities should continue; he explains potential benefits and hazards.

1501 Kidd, James Robbins. FINANCING CONTINUING EDUCATION. New York: Scarecrow Press, 1962. 209 p.

Analysis of the growing problem of adult education financing, with a call for extensive federal support.

1502 Kiely, Margaret. COMPARISONS OF STUDENTS OF TEACHERS COL-LEGES AND STUDENTS OF LIBERAL-ARTS COLLEGES. Contributions to Education No. 440. New York: Teachers College, Columbia University, 1931. 147 p.

Found many similarities between liberal arts students and teachers' college students. Concluded that teacher training institutions should include more arts courses and that liberal arts colleges should stop opposing professional training for teachers.

1503 Kimmons, Willie James. BLACK ADMINISTRATORS IN PUBLIC AND COMMUNITY COLLEGES: SELF-PERCEIVED ROLE AND STATUS. New York: Carleton Press, 1977. 202 p.

Studied black administrators' attitudes toward their jobs, relationships with colleagues, and personal and professional backgrounds. Found that attitudes varied with the racial composition of the institutions where black administrators worked.

1504 Kinder, James S. THE INTERNAL ADMINISTRATION OF THE LIBERAL ARTS COLLEGE. Contributions to Education No. 597. New York: Teachers College, Columbia University, 1934. 160 p.

Analyzed administration at 116 colleges and universities. Listed seventeen principles of administration and discussed how institutions studied were employing them.

1505 King, Lauriston R. THE WASHINGTON LOBBYISTS FOR HIGHER EDU-CATION. Lexington, Mass.: D.C. Heath and Co., 1975. 127 p.

Describes the Washington-based higher education lobbies; reviews historically the growth of major higher education associations and differences between them.

1506 Kinley, David. THE AUTOBIOGRAPHY OF DAVID KINLEY. Urbana: University of Illinois Press, 1949. 167 p.

Scottish-born (1861) Kinley, educated in the United States,

served the University of Illinois in many posts, including president (1920-30).

1507 Kinsella, Susan. FOOD ON CAMPUS: A RECIPE FOR ACTION. Emmaus, Pa.: Rodale Press, 1978. 160 p.

Many college food services provide nutritionally inadequate food. Proposes ways students can improve their cafeterias' quality. Explains how many campus cafeterias are managed and includes questions to use in evaluating food quality.

1508 Kintzer, Frederick C. ARTICULATION AND TRANSFER, TOPICAL PAPER NO. 59. Los Angeles: ERIC Clearinghouse for Junior Colleges, University of California, 1977. 46 p.

State and federal funding policies and higher education curricular factors affecting student transfer options. Examines government guidelines for: (1) transferring credits and courses, and (2) awarding formal credit to adults in nontraditional education programs.

1509 _____. MIDDLEMAN IN HIGHER EDUCATION: IMPROVING ARTICULATION AMONG HIGH SCHOOL, COMMUNITY COLLEGE, AND SENIOR INSTITUTIONS. San Francisco: Jossey-Bass Publishers, 1973. 188 p.

Policies and problems of each state and Canadian province in the upward transfer of students from high school to junior college to senior college.

1510 Kirk, Russell Amos. ACADEMIC FREEDOM: AN ESSAY IN DEFINITION. Chicago: Henry Regnery, 1955. 210 p.

Examines academic freedom, which author calls a precious inheritance that must be saved for future generations.

1511 _____. DECADENCE AND RENEWAL IN THE HIGHER LEARNING: AN EPISODIC HISTORY OF AMERICAN UNIVERSITY AND COLLEGE SINCE 1953. South Bend, Ind.: Gateway Editions, 1978. 354 p.

Labels as decadent the multiversity and the typical campus which by 1977 was a place for "fun and games." Feeling hopeful because he thinks higher education can hardly get worse, Kirk favors reforms such as the external degree and the "free" colleges which hold classes off-campus.

1512 Kirschner, Alan H. UNITED NEGRO COLLEGE FUND STATISTICAL REPORT OF THE MEMBER INSTITUTIONS. New York: United Negro College Fund, 1978. 51 p.

Enrollment, degrees, faculty, and financial data on forty-one member institutions.

1513 Kitzhaber, Albert R. THEMES, THEORIES, AND THERAPY: THE TEACH-
ING OF WRITING IN COLLEGE. New York: McGraw-Hill Book Co.,
1963. 175 p.

> President of the National Council of Teachers of English gives
> history, critique, and recommendations for improving college
> freshman composition course.

1514 Kitzhaber, Albert R., et al. EDUCATION FOR COLLEGE: IMPROVING THE
HIGH SCHOOL CURRICULUM. New York: Ronald Press Co., 1961. 195 p.

> Report on the 1958-59 Portland, Oregon, study of what sub-
> jects high school students should be taught in preparation for
> college.

1515 Klassen, Frank H., and Gollnick, Donna M., eds. PLURALISM AND THE
AMERICAN TEACHER: ISSUES AND CASE STUDIES. Washington, D.C.:
American Association of Colleges for Teacher Education, 1977. 252 p.

> Eleven papers on multicultural education in teacher education.

1516 Klein, Barry T., ed. GUIDE TO AMERICAN EDUCATIONAL DIRECTO-
RIES. 4th ed. Rye, N.Y.: Todd Publications, 1976. 364 p.

> Lists by subject over 2,500 education information directories
> which describe colleges and universities, employment services,
> financial aid, government agencies, libraries, museums, re-
> search groups, and members of academic disciplines and the
> professions.

1517 Kline, Morris. WHY THE PROFESSOR CAN'T TEACH: MATHEMATICS
AND THE DILEMMA OF UNIVERSITY EDUCATION. New York: St.
Martin's Press, 1978. 288 p.

> Fundamental conflict between research and teaching, as exem-
> plified in college mathematics departments. The author be-
> lieves teaching is a valid specialization in itself. Recommends
> separating graduate and undergraduate education, and having
> research universities discontinue undergraduate education.

1518 Klineberg, Otto. INTERNATIONAL EDUCATIONAL EXCHANGE: AN
ASSESSMENT OF ITS NATURE AND ITS PROSPECTS. Atlantic Highlands,
N.J.: Humanities Press, 1977. 270 p.

> Describes, compares, and assesses benefits of study-abroad pro-
> grams in France, Great Britain, India, Japan, the United States,
> West Germany, and Yugoslavia.

1519 Klineberg, Otto, et al. STUDENTS, VALUES, AND POLITICS: A CROSS-
CULTURAL COMPARISON. New York: Free Press, 1978. 342 p.

Survey of ten thousand young people in eleven countries in 1969-70 found some common attitudes, such as opposition to racism and nationalism. But other strikingly different views were held about the university, political and social systems, and cultural and moral values.

1520 Klopf, Gordon John. COLLEGE STUDENT GOVERNMENT. 4th ed. New York: Harper and Brothers, 1960. 105 p.

Student government manual prepared for the National Student Association on: (1) developing student leadership, (2) student participation in college administration, and (3) college staff and student relations.

1521 Klotsche, J. Martin. THE URBAN UNIVERSITY: AND THE FUTURE OF OUR CITIES. New York: Harper and Row, 1966. 149 p.

Study of urban universities, which enroll about half of U.S. higher education students, by the chancellor, University of Wisconsin-Milwaukee; on trends, special roles, and proposals for new courses.

1522 Knapp, Joan, and Hamilton, I. Bruce. THE EFFECT OF NONSTANDARD UNDERGRADUATE ASSESSMENT AND REPORTING PRACTICES ON THE GRADUATE SCHOOL ADMISSIONS PROCESS. Princeton, N.J.: Educational Testing Service, 1979. 64 p.

Study of thirty-five graduate schools on such problems as credit by examination, prior learning, field experience, narrative transcripts, and pass-fail grading.

1523 Knapp, Robert H. THE ORIGINS OF AMERICAN HUMANISTIC SCHOLARS. Englewood Cliffs, N.J.: Prentice-Hall, 1964. 172 p.

Studied U.S. doctoral graduates in history, English, languages, fine arts, and music, from 1936 to 1959. Found that the humanities are dominated by eastern institutions which mistakenly define objectives too narrowly and extend graduate programs too long.

1524 Knapp, Robert H., and Goodrich, H.B. ORIGINS OF AMERICAN SCIENTISTS. Chicago: University of Chicago Press, 1952. 450 p.

Found in study of 489 U.S. undergraduate colleges that most future science Ph.D.s attended small private liberal arts colleges with high faculty-student ratio; these strongly support the science faculty and include at least one distinguished teacher.

1525 Knapp, Robert H., and Greenbaum, Joseph J. THE YOUNGER AMERICAN SCHOLAR: HIS COLLEGIATE ORIGINS. Chicago: University of Chicago Press, 1953. 122 p.

Studied post-1946 Ph.D.s in humanities, social sciences, and natural sciences from twenty-five graduate schools which grant most U.S. doctorates. Found that most attended high-cost eastern undergraduate institutions, a concentration of which the authors disapproved.

1526 Knauth, E. Frederic. COLLEGE BUSINESS MANAGER. New York: New York University Press, 1955. 166 p.

Study of eighty-nine chief business officers of small, liberal, independent colleges.

1527 Knepper, Edwin G. THE HISTORY OF BUSINESS EDUCATION IN THE UNITED STATES. Ann Arbor, Mich.: Edwards Brothers, 1941. 221 p.

History of U.S. business education: the rise of business schools (1852-93), the impact of the typewriter (perfected 1873), and the twentieth century when business courses moved into post-secondary institutions.

1528 Knepper, George W. NEW LAMPS FOR OLD, A CENTENNIAL PUBLI-CATION: ONE HUNDRED YEARS OF URBAN EDUCATION AT THE UNI-VERSITY OF AKRON. Akron, Ohio: University of Akron Press, 1970. 407 p.

Centennial history focusing on administrators, benefactors, student life, general education, and prospects for municipal universities.

1529 Knight, Douglas M., ed. THE FEDERAL GOVERNMENT AND HIGHER EDUCATION. Englewood Cliffs, N.J.: Prentice-Hall, 1960. 208 p.

History and problems of federal aid to higher education, with recommendations.

1530 Knight, Edgar W. WHAT COLLEGE PRESIDENTS SAY. Chapel Hill: University of North Carolina Press, 1940. 377 p.

Statements by college presidents (1827-1940) on important aspects of higher education: faculty relations and societal obligations. Concluding summary.

1531 Knight, Edgar W., and Hall, Clifton L. READINGS IN AMERICAN EDU-CATIONAL HISTORY. New York: Appleton-Century-Crofts, 1951. 799 p.

Excellent compilation with comments on U.S. educational history documents, including origins of colonial colleges, early and important state universities, foundations aiding higher education, early women's colleges, and other aspects of higher education.

1532 Knipp, Anna Heubeck, and Thomas, Thaddeus P. THE HISTORY OF GOUCHER COLLEGE. Baltimore, Md.: Goucher College, 1938. 659 p.

> Goucher's first fifty years, reflecting changes in women's education.

1533 Knoell, Dorothy M. BLACK STUDENT POTENTIAL. New York: American Association of Junior Colleges, 1970. 78 p.

> College attendance in 1968 of black and white high school graduates in five cities. In three cities the attendance rate was lower for blacks, but those blacks in college (many of them junior colleges) received much parental encouragement.

1534 _____. PEOPLE WHO NEED COLLEGE: A REPORT ON STUDENTS WE HAVE YET TO SERVE. Washington, D.C.: American Association of Junior Colleges, 1970. 182 p.

> Attitudes, characteristics, and potential of one thousand urban black community college students. Recommends identifying less able students in high school and developing community college programs to help them succeed.

1535 _____. TOWARD EDUCATIONAL OPPORTUNITY FOR ALL. Albany: State University of New York, 1966. 220 p.

> Unmet postsecondary education needs which the State University of New York might meet through two-year colleges. Wants improved counseling, universities to offer remedial work, and more opportunities in existing two-year colleges.

1536 Knoell, Dorothy M., and McIntyre, Charles. PLANNING COLLEGES FOR THE COMMUNITY. San Francisco: Jossey-Bass Publishers, 1974. 149 p.

> Guide to developing more efficient community college master plans. Shows how to increase access to college and how to provide a variety of adult education.

1537 Knoell, Dorothy M., and Medsker, Leland L. FROM JUNIOR TO SENIOR COLLEGE: A NATIONAL STUDY OF THE TRANSFER STUDENT. Washington, D.C.: American Council on Education, 1965. 102 p.

> Evaluates the junior college function by assessing characteristics and performance of transfers to four-year colleges.

1538 Knoll, Robert E., and Brown, Robert D. EXPERIMENT AT NEBRASKA: THE FIRST TWO YEARS OF A CLUSTER COLLEGE. Lincoln: University of Nebraska, 1972. 127 p.

> Tribulations of innovative University of Nebraska lower division

undergraduate residential program whose curriculum theme was "The Nature of Change."

1539 Knorr, Owen A., ed. LONG-RANGE PLANNING IN HIGHER EDUCA-TION. Boulder, Colo.: Western Interstate Commission for Higher Education, 1965. 128 p.

Conference papers on higher education planning; discussed design and change in higher education, autonomy and coordination, housing educational programs, financial planning, and systems analysis in planning.

1540 Knorr, Owen A., and Minter, W. John, eds. ORDER AND FREEDOM CAMPUS. Boulder, Colo.: Western Interstate Commission on Higher Education, 1965. 100 p.

Well-known educators and student activists discussed changing patterns of university authority, student unrest, and the 1964 Berkeley revolt.

1541 Knowles, Asa S., ed. HANDBOOK OF COLLEGE AND UNIVERSITY ADMINISTRATION. 2 vols. New York: McGraw-Hill Book Co., 1970. 1,100 p., 1,300 p.

Encyclopedic view of higher education administration operating procedures and practices. Volume one, on general administration: legal aspects, governing boards, and institutional research; volume two, on academic administration: admissions, learning resources, and student personnel administration.

1542 _____. THE INTERNATIONAL ENCYCLOPEDIA OF HIGHER EDUCATION. 10 vols. San Francisco: Jossey-Bass Publishers, 1977. 5,208 p.

Omnibus, comprehensive, A-Z coverage of all aspects of higher education in the United States and abroad, including history, operating characteristics, finance, legal, and all other aspects of all kinds of higher education institutions, related organizations and centers, public and private concerns, and state-federal-regional relations in every major world country and geographical area.

1543 Knowles, Asa S., et al. HANDBOOK OF COOPERATIVE EDUCATION. San Francisco: Jossey-Bass Publishers, 1971. 386 p.

Higher education students in work experiences: its history, values, objectives, types of programs, administration, and relevance to women and minorities; facts and illustrations are drawn from Northeastern University where Knowles is president, but with wide U.S. application and some developments in Canada and England discussed.

1544 Knowles, John H., ed. VIEWS OF MEDICAL EDUCATION AND MEDI-
CAL CARE. Cambridge, Mass.: Harvard University Press, 1968. 178 p.

Essays on the shortage of competent medical education faculty
and the need for behavioral and social science in medical
training.

1545 Knowles, Malcolm S. THE ADULT EDUCATION MOVEMENT IN THE
UNITED STATES. New York: Holt, Rinehart and Winston, 1962. 335 p.

Comprehensive history of adult education from the colonial
period. Part 1, influence of social change and adult education's effect on national culture. Part 2, organizations which
coordinate adult education. Part 3, future trends.

1546 Knox, Alan Boyd. ADULT DEVELOPMENT AND LEARNING: A HAND-
BOOK ON INDIVIDUAL GROWTH AND COMPETENCE IN THE ADULT
YEARS FOR EDUCATION AND THE HELPING PROFESSIONS. San Fran-
cisco: Jossey-Bass Publishers, 1977. 679 p.

Information on the most effective circumstances for adult education, changes in learning abilities with age, and the effect
of family, social activities, education, occupation, personality,
and health on development and learning.

1547 Koch, Carl, and Brazil, James M. STRATEGIES FOR TEACHING THE
COMPOSITION PROCESS. Urbana, Ill.: National Council of Teachers
of English, 1978. 108 p.

Practical tips for teaching writing to high school and college
students, including choosing a topic, writing, and criticizing
the essay.

1548 Koch, James V., and Chizmar, John R., Jr. THE ECONOMIC EFFECTS
OF AFFIRMATIVE ACTION. Lexington, Mass.: Lexington Books, 1976.
158 p.

Involves salary increments for women faculty members at Illinois State University. Describes a general method of evaluating
such an affirmative action program.

1549 Koch, Vivienne. CHANGE OF LOVE. New York: McDowell, Obolensky,
1960. 216 p.

Novel about a southern university professor as a Fulbright fellow; depicts American academic culture abroad.

1550 Koefod, Paul E. THE WRITING REQUIREMENTS FOR GRADUATE DE-
GREES. Englewood Cliffs, N.J.: Prentice-Hall, 1964. 268 p.

The milieu in which academic writing is done. Essays on research and creativity; has lists of model doctoral dissertations and master's theses.

1551 Koerner, James D. THE MISEDUCATION OF AMERICAN TEACHERS. Boston: Houghton Mifflin Co., 1963. 360 p.

Critical appraisal of teacher education programs and suggestions for upgrading their curriculum.

1552 Kolstoe, Oliver P. COLLEGE PROFESSORING: OR, THROUGH ACADEMIA WITH GUN AND CAMERA. Carbondale: Southern Illinois University Press, 1975. 150 p.

Comical look at the life of a college professor, from being hired to coping as a scholar.

1553 Koltai, Leslie, ed. MERGING THE HUMANITIES. San Francisco: Jossey-Bass Publishers, 1975. 105 p.

About teaching humanities in community colleges. Includes methods for enlivening courses and integrating the humanities with communication skills.

1554 Komarovsky, Mirra. WOMEN IN THE MODERN WORLD: THEIR EDUCATION AND THEIR DILEMMAS. Boston: Little, Brown and Co., 1953. 319 p.

Discussion of varying roles at different periods, the impact of technology, increasing opportunity for careers, and the effect of these factors on higher education. Chapter on "Towards a Philosophy of Women's Education."

1555 Koon, Jeff, ed. LOWER DIVISION EDUCATION AT BERKELEY: THE STUDENTS' ASSESSMENT. Berkeley: Associated Students, University of California, 1978. 60 p.

Student evaluations of lower division programs in five colleges at University of California, Berkeley.

1556 Koos, Leonard V. THE COMMUNITY COLLEGE STUDENT. Gainesville: University of Florida Press, 1970. 580 p.

Synthesizes research findings and descriptive literature to profile community college students: (1) physical, mental, and social development; (2) aptitudes, academic competence, and personal problems; and (3) implications for curriculum development and student personnel services.

1557 _____. INTEGRATING HIGH SCHOOL AND COLLEGE. New York: Harper and Brothers, 1946. 208 p.

A plea to combine the last two high school years with the first two years of college. Cites examples at the undergraduate college of the University of Chicago and at Pasadena (California) Junior College.

1558 Kopenhaver, Lillian Lodge, and Click, J. William. ETHICS AND RE-SPONSIBLITIES OF ADVISING COLLEGE STUDENT PUBLICATIONS. Athens, Ohio: National Council of College Publications Advisers, 1978. 52 p.

Guide for advisers for student newspapers, magazines, and yearbooks, including codes of ethics and professional standards.

1559 Kotschnig, Walter M. UNEMPLOYMENT IN THE LEARNED PROFESSIONS. London: Oxford University Press, 1937. 347 p.

Study of worldwide unemployment among college graduates. Discusses the great desire for higher education, overcrowding of universities, and country-by-country problems of the learned professions. Describes attempts to balance educational output with professional and social needs.

1560 Kotschnig, Walter M., and Prys, Elined, eds. THE UNIVERSITY IN A CHANGING WORLD, A SYMPOSIUM. London: Oxford University Press, 1932. 244 p.

Concept of universities in France, Germany, Britain, the United States, Italy, and the Soviet Union. One essayist scores American universities as lacking purposes or values, in contrast to foreign universities.

1561 Kozma, Robert B., et al. INSTRUCTIONAL TECHNIQUES IN HIGHER EDUCATION. Englewood Cliffs, N.J.: Educational Technology Publications, 1978. 419 p.

Handbook explaining more than a dozen teaching methods for college and university faculty members.

1562 Kozol, Jonathan. THE FUME OF POPPIES. Boston: Houghton Mifflin Co., 1958. 181 p.

Novel about Harvard college students in and out of love.

1563 Kraft, Leonard E., and Casey, John P., eds. ROLES IN OFF-CAMPUS STUDENT TEACHING. Champaign, Ill.: Stipes Publishing Co., 1967. 318 p.

Readings on the roles of student teachers, cooperating teachers, and college supervisors.

1564 Kramer, Howard C., and Gardner, Robert E. ADVISING BY FACULTY. Washington, D.C.: National Education Association, 1977. 56 p.

Guidelines for faculty members who are academic advisers for students.

1565 Kramer, Rena, et al. DISTRIBUTION OF GRADES: 1972. New York: City University of New York, 1974. 37 p.

Study of grade distribution at four-year colleges of City University of New York.

1566 Krathwohl, David Reading, et al. TAXONOMY OF EDUCATIONAL OBJECTIVES: THE CLASSIFICATION OF EDUCATIONAL GOALS. HANDBOOK 2. AFFECTIVE DOMAIN. New York: David McKay Co., 1964. 196 p.

Analysis of educational goals applied to higher education.

1567 Krichmar, Albert, et al. THE WOMEN'S MOVEMENT IN THE SEVENTIES: AN INTERNATIONAL ENGLISH-LANGUAGE BIBLIOGRAPHY. Metuchen, N.J.: Scarecrow Press, 1977. 875 p.

Over 8,600 partially annotated books, reports, articles, and dissertations on women's activities in nearly one hundred countries. Many of the entries are on women's education, including higher education, in the United States and abroad.

1568 Kriegel, Leonard. WORKING THROUGH: A TEACHER'S JOURNEY IN THE URBAN UNIVERSITY. New York: Saturday Review Press, 1972. 210 p.

Author describes and compares problems of four New York City universities where he taught: Columbia University, New York University, City University of New York, and Long Island University.

1569 Kruytbosch, Carlos E., and Messinger, Sheldon L., eds. THE STATE OF THE UNIVERSITY: AUTHORITY AND CHANGE. Beverly Hills, Calif.: Sage Publications, 1970. 379 p.

Essays, both liberal and conservative, about unrest at University of California at Berkeley, the nature of the university, students, research, the presidency, and faculty participation in governance.

1570 Kuder, Merle S. TRENDS OF PROFESSIONAL OPPORTUNITIES IN THE LIBERAL ARTS COLLEGE. Contributions to Education No. 717. New York: Teachers College, Columbia University, 1937. 236 p.

Fifty-year analysis of catalogs (1883-1934) from eleven New

England independent liberal arts colleges shows trends in employment, faculty duties, promotion, tenure, and training of teachers and other personnel. Found rapid growth of non-teaching positions, tendency toward increased specialization, greater number of faculty with Ph.D. degrees, more women teachers in coeducational institutions, and delay in women faculty promotions.

1571 Kuder, Merle S., and McClane, Douglas V., eds. MAPPING YOUR EDUCATION. Portland, Oreg.: Abbott, Kerns, and Bell Co., 1947. 210 p.

Discusses career planning and higher education and provides information on fourteen colleges in Oregon and fifteen colleges in Washington.

1572 Kuhlman, A.F. COLLEGE AND UNIVERSITY LIBRARY SERVICE. Chicago: American Library Association, 1937. 159 p.

Trends, standards, reserve book systems, regional bibliography, indexes and abstracts of periodical literature, and the education of librarians for higher education library services.

1573 _____ . THE NORTH TEXAS REGIONAL LIBRARIES: AN INQUIRY INTO THE FEASIBILITY AND DESIRABILITY OF DEVELOPING THEM AS A CO-OPERATIVE ENTERPRISE. Nashville, Tenn.: George Peabody College for Teachers Press, 1943. 85 p.

Survey of library needs of six North Texas higher education institutions, with recommendations for regional cooperation.

1574 Kuklick, Bruce. THE RISE OF AMERICAN PHILOSOPHY: CAMBRIDGE, MASSACHUSETTS, 1860–1930. New Haven, Conn.: Yale University Press, 1977. 720 p.

Author shows that Harvard philosophers Charles S. Peirce, William James, Josiah Royce, George Santayana, Alfred North Whitehead, and C.I. Lewis influenced an important period in U.S. intellectual history; that from this group arose American pragmatism; and from their students came founders and faculty of major U.S. university philosophy departments.

1575 Kunen, James S. THE STRAWBERRY STATEMENT. New York: Random House, 1969. 176 p.

Personal account of 1968 Columbia University student riots.

1576 Kunz, James W. HOW TO RECRUIT HIGH SCHOOL STUDENTS. Kansas City, Mo.: National Research Center for College and University Admissions, 1979. 52 p.

A guide to using direct mail to recruit college students.

1577 Ladd, Dwight R. CHANGE IN EDUCATIONAL POLICY: SELF-STUDIES IN SELECTED COLLEGES AND UNIVERSITIES. New York: McGraw-Hill Book Co., 1970. 231 p.

Reviews, evaluates, and considers the feasibility of change suggested in self-studies made in the 1960s by eleven universities: Michigan State, Duke, Brown, Stanford, UCLA, Berkeley, and others.

1578 Ladd, Everett Carll, Jr., and Lipset, Seymour Martin. THE DIVIDED ACADEMY: PROFESSORS AND POLITICS. New York: McGraw-Hill Book Co., 1975. 407 p.

Data from 600,000 faculty in 1969 and updated 1972 find most to be politically left of center, and affected by their academic discipline, ideology, age, and religion.

1579 _____. PROFESSORS, UNIONS, AND AMERICAN HIGHER EDUCATION. Washington, D.C.: American Enterprise Institute for Public Policy Research, 1973. 124 p.

Relationships between unionization and higher education, containing faculty opinion, characteristics of unionized faculty, and other related facts.

1580 LaFauci, Horatio M., and Richter, Peyton E. TEAM TEACHING AT THE COLLEGE LEVEL. New York: Pergamon Press, 1970. 157 p.

Examines team teaching used in limited courses at Boston University's College of Basic Studies.

1581 Lahti, Robert E. INNOVATIVE COLLEGE MANAGEMENT: IMPLEMENTING PROVEN ORGANIZATIONAL PRACTICE. San Francisco: Jossey-Bass Publishers, 1973. 182 p.

A college president says that professional managerial techniques can result in increased productivity and organizational efficiency. Advocates management by objective; annotated bibliography.

1582 Lambert, Richard D., and Bressler, Marvin. INDIAN STUDENTS ON AN AMERICAN CAMPUS. Minneapolis: University of Minnesota Press, 1956. 122 p.

Found among nineteen South Asian students at the University of Pennsylvania, observed from one to three years, that their cultural and political backgrounds influenced them as students, tourists, and "ambassadors."

1583 Lambie, Morris Bryan, ed. UNIVERSITY TRAINING FOR THE NATIONAL SERVICE. Minneapolis: University of Minnesota Press, 1932. 325 p.

> Conference examined attitudes and responsibilities of universities which train and recruit students for government service careers.

1584 Lamont, Lansing. CAMPUS SHOCK: A FIRSTHAND REPORT ON COLLEGE LIFE TODAY. New York: E.P. Dutton, 1979. 144 p.

> From 675 interviews on eight ivy league campuses plus the universities of Michigan, Chicago, Stanford, and Berkeley, former TIME correspondent reports alarming rise of campus rape, robbery, racial distrust, crowding, cheating, loneliness, grade grubbing, sexual anxiety, blasting stereo noise, and numbing unemployment fears. His proposed reforms include rewarding committed teaching, reducing grading inequities, defusing racial tension, and reinstating single-sex dorms.

1585 Lancaster, Otis E. EFFECTIVE TEACHING AND LEARNING. New York: Gordon and Breach, Science Publishers, 1974. 358 p.

> Overview of the teaching-learning process; for engineering faculties but useful for other fields.

1586 Landeen, William M. E.O. HOLLAND AND THE STATE COLLEGE OF WASHINGTON, 1916-1944. Pullman: State College of Washington, 1958. 454 p.

> Administration and development of the State College of Washington during Ernest Otto Holland's presidency (1916-45).

1587 Landini, Richard G., and Douglas, Patricia P., eds. QUALITY IN HIGHER EDUCATION IN TIMES OF FINANCIAL STRESS. Corvallis: Oregon State University Press, 1976. 80 p.

> Conference on how higher education institutions can survive financial stress.

1588 Landrith, Harold F. INTRODUCTION TO THE COMMUNITY JUNIOR COLLEGE. Danville, Ill.: Interstate Printers and Publishers, 1971. 321 p.

> Faculty discussions on the role and problems of community and junior colleges.

1589 Lane, Harlan L., and Taylor, John H., eds. RESEARCH CONFERENCE ON SOCIAL SCIENCE METHODS AND STUDENT RESIDENCES. Ann Arbor: University of Michigan, 1965. 254 p.

> Social science methodology in studying significant problems about college dormitory life.

1590 Lane, Wheaton J., ed. PICTORIAL HISTORY OF PRINCETON. Princeton, N.J.: Princeton University Press, 1947. 200 p.

Pictures and commentary about the social history of Princeton University, issued at its bicentennial; reflect national political crises, intellectual currents, artistic tastes, and life styles.

1591 Langford, Glenn. TEACHING AS A PROFESSION: AN ESSAY IN THE PHILOSOPHY OF EDUCATION. Totowa, N.J.: Rowman and Littlefield, 1978. 126 p.

Education as practiced by professional teachers is analyzed and parallels are drawn with the legal and medical professions.

1592 Lanier, Lyle H., and Andersen, Charles J. A STUDY OF THE FINANCIAL CONDITION OF COLLEGES AND UNIVERSITIES: 1972-1975. Washington, D.C.: American Council on Education, 1975. 102 p.

Analyzed effects of national inflation-recession conditions on institutions of higher education.

1593 Laque, Carol Feiser, and Sherwood, Phyllis A. A LABORATORY APPROACH TO WRITING. Champaign, Ill.: National Council of Teachers of English, 1977. 135 p.

Emphasizes learning by doing and presents methods, techniques, and exercises for teaching writing in high school and college.

1594 Laqueur, Walter Z., and Labedz, Leopold, eds. THE STATE OF SOVIET STUDIES. Cambridge: MIT Press, 1965. 177 p.

Essays on Soviet studies in the United States and Western Europe; also on American students and American studies in the Soviet Union.

1595 Larson, Jens Frederick, and Palmer, Archie MacInnes. ARCHITECTURAL PLANNING OF THE AMERICAN COLLEGE. New York: McGraw-Hill Book Co., 1933. 181 p.

On choosing the architect and planning the campus and the individual buildings of a liberal arts college; with drawings and photographs.

1596 Lathem, Edward Connery, ed. JOHN SLOAN DICKEY: THE DARTMOUTH EXPERIENCE. Hanover, N.H.: University Press of New England, 1978. 308 p.

Speeches by the president of Dartmouth, 1945-70.

1597 Laudicina, Robert A., and Tramutola, Joseph L., Jr. A LEGAL OVER-

VIEW OF THE NEW STUDENT: AS EDUCATIONAL CONSUMER, CITI-
ZEN, AND BARGAINER. Springfield, Ill.: Charles C Thomas, Publisher,
1977. 299 p.

> Readings on the legal relationships between students and col-
> leges.

1598 Lauwerys, Joseph A., and Scanlon, David G., eds. EXAMINATIONS:
WORLD YEAR BOOK OF EDUCATION 1969. New York: Harcourt,
Brace and World, 1969. 404 p.

> Examination systems and their effects in various countries dis-
> cussed and compared.

1599 Lavin, David E. THE PREDICTION OF ACADEMIC PERFORMANCE: A
THEORETICAL ANALYSIS AND REVIEW OF RESEARCH. New York: Russell Sage Foundation, 1965. 182 p.

> Interprets in psychosociological context over three hundred
> studies (done 1953–61) about predicting college students' aca-
> demic achievement. Suggests future research needs.

1600 _____. STUDENT RETENTION AND GRADUATION AT THE CITY UNI-
VERSITY OF NEW YORK: SEPTEMBER, 1970: ENROLLEES THROUGH
SEVEN SEMESTERS. New York: City University of New York, 1974.
37 p.

> Effects of CUNY's open admissions policy since its September
> 1970 inception.

1601 Lawrence, G. Ben, and Service, Allan L., eds. QUANTITATIVE AP-
PROACHES TO HIGHER EDUCATION MANAGEMENT. Washington, D.C.:
American Association for Higher Education, 1978. 91 p.

> Discusses the origin of resource management in higher educa-
> tion. Advocates standardization of managerial goals and or-
> ganizational principles.

1602 Lawrence, Marcia. HOW TO TAKE THE SAT: SCHOLASTIC APTITUDE
TEST. New York: New American Library, 1979. 372 p.

> "How-to" guide for taking the college admissions test.

1603 Layton, Elizabeth N. SURVEYS OF HIGHER EDUCATION IN THE UNITED
STATES, 1937-1949. Washington, D.C.: U.S. Office of Education, 1949.
24 p.

> An annotated list of higher education surveys; those dealing
> with faculty and teaching methods are listed separately.

1604 Lazarsfeld, Paul F., and Thielens, Wagner, Jr. THE ACADEMIC MIND:

SOCIAL SCIENTISTS IN A TIME OF CRISIS: WITH A FIELD REPORT BY DAVID RIESMAN. Glencoe, Ill.: Free Press, 1958. Reprint. New York: Arno Press, 1976. 464 p.

Assesses impact on U.S. social scientists of loyalty oaths, professional informers, attacks on members of suspect organizations, and other McCarthy era intellectual freedom threats.

1605 Leacock, Stephen. THE PURSUIT OF KNOWLEDGE. New York: Liveright Publishing Corp., 1934. 48 p.

Noted humorist and professor at McGill University discusses freedom and compulsion in education, university entrance requirements, examinations, and the teaching of English literature.

1606 _____. TOO MUCH COLLEGE. New York: Dodd, Mead and Co., 1939. 255 p.

Humorist looks at college education: academic red tape, scholastic tradition, education jargon, and pseudoscience.

1607 Learned, William S., and Wood, Ben D. THE STUDENT AND HIS KNOWLEDGE. New York: Carnegie Foundation for the Advancement of Teaching, 1938. 406 p.

Data from thousands of high school seniors and college sophomores showed a very low correlation between credit hours earned and actual knowledge retained. Recommended that college programs include experiences to help students integrate knowledge.

1608 Le Duc, Thomas. PIETY AND INTELLECT AT AMHERST COLLEGE, 1865-1912. New York: Columbia University Press, 1946. Reprint. New York: Arno Press, 1969. 165 p.

Intellectual history of Amherst, as seen in change from training clergymen to a liberal arts education.

1609 Lee, Barbara A. COLLECTIVE BARGAINING IN FOUR-YEAR COLLEGES. Washington, D.C.: American Association for Higher Education, 1978. 78 p.

Development of collective bargaining and its impact on college decision making.

1610 Lee, Calvin B.T. THE CAMPUS SCENE, 1900-1970: CHANGING STYLES IN UNDERGRADUATE LIFE. New York: David McKay and Co., 1970. 178 p.

Social history of student life--fads and fashions--with a description of 1960s student unrest.

1611 _____, ed. IMPROVING COLLEGE TEACHING. Washington, D.C.: American Council on Education, 1967. 407 p.

> On college curriculum, teaching, faculty evaluation, effective instructional methods, teaching versus research, and in-service training. Authors include Logan Wilson, William Arrowsmith, Allan Cartter, and Robert Nisbet.

1612 Lee, Edwin Augustus. THE DEVELOPMENT OF PROFESSIONAL PROGRAMS OF EDUCATION IN SIX SELECTED UNIVERSITIES OF THE UNITED STATES. New York: 1925. 125 p.

> Author observed growing professionalism in schools of education at the Universities of Iowa, Michigan, and Missouri, and at Harvard, Stanford, and the University of Chicago.

1613 Lee, Eugene C., and Bowen, Frank M. MANAGING MULTICAMPUS SYSTEMS: EFFECTIVE ADMINISTRATION IN AN UNSTEADY STATE. San Francisco: Jossey-Bass Publishers, 1975. 172 p.

> How nine multicampus institutions are coping with less money and fewer students. On academic planning, budgeting, and strategies for faculty retrenchment and renewal.

1614 _____. THE MULTICAMPUS UNIVERSITY: A STUDY OF ACADEMIC GOVERNANCE. New York: McGraw-Hill Book Co., 1971. 481 p.

> Origins, administration, operations, procedures, strengths, weaknesses, and the state legislature as ultimate coordinating agency of multicampus universities (having at least two four-year colleges in separate locations).

1615 Lee, Joel M., and Hamilton, Beth A., eds. AS MUCH TO LEARN AS TO TEACH: ESSAYS IN HONOR OF LESTER ASHEIM. Hamden, Conn.: Shoe String Press, 1979. 273 p.

> Academic libraries and their service to professional education; essays honoring University of North Carolina library science professor.

1616 Lee, W. Storrs. GOD BLESS OUR QUEER OLD DEAN. New York: G.P. Putnam's Sons, 1959. 256 p.

> Amusing yet analytical book on the functions, duties, and responsibilities of a student personnel dean by a former Middlebury College dean of men.

1617 Leemon, Thomas A. THE RITES OF PASSAGE IN A STUDENT CULTURE: A STUDY OF THE DYNAMICS OF TRANSITION. New York: Teachers College Press, 1972. 215 p.

Applied Arnold Van Gennep's 1909 anthropological theory to how a student becomes a member of a college fraternity. Implications about personality and social organization.

1618 Leggett, Glenn. YEARS OF TURMOIL, YEARS OF CHANGE: SELECTED PAPERS OF A COLLEGE PRESIDENT, 1965-1975. Danville, Ill.: Interstate Printers and Publishers, 1978. 214 p.

Former president of Grinnell College on such topics as academic governance and student life.

1619 Lehman, Benjamin Harrison. WILD MARRIAGE. New York: Harper and Brothers, 1925. 324 p.

Novel about a Harvard professor's family scandal.

1620 Lehrer, Stanley, ed. LEADERS, TEACHERS, AND LEARNERS IN ACADEME: PARTNERS IN THE EDUCATIONAL PROCESS. New York: Appleton-Century-Crofts, 1970. 565 p.

Articles on higher education administration, faculty, students, and the art of teaching.

1621 Leider, Robert. THE A'S AND B'S OF MERIT SCHOLARSHIPS: A GUIDE TO CURRENT PROGRAMS, 1978/79. Alexandria, Va.: Octameron Associates, 1978. 32 p.

Major merit awards offered by federal and state governments, private organizations, and colleges.

1622 Leigh, Robert D., ed. MAJOR PROBLEMS IN THE EDUCATION OF LIBRARIANS. New York: Columbia University Press, 1954. 116 p.

Five major problems in educating librarians and how they might be solved, as discussed in a Columbia University School of Library Service seminar.

1623 Leitch, Alexander, ed. A PRINCETON COMPANION. Princeton, N.J.: Princeton University Press, 1978. 559 p.

Reference book on Princeton life, past and present: biographies of prominent administrators, trustees, faculty, and alumni; histories of academic department and research units; accounts of best-known buildings; and descriptions of libraries.

1624 Leland, Carole A., and Lozoff, Marjorie M. COLLEGE INFLUENCES ON THE ROLE DEVELOPMENT OF FEMALE UNDERGRADUATES. Stanford, Calif.: Institute for the Study of Human Problems, Stanford University, 1969. 100 p.

After reviewing twenty years' research on college women's educational and occupational development, study focused on the autonomy (self-development) of forty-nine able Stanford University women students, refuting the view that women with homogeneous backgrounds have similar educational needs.

1625 LeMelle, Tilden J., and LeMelle, Wilbert J. THE BLACK COLLEGE: A STRATEGY FOR RELEVANCY. New York: Praeger Publishers, 1969. 144 p.

To strengthen black colleges: merge neighboring small colleges; form consortia to coordinate planning, research, and faculty exchange; establish a national center to revise curriculum along manpower needs; and decentralize decision making away from president's office.

1626 Lemlech, Johanna, and Marks, Merle B. THE AMERICAN TEACHER: 1776-1976. Fastback No. 76. Bloomington, Ind.: Phi Delta Kappa, 1976. 38 p.

Historical profile of the evolution of the teaching profession.

1627 Lenning, Oscar T. THE BENEFITS CRISIS IN HIGHER EDUCATION. Washington, D.C.: American Association for Higher Education, 1974. 62 p.

Reviews recent literature on how higher education benefits individual students and the larger society. Proposes a model for ordering priorities and calls for a theoretical approach to the outcomes of higher education.

1628 _____, ed. IMPROVING EDUCATIONAL OUTCOMES. San Francisco: Jossey-Bass Publishers, 1976. 105 p.

On changing institutional policies to improve campus life and to help high-risk students.

1629 Lenning, Oscar T., and Cooper, Edward M. GUIDEBOOK FOR COLLEGES AND UNIVERSITIES: PRESENTING INFORMATION TO PROSPECTIVE STUDENTS. Boulder, Colo.: National Center for Higher Education Management Systems, 1978. 84 p.

Ways to provide college information to prospective students in compliance with the student consumer information section of the 1976 Higher Education Act Amendments.

1630 Leonard, Eugenie Andruss. PROBLEMS OF FRESHMAN COLLEGE GIRLS. New York: Teachers College, Columbia University, 1932. 139 p.

Found that pre-college experiences to develop self-reliance and independence would ease freshman girls' social adjustment to college life.

1631 Lepchenske, George L., and Harcleroad, Fred F. ARE LIBERAL ARTS COLLEGES PROFESSIONAL SCHOOLS? A RESTUDY. Tucson: University of Arizona, 1978. 34 p.

Follow-up study, conducted since 1957, of curricula in 1900 and 1957 at fifty liberal arts colleges.

1632 Lerner, Marguerite Rush. MEDICAL SCHOOL: THE INTERVIEW AND THE APPLICANT. Woodbury, N.Y.: Barron's Educational Series, 1977. 160 p.

Guide for would-be medical students which describes the application process and how it works.

1633 LeRoy, Lauren, and Lee, Philip R., eds. DELIBERATIONS AND COM-PROMISE: THE HEALTH PROFESSIONS EDUCATIONAL ASSISTANCE ACT OF 1976. Cambridge, Mass.: Ballinger Publishing Co., 1978. 469 p.

Hearings of the 1976 Health Professions Educational Assistance Act on supply of physicians, medical specialties, and federal support for medical education.

1634 Leslie, David W. CONFLICT AND COLLECTIVE BARGAINING. Washington, D.C.: American Association for Higher Education, 1976. 70 p.

Compared methods for resolving faculty members' grievances used by collective bargaining universities to those used by non-unionized institutions.

1635 Leslie, Larry L., and Miller, Howard F., Jr. HIGHER EDUCATION AND THE STEADY STATE. Washington, D.C.: American Association for Higher Education, 1974. 58 p.

Using business terminology, concluded that--despite efforts at new products, production methods, and markets--higher education is facing a no-growth situation.

1636 Leslie, Warren. LOVE OR WHATEVER IT IS. New York: McGraw-Hill Book Co., 1960. 335 p.

Novel about faculty, students, and townspeople in a New England college town caught up in a murder.

1637 Lester, Richard A. ANTIBIAS REGULATION OF UNIVERSITIES: FACULTY PROBLEMS AND THEIR SOLUTIONS. New York: McGraw-Hill Book Co., 1974. 168 p.

Suggests ways to apply and improve higher education affirmative action programs.

1638 Letter, Sidney S., ed. TIME HAS COME TODAY. New York: Teachers College, Columbia University, 1970. 111 p.

Papers include one by William Arrowsmith and Jack T. Johnson on a philosophical dimension and purposeful framework for higher education.

1639 Levenstein, Aaron, ed. THE UNIQUENESS OF COLLECTIVE BARGAIN-ING IN HIGHER EDUCATION. New York: National Center for the Study of Collective Bargaining in Higher Education, Baruch College, City University of New York, 1979. 112 p.

Impact of collective bargaining on institutional governance, differences between bargaining at public and private colleges, financial issues, and strikes.

1640 Lever, Janet, and Schwartz, Pepper. WOMEN AT YALE: LIBERATING A COLLEGE CAMPUS. Indianapolis: Bobbs-Merrill, 1971. 274 p.

Impact women students have made on Yale University and the effect on the women themselves.

1641 Lever, William Edward. HOW TO OBTAIN MONEY FOR COLLEGE: A COMPLETE GUIDE TO THE SOURCES OF FINANCIAL AID FOR EDUCA-TION. New York: Arco Publishing Co., 1976. 176 p.

Guide to federal, state, and local sources for college finan-cial aid: lists postsecondary institutions eligible for Basic Edu-cation Opportunity Grants, describes and gives addresses of federal Guaranteed Loan Program agencies, and lists other state agencies administering financial aid programs.

1642 Levi, Albert William. GENERAL EDUCATION IN THE SOCIAL STUDIES. Washington, D.C.: American Council on Education, 1948. 336 p.

To prepare good citizens, outlines a required two-year college social studies course designed by seven social scientists repre-senting twenty-two cooperating colleges.

1643 _____. THE HUMANITIES TODAY. Bloomington: Indiana University Press, 1970. 96 p.

Essays attempt to define the humanities and establish their place in higher education.

1644 Levi, Edward Hirsch. POINT OF VIEW: TALKS ON EDUCATION. Chi-cago: University of Chicago Press, 1970. 186 p.

University of Chicago's president affirms the traditional role of higher education.

1645 Levine, Arthur. HANDBOOK ON UNDERGRADUATE CURRICULUM. San Francisco: Jossey-Bass Publishers, 1978. 662 p.

Part one is on tests and grades, general education, and methods of instruction. Part two gives a philosophical, institutional, historical, and cultural framework for these curriculum concerns.

1646 _____. THE LIFE AND DEATH OF INNOVATION IN HIGHER EDUCATION. Buffalo: Faculty of Educational Studies, State University of New York, 1979. 70 p.

Case study of change in colleges at the State University of New York, Buffalo.

1647 Levine, Arthur E., and Weingart, John R. REFORM OF UNDERGRADUATE EDUCATION. San Francisco: Jossey-Bass Publishers, 1973. 160 p.

Studied undergraduate advising systems, general education, and student-centered experiments at twenty-six institutions, among them Antioch, Berkeley, Eckerd, Harvard, St. John's, and University of Wisconsin-Green Bay.

1648 Lewis, Lionel Stanley. SCALING THE IVORY TOWER: MERIT AND ITS LIMITS IN ACADEMIC CAREERS. Baltimore, Md.: Johns Hopkins University Press, 1975. 238 p.

Sociological study of higher education faculty appointment and advancement in Britain, France, and the United States. Found publications and teaching abilities less important than hard work, conscientiousness, ability to get along with colleagues, and family circumstances.

1649 Lewis, Marianna O., ed. THE FOUNDATION DIRECTORY. New York: Foundation Center, 1977. 661 p.

Directory of over 2,800 award-granting foundations.

1650 Lewis, Sinclair. ARROWSMITH. New York: Harcourt, Brace and Co., 1925. 448 p.

Novel about idealistic student Martin Arrowsmith's medical career.

1651 Lewis, Wells. THEY STILL SAY NO. New York: Farrar and Rinehart, 1939. 306 p.

Novel of a student during four years at Harvard who then went to work in Mexico.

1652 Lewis, Wilmarth Sheldon. TUTORS' LANE. New York: Alfred A. Knopf, 1922. 164 p.

A novel about a young English instructor in a New England college who competes for the hand of the dean's niece against another senior colleague with family and wealth.

1653 Liebert, Robert. RADICAL AND MILITANT YOUTH: A PSYCHOANA-LYTIC INQUIRY. New York: Praeger Publishers, 1971. 257 p.

Psychoanalyst's study of student protesters in the April 1968 Columbia University crisis shows that events paralleled a significant period in their psychological development.

1654 Lifton, Robert Jay, ed. THE WOMAN IN AMERICA. Boston: Houghton Mifflin Co., 1965. 293 p.

Part played by education, particularly higher education, in careers of such prominent women as Jane Addams, Eleanor Roosevelt, and Lillian Wald.

1655 Light, Donald, Jr., et al. THE DYNAMICS OF UNIVERSITY PROTEST. Chicago: Nelson-Hall, 1977. 198 p.

Causes of 1960s student unrest examined by six social scientists.

1656 Ligon, Ernest M. A GREATER GENERATION. New York: Macmillan Co., 1948. 157 p.

Aims, methods, and results of the Union College (Schenectady, New York) Character Research Project; author believes character can be taught.

1657 Ligon, J. Frank, ed. CONFRONTATIONS: PROCEEDINGS, THIRTY-FIRST ANNUAL PACIFIC NORTHWEST CONFERENCE ON HIGHER EDU-CATION. Corvallis: Oregon State University Press, 1970. 240 p.

Late 1960s campus confrontations arising from black protests and student unrest.

1658 Lincoln, Freeman. NOD. New York: Coward-McCann, 1933. 289 p.

Novel about a Harvard student whose graduation with honors is interrupted.

1659 Lindgren, Henry Clay. THE PSYCHOLOGY OF COLLEGE SUCCESS: A DYNAMIC APPROACH. New York: John Wiley and Sons, 1969. 141 p.

How to succeed in college: learning strategies, reading and writing skills, what to do about failure, and other problems.

1660 Lindquist, Everet Franklin, ed. EDUCATIONAL MEASUREMENT. Washington, D.C.: American Council on Education, 1951. 819 p.

Textbook on the theory and technique of educational measurement.

1661 Lindsey, Margaret, et al. INQUIRY INTO TEACHING BEHAVIOR OF SUPERVISORS IN TEACHER EDUCATION LABORATORIES. New York: Teachers College Press, 1969. 272 p.

> Roles of college supervisors and cooperating teachers in preparing students for teaching.

1662 Lineberry, William P., ed. COLLEGES AT THE CROSSROADS. New York: H.W. Wilson Co., 1966. 186 p.

> Analysis of such contemporary higher education problems as teaching versus research, faculty tenure, and student needs.

1663 Linn, James Weber. THIS WAS LIFE. Indianapolis: Bobbs-Merrill Co., 1936. 304 p.

> Novel about University of Chicago life in 1893-94, soon after its founding, by author who taught there. Contrasts Ivy League with mass coeducational higher education.

1664 _____. WINDS OVER THE CAMPUS. Indianapolis: Bobbs-Merrill Co., 1936. 344 p.

> Novel's hero, a University of Chicago undergraduate in THIS WAS LIFE (above), fights for academic freedom as a professor at the same university in the 1930s.

1665 Linn, Robert L. GRADE ADJUSTMENTS FOR PREDICTION OF ACADEMIC PERFORMANCE: A REVIEW. Princeton, N.J.: Educational Testing Service, 1965. 27 p.

> Concludes that any technique used to equalize grades from different high schools does not greatly affect the use of grades in predicting college academic success.

1666 Linn, Robert L., et al. A GUIDE TO RESEARCH DESIGN: INSTITUTIONAL RESEARCH PROGRAM FOR HIGHER EDUCATION. Princeton, N.J.: Educational Testing Service, 1965. 53 p.

> Guidelines for institutional research: using human resources, using specific tests and other instruments, and interpreting results.

1667 Lins, L. Joseph. METHODOLOGY OF ENROLLMENT PROJECTIONS FOR COLLEGES AND UNIVERSITIES. Washington, D.C.: American Council on Education, American Association of Collegiate Registrars and Admissions Officers, 1960. 67 p.

> Techniques for estimating future enrollment levels, locally and statewide.

1668 _____, ed. THE ROLE OF INSTITUTIONAL RESEARCH IN PLANNING. Madison: University of Wisconsin, 1963. 174 p.

    Reports on ongoing institutional research including student follow-up studies, mobility studies, and decision-making studies.

1669 Lipset, Seymour Martin, and Altbach, Philip G., eds. STUDENTS IN REVOLT. Boston: Houghton Mifflin Co., 1969. 561 p.

    Case studies of 1960s student dissent in several countries; shows student movements to be diverse and complex, some motivated by local events rather than national and international problems. Article on U.S. student left raises the possibility of massive conservative backlash.

1670 Lipset, Seymour Martin, and Riesman, David. EDUCATION AND POLITICS AT HARVARD. New York: McGraw-Hill Book Co., 1975. 440 p.

    Study of the history and curriculum of Harvard. Stresses the key role of faculty in institutional governance. Shows that dissension and unrest, not unique to the sixties, has been typical at Harvard.

1671 Lipset, Seymour Martin, and Wolin, Sheldon S., eds. THE BERKELEY STUDENT REVOLT: FACTS AND INTERPRETATIONS. Garden City, N.Y.: Doubleday and Co., 1965. 585 p.

    The 1964-65 University of California at Berkeley student riots, using documents and empirical research; balanced view edited by two Berkeley faculty members.

1672 Lipsky, Eleazar. THE SCIENTISTS. New York: Appleton-Century-Crofts, 1959. 375 p.

    A novel with flashbacks about a court battle between a university scientist soon to win a research center and a possible Nobel Prize and his antagonist, a former professor claiming that the scientific breakthrough was stolen from his own pioneer work.

1673 Litt, Edgar. THE PUBLIC VOCATIONAL UNIVERSITY: CAPTIVE KNOWLEDGE AND PUBLIC POWER. New York: Holt, Rinehart and Winston, 1969. 159 p.

    Political scientist asserts that state universities are inextricably influenced by federal government interests.

1674 Litwak, Leo, and Wilner, Herbert. COLLEGE DAYS IN EARTHQUAKE COUNTRY: ORDEAL AT SAN FRANCISCO STATE, A PERSONAL RECORD. New York: Random House, 1972. 235 p.

Two liberal English professors' sensitive, personal accounts of the 1968 crisis at San Francisco State.

1675 Lively, Charles E., and Preiss, Jack J. CONSERVATION EDUCATION IN AMERICAN COLLEGES. New York: Ronald Press Co., 1957. 267 p.

Report of a 1954-55 national survey of the status of the teaching of conservation in U.S. colleges and universities.

1676 Liveright, Alexander Albert. A STUDY OF ADULT EDUCATION IN THE UNITED STATES. Brookline, Mass.: Center for the Study of Liberal Education for Adults at Boston University, 1968. 138 p.

U.S. adult education overview recommends better degree programs, more trained faculty, more financial support from the federal government and universities, and innovations in reaching and teaching adults.

1677 Livesey, Herbert B. THE PROFESSORS: WHO THEY ARE, WHAT THEY DO, WHAT THEY REALLY WANT AND WHAT THEY NEED. New York: Charterhouse, 1975. 343 p.

Depicts professors as well paid, underworked, critical of society, and somewhat pompous.

1678 Livesey, Herbert B., and Robbins, Gene A. GUIDE TO AMERICAN GRADUATE SCHOOLS. 2d ed. New York: Viking Press, 1970. 410 p.

For each institution, listed alphabetically, gives location, general characteristics, admissions requirements, financial aid, degree requirements, and fields of study.

1679 Lloyd, Arthur Y. PUBLIC HIGHER EDUCATION IN KENTUCKY: REPORT TO THE COMMITTEE ON FUNCTIONS AND RESOURCES OF STATE GOVERNMENT. Frankfort, Ky.: Legislative Research Commission, 1952. 185 p.

Survey of the organization and administration of Kentucky's six state-controlled institutions of higher education.

1680 Lloyd-Jones, Esther McDonald, and Estrin, Herman A., eds. THE AMERICAN STUDENT AND HIS COLLEGE. Boston: Houghton Mifflin, 1967. 384 p.

Contemporary campus culture, student rights, and responsibilities, and other issues from news stories, speeches, and other popular sources.

1681 Lloyd-Jones, Esther McDonald, and Smith, Margaret R. STUDENT PERSONNEL PROGRAM FOR HIGHER EDUCATION. New York: McGraw-Hill Book Co., 1938. 332 p.

Outline of higher education student personnel work based on concern for the well-rounded growth of each individual student.

1682 _____, eds. STUDENT PERSONNEL WORK AS DEEPER TEACHING. New York: Harper and Brothers, 1954. 361 p.

Emphasizes that student personnel work should aim first at helping the full development of individual students; but this goal is often ignored because of specialization among student personnel workers.

1683 Lockmiller, David Alexander. THE CONSOLIDATION OF THE UNIVERSITY OF NORTH CAROLINA. Raleigh: University of North Carolina Press, 1942. 160 p.

The 1931 consolidation of the State College of Agriculture and Engineering at Raleigh and the Woman's College at Greensboro with the University of North Carolina.

1684 _____. SCHOLARS ON PARADE; COLLEGES, UNIVERSITIES, COSTUMES AND DEGREES. New York: Macmillan Co., 1969. 290 p.

Anecdotal chronology of the development of such features of academia as degrees, robes, and ceremonies.

1685 Lodgson, Guy William. THE UNIVERSITY OF TULSA: A HISTORY, 1882-1972. Norman: University of Oklahoma Press for the Oklahoma Heritage Association, 1977. 358 p.

Founded as Presbyterian School for Indian Girls; major social and economic influences (including the discovery of petroleum) that shaped University of Tulsa's development.

1686 Loeb, Judith, ed. FEMINIST COLLAGE: EDUCATING WOMEN IN THE VISUAL ARTS. New York: Teachers College Press, 1979. 320 p.

Changing world of visual arts education for women. Contributors (among them Margaret Mead) from various fields related to the visual arts consider feminism's effect on art.

1687 Logan, Rayford W. HOWARD UNIVERSITY: THE FIRST HUNDRED YEARS, 1867-1967. New York: New York University Press, 1969. 658 p.

Centennial history: founded 1867 by the Freedman's Bureau (with no reference to segregation), named for General O.O. Howard, first president as well as Freedman's Bureau head, and its professional schools which expanded opportunities to blacks who, by 1900, were in a majority.

1688 Lomask, Milton. A MINOR MIRACLE: AN INFORMAL HISTORY OF THE NATIONAL SCIENCE FOUNDATION. Washington, D.C.: Government Printing Office, 1976. 285 p.

> Legislative debates and compromises that led to the National Science Foundation Act of 1950; styles and personalities of its four directors; its expanding responsibilities; and the controversy over its role in national science policy.

1689 Lombardi, John. MANAGING FINANCES IN COMMUNITY COLLEGES. San Francisco: Jossey-Bass Publishers, 1973. 145 p.

> Suggests strategies for increasing funding, controlling expenditures, and more efficient resource allocation for two-year colleges.

1690 _____. NONCAMPUS COLLEGES: NEW GOVERNANCE PATTERNS FOR OUTREACH PROGRAMS. Los Angeles: ERIC Clearinghouse for Junior Colleges, University of California, 1978. 74 p.

> Functions, characteristics, and comparison of eight colleges without campuses: faculties, financing, student bodies, locations, and facilities.

1691 _____. PART-TIME FACULTY IN COMMUNITY COLLEGES. Los Angeles: ERIC Clearinghouse for Junior Colleges, University of California, 1976. 58 p.

> Use of part-time faculty and their working conditions in two-year colleges.

1692 London, Howard B. THE CULTURE OF A COMMUNITY COLLEGE. New York: Praeger Publishers, 1978. 181 p.

> Challenges traditional view that the community college provides working class students with upward mobility. Based on interviews and other firsthand sources during a year's study of a new northeastern urban two-year college.

1693 Long, John D. NEEDED EXPANSION OF FACILITIES FOR HIGHER EDUCATION--1958-70: HOW MUCH WILL IT COST? Washington, D.C.: American Council on Education, 1958. 46 p.

> Estimates physical facilities higher education institutions will likely need by 1970 and the probable cost.

1694 Lopate, Carol. WOMEN IN MEDICINE. Baltimore, Md.: Johns Hopkins University Press, 1968. 204 p.

> Problems women medical students face, such as lack of financial aid, inadequate child-care facilities, and rigid scheduling, and their reluctance to press for change. Sees improved con-

ditions as U.S. society abandons sex-role stereotypes.

1695 Lopez, Ronald W., et al. CHICANOS IN HIGHER EDUCATION: STATUS AND ISSUES. Los Angeles: Chicano Studies Center Publications, University of California, 1976. 199 p.

> Descriptive and statistical data from census reports and civil rights documents. Includes high school completion rates, undergraduate and graduate enrollments, and funding figures.

1696 Lord, Milton E., et al. MODERN EDUCATION AND HUMAN VALUES. Pittsburgh, Pa.: University of Pittsburgh Press, 1957. 128 p.

> Lectures on human values, with one by lawyer Robert E. Mathews, stating that professional schools must instill moral responsibility along with professional content.

1697 Louttit, Chauncey McKinley, et al. OPEN DOOR TO EDUCATION. Urbana: University of Illinois Press, 1951. 64 p.

> On the short-lived Galesburg "G. I." division of the University of Illinois designed for many veterans entering higher education. It closed when the need was met, but while operating, maintained the quality of education of the Urbana campus.

1698 Love, Donald M. HENRY CHURCHILL KING OF OBERLIN. New Haven, Conn.: Yale University Press, 1956. 300 p.

> King (1858-1934) attended Oberlin and Harvard and studied in Germany; he returned to teach at Oberlin and then served as president, 1902-27.

1699 Lovejoy, Clarence E. LOVEJOY'S COLLEGE GUIDE. 14th ed. New York: Simon and Schuster, 1979. 386 p.

> Section one has articles on higher education expenses, financial aid, admissions, and choosing a college. Section two lists career fields (such as advertising) and colleges offering courses in each field. Section three briefly describes thirty-six hundred U.S. colleges and universities.

1700 Lovell, John P. NEITHER ATHENS NOR SPARTA? THE AMERICAN SERVICE ACADEMIES IN TRANSITION. Bloomington: Indiana University Press, 1979. 362 p.

> History and development of U.S. service academies. Shows differences and similarities. Cites as the key dilemma the combination of four years of undergraduate education with military training and professionalization. Suggests alternatives (for example, service academies as postgraduate institutions only).

1701 Lovett, Robert Morss. ALL OUR YEARS: THE AUTOBIOGRAPHY OF ROBERT MORSS LOVETT. New York: Viking Press, 1948. 373 p.

Self-portrait of a professor of English, who traveled widely and was a regular contributor to the NEW REPUBLIC.

1702 Lowell, A. Lawrence. AT WAR WITH ACADEMIC TRADITIONS IN AMERICA. Cambridge, Mass.: Harvard University Press, 1934. 357 p.

Major papers during Lowell's presidency of Harvard University (1909-33), where he strengthened undergraduate education, reduced electives, developed the tutorial system and comprehensive examinations, and introduced freshman dormitories and the house plan.

1703 _____. WHAT A UNIVERSITY PRESIDENT HAS LEARNED. New York: Macmillan and Co., 1938. 150 p.

Autobiography of former Harvard University president (1909-33) and of the problems he encountered.

1704 Lowry, Howard F. COLLEGE TALKS. New York: Oxford University Press, 1969. 177 p.

Speeches of the former president of the College of Wooster, Ohio.

1705 _____. THE MIND'S ADVENTURE: RELIGION AND HIGHER EDUCATION. Philadelphia: Westminster Press, 1950. 154 p.

College of Wooster president believes religion and religious values should be integral part of liberal education.

1706 Loye, David. THE LEADERSHIP PASSION: A PSYCHOLOGY OF IDEOLOGY. San Francisco: Jossey-Bass Publishers, 1977. 249 p.

What constitutes leadership and how it can be developed and discovered; explored in part through campus political activities of elites at Princeton University.

1707 Lubbers, Irwin J. COLLEGE ORGANIZATION AND ADMINISTRATION. Evanston, Ill.: Northwestern University, School of Education, 1932. 155 p.

Survey of 180 U.S. colleges on the organization and administration of liberal arts colleges.

1708 Luck, Michael F., and Tolle, Donald J. COMMUNITY COLLEGE DEVELOPMENT: ALTERNATIVE FUND-RAISING STRATEGIES. Indianapolis: R and R Newkirk, 1978. 167 p.

On establishing and operating foundations and fund-raising programs for public two-year colleges.

1709 Luckey, George Washington Andrew. THE PROFESSIONAL TRAINING OF SECONDARY TEACHERS IN THE UNITED STATES. New York: Macmillan and Co., 1903. 391 p.

> Historical study describes the rise of normal schools and of education departments in colleges and universities. Appendix tells the history of teacher education at the University of Nebraska.

1710 Lukac, George, ed. ALOUD TO ALMA MATER. New Brunswick, N.J.: Rutgers University Press, 1966. 241 p.

> Informal bicentennial history of Rutgers University through documents, diary entries, and reminiscences.

1711 Lumbard, Charles G. SENIOR SPRING. New York: Simon and Schuster, 1954. 243 p.

> Novel about an architectural senior at a university modeled after the University of California, Berkeley.

1712 Lumsdaine, Arthur A., and Glaser, R., eds. TEACHING MACHINES AND PROGRAMMED LEARNING; A SOURCE BOOK. Washington, D.C.: National Education Association, 1960. 724 p.

> Role of programmed materials in teaching at all levels, including higher education.

1713 Lunden, Walter A. THE DYNAMICS OF HIGHER EDUCATION. Pittsburgh, Pa.: Pittsburgh Printing Co., 1939. 402 p.

> Sociological and historical overview of higher education as a social institution. Includes such aspects as social stratification within institutions and faculty mobility.

1714 Lunn, Harry H., Jr. THE STUDENT'S ROLE IN COLLEGE POLICY-MAKING. Washington, D.C.: American Council on Education, 1957. 100 p.

> On student participation in general government, academic administration, and student personnel administration of higher education institutions.

1715 Lurie, Alison. LOVE AND FRIENDSHIP. New York: Macmillan and Co., 1962. 314 p.

> Novel about the wife of a humanities professor at a New England college.

1716 Lurie, Edward. LOUIS AGASSIZ: A LIFE IN SCIENCE. Chicago: University of Chicago Press, 1960. 449 p.

Psychoanalytic biography of Swiss-born naturalist Agassiz (1807–73), who moved to the United States in 1848 to teach at Harvard, where he founded the zoology museum.

1717 Lutz, Alma. EMMA WILLARD: DAUGHTER OF DEMOCRACY. Boston: Houghton Mifflin, 1929. 291 p.

Biography of Emma Hart Willard (1787-1870), author of PLAN FOR IMPROVING FEMALE EDUCATION (1818), which called for state aid to women's education; and founder (1821)--without state aid--of Troy (New York) Female Seminary, after 1895 called the Emma Willard School. She developed textbooks, trained teachers who advanced women's education nationally, and proved the value of higher education for women.

1718 Lyle, Guy Redfers. CLASSIFIED LIST OF PERIODICALS FOR THE COLLEGE LIBRARY. Boston: F.W. Faxon Co., 1934. 102 p.

List of periodicals for college libraries compiled by the then librarian at Antioch College, Ohio.

1719 _____. COLLEGE LIBRARY PUBLICITY. Boston: F.W. Faxon Co., 1935. 113 p.

How to explain library needs and services to college administrators and others the library serves.

1720 _____. THE LIBRARIAN SPEAKING; INTERVIEWS WITH UNIVERSITY LIBRARIANS. Athens: University of Georgia Press, 1970. 206 p.

Interviews with distinguished college librarians about major higher education library problems.

1721 _____. THE PRESIDENT, THE PROFESSOR, AND THE COLLEGE LIBRARY. New York: H.W. Wilson Co., 1963. 88 p.

Speeches by the then Emory University librarian about the relation between the library and the university.

1722 Lyle, Guy Redfers, et al. THE ADMINISTRATION OF THE COLLEGE LIBRARY. New York: H.W. Wilson Co., 1944. 601 p.

Guide to college library problems.

1723 Lynd, Helen Merrell. FIELD WORK IN COLLEGE EDUCATION. New York: Columbia University Press, 1945. 302 p.

Place of field work in the Sarah Lawrence College curriculum; illustrates its value to students, the college, and the community.

1724 Lyons, Gene M., and Masland, John W. EDUCATION AND MILITARY LEADERSHIP. Princeton, N.J.: Princeton University Press, 1959. 283 p.

Strengths and weaknesses of higher education ROTC in preparing military commissioned officers.

1725 Lyons, John O. THE COLLEGE NOVEL IN AMERICA. Carbondale: Southern Illinois University Press, 1962. 208 p.

Novels about U.S. college and university life, including students, faculty, administrators, college and university towns, fraternities, sports, and mores. Bibliography of 215 novels (1829-1962), with chapters on academic freedom, eccentricities of academicians, and double standards in women's education and careers. Novels are set in fictional, thinly disguised, or actual colleges and universities.

1726 Lyons, Louis M., ed. THE NIEMAN FELLOWS REPORT. Cambridge, Mass.: Harvard University Press, 1948. 135 p.

Report on the first ten years of Nieman Fellowships to improve U.S. journalism, largely in the words of the fellows, practicing journalists granted one year's study at Harvard.

1727 Lysaught, Jerome P. AN ABSTRACT FOR ACTION. New York: McGraw-Hill Book Co., 1970. 167 p.

National Commission for the Study of Nursing Education report. Recognizes low public esteem for nursing. Concludes that nursing education is done best in universities. Urges statewide planning for nursing education.

1728 McAfee, Joseph Ernest. COLLEGE PIONEERING: PROBLEMS AND PHASES OF THE LIFE AT PARK COLLEGE DURING ITS EARLY YEARS. Kansas City, Mo.: Alumni Parkana Committee, 1938. 264 p.

Author's founding of Park College, United Presbyterian liberal arts college in Kansas City, Missouri.

1729 McAllester, Susan, ed. A CASE FOR EQUITY: WOMEN IN ENGLISH DEPARTMENTS. Urbana, Ill.: National Council of Teachers of English, 1971. 100 p.

About discriminatory practices against women students and women faculty members in higher education.

1730 McAllister, Charles E. INSIDE THE CAMPUS: MR. CITIZEN LOOKS AT HIS UNIVERSITIES. New York: Fleming H. Revell Co., 1948. 247 p.

Recommendations based on interviews on eighty-nine state and twelve private campuses: (1) legislatures should appropriate lump sums to colleges, (2) faculty salaries should be competitive, (3) universities should pay faculty expenses to scholarly meetings, and (4) state institutions should be active in the American Council on Education.

1731 McAllister, Ethel M. AMOS EATON, SCIENTIST AND EDUCATOR, 1776-1842. Philadelphia: University of Pennsylvania Press, 1941. 587 p.

Eaton, founder of Rensselaer Polytechnic Institute, Troy, New York, also established the first chain of science laboratories in the United States.

1732 Macauley, Robie. THE DISGUISES OF LOVE. New York: Random House, 1952. 282 p.

Novel, showing the influence of Virginia Woolf, about a psychology professor's extramarital complications.

1733 McBee, Mary Louise, and Blake, Kathryn A., eds. THE AMERICAN WOMAN: WHO WILL SHE BE? Beverly Hills, Calif.: Glencoe Press, 1974. 164 p.

Papers include K. Patricia Cross, "The Education of Women Today and Tomorrow," urging higher education opportunities for all women.

1734 McCabe, Joseph E. YOUR FIRST YEAR AT COLLEGE: LETTERS TO A COLLEGE FRESHMAN. Philadelphia: Westminster Press, 1967. 93 p.

Encouraging and cautionary letters from father to son in college about family's financial and emotional investments, fraternities, social life, the girl back home, and other matters.

1735 McCallum, John D. COLLEGE BASKETBALL, U.S.A.: SINCE 1892. New York: Stein and Day, 1979. 308 p.

History of college basketball, including well-known players and coaches.

1736 McCarthy, Mary Theresa. THE GROVES OF ACADEME. New York: Harcourt, Brace and Co., 1952. 302 p.

Satirical novel of a struggle between a college president and a professor.

1737 McCarty, Donald James, et al. NEW PERSPECTIVES ON TEACHER EDUCATION. San Francisco: Jossey-Bass Publishers, 1973. 255 p.

Such teacher education problems as rigidity of relationship between schools of education and public school systems, the educational establishment's resistance to change, effects of state and federal intervention, teacher accrediting, and needed curricular changes.

1738 McCaul, Margaret E. GUIDANCE FOR COLLEGE STUDENTS. Scranton, Pa.: International Textbook Co., 1939. 231 p.

> Problems of college life and work, personality development, and choosing a vocation.

1739 Maccia, Elizabeth Steiner, et al. WOMEN AND EDUCATION. Springfield, Ill.: Charles C Thomas, Publisher, 1975. 381 p.

> Contributors Florence Howe, David Riesman, Sheila Tobias, and others on education and the bias against women.

1740 McCluskey, Neil G., ed. THE CATHOLIC UNIVERSITY: A MODERN APPRAISAL. Notre Dame, Ind.: University of Notre Dame Press, 1970. 375 p.

> Essays stress joint goals of exemplifying Catholicity while maintaining academic freedom in Catholic higher education.

1741 McConnaughey, James Parker. VILLAGE CHRONICLE. New York: Farrar and Rinehart, 1936. 357 p.

> Novel about intellectual life in a North Carolina university town, transparently Chapel Hill.

1742 McConnell, Thomas Raymond. A GENERAL PATTERN FOR AMERICAN PUBLIC HIGHER EDUCATION. New York: McGraw-Hill Book Co., 1962. 198 p.

> Suggests that in the following ten years universities should serve needs of advanced undergraduate and graduate students while state colleges should serve those with lower potential.

1743 _____. STUDIES IN HIGHER EDUCATION: BIENNIAL REPORT OF THE COMMITTEE ON EDUCATIONAL RESEARCH, 1940-42. Minneapolis: University of Minnesota Press, 1944. 126 p.

> Self-analysis of various phases of the University of Minnesota identified such problems as faculty members' long working hours (over fifty hours per week) and curricular needs.

1744 _____. THE REDISTRIBUTION OF POWER IN HIGHER EDUCATION. Berkeley: Center for Research and Development in Higher Education, University of California, 1971. 67 p.

> Sees changes in university governance resulting from new personal and social values; feels that academic freedom is endangered; and predicts long period of unrest.

1745 McConnell, Thomas Raymond, and Edelstein, Stewart. CAMPUS GOVERNANCE AT BERKELEY: A STUDY IN JURISDICTIONS. Berkeley: Center for Research and Development in Higher Education, University of California, 1977. 72 p.

> Changes in campus governance by faculty members, students, and administrators at the University of California, Berkeley, 1966–75.

1746 McConnell, Thomas Raymond, and Mortimer, Kenneth. THE FACULTY IN UNIVERSITY GOVERNANCE. Berkeley: Center for Research and Development in Higher Education, University of California, 1971. 201 p.

> Studies of faculty senates at the Universities of California at Berkeley, Minnesota, and Fresno State College. Critical of separate formal jurisdictions for administration and faculty; sees conflict in relationships between faculty and boards of trustees; and concludes that shared responsibility is the best form of academic governance.

1747 McConnell, Thomas Raymond, and Willey, Malcolm M., eds. HIGHER EDUCATION AND THE WAR. Philadelphia: American Academy of Political and Social Science, 1944. 207 p.

> Discusses educational rebuilding problems, especially in higher education, that would follow World War II, such as enrollment planning, credit for military experience, student counseling, and financial support.

1748 McCord, David. IN SIGHT OF SEVER: ESSAYS FROM HARVARD. Cambridge, Mass.: Harvard University Press, 1963. 298 p.

> On the professors, personalities, and events which made Harvard the cultural and educational center of New England.

1749 McCormack, Wayne, ed. THE BAKKE DECISION: IMPLICATIONS FOR HIGHER EDUCATION ADMISSIONS. Washington, D.C.: American Council on Education, 1978. 61 p.

> U.S. Supreme Court decision and higher education implications of University of California, Davis, Bakke case on reverse discrimination in medical education.

1750 McCormick, Richard P. RUTGERS: A BICENTENNIAL HISTORY. New Brunswick, N.J.: Rutgers University Press, 1966. 336 p.

> Precariously founded as Queen's College by the Dutch Reformed Church, modern Rutgers arose from 1862 Morrill Act aid, and in 1956 became "The State University" of New Jersey.

1751 McCoy, Charles S. THE RESPONSIBLE CAMPUS: TOWARD A NEW IDENTITY FOR THE CHURCH-RELATED COLLEGE. Nashville, Tenn.: United Methodist Church, 1972. 168 p.

Recommends that church colleges be part of a pluralistic system of U.S. higher education, rather than a group apart. Calls for better trustees, student involvement in policy making, and more attention to learning.

1752 McCrum, Blanche Prichard. AN ESTIMATE OF STANDARDS FOR A COLLEGE LIBRARY. Lexington, Va.: Harold Lauck Journalism Laboratory Press, Washington and Lee University, 1937. 166 p.

Place of the library in educational programs, book collection, staff, budget, catalog, faculty relations, student relations, and the library building.

1753 McCune, Shirley D. COMPLYING WITH TITLE IX: THE FIRST TWELVE MONTHS. Washington, D.C.: Resource Center on Sex Roles in Education, 1976. 34 p.

Sex bias law affecting higher education institutions; requirements and implementation.

1754 _____ . COMPLYING WITH TITLE IX: IMPLEMENTING INSTITUTIONAL SELF-EVALUATION. Washington, D.C.: Resource Center on Sex Roles in Education, 1976. 140 p.

Institutional self-evaluation in women's access to courses, counseling, marital and parental status, athletics, financial assistance, employment, and treatment as students.

1755 McCune, Shirley D., and Matthews, Martha. PROGRAMS FOR EDUCATIONAL EQUITY: SCHOOLS AND AFFIRMATIVE ACTION. Washington, D.C.: Government Printing Office, 1975. 56 p.

Higher education equity for women and minorities; includes legal background and monitoring programs for affirmative action.

1756 McDonald, Edward D., and Hinton, Edward M. DREXEL INSTITUTE OF TECHNOLOGY, 1891-1941. Philadelphia: Drexel Institute of Technology, 1942. 336 p.

History of Drexel Institute of Technology and its progress toward granting collegiate degrees.

1757 McDowell, Tremaine. AMERICAN STUDIES. Minneapolis: University of Minnesota Press, 1948. 96 p.

Found that thirty U.S. colleges and universities offered American Studies programs, consisting mainly of U.S.-related history, literature, anthropology, art, economics, education, geography, music, natural science, philosophy, political science, religion, and sociology; that sixty institutions offered B.A. degrees in

American Civilization, while fifteen institutions offered the
M.A. and Ph.D. degrees.

1758 McEvoy, James, and Miller, Abraham, eds. BLACK POWER AND STU-
DENT REBELLION. Belmont, Calif.: Wadsworth Publishing Co., 1969.
440 p.

Stokeley Carmichael, Roy Wilkins, S.I. Hayakawa, Daniel
Bell, Max Rafferty, and others write on the roots, scope, and
implications of student protest and campus unrest.

1759 McFadden, Dennis N., et al., eds. USHER REDESIGN MODEL. Columbus, Ohio: Battelle Center for Improved Education, 1975. 402 p.

Model for involving the entire educational community in the
redesign of college management systems.

1760 McFarlane, William Hugh, and Wheeler, Charles L. LEGAL AND POLIT-
ICAL ISSUES OF STATE AID FOR PRIVATE HIGHER EDUCATION. Atlanta: Southern Regional Education Board, 1971. 78 p.

Need for and legal aspects of state support for private higher
education. Justifies such support as overcoming state monopo-
ly of education.

1761 McGee, Reece Jerome. ACADEMIC JANUS: THE PRIVATE COLLEGE
AND ITS FACULTY. San Francisco: Jossey-Bass Publishers, 1971. 264 p.

Sociological analysis of eleven liberal arts colleges and their
faculty mobility. Recommends that such colleges recruit re-
search-oriented professors who can prepare students for graduate school.

1762 McGill, Samuel H. THE CONTRIBUTION OF THE CHURCH-RELATED
COLLEGE TO THE PUBLIC'S GOOD. Washington, D.C.: Association
of American Colleges, 1970. 113 p.

Essays on church-related colleges, their contributions to a humane society, and their useful counteraction to the sameness
of public colleges.

1763 McGinnis, Frederick Alphonso. HISTORY AND AN INTERPRETATION OF
WILBERFORCE UNIVERSITY. Blanchester, Ohio: Brown Publishing Co.,
1941. 215 p.

History of Wilberforce University (one of two historically black
northern colleges), its contributions, and tensions caused by
denominational politics and by joint support and control by the
State of Ohio and the African Methodist Episcopal Church.

1764 McGlothlin, William J. THE PROFESSIONAL SCHOOLS. New York:

Center for Applied Research in Education, 1964. 118 p.

Analysis of higher education for twenty professions. Examined need for: (1) enrolling more students despite high admissions requirements, (2) more liberal education in professional programs, and (3) meeting mounting costs.

1765 McGrane, Reginald C. THE UNIVERSITY OF CINCINNATI: A SUCCESS STORY IN URBAN HIGHER EDUCATION. New York: Harper and Row, 1963. 364 p.

University of Cincinnati history; founding of its various divisions; and the influence of its philanthropists, faculty, and civic leaders. Discusses urban education problems.

1766 McGrath, Earl James. EDUCATION: THE WELLSPRING OF DEMOCRACY. University: University of Alabama Press, 1951. 139 p.

Speeches by the then U.S. Commissioner of Education on scholarships to qualified needy college students and the need for a comprehensive national survey of community colleges.

1767 _____. GENERAL EDUCATION AND THE PLIGHT OF MODERN MAN. Tucson: Program in Liberal Studies, University of Arizona, 1977. 182 p.

Recommends changes in liberal arts education to equip students to cope with a complex world, rather than be mere skilled specialists.

1768 _____. THE GRADUATE SCHOOL AND THE DECLINE OF LIBERAL EDUCATION. New York: Teachers College, Columbia University, 1959. 65 p.

Recommends changing graduate schools so that liberal education can flourish, research receive less emphasis, and dynamic teaching be rewarded.

1769 _____. MEMO TO A COLLEGE FACULTY MEMBER. New York: Columbia University Press, 1961. 54 p.

Calls on faculty members to oppose proliferation of course offerings in the interest of efficient and effective higher education.

1770 _____. THE PREDOMINANTLY NEGRO COLLEGES AND UNIVERSITIES IN TRANSITION. New York: Teachers College, Columbia University, 1965. 204 p.

Study of 120 black colleges, their characteristics, needs, and prospects; concludes that they need large-scale federal assistance.

1771 _____. SHOULD STUDENTS SHARE THE POWER? A STUDY OF THEIR ROLE IN COLLEGE AND UNIVERSITY GOVERNANCE. Philadelphia: Temple University Press, 1970. 124 p.

Pros, cons, and background of student participation in academic governance; shows that when given such responsibility students have done well.

1772 _____, ed. COMMUNICATION IN GENERAL EDUCATION. Dubuque, Iowa: William C. Brown Co., 1949. 244 p.

Recommends curriculum for teaching symbols needed to communicate the cultural heritage. Such courses would synthesize English, speech, and aspects of social psychology.

1773 _____. COOPERATIVE LONG-RANGE PLANNING IN LIBERAL ARTS COLLEGES. New York: Teachers College, Columbia University, 1964. 108 p.

Report of liberal arts college presidents about improving instruction.

1774 _____. THE HUMANITIES IN GENERAL EDUCATION. Dubuque, Iowa: William C. Brown Co., 1949. 308 p.

Eighteen humanities curricular plans. Identifies trends and concludes that humanities programs should help students become mature and well-integrated persons.

1775 _____. THE LIBERAL ARTS COLLEGE'S RESPONSIBILITY FOR THE INDIVIDUAL STUDENT. New York: Teachers College, Columbia University, 1966. 122 p.

Liberal arts college presidents take a progressive, student-centered view of liberal education.

1776 _____. PROSPECT FOR RENEWAL: THE FUTURE OF THE LIBERAL ARTS COLLEGE. San Francisco: Jossey-Bass Publishers, 1972. 160 p.

Lectures by Harold Mendelsohn, Nevitt Sanford, the editor, and others on the roles of faculty members and students and on the survival of small liberal arts colleges.

1777 _____. SCIENCE IN GENERAL EDUCATION. Dubuque, Iowa: William C. Brown Co., 1948. 400 p.

Examines higher education science curriculum problems of poor teaching, and inappropriate teaching materials.

1778 _____. SOCIAL SCIENCE IN GENERAL EDUCATION. Dubuque, Iowa: William C. Brown Co., 1948. 286 p.

"How-to" guide to changing the higher education social science curriculum; describes programs used at twenty colleges.

1779 _____. UNIVERSAL HIGHER EDUCATION: A PLAN FOR A NEW EDUCATIONAL PATTERN. New York: McGraw-Hill Book Co., 1966. 258 p.

On ways to provide postsecondary education for a majority of college-age youth. Topics: philosophy, admissions policies, and needs for new community colleges. Contributors: Henry Steele Commager, Algo Henderson, Harold Howe, T.R. McConnell, Daniel Patrick Moynihan, and others.

1780 McGrath, Earl James, and Russell, Charles H. ARE LIBERAL ARTS COLLEGES BECOMING PROFESSIONAL SCHOOLS? New York: Teachers College, Columbia University, 1958. 26 p.

Examines post-1870 developments in fifty liberal arts colleges. Concludes that they combine vocational training with liberal education, a trend that will grow.

1781 McGrath, Earl James, et al. TOWARD GENERAL EDUCATION. New York: Macmillan Co., 1948. 224 p.

Ten University of Iowa professors explore the meaning and purpose of general education.

1782 McGuigan, Dorothy Gies. A DANGEROUS EXPERIMENT: 100 YEARS OF WOMEN AT THE UNIVERSITY OF MICHIGAN. Ann Arbor: Center for the Continuing Education of Women, University of Michigan, 1970. 136 p.

University's centennial history of coeducation, 1870-1970; controversy about admitting women; problems encountered by early women students, including women medical students; and establishment of dean of women. Review of current status shows continuing discrimination against women as students, teachers, and administrators.

1783 _____, ed. NEW RESEARCH ON WOMEN AND SEX ROLES AT THE UNIVERSITY OF MICHIGAN. Ann Arbor: Center for Continuing Education of Women, University of Michigan, 1976. 403 p.

Recent research on women by University of Michigan faculty, students, and former students. Includes chapter on the problems of women in higher education.

1784 McHale, Kathryn, and Speek, Frances Valiant, eds. HOUSING COLLEGE STUDENTS. Washington, D.C.: American Association of University Women, 1934. 96 p.

On- and off-campus housing, mainly for women: dormitory designs, equipment, food services, and student dietary practices. Papers include housing plans of some dozen colleges and universities.

1785 McHenry, Dean Eugene, et al. ACADEMIC DEPARTMENTS: PROBLEMS, VARIATIONS, AND ALTERNATIVES. San Francisco: Jossey-Bass Publishers, 1977. 240 p.

Evaluates higher education departments in the United States and Britain; describes alternative type departments at the Universities of Wisconsin (Green Bay) and California (Santa Cruz), Hampshire College, and Evergreen State College.

1786 Machlup, Fritz. EDUCATION AND ECONOMIC GROWTH. Lincoln: University of Nebraska Press, 1970. 106 p.

Concludes that: (1) increased education adds to income; (2) ability affects income differentials more than does education; (3) rising numbers of educated persons depress the income effect of education; and (4) increased education has less economic effect on blacks than on whites.

1787 _____. THE PRODUCTION AND DISTRIBUTION OF KNOWLEDGE IN THE UNITED STATES. Princeton, N.J.: Princeton University Press, 1962. 416 p.

Explores how knowledge is produced. Examines education, research, development, media, information machines, and information services according to their use of resources, productivity, and contribution to knowledge. Sees knowledge as a form of wealth with its own market value. Suggests reforms (ten years, instead of twelve, for public education); and analyzes effects of informal education.

1788 McInerny, Ralph. SPINNAKER. South Bend, Ind.: Gateway Editions, 1977. 176 p.

Novel about college life in the 1960s by author-professor at a large midwestern university.

1789 MacIver, Robert Morrison. ACADEMIC FREEDOM IN OUR TIMES. New York: Columbia University Press, 1955. 329 p.

Written during the 1950s McCarthy anticommunist era; author defines and defends academic freedom for student, teacher, university, and social welfare.

1790 Mackay, Maxine. STATUS OF WOMEN COMMITTEE: FACULTY REPORT. Tampa: American Association of University Women, Tampa, Florida, 1970. 31 p.

Study of sex discrimination in the state university system of Florida.

1791 McKeachie, Wilbert James. TEACHING TIPS: A GUIDEBOOK FOR THE BEGINNING COLLEGE TEACHER. 7th ed. Lexington, Mass.: D.C. Heath, 1978. 338 p.

On course preparation, traditional and innovative teaching methods, examinations, grading, discipline, counseling, motivation, and student rating of faculty.

1792 McKeefery, William James. PARAMETERS OF LEARNING; PERSPECTIVES IN HIGHER EDUCATION TODAY. Carbondale: Southern Illinois University Press, 1970. 169 p.

Relates educational process to predicting educational outcomes. Useful chapter on using media in college teaching.

1793 Macken, E., et al. HOME-BASED EDUCATION: NEEDS AND TECHNOLOGICAL OPPORTUNITIES. Washington, D.C.: National Institute of Education, 1976. 130 p.

Pursuing education at home by correspondence courses, television, and computer-assisted instruction.

1794 MacKenney, Loren C., et al., eds. A STATE UNIVERSITY SURVEYS THE HUMANITIES. Chapel Hill: University of North Carolina Press, 1945. 262 p.

Part 1: though they have lost their once-commanding position, the humanities continue to enrich students at the University of North Carolina, Chapel Hill; part 2: humanistic and non-humanistic aspects of eleven subjects taught; part 3: Norman Foerster on the future of the humanities in state universities.

1795 MacKenzie, Norman Archibald McRae, et al. OPEN LEARNING: SYSTEMS AND PROBLEMS IN POST-SECONDARY EDUCATION. Paris: UNESCO, 1976. 498 p.

Describes in thirteen countries, including the United States, such alternative higher education experiments as Britain's Open University (home study by BBC television, radio, and textbooks).

1796 MacKenzie, Ossian, et al. CORRESPONDENCE INSTRUCTION IN THE UNITED STATES. New York: McGraw-Hill Book Co., 1968. 261 p.

History of private and university correspondence study; current problems in finance, staffing, public relations, credit, and accreditation; future developments; and competition from new media.

1797 McKinney, Richard I. RELIGION IN HIGHER EDUCATION AMONG NEGROES. New Haven, Conn.: Yale University Press, 1945. 165 p.

Historical function of religious emphasis in black colleges (which mainly prepared preachers and teachers) and its effect on current black students in a more secular society.

1798 McLachlan, James. PRINCETONIANS 1748–1768: A BIOGRAPHICAL DICTIONARY. Princeton, N.J.: Princeton University Press, 1976. 706 p.

Biographical dictionary of Princeton's 338 earliest students, presenting twenty-seven categories of available information, including family relationships, education, and occupations.

1799 Maclean, John. HISTORY OF THE COLLEGE OF NEW JERSEY FROM ITS ORIGIN IN 1746 TO THE COMMENCEMENT OF 1854. 2 vols. Philadelphia: J.B. Lippincott and Co., 1877. Reprint. 2 vols. in 1. New York: Arno Press, 1969.

Princeton University history, 1746–1854, and the alumni leadership role in the early republic.

1800 McLean, Joseph E., ed. THE PUBLIC SERVICE AND UNIVERSITY EDUCATION. Princeton, N.J.: Princeton University Press, 1949. 246 p.

Lectures on the responsibility of higher education institutions to prepare students for public service careers.

1801 McLean, Milton D., ed. RELIGIOUS STUDIES IN PUBLIC UNIVERSITIES. Carbondale: Southern Illinois University, 1967. 266 p.

Part 1: on higher education religious studies. Part 2: religious studies programs in 135 public and eleven private institutions.

1802 McLean, Milton D., and Kimber, Harry H. TEACHING OF RELIGION IN STATE UNIVERSITIES: DESCRIPTIONS OF PROGRAMS IN TWENTY-FIVE INSTITUTIONS. Ann Arbor: University of Michigan, 1960. 117 p.

Concludes that: (1) academic preparation of religious studies faculty is comparable to that of other faculty members; and (2) student enrollment is high when compared with enrollment in other elective courses.

1803 McLean, Sandi, ed. THE CHANGING ROLE OF THE COLLEGE PRESIDENCY: ESSAYS ON GOVERNANCE. Washington, D.C.: American Association of State Colleges and Universities, 1974. 25 p.

Essays on the college presidency by William C. Friday, Stanley O. Ikenberry, and others.

1804 McLeish, John. STUDENTS' ATTITUDES AND COLLEGE ENVIRONMENTS. Cambridge, Engl.: Cambridge Institute of Education, 1970. 251 p.

> Student attitudes at ten colleges of the Cambridge (England) Institute of Education compared with education students' attitudes in several other countries including the United States.

1805 McLure, Gail Thomas, and McLure, John W. WOMEN'S STUDIES. West Haven, Conn.: National Education Association, 1977. 80 p.

> The role women's studies in higher education can play in ending sex-role stereotyping in schools. Suggests needed curriculum changes.

1806 McMahon, Ernest E. THE EMERGING EVENING COLLEGE: A STUDY OF FACULTY ORGANIZATIONS AND ACADEMIC CONTROL IN TEN EASTERN UNIVERSITY EVENING COLLEGES. New York: Teachers College, Columbia University, 1960. 163 p.

> Evolution, problems, and opportunities of city evening colleges.

1807 McMahon, Walter W. INVESTMENT IN HIGHER EDUCATION. Lexington, Mass.: Lexington Books, 1974. 200 p.

> Financial investments and dividends of higher education; a technical and mathematical study.

1808 McManis, Gerald L., and Harvey, L. James. PLANNING, MANAGEMENT, AND EVALUATION SYSTEMS IN HIGHER EDUCATION. Littleton, Colo.: Ireland Educational Corp., 1978. 97 p.

> Explains P.M.E., M.B.O., P.P.B., and zero-based budgeting for higher education.

1809 McMurrin, Sterling M., ed. ON THE MEANING OF THE UNIVERSITY. Salt Lake City: University of Utah Press, 1976. 123 p.

> Essays look at choices confronting higher education and the country. Contributors include the editor, Eric Ashby, Brand Blanshard, T.R. McConnell, and Mina Rees.

1810 McNally, William James. THE BARB. New York: G.P. Putnam's Sons, 1923. 389 p.

> Novel about a young professor who comes to a midwestern university to teach after several years in a more scholarly European atmosphere.

1811 MacRae, Donald. DWIGHT CRAIG. Boston: Houghton Mifflin Co., 1947. 398 p.

Novel about a western university president trying to live down early career, when he climbed by victimizing others.

1812 McVey, Frank LeRond. A UNIVERSITY IS A PLACE--A SPIRIT. Lexington: University of Kentucky Press, 1944. 458 p.

Addresses on university problems when McVey (1869-1953) was president of the University of North Dakota (1909-17) and then the University of Kentucky (1917-40).

1813 McVey, Frank LeRond, and Hughes, Raymond M. PROBLEMS OF COLLEGE AND UNIVERSITY ADMINISTRATION. Ames: Iowa State College Press, 1952. 326 p.

Two president emeriti of state universities on higher education problems, including staff recruitment, pensions, sabbatical leave, teaching, research, fellowships, and participants in governance.

1814 McWhinnie, Ralph E., ed. THOSE GOOD YEARS AT WYOMING U. Casper, Wyo.: Prairie Publishing Co., 1965. 334 p.

Reminiscences and anecdotes by 113 University of Wyoming alumni on faculty, fellow students, and academic and athletic events going back to the university's founding; edited by former registrar and admissions director.

1815 Madison University. THE FIRST HALF CENTURY OF MADISON UNIVERSITY (1819-1869). New York: Sheldon, 1872. 503 p.

Fiftieth anniversary volume with sketches of 1,100 alumni. Later Colgate University, Hamilton, New York.

1816 Madsen, David. THE NATIONAL UNIVERSITY: ENDURING DREAM OF THE USA. Detroit: Wayne State University Press, 1966. 178 p.

Efforts toward a national university since George Washington proposed it in 1775 to the 1961 chartering of a foundation to encourage its establishment. Pros and cons. Concludes that the idea failed because of public indifference but that it came in the back door via increased federal influence on higher education.

1817 Mahoney, Margaret, ed. THE ARTS ON CAMPUS: THE NECESSITY FOR CHANGE. Greenwich, Conn.: New York Graphic Society, 1970. 143 p.

On the need to integrate the arts into general higher education; backs the idea that the arts in the university must become as professionally based as other disciplines and work toward developing an "artist-teacher-scholar."

1818 Maine. University. SURVEY OF HIGHER EDUCATION IN MAINE. Orono: 1932. 430 p.

Statistical survey of higher education in Maine. Views Maine's needs for graduate work, agricultural education, women's education, and scholarships.

1819 Malamud, Bernard. A NEW LIFE. New York: Farrar, Straus and Cudahy, 1961. 367 p.

Novel about antiintellectualism in an Oregon state agricultural college (author taught at Oregon State College), a charge made by a vulnerable New York English instructor hired for one year to replace a fired radical instructor.

1820 Mallery, David. FERMENT ON THE CAMPUS: AN ENCOUNTER WITH THE NEW COLLEGE GENERATION. New York: Harper and Row, 1966. 147 p.

Author's survey of student opinion at seven colleges and universities on student-administration and student-faculty relations; international, political, and local community involvement; fraternity-sorority influence, and other matters troubling student activists.

1821 Malnig, Lawrence R., and Morrow, Sandra L. WHAT CAN I DO WITH A MAJOR IN . . . ? Jersey City, N.J.: Saint Peters College Press, 1975. 101 p.

Twenty-year follow-up study of jobs held by ten thousand college graduates who majored in twenty-one fields. Useful for career planning.

1822 Malone, Dumas. EDWIN A. ALDERMAN: A BIOGRAPHY. Garden City, N.Y.: Doubleday, Doran and Co., 1940. 392 p.

Alderman (1861-1931) helped found the University of North Carolina, Greensboro, and was president of University of North Carolina at Chapel Hill, Tulane University, and the University of Virginia.

1823 Manchester, Frederick, and Shephard, Odell. IRVING BABBITT: MAN AND TEACHER. New York: G.P. Putnam's Sons, 1941. 337 p.

Babbitt (1865-1933) taught languages at Montana and Williams Colleges and at Harvard; as leading humanist he wanted college to promote wisdom and character and not train for power and service.

1824 Manchester, William Raymond. THE LONG GAINER. Boston: Little, Brown and Co., 1961. 495 p.

Novel about a college president whose campaign for state governor is threatened by an undergraduate scandal.

1825 Mandell, Richard D. THE PROFESSOR GAME. Garden City, N.Y.:
Doubleday and Co., 1977. 274 p.

Exposé of college professors who, author claims, have small
teaching loads, big salaries, and assorted grants. Discusses
money, power, sex, salaries, and sabbaticals; says most professors lack interest in the mind or the education of youth.

1826 Mangum, Garth L., ed. THE MANPOWER REVOLUTION: ITS POLICY
CONSEQUENCES. Garden City, N.Y.: Doubleday and Co., 1965.
580 p.

U.S. Senate subcommittee hearings on technology's impact on
labor force skills; problems of training and retraining as technology changes.

1827 Manier, Edward, and Houck, John W., eds. ACADEMIC FREEDOM AND
THE CATHOLIC UNIVERSITY. South Bend, Ind.: Fides Publishers, 1967.
225 p.

On academic freedom and clashes with ecclesiastical authorities in U.S. Roman Catholic universities.

1828 Manley, Robert N. CENTENNIAL HISTORY OF THE UNIVERSITY OF
NEBRASKA. Vol 1. FRONTIER UNIVERSITY (1869-1919). Lincoln: University of Nebraska Press, 1969. 331 p.

Early history of the University of Nebraska. Appendix includes
charter, names of chancellors and regents, chronology of
buildings, essay on sources, and index.

1829 Mann, Georg. DOLLAR DIPLOMA. New York: Macmillan Co., 1960.
204 p.

Satirical novel told through the editor of a university press
about fund raising and curriculum conflicts.

1830 Mann, Richard D., et al. THE COLLEGE CLASSROOM: CONFLICT,
CHANGE, AND LEARNING. New York: Wiley-Interscience, 1970.
389 p.

Complex psychological analysis of college teaching. Identifies
eight student types and teacher roles. Says that faculty members should share experiences and cooperate in order to improve
their teaching.

1831 Manning, Winton H., et al. SELECTIVE ADMISSIONS IN HIGHER EDU-
CATION. San Francisco: Jossey-Bass Publishers, 1977. 256 p.

Explores whether racial or ethnic minority status may be explicitly considered in admitting students. Cites Bakke case. Gives guidelines and recommendations for policymakers.

1832 Marbut, Ann. THE TARNISHED TOWER. New York: David McKay Co., 1957. 283 p.

Novel about a young professor's unprincipled attempt to take over a southern university from its weak president.

1833 Marchant, Maurice P. PARTICIPATIVE MANAGEMENT IN ACADEMIC LIBRARIES. Westport, Conn.: Greenwood Press, 1977. 260 p.

Suggests staff participation in decision making and planning for academic libraries.

1834 Marcy, Willard, ed. PATENT POLICY: GOVERNMENT, ACADEMIC, AND INDUSTRY CONCEPTS. Washington, D.C.: American Chemical Society, 1978. 173 p.

About University of California's patent program, patent policies of other institutions, and potential economic benefits from patents.

1835 Margolis, John D., ed. THE CAMPUS IN THE MODERN WORLD: TWENTY-FIVE ESSAYS. New York: Macmillan Co., 1969. 381 p.

Jacques Barzun, Arthur Bestor, T.S. Eliot, Robert M. Hutchins, and others support the Great Books and other classical traditions in higher education.

1836 Mark, Jorie Lester. PARAPROFESSIONALS IN EDUCATION. New York: Bank Street College of Education, 1978. 108 p.

Programs for training public school paraprofessionals are compared with the ideas of educational reformers; recommends standardizing methods for training paraprofessionals.

1837 Marks, Percy. THE PLASTIC AGE. New York: Century Co., 1924. 332 p.

Novel about the disillusion of college youth in the 1920s, a contrast between the purity and innocence of youth and the essential worldliness of an Ivy League college that might be Dartmouth (where the author taught).

1838 _____. THE UNWILLING GOD. New York: Harper and Brothers, 1929. 338 p.

Novel about a hard working youth from a poor family who wins a football scholarship but fumes at professors' incompeten-

cies and other students' snobbery and frivolity--until he wins
their acclaim as a sports hero.

1839 Marksberry, Mary Lee, and Louttit, Chauncey McKinley. UNIVERSITY
WOMEN'S OPINIONS ON THEIR EDUCATION. Urbana: Committee on
Education for Women, University of Illinois, 1951. 28 p.

University of Illinois alumnae said that their college programs
were satisfactory for career training, but less satisfactory for
marriage and homemaking. Most with careers were in teaching.

1840 Marpiner, Ernest C. THE MAN OF MAYFLOWER HILL: A BIOGRAPHY
OF FRANKLIN W. JOHNSON. Waterville, Maine: Colby College Press,
1967. 137 p.

Johnson (1870-1956) was education professor at Teachers College, Columbia University, and then president of Colby College.

1841 Marquis Academic Media. YEARBOOK OF HIGHER EDUCATION 1977-
78. 9th ed. Chicago: 1977. 700 p.

Descriptive and statistical directory of U.S. higher education.

1842 Marrin, Albert. NICHOLAS MURRAY BUTLER. Boston: Twayne Publishers,
1976. 226 p.

Butler (1862-1947), president of Columbia University, 1902-45,
was influential academic statesman, and supporter of international arbitration and the Carnegie Endowment for International
Peace.

1843 Marshall, Edna M. EVALUATION OF TYPES OF STUDENT TEACHING.
Contributions to Education No. 488. New York: Teachers College,
Columbia University, 1932. 91 p.

Measured teaching success of three types of student teaching.
Concluded that the longer student teaching program was more
efficient.

1844 Marshall, Howard D. THE MOBILITY OF COLLEGE FACULTIES. New
York: Pageant Press, 1964. 152 p.

Found college faculty mobility to be great because demand--
especially for older scholars--was very high.

1845 Marshall, Max S. TWO SIDES TO A TEACHER'S DESK. New York:
Macmillan Co., 1951. 284 p.

A professor's personal philosophy of education--which stresses
helping students to help themselves--and his views about classroom techniques and evaluation.

1846 Marston, Everett Carter. TAKE THE HIGH GROUND. Boston: Little, Brown and Co., 1954. 243 p.

> Novel about a year in the life of an English instructor who goes from the University of Chicago and war service to a New England college.

1847 Martin, Warren Bryan. CONFORMITY: STANDARDS AND CHANGE IN HIGHER EDUCATION. San Francisco: Jossey-Bass Publishers, 1969. 264 p.

> After studying four liberal arts colleges and four universities, author concludes that American higher education is conformist, that the controlling value is professionalism, and that desired diversity can come from careful planning and commitment to values rather than to professional standards.

1848 _____. REDEFINING SERVICE, RESEARCH, AND TEACHING. San Francisco: Jossey-Bass Publishers, 1977. 104 p.

> Proposes more effective linkage of higher education's three traditional goals: teaching, research, and service. Says that service should be emphasized more and defined broadly.

1849 Martorana, S.V., and Kuhns, Eileen. MANAGING ACADEMIC CHANGE. INTERACTIVE FORCES AND LEADERSHIP IN HIGHER EDUCATION. San Francisco: Jossey-Bass Publishers, 1975. 218 p.

> Authors present twenty-four recent innovations in higher education, such as degree by examination, talkback television, and a three-year baccalaureate program. They examine results of innovations and propose a theory for managing change.

1850 Martorana, S.V., and Nespoli, Lawrence A. REGIONALISM IN AMERICAN POSTSECONDARY EDUCATION: CONCEPTS AND PRACTICES. University Park: Center for the Study of Higher Education, Pennsylvania State University, 1978. 334 p.

> Higher education cooperative arrangements in various U.S. geographic areas.

1851 Martorana, S.V., et al., eds. ACCOMMODATING CHANGE IN POSTSECONDARY OCCUPATIONAL EDUCATION. University Park: Center for the Study of Higher Education, Pennsylvania State University, 1977. 79 p.

> Relation of career education to postsecondary occupational education and the shifts in cultural attitudes and facilities needed to achieve lifelong learning.

1852 Martyn, Kenneth A. INCREASING OPPORTUNITIES FOR DISADVANTAGED STUDENTS: FINAL REPORT. Los Angeles: California State College at Los Angeles, 1969. 225 p.

Recommendations to California's Joint Committee on Higher Education for assisting minority students in overcoming barriers to higher education.

1853 Masland, John W., and Radway, Laurence I. SOLDIERS AND SCHOLARS: MILITARY EDUCATION AND NATIONAL POLICY. Princeton, N.J.: Princeton University Press, 1957. 530 p.

Analysis of undergraduate officer education at all three service academies. Considers goal of military education to produce both soldiers and statesmen.

1854 Mason, Carleton D. ADAPTATIONS OF INSTRUCTION TO INDIVIDUAL DIFFERENCES IN THE PREPARATION OF TEACHERS IN NORMAL SCHOOLS AND TEACHERS COLLEGES. New York: Teachers College, Columbia University, 1940. 279 p.

Used data from administrators, faculty, and students at teachers colleges to assess their effectiveness in training educational leaders.

1855 Mason, Henry L. COLLEGE AND UNIVERSITY GOVERNMENT: A HANDBOOK OF PRINCIPLE AND PRACTICE. New Orleans: Tulane University, 1972. 175 p.

Summarized writings during 1958 through 1972 on the roles of trustees, administrators, faculties, senates, and students in higher education governance.

1856 Mason, Thomas R., ed. ASSESSING COMPUTER-BASED SYSTEMS MODELS. San Francisco: Jossey-Bass Publishers, 1976. 112 p.

Role of computer models in higher education planning and management.

1857 Mathews, Lois Kimball. THE DEAN OF WOMEN. Boston: Houghton Mifflin Co., 1915. 275 p.

Early book on the dean of women in American colleges and universities. Chapters on student living conditions, employment, vocational guidance, social life, discipline, and intellectual life.

1858 Mattfeld, Jacquelyn A., and Van Aken, Carol G., eds. WOMEN AND THE SCIENTIFIC PROFESSIONS: THE M.I.T. SYMPOSIUM ON AMERICAN WOMEN IN SCIENCE AND ENGINEERING. Cambridge: MIT Press, 1965. 250 p.

On the role of women in scientific professions. Explores personal, social, and economic factors in professional careers for women; looks at status of women in industry and the academic world; discusses problems of female employment and the prospects for women in the scientific professions.

1859 Matthews, Donald R., and Prothro, James W. NEGROES AND THE NEW SOUTHERN POLITICS. New York: Harcourt, Brace and World, 1966. 551 p.

Chapter on black college students who become black political elites in this analysis of blacks in southern politics and the antisegregation movement.

1860 Mauer, George J., ed. CRISES IN CAMPUS MANAGEMENT: CASE STUDIES IN THE ADMINISTRATION OF COLLEGES AND UNIVERSITIES. New York: Praeger Publishers, 1976. 266 p.

Nineteen case studies of problems in higher education governance. Editor says administrators need training in campus management techniques. Proposes creating an Academy for Higher Education Administration as a center to help solve governance problems.

1861 Maxwell, Martha. IMPROVING STUDENT LEARNING SKILLS: A COMPREHENSIVE GUIDE TO SUCCESSFUL PRACTICES AND PROGRAMS FOR INCREASING THE PERFORMANCE OF UNDERPREPARED STUDENTS. San Francisco: Jossey-Bass Publishers, 1979. 500 p.

Guide to organizing, staffing, supporting, and evaluating effective programs for underprepared students. Separate chapters on improving student skills in mathematics, science, writing, speaking, reading, and studying.

1862 Maxwell, William. THE FOLDED LEAF. New York: Harper and Brothers, 1945. 310 p.

Novel set in a Big Ten university about two friends from the same Wisconsin town and high school. Has much about fraternity life, college sports, love, and a suicide attempt.

1863 Mayer, Frederick. CREATIVE UNIVERSITIES. Boston: Twayne Publishers, 1961. 112 p.

Sees ultimate function of the university as creating a perfect society. Criticizes universities as excessively vocation-oriented.

1864 _____. NEW DIRECTIONS FOR THE AMERICAN UNIVERSITY. Washington, D.C.: Public Affairs Press, 1957. 52 p.

Wants change in university administration to reflect more concern about the inner development of students which author

thinks is more important than the concern for lowered standards of education.

1865 Mayhew, Lewis B. ARROGANCE ON CAMPUS. San Francisco: Jossey-
Bass Publishers, 1970. 155 p.

American higher education problems in light of campus unrest
during late 1960s; sees students, faculty, and administration
as arrogant and in need of reform in curriculum, campus life,
and governance.

1866 _____. THE CARNEGIE COMMISSION ON HIGHER EDUCATION: A
CRITICAL ANALYSIS OF THE REPORTS AND RECOMMENDATIONS. San
Francisco: Jossey-Bass Publishers, 1973. 441 p.

Invaluable summary, review, critique, and synthesis of the
Commission's over fifty reports and documents for improving
and reshaping U.S. higher education.

1867 _____. CHANGING PRACTICES IN EDUCATION FOR THE PROFES-
SIONS. Atlanta: Southern Regional Education Board, 1971. 82 p.

Sees reform in professional education in more clinical experience, more emphasis upon social and behavioral sciences, and
a move toward free election of courses.

1868 _____. COLLEGES TODAY AND TOMORROW. San Francisco: Jossey-
Bass Publishers, 1969. 255 p.

Surveys U.S. higher education, future trends, university government relations, student problems, and curriculum reform;
sees increasing size and neglect of undergraduate teaching as
inevitable but points out that cluster colleges will help.

1869 _____. CONTEMPORARY COLLEGE STUDENTS AND THE CURRICULUM.
Atlanta: Southern Regional Education Board, 1969. 86 p.

Curriculum and instruction fail to meet college student needs,
partly due to student unrest, putting faculty research and publications ahead of curriculum decisions, and putting graduate
over undergraduate education; thinks there is neglect of the
total development of the student.

1870 _____. GRADUATE AND PROFESSIONAL EDUCATION, 1980: A SUR-
VEY OF INSTITUTIONAL PLANS. New York: McGraw-Hill Book Co.,
1970. 38 p.

Projects that the United States will produce seventy thousand
Ph.D.s by 1980. Discusses rapid growth of humanistic fields
over scientific fields in graduate programs; cites federal policy
as aiding increased institutional interest in graduate education.

1871 _____. HIGHER EDUCATION FOR OCCUPATIONS. Atlanta: Southern Regional Education Board, 1974. 140 p.

> Discusses and plans relevant curriculum in U.S. undergraduate education for occupational, vocational, or career students.

1872 _____. LEGACY OF THE SEVENTIES: EXPERIMENT, ECONOMY, EQUALITY, AND EXPEDIENCY IN AMERICAN HIGHER EDUCATION. San Francisco: Jossey-Bass Publishers, 1977. 366 p.

> Nontraditional education arose about 1968-70 in reaction to traditional higher education meritocracy, selectivity, campus autonomy, and professorial primacy. Based on the belief in educational opportunity for all at every age and especially for adults and part-time students, this trend is now in decline because higher education is not an agency for social reform, is not a remedial substitute for basic education, cannot long appeal to transitory constituencies, costs too much, and traditional higher education can and will absorb less controversial features.

1873 _____. THE LITERATURE OF HIGHER EDUCATION 1971. San Francisco: Jossey-Bass Publishers, 1971. 162 p.

> Reviews over 150 of the year's higher education books under categories of governance, history, campus unrest, institutional differences, proceedings, teaching and professional procedures, curriculum, and economic analyses. Also evaluates in one essay higher education literature, 1965-70.

1874 _____. THE LITERATURE OF HIGHER EDUCATION 1972. San Francisco: Jossey-Bass Publishers, 1972. 184 p.

> Evaluative summaries of higher education books published in 1971 (plus some from earlier years) arranged under trends, administration, organization, governance, student protest, students and their affairs, curricular and instructional concerns, educational opinion and policy, types of institutions, faculty and their affairs, history, and bibliographies.

1875 _____. REFORM IN GRADUATE EDUCATION. Atlanta: Southern Regional Education Board, 1972. 182 p.

> On changes, innovations, and reforms in graduate education in the arts and sciences. Reviews essential literature on graduate education; chapters on curriculum, instruction, structure, organization, preparing college teachers, issues, and guidelines for change.

1876 _____. THE SMALLER LIBERAL ARTS COLLEGE. New York: Center of Applied Research in Education, 1962. 113 p.

Author blames failure of small liberal arts colleges to become
centers of intellectual and cultural activity to wrong geographic location, limited staff, and limited research funds.

1877 _____, ed. GENERAL EDUCATION: AN ACCOUNT AND APPRAISAL;
A GUIDE FOR COLLEGE FACULTIES. New York: Harper and Row, 1960.
212 p.

On general education's strengths, weaknesses, and prospects.
Looks at such aspects as administrative practices, curricular
problems, and faculty and teaching quality.

1878 _____. HIGHER EDUCATION IN THE REVOLUTIONARY DECADES.
Berkeley, Calif.: McCutchan Publishers, 1967. 466 p.

Effect on higher education of post-World War II population ex-
plosion, growth of cybernetics, revolt of colonial peoples,
development of modern weapons systems, growth of technology
and automation, and increases in knowledge.

1879 Mayhew, Lewis B., and Ford, Patrick J. CHANGING THE CURRICULUM.
San Francisco: Jossey-Bass Publishers, 1971. 188 p.

Ways for administrators and faculty to reform undergraduate
curricula to meet more effectively students' developmental
needs.

1880 _____. REFORM IN GRADUATE AND PROFESSIONAL EDUCATION.
San Francisco: Jossey-Bass Publishers, 1974. 254 p.

Sees more evidence of reform in professional schools than in
the arts and sciences; explores reforms in curriculum, clinical
and field experience, reorganizing student time, technology,
research, and independent study.

1881 Maynard, James. SOME MICROECONOMICS OF HIGHER EDUCATION:
ECONOMICS OF SCALE. Lincoln: University of Nebraska Press, 1971.
186 p.

There is an enrollment size below which costs are excessive
and above which proportionate economies do not operate. Very
large campuses are uneconomical. Recommends that new institutions be established only if they will quickly attain an economically viable enrollment.

1882 Mayo, G. Douglas, and Claxton, Charles S. IMPROVING COLLEGE
TEACHING. Memphis, Tenn.: Center for Instructional Service and Research, Memphis State University, 1978. 69 p.

Conference of Tennessee colleges and universities to improve
teaching in various disciplines.

1883 Mayor, John R., and Swartz, Willis G. ACCREDITATION IN TEACHER EDUCATION: ITS INFLUENCE ON HIGHER EDUCATION. Washington, D.C.: National Commission on Accrediting, 1965. 311 p.

> Part I: history and problems related to accreditation in teacher education; part II: influences of teacher education accreditation on higher education; and part III: recommendations for teacher education accreditation at the state, regional, and national levels.

1884 Mayville, William V. INTERDISCIPLINARITY: THE MUTABLE PARADIGM. Washington, D.C.: American Association for Higher Education, 1979. 72 p.

> History and development of interdisciplinary programs in U.S. colleges and universities, with specific illustrations.

1885 Mead, Margaret. BLACKBERRY WINTER: MY EARLIER YEARS. New York: William Morrow and Co., 1972. 305 p.

> Autobiography of American anthropologist during her first thirty-seven years (1902-39). Tells of her childhood, schooling, higher education at Barnard College and Columbia University, marriages, and pioneering field experiences.

1886 Mead, Margaret, and Balgley, Frances. AMERICAN WOMEN. THE RE-PORT OF THE PRESIDENT'S COMMISSION ON THE STATUS OF WOMEN AND OTHER PUBLICATIONS OF THE COMMISSION. New York: Charles Scribner's Sons, 1965. 274 p.

> Chapter on education and many index entries on all school levels especially higher education, education for mature women, counseling, guidance, and vocational training.

1887 Meader, James Laurence. NORMAL SCHOOL EDUCATION IN CONNEC-TICUT. Contributions to Education No. 307. New York: Teachers College, Columbia University, 1928. 96 p.

> Brief history of Connecticut public schools and the founding of a teacher training school, a cooperative plan for teacher education, and results of a statistical study of Connecticut teacher education.

1888 Means, Howard B., and Semas, Philip W., eds. FACULTY COLLECTIVE BARGAINING, SECOND EDITION. Washington, D.C.: Editorial Projects for Education, 1976. 157 p.

> News, facts, and figures on collective bargaining in higher education. Includes faculty attitudes toward bargaining, campus elections, strikes, a glossary, summaries of pertinent legislation, court decisions, National Labor Relations Board rulings, and a bibliography.

1889 Mechanic, David. STUDENTS UNDER STRESS: A STUDY IN THE SO-
CIAL PSYCHOLOGY OF ADAPTATION. New York: Free Press of Glencoe, 1962. 231 p.

> Physiological and social aspects as well as psychoanalytical
> mechanisms used by twenty-two graduate students under stress
> while taking critical examinations.

1890 Mecklin, John W. MY QUEST FOR FREEDOM. New York: Charles
Scribner's Sons, 1945. 293 p.

> Professor who taught at Lafayette College, University of Pitts-
> burgh, and Dartmouth College tells of his experiences with
> pragmatic philosophy.

1891 Medical College of Virginia. PROBLEMS OF COLLEGIATE SUCCESS OR
FAILURE WITH PARTICULAR REFERENCE TO PROFESSIONAL SCHOOLS
OF MEDICINE. Richmond: 1949. 124 p.

> Characteristics of dropouts from twenty-two classes (1926-49)
> at the Medical College of Virginia. Concluded that students
> likely to succeed had above average aptitude test scores, came
> from urban communities, from universities instead of colleges,
> and from northern rather than southern preparatory schools.

1892 Medsker, Leland L. THE JUNIOR COLLEGE: PROGRESS AND PROSPECT.
New York: McGraw-Hill Book Co., 1960. 367 p.

> Evaluates critically junior colleges. Says that they are failing
> to give adequate terminal education, educational and voca-
> tional guidance, and general education. Recommends that
> junior colleges develop their own identity and coordinate their
> operations with their objectives.

1893 Medsker, Leland L., and Tillery, Dale. BREAKING THE ACCESS BAR-
RIERS: A PROFILE OF TWO-YEAR COLLEGES. New York: McGraw-
Hill Book Co., 1971. 183 p.

> History of the two-year college movement, statistics, student
> characteristics, curricular programs, administration, staffing,
> financing, and planning. Recommends more state and federal
> financial support, student aid, and a nationwide program to
> develop faculty and administrators.

1894 Medsker, Leland L., and Trent, James W. THE INFLUENCE OF DIFFER-
ENT TYPES OF PUBLIC HIGHER INSTITUTIONS ON COLLEGE ATTEN-
DANCE FROM VARYING SOCIOECONOMIC AND ABILITY LEVELS.
Berkeley: Center for Research and Development in Higher Education, Uni-
versity of California, 1965. 110 p.

> Found among ten thousand 1959 high school graduates that the

most important factors affecting their college attendance were parents who encourage their college plans and easy access to a junior college, especially for low socioeconomic students.

1895 Meeth, L. Richard. QUALITY EDUCATION FOR LESS MONEY: A SOURCEBOOK FOR IMPROVING COST EFFECTIVENESS. San Francisco: Jossey-Bass Publishers, 1974. 206 p.

Studied sixty-six reputable but nonprestigious undergraduate church-related colleges. Recommended that such colleges use institutional research and planning to achieve efficiency and effectiveness.

1896 _____, ed. SELECTED ISSUES IN HIGHER EDUCATION: AN ANNO-TATED BIBLIOGRAPHY. New York: Teachers College Press, 1965. 212 p.

Over 1,000 annotated books and articles, 1955-65, on U.S. college and university policymaking, operations, curriculum, teaching, administration, finance, and business management.

1897 Mehnert, Klaus. TWILIGHT OF THE YOUNG: THE RADICAL MOVE-MENTS OF THE 1960'S AND THEIR LEGACY. New York: Holt, Rine-hart and Winston, 1977. 428 p.

Commentary on 1960s radical movements by a journalist-teacher-lecturer and world traveler who sees the upheaval as a global phenomenon caused by a "break in time," between the indus-trial age and the atomic era.

1898 Meier, Gretl S. JOB SHARING: A NEW PATTERN FOR QUALITY OF WORK AND LIFE. Kalamazoo, Mich.: W.E. Upjohn Institute for Em-ployment Research, 1979. 187 p.

Job sharing, where two higher education faculty members joint-ly hold one position.

1899 Meigs, Cornelia L. WHAT MAKES A COLLEGE? A HISTORY OF BRYN MAWR. New York: Macmillan Co., 1956. 277 p.

History of the small prestigious liberal arts college for women founded in 1885 by Quaker Joseph Taylor, as recorded by a professor emerita and official college historian.

1900 Meiklejohn, Alexander. EDUCATION BETWEEN TWO WORLDS. New York: Harper and Brothers, 1942. 303 p.

Humanist's account of the slow decay of liberal education in the face of state control of schooling and the influence of John Dewey's philosophy.

1901 _____. THE EXPERIMENTAL COLLEGE. New York: Harper and Brothers, 1932. Reprint. New York: Arno Press, 1972. 421 p.

> Description by the originator of the Experimental College of the University of Wisconsin from its beginning in 1927, its philosophy, successes and failures, and the teaching methods used to nurture in students "a humane and responsible intelligence."

1902 Meland, Bernard E. HIGHER EDUCATION AND THE HUMAN SPIRIT. Chicago: University of Chicago Press, 1953. 204 p.

> Defends the place of religion among the liberal arts and says humanities should be the core of the undergraduate curriculum.

1903 Melzer, John H. PHILOSOPHY IN THE CLASSROOM: A REPORT. Lincoln: University of Nebraska Press, 1954. 192 p.

> Teaching philosophy in higher education; course content and practical problems based on responses from many philosophy professors.

1904 Menacker, Julius. FROM SCHOOL TO COLLEGE: ARTICULATION AND TRANSFER. Washington, D.C.: American Council on Education, 1975. 229 p.

> On students' transition to college and on improving college placement. For college admissions officers, high school counselors, students, and parents.

1905 Menashe, Louis, and Radosh, Ronald, eds. TEACH-INS: U.S.A.; REPORTS, OPINIONS, DOCUMENTS. New York: Praeger Publishers, 1967. 349 p.

> Captures the 1965 antiwar academic protests in speeches, recollections, and other documents from campus teach-ins.

1906 Menges, Robert J. TEACHING-LEARNING EXPERIENCES FOR COLLEGE STUDENTS AND OTHER ADULTS: A SELECTED ANNOTATED BIBLIOGRAPHY. Evanston, Ill.: Center for the Teaching Professions, Northwestern University, 1979. 74 p.

> Annotates about four hundred publications on postsecondary teaching and learning.

1907 Merton, Robert K., et al., eds. THE STUDENT-PHYSICIAN: INTRODUCTORY STUDIES IN THE SOCIOLOGY OF MEDICAL EDUCATION. Cambridge, Mass.: Harvard University Press, 1957. 360 p.

> Sociological study of medical student's idea of what a physician is, reasons for choosing medicine, and changing image

of the profession while in medical school. Students and faculty at medical schools of Cornell, the University of Pennsylvania, and Western Reserve participated.

1908 Messick, Samuel, et al. INDIVIDUALITY IN LEARNING: IMPLICATIONS OF COGNITIVE STYLES AND CREATIVITY FOR HUMAN DEVELOPMENT. San Francisco: Jossey-Bass Publishers, 1976. 382 p.

Examines students' different ways of learning, deplores overemphasis on scholastic aptitude, and suggests that educators use individualized instruction to fit students' styles of learning (as affected by such factors as sex and ethnicity).

1909 Metcalf, Keyes D., et al. THE PROGRAM OF INSTRUCTION IN LIBRARY SCHOOLS. Urbana: University of Illinois Press, 1943. 140 p.

Recommends more graduate-level instruction, more emphasis on research and advanced study, and one administrator for both university library and library school.

1910 Metzger, Walter P., ed. THE AMERICAN CONCEPT OF ACADEMIC FREEDOM INFORMATION: A COLLECTION OF ESSAYS AND REPORTS. New York: Arno Press, 1977. 300 p.

Evolution of ideas about academic freedom during 1885-1973 by John Dewey, Charles W. Eliot, Arthur Lovejoy, the American Association of University Professors, and the American Philosophical Society.

1911 _____. THE CONSTITUTIONAL STATUS OF ACADEMIC FREEDOM. New York: Arno Press, 1977. 600 p.

Court rulings and commentary on famous academic freedom cases, 1925-74, including the Tennessee Scopes trial and the Bertrand Russell case.

1912 _____. PROFESSORS ON GUARD: THE FIRST AAUP INVESTIGATIONS. New York: Arno Press, 1977. 267 p.

Historic investigations of academic freedom cases during 1915-17 by philosopher Arthur O. Lovejoy for the American Association of University Professors, of which he was principal organizer.

1913 _____. READER ON THE SOCIOLOGY OF THE ACADEMIC PROFESSION. New York: Arno Press, 1977. 450 p.

Articles from 1940 to 1974 by David Riesman, Talcott Parsons, and Logan Wilson on higher education structure, careers of professors, governance, and collective bargaining.

1914 Metzger, Walter F., et al. DIMENSIONS OF ACADEMIC FREEDOM.
Urbana: University of Illinois Press, 1969. 121 p.

Explores academic freedom in historical perspective. Metzger
finds AAUP's 1915 definition of academic freedom inadequate
for contemporary situations.

1915 Metzler, John H. COLLECTIVE BARGAINING FOR COMMUNITY COL-
LEGES. Washington, D.C.: Association of Community College Trustees,
1977. 110 p.

Explains the collective bargaining process; aids community college presidents and trustees to negotiate with faculty and staff.

1916 Metzler, Ken. CONFRONTATION: THE DESTRUCTION OF A COL-
LEGE PRESIDENT. Plainview, N.Y.: Nash Publishing Corp., 1973.
337 p.

Explores activist student splinter groups, disenchanted alumni,
frugal state legislature, and unsympathetic governor as con-
tributing factors in the disablement and death of the acting
president of the University of Oregon.

1917 Meyer, Annie Nathan. BARNARD BEGINNINGS. Boston: Houghton
Mifflin Co., 1935. 196 p.

Author's and other ambitious New York City women's struggle
to found in 1889 Barnard College as an undergraduate college
of Columbia College.

1918 Meyer, Peter. AWARDING COLLEGE CREDIT FOR NON-COLLEGE
LEARNING. San Francisco: Jossey-Bass Publishers, 1975. 195 p.

About awarding college credit for learning gained before college admission and not measurable by standardized tests. Analyzes how such credit is granted at more than one hundred U.S.
colleges. Suggests how to award such credit. Recommends a
National Center for Assessment of Prior Learning.

1919 Meyerson, Martin, and Winegrad, Dilys. GLADLY LEARN AND GLADLY
TEACH: FRANKLIN AND HIS HEIRS AT THE UNIVERSITY OF PENNSYL-
VANIA, 1740-1976. Philadelphia: University of Pennsylvania Press, 1978.
263 p.

History of the University of Pennsylvania told through biographies of outstanding professors.

1920 Mezirow, Jack. EDUCATION FOR PERSPECTIVE TRANSFORMATION:
WOMEN'S RE-ENTRY PROGRAMS IN COMMUNITY COLLEGES. New
York: Center for Adult Education, Teachers College, Columbia University,
1978. 59 p.

Assesses and proposes improvements in community college programs which serve women returning to college.

1921 Miami-Dade Community College. GENERAL EDUCATION IN A CHANG-
ING SOCIETY: GENERAL EDUCATION PROGRAM, BASIC SKILLS RE-
QUIREMENTS, STANDARDS OF ACADEMIC PROGRESS AT MIAMI-DADE
COMMUNITY COLLEGE. Miami, Fla.: 1978. 105 p.

Three-year study of Miami-Dade College; asks for improvements
in the general education core curriculum.

1922 Michie, Allan, et al. THE UNIVERSITY LOOKS ABROAD: APPROACHES
TO WORLD AFFAIRS AT SIX AMERICAN UNIVERSITIES: A REPORT FROM
EDUCATION AND WORLD AFFAIRS. New York: Walker and Co., 1966.
300 p.

International programs at Cornell, Indiana, Michigan State,
Stanford, and Tulane Universities and at the University of Wisconsin. Guidelines for future international programs.

1923 Michigan. Office of Veterans Affairs. A SURVEY OF DEGREE-GRANT-
ING INSTITUTIONS APPROVED FOR PARTICIPATION IN THE SERVICE-
MAN'S READJUSTMENT ACT OF 1944: PART I, COLLEGES AND UNI-
VERSITIES OF THE STATE OF MICHIGAN. Lansing: 1944. 56 p.

Describes the nineteen colleges and universities in Michigan
eligible to provide education for veterans under the 1944 G.I.
Bill.

1924 Michigan. State University. Institute of Research on Overseas Programs.
THE INTERNATIONAL PROGRAMS OF AMERICAN UNIVERSITIES: AN
INVENTORY AND ANALYSIS. East Lansing: 1958. 323 p.

Describes overseas programs of nearly 2,000 U.S. higher education institutions.

1925 Michigan. University. Center for Continuing Education of Women.
WOMEN ON CAMPUS: 1970; A SYMPOSIUM. Ann Arbor: 1970. 65 p.

Barriers to women, including black women, at the University
of Michigan.

1926 _____. Center for the Study of Higher Education, School of Education.
STRUCTURE AND EMERGENCE. Ann Arbor: 1977. 114 p.

Symposium on innovation in undergraduate education. How
changes have been made in colleges and universities and how
new knowledge about innovation can be disseminated.

1927 _____. School of Library Sciences. WOMEN IN THE LIBRARY PRO-

FESSION: LEADERSHIP ROLES AND CONTRIBUTIONS. Ann Arbor:
1971. 34 p.

Papers on women in the library profession.

1928 Mickelson, Joel C., ed. AMERICAN PERSONALITY AND THE CREATIVE
ARTS. Minneapolis: Burgess Publishing Co., 1969. 180 p.

History of the development of American studies courses, with
implications for other interdisciplinary fields, such as black
studies.

1929 Middleberg, Maurice I. MORAL EDUCATION AND STUDENT DEVELOP-
MENT DURING THE COLLEGE YEARS: A SELECTIVE ANNOTATED BIB-
LIOGRAPHY. Tucson: Program in Liberal Studies, University of Arizona,
1977. 61 p.

Annotated readings on the effects of college education on student's personality and values, theories on moral development,
and the philosophical problems of teaching morality.

1930 Middlebrook, William T. HOW TO ESTIMATE THE BUILDING NEEDS OF
A COLLEGE OR UNIVERSITY: A DEMONSTRATION OF METHODS DEVEL-
OPED AT THE UNIVERSITY OF MINNESOTA. Minneapolis: University
of Minnesota Press, 1958. 170 p.

Instrument author developed to determine University of Minnesota building needs and its applicability at other colleges and
universities.

1931 Miers, Earl Schenck. THE IVY YEARS. New Brunswick, N.J.: Rutgers
University Press, 1945. 229 p.

Realistic autobiographical novel set at Rutgers University.

1932 Miles, Edward V. MANUAL OF TEACHERS COLLEGE ACCOUNTING.
Washington, D.C.: American Council on Education, 1940. 190 p.

Handbook for improving accounting practices at teachers colleges.

1933 Miles, Michael W. THE RADICAL PROBE: THE LOGIC OF STUDENT
REBELLION. New York: Atheneum Press, 1971. 311 p.

Says 1960s student protests will have long-range significance
because they were broadbased moral reaction to a sick society.
Believes such movements should direct their efforts against the
power elite which controls U.S. society.

1934 Millay, Kathleen Young. AGAINST THE WALL. New York: Macaulay
Co., 1929. 442 p.

Novel about a small-town girl from Maine who wins a scholarship to a famous woman's college, recognizably Vassar, but
rebels and leaves because of snobbery and backbiting.

1935 Millbank Memorial Fund Commission. HIGHER EDUCATION FOR PUBLIC
HEALTH: A REPORT OF THE MILLBANK MEMORIAL FUND COMMISSION.
New York: Prodist, Watson Academic Publications, 1977. 218 p.

Recommends reorganizing and improving health education programs at universities and schools of public health.

1936 Miller, Eugene. BARRON'S GUIDE TO GRADUATE BUSINESS SCHOOLS,
EASTERN EDITION. Woodbury, N.Y.: Barron's Educational Series, 1978.
342 p.

Describes each institution's academic community, calendar, programs, admissions, costs, financial aid, library, placement,
and recruiting activities. Introduction describes various Master's degrees in Business Administration and application procedures.

1937 Miller, Howard. THE REVOLUTIONARY COLLEGE: AMERICAN PRES-
BYTERIAN HIGHER EDUCATION, 1707-1837. New York: New York
University Press, 1976. 381 p.

Historical contributions to religion and higher education of
Presbyterians, the most active denomination outside of New
England. Often, theirs were the first higher education schools
in the middle and southern states. Much on Princeton, begun
1746 as the College of New Jersey.

1938 Miller, J. Hillis, and Allen, John S. VETERANS CHALLENGE THE COL-
LEGES: THE NEW YORK PROGRAM. New York: King's Crown Press,
1947. 150 p.

Problems at ninety-two New York colleges when World War II
veterans caused enrollments to mount. How state and federal
agencies and higher education institutions collaborated to set
up emergency facilities.

1939 Miller, J. Hillis, and Brooks, Dorothy V.N. THE ROLE OF HIGHER
EDUCATION IN WAR AND AFTER. New York: Harper and Brothers,
1944. 222 p.

Impact of World War II on higher education enrollments, faculty leaves of absence and replacement, student acceleration,
and curriculum. Says some changes were inevitable, especially
within junior colleges. Recommends further changes, especially more scholarships for needy students.

1940 Miller, James L., Jr. STATE BUDGETING FOR HIGHER EDUCATION:

THE USE OF FORMULAS AND COST ANALYSIS. Ann Arbor: Institute of Public Administration, University of Michigan, 1965. 228 p.

> Describes five states' 1963 procedures in making formulas for budget requests and cost analyses as they worked out appropriations for public higher education.

1941 Miller, Jerry W., and Mills, Olive, eds. CREDENTIALING EDUCATIONAL ACCOMPLISHMENT. Washington, D.C.: American Council on Education, 1978. 255 p.

> Role higher education institutions play in granting credentials—especially degrees. Recommends changes that will clarify the meaning of credentials and assure that institutions are consistent in awarding them. Says that traditional degrees should be accompanied by a narrative description of each student's work.

1942 Miller, Kathryn Naomi. THE SELECTION OF UNITED STATES SERIAL DOCUMENTS FOR LIBERAL ARTS COLLEGES. New York: H.W. Wilson Co., 1937. 364 p.

> Compares opinions on selection of U.S. serial documents by instructors from eighty-one colleges with selection opinions of college librarians.

1943 Miller, Michael V., and Gilmore, Susan, eds. REVOLUTION AT BERKELEY: THE CRISIS IN AMERICAN EDUCATION. New York: Dell Publishing Co., 1965. 348 p.

> Partisan articles on the 1964–65 University of California, Berkeley, student riots.

1944 Miller, Nolan. MERRY INNOCENTS. New York: Harper and Brothers, 1947. 239 p.

> Novel about prejudice affecting a professor's family maid in a midwestern town.

1945 _____. WHY I AM SO BEAT. New York: G.P. Putnam's Sons, 1954. 213 p.

> Novel in the first person about a freshman at a large city university worried over World War II draft.

1946 Miller, Richard I. THE ASSESSMENT OF COLLEGE PERFORMANCE: A HANDBOOK OF TECHNIQUES AND MEASURES FOR INSTITUTIONAL SELF-EVALUATION. San Francisco: Jossey-Bass Publishers, 1979. 374 p.

> Criteria for using existing staff and funds to evaluate such key functions as faculty, learning, curriculum, administration, and

financial management. Includes rating forms often used and recent studies done by various institutions.

1947 _____. DEVELOPING PROGRAMS FOR FACULTY EVALUATION. San Francisco: Jossey-Bass Publishers, 1974. 248 p.

Procedures for starting a valid system of faculty evaluation; discusses the validity and reliability of student evaluation of teaching and stresses classroom teaching as one of nine major aspects to be evaluated.

1948 _____. EVALUATING FACULTY PERFORMANCE. San Francisco: Jossey-Bass Publishers, 1972. 145 p.

Guide to faculty evaluation which emphasizes teaching effectiveness as one of nine categories to be evaluated mainly by student views. Includes sample appraisal forms.

1949 Miller, Russell E. LIGHT ON THE HILL: A HISTORY OF TUFTS COLLEGE, 1852-1952. Boston: Beacon Press, 1966. 734 p.

Tuft's centennial history explores religious (founded by Universalists), financial, and administrative aspects of its growth as a small, high quality university.

1950 Miller, Stephen J. PRESCRIPTION FOR LEADERSHIP: TRAINING FOR THE MEDICAL ELITE. Chicago: Aldine Publishing Co., 1970. 256 p.

Concluded that, as residents in the Harvard Medical Unit of Boston City Hospital, young doctors become part of a national medical elite; and that medical internship helps develop one's self-concept as a professional and one's knowledge of actual clinical procedures.

1951 Miller, Theodore Kay, and Prince, Judith S. THE FUTURE OF STUDENT AFFAIRS: A GUIDE TO STUDENT DEVELOPMENT FOR TOMORROW'S HIGHER EDUCATION. San Francisco: Jossey-Bass Publishers, 1976. 220 p.

Analyzes ideas of Erik Erikson, Robert Havighurst, and others about higher education's role in producing change in the individual student. Suggests practical ways student services staff can build programs to enhance student development.

1952 Miller, Warren. THE BRIGHT YOUNG THINGS. Boston: Little, Brown and Co., 1958. 240 p.

Novel about students in a New England women's college maturing and falling in love.

1953 Millett, Fred B. PROFESSOR: PROBLEMS AND REWARDS IN COLLEGE TEACHING. New York: Macmillan Co., 1961. 189 p.

> For those considering college teaching, outlines training, activities, and responsibilities of mainly humanities professors and cites advantages and disadvantages of academic life.

1954 _____. THE REBIRTH OF LIBERAL EDUCATION. New York: Harcourt, Brace and Co., 1945. 179 p.

> Concludes that humanities teaching--weakened by vocationalism and by cafeteria-style electives--must be strengthened by developing thoroughly integrated, broadly based humanities courses.

1955 Millett, John David. DECISION MAKING AND ADMINISTRATION IN HIGHER EDUCATION. Kent, Ohio: Kent State University Press, 1968. 161 p.

> About decision making, planning, systems analysis, financing, and internal communication in higher education administration. Found two major changes occurring: government agencies have increasing authority, and faculty and students are having more influence on academic policy.

1956 _____. FINANCING HIGHER EDUCATION IN THE UNITED STATES: THE STAFF REPORT OF THE COMMISSION ON FINANCING HIGHER EDUCATION. New York: Columbia University Press, 1952. 503 p.

> Concludes that states--not the federal government--must take major responsibility for adequate financing of public institutions and that private institutions must rely on benefactions.

1957 _____. HIGHER EDUCATION AND THE 1980'S. Washington, D.C.: Academy for Educational Development, 1978. 43 p.

> Notes changes in enrollments and in state and federal policies toward higher education. Urges colleges and universities to develop policies for the predicted 1980s slump.

1958 _____. HIGHER EDUCATION PLANNING: A REPORT OF EXPERIENCE AND A FORECAST OF STRATEGIES FOR CHANGE. Washington, D.C.: Academy for Educational Development, 1979. 36 p.

> Report of a project to improve management and leadership in colleges and universities.

1959 _____. NEW STRUCTURES OF CAMPUS POWER: SUCCESS AND FAILURES OF EMERGING FORMS OF INSTITUTIONAL GOVERNANCE. San Francisco: Jossey-Bass Publishers, 1978. 294 p.

After studying thirty instances of joint student-faculty-administration campus wide governance, author is critical because of failure in purpose, budget, management, and program evaluation. He suggests stronger emphasis on president's leadership and management, and use of campus-wide governance only in an advisory capacity.

1960 _____. POLITICS AND HIGHER EDUCATION. University: University of Alabama Press, 1975. 147 p.

Author's experiences as a public university president and as chief executive officer of Ohio's coordinating board for higher education. Believes that politics and education do mix. Discusses federal funding, the state board of regents, support for the development of a state higher education system, and higher education's need for political spokesmen.

1961 _____, ed. MANAGING TURBULENCE AND CHANGE. San Francisco: Jossey-Bass Publishers, 1977. 100 p.

Describes expected changes in higher education and advises on how to handle the changes.

1962 Millett, John David, et al. WHAT IS A COLLEGE FOR? Washington, D.C.: Public Affairs Press, 1961. 48 p.

August Heckscher, Robert M. Hutchins, Max Lerner, David Shepard, and Mark Van Doren conclude that a college's true function is to advance human talent and to help us be our best selves.

1963 Millett, Kate. SEXUAL POLITICS. Garden City, N.Y.: Doubleday and Co., 1970. 512 p.

Wide-ranging survey of how and why women have been put into subordinate roles. Many index entries on women's education at all levels in the United States and the Soviet Union. Criticizes treatment of women by writers D.H. Lawrence and Norman Mailer.

1964 Mills, C. Wright. SOCIOLOGY AND PRAGMATISM: THE HIGHER LEARNING IN AMERICA. New York: Paine-Whitman, 1964. 475 p.

Famed sociology professor Mills's (1916-62) published 1941 dissertation. He analyzed pragmatism's relation to U.S. society through writings of Charles Peirce, William James, and John Dewey. He believed power lies with the military-industrial elite. He believed "higher learning" should be the important link between schools and U.S. society.

1965 Mills, Gail A. ACCOUNTING MANUAL FOR COLLEGE. Princeton, N.J.: Princeton University Press, 1937. 165 p.

Princeton University bursar outlines an accounting system for a liberal arts college and tells how to adapt it for a small or large institution.

1966 Mills, Henry C., et al. STUDIES IN ARTICULATION OF HIGH SCHOOL AND COLLEGE, WITH SPECIAL REFERENCE TO THE SUPERIOR STUDENT. Buffalo, N.Y.: University of Buffalo, 1934. 319 p.

Advocates special guidance in high school to prepare for the transition to college. Includes analysis of the superior student and predictions of college performance.

1967 Mills, Herbert Elmer, et al. COLLEGE WOMEN AND THE SOCIAL SCIENCES. New York: John Day Co., 1934. 324 p.

In honor of Mills's forty years as Vassar economics professor, his former students describe the uses they have made of their study of economics.

1968 Milner, Clyde A. THE DEAN OF THE SMALL COLLEGE. Boston: Christopher Publishing House, 1936. 151 p.

Views the small college dean in context of a Christian philosophy of education. Lists duties deans reported having and ones they said they should have.

1969 Milner, Murray. EFFECTS OF FEDERAL AID TO HIGHER EDUCATION ON SOCIAL AND EDUCATIONAL INEQUALITY. New York: Center for Policy Research, 1970. 204 p.

On federal aid to higher education students. Author believes upper income groups are helped more than low income students. Concludes that inequality will continue.

1970 Milton, Ohmer. ALTERNATIVES TO THE TRADITIONAL: HOW PROFESSORS TEACH AND HOW STUDENTS LEARN. San Francisco: Jossey-Bass Publishers, 1972. 156 p.

Research findings on traditional and alternative methods of education. Says neither is superior. Traditional education places little responsibility on students and grading systems are ambiguous. Is cautiously optimistic about such alternatives as off-campus experimental education, cluster colleges, interdisciplinary courses, and especially the learning resources center concept.

1971 Milton, Ohmer, and Shoben, Edward Joseph, Jr., eds. LEARNING AND THE PROFESSORS. Athens: Ohio University Press, 1968. 216 p.

John W. Gardner, Logan Wilson, and others examine difficulties facing professors. They present research findings about faculty, students, values, and other teaching-learning matters.

1972 Milton, Ohmer, et al. ON COLLEGE TEACHING: A GUIDE TO CONTEMPORARY PRACTICES. San Francisco: Jossey-Bass Publishers, 1978. 404 p.

Includes such new approaches to college teaching as Personalized Systems of Instruction, teaching with computers, learning contracts, competency-based instruction, case studies, field experience, lecturing, testing, and discussions. Also discusses working with older students and evaluating college teachers.

1973 Mims, Edwin. CHANCELLOR KIRKLAND OF VANDERBILT. Nashville, Tenn.: Vanderbilt University Press, 1940. 362 p.

James Hampton Kirkland (1859-1939) as chancellor of Vanderbilt University, 1893-1937, his struggle to remove Vanderbilt from rigid church control, and his special success with Vanderbilt's medical school.

1974 _____. HISTORY OF VANDERBILT UNIVERSITY. Nashville, Tenn.: Vanderbilt University Press, 1946. Reprint. New York: Arno Press, 1977. 497 p.

Vanderbilt English professor traces the growth of the small Methodist seminary in Nashville to multiversity status, following Cornelius Vanderbilt's endowment in 1873. Stresses the struggle over church and lay control.

1975 Mingle, James R. FACT BOOK ON HIGHER EDUCATION IN THE SOUTH, 1977 AND 1978. Atlanta: Southern Regional Education Board, 1978. 77 p.

Information on finances, enrollments, access, and participation in higher education for fourteen southern states.

1976 Minnesota. University. THE EFFECTIVE GENERAL COLLEGE CURRICULUM AS REVEALED BY EXAMINATIONS. Minneapolis: University of Minnesota Press, 1937. 427 p.

Review of the courses, testing, and evaluation of the General College of the University of Minnesota.

1977 Minnesota Higher Education Coordinating Board. DIRECTORY OF MINNESOTA NON-BACCALAUREATE POST-SECONDARY EDUCATIONAL PROGRAMS. St. Paul: 1978. 57 p.

Listing of over 1,400 nonbaccalaureate postsecondary programs which require less than four years to complete.

1978 Minnigerode, Meade. THE BIG YEAR: A COLLEGE STORY. New York: G.P. Putnam's Sons, 1921. 287 p.

Novel about student life in a thinly disguised Yale College.

1979 Minogue, Kenneth R. THE CONCEPT OF A UNIVERSITY. Los Angeles: University of California Press, 1973. 231 p.

Echoes conservative views of Cardinal Newman and Robert M. Hutchins about the intellectual nature of the university; disavows those who want the university to transform society and to focus on vocational and professional ends.

1980 Minter, W. John, ed. CAMPUS AND CAPITOL: HIGHER EDUCATION AND THE STATE. Boulder, Colo.: Western Interstate Commission for Higher Education, 1966. 192 p.

On the growing interdependence between government and higher education. Sees federal influence as a threat to the autonomy of individual colleges.

1981 _____. THE INDIVIDUAL AND THE SYSTEM: PERSONALIZING HIGHER EDUCATION. Boulder, Colo.: Western Interstate Commission for Higher Education, 1967. 187 p.

On changes and reforms in higher education, curriculum experiments, characteristics of students and faculty, student personnel services, use of computers, and changing values.

1982 Minter, W. John, and Snyder, Patricia O., eds. VALUE CHANGE AND POWER CONFLICT IN HIGHER EDUCATION. Berkeley: Center for Research and Development in Higher Education, University of California, 1970. 128 p.

Papers on critical issues, major problems, and power conflicts in U.S. universities.

1983 Minter, W. John, and Thompson, Ian M., eds. COLLEGES AND UNIVERSITIES AS AGENTS OF SOCIAL CHANGE. Boulder, Colo.: Western Interstate Commission for Higher Education, 1968. 148 p.

Some contributors fear the loss of the university's individuality and character in taking stands on social issues. Others agree that the university should promote free thought and discussion but differ on how best to do this.

1984 Missouri. Department of Higher Education. REPORT OF THE TASK FORCE ON OFF-CAMPUS EDUCATION. Jefferson City, Mo.: 1978. 47 p.

Results of a study on quality and duplication of off-campus courses in Missouri.

1985 Mitchell, Betty Jo, et al. COST ANALYSIS OF LIBRARY FUNCTIONS: A TOTAL SYSTEM APPROACH. Greenwich, Conn.: Jai Press, 1978. 192 p.

> Details the program at California State University, Northridge, for determining library costs.

1986 Mitchell, Janet A., ed. HIGHER EDUCATION EXCHANGE 78/79. Philadelphia: J.B. Lippincott, 1978. 766 p.

> Essential information on thirty-two hundred U.S. and Canadian higher education institutions, twenty-five hundred accredited postsecondary proprietary institutions, four thousand suppliers of goods and services, two hundred thousand administrators and faculty, and thirteen hundred associations and agencies.

1987 Mitchell, Joyce Slayton. I CAN BE ANYTHING: COLLEGES AND CAREERS FOR YOUNG WOMEN. Rev. ed. New York: Bantam Books, 1978. 327 p.

> Describes 150 careers for women from accountant to zoologist, the education needed, salaries, number of women in each field, the future for women, names of colleges awarding degrees in the fields, where to get more information, recommended readings, addresses of schools, colleges, and universities.

1988 _____. STOPOUT! WORKING WAYS TO LEARN. Garrett Park, Md.: Garrett Park Press, 1978. 214 p.

> For that half of all college students who temporarily drop out (most return to get a degree), this directory lists 138 government, nonprofit, and other agencies and opportunities where dropouts (or stopouts) can find out-of-college work.

1989 Mitchell, Juliet. WOMAN'S ESTATE. New York: Pantheon Books, 1971. 182 p.

> Shows origin of women's protests in part as a consequence of higher education. Relates women's education to the women's liberation movement in the United States, Britain, Holland, Sweden, and France.

1990 Mitchell, Ronald Elwy. DESIGN FOR NOVEMBER. New York: Harper and Brothers, 1947. 282 p.

> Novel about a college faculty member in a small midwestern town.

1991 Mitchner, Stuart. LET ME BE AWAKE. New York: Thomas Y. Crowell Co., 1959. 305 p.

This college novel contest winner is about an Indiana high school graduate at a small Pennsylvania college.

1992 Mitterling, Philip I., ed. PROCEEDINGS OF THE CONFERENCE ON TALENTED WOMEN AND THE AMERICAN COLLEGE. NEEDED RESEARCH ON ABLE WOMEN IN HONORS PROGRAMS, COLLEGE AND SOCIETY. Washington, D.C.: U.S. Office of Education, 1964. 141 p.

Papers by Bruno Bettelheim, Diana Trilling, David Riesman, and Paul A. Heist on talented college women.

1993 Modern Language Association. Commission on the Status of Women. ACADEMIC WOMEN, SEX DISCRIMINATION AND THE LAW. Rev. ed. New York: 1975. 30 p.

About such laws as Women's Educational Equity Act, Equal Pay Act of 1963, and Executive Order 11246. Discusses how to use the law through grievance procedures and enforce affirmative action for women in higher education.

1994 Modern Language Association. Publications Center. MLA HANDBOOK FOR WRITERS OF RESEARCH PAPERS, THESES, AND DISSERTATIONS. New York: 1977. 163 p.

Reference for graduate and undergraduate students doing research papers. Based on the MLA Style Sheet.

1995 Monroe, Charles R. PROFILE OF THE COMMUNITY COLLEGE: A HANDBOOK. San Francisco: Jossey-Bass Publishers, 1972. 435 p.

Community college history, philosophy, goals, fiscal structure, and general organization.

1996 Monroe, Walter S. TEACHING-LEARNING THEORY AND TEACHER EDUCATION, 1890-1950. Urbana: University of Illinois Press, 1952. 426 p.

Changes and controversies in teaching-learning theory and in teacher education purposes and practices.

1997 _____, ed. ENCYCLOPEDIA OF EDUCATIONAL RESEARCH: A PROJECT OF THE AMERICAN EDUCATIONAL RESEARCH ASSOCIATION. New York: Macmillan Co., 1950. 1,520 p.

Includes several articles on college faculty and college teaching.

1998 Monroe, Will S. EDUCATIONAL LABORS OF HENRY BARNARD: A STUDY IN THE HISTORY OF AMERICAN PEDAGOGY. Syracuse, N.Y.: C.W. Bardeen, 1893. 35 p.

Barnard (1811-1900), Yale graduate, was Connecticut and Rhode Island state school superintendent, U.S. Commissioner of Education, University of Wisconsin chancellor (1858–60), and St. John's College president (1866–67).

1999 Montefiore, Alan, ed. NEUTRALITY AND IMPARTIALITY: THE UNIVERSITY AND POLITICAL COMMITMENT. New York: Cambridge University Press, 1975. 292 p.

Conservative professors, reacting against late 1960s campus activism, assert traditional norms of academic neutrality, impartiality, autonomy, and the need to limit academic tolerance.

2000 Montgomery, James R., ed. PROCEEDINGS OF THE RESEARCH CONFERENCE ON COLLEGE DROPOUTS. Knoxville: University of Tennessee, 1964. 83 p.

Discussion of higher education policies that encourage dropouts, their early warning signs, ways to reduce their number, and help for those who have dropped out.

2001 Montgomery, Robert N., ed. THE WILLIAM RAINEY HARPER MEMORIAL CONFERENCE. Chicago: University of Chicago Press, 1938. 167 p.

On responsibilities of liberal arts colleges and on the ideas of William Rainey Harper (1856–1906), University of Chicago's first president (1890–1906).

2002 Montross, Lois Seyster. THE PERFECT PAIR. Garden City, N.Y.: Doubleday, Doran and Co., 1934. 311 p.

Novel about two successful college students who fall in and out of love.

2003 Montross, Lynn, and Montross, Lois Seyster. FRATERNITY ROW. New York: George H. Doran Co., 1926. 308 p.

Sixteen satirical stories about midwestern university students, faculty, and administration.

2004 _____. TOWN AND GOWN. New York: George H. Doran Co., 1923. 283 p.

Novel about life in a coeducational midwestern university.

2005 Mood, Alexander McFarlane. THE FUTURE OF HIGHER EDUCATION: SOME SPECULATIONS AND SUGGESTIONS. New York: McGraw-Hill Book Co., 1973. 166 p.

Innovative suggestions for improving undergraduate studies, including one year residency, video cassettes instead of lectures, nontechnical courses and language, and apprenticeship training. Favors no entrance requirements and lifelong learning in community colleges.

2006 Moody, Ann. COMING OF AGE IN MISSISSIPPI. New York: Dial
Press, 1968. 345 p.

> Autobiography of militant black girl going to school and col-
> lege in Mississippi.

2007 Moon, Rexford G., Jr. STUDENT FINANCIAL AID IN THE UNITED
STATES: ADMINISTRATION AND RESOURCES. Princeton, N.J.: College Entrance Examination Board, 1963. 47 p.

> Analysis of the approximately $700 million in financial aid
> awarded to U.S. college and university students.

2008 Moor, James R., Jr. THE DEMAND FOR HIGHER EDUCATION IN MICH-
IGAN: PROJECTIONS TO THE YEAR 2000. Lansing, Mich.: Presidents
Council, State Colleges and Universities, 1978. 103 p.

> Michigan enrollment forecasts to the end of the century.

2009 Moore, Charles Guy. THE CAREER GAME. New York: National Institute of Career Planning, 1977. 267 p.

> How college students can identify career interests, obtain in-
> formation about a field from those working in it, and secure
> a desirable job.

2010 Moore, Donald R. MONEY FOR COLLEGE! HOW TO GET IT. Woodbury, N.Y.: Barron's Educational Series, 1979. 276 p.

> Lists federal and state sources of college student financial aid.
> Has a section for women and minority groups.

2011 Moore, John W., and Patterson, Robert A. PENNSYLVANIA COMMUNITY
COLLEGE FACULTY: ATTITUDES TOWARD FACULTY BARGAINING. Uni-
versity Park: Center for the Study of Higher Education, Pennsylvania State
University, 1971. 60 p.

> Pennsylvania community college faculty attitudes toward col-
> lective bargaining. They supported the idea of collective bar-
> gaining but were ambivalent about using strikes.

2012 Moore, Philip Samuel. A CENTURY OF LAW AT NOTRE DAME. Notre
Dame, Ind.: University of Notre Dame Press, 1969. 177 p.

> History of Notre Dame's law school, curriculum changes, and
> other developments.

2013 Moore, William, Jr. AGAINST THE ODDS: THE HIGH RISK STUDENT
IN THE COMMUNITY COLLEGE. San Francisco: Jossey-Bass Publishers,
1970. 244 p.

Criticizes community colleges for failing to meet the needs of the "high-risk" student. Has practical suggestions for creating an adequate program for students with diverse backgrounds and capabilities.

2014 _____. BLIND MAN ON A FREEWAY: THE COMMUNITY COLLEGE ADMINISTRATOR. San Francisco: Jossey-Bass Publishers, 1971. 173 p.

Recommends that a specialized training program be offered for community college administrators.

2015 Moore, William, Jr., and Wagstaff, Lonnie H. BLACK EDUCATORS IN WHITE COLLEGES: PROGRESS AND PROSPECTS. San Francisco: Jossey-Bass Publishers, 1974. 226 p.

Survey of over three thousand black professionals working at white colleges showed that racial and cultural divisions still exist, particularly among community college staff members. Chapter on black women faculty and administrators, their salary discrepancies, and unique social pressures they experienced.

2016 Moos, Malcolm, and Rourke, Francis E. THE CAMPUS AND THE STATE. Baltimore, Md.: Johns Hopkins University Press, 1959. 414 p.

Impact of state administrative controls (since 1917) on the freedom of state colleges and universities. Found that public higher education has lost much autonomy.

2017 Moos, Rudolf H. EVALUATING EDUCATIONAL ENVIRONMENTS: PROCEDURES, MEASURES, FINDINGS, AND POLICY IMPLICATIONS. San Francisco: Jossey-Bass Publishers, 1979. 334 p.

Considers how changes in higher education institutional policies, residence facilities, and classroom activities might reduce student apathy, alienation, absenteeism, and attrition.

2018 Moran, Gerald P. PRIVATE COLLEGES: THE FEDERAL TAX SYSTEM AND ITS IMPACT. Toledo, Ohio: Center for the Study of Higher Education, 1977. 88 p.

Impact of the federal tax system on the operation and growth of private colleges and universities.

2019 Morey, Lloyd. THE STATE-SUPPORTED UNIVERSITY. Carbondale: Southern Illinois University Press, 1961. 112 p.

Former University of Illinois president on the state-supported university, what makes an educated person, and the relationship of higher education and national welfare.

2020 Morgan, Arthur Ernest. OBSERVATIONS. Comp. by Vivian H. Bresnehen. Yellow Springs, Ohio: Antioch College Press, 1968. 324 p.

> Ideas of Arthur Morgan (1878-1975), first chairman of the Tennessee Valley Authority and president of Antioch College, 1920-36.

2021 Morgan, Gordon D. THE GHETTO COLLEGE STUDENT: A DESCRIPTIVE ESSAY ON COLLEGE YOUTH FROM THE INNER CITY. Iowa City: American College Testing Program, 1970. 64 p.

> Interviews with inner-city college students describing problems and conditions that influence their education.

2022 Morgan, John. A DISCOURSE UPON THE INSTITUTION OF MEDICAL SCHOOLS IN AMERICA. Philadelphia: W. Bradford, 1765. Reprint. New York: Arno Press, 1975. 63 p.

> Commencement address, 1765, College of Philadelphia, later the University of Pennsylvania, supporting the founding of schools of medicine.

2023 Morgenstern, Oskar. THE QUESTION OF NATIONAL DEFENSE. New York: Random House, 1959. 306 p.

> Emphasizes the need for universities to raise technological and intellectual standards to meet the Soviet threat.

2024 Morison, Robert S. STUDENTS AND DECISION MAKING, WITH COMMENTS BY IAN MACNEIL. New York: Public Affairs Press, 1970. 136 p.

> Notes the uncertainty of purpose higher education institutions face, evolving decentralized collegiate administration, and the need for a greater student role in decision making.

2025 _____, ed. THE CONTEMPORARY UNIVERSITY: U.S.A. Boston: Houghton Mifflin Co., 1966. 364 p.

> Broad, optimistic view of U.S. higher education based on an American Association of Arts and Sciences conference.

2026 Morison, Samuel Eliot. THE TERCENTENNIAL HISTORY OF HARVARD COLLEGE AND UNIVERSITY, 1636-1936. 5 vols. Cambridge, Mass.: Harvard University Press, 1930-36. 472 p., 707 p. (2 vols. in 1), 724 p., 660 p.

> Most comprehensive history of Harvard and probably of any U.S. university.

2027 _____. THREE CENTURIES OF HARVARD, 1636-1936. Cambridge, Mass.: Harvard University Press, 1936. 512 p.

Abridged history of Harvard from its founding through the first years of James Bryant Conant's presidency, which extended from 1933 to 1953.

2028 Morrill, James Lewis. THE ONGOING STATE UNIVERSITY. Minneapolis: University of Minnesota Press, 1960. 143 p.

Eloquent support of land-grant colleges' emphasis on combining practical knowledge with a liberal education, by former University of Minnesota president, 1945-60.

2029 Morris, Ira. THE PAPER WALL. New York: Alfred A. Knopf, 1961. 302 p.

Novel about an English professor's betrayal of a colleague in a case of academic freedom and his sabbatical leave in Japan to escape his conscience.

2030 Morris, William H., ed. EFFECTIVE COLLEGE TEACHING: THE QUEST FOR RELEVANCE. Washington, D.C.: American Council on Education, 1970. 162 p.

On teaching various disciplines by authorities in each field. Discusses such issues as pass-fail, testing, student rapport, content emphasis, and college administration.

2031 Morrison, Bakewell. CHARACTER FORMATION IN COLLEGE. Milwaukee, Wis.: Bruce Publishing Co., 1938. 214 p.

Guidance suggestions for college students.

2032 Morrison, D. Grant, et al. THE TWO-YEAR COMMUNITY COLLEGE: AN ANNOTATED LIST OF UNPUBLISHED STUDIES AND SURVEYS, 1957-61. Washington, D.C.: Government Printing Office, 1963. 41 p.

Annotated bibliography of 270 items about two-year colleges.

2033 Morrison, Henry C. SCHOOL AND COMMONWEALTH: ADDRESSES AND ESSAYS. Chicago: University of Chicago Press, 1937. 238 p.

University of Chicago professor of education (1919-37) and laboratory school director on problems of higher education, administration, school finance, curriculum, and educational theory.

2034 Morrison, Robert H. INTERNAL ADMINISTRATIVE ORGANIZATION IN TEACHERS COLLEGES. New York: Teachers College, Columbia University, 1933. 183 p.

Organizational structure of 150 teachers colleges; used twenty criteria to evaluate practices, a pattern administrators can follow in institutional self-study.

2035 Morrison, Theodore. THE STONES OF THE HOUSE. New York: Viking Press, 1953. 375 p.

> First of three novels about an acting president at a small university and his precarious incumbency.

2036 _____. TO MAKE A WORLD. New York: Viking Press, 1957. 408 p.

> Sequel novel to Morrison's THE STONES OF THE HOUSE (see above); about a university president's assistant who negotiates with a foundation.

2037 _____. THE WHOLE CREATION. New York: Viking Press, 1962. 405 p.

> Author's third college novel in sequence; about a biology professor and a writer who becomes a university lecturer.

2038 Morrison, Wilma. THE SCHOOL RECORD: ITS USE AND ABUSE IN COLLEGE ADMISSIONS. New York: College Entrance Examination Board, 1961. 15 p.

> Value of school records when used by college admissions offices, and how to prevent misuse of this information.

2039 Morsch, William. STATE COMMUNITY COLLEGE SYSTEMS: THEIR ROLE AND OPERATION IN SEVEN STATES. New York: Praeger Publishers, 1971. 149 p.

> Community college systems in California, Florida, New York, Michigan, Illinois, Washington, and Texas.

2040 Morse, Horace T., ed. GENERAL EDUCATION IN TRANSITION: A LOOK AHEAD. Minneapolis: University of Minnesota Press, 1951. 310 p.

> Trends, proposed future steps, and implications for college programs of general education.

2041 Morse, William G. PARDON MY HARVARD ACCENT. New York: Farrar and Rinehart, 1941. 364 p.

> Autobiography of Harvard purchasing agent who developed Harvard's purchasing department.

2042 Mortimer, Kenneth P., ed. FACULTY BARGAINING, STATE GOVERNMENT, AND CAMPUS AUTONOMY. Denver: Education Commission of the States, 1976. 106 p.

> Collective bargaining practices in eight states; emphasizes legislation, procedures, and relations between state governments and campuses under collective bargaining.

2043 Mortimer, Kenneth P., and Leslie, David W., eds. INSTITUTIONAL SELF-STUDY AT THE PENNSYLVANIA STATE UNIVERSITY. University Park: Center for the Study of Higher Education, Pennsylvania State University, 1970. 157 p.

> Lists agencies engaged in institutional research at Penn State. Discusses the value of such research. Reviews the history of institutional research from its nineteenth-century origins.

2044 Mortimer, Kenneth P., and McConnell, Thomas Raymond. SHARING AUTHORITY EFFECTIVELY: PARTICIPATION, INTERACTION, AND DISCRETION. San Francisco: Jossey-Bass Publishers, 1977. 322 p.

> Analyzes the bases of authority and legitimacy in campus decision making from the view of the 1960s campus upheaval. States problems and offers suggestions for dealing with them. Discusses faculty senates, faculty unions, and the increased influence of federal, state, and system levels of governance.

2045 Mortimer, Kenneth P., and Richardson, Richard C., Jr. GOVERNANCE IN INSTITUTIONS WITH FACULTY UNIONS: SIX CASE STUDIES. University Park: Center for the Study of Higher Education, Pennsylvania State University, 1977. 190 p.

> Examines unionized faculties in two community colleges and four four-year colleges and their use of collective bargaining. Explores the idea that faculty collective bargaining causes new tensions between faculty members and administrators.

2046 Mosher, Edith K., and Wagoner, Jennings L., Jr., eds. THE CHANGING POLITICS OF EDUCATION: PROSPECTS FOR THE 1980'S. Berkeley, Calif.: McCutchan Publishers, 1978. 359 p.

> On litigation, education lobbies, state control, affirmative action enforcement, and other political issues facing higher education.

2047 Mosmann, Charles John. ACADEMIC COMPUTERS IN SERVICE: EFFECTIVE USES FOR HIGHER EDUCATION. San Francisco: Jossey-Bass Publishers, 1973. 186 p.

> Surveys computer use in administration, research, and instruction; kinds of computing available; and other aspects of computer management.

2048 Moulton, Phillips P. ENHANCING THE VALUES OF INTERCOLLEGIATE ATHLETICS AT SMALL COLLEGES. Ann Arbor: Center for the Study of Higher Education, University of Michigan, 1978. 108 p.

> Solutions to problems arising from men's spectator sports at small colleges.

2049 Mount Holyoke College. THE CENTENARY OF MOUNT HOLYOKE COL-
LEGE. South Hadley, Mass.: 1937. 195 p.

> Addresses on the centennial of Mount Holyoke College,
> founded by Mary Lyon in 1837, are by such women leaders
> as Mary Beard, Virginia Gildersleeve, and Frances Perkins.

2050 Mowry, William A. RECOLLECTIONS OF A NEW ENGLAND EDUCA-
TOR. Morristown, N.J.: Silver Burdett, 1908. 292 p.

> Author's recollections of Brown University, teachers' institutes,
> and other educational experiences.

2051 Moxon, Rosamond Sawyer, and Peabody, Mabel Clarke. TWENTY-FIVE
YEARS: TWO ANNIVERSARY SKETCHES OF NEW JERSEY COLLEGE FOR
WOMEN. New Brunswick: New Jersey College for Women, Rutgers Uni-
versity, 1943. 74 p.

> Historical sketch of what is now Douglass College, one of nine
> undergraduate colleges of Rutgers University, founded for wom-
> en in 1918 by the New Jersey State Federation of Women's
> Clubs under the leadership of Mabel Smith Douglass. Analyzes
> the status of alumnae.

2052 Mueller, Gustav Emil. EDUCATION LIMITED. Norman: University of
Oklahoma Press, 1949. 141 p.

> Calls for broadening liberal education to include moral, esthe-
> tic, and philosophical dimensions.

2053 Mueller, Kate Hevner. EDUCATING WOMEN FOR A CHANGING
WORLD. Minneapolis: University of Minnesota Press, 1954. 302 p.

> Former dean of women who recognized that women's changing
> roles would require changes in their higher education. Chap-
> ters on educating for earning, dating, mating, homemaking,
> citizenship, politics, and leisure.

2054 Muller, Leo C., and Muller, Ouida Gean. COLLEGE FOR COEDS.
New York: Pittman Publishing, 1960. 201 p.

> Designed to help high school girls and their parents find an-
> swers about college education, choosing a college, academic
> life, and social life.

2055 _____, eds. NEW HORIZONS FOR COLLEGE WOMEN. Washington,
D.C.: Public Affairs Press, 1960. 128 p.

> Seventy-fifth anniversary of Mississippi State College for Wom-
> en, the first publicly supported women's college in America,
> and a concluding plea for greater financial aid to women's
> higher education.

2056 Mumford, Lewis. MY WORKS AND DAYS: A PERSONAL CHRONICLE. New York: Harcourt Brace Jovanovich, 1979. 545 p.

> Memoir of famed urban analyst, city planner, architectural critic, and social philosopher of urban society (born 1895). He attended City College of New York and held visiting professorships at North Carolina State College, the University of Pennsylvania, and MIT.

2057 Munday, Leo A., and Davis, Jeanne C. VARIETIES OF ACCOMPLISHMENT AFTER COLLEGE: PERSPECTIVES ON THE MEANING OF ACADEMIC TALENT. Iowa City: American College Testing Program, 1974. 21 p.

> Found no correlation between the accomplishments of young adults two years after college and their college admission data.

2058 Munitz, Barry. LEADERSHIP IN COLLEGES AND UNIVERSITIES: ASSESSMENT AND SEARCH. Oak Brook, Ill.: Johnson Associates, 1977. 53 p.

> Handbook for evaluating the relationship between college chief executive officers and their governing boards.

2059 Munroe, Ruth Learned. PREDICTION OF THE ADJUSTMENT AND ACADEMIC PERFORMANCE OF COLLEGE STUDENTS. Stanford, Calif.: Stanford University Press, 1945. 104 p.

> Rorschach test and its use in conjunction with intelligence tests to predict college students' success.

2060 _____. TEACHING THE INDIVIDUAL. New York: Columbia University Press, 1942. 353 p.

> Report on individualizing instruction based on records of over one hundred students at Sarah Lawrence College.

2061 Murphy, Judith, and Florio, Carol. NEVER TOO OLD TO TEACH. New York: Academy for Educational Development, 1978. 115 p.

> Study of men and women over sixty who are teaching in schools, colleges, and other institutions.

2062 Murphy, Judith, and Jones, Loona. RESEARCH IN ARTS EDUCATION: A FEDERAL CHAPTER. Washington, D.C.: Arts and Humanities Staff, Office of Education, 1978. 86 p.

> Summary of recent research in higher education arts education done under the Office of Education's arts and humanities program.

2063 Murphy, Lois B., and Raushenbush, Esther, eds. ACHIEVEMENT IN THE COLLEGE YEARS. New York: Harper and Row, 1960. 240 p.

About the intellectual and personal growth of eighty-five Sarah Lawrence students from college entrance until two years after graduation.

2064 Murphy, Thomas P., ed. UNIVERSITIES IN THE URBAN CRISIS. Port Washington, N.Y.: Dunellen Publishing Co., 1975. 418 p.

On higher education's involvement in urban concerns--government, community, and students--and the future of urban higher education.

2065 Murphy, William Michael, and Bruckner, D.J.R., eds. THE IDEA OF THE UNIVERSITY OF CHICAGO: SELECTIONS FROM THE PAPERS OF THE FIRST EIGHT CHIEF EXECUTIVES OF THE UNIVERSITY OF CHICAGO. Chicago: University of Chicago Press, 1976. 533 p.

University of Chicago's first eight presidents' papers reflect changing times and varying leadership styles during eighty years.

2066 Mushkin, Selma J., ed. ECONOMICS OF HIGHER EDUCATION. Washington, D.C.: U.S. Office of Education, 1962. 406 p.

Reviews past higher education economics and forecasts problems facing colleges because of rising enrollments caused by post-World War II baby boom.

2067 Muskingum College Faculty. A COLLEGE LOOKS AT ITS PROGRAM. New Concord, Ohio: Muskingum College, 1937. 326 p.

Muskingum College faculty members report on their experimental courses, testing, curriculum, administration, and objectives.

2068 Myers, William Starr, ed. WOODROW WILSON: SOME PRINCETON MEMORIES. Princeton, N.J.: Princeton University Press, 1946. 91 p.

Reminiscences by seven of Woodrow Wilson's Princeton colleagues on his reorganization of educational policy under the preceptorial system and his effort to introduce the "Quad Plan" for coordinating social and intellectual life at Princeton.

2069 Nabokov, Vladimir. PALE FIRE. New York: G.P. Putnam's Sons, 1962. 315 p.

Fantasy novel in poetic form and commentary on the poem about a deposed king in New England college town setting.

2070 _____. PNIN. Garden City, N.Y.: Doubleday and Co., 1957. 191 p.

Novel about emigré Russian professor in an upstate New York college.

2071 Nagai, Michio. AN OWL BEFORE DUSK. Berkeley, Calif.: Carnegie Commission on Higher Education, 1976. 49 p.

Tokyo University education lecturer and later Japan's Minister of Education gives his impressions of U.S. and world university students since the 1950s.

2072 Nash, Arnold S., ed. THE CHOICE BEFORE THE HUMANITIES. Durham, N.C.: Regional Education Laboratory for the Carolinas and Virginia, 1969. 153 p.

Papers on the extent of need for the humanities in higher education.

2073 Nash, Paul. MODELS OF MAN: EXPLORATIONS IN THE WESTERN EDUCATIONAL TRADITION. New York: John Wiley and Sons, 1969. 470 p.

Philosophical models of educated Western man from Socrates to Professor B.F. Skinner.

2074 Nash, Willard L. MILITARY SCIENCE AND TACTICS AND PHYSICAL EDUCATION. Contributions to Education No. 614. New York: Teachers College, Columbia University, 1934. 129 p.

Found physical education departments doing a more credible job than military training departments. Compared aims and objectives of those departments in colleges and universities.

2075 Nathan, Harriet, and Scott, Stanley, eds. EXPERIMENT AND CHANGE IN BERKELEY: ESSAYS ON CITY POLITICS, 1950-1975. Berkeley: Institute of Governmental Studies, University of California, 1979. 501 p.

Twenty-five year relationship between the Berkeley campus and the city of Berkeley, including student demonstrations at People's Park.

2076 Nathan, Maud. ONCE UPON A TIME AND TODAY. New York: G.P. Putnam's Sons, 1933. 327 p.

Autobiography of a wealthy Jewish socialite, woman suffragist, and a founder of Barnard College (born 1862).

2077 Nathan, Robert Gruntal. MR. WHITTLE AND THE MORNING STAR. New York: Alfred A. Knopf, 1947. 175 p.

Novel about a professor in a small college who goes through a crisis of middle age.

2078 _____. PETER KINDRED. New York: Duffield and Co., 1920. 526 p.

Novel of a wealthy youth who goes from Phillips Exeter to Harvard, is influenced by an economics professor, and marries a Radcliffe student.

2079 National Academy of Sciences. TOWARD BETTER UTILIZATION OF SCIENTIFIC AND ENGINEERING TALENT: A PROGRAM FOR ACTION. Washington, D.C.: Committee on Utilization of Scientific and Engineering Manpower, 1964. 183 p.

On the dislocation in engineering and science careers caused by the switch-over to space technology. Recommends that colleges and universities update engineering and science education to fit technological demands.

2080 National Academy of Sciences, et al. CAREER OF PH.D.'S: ACADEMIC VERSUS NONACADEMIC. A SECOND REPORT ON FOLLOW-UP DOCTORATE COHORTS, 1935-1960. Washington, D.C.: 1968. 106 p.

Compared career patterns of Ph.D. men and women, 1935-60, on salaries, academic progress, teaching, research, graduate education, and doctoral fields. Mainly, women were behind men, but a larger proportion of women than men received postdoctoral fellowships.

2081 National Alliance of Businessmen. DIRECTORY OF PREDOMINANTLY BLACK COLLEGES AND UNIVERSITIES IN THE UNITED STATES OF AMERICA. Washington, D.C.: 1972. 91 p.

Lists key administrators, enrollments, and degrees given at eighty-five mainly black colleges and universities.

2082 National Association for Women Deans, Administrators, and Counselors. A GRIEVANCE HANDBOOK FOR WOMEN EDUCATORS. Washington, D.C.: 1977. 35 p.

Guidelines for women teachers who wish to file grievances against their employers. Reviews federal regulations that prohibit sex discrimination.

2083 _____. RESIDENCE HALLS FOR WOMEN STUDENTS; ADMINISTRATIVE PRINCIPLES AND PROCEDURES. Washington, D.C.: 1947. 95 p.

Theory and practices in women's college residence halls; staff selection and organization, group living, student government, house administration, and food and building problems.

2084 National Association of College and University Business Officers. CAMPUS ENERGY MANAGEMENT PROJECTS. Washington, D.C.: 1979. 58 p.

Energy-saving measures used by sixty U.S. and Canadian colleges and universities.

2085 _____. ENERGY MANAGEMENT FOR COLLEGES AND UNIVERSITIES. Washington, D.C.: 1977. 140 p.

To help college and university administrators plan and manage effective energy programs. Discusses ways to conserve energy and the nature of national and international energy supply and demand.

2086 _____. "FINAL" TITLE IX REGULATIONS ISSUED BY OCR. Washington, D.C.: 1975. 21 p.

U.S. Department of HEW regulations for implementing Title IX of the 1972 Education Act amendments.

2087 _____. GOVERNMENT CONTRACTS AND GRANTS FOR RESEARCH, REVISION ONE: A GUIDE FOR COLLEGES AND UNIVERSITIES. Washington, D.C.: 1977. 35 p.

Explains clauses in federal contracts to help college and university administrators of federally sponsored programs.

2088 _____. GUIDE TO THE SECTION 504 SELF-EVALUATION FOR COLLEGES AND UNIVERSITIES. Washington, D.C.: 1978. 127 p.

Guide, approved by the U.S. Office for Civil Rights, to help colleges and universities comply with Section 504 of the 1973 Rehabilitation Act, which requires equal educational opportunities for handicapped persons.

2089 _____. PATENT AND COPYRIGHT POLICIES AT SELECTED UNIVERSITIES. Washington, D.C.: 1978. 87 p.

Patent and copyright policies of thirteen universities; two supplements suggest what should appear in any such policy.

2090 _____. RESULTS OF THE 1977 NACUBO COMPARATIVE PERFORMANCE STUDY AND INVESTMENT QUESTIONNAIRE. Washington, D.C.: 1978. 96 p.

Information on endowment funds of 148 colleges and universities.

2091 National Association of Foreign Student Advisors. HANDBOOK FOR COUNSELORS OF STUDENTS ABROAD. New York: 1949. 214 p.

History of international student exchanges, counselors' qualifications, barriers to participation in campus life, group activities, counseling, laws and regulations, and suggestions for teaching English.

2092 National Association of Independent Colleges and Universities. FEDERAL STUDENT ASSISTANCE AND CATEGORICAL PROGRAMS. Washington, D.C.: 1978. 145 p.

> Describes forty federal college student assistance programs and their funding history.

2093 National Association of State Universities and Land-Grant Colleges, and American Association of State Colleges and Universities. RECOMMENDATIONS FOR NATIONAL ACTION AFFECTING HIGHER EDUCATION. Washington, D.C.: 1968. 20 p.

> Recommends expanding post-secondary educational opportunity, more programs for disadvantaged students, more national institutional grants, more student aid, and more funding for academic facilities and housing.

2094 National Association of Student Financial Aid Administrators. CHARACTERISTICS AND ATTITUDES OF THE FINANCIAL AID ADMINISTRATOR: A REPORT ON THE SURVEY OF THE PROFESSION IN 1977. Washington, D.C.: 1978. 189 p.

> Information on personal and job characteristics, attitudes, salaries, external contacts, and professional development of college financial aid administrators.

2095 National Board on Graduate Education. GRADUATE EDUCATION: PURPOSES, PROBLEMS, AND POTENTIAL. Washington, D.C.: 1974. 18 p.

> National Board's views of and solutions for purposes and problems of graduate education.

2096 National Catholic Educational Association. MINISTRY OF FACULTY IN THE CATHOLIC COLLEGE/UNIVERSITY. Washington, D.C.: 1978. 32 p.

> Articles on theology, economics, sociology, and philosophy of Catholic university faculties.

2097 National Center for Education Statistics. THE CONDITION OF EDUCATION. 2 vols. Washington, D.C.: Government Printing Office, 1978. 315 p., 19 p.

> Facts and figures about students, schools, and finances at all levels, including higher education.

2098 _____. NATIONAL LONGITUDINAL STUDY OF THE HIGH SCHOOL CLASS OF 1972: A CAPSULE DESCRIPTION OF FIRST FOLLOWUP SURVEY DATA. Washington, D.C.: Government Printing Office, 1976. 43 p.

> About the higher education and work activities of 1972 high school graduates.

2099 National Center for Public Service Internship Programs. DIRECTORY OF PUBLIC SERVICE INTERNSHIPS: OPPORTUNITIES FOR THE GRADUATE, POST GRADUATE, AND MID-CAREER PROFESSIONAL. Washington, D.C.: 1976. 159 p.

> Describes internship programs' objectives, recruitment, selection, admission, and remuneration.

2100 National Center for the Study of Collective Bargaining in Higher Education. DIRECTORY OF BARGAINING AGENTS AND CONTRACTS IN HIGHER EDUCATION. New York: Baruch College, CUNY, 1977. 22 p.

> Lists colleges and universities with collective bargaining contracts, names the union involved, and the contract duration.

2101 National Commission on Accrediting. PROCEDURES OF ACCREDITING EDUCATION IN THE PROFESSIONS. Washington, D.C.: 1964.

> Describes accrediting procedures used and criteria developed in national organizations of thirty professions, including art, chemistry, nursing, and law. Details about eligibility, team visits, appeal procedures, and costs.

2102 National Committee on Standard Reports for Institutions of Higher Education. FINANCIAL REPORTS FOR COLLEGES AND UNIVERSITIES. Chicago: University of Chicago Press, 1935. 285 p.

> To achieve uniformity in higher education accounting reports, this report suggests a sectionalized balance sheet of assets, liabilities, and surpluses of all funds.

2103 National Committee on the Preparation of a Manual on College and University Business Administration. COLLEGE AND UNIVERSITY BUSINESS ADMINISTRATION. Vol. 11. Washington, D.C.: American Council on Education, 1955. 267 p.

> Business administration concerns of higher education institutions, such as maximum plant utilization, expenditure controls, and standardized accounting.

2104 National Committee on the Revision of College and University Business Administrations. COLLEGE AND UNIVERSITY BUSINESS ADMINISTRATION. Washington, D.C.: American Council on Higher Education, 1968. 311 p.

> Information and guidance for the higher education business officer about areas in which he has primary responsibility.

2105 National Convention on Work and the College Student, 1st, Southern Illinois University at Carbondale, 1975. WORK AND THE COLLEGE STUDENT: PROCEEDINGS. Edited by Roland Keene, et al. Carbondale: Southern Illinois University Press, 1976. 466 p.

Conference papers on student work activities and the relationship between student work and learning in higher education.

2106 National Council of Administrative Women in Education of the National Education Association. ADMINISTRATIVE WOMEN IN HIGHER EDUCATION. Washington, D.C.: 1952. 29 p.

Data from 971 public and private U.S. higher education institutions: (1) 27.6 percent of administrative positions were held by women; (2) fewer than 10 percent of deans, business managers, vice presidents, presidents, and provosts were women; and (3) one-third of governing boards had no women, while women composed only 12 percent of those boards having women.

2107 _____. WANTED--MORE WOMEN IN EDUCATIONAL LEADERSHIP. Washington, D.C.: 1965. 28 p.

Research on women in elementary, secondary, and higher education showed a decline in numbers and status, 1945-65.

2108 National Council of Teachers of English. AN ANNOTATED LIST OF TRAINING PROGRAMS FOR COMMUNITY COLLEGE ENGLISH TEACHERS. Urbana, Ill.: 1977. 58 p.

For the more than forty U.S. programs which train English teachers for two-year colleges, gives program information, student requirements, and methods of program planning and evaluation.

2109 National Education Association. THE STATUS OF WOMEN FACULTY AND ADMINISTRATORS IN HIGHER EDUCATION INSTITUTIONS, 1971-72. Washington, D.C.: 1973. 8 p.

Information by sex about faculty salaries, tenure status, and the number of persons and their salaries in administrative positions.

2110 NATIONAL FACULTY DIRECTORY, 1980. 10th ed. Detroit: Gale Research Co., 1979. 2,668 p.

Alphabetical listing of more than 480,000 faculty members in U.S. and Canadian two-year and four-year colleges and universities.

2111 National League for Nursing. CURRICULUM PROCESS FOR DEVELOPING OR REVISING A BACCALAUREATE NURSING PROGRAM. New York: 1978. 65 p.

Papers on a revised curriculum for educators of nurses.

2112 _____. DEVELOPMENT OF COMPETENCIES IN ASSOCIATE DEGREE NURSING: A NURSING SERVICE PERSPECTIVE. New York: 1978. 14 p.

Three views of the competencies that can be expected of associate degree nursing graduates.

2113 _____. DOCTORAL PROGRAMS IN NURSING, 1978-79. New York: 1979. 8 p.

Institutions, administrators, areas of study, and degrees offered by doctoral nursing programs in thirteen states and the District of Columbia.

2114 _____. EVALUATION OF STUDENTS IN BACCALAUREATE NURSING PROGRAMS. New York: 1978. 98 p.

Instructors' methods for evaluating clinical work of baccalaureate nursing students.

2115 _____. IMPLEMENTATION OF CONTINUING EDUCATION IN NURSING. New York: 1979. 21 p.

Ways to design and begin continuing education programs for nurses at regional and state levels.

2116 _____. LONGITUDINAL AND GRADUATE FOLLOW-UP STUDIES IN ASSOCIATE DEGREE EDUCATION. New York: 1978. 23 p.

On nursing research at Purdue University and Tarrant County (Texas) Junior College that might affect curriculum and student retention.

2117 _____. NURSING ADMINISTRATION: PRESENT AND FUTURE. New York: 1979. 29 p.

Curriculum and teaching techniques for training nursing administrators.

2118 _____. NURSING DATA BOOK: STATISTICAL INFORMATION ON NURSING EDUCATION AND NEWLY LICENSED NURSES. New York: 1979. 86 p.

Nursing information compiled from periodic surveys.

2119 _____. PROMOTING STUDENT RETENTION IN A NURSING PROGRAM. New York: 1978. 18 p.

Ways faculty members and students can encourage students to stay in nursing programs.

2120 _____ . SOME STATISTICS ON BACCALAUREATE AND HIGHER DEGREE PROGRAMS IN NURSING, 1974-75. New York: 1977. 18 p.

> Tables show the number of nursing students enrolled in graduate and undergraduate degree programs.

2121 _____ . STATE-APPROVED SCHOOLS OF NURSING: L.P.N./L.V.N., 1977. New York: 1978. 87 p.

> Lists accredited institutions that award diplomas to practical nurses and vocational nurses and gives enrollment and admissions information.

2122 _____ . TOWARD EXCELLENCE IN NURSING EDUCATION: A GUIDE FOR DIPLOMA SCHOOL IMPROVEMENT. 3d ed. New York: 1977. 58 p.

> Guide for developing and improving programs, services, and curricula of nursing schools; on the administration, organization, and philosophy of nursing education.

2123 _____ . TRENDS, ISSUES AND IMPLICATIONS IN STUDENT SELECTION. New York: 1978. 30 p.

> On legal and ethical issues in admissions to nursing programs.

2124 National Liaison Committee on Foreign Student Admissions. THE FOREIGN GRADUATE STUDENT: PRIORITIES FOR RESEARCH AND ACTION. New York: College Entrance Examination Board, 1971. 98 p.

> Report calling for new admissions policies for foreign graduate students and for more systematic research, especially on financial aid and master's degree programs. Urged continued government fellowship programs and continued appreciation of foreign students' contributions.

2125 National Manpower Council. STUDENT DEFERMENT AND NATIONAL MANPOWER POLICY. New York: Columbia University Press, 1952. 102 p.

> Topics: operation of student deferment policy, effect of compulsory military service on college finances, history of deferment and classification policy, and the relationship between democratic values and U.S. student deferment policy.

2126 _____ . WOMANPOWER. New York: Columbia University Press, 1957. 371 p.

> Discusses secondary and higher education of women, the teaching profession, and sex labels in professions, as well as adult education, commercial education, home economics, and training programs.

2127 National Research Council. THE INVISIBLE UNIVERSITY: POST-DOCTORAL EDUCATION IN THE UNITED STATES. Washington, D.C.: National Academy of Sciences, 1969. 310 p.

> Who postdoctoral fellows are, how chosen, where concentrated, what they do, and their contributions. Recommends more careful selection of fellows and their supervisors, more provisions for teaching and administrative experience, and more record keeping of their subsequent careers.

2128 National Science Foundation. EDUCATION AND EMPLOYMENT SPE-CIALIZATION IN 1952 OF JUNE 1951 COLLEGE GRADUATES. Washington, D.C.: Government Printing Office, 1955. 78 p.

> Found among forty-nine thousand June 1951 college graduates that over two-thirds were employed in 1952, most in jobs related to their college education but not necessarily in specific technical fields of their training.

2129 _____. EXPENDITURES FOR SCIENTIFIC AND ENGINEERING ACTIVI-TIES AT UNIVERSITIES AND COLLEGES, FISCAL YEAR 1973. Washington, D.C.: Government Printing Office, 1973. 107 p.

> Research expenditures in the sciences and engineering by sources of funds, fields of science, and kinds of research. Institutions grouped by highest degree offered, type of control, and size of their federal and total expenditures.

2130 _____. FEDERAL SUPPORT TO UNIVERSITIES, COLLEGES, AND SE-LECTED NONPROFIT INSTITUTIONS, FISCAL YEAR 1974. Washington, D.C.: Government Printing Office, 1976. 71 p.

> How much federal money was awarded directly to individual colleges and universities in 1974.

2131 _____. GRADUATE SCIENCE EDUCATION: STUDENT SUPPORT AND POSTDOCTORALS, FALL 1974. Washington, D.C.: Government Printing Office, 1976. 87 p.

> Statistics on financial aid to graduate students in sciences and engineering at doctorate-granting institutions, including characteristics of students, types and sources of financial support, and enrollment trends.

2132 _____. TWO YEARS AFTER THE COLLEGE DEGREE: WORK AND FUR-THER STUDY PATTERNS. A REPORT ON A 1960 SURVEY OF 1958 COL-LEGE GRADUATES PREPARED BY THE BUREAU OF SOCIAL SCIENCE RE-SEARCH, INC., FOR THE NATIONAL SCIENCE FOUNDATION. Washington, D.C.: Government Printing Office, 1963. 335 p.

> Surveys work and further study activities of forty thousand June

1958 graduates with bachelor's, master's, and professional degrees from twelve hundred institutions. Median salaries reported by degrees held and by occupation.

2133 National University Extension Association. GUIDE TO INDEPENDENT STUDY THROUGH CORRESPONDENCE INSTRUCTION. Washington, D.C.: 1975. 44 p.

Correspondence courses in fifty-six subject areas at all school levels by seventy-three accredited higher education members of the National University Extension Association. Data on credits, degrees, special services, and programs.

2134 Nearing, Scott. EDUCATIONAL FRONTIERS: A BOOK ABOUT SIMON NELSON PATTEN AND OTHER TEACHERS. New York: Seltzer, 1925. 250 p.

Describes Simon Patten's work as University of Pennsylvania economics professor, his teaching skills, economic theories, writings, interest in public questions, and his forced retirement for alleged World War I pro-Germanism.

2135 Neckers, James W. THE BUILDING OF A DEPARTMENT: CHEMISTRY AT SOUTHERN ILLINOIS UNIVERSITY, 1927-1967. Carbondale: Southern Illinois University Press, 1979. 187 p.

Firsthand account by a chemistry professor of the development of his university department over four decades.

2136 Neff, Wanda Fraiken. LONE VOYAGERS. Boston: Houghton Mifflin Co., 1929. 286 p.

Novel of professors, their wives, and academic competition at a disguised University of Minnesota.

2137 Neilson, William Allan, ed. CHARLES W. ELIOT: THE MAN AND HIS BELIEFS. New York: Harper and Brothers, 1926. 790 p.

Brief biographical account of Eliot (1834-1926) and his selected papers during his Harvard University presidency (1869-1909).

2138 Nelson, M. Janice, ed. CLINICAL PERSPECTIVES IN NURSING RESEARCH: RELEVANCE, SUFFERING, RECOVERY. New York: Teachers College Press, 1978. 95 p.

Three research reports, with critiques, on use of the clinical laboratory, nurses' perceptions of patients' suffering, and patients' definitions of recovery.

2139 Nemerov, Howard. THE HOMECOMING GAME. New York: Simon and Schuster, 1957. 246 p.

Novel about a history professor who fails the leading football player on the eve of an important game and the resulting complications.

2140 Nenninger, Timothy K. THE LEAVENWORTH SCHOOLS AND THE OLD ARMY: EDUCATION, PROFESSIONALISM, AND THE OFFICER CORPS OF THE UNITED STATES ARMY, 1881-1918. Westport, Conn.: Greenwood Press, 1978. 173 p.

History of military education at Fort Leavenworth from the School of Application, which trained junior officers, to the Army School of the Line and the Army Staff College, which prepared officers for general staff duties and high command.

2141 Ness, Frederic W. AN UNCERTAIN GLORY: LETTERS OF CAUTIOUS BUT SOUND ADVICE TO STANLEY, A DEAN-IN-WAITING, FROM C.F. COLTSWOOD, A PRESIDENT-AT-LARGE. San Francisco: Jossey-Bass Publishers, 1971. 154 p.

Letters from a fictional college president to a young aspirant to an academic administration career discuss everything from academic freedom and faculty unionism to sex on campus.

2142 _____, ed. A GUIDE TO GRADUATE STUDY: PROGRAMS LEADING TO THE PH.D. DEGREE. Washington, D.C.: Association of American Colleges, 1957. 336 p.

Advice for undergraduates about who should go to graduate school, how to prepare and gain admission, and how to finance graduate study. Lists universities and colleges where specific fields (Ph.D.) are offered.

2143 Netcher, Jack R. A MANAGEMENT MODEL FOR COMPETENCY-BASED HPER PROGRAMS. St. Louis: C.V. Mosby Co., 1977. 127 p.

Plan for designing and developing health, physical education, and recreational programs in colleges and universities. Methods for managing the programs, selecting and training faculty members, and determing course content and evaluation methods.

2144 Neuls-Bates, Carol, ed. THE STATUS OF WOMEN IN COLLEGE MUSIC: PRELIMINARY STUDIES. Binghamton: College Music Society, State University of New York, 1977. 34 p.

Papers on such topics as hiring and promotion, research on women in music, foundation support for women, women in musicology, and black women in teaching.

2145 Neumann, Franz L., et al. THE CULTURAL MIGRATION: THE EURO-

PEAN SCHOLAR IN AMERICA. Philadelphia: University of Pennsylvania Press, 1953. Reprint. New York: Arno Press, 1977. 156 p.

Five emigrè scholars compare the European academic culture they left with U.S. academic culture. Neumann examines the history of intellectual exile. Henri Peyre views scholarly expression in adopted languages, Erwin Panofsky discusses U.S. contribution to art history, and Paul Tillich tells of discovering in the United States that German theology did not encompass all of Protestant theology.

2146 Nevins, Allan. THE STATE UNIVERSITIES AND DEMOCRACY. Urbana: University of Illinois Press, 1962. 171 p.

Centennial history of land-grant institutions since the 1862 Morrill Land Grant Act. Records such early hardships as financial mismanagement, popular opposition, and religious censure. Tells of their present prestige.

2147 Newcomb, Theodore M. PERSONALITY AND SOCIAL CHANGE: ATTITUDE FORMATION IN A STUDENT COMMUNITY. New York: Dryden Press, 1943. 225 p.

Research on changes in attitudes of Bennington College students toward the New Deal, 1935-39; author found students became more progressive while in college.

2148 Newcomb, Theodore M., and Wilson, Everett K., eds. COLLEGE PEER GROUPS: PROBLEMS AND PROSPECTS FOR RESEARCH. Chicago: Aldine Publishing Co., 1966. 303 p.

Contributors James S. Coleman, David Riesman, and others on college peer group influence.

2149 Newcomb, Theodore M., et al. PERSISTENCE AND CHANGE: BENNINGTON COLLEGE AND ITS STUDENTS AFTER TWENTY-FIVE YEARS. New York: John Wiley and Sons, 1967. 292 p.

Follow-up study twenty-five years after Newcomb's PERSONALITY AND SOCIAL CHANGE: ATTITUDE FORMATION IN A STUDENT COMMUNITY (see above) found that most graduates between 1938 and 1961 retained about the same attitudes they held as Bennington seniors. Study identifies the persistent effects of a particular pattern of college education on student attitudes.

2150 Newcomer, James, et al. LIBERAL EDUCATION AND PHARMACY. New York: Teachers College, Columbia University, 1960. 125 p.

In 1960 found that liberal arts studies composed 14.3 percent of the curriculum of accredited pharmacy schools.

2151 Newcomer, Mabel. A CENTURY OF HIGHER EDUCATION FOR AMERI-
CAN WOMEN. New York: Harper and Brothers, 1959. 266 p.

This history of women's higher education attributes its late
nineteenth-century expansion to such factors as the need for
teachers and U.S. industrialization. Reviews past and recent
controversies.

2152 Newfield, Jack. A PROPHETIC MINORITY. New York: Signet Books,
1966. 158 p.

On the New Left by the then-editor of VILLAGE VOICE and
member of Students for a Democratic Society. Calls the New
Left movement an ethical revolt against poverty, war, racism,
and dehumanization caused by the modern corporate state.
Critical of some radicals for their nihilism and antiintellectualism.

2153 New Hampshire. University. HISTORY OF THE UNIVERSITY OF NEW
HAMPSHIRE, 1866-1941, WITH A FOREWORD BY PRESIDENT ENGLE-
HARDT. Durham: University of New Hampshire, 1941. 333 p.

History of the University of New Hampshire from its founding,
its early experiences in agricultural education, its problems
in World War I, and its transformation from a college to a
university.

2154 Newman, Frank, et al. REPORT ON HIGHER EDUCATION. Washington,
D.C.: U.S. Office of Education, 1971. 130 p.

Problems and changes needed in higher education. Recommends
modification of attendance patterns, more off-campus education,
and more opportunities for women and minorities.

2155 Newsom, Carroll V. A UNIVERSITY PRESIDENT SPEAKS OUT: ON CUR-
RENT EDUCATION. New York: Harper and Brothers, 1961. 118 p.

Reflections of a university president, formerly a mathematics
professor, on how higher education can develop richly varied,
well educated individuals.

2156 New York University. THE OBLIGATION OF UNIVERSITIES TO THE
SOCIAL ORDER. New York: New York University Press, 1932. 503 p.

Conference papers and discussions concluded that universities
should lead in changing the world.

2157 Niblett, W. Roy. UNIVERSITIES BETWEEN TWO WORLDS. New York:
Halsted Press, 1974. 179 p.

Author insists that universities must be concerned about values, especially as they affect the relationship between knowledge and experience.

2158 _____, ed. HIGHER EDUCATION: DEMAND AND RESPONSE. San Francisco: Jossey-Bass Publishers, 1970. 267 p.

Papers of U.S., British, and Canadian theorists about higher education issues.

2159 Niblett, W. Roy, and Butts, R. Freeman, eds. UNIVERSITIES FACING THE FUTURE: AN INTERNATIONAL PERSPECTIVE. San Francisco: Jossey-Bass Publishers, 1972. 400 p.

Essays on higher education in many countries, including the United States; on such themes as mass post-secondary education and comprehensive universities.

2160 Nicholas, Russell C., ed. STAFF DEVELOPMENT. Cupertino, Calif.: De Anza College Learning Center, 1978. 41 p.

Bibliography of materials published between 1970 and 1976 on improving the staff of educational institutions.

2161 Nichols, David C., ed. PERSPECTIVES ON CAMPUS TENSIONS: PAPERS PREPARED FOR THE SPECIAL COMMITTEE ON CAMPUS TENSIONS. Washington, D.C.: American Council on Education, 1970. 219 p.

On the crisis in higher education and the discontents of students, faculty, administrators, and trustees. Contributors: Kenneth Boulding, William Birenbaum, Judson Jerome, J.L. Zwingle, Seymour Lipset, Kenneth Keniston, Clark Kerr, and others.

2162 Nichols, David C., and Mills, Olive, eds. THE CAMPUS CRISIS. Washington, D.C.: American Council on Education, 1970. 309 p.

The Council's October 1969 meeting included a call for open admissions and a black speaker's unease about black studies programs because they did not help blacks fit into leadership positions in government and education.

2163 Nicholson, Lionell S. THE LAW SCHOOLS OF THE UNITED STATES. Baltimore, Md.: Lord Baltimore Press, 1958. 245 p.

Statistical and analytical report for the Survey of the Legal Profession; used data from 136 completed questionnaires and visits to 160 law schools.

2164 Nisbet, Robert. THE DEGRADATION OF THE ACADEMIC DOGMA: THE UNIVERSITY IN AMERICA, 1945-1970. New York: Basic Books, 1971. 252 p.

British sociologist urges U.S. higher education to return to its traditional teaching and research roles and disengage from outside funding and politicization.

2165 Nitsch, Wolfgang, et al. SOCIAL SCIENCE RESEARCH ON HIGHER EDUCATION AND UNIVERSITIES: PART II: ANNOTATED BIBLIOGRAPHY. The Hague, Netherlands: Mouton and Co., 1970. 802 p.

Brief annotations (8,287) of worldwide (United States included) books, reports, and articles on higher education; arranged under various subject headings.

2166 Noble, Jeanne L. THE NEGRO WOMAN'S COLLEGE EDUCATION. New York: Teachers College, Columbia University, 1956. 163 p.

Surveyed educational experiences, social background, and current social lives of four hundred black women college graduates in six U.S. cities. Interviewed part of these graduates in prominent positions. Analyzed earlier surveys. Historical review of higher education for black women.

2167 Nolfi, George J., Jr., ed. CURRENT CAMPUS ISSUES. Cambridge, Mass.: University Consultants, 1969. 126 p.

College and university administrators' papers on the student role in governance, resource management, financial planning, and federal influence on higher education policy.

2168 Nolfi, George J., Jr., et al. EXPERIENCES OF RECENT HIGH SCHOOL GRADUATES: THE TRANSITION TO WORK OR POSTSECONDARY EDUCATION. Lexington, Mass.: Lexington Books, 1978. 211 p.

Studied the expectations and experiences of twenty-three thousand students from thirteen hundred high schools during the two years following high school graduation.

2169 Nordly, Carl L. THE ADMINISTRATION OF INTRAMURAL ATHLETICS FOR MEN IN COLLEGES AND UNIVERSITIES. Contributions to Education No. 716. New York: Teachers College, Columbia University, 1937. 134 p.

Recommended procedures for improving administration of intramural athletic programs and administrative policies in selected colleges and universities.

2170 Norris, Donald M., et al. MANPOWER STUDIES IN POSTSECONDARY EDUCATION. Washington, D.C.: American Association for Higher Education, 1978. 53 p.

Critically reviews recent manpower supply and demand projections applied to post-secondary education and suggests how to make better use of such studies.

2171 North, Walter M. THE RELATIONSHIP OF AID TO FEE INCREASES AND ENROLLMENT GROWTH. Bloomington, Ind.: Midwest Association of Student Financial Aid Administrators, 1970. 60 p.

Examines the policy of easing higher education financial problems by increasing both enrollment and student fees. Cautions against such a policy because it produces more need for student financial aid.

2172 Norton, Arthur O., ed. THE FIRST STATE NORMAL SCHOOL IN AMERICA: THE JOURNALS OF CYRUS PEIRCE AND MARY SWIFT. Cambridge, Mass.: Harvard University Press, 1926. Reprint. New York: Arno Press, 1976. 299 p.

Documentary history of the first U.S. normal school, Framingham, Massachusetts, 1839-1841, including journals of Principal Cyrus Peirce and early student Mary Swift.

2173 Norwood, William Frederick. MEDICAL EDUCATION IN THE UNITED STATES BEFORE THE CIVIL WAR. Philadelphia: University of Pennsylvania Press, 1944. Reprint. New York: Arno Press, 1972. 487 p.

U.S. medical education history from early apprenticeship to the 1765 opening of the first medical school (now the University of Pennsylvania School of Medicine) and to the Civil War. By 1800, twelve institutions granted medical degrees and others sprang up rapidly. Includes historical sketches of individual medical schools.

2174 Nosow, Sigmund. PROFESSIONAL SELF IMAGES AND ORGANIZATION ORIENTATIONS OF A GENERAL EDUCATION FACULTY. East Lansing: University College, Michigan State University, 1969. 174 p.

Sociological study of faculty at Michigan State's University College (perhaps the oldest U.S. university-connected general education college). Found older faculty generally satisfied but younger faculty favored offering courses more closely related to their own professional training.

2175 Nosow, Sigmund, and Clark, Frederick R. GOALS/AIMS/OBJECTIVES: DUQUESNE UNIVERSITY, A CASE STUDY. Atlantic Highlands, N.J.: Humanities Press, 1977. 243 p.

Relates specific policies at Catholic Duquesne University to the purposes of Catholic higher education.

2176 Novak, Steven J. THE RIGHTS OF YOUTH: AMERICAN COLLEGES AND STUDENT REVOLT, 1798-1815. Cambridge, Mass.: Harvard University Press, 1977. 218 p.

Early U.S. college student activism, most of it on local issues and dealt with harshly by administrators. Describes thirteen major confrontations at Dartmouth, Harvard, Yale, Princeton, William and Mary, and others; says reaction contributed to campus conservatism.

2177 Nowlan, James Dunlap. THE POLITICS OF HIGHER EDUCATION: LAWMAKERS AND THE ACADEMY IN ILLINOIS. Urbana: University of Illinois Press, 1976. 109 p.

Four case studies on how the Illinois state legislature (author was member) dealt with such higher education issues during 1969-72 as student unrest, budgeting, tuition, and aid to private institutions. Also on the role of the governor, Bureau of the Budget, Illinois Board of Higher Education, various university campuses, and special interest groups.

2178 Nye, Russell B., et al., eds. CRISES ON CAMPUS. Bowling Green, Ohio: Bowling Green State University, 1971. 211 p.

Articles on topics from black studies to the 1940s radical folksong movement.

2179 Nyquist, Ewald B., et al. COLLEGE LEARNING, ANYTIME, ANYWHERE. New York: Harcourt Brace Jovanovich, 1977. 164 p.

Ways to earn credits and a college degree by off-campus study and special examinations. Describes external degree programs at New Jersey's Thomas A. Edison College, the Connecticut Board for State Academic Awards, and New York State's Regents External Degree Program.

2180 Oaks, Dallin, et al. PRIVATE HIGHER EDUCATION: THE JOB AHEAD. Malibu, Calif.: American Association of Presidents of Independent Colleges and Universities, Pepperdine University, 1976. 31 p.

Papers on government and private higher education, legal and legislative problems, morality, and private higher education and the public interest.

2181 O'Banion, Terry. ORGANIZING STAFF DEVELOPMENT PROGRAMS THAT WORK. Washington, D.C.: American Association of Community and Junior Colleges, 1979. 32 p.

Suggestions for staff development in community colleges.

2182 _____. TEACHERS FOR TOMORROW: STAFF DEVELOPMENT IN THE COMMUNITY-JUNIOR COLLEGE. Tucson: University of Arizona Press, 1972. 185 p.

Junior college history, characteristics, curriculum, teacher recruitment, and staffing.

2183 _____, ed. DEVELOPING STAFF POTENTIAL. San Francisco: Jossey-Bass Publishers, 1977. 124 p.

> Methods for encouraging untapped potential of entire community college staff.

2184 O'Banion, Terry, and Thurston, Alice, eds. STUDENT DEVELOPMENT PROGRAMS IN THE COMMUNITY JUNIOR COLLEGE. New York: Prentice-Hall, 1972. 235 p.

> Articles on student counseling programs in the junior college. For counselors and teachers; stresses communication of values, course content, and achievement in practical and vocational fields.

2185 O'Connell, Thomas E. COMMUNITY COLLEGES: A PRESIDENT'S VIEW. Urbana: University of Illinois Press, 1968. 172 p.

> Background and role of the multipurpose junior or community college as rapidly growing part of higher education. Chapters on students, campus, president, how to start a community college, and campus planning.

2186 O'Connor, Thomas J. FOLLOW-UP STUDIES IN JUNIOR COLLEGES. Washington, D.C.: American Association of Junior Colleges, 1965. 75 p.

> Encourages follow-up studies (i.e., implementing recommended improvements) to upgrade two-year college programs and services.

2187 Odegaard, Charles E. MINORITIES IN MEDICINE: FROM RECEPTIVE PASSIVITY TO POSITIVE ACTION 1966-76. New York: Josiah Macy, Jr. Foundation, 1977. 163 p.

> Efforts and effects of U.S. medical schools to recruit and specially educate minority students.

2188 Offner, Herman Leroy. ADMINISTRATIVE PROCEDURES FOR CHANGING CURRICULUM PATTERNS FOR SELECTED STATE TEACHERS COLLEGES. Contributions to Education No. 898. New York: Teachers College, Columbia University, 1944. 145 p.

> Historical study of curriculum-making process in New Jersey, New York, and Pennsylvania teachers colleges, 1844-1942. Recommends a model curriculum revision plan.

2189 Ogilvie, William, and Raines, Max R., eds. PERSPECTIVES ON THE COMMUNITY JUNIOR COLLEGE. New York: Appleton-Century-Crofts, 1971. 635 p.

> Historic uniqueness and increasingly professionalized staffs of

U.S. two-year colleges, which provide general, vocational, and adult education.

2190 O'Hara, William T., and Hill, John G., Jr. THE STUDENT/THE COL-LEGE/THE LAW. New York: Teachers College Press, 1972. 220 p.

Summarizes laws affecting college admissions, confidentiality of records, due process, and other college student-related issues. Each chapter has illustrative court cases.

2191 O'Hearne, John J. COUNSELORS AND FINANCIAL AID: HELPING STUDENTS PLAN FOR COLLEGE. New York: College Board Publications, 1975. 36 p.

Historic and contemporary view of college student financial aid; plus student needs, expenses, budgeting, aid available, and under what conditions.

2192 Ohio. Board of Regents. OHIO MASTER PLAN FOR PUBLIC POLICY IN HIGHER EDUCATION. Columbus: 1971. 89 p.

Recommends: changed admissions policies, new junior colleges, job education centers at two-year colleges for high school graduates and dropouts, state aid to private institutions, and increased state support.

2193 _____. SPACE PLANNING GUIDELINES FOR THE PUBLIC UNIVERSITIES IN OHIO. Columbus:' 1974. 58 p.

Manual on private and public higher education planning for Ohio.

2194 Ohio. State University. Columbus. REPORT OF THE AD HOC COM-MITTEE TO REVIEW THE STATUS OF WOMEN AT THE OHIO STATE UNI-VERSITY, PHASES I AND II. Columbus: 1972. 360 p.

Status of women administrative and professional employees as to recruitment, appointment, promotion, tenure, salaries, and benefits.

2195 Ohio University. Athens. Center for Afro-American Studies. AFRO-AMERICAN STUDIES AND CONTEMPORARY ISSUES. 3 vols. Athens: 1972. 83 p., 103 p., 97 p.

Detailed guide and manual for college and university black study courses.

2196 Ohmann, Richard Malin, ed. TEACHING ENGLISH IN TWO-YEAR COL-LEGES: THREE SUCCESSFUL PROGRAMS. Urbana, Ill.: National Council of Teachers of English, 1974. 136 p.

Profiles of English programs at three two-year colleges: an inner city black college, a southern rural college, and a big city northern college.

2197 Ohmann, Richard Malin, and Coley, W.B., eds. IDEAS FOR ENGLISH 101: TEACHING WRITING IN COLLEGE. Urbana, Ill.: National Council of Teachers of English, 1975. 234 p.

Tactics and strategies on teaching college freshman English.

2198 Oinas, Felix J., ed. LANGUAGE TEACHING TODAY: REPORT OF THE LANGUAGE LABORATORY CONFERENCE HELD AT INDIANA UNIVERSITY, JANUARY 22-23, 1960. Bloomington: Indiana University Research Center in Anthropology, Folklore, and Linguistics, 1960. 221 p.

Papers on establishing, using, and improving language laboratories at all school levels.

2199 Olin, Helen R. THE WOMEN OF A STATE UNIVERSITY: AN ILLUSTRATION OF THE WORKING OF COEDUCATION IN THE MIDDLE WEST. New York: G.P. Putnam, 1909. 308 p.

How coeducation flourished at University of Wisconsin.

2200 Olson, Keith W. THE G.I. BILL, THE VETERANS, AND THE COLLEGES. Lexington: University Press of Kentucky, 1974. 139 p.

Concludes that the dominant motive of the originators of the G.I. Bill was anxiety about the economy, and that they did not anticipate its actual consequences: veterans' academic successes and the growth of higher education.

2201 Oltman, Ruth M. CAMPUS 1970--WHERE DO WOMEN STAND? RESEARCH REPORT OF A SURVEY ON WOMEN IN ACADEME. Washington, D.C.: American Association of University Women, 1970. 25 p.

Inequalities of women in higher education as students, administrators, faculty, and trustees.

2202 O'Neil, Robert M. DISCRIMINATING AGAINST DISCRIMINATION: PREFERENTIAL ADMISSIONS AND THE DEFUNIS CASE. Bloomington: Indiana University Press, 1976. 271 p.

Discusses and takes issue with white Marco DeFunis who sued the University of Washington for rejecting his law school application (1971), while admitting less qualified minorities. Lawyer-author favors preferential admissions for minorities as compensation for past discrimination; connects minority under-representation with urban violence.

2203 O'Neil, Robert M., et al. NO HEROES, NO VILLAINS: NEW PER-
SPECTIVES ON KENT STATE AND JACKSON STATE UNIVERSITY. San
Francisco: Jossey-Bass Publishers, 1972. 173 p.

> Analysis of student protest deaths at Kent and Jackson State
> Universities in 1970. Describes roles of the university, its
> administrators and faculties before, during, and after the trag-
> edies.

2204 O'Neill, Barbara Powell. CAREERS FOR WOMEN AFTER MARRIAGE
AND CHILDREN. New York: Macmillan Co., 1965. 401 p.

> Case studies of women in various fields, why and how they
> entered those fields, and higher education institutions offering
> training for such fields as teaching, library work, social work,
> counseling, health fields, engineering, math, science, law,
> city planning, and architecture.

2205 O'Neill, Mary Berenice. AN EVALUATION OF THE CURRICULA OF A
SELECTED GROUP OF CATHOLIC WOMEN'S COLLEGES. St. Louis, Mo.:
Sisters of St. Joseph of Carondelet, 1942. 390 p.

> Studied entrance requirements, aims, and curriculum of nine
> Catholic women's colleges.

2206 Orcutt, William Dana. WALLACE CLEMENT SABINE: A STUDY IN
ACHIEVEMENT. Norwood, Mass.: Plimpton Press, 1933. 376 p.

> Sabine (1868-1919), creator of the science of architectural
> acoustics, was Harvard physics and mathematics professor and
> dean.

2207 Organization for Economic Co-operation and Development. HIGHER EDU-
CATION AND THE DEMAND FOR SCIENTIFIC MANPOWER IN THE
UNITED STATES. Paris: 1963. 102 p.

> Visiting team of international educators examined supply and
> demand for U.S. scientists, higher education structure, teaching
> quality, effect of federal funding, and educational help to
> developing countries. Concluding discussion of findings with
> the international examiners, U.S. delegation, and other OECD
> representatives.

2208 Orlans, Harold. THE EFFECTS OF FEDERAL PROGRAMS ON HIGHER
EDUCATION. Washington, D.C.: Brookings Institution, 1962. 361 p.

> Studied thirty-six higher education institutions and found that
> heavy federal spending on sciences: (1) had not increased en-
> rollments in sciences within the liberal arts curriculum; and
> (2) had not caused brightest students to abandon social sciences
> and humanities to enter scientific fields.

2209 _____. THE NONPROFIT RESEARCH INSTITUTE: ITS ORIGIN, OPERA-TION, PROBLEMS, AND PROSPECTS. New York: McGraw-Hill Book Co., 1972. 243 p.

> Nonprofit research institutes and their relations with universities. Found such institutes vital to science and engineering. Their main problems are intellectual isolation and financial instability. Recommends their management by a consortium of universities.

2210 _____. PRIVATE ACCREDITATION AND PUBLIC ELIGIBILITY. Lexington, Mass.: Lexington Books, 1975. 261 p.

> Discusses the U.S. Office of Education's role in regulating private accrediting agencies. Concludes that the present interaction between private accreditation and federal fund eligibility is adequate but there is a need to reduce defects.

2211 O'Rourke, John T., and Miner, Leroy M.S. DENTAL EDUCATION IN THE UNITED STATES. Philadelphia: W.B. Saunders Co., 1941. 367 p.

> History of American dentistry, its changing curriculum, dental research, and the relationship of dentistry to medicine and the public.

2212 Orwig, M.D., ed. FINANCING HIGHER EDUCATION: ALTERNATIVES FOR THE FEDERAL GOVERNMENT. Iowa City: American College Testing Program, 1971. 390 p.

> Papers on efficient allocation of resources, equalizing opportunities, and alternate ways of financing (especially full cost pricing versus free public education). Reviews increased federal participation and political implications.

2213 Osgood, Charles G., et al. THE MODERN PRINCETON. Princeton, N.J.: Princeton University Press, 1947. 160 p.

> Essays on Princeton since 1896 by seven Princetonians, including Osgood, Christian Gauss, and Hugh S. Taylor, on undergraduate life, scholarship and research, architecture, board of trustees, and alumni.

2214 Ostheimer, Richard. STUDENT CHARGES AND FINANCING HIGHER EDUCATION: A STAFF STUDY FOR THE COMMISSION ON FINANCING HIGHER EDUCATION. New York: Columbia University Press, 1953. 217 p.

> Study on the effects raising student charges would have on revenues, equality of educational opportunity, enrollment, and quality of education. Concluded that modest student fee increase would benefit higher education finances.

2215 O'Toole, James. WORK, LEARNING, AND THE AMERICAN FUTURE. San Francisco: Jossey-Bass Publishers, 1977. 238 p.

Favors a lifelong systematic integration of work and learning. Advocates fusing liberal and technical education.

2216 O'Toole, Simon. CONFESSIONS OF AN AMERICAN SCHOLAR. Minneapolis: University of Minnesota Press, 1970. 111 p.

Autobiographical account of becoming a full professor, gaining some establishment fame, and eventually becoming disillusioned with U.S. higher education.

2217 Ott, Mary Diederich. ANALYSIS OF DOCTOR'S DEGREES AWARDED TO MEN AND TO WOMEN, 1970-71 THROUGH 1974-75. Washington, D.C.: Government Printing Office, 1977. 56 p.

Analyzes the number of doctoral degrees awarded, their distribution within the disciplines, by regions, and between public and private institutions.

2218 Otten, C. Michael. UNIVERSITY AUTHORITY AND THE STUDENT: THE BERKELEY EXPERIENCE. Berkeley: University of California Press, 1970. 222 p.

History of student-institutional relations in U.S. higher education. From early paternalism to growing twentieth-century bureaucracy, which students challenged. Sociological interpretation of late 1960s Berkeley student uprising. Predicts greater student participation in governance.

2219 Otto, Max C., et al. WILLIAM JAMES: THE MAN AND THE THINKER. Madison: University of Wisconsin Press, 1942. 147 p.

Lectures on the centenary of James's birth by Otto, Boyd Bode, John Dewey, D.S. Miller, and Norman Cameron.

2220 THE OVERSEAS SELECTION OF FOREIGN STUDENTS. New York: Education and World Affairs, 1966. 40 p.

Identifies principal agencies that screen foreign students in their own countries. Recommends a quasi-public agency to improve counseling, evaluating, and testing of foreign students before they come to the United States.

2221 Owen, Wyn F., and Antione, George H., eds. GUIDE TO GRADUATE STUDY IN ECONOMICS AND AGRICULTURAL ECONOMICS: UNITED STATES OF AMERICA AND CANADA. 4th ed. Homewood, Ill.: Richard D. Irwin, 1977. 328 p.

U.S. and selected foreign universities offering advanced degrees in economics and agricultural economics: admissions, programs of study, special programs, interdisciplinary programs, and degrees awarded.

2222 Ozmon, Howard, ed. CONTEMPORARY CRITICS OF EDUCATION. Danville, Ill.: Interstate Printers and Publishers, 1970. 223 p.

Critics Arthur Bestor, Jerome S. Bruner, Robert M. Hutchins, Paul Goodman, James D. Koerner, Hyman G. Rickover, Max Rafferty, and others on education at all levels, especially higher education.

2223 Pace, Charles Robert. COLLEGE AND UNIVERSITY ENVIRONMENTAL SCALES: TECHNICAL MANUAL. Princeton, N.J.: Educational Testing Service, 1963. 81 p.

On using scales to measure student attitudes about college life, facilities, faculty, instruction, examinations, and other campus features.

2224 _____. THE DEMISE OF DIVERSITY? A COMPARATIVE PROFILE OF EIGHT TYPES OF INSTITUTIONS. Berkeley, Calif.: Carnegie Commission on Higher Education, 1974. 131 p.

Institutions of higher education with the most distinctive qualities are declining in enrollments while others are attracting increasing numbers.

2225 _____. EDUCATION AND EVANGELISM: A PROFILE OF PROTESTANT COLLEGES. New York: McGraw-Hill Book Co., 1972. 120 p.

Compares eighty-eight Protestant colleges of three types: those formerly Protestant, now independent; those with major denominational connections; and those associated with evangelical, fundamentalist churches.

2226 _____. THEY WENT TO COLLEGE: STUDY OF 951 FORMER UNIVERSITY STUDENTS. Minneapolis: University of Minnesota Press, 1941. 148 p.

Survey of 951 University of Minnesota students, graduates and nongraduates, their activities, attitudes, problems, personal lives, home, family, vocation, and sociocivic affairs. Found apathy and failure to appreciate interrelationships among problems. Author called for revised educational programs.

2227 _____, ed. EVALUATING LEARNING AND TEACHING. San Francisco: Jossey-Bass Publishers, 1973. 110 p.

On teaching, learning, and evaluation. Cites advantages and disadvantages of existing evaluation systems and describes most promising new systems.

2228 Pacific Northwest Conference on Higher Education. QUALITY IN HIGHER EDUCATION IN TIMES OF FINANCIAL STRESS. Corvallis: Oregon State University Press, 1976. 80 p.

Conference papers on how to maintain higher education quality despite severe budget cuts.

2229 Page, Robert G., and Littlemeyer, Mary H. CONFERENCE ON THE OPTIMAL PREPARATION FOR THE STUDY OF MEDICINE, 1967. Chicago: University of Chicago Press, 1969. 287 p.

Explores the changing qualifications of entering medical students, admissions requirements, and curricular developments.

2230 Palinchak, Robert. THE EVOLUTION OF THE COMMUNITY COLLEGE. Metuchen, N.J.: Scarecrow Press, 1973. 364 p.

Synthesizes research on the community college movement; assesses its place in higher education.

2231 Palmer, Archie M., and Holton, Grace. COLLEGE INSTRUCTION IN ART. New York: Association of American Colleges, 1934. 62 p.

Commentary from U.S. art educators on the status of college art instruction and needed developments.

2232 Palola, Ernest G., and Padgett, William. PLANNING FOR SELF-RENEWAL: A NEW APPROACH TO PLANNED ORGANIZATIONAL CHANGE. Berkeley: Center for Research and Development in Higher Education, University of California, 1971. 118 p.

University planning in four states. Concluded that self-renewal is aided by strong leadership, wide participation in the planning process, and use of outside experts. Suggested planning model.

2233 Pangburn, Jessie M. THE EVOLUTION OF THE AMERICAN TEACHERS COLLEGE. New York: Teachers College, Columbia University, 1932. 140 p.

Forty-year history (1890-1930) of teacher education stresses changes in curriculum and faculty quality.

2234 Pannell, Anne Gary, and Wyatt, Dorothea E. JULIA S. TUTWILER AND SOCIAL PROGRESS IN ALABAMA. University: University of Alabama Press, 1961. 158 p.

Biography of Tutwiler (1841-1916), Livingston College president, now Livingston (Alabama) University, advocate of vocational and higher education for women, and proponent of prison reform.

2235 Panos, Robert J., and Astin, Alexander W. THEY WENT TO COLLEGE: A DESCRIPTIVE SUMMARY OF THE CLASS OF 1965. Washington, D.C.: American Council on Education, Office of Research, 1967. 34 p.

> Personal backgrounds and college experiences of a national student sample in 246 colleges and universities.

2236 Papillon, Cassian Edmund. THE PRINCIPLES OF ENTRANCE REQUIRE-MENTS OF CATHOLIC COLLEGES IN THE UNITED STATES. Washington, D.C.: Catholic University of America Press, 1949. 246 p.

> Used findings from a survey of 109 Catholic four-year colleges to establish principles for setting entrance requirements. Recommended acceptance of experience and skills for conventional entrance requirements.

2237 Paredes, Americo, ed. HUMANIDAD: ESSAYS IN HONOR OF GEORGE I. SANCHEZ. Los Angeles: Chicano Studies Center Publications, University of California, 1976. 144 p.

> On Chicano studies and education; University of Texas professor George I. Sanchez (1906-72) early attacked the cultural bias of testing and other discriminatory aspects of U.S. education.

2238 Parekh, Satish B. LONG-RANGE PLANNING: AN INSTITUTION-WIDE APPROACH TO INCREASING ACADEMIC VITALITY. New Rochelle, N.Y.: Change Magazine Press, 1977. 77 p.

> Model planning program to help administrators and faculty define institutions' academic purposes, assign responsibilities, determine financial and manpower resources, and evaluate efforts.

2239 _____, ed. PLANNING FOR IMPLEMENTATION. New York: Phelps-Stokes Fund, 1976. 108 p.

> Conference papers on college and university planning.

2240 Park, Clyde W. AMBASSADOR TO INDUSTRY: THE IDEA AND LIFE OF HERMAN SCHNEIDER. Indianapolis, Ind.: Bobbs-Merrill Co., 1943. 324 p.

> Schneider (1872-1939), University of Cincinnati professor (1903-06), engineering dean (1906-29), and president (1929-32), began alternating work experience in one's major field with study and was known as the father of cooperative higher education.

2241 Park, Joe, ed. THE RISE OF AMERICAN EDUCATION: AN ANNOTATED BIBLIOGRAPHY. Evanston, Ill.: Northwestern University Press, 1965. 216 p.

Annotates fifty-eight U.S. higher education books plus biographies and other items on related topics.

2242 Parker, Clyde A., ed. ENCOURAGING DEVELOPMENT IN COLLEGE STUDENTS. Minneapolis: University of Minnesota Press, 1979. 295 p.

Explains personality theories. Gives specific programs to help students mature during their college years.

2243 Parker, Franklin. GEORGE PEABODY: A BIOGRAPHY. Nashville, Tenn.: Vanderbilt University Press, 1971. 233 p.

Peabody's (1795-1869) Education Fund (1862) for southern states went to normal schools, including George Peabody College for Teachers, part of Vanderbilt University, Nashville. He endowed anthropology at Yale's and Harvard's Peabody Museums (1866); financed the education of nephew Othniel Charles Marsh (1831-99), first U.S. paleontology professor (Yale); and endowed Peabody Conservatory of Music, Baltimore.

2244 Parker, Franklin, et al. THE JUNIOR AND COMMUNITY COLLEGE: A BIBLIOGRAPHY OF DOCTORAL DISSERTATIONS: 1918-1963. Washington, D.C.: American Association of Junior Colleges, 1965. 47 p.

Over six hundred unannotated dissertations on the junior and community college arranged under fourteen categories.

2245 Parker, Franklin, and Parker, Betty June, eds. AMERICAN DISSERTATIONS ON FOREIGN EDUCATION. 11 vols. Troy, N.Y.: Whitston Publishing Co., 1971-1979. Various paginations.

Many of the thousands of U.S. and Canadian dissertations listed, abstracted, and indexed by subject in each of the eleven volumes published so far (world coverage is anticipated) compare U.S. education at all levels, including higher education, with counterpart aspects in other countries. Refers to many specific U.S. colleges and universities.

2246 _____. EDUCATION IN PUERTO RICO AND OF PUERTO RICANS IN U.S.A.: ABSTRACTS OF AMERICAN DOCTORAL DISSERTATIONS. San Juan, Puerto Rico: Inter American University Press, 1978. 601 p.

Many of the 284 U.S. and Canadian dissertations listed, abstracted, and indexed by subject are on some aspect of higher education, including women's education. Refers to many specific higher education institutions.

2247 _____. WOMEN'S EDUCATION--A WORLD VIEW: ANNOTATED BIBLIOGRAPHY OF DOCTORAL DISSERTATIONS. Vol. 1. Westport, Conn.: Greenwood Press, 1979. 470 p.

Many of the U.S. and Canadian dissertations listed, annotated, and indexed by subject are on U.S. higher education, including specific colleges and universities, and on women educated for various professions: nurses, physicians, others. Volume two in preparation will include books and reports on women's education, including U.S. higher education.

2248 Parker, Gail Thain, and Hawes, Gene R. COLLEGE ON YOUR OWN. New York: Bantam Books, 1978. 432 p.

Self-study college education guide, with reading program of major books in each field.

2249 Parker, James Reid. ACADEMIC PROCESSION. New York: Harcourt, Brace and Co., 1937. 281 p.

Short stories about typical small New England college faculty types: humorless scientist, superficial literati, self-important faculty marshall, wives aspiring to culture, faculty club politics, and groveling before the trustees.

2250 Parker, Orin D. CULTURAL CLUES TO THE MIDDLE EASTERN STUDENT. Washington, D.C.: American Friends of the Middle East, 1976. 18 p.

Problems Middle East students are likely to have in U.S. universities, and ways to ease their adjustment.

2251 Parsons, Kermit Carlyle. THE CORNELL CAMPUS: A HISTORY OF ITS PLANNING AND DEVELOPMENT. Ithaca, N.Y.: Cornell University Press, 1968. 336 p.

In the spirit of the 1862 Morrill Act, founder Ezra Cornell determined that Cornell University would serve rural and urban working class youths. First president, Andrew Dickson White, extended the curriculum to include scientific and professional courses.

2252 Parsons, Talcott, and Platt, Gerald M. THE AMERICAN UNIVERSITY. Cambridge, Mass.: Harvard University Press, 1973. 463 p.

Development, current status, and a theoretical model of the university in its societal context. Discusses students, general education, professional schools, the nature of the university system, and its role in intellectual life.

2253 Partch, Clarence Elmar. FACILITIES NEEDED FOR HIGHER EDUCATION. New Brunswick, N.J.: Rutgers University, 1948. 71 p.

Predicts enrollment trends to 1960 for each state and projects facilities needed.

2254 Passell, Peter, and Ross, Leonard. STATE POLICIES AND FEDERAL PRO-
GRAMS: PRIORITIES AND CONSTRAINTS. New York: Praeger Publishers, 1978. 168 p.

> State and federal relations in California before 1975 as they
> affected fiscal policy for education, including higher educa-
> tion, medical-welfare programs, and unemployment insurance.

2255 Patterson, Franklin Kessel. COLLEGES IN CONSORT: INSTITUTIONAL
COOPERATION THROUGH CONSORTIA. San Francisco: Jossey-Bass
Publishers, 1974. 182 p.

> Studied fifty-five consortia. Found them weakened by partici-
> pating colleges' traditional autonomy and by administrators'
> concern with their own institutions. Recommended that consor-
> tia establish governing boards independent of institutions they
> serve.

2256 Patterson, Samuel W. HUNTER COLLEGE: EIGHTY-FIVE YEARS OF
SERVICE. New York: Lantern Press, 1955. 263 p.

> Informal history of Hunter College, New York, with emphasis
> on the personalities of the men and women who led in pro-
> viding education for women.

2257 Pattillo, Manning M., Jr., and MacKenzie, Donald M. CHURCH-
SPONSORED HIGHER EDUCATION IN THE UNITED STATES; REPORT OF
THE COMMISSION ON CHURCH COLLEGES AND UNIVERSITIES. Wash-
ington, D.C.: American Council on Education, 1966. 309 p.

> Evaluations of 817 U.S. church-supported colleges' curricula,
> finance, and personnel. Concluded that in a decade the col-
> leges improved academically and financially.

2258 Patton, Carl V. ACADEMIA IN TRANSITION: MID-CAREER CHANGE
OR EARLY RETIREMENT. Cambridge, Mass.: Abt Books, 1979. 212 p.

> Early retirement impact on professors' careers and personal lives;
> on universities' manpower and fiscal structures; early retirement
> incentives; and early retirement human, legal, and administra-
> tive consequences.

2259 Patton, Leslie Karr. THE PURPOSES OF CHURCH-RELATED COLLEGES.
Contributions to Education No. 783. New York: Teachers College,
Columbia University, 1940. 287 p.

> Aims of small church-related colleges (up to six hundred stu-
> dents) in four periods during 1857-1921. Identified such influ-
> ences as Jefferson's and Franklin's utilitarianism, Dartmouth
> Case which reduced fear of state domination; advancing fron-
> tier, and growth of philanthropy. Discusses implications of

three major aims: citizenship and society, individual growth, and development of Christian character.

2260 Paulsen, Frank Robert, ed. HIGHER EDUCATION: DIMENSIONS AND DIRECTIONS. Tucson: University of Arizona Press, 1970. 179 p.

Essays about liberal studies and philosophy of education.

2261 Payne, Charles E. JOSIAH BUSHNELL GRINNELL. Iowa City: State Historical Society of Iowa, 1938. 338 p.

Vermont-born Grinnell (1821-91), abolitionist who moved to Iowa in 1854, founded the town of Grinnell, and persuaded Iowa College to relocate there. He aided John Brown, helped found the Iowa Republican Party, was state senator and U.S. congressman, and promoted railroads and better agricultural practices in Iowa. To honor him Iowa College in 1909 was renamed Grinnell College.

2262 Peabody, Francis Greenwood. EDUCATION FOR LIFE. Garden City, N.Y.: Doubleday, 1919. 393 p.

Early history of black, private, and nonsectarian Hampton Institute, Hampton, Virginia.

2263 Peairs, Richard H., ed. AVOIDING CONFLICT IN FACULTY PERSONNEL PRACTICES. San Francisco: Jossey-Bass Publishers, 1974. 102 p.

Advice on faculty codes, grievance procedures, and fairness in resolving conflict.

2264 Peare, Catherine Owens. MARY McLEOD BETHUNE. New York: Vanguard Press, 1951. 219 p.

Bethune (1875-1955), black educator who in 1904 founded a girls' school in Daytona Beach, Florida, which in 1923 merged with Cookman Institute to form Bethune-Cookman College. In 1935 she founded the National Council of Negro Women.

2265 Pearson, Richard. THE OPENING DOOR: A REVIEW OF NEW YORK STATE'S PROGRAMS OF FINANCIAL AID FOR COLLEGE STUDENTS. New York: College Entrance Examination Board, 1967. 89 p.

Relationship between access to higher education and student financial aid programs in New York state.

2266 Peck, Elisabeth S. BEREA'S FIRST CENTURY 1855-1955. Lexington: University of Kentucky Press, 1955. 217 p.

Centennial history of Berea College, Kentucky, founded 1855 by abolitionist John G. Fee. Independent, nonsectarian, serving poor mountain youth; has a labor program which requires students (no tuition) to work at least ten hours weekly for the college.

2267 Peirce, Adah. VOCATIONS FOR WOMEN. New York: Macmillan Co., 1933. 329 p.

Career guidance for college women; on many professions, employment opportunities, training requirements, and other details.

2268 Pell, Arthur R. CHOOSING A COLLEGE MAJOR: BUSINESS. New York: David McKay Co., 1979. 183 p.

Guide for students interested in business administration, marketing, accounting, finance, and data processing.

2269 Peltason, Jack Walter, and Massengale, Marcy V., eds. STUDENTS AND THEIR INSTITUTIONS: A CHANGING RELATIONSHIP. Washington, D.C.: American Council on Education, 1978. 201 p.

Ernest Boyer, John Silber, Harold Hodgkinson, and others on implications of declining higher education enrollments, new programs for nontraditional and adult students, and costs and benefits of a degree.

2270 Pember, Timothy. SWANSON. New York: Harcourt, Brace and Co., 1951. 280 p.

Novel about a California college professor who was a conscientious objector to war, was charged falsely with a crime, and descended to skid row.

2271 Penney, James F. PERSPECTIVE AND CHALLENGE IN COLLEGE PERSONNEL WORK. Springfield, Ill.: Charles C Thomas Publisher, 1972. 93 p.

Changes in the student personnel field since the 1930s; examines the prevailing philosophy and practices in U.S. higher education.

2272 Pennman, Kenneth A. PLANNING PHYSICAL EDUCATION AND ATHLETIC FACILITIES IN SCHOOLS. New York: John Wiley and Sons, 1977. 443 p.

On school and college athletic facilities and equipment; for physical education students, administrators, school planners, architects, and architectural students.

2273 Pennsylvania Commission for United Ministries in Higher Education. THE CHURCH'S MINISTRY IN HIGHER EDUCATION IN PENNSYLVANIA: THE

NEXT TEN YEARS. Berwyn, Pa.: 1978. 32 p.

Two papers on the future of the church's ministry to Pennsylvania higher education.

2274 Pentony, DeVere, et al. UNFINISHED REBELLIONS. San Francisco: Jossey-Bass Publishers, 1971. 315 p.

Background of 1968-69 San Francisco State student strike; public reaction to student rebellion, problems of minority education, and challenges to faculty governance.

2275 Perel, William M., and Vairo, Philip D. URBAN EDUCATION: PROBLEMS AND PROSPECTS. New York: David McKay Co., 1969. 145 p.

Says urban universities, urban adult education, and other city schooling are poorly supported because of white flight to suburbs and rural power in state legislatures. Calls for reversal of this trend if cities' ills are to be cured.

2276 Perkins, Dexter. YIELD OF THE YEARS: AN AUTOBIOGRAPHY. Boston: Little, Brown and Co., 1969. 245 p.

Autobiography of Perkins (1889-), history professor at the University of Rochester and Cornell University.

2277 Perkins, James A. THE UNIVERSITY IN TRANSITION. Princeton, N.J.: Princeton University Press, 1966. 90 p.

Cornell University president on problems of U.S. higher education: teaching, research, application of knowledge, internal cohesion, and the identity crisis posed by growing governmental involvement.

2278 Perkins, John A. PLAIN TALK FROM A CAMPUS. Newark: University of Delaware Press, 1959. 195 p.

University of Delaware president on public higher education, more federal aid, public service and higher education, and future prospects.

2279 Perry, Bliss. AND GLADLY TEACH: REMINISCENCES. Boston: Houghton Mifflin Co., 1935. 315 p.

Autobiography of English literature Professor Perry (1860-1954), his student years at Williams College and in Germany; his career as editor, novelist, and biographer; and his teaching at Williams College (1886-93), Princeton (1893-1900), and Harvard (1904-30), whose faculty, atmosphere, and programs he describes.

2280 Perry, Charles M. HENRY PHILIP TAPPAN: PHILOSOPHER AND UNI-
VERSITY PRESIDENT. Ann Arbor: University of Michigan Press, 1933.
Reprint. New York: Arno Press, 1972. 475 p.

Tappan (1805-81), first president of the University of Michigan
(1852-63), established the German elective pattern, put science
on an equal basis with the classics, and gave students much
freedom. His leadership, though fought by many in Michigan,
made the University of Michigan a model for other state universities.

2281 Perry, Richard R., and Hall, W. Frank IV, eds. THE ORGANIZED OR-
GANIZATION: THE AMERICAN UNIVERSITY AND ITS ADMINISTRA-
TION. Toledo, Ohio: University of Toledo, 1971. 135 p.

Essays on the history, stresses, and directions of college administration.

2282 Perry, William G., Jr. FORMS OF INTELLECTUAL AND ETHICAL DEVEL-
OPMENT IN THE COLLEGE YEARS. New York: Holt, Rinehart and
Winston, 1970. 256 p.

Used interviews for this research into students' personal development.

2283 Persons, Christopher Edgar. PUBLIC RELATIONS FOR COLLEGES AND
UNIVERSITIES: A MANUAL OF PRACTICAL PROCEDURE. Stanford,
Calif.: Stanford University Press, 1946. 61 p.

Advertising agency executive outlines steps for an effective
higher education public relations program.

2284 Perutz, Kathrin. THE GARDEN. New York: Atheneum Publishers, 1962.
185 p.

Novel about a permissive Eastern girls' college.

2285 Pervin, Lawrence A., et al., eds. THE COLLEGE DROPOUT AND THE
UTILIZATION OF TALENT. Princeton, N.J.: Princeton University Press,
1966. 260 p.

Educators, psychiatrists, and social scientists on college dropouts' problems: influencing factors, family attitudes, personality traits related to students' difficulties, psychiatric treatment, and decisions on readmission.

2286 Petersen, Renee, and Petersen, William. UNIVERSITY ADULT EDUCA-
TION: A GUIDE TO POLICY. New York: Harper and Brothers, 1960.
288 p.

Functions, principles, and problems of adult education in the context of higher education purposes. Calls on universities to define more carefully their role in the continuing education of adults.

2287 Peterson, Houston, ed. GREAT TEACHERS: PORTRAYED BY THOSE WHO STUDIED UNDER THEM. New Brunswick, N.J.: Rutgers University Press, 1946. 351 p.

Essays on twenty-five great nineteenth- and early twentieth-century teachers, most of whom taught in colleges or universities, including Louis Agassiz, John Dewey, Mark Hopkins, William James, Lizzie Moore, Anne M. Sullivan, Frederick Jackson Turner, and Woodrow Wilson.

2288 Peterson, Marvin W., ed. BENEFITING FROM INTERINSTITUTIONAL RESEARCH. San Francisco: Jossey-Bass Publishers, 1976. 108 p.

Effects of cross-institutional research; i.e., research done jointly by two or more colleges or universities.

2289 Peterson, Marvin W., et al. BLACK STUDENTS ON WHITE CAMPUSES: THE IMPACTS OF INCREASED BLACK ENROLLMENTS. Ann Arbor: Institute for Social Research, University of Michigan, 1978. 388 p.

Examines remedial programs, conflicts, and changes when blacks were rapidly admitted to thirteen white campuses in the 1960s and early seventies. Reasons for the success or failure of these minority programs are pinpointed and problems of incorporating new programs discussed.

2290 Peterson, Richard E., and Bilorusky, John A. MAY 1970: THE CAMPUS AFTERMATH OF CAMBODIA AND KENT STATE. Berkeley, Calif.: Carnegie Commission on Higher Education, 1971. 177 p.

Authors concluded that reforms in higher education were accelerated by student protests.

2291 Peterson, Richard E., et al. LIFELONG LEARNING IN AMERICA: AN OVERVIEW OF CURRENT PRACTICES, AVAILABLE RESOURCES, AND FUTURE PROSPECTS. San Francisco: Jossey-Bass Publishers, 1979. 532 p.

Guide to policies (local, state, and federal), programs, practices, trends, and resources in lifelong learning.

2292 Peterson, Shailer. PREPARING TO ENTER PHARMACY SCHOOL. Manchaca, Tex.: Sterling Swift Publishing Co., 1978. 295 p.

Overview of admissions process for pharmacy education; suggests a pre-pharmacy curriculum, stresses the demands of pharmacy education, and tells of pharmacy career opportunities.

2293 PETERSON'S ANNUAL GUIDE TO GRADUATE STUDY, 1978. 5 vols.
Princeton, N.J.: Peterson's Guides, 1978. 504 p., 839 p., 1,271 p.,
503 p., 501 p.

> Volume 1 lists 1,350 U.S. and Canadian graduate institutions
> and 188 programs of study. Remaining volumes give details,
> by field, about graduate programs: volume 2, humanities and
> social sciences; volume 3, biological, agricultural, and health
> sciences; volume 4, physical sciences; and volume 5, engi-
> neering and applied sciences.

2294 PETERSON'S ANNUAL GUIDE TO UNDERGRADUATE STUDY, 1978.
Princeton, N.J.: Peterson's Guides, 1978. 1,571 p.

> Describes U.S. and Canadian two- and four-year colleges and
> 122 major fields. Includes each institution's academic facili-
> ties, costs, admission requirements, and financial aid.

2295 Pfnister, Allan O. PLANNING FOR HIGHER EDUCATION: BACK-
GROUND AND APPLICATION. Boulder, Colo.: Westview Press, 1976.
354 p.

> Predicts trends in college enrollments, student characteristics,
> curriculum reforms, and administrative and financial problems.
> Advises administrators and faculty members on improving
> planning.

2296 Phelps, William Lyon. AUTOBIOGRAPHY WITH LETTERS. New York:
Oxford University Press, 1939. 986 p.

> Phelps (1865-1943), Yale literature professor (1892-1933),
> taught pioneering novel and contemporary drama courses. Let-
> ters with literary figures compose most of book.

2297 Phillips, Ione. THE ADDED DIMENSION: STATE AND LAND-GRANT
UNIVERSITIES SERVING STATE AND LOCAL GOVERNMENT. Washing-
ton, D.C.: National Association of State Universities and Land-Grant
Colleges, 1977. 96 p.

> Efforts of National Association of State Universities and Land-
> Grant Colleges to provide their state and local governments
> with the scientific and technological information to help in
> land-use planning, energy conservation and development, trans-
> portation policy, health care, and other areas.

2298 Pierce, Anna Eloise. DEANS AND ADVISERS OF WOMEN AND GIRLS.
New York: Professional and Technical Press, 1928. 636 p.

> Examines women's education and the preparation and duties of
> women deans and advisers.

2299 Pierce, Barbara Hanson. JUNIOR YEAR IN BRITAIN: WHERE TO GO, HOW TO APPLY, WHAT TO EXPECT. Princeton, N.J.: Peterson's Guides, 1979. 151 p.

> Guide to British universities that accept U.S. undergraduates for short-term study.

2300 Pierson, Frank C., et al. THE EDUCATION OF AMERICAN BUSINESS-MEN. New York: McGraw-Hill Book Co., 1959. 740 p.

> Study of weaknesses in undergraduate business education, with recommendations for improved objectives, methods, and teacher preparation. Found graduate programs generally effective.

2301 Pierson, George Wilson. YALE: THE UNIVERSITY COLLEGE, 1921-1937. New Haven, Conn.: Yale University Press, 1955. 740 p.

> Yale history from 1921 to 1937, and its evolution to a university. Shows rapid changes in administration and enrollments and corresponding academic improvement.

2302 _____. YALE COLLEGE: AN EDUCATIONAL HISTORY, 1871-1921. New Haven, Conn.: Yale University Press, 1952. 773 p.

> Yale history from 1871 to 1921, chronological and topical. Includes educational problems; relations with alumni; and influences of presidents, deans, and great teachers. Thesis is that Yale preserved old ideals and purposes while adapting to changing needs.

2303 Pierson, Irene. CAMPUS CUES. Danville, Ill.: Interstate Printers and Publishers, 1956. 147 p.

> Social deportment and etiquette for college students.

2304 Pierson, Mary Bynum. GRADUATE WORK IN THE SOUTH. Chapel Hill: University of North Carolina Press, 1947. 265 p.

> History of southern graduate education. Details graduate programs at the Universities of Georgia, North Carolina, Texas, Virginia, at Duke and Vanderbilt Universities, and at Nashville's Peabody College. Cites such problems as inadequate libraries and financial support and heavy teaching loads. Chapter on inadequate black graduate education. Cites poverty and conservatism as major barriers to strong graduate programs in the South.

2305 Pine, Hester. BEER FOR THE KITTEN. New York: Farrar and Rinehart, 1939. 312 p.

> Satirical novel of life in a small New England college town (author is wife of a college professor).

2306 Pitcher, Barbara. A FURTHER STUDY FOR PREDICTING LAW SCHOOL GRADES FOR FEMALE LAW STUDENTS. Princeton, N.J.: Educational Testing Service, 1976.

> Examines the validity of using the Law School Admission Test, undergraduate grades, and writing ability to predict law school grades of female students.

2307 Pitcher, Robert W., and Blaushild, Babette. WHY COLLEGE STUDENTS FAIL. New York: Funk and Wagnalls, 1970. 271 p.

> Analyzes causes of college student failure. Says college success comes with motivation, maturity, and improved language skills. Recommends ways traditional college programs might better serve students.

2308 Pittsburgh. University. Advisory Council on Women's Opportunities. PROGRESS REPORT TO THE CHANCELLOR. Pittsburgh, Pa.: 1970. 14 p.

> Recommendations for ending sex discrimination at University of Pittsburgh.

2309 PLANNING, PROGRAMMING, BUDGETING SYSTEMS IN ACADEMIC LIBRARIES: AN EXPLORATORY STUDY OF PPBS IN UNIVERSITY LIBRARIES HAVING MEMBERSHIP IN THE ASSOCIATION OF RESEARCH LIBRARIES. Edited by Harold Chester Young. Detroit: Gale Research Co., 1977. 227 p.

> Study of the planning, programming, and budgeting systems useful in efficient financial management in university libraries.

2310 Plant, Walter T. PERSONALITY CHANGES ASSOCIATED WITH A COLLEGE EDUCATION. San Jose, Calif.: San Jose State College, 1962. 83 p.

> Study of students' personality change in proportion to the quantity of college attendance.

2311 Plochmann, George Kimball. THE ORDEAL OF SOUTHERN ILLINOIS UNIVERSITY. Carbondale: Southern Illinois University Press, 1959. 662 p.

> History of Southern Illinois University's problems common to many similar state institutions--tightfisted legislators, provincialism, faculty recruitment, and the ordeal of evolving from normal school to university.

2312 Podolsky, Arthur, and Smith, Carolyn R. EDUCATION DIRECTORY, COLLEGES AND UNIVERSITIES 1977-78. Washington, D.C.: Government Printing Office, 1978. 558 p.

Annual directory of all U.S. two-year and above higher education institutions. Information: address, tuition and fees, control or affiliation, programs, accreditation, and names and titles of principal officers.

2313 Politelia, Dario, ed. DIRECTORY OF THE COLLEGE STUDENT PRESS IN AMERICA, FOURTH EDITION, 1977-78. New York: Oxbridge Communications, 1977. 654 p.

Lists essential information on 5,499 college magazines, newspapers, and yearbooks.

2314 Pollard, Lucille Addison. WOMEN ON COLLEGE AND UNIVERSITY FACULTIES: A HISTORICAL SURVEY AND A STUDY OF THEIR PRESENT ACADEMIC STATUS. New York: Arno Press, 1977. 336 p.

Surveys the early employment of women on college faculties and subsequent employment trends.

2315 Poole, Herbert, ed. ACADEMIC LIBRARIES BY THE YEAR 2000: ESSAYS HONORING JERROLD ORNE. New York: R.R. Bowker Co., 1978. 205 p.

About university libraries in the future; essays honoring retiring librarian Orne (1911-) at the University of North Carolina, Chapel Hill; short biography and bibliography of his writings.

2316 Porter, Harold Everett. PEPPER. New York: Century Co., 1915. 316 p.

Short stories on the frivolous side of Harvard undergraduate life.

2317 Porter, Noah. THE AMERICAN COLLEGES AND THE AMERICAN PUBLIC. New Haven, Conn.: C.C. Chatfield and Co., 1870. Reprint. New York: Arno Press, 1978. 285 p.

Conservative Noah Porter (Yale philosophy professor, 1846-71, and president, 1871-86) defended the traditional course system and resisted as hasty many academic changes, particularly the elective systems.

2318 Portman, David N. THE UNIVERSITIES AND THE PUBLIC: A HISTORY OF HIGHER ADULT EDUCATION IN THE UNITED STATES. Chicago: Nelson-Hall Publishers, 1979. 214 p.

History of U.S. adult higher education from its nineteenth-century origins in the Chautauqua movement and university extension experiments to today's evening colleges, summer sessions, and liberal arts colleges' adult programs.

2319 Potter, David. DEBATING IN THE COLONIAL CHARTERED COLLEGES:
AN HISTORICAL SURVEY, 1642-1900. Contributions to Education No.
899. New York: Teachers College, Columbia University, 1944. 158 p.

> History of debating in the nine colonial colleges to 1900; in-
> cludes questions debated during different periods and changes
> in debating styles.

2320 Pottker, Janice, and Fishel, Andrew, eds. SEX BIAS IN THE SCHOOLS:
THE RESEARCH EVIDENCE. Rutherford, N.J.: Fairleigh Dickinson University Press, 1977. 571 p.

> Research techniques used to document sex discrimination and
> its effect at all school levels. Other topics are women in
> academic governance, continuing education for women, and
> sex bias in college admissions.

2321 Powell, John R., et al. THE PERSONNEL ASSISTANT IN COLLEGE
RESIDENCE HALLS. Boston: Houghton Mifflin Co., 1969. 215 p.

> Handbook for students employed as personnel assistants in col-
> lege residence halls.

2322 Power, Edward John. A HISTORY OF CATHOLIC HIGHER EDUCATION
IN THE UNITED STATES. Milwaukee, Wis.: Bruce Publishing Co., 1958.
383 p.

> Historical study stressing Catholic men's colleges (women's col-
> leges were modeled after them). Appendix includes a list by
> states of men's and women's colleges.

2323 Powers, Thomas F., ed. EDUCATING FOR CAREERS: POLICY ISSUES
IN A TIME OF CHANGE. University Park: Pennsylvania State University Press, 1977. 190 p.

> Papers on career education and on vocational training versus
> liberal arts.

2324 Prator, Ralph. THE COLLEGE PRESIDENT. New York: New York Center for Applied Research in Education, 1963. 118 p.

> History of the college presidency; qualifications and functions.

2325 Pratt, Arden L. ENVIRONMENTAL EDUCATION IN THE COMMUNITY
COLLEGE. Washington, D.C.: American Association of Junior Colleges,
1971. 112 p.

> Cautions that environmental education may be a fad, describes
> kinds of programs being offered, and reminds those planning
> job-related environmental education courses to investigate their
> state's standards.

2326 President's Commission on Campus Unrest. THE REPORT OF THE PRESI-
DENT'S COMMISSION ON CAMPUS UNREST: INCLUDING SPECIAL
REPORTS: THE KILLINGS AT JACKSON STATE, THE KENT STATE TRAG-
EDY. Washington, D.C.: Government Printing Office, 1970. 537 p.
New York: Arno Press, 1970. 537 p.

> The Scranton Commission, named to investigate the 1970 Kent
> State and Jackson State tragedies, deals with causes and im-
> pact of campus unrest. Also has a section on the evolution
> of the black student movement. Call for understanding, recon-
> ciliation, and shared national commitment.

2327 President's Committee on Education Beyond the High School. THE
STRENGTH TO MEET OUR NATIONAL NEED. Washington, D.C.: American Council on Education, 1956. 125 p.

> Report on such topics as need for more community colleges,
> salvaging talent, adult education, and ending barriers to equal
> education.

2328 Price, Louise. CREATIVE GROUP WORK ON THE CAMPUS. New York:
Teachers College, Columbia University, 1941. 437 p.

> On the development of group processes in student life at
> Stephens College and Stanford University.

2329 Priest, Bill J., and Pickelman, John E. INCREASING PRODUCTIVITY
IN THE COMMUNITY COLLEGE: AN ACTION-ORIENTED APPROACH.
Washington, D.C.: American Association of Community and Junior Col-
leges, 1976. 36 p.

> Guide on efficient management for community colleges. Based
> on a study of the Dallas County Community College District.

2330 Professional Societies Committee of the Study Commission on Undergraduate Education and the Education of Teachers. A TIME HALF DEAD AT
THE TOP: PROFESSIONAL SOCIETIES AND THE REFORM OF SCHOOL-
ING IN AMERICA, 1955-75. Lincoln: Nebraska Curriculum Development Center, University of Nebraska, 1976. 293 p.

> Inner workings of such professional societies as Mathematical
> Association of America and the American Institute of Physics,
> their relations with the federal government, and their role in
> educational reform.

2331 Proia, Nicholas C., ed. BARRON'S HANDBOOK OF COLLEGE TRANS-
FER INFORMATION. Woodbury, N.Y.: Barron's Educational Series,
1975. 297 p.

> Charts by state and institution provide transfer information on
> thirteen hundred U.S. colleges and universities. Subheadings

include student services, career planning, personal development, and programs for women.

2332 Proia, Nicholas C., and DiGaspari, Vincent M., eds. BARRON'S HAND-
BOOK OF AMERICAN COLLEGE FINANCIAL AID. Woodbury, N.Y.:
Barron's Educational Series, 1974. 508 p.

Charts by state and institution list seventeen categories of student financial aid along with application requirements.

2333 _____. BARRON'S HANDBOOK OF JUNIOR AND COMMUNITY COL-
LEGE FINANCIAL AID. Woodbury, N.Y.: Barron's Educational Series,
1971. 704 p.

Lists types of aid available at over eight hundred two-year
colleges and how to apply for it.

2334 Project on Noncollegiate Sponsored Instruction. A GUIDE TO EDUCA-
TIONAL PROGRAMS IN NONCOLLEGIATE ORGANIZATIONS. Washington, D.C.: American Council on Education, 1976. 193 p.

Lists over six hundred U.S. noncollegiate courses offered by
thirty-eight groups such as businesses, industries, labor unions,
government agencies, and professional and voluntary agencies.
Gives advice to help colleges and universities award equivalent credit in degree programs.

2335 Propst, Robert L., and Propst, Claudia G. THE UNIVERSITY OF MASSA-
CHUSETTS DORMITORY EXPERIMENT. Ann Arbor, Mich.: Herman Miller Research Corp., 1974. 95 p.

Behavior and attitudes of students toward living in a high-rise
dormitory. Gives causes of student dissatisfaction. Describes
an experiment comparing an innovative with a traditional living
arrangement.

2336 Pruette, Lorine. G. STANLEY HALL: A BIOGRAPHY OF A MIND. New
York: Appleton, 1926. 267 p.

Pioneer psychologist Hall (1844-1924), on completing his Harvard Ph.D., studied theology and philosophy in New York and
Germany (1868-71), taught for six years, and returned to Germany (1878-80) to study mainly psychology. He taught at
Johns Hopkins University (1881-88), where he established a
psychology laboratory, was first president of the American Psychological Association (1881), founder of the Child Study Association (1888), and first president and psychology professor at
Clark University (1888-1919).

2337 Pullias, Earl V., et al. TOWARD EXCELLENCE IN COLLEGE TEACHING.
Dubuque, Iowa: William C. Brown Co., 1963. 133 p.

A psycho-philosophical approach to college teaching, including critical thinking, value judgments, and personality development.

2338 Puner, Helen Walker. NOT WHILE YOU'RE A FRESHMAN: A CHAPTER IN THE LIFE OF MONOLOGUE. New York: Coward-McCann, 1965. 191 p.

An American mother's tongue-in-cheek meandering notes to her college freshman daughter.

2339 Pusey, Nathan M. THE AGE OF THE SCHOLAR: OBSERVATIONS ON EDUCATION IN A TROUBLED DECADE. Cambridge, Mass.: Belknap Press of Harvard University Press, 1963. 210 p.

Speeches by Harvard's president on such perennial higher education questions as the nature of free inquiry, scientists' role, public versus private universities, teacher education, and academic freedom.

2340 _____. AMERICAN HIGHER EDUCATION, 1945-1970: A PERSONAL REPORT. Cambridge, Mass.: Harvard University Press, 1978. 204 p.

Harvard's president emeritus reminisces about post U.S. higher education, its role in world affairs, graduate education and research developments, 1950s anticommunist hysteria, and 1960s student unrest.

2341 Pusey, William W. THE INTERRUPTED DREAM: THE EDUCATIONAL PROGRAM AT WASHINGTON COLLEGE, 1850-1880. Lexington, Va.: Liberty Hall Press, 1976. 64 p.

History of Washington College (now Washington and Lee University) during the thirty years surrounding the Civil War. Compares its curriculum to that of other colleges.

2342 Putt, S. Gorley, ed. COUSINS AND STRANGERS: COMMENTS ON AMERICA BY COMMONWEALTH FUND FELLOWS FROM BRITAIN, 1946-1952. Cambridge, Mass.: Harvard University Press, 1956. 222 p.

British graduate students' comments on U.S. traits, manners, and mainly academic life.

2343 Quay, Richard H. RESEARCH IN HIGHER EDUCATION: A GUIDE TO SOURCE BIBLIOGRAPHIES. New York: College Entrance Examination Board, 1976. 54 p.

A 572-item partially annotated bibliography of bibliographies and reviews of the literature on higher education appearing between 1960 and 1975, arranged under such subheadings as social policy and politics and higher education.

2344 Quincy, Josiah. THE HISTORY OF HARVARD UNIVERSITY. 2 vols. Cambridge, Mass.: Owen, 1840. Reprint. New York: Arno Press, 1977. 612 p., 728 p.

> Harvard's first two hundred years based on original sources written by Quincy while its president. Topics: rise of lay control, early tenure policies, and free inquiry despite sectarian dogma. Appendix contains documents.

2345 Quindry, Kenneth E., and Currence, Mary G. STATE AND LOCAL REVENUE POTENTIAL, 1974. Atlanta: Southern Regional Education Board, 1976. 117 p.

> State-by-state data on public revenues for higher education and an analysis of future taxing potential.

2346 Radcliffe College Committee on Graduate Education for Women. GRADUATE EDUCATION FOR WOMEN: THE RADCLIFFE PH.D.: A REPORT BY A FACULTY-TRUSTEE COMMITTEE. Cambridge, Mass.: Harvard University Press, 1956. 135 p.

> Surveyed 522 Radcliffe Ph.D. recipients, from 1901 to 1951, on scholarly achievement, professional lives, and marriage. Half reported sex bias in their professions. Those who married had difficulty combining domestic and professional duties.

2347 Rader, Benjamin G. THE ACADEMIC MIND AND REFORM: THE INFLUENCE OF RICHARD T. ELY IN AMERICAN LIFE. Lexington: University of Kentucky Press, 1966. 276 p.

> Ely (1854-1943), who earned a Ph.D. in Heidelberg, Germany, taught at Johns Hopkins (1881-92), was University of Wisconsin economics chairman (1892-1925), helped found the American Economics Association (1885), and published twenty books including a leading textbook. Critical of classical economics and big business; his ideas strengthened labor and influenced Wisconsin's progressives.

2348 Rader, Hannelore B. WOMEN IN HIGHER EDUCATION ADMINISTRATION: ANNOTATED BIBLIOGRAPHY. Washington, D.C.: National Association for Women Deans, Administrators, and Counselors, 1977. 12 p.

> Annotated list of articles, studies, and surveys on women administrators in higher education.

2349 Raiborn, Mitchell H. FINANCIAL ANALYSIS CF INTERCOLLEGIATE ATHLETICS. Kansas City, Mo.: National Collegiate Athletic Association, 1970. 127 p.

> Only big time football schools break even on intercollegiate programs; student attendance at athletic events has decreased while public attendance has increased.

2350 Raines, Max R. DEVELOPING CONSTITUENCY PROGRAMS IN COM-
MUNITY COLLEGES. Washington, D.C.: American Association of Community and Junior Colleges, 1977. 64 p.

> Community colleges must understand their various constituencies
> in order to provide effective educational services; offers a
> planning model for assessing needs.

2351 Rainey, Homer P. THE TOWER AND THE DOME: A FREE UNIVERSITY
VERSUS POLITICAL CONTROL. Boulder, Colo.: Pruett Publishing Co.,
1971. 151 p.

> Former University of Texas at Austin president (1939-44) tells
> his side of the fight with regents and the Texas legislature
> over academic freedom and political interference which led
> to his dismissal.

2352 Rainsford, George N. CONGRESS AND HIGHER EDUCATION IN THE
NINETEENTH CENTURY. Knoxville: University of Tennessee Press, 1972.
156 p.

> This political history of nineteenth-century federal legislation
> concludes that congressional aid of higher education has most
> often been a by-product of other programs such as sale of pub-
> lic lands, accommodation of special interest groups, or strength-
> ening national defense.

2353 Ramaley, Judith A., ed. COVERT DISCRIMINATION AND WOMEN IN
THE SCIENCES. Boulder, Colo.: Westview Press, 1978. 123 p.

> Essays sponsored by the American Association for the Advance-
> ment of Science on cultural biases, some hidden and uncon-
> scious, which affect women's professional development.

2354 Rammelkamp, Charles Henry. ILLINOIS COLLEGE: A CENTENNIAL HIS-
TORY, 1829-1929. New Haven, Conn.: Yale University Press, 1928.
605 p.

> Illinois College (Jacksonville) president tells of eight presidents'
> administrations, the college's place in the antislavery move-
> ment, and the founding of Illinois' first medical school.

2355 Rand, Christopher. CAMBRIDGE, U.S.A.: HUB OF A NEW WORLD.
New York: Oxford University Press, 1964. 195 p.

> Based on NEW YORKER articles about the power, money, pres-
> tige, and influence of the Harvard-MIT educational complex.

2356 Raney, M. Llewellyn. THE UNIVERSITY LIBRARIES. Chicago: University of Chicago Press, 1933. 250 p.

Survey, 1929-33, of the adequacy and future needs of the University of Chicago library collections found that one and a half million volumes should be added.

2357 Rapoport, Roger, and Kirshbaum, Laurence J. IS THE LIBRARY BURNING? New York: Random House, 1969. 180 p.

Campus turmoil is examined by two recently graduated college students.

2359 Rarig, Emory W., Jr., ed. THE COMMUNITY JUNIOR COLLEGE: AN ANNOTATED BIBLIOGRAPHY. New York: Teachers College Press, 1966. 113 p.

Annotated bibliography of over three hundred books and articles on community junior college history, purpose, administration, programs, personnel, facilities, research, and students.

2360 Rasey, Marie I. THIS IS TEACHING. New York: Harper and Brothers, 1950. 218 p.

Illustrates how progressive concepts of education can be used in college teaching.

2361 Ratterman, P.H. THE EMERGING CATHOLIC UNIVERSITY: WITH A COMMENTARY ON THE JOINT STATEMENT ON THE RIGHTS AND FREEDOMS OF STUDENTS. New York: Fordham University Press, 1968. 177 p.

Xavier University (Cincinnati) vice president discusses basic philosophical changes affecting relations between Catholic universities and their students. Appendix has commentary on the Joint Statement on the Rights and Freedoms of Students.

2362 Rattigan, Bernard T. A CRITICAL STUDY OF THE GENERAL EDUCATION MOVEMENT. Washington, D.C.: Catholic University of America Press, 1952. 247 p.

History of the general education movement, emphasizing its implications for Catholic higher education.

2363 Rauh, Morton A. COLLEGE AND UNIVERSITY TRUSTEESHIP. Yellow Springs, Ohio: Antioch Press, 1959. 112 p.

Responsibilities and issues which face academic trustees.

2364 _____. THE TRUSTEESHIP OF COLLEGES AND UNIVERSITIES. New York: McGraw-Hill Book Co., 1969. 160 p.

Higher education trustee functions, based on a survey of fifty-four hundred trustees of private, public, state, and religious institutions.

2365 Raushenbush, Esther. LITERATURE FOR INDIVIDUAL EDUCATION. New York: Columbia University Press, 1942. 262 p.

Freshman exploratory courses in literature used for guidance at Sarah Lawrence College, where students were first introduced through realistic fiction to poverty and crime. Author suggests such themes as religion and society and the literature of minority groups to broaden student horizons.

2366 _____. THE STUDENT AND HIS STUDIES. Middletown, Conn.: Wesleyan University Press, 1964. 185 p.

Interviewed 170 students at eight colleges and did case studies of four students on their intellectual growth. Concluded that because of massive size and faculty research large institutions should explore innovations such as satellite colleges to help individual students find themselves intellectually.

2367 _____, ed. PSYCHOLOGY FOR INDIVIDUAL EDUCATION. New York: Columbia University Press, 1942. 306 p.

Role of an exploratory psychology course at Sarah Lawrence College to help students achieve emotional and intellectual maturity.

2368 Ray, Anna Chapin. ACKROYD OF THE FACULTY. Boston: Little, Brown and Co., 1907. 311 p.

Novel of a young instructor in a great university who must overcome poverty to win the cultured daughter of his department chairman.

2369 Ray, Robert F. ADULT PART-TIME STUDENTS AND THE C.I.C. UNIVERSITIES. Iowa City: Division of Continuing Education, State University of Iowa, 1977. 424 p.

Courses and programs offered to adult part-time students at eleven midwestern universities.

2370 Reardon, Robert C., and Burck, Harman D., eds. FACILITATING CAREER DEVELOPMENT: STRATEGIES FOR COUNSELORS. Springfield, Ill.: Charles C Thomas, Publishers, 1976. 315 p.

On counseling techniques useful in vocational guidance.

2371 Reck, W. Emerson. THE CHANGING WORLD OF COLLEGE RELATIONS: HISTORY AND PHILOSOPHY, 1917-1975. Washington, D.C.: Council for Advancement and Support of Education, 1977. 466 p.

History and philosophy of the public relations concept in higher education.

2372 _____. PUBLIC RELATIONS: A PROGRAM FOR COLLEGES AND UNI-VERSITIES. New York: Harper and Brothers, 1946. 286 p.

Analysis of public relations programs for institutions of higher education.

2373 _____, ed. COLLEGE PUBLICITY MANUAL. New York: Harper and Brothers, 1948. 246 p.

Guidebook, by eighteen experienced higher education public relations specialists.

2374 Redfield, Margaret Park, ed. THE SOCIAL USES OF SOCIAL SCIENCE: THE PAPERS OF ROBERT REDFIELD. Vol. 2. Chicago: University of Chicago Press, 1963. 287 p.

Papers of University of Chicago anthropologist and dean of social sciences on such topics as the educational experience and the university and society.

2375 Reece, Ernest J. THE CURRICULUM IN LIBRARY SCHOOLS. New York: Columbia University Press, 1936. 220 p.

Analyzes librarians' duties and recommends that the library science curriculum train students for specific functions.

2376 _____. PROGRAMS FOR LIBRARY SCHOOLS. New York: Columbia University Press, 1943. 64 p.

Practical and philosophical approach to training librarians, with specific recommendations on course content and program sequence.

2377 _____. THE TASK AND TRAINING OF LIBRARIANS. New York: King's Crown Press, 1949. 91 p.

Recommendations from librarians, education consultants, and professors for changes in library science curricula, based on a 1947 Columbia University School of Library Science investigation.

2378 Reed, Anna Y., et al. THE EFFECTIVE AND THE INEFFECTIVE COLLEGE TEACHER: A STUDY MADE FOR THE NATIONAL PERSONNEL SERVICE, INC. New York: American Book Co., 1935. 344 p.

College teaching study based on the literature and data from several hundred liberal arts and teacher education colleges. Includes personality characteristics of effective and ineffective faculty.

2379 Reed, Germaine M. DAVID FRENCH BOYD: FOUNDER OF LOUISIANA STATE UNIVERSITY. Baton Rouge: Louisiana State University Press, 1977. 315 p.

> Virginia-born Boyd (1834-99), a founder, president (1876-80, 1884-86), and professor at Louisiana State University, earlier taught in and then headed the Louisiana State Seminary of Learning, which merged with other schools to form Louisiana State University. He also pioneered in industrial and technical education in the South.

2380 Reeves, Floyd W., ed. ON GETTING INTO COLLEGE: A STUDY OF DISCRIMINATIONS IN COLLEGE ADMISSIONS. Washington, D.C.: American Council on Education, 1949. 99 p.

> Study of white 1947 high school graduates admitted to college showed economic, sex, religious, and other barriers. Only 56 percent of Jewish applicants were accepted compared to 67 percent of Catholics, and 67 percent of Protestants, although twice as many Jews in proportion to their numbers applied. Of all 1947 graduates, 35 percent applied for college and 87 percent of applicants were admitted. Concluded that more two-year public community colleges are needed.

2381 Reeves, Floyd W., and Russell, John Dale. ADMISSION AND RETENTION OF UNIVERSITY STUDENTS. Chicago: University of Chicago Press, 1933. 360 p.

> Examines the effectiveness of various selection criteria among University of Chicago undergraduates and graduates (including graduate students in education and in law). Includes a section on transfer students and has extensive conclusions. (One of a series of grant-aided University of Chicago internal surveys).

2382 _____. THE ALUMNI OF THE COLLEGES. Chicago: University of Chicago Press, 1932. 126 p.

> Study of college curriculum effectiveness based on alumni evaluation of their academic experiences.

2383 _____. SOME UNIVERSITY STUDENT PROBLEMS. Chicago: University of Chicago Press, 1933. 194 p.

> Survey of University of Chicago student aid and living conditions.

2384 Reeves, Floyd W., et al. CLASS SIZE AND UNIVERSITY COST. Chicago: University of Chicago Press, 1933. 229 p.

University of Chicago survey into efficient utilization of instructional and physical resources.

2385 _____. INSTRUCTIONAL PROBLEMS IN THE UNIVERSITY. Chicago: University of Chicago Press, 1933. 245 p.

Historical review of the University of Chicago curriculum, evolution of its then new curriculum plan, some campus educational experiments, and work of the university's laboratory schools.

2386 _____. THE ORGANIZATION AND ADMINISTRATION OF THE UNIVERSITY. Chicago: University of Chicago Press, 1933. 151 p.

Faculty study of University of Chicago administrative organization concluded that faculty should not be involved in administrative and executive functions.

2387 _____. TRENDS IN UNIVERSITY GROWTH. Chicago: University of Chicago Press, 1933. 242 p.

Trends in University of Chicago's enrollments, degrees conferred, faculty, finances, and other data for selected years before 1918-19 and annually afterwards.

2388 _____. UNIVERSITY EXTENSION SERVICES. Chicago: University of Chicago Press, 1933. 173 p.

Concludes that, as a private institution, the University of Chicago should emphasize research into extension work. Recommends that an assistant to the president coordinate off-campus services.

2389 _____. THE UNIVERSITY FACULTY. Chicago: University of Chicago Press, 1933. 326 p.

Concluded that heavy University of Chicago teaching loads discouraged research and that inbreeding was a problem since over half the faculty held University of Chicago degrees.

2390 _____. UNIVERSITY PLANT FACILITIES. Chicago: University of Chicago Press, 1933. 154 p.

University of Chicago study of its plant facilities to determine building needs.

2391 Reich, Warren T., ed. ENCYCLOPEDIA OF BIOETHICS. 4 vols. New York: Free Press, 1978.

> Contains 314 articles about religious and ethical questions raised by research and medical practices affecting human life and behavior.

2392 Reid, Mary Eliza, ed. THIRTY-FIVE YEARS OF WEST VIRGINIA STATE NURSES' ASSOCIATION: A HISTORY OF NURSING IN WEST VIRGINIA. Charleston: West Virginia State Nurses' Association, 1941. 87 p.

> Brief history of West Virginia nursing schools, scholarship aid, and training programs.

2393 Reinert, Paul Clare. FACULTY TENURE IN COLLEGES AND UNIVER-SITIES FROM 1900 TO 1940. St. Louis: St. Louis University Press, 1946. 138 p.

> Historical study of ten state, ten private, and ten Catholic institutions found that an average faculty member stayed in one position 5.86 years.

2394 _____. THE URBAN CATHOLIC UNIVERSITY. New York: Sheed and Ward, 1970. 182 p.

> Jesuit university president (St. Louis University) comments on urban Catholic higher education.

2395 Renetzky, Alvin, ed. YEARBOOK OF HIGHER EDUCATION 1969. Los Angeles: Academic Media, 1969. 858 p.

> Part 1 lists twenty-six hundred colleges and universities with officers, enrollment, calendar; part 2, statistical information: staff, degrees, federal support, salaries; part 3, regional associations, support programs, legislation, glossary. Issued annually.

2396 Research Resources Information Center. MINORITY BIOMEDICAL SUPPORT PROGRAM: A DIRECTORY OF THE RESEARCH PROJECTS. Rockville, Md.: 1978. 68 p.

> Lists university biomedical research projects federally funded to increase ethnic minority employment in such work.

2397 RESEARCH UNIVERSITIES AND THE NATIONAL INTEREST: A REPORT FROM FIFTEEN UNIVERSITY PRESIDENTS. Naugatuck, Conn.: Ford Foundation, 1977. 148 p.

> Urges a stronger bond between major research universities and the federal government.

2398 Resnick, William C., and Heller, David H., eds. ON YOUR OWN IN COLLEGE. Columbus, Ohio: Charles E. Merrill Books, 1963. 275 p.

> James Thurber, Robert M. Hutchins, Harold Taylor, Ernest Havemann, and others write on college students, their attitudes and behaviors, conditions for effective study, and the college as a social institution.

2399 Rever, Philip R. SCIENTIFIC AND TECHNICAL CAREERS: FACTORS INFLUENCING DEVELOPMENT DURING THE EDUCATIONAL YEARS. Iowa City: American College Testing Program, 1973. 198 p.

> Suggests topics and directions of future research on factors that influence students to choose science and technology careers.

2400 _____, ed. OPEN ADMISSIONS AND EQUAL ACCESS. Iowa City: American College Testing Program, 1971. 109 p.

> Papers collectively challenge the goal of universal higher education. Example: Theodore Newcomb says that if a university is going to have open admissions, it must be prepared to change drastically.

2401 Reynolds, James W. THE COMPREHENSIVE JUNIOR COLLEGE CURRICULUM. Berkeley, Calif.: McCutchan Publishers, 1969. 227 p.

> On junior college curricula, including student use of library resources.

2402 Rich, Catherine R., ed. PROBLEMS OF REGISTRARS AND ADMISSIONS OFFICERS IN HIGHER EDUCATION. Washington, D.C.: Catholic University of America Press, 1955. 208 p.

> Papers on the development of the registrar's office, college and university record keeping, publicity and public relations, and professional preparation of registrars and admissions officers.

2403 Rich, Catherine R., and Garrett, Thomas A., eds. PHILOSOPHY AND PROBLEMS OF COLLEGE ADMISSIONS. Washington, D.C.: Catholic University Press of America, 1963. 232 p.

> Papers on the college admissions process, including one by Ewald Nyquist cautioning against taking objective norms too seriously.

2404 Rich, Harvey E., and Jolicoeur, Pamela M. STUDENT ATTITUDES AND ACADEMIC ENVIRONMENTS: A STUDY OF CALIFORNIA HIGHER EDUCATION. New York: Praeger Publishers, 1978. 120 p.

> Impact of twelve California colleges and universities on stu-

dents' satisfaction with campus experience, personal development, values, religion, and sociopolitical attitudes.

2405 Richards, Robert K. CONTINUING MEDICAL EDUCATION: PERSPEC-
TIVES, PROBLEMS, PROGNOSIS. New Haven, Conn.: Yale University
Press, 1978. 214 p.

Author predicts mandatory relicensing and hence continuing
education of physicians. Wants states to develop continuing
medical education plans and to review M.D. accreditation
process.

2406 Richardson, Leroy Parker. UNDERGRADUATE CURRICULUM IMPROVE-
MENT. Durham, N.C.: National Laboratory for Higher Education, 1971.
49 p.

Various views toward proposed undergraduate curricular reforms.
Agreed that course proliferation is undesirable, that comprehensive framework for considering curriculum is needed, and
that curriculum planning should involve management analysis.

2407 Richardson, Richard C., Jr., ed. REFORMING COLLEGE GOVERNANCE.
San Francisco: Jossey-Bass Publishers, 1975. 97 p.

On community college governance and such topics as multicampus governance needs and the value of a human relations
approach to governance.

2408 Richardson, Richard C., Jr., et al. GOVERNANCE FOR THE TWO-YEAR
COLLEGE. Englewood Cliffs, N.J.: Prentice-Hall, 1972. 245 p.

Advocates participatory governance by faculty, students, and
administrators based on compromise and consensus. Discusses
relation between behavioral science and participatory management. Proposes ways to evaluate such governance.

2409 Richman, Barry M., and Farmer, Richard N. LEADERSHIP, GOALS, AND
POWER IN HIGHER EDUCATION. San Francisco: Jossey-Bass Publishers,
1974. 364 p.

Explores ways of managing colleges and universities. Case
studies offer examples of viable management systems and strategies, good and ill-conceived goals, and power relationships.

2410 Rider, Fremont. THE SCHOLAR AND THE FUTURE OF THE RESEARCH
LIBRARY. New York: Hadham Press, 1944. 236 p.

Author, librarian at Wesleyan University (Connecticut), early
proposed that research libraries use microprint (as today's micro-
fiche) for little used but still accessible scholarly books.

2411 Rieke, Robert. A RETROSPECTIVE VISION: THE UNIVERSITY OF NORTH CAROLINA AT CHARLOTTE, 1965-1975. Charlotte: Development Office, University of North Carolina, 1977. 121 p.

> History department chairman's personal account of the first ten years (1965-75) of the University of North Carolina, Charlotte. Effect of state politics, administrative projects, and influence of antiwar campus unrest.

2412 Riendeau, Albert J. THE ROLE OF THE ADVISORY COMMITTEE IN OC-CUPATIONAL EDUCATION IN THE JUNIOR COLLEGE. Washington, D.C.: American Association of Junior Colleges, 1967. 75 p.

> Describes role, structure, function, and organization of advisory committees (composed of outside industry personnel) in developing vocationally oriented junior college programs.

2413 Riesman, David. CONSTRAINT AND VARIETY IN AMERICAN EDUCA-TION. Lincoln: University of Nebraska Press, 1956. 160 p.

> Sociologist looks at education as a social institution with emphasis on sources of leadership and forces that constrain freedom. One effect is that colleges and universities imitate one another instead of being experimental and innovative.

2414 Riesman, David, et al. ACADEMIC VALUES AND MASS EDUCATION: THE EARLY YEARS OF OAKLAND AND MONTEITH. Garden City, N.Y.: Doubleday, 1970. 332 p.

> First ten years of two commuter colleges, Oakland College of Michigan State University and Monteith College of Wayne State University. Found that they were alike in being connected with stable institutions whose main administrator strongly supported them. Subordinates, who determined curriculum and other important matters, were crucial to their success.

2415 Riesman, David, and Stadtman, Verne A., eds. ACADEMIC TRANSFOR-MATION: SEVENTEEN INSTITUTIONS UNDER PRESSURE. New York: McGraw-Hill Book Co., 1973. 489 p.

> Impact of student protest on seventeen colleges and universities.

2416 Rigby, Barry D., ed. SHORT-TERM TRAINING FOR SOCIAL DEVELOP-MENT: THE PREPARATION OF FRONT-LINE WORKERS AND TRAINERS. New York: International Association of Schools of Social Work, 1978. 84 p.

> Stresses training that social workers will need to perform specific tasks in rural and urban areas.

2417 Riker, Harold C. PLANNING FUNCTIONAL COLLEGE HOUSING. New

York: Bureau of Publications, Teachers College, Columbia University, 1956. 240 p.

Says college housing should provide an environment for student growth. Recommends procedures for planning residence halls.

2418 Riley, Gary L., and Baldridge, J. Victor, eds. GOVERNING ACADEMIC ORGANIZATIONS: NEW PROBLEMS, NEW PERSPECTIVES. Berkeley, Calif.: McCutchan Publishers, 1977. 347 p.

Discusses colleges and universities as complex organizations; issues related to innovation and change; vested interests of students, administrators, faculty, and trustees; and collective bargaining in various types of higher education institutions.

2419 Riley, John W., Jr., et al. THE STUDENT LOOKS AT HIS TEACHER. New Brunswick, N.J.: Rutgers University Press, 1950. 166 p.

A rating scale was developed at Brooklyn College, using student conceptions of the ideal teacher. Individual professors were the only ones to see evaluations of their teaching.

2420 Risenhoover, Morris, and Blackburn, Robert T., eds. ARTISTS AS PROFESSORS: CONVERSATIONS WITH MUSICIANS, PAINTERS, SCULPTORS. Urbana: University of Illinois Press, 1976. 217 p.

Nineteen artists in residence at nine universities, interviewed intensively, were generally positive about their situations and pleased at the recognition implicit in their posts.

2421 Ritchie, Andrew Carnduff. THE VISUAL ARTS IN HIGHER EDUCATION. New Haven, Conn.: College Art Association and Yale University Press, 1966. 195 p.

A look at art, art history, and art museums at U.S. colleges.

2422 Ritchie, Miller Alfred Franklin. THE COLLEGE PRESIDENCY: INITIATION INTO THE ORDER OF THE TURTLE. New York: Philosophical Library, 1970. 179 p.

Ritchie's candid memoirs as president of two liberal arts colleges--Hartwick College, Oneonta, New York, and Pacific University, Forest Grove, Oregon.

2423 Ritterbush, Philip C., ed. LET THE ENTIRE COMMUNITY BECOME OUR UNIVERSITY. Washington, D.C.: Acropolis Books, 1973. 227 p.

Essays on off-campus study and institutional change in U.S. higher education.

2424 Rivlin, Alice M. THE ROLE OF THE FEDERAL GOVERNMENT IN FI-

NANCING HIGHER EDUCATION. Washington, D.C.: Brookings Institution, 1961. 179 p.

Reviews the history of federal involvement in land-grant institutions; federal involvement in research, student aid, military academies, and other programs; gives pros and cons of federal subsidies; and endorses federal aid to undergraduate education and to graduate research.

2425 Rivlin, Harry N., et al., eds. THE FIRST YEARS IN COLLEGE: PREPARING STUDENTS FOR A SUCCESSFUL COLLEGE CAREER. Boston: Little, Brown and Co., 1965. 605 p.

For high school students who expect to enter a liberal arts college, twenty-two professors wrote introductions to their academic fields.

2426 Roach, Helen P. HISTORY OF SPEECH EDUCATION AT COLUMBIA COLLEGE, 1754-1940. Contributions to Education No. 963. New York: Teachers College, Columbia University, 1950. 134 p.

Nearly two hundred-year history of speech education at Columbia. During 1811 to 1958, except for student literary societies, speech instruction was ignored. Tells of curricular programs in speaking, reading, speech correction, and dramatics.

2427 Robbins, Martin D., et al. WHO RUNS THE COMPUTER?--STRATEGIES FOR MANAGEMENT OF COMPUTERS IN HIGHER EDUCATION. Boulder, Colo.: Westview Press, 1976. 102 p.

On uses and management of computers on university campuses.

2428 Robbins, Paula I. SUCCESSFUL MIDLIFE CAREER CHANGE: SELF-UNDERSTANDING AND STRATEGIES FOR ACTION. New York: AMACOM, 1979. 268 p.

Includes chapter on higher education as transition to career change or to retirement.

2429 Robbins, Rainard B. COLLEGE PLANS FOR RETIREMENT INCOME. New York: Columbia University Press, 1940. 253 p.

Reviews various higher education retirement income plans. Appendix contains a schedule of teachers' insurance and annuity association plans.

2430 Roberts, Dayton Y., ed. JUNIOR COLLEGE LOCAL AND STATE RELATIONS. Gainesville: Institute of Higher Education, University of Florida, 1968. 66 p.

Papers on junior college public relations and such specific

aspects as educational reporting, state and local relations, and financial management.

2431 _____. LEGAL ISSUES IN HIGHER EDUCATION, 1960-1970: A SE-LECTED BIBLIOGRAPHY. Gainesville: Institute of Higher Education, University of Florida, 1971. 36 p.

Professional and popular writings on legal aspects of higher education, 1960-70, are briefly annotated.

2432 Robertson, D.B., ed. POWER AND EMPOWERMENT IN HIGHER EDUCATION: STUDIES IN HONOR OF LOUIS SMITH. Lexington: University Press of Kentucky, 1978. 158 p.

Essays by faculty members and administrators on the meaning of power in higher education. Published to honor Louis Smith, longtime professor and academic dean at Berea College, Kentucky.

2433 Robinson, Edgar Eugene. INDEPENDENT STUDY IN THE LOWER DIVISION AT STANFORD UNIVERSITY, 1931-1937. Stanford, Calif.: Stanford University Press, 1937. 90 p.

Origin and development of Stanford's lower division independent study program, case studies of participating students, and faculty reaction to the program.

2434 Robinson, Edgar Eugene, and Edwards, Paul Carroll, eds. THE MEMOIRS OF RAY LYMAN WILBUR: 1875-1949. Stanford, Calif.: Stanford University Press, 1960. 687 p.

Includes Wilbur's long service as Stanford's first medical school dean (1911-16), university president (1916-43), and Secretary of the Interior in President Hoover's cabinet (1929-33).

2435 Robinson, Lora H. INSTITUTIONAL ANALYSIS OF SEX DISCRIMINATION: A REVIEW AND ANNOTATED BIBLIOGRAPHY. Washington, D.C.: National Institute of Education, 1973. 10 p.

College faculty women's salaries, promotions, and tenure; annotated bibliography of studies on women's status at seventeen U.S. universities.

2436 _____. THE STATUS OF ACADEMIC WOMEN. Washington, D.C.: ERIC Clearinghouse on Higher Education, George Washington University, 1971. 26 p.

Examines several major studies on academic women; lists annotated reports on women's status at sixty-five colleges and universities; and describes twenty-five projects concerned with the establishment of committees, task forces, and study groups on the status of academic women.

2437 _____ . WOMEN'S STUDIES: COURSES AND PROGRAMS FOR HIGHER EDUCATION. Washington, D.C.: American Association for Higher Education, 1973. 48 p.

Background of women's studies programs; lists thirty-two campuses offering such programs.

2438 Robson, William A. THE UNIVERSITY TEACHING OF THE SOCIAL SCIENCES: POLITICAL SCIENCE. New York: Columbia University Press, 1954. 249 p.

State of political science teaching in ten countries, including the United States, Canada, Mexico, Britain, France, and India. Author sees overspecialization as the greatest threat to political science here and elsewhere.

2439 Roche, George C. III. THE BALANCING ACT: QUOTA HIRING IN HIGHER EDUCATION. La Salle, Ill.: Open Court Publishing Co., 1974. 92 p.

Hillsdale College, Michigan, president asserts that affirmative action threatens higher education integrity. Standards of excellence cannot be maintained if colleges lose control of admissions. Renounces the quota system which federal guidelines imply. College applicants should be judged solely on individual merit. Chapter on hiring women faculty.

2440 Rockart, John Fralick, and Morton, Michael S. Scott. COMPUTERS AND THE LEARNING PROCESS IN HIGHER EDUCATION. New York: McGraw-Hill Book Co., 1975. 356 p.

Computers' role in the learning process, cost effectiveness, administrative and faculty attitudes and policies toward computer learning, and an evaluation of computer-based learning programs.

2441 Rodgers, Walter P. ANDREW D. WHITE AND THE MODERN UNIVERSITY. Ithaca, N.Y.: Cornell University Press, 1942. 259 p.

White (1832-1918), graduate of Yale, the Sorbonne, and the University of Berlin, taught at the University of Michigan (1857-64); as New York state senator supported the founding of Cornell University and was its first president (1865-85).

2442 Rogan, Donald L. CAMPUS APOCALYPSE: THE STUDENT SEARCH TODAY. New York: Seabury Press, 1969. 154 p.

Kenyon College campus chaplain contends that such late 1960s student mores and concerns as activism, relevance, and revolution are comparable to religion's concern with salvation.

2443 Rogers, Carl R. FREEDOM TO LEARN. Columbus, Ohio: Charles E. Merrill Co., 1969. 358 p.

> Rogers, leading nondirective, client-centered psychotherapist, would like to restore freedom and remove tension from learning. Contains his essay on "Revolutionary Program for Graduate Education."

2444 Rogers, Dorothy. OSWEGO: FOUNTAINHEAD OF TEACHER EDUCATION: A CENTURY IN THE SHELDON TRADITION. New York: Appleton-Century-Crofts, 1961. 305 p.

> Edward Austin Sheldon (1823-97), founded in 1859 the Oswego State Normal and Training School, brought Pestalozzian teachers from England and the continent to Oswego, which became the major U.S. teacher training institution and the center of Pestalozzian object teaching method.

2445 Rogers, Francis Millet. HIGHER EDUCATION IN THE UNITED STATES: A SUMMARY VIEW. Cambridge, Mass.: Harvard University Press, 1952. 54 p.

> Lectures given in Brazil on U.S. higher education.

2446 THE ROLE OF THE UNIVERSITY IN PROMOTING CHANGE. Ithaca, N.Y.: Cornell University, 1962. 55 p.

> Universities must confront social and economic implications of automation, the challenging needs of less developed countries, and design short-term adult programs to meet continuing education needs.

2447 Roose, Kenneth D., and Andersen, Charles J. A RATING OF GRADUATE PROGRAMS. Washington, D.C.: American Council on Education, 1970. 115 p.

> Identifies distinguished graduate programs and suggests need to upgrade such programs elsewhere.

2448 Root, Edward Merrill. COLLECTIVISM ON THE CAMPUS: THE BATTLE FOR THE MIND IN AMERICAN COLLEGES. New York: Devin-Adair Co., 1955. 403 p.

> This conservative McCarthy era attack charges U.S. higher education with harboring socialists and communists.

2449 Roper, Elmo. FACTORS AFFECTING THE ADMISSION OF HIGH SCHOOL SENIORS TO COLLEGE. Washington, D.C.: American Council on Education, 1949. 312 p.

> Found religious discrimination, especially against Jews, among

1947 high school graduates who applied to northeast colleges. Because barriers were fewest in hometown colleges, study concluded that more two-year community colleges are needed. Companion to Reeves, Floyd D., ON GETTING INTO COLLEGE: A STUDY OF DISCRIMINATIONS IN COLLEGE ADMISSION. See No. 2380.

2450 Rose, Arnold M. LIBEL AND ACADEMIC FREEDOM: A LAWSUIT AGAINST POLITICAL EXTREMISTS. Minneapolis: University of Minnesota Press, 1968. 287 p.

Autobiographical account of the libel suit sociology professor Rose brought against those attacking him as a Communist. Rose collaborated on Gunnar Myrdal's AN AMERICAN DILEMMA, 1942.

2451 Rose, Clare, ed. MEETING WOMEN'S NEW EDUCATIONAL NEEDS. San Francisco: Jossey-Bass Publishers, 1975. 102 p.

Ways colleges can reinforce women's educational aspirations and eliminate barriers. Examples involve counseling, financial aid, course scheduling, skills training, and liberal arts.

2452 Rose, Clare, and Nyre, Glenn F. ACCESS AND ASSISTANCE: THE STUDY OF EOP/EOPS IN CALIFORNIA'S PUBLIC INSTITUTIONS OF HIGHER EDUCATION. 2 vols. Los Angeles: Evaluation and Training Institute, 1977. 573 p.

Study of Extended Opportunity Programs and Services for economically disadvantaged students at California higher education institutions. Examines students' racial and ethnic backgrounds and their unmet financial needs. Tells how programs are administered and suggests ways to distribute student financial aid. Case studies from twenty-six institutions.

2453 Rosecrance, Francis C. THE AMERICAN COLLEGE AND ITS TEACHERS. New York: Macmillan Co., 1962. 316 p.

Overview of higher education for beginning faculty members or those considering college teaching. Brief history of U.S. higher education. Looks at innovative curricula. Discusses professors' responsibilities and faculty evaluation.

2454 Rosen, Charles. SCANDALS OF '51: HOW THE GAMBLERS ALMOST KILLED COLLEGE BASKETBALL. New York: Holt, Rinehart and Winston, 1978. 262 p.

Account of players, coaches, and gamblers involved in fixing college basketball games in the late 1940s and early 1950s.

2455 Rosenberg, Marie Barovic, and Bergstrom, Len V., eds. WOMEN AND SOCIETY: A CRITICAL REVIEW OF THE LITERATURE WITH A SELECTED ANNOTATED BIBLIOGRAPHY. Beverly Hills, Calif.: Sage Publications, 1975. 354 p.

   Includes many briefly annotated books and other sources on women's education and women's colleges among the thirty-six hundred entries.

2456 Rosenkranz, Richard. ACROSS THE BARRICADES. Philadelphia: J.B. Lippincott Co., 1971. Irregular paging.

   Description by involved student of events and personalities in the Avery Hall Commune during the 1968 Columbia University confrontation. Includes academic matters.

2457 Rosentreter, Frederick M. THE BOUNDARIES OF THE CAMPUS: A HISTORY OF THE UNIVERSITY OF WISCONSIN EXTENSION DIVISION 1885-1945. Madison: University of Wisconsin Press, 1957. 210 p.

   History of a leading extension program, with accounts of farmers' institutes, correspondence courses, health education, and educational broadcasting.

2458 Ross, Earle D. DEMOCRACY'S COLLEGE: THE LAND-GRANT MOVEMENT IN THE FORMATIVE STAGE. Ames: Iowa State College Press, 1942. Reprint. New York: Arno Press, 1969. 267 p.

   Origin and early years of the 1862 Land Grant College Act introduced by U.S. Senator Justin F. Morrill of Vermont. Chapters on the industrial movement, the forces which induced federal intervention in higher education through the land grant colleges, their curriculum, students, and advantages.

2459 _____. A HISTORY OF THE IOWA STATE COLLEGE OF AGRICULTURE AND MECHANICS ARTS. Ames: Iowa State College Press, 1942. 451 p.

   History of what is now Iowa State University in relation to Iowa's agricultural and industrial development, internal and external politics, administrative difficulties, and resolution of liberal and vocational conflicts.

2460 Ross, Edward Alsworth. SEVENTY YEARS OF IT: AN AUTOBIOGRAPHY. New York: D. Appleton Century Co., 1936. Reprint. New York: Arno Press, 1977. 341 p.

   Ross (1866-1951) taught sociology at Johns Hopkins, University of Indiana, Cornell, Stanford, and the Universities of Nebraska and Wisconsin.

2461 Ross, Marion, ed. RELIGION AND THE CAMPUS. Oakland, Calif.: Mills College, 1965. 47 p.

Robert Nisbet, George Hedley, and Ernest Gordon write on religion, with implications for college students.

2462 Ross, Murray G. THE UNIVERSITY: THE ANATOMY OF ACADEME. New York: McGraw-Hill Book Co., 1976. 310 p.

Readable comparison of university development in England, Canada, and the United States; mainly in the 1960s and 1970s; by York University (Canada) president.

2463 _____, ed. NEW UNIVERSITIES IN THE MODERN WORLD. New York: St. Martin's Press, 1966. 190 p.

Case studies of establishing new universities in the United States, Britain, Canada, India, and elsewhere. Includes details on each university's origin, staff recruitment problems, and initial difficulties.

2464 Ross, Nancy Wilson. TAKE THE LIGHTNING. New York: Harcourt, Brace and Co., 1940. 314 p.

Novel about a young psychologist who teaches in a western college.

2465 Rossi, Alice S., and Calderwood, Ann, eds. ACADEMIC WOMEN ON THE MOVE. New York: Russell Sage Foundation, 1973. 560 p.

Articles on women teachers at all levels, particularly higher education; their careers as students, researchers, faculty, and administrators; and the dilemma of black women in higher education.

2466 Rossmann, Jack E., et al. OPEN ADMISSIONS AT CITY UNIVERSITY OF NEW YORK: AN ANALYSIS OF THE FIRST YEAR. Englewood Cliffs, N.J.: Prentice-Hall, 1975. 265 p.

Brief history of open admissions at CUNY. Study of motivation and achievements of open admissions students during their first year, fall 1970 to fall 1971. Found that white ethnics benefited more than blacks and Puerto Ricans.

2467 Roszak, Theodore, ed. THE DISSENTING ACADEMY. New York: Pantheon Books, 1968. 304 p.

Essays on the state of the university reflect late 1960s suspicion of government, military, and industrial influence in higher education.

2468 Roth, Roberta, and Walwada, Mark. AMERICAN URBAN STUDIES PROGRAMS: AN INVENTORY AND ANALYSIS OF UNDERGRADUATE AND

GRADUATE URBAN STUDIES PROGRAMS. Buffalo, N.Y.: Office of Urban Affairs, State University of New York, 1973. 96 p.

Inventory of graduate urban university programs includes number and kinds of students, faculty, facilities, programs, degrees offered, and special teaching methods.

2469 Rothchild, John, and Wolf, Susan. THE CHILDREN OF THE COUNTER-CULTURE. Garden City, N.Y.: Doubleday, 1976. 207 p.

Author's personal odyssey visiting campus protesters and drop-outs of the 1960s to see how they were living, what they were thinking, and how they were raising their children in the 1970s; visits to Synanon, Hare Krishna, and other commune groups.

2470 Rothman, Sheila M. WOMAN'S PROPER PLACE: A HISTORY OF CHANGING IDEALS AND PRACTICES, 1870 TO THE PRESENT. New York: Basic Books, 1978. 322 p.

Changing norms that have propelled women into the American mainstream, including higher education and the professions. Interesting sections on Vassar, Smith, and other women's col-leges; also women's role in urban reform (Jane Addams of Hull House and other settlement houses).

2471 Roueche, John E. SALVAGE, REDIRECTION, OR CUSTODY? REMEDIAL EDUCATION IN THE COMMUNITY JUNIOR COLLEGE. Washington, D.C.: American Association of Junior Colleges, 1968. 67 p.

Critical of remedial programs in community colleges for failing to overcome student deficiencies and for ignoring evaluative research on such programs.

2472 _____, ed. INCREASING BASIC SKILLS BY DEVELOPMENTAL STUDIES. San Francisco: Jossey-Bass Publishers, 1977. 104 p.

How to develop poorly prepared college students' basic aca-demic skills through tutoring, counseling, special courses, and learning centers.

2473 Roueche, John E., and Boggs, John R. JUNIOR COLLEGE INSTITU-TIONAL RESEARCH: THE STATE OF THE ART. Washington, D.C.: American Association of Junior Colleges, 1968. 66 p.

Surveys institutional research in seventy junior colleges. Says that successful institutional research programs depend on the commitment of junior college presidents.

2474 Roueche, John E., and Kirk, R. Wade. CATCHING UP: REMEDIAL EDUCATION. San Francisco: Jossey-Bass Publishers, 1973. 106 p.

Selected innovative remedial programs, key ingredients in their success, and ways similar programs might be set up to help high-risk students.

2475 Roueche, John E., and Pitman, John C. A MODEST PROPOSAL: STUDENTS CAN LEARN. San Francisco: Jossey-Bass Publishers, 1972. 142 p.

Instructional and institutional change in the community college. Recommends using programmed instruction and noncompetitive student evaluation.

2476 Roueche, John E., and Snow, Jerry J. OVERCOMING LEARNING PROBLEMS: A GUIDE TO DEVELOPMENTAL EDUCATION IN COLLEGE. San Francisco: Jossey-Bass Publishers, 1977. 188 p.

Successful remedial programs in U.S. two-year and four-year colleges, practices that have improved retention and achievement of high-risk or nontraditional students, and suggestions for organizing and implementing such programs.

2477 Roueche, John E., et al. ACCOUNTABILITY AND THE COMMUNITY COLLEGE: DIRECTIONS FOR THE 70'S. Washington, D.C.: American Association of Junior Colleges, 1971. 46 p.

Internal and external devices for evaluating junior colleges; urges accountability as necessary for gaining continued public support.

2478 Rourke, Francis E., and Brooks, Glenn E. THE MANAGERIAL REVOLUTION IN HIGHER EDUCATION. Baltimore, Md.: Johns Hopkins University Press, 1966. 182 p.

Analyzes the impact of managerial techniques on U.S. higher education administration. Discusses computers, automation, institutional research, and their effects on policymaking.

2479 Rowe, Frederick B. CHARACTERISTICS OF WOMEN'S COLLEGE STUDENTS. Atlanta: Southern Regional Education Board, 1964. 55 p.

Describes student and institutional characteristics at three women's colleges.

2480 Rowe, Henry K. A CENTENNIAL HISTORY: 1837-1937, COLBY ACADEMY, COLBY JUNIOR COLLEGE. New London, N.H.: Colby Junior College, 1937. 435 p.

Colby (New London, New Hampshire) began as a coeducational academy and in 1932 became a junior college for women. Deals with the poverty around Colby, illustrative of the school's struggle to survive.

2481 Rowland, A. Westley, ed. HANDBOOK OF INSTITUTIONAL ADVANCE-
MENT: A PRACTICAL GUIDE TO COLLEGE AND UNIVERSITY RELA-
TIONS, FUND RAISING, ALUMNI RELATIONS, GOVERNMENT RELA-
TIONS, PUBLICATIONS, AND EXECUTIVE MANAGEMENT FOR CON-
TINUED ADVANCEMENT. San Francisco: Jossey-Bass Publishers, 1977.
577 p.

> Omnibus, ambitious compilation of essential information to
> help colleges and universities capture and hold public, pri-
> vate, and government support and goodwill despite criticism
> and financial stringency.

2482 Ruddick, Sara, and Daniels, Pamela, eds. WORKING IT OUT: TWENTY-
THREE WOMEN WRITERS, ARTISTS, SCIENTISTS AND SCHOLARS TALK
ABOUT THEIR LIVES AND WORK. New York: Pantheon Books, 1977.
343 p.

> New feminist thinking. Evelyn Fox Keller describes difficulties
> in getting a Harvard physics department Ph.D. Experimental
> psychologist Naomi Weisstein also faced Harvard barriers and
> difficulties in getting an academic job. Women scientists re-
> port more difficulties than those in liberal arts.

2483 Rudolph, Frederick. THE AMERICAN COLLEGE AND UNIVERSITY, A
HISTORY. New York: Alfred A. Knopf, 1962. 516 p.

> Readable, interpretive history of U.S. higher education, with
> a chapter on the higher education of women.

2484 _____. CURRICULUM: A HISTORY OF THE AMERICAN UNDERGRADU-
ATE COURSE OF STUDY SINCE 1636. San Francisco: Jossey-Bass Publishers, 1977. 362 p.

> Relates, historically, college courses to social trends and his-
> toric events. Interprets the impact of past curriculum develop-
> ments on current practices.

2485 _____. MARK HOPKINS AND THE LOG: WILLIAMS COLLEGE, 1836-
1872. New Haven, Conn.: Yale University Press, 1956. 267 p.

> Social history of Williams College, Williamstown, Massachusetts,
> during the presidency of Mark Hopkins, more moralist than
> scholar. Describes the gradual change in the student body.

2486 Rudy, Willis Solomon. THE COLLEGE OF THE CITY OF NEW YORK: A
HISTORY, 1847-1947. New York: City College Press, 1949. Reprint.
New York: Arno Press, 1977. 492 p.

> Centennial history of the first major U.S. municipal university,
> distinguished for educating many foreign born and their off-
> spring who contributed to national life out of proportion to
> their numbers.

2487 Rugg, Harold Ordway. TEACHER OF TEACHERS: FRONTIERS OF THEORY AND PRACTICE IN TEACHER EDUCATION. New York: Harper and Row, 1952. 308 p.

> Leading social reconstructionist at Columbia University (1920–51), Rugg (1886–1960) called on teacher educators to creatively prepare teachers to lead society through technological change and to help reintegrate American culture.

2488 Ruml, Beardsley. MEMO TO A COLLEGE TRUSTEE: A REPORT ON FINANCIAL AND STRUCTURAL PROBLEMS OF THE LIBERAL COLLEGE. New York: McGraw-Hill Book Co., 1959. 94 p.

> Liberal arts colleges should avoid course proliferation, raise the student-faculty ratio, and with money saved increase faculty salaries.

2489 Runkel, Philip, et al., eds. THE CHANGING COLLEGE CLASSROOM. San Francisco: Jossey-Bass Publishers, 1969. 359 p.

> College teachers' attempts to involve students in meaningful learning experiences, most often by trying to get greater integration between student values or feelings and intellect.

2490 Rush, Charles E., ed. LIBRARY RESOURCES OF THE UNIVERSITY OF NORTH CAROLINA: A SUMMARY OF FACILITIES FOR STUDY AND RESEARCH. Chapel Hill: University of North Carolina Press, 1945. 264 p.

> Chapters by curators of special collections and faculty members who use them. History of the library, facilities for cooperation with other North Carolina libraries, and details about the Collection of North Carolinians and the Southern Historical Collection.

2491 Rushing, William A. THE PSYCHIATRIC PROFESSIONS. POWER, CONFLICT, AND ADAPTATION IN A PSYCHIATRIC HOSPITAL STAFF. Chapel Hill, N.C.: University of North Carolina Press, 1964. 267 p.

> Social-psychological problems of professional personnel in a university medical school's psychiatry department.

2492 Rusk, James J., and Leslie, Larry L. THE SETTING OF TUITION IN PUBLIC HIGHER EDUCATION. Tucson: Center for the Study of Higher Education, University of Arizona, 1979. 17 p.

> Analyzes factors that determine tuition levels among major state universities.

2493 Ruskin, Robert S. PERSONALIZED SYSTEM OF INSTRUCTION: AN EDUCATIONAL ALTERNATIVE. Washington, D.C.: American Association for Higher Education, 1974. 44 p.

Brief history and characteristics of personalized system of instruction. Describes a typical classroom, reviews research, and speculates on the future of such personalized programs.

2494 Russell, James Earl. FEDERAL ACTIVITIES IN HIGHER EDUCATION AFTER THE SECOND WORLD WAR. New York: King's Crown Press, 1951. 257 p.

World War II federal involvement in higher education most often consisted of aid to special groups of individuals or aid for some special purposes. Concern for colleges and universities was secondary.

2495 _____. FOUNDING TEACHERS COLLEGE. New York: Teachers College, Columbia University, 1937. 106 p.

On the development of Teachers College, which in 1897 became part of Columbia University, despite the university's resistance. Named dean in 1897, Russell led it to eminence among professional schools of education, enrolling in 1927 when he retired nearly 5,000 students taught by such professors as John Dewey, William Heard Kilpatrick, and Edward L. Thorndike.

2496 Russell, John Dale. THE FINANCE OF HIGHER EDUCATION. Chicago: University of Chicago Press, 1954. 416 p.

Handbook for administrators on the effective business and financial management of higher education institutions.

2497 _____, ed. HIGHER EDUCATION IN THE POSTWAR PERIOD. Chicago: University of Chicago Press, 1944. 169 p.

Conference papers concerned with higher education planning for postwar changes.

2498 _____. THE OUTLOOK FOR HIGHER EDUCATION. Chicago: University of Chicago Press, 1939. 256 p.

Conference papers by University of Cincinnati president Raymond Walters on student enrollment trends and by Leonard V. Koos of the University of Chicago on the conflict between university extension departments and the junior college movement.

2499 _____. PROBLEMS OF FACULTY PERSONNEL. Chicago: University of Chicago Press, 1946. 146 p.

Conference papers examine faculty personnel issues in U.S. colleges and universities.

2500 Russell, John Dale, and Doi, James I. MANUAL FOR STUDIES OF SPACE UTILIZATION IN COLLEGES AND UNIVERSITIES. Athens, Ohio: American Association of Collegiate Registrars and Admissions Officers, 1957. 130 p.

Manual for analyzing space use and determining space needs. Presents norms derived from space utilization studies.

2501 Russell, John Dale, and Mackenzie, Donald, eds. EMERGENT RESPONSIBILITIES IN HIGHER EDUCATION. Chicago: University of Chicago Press, 1945. 142 p.

Administration and curriculum problems are dominant concerns in these conference papers.

2502 Russell, John Dale, and Reeves, Floyd W. FINANCE. Chicago: University of Chicago Press, 1935. 133 p.

Compared per student expenditure, income sources (especially student fees), and financial stability of fifty-seven cooperating institutions. Discussed how finances relate to accreditation.

2503 Russell, John M. GIVING AND TAKING: ACROSS THE FOUNDATION DESK. New York: Teachers College Press, 1977. 90 p.

Forty-year president of a philanthropic foundation writes on the philosophy and organization of independent foundations. Offers advice to both foundation personnel and higher education persons who seek foundation grants.

2504 Russell, Phillips. THE WOMAN WHO RANG THE BELL: THE STORY OF CORNELIA PHILLIPS SPENCER. Chapel Hill: University of North Carolina Press, 1949. 293 p.

Spencer, friend of the University of North Carolina at Chapel Hill (where her father taught) and at Greensboro, opposed post-Civil War radical control of the university. After the 1870 closing of the Chapel Hill campus, she fought for its reopening. Both institutions later named buildings for her.

2505 Russell, William F., and Elliott, Edward C., eds. THE RISE OF A UNIVERSITY. 2 vols. New York: Columbia University Press, 1937. 415 p., 515 p.

Columbia University annual report selections by Frederick A.P. Barnard (president, 1864-89) and Nicholas Murray Butler (president, 1901-45). On administration, women's education, professional education, graduate education, and university extension.

2506 Ryan, Will Carson. STUDIES IN EARLY GRADUATE EDUCATION. New York: Carnegie Foundation for the Advancement of Teaching, 1939. Reprint. New York: Arno Press, 1971. 167 p.

Early centers of U.S. graduate education: Johns Hopkins and

Clark Universities and the University of Chicago. Elements that contributed to their significance and implications for contemporary graduate education.

2507 Sachar, Abram Leon. A HOST AT LAST. Boston: Atlantic-Little, Brown, 1976. 308 p.

Sachar's (1899--) autobiography tells of the founding of Brandeis University, Massachusetts, and of his twenty years as its first president (1948-68).

2508 Sack, Saul. HISTORY OF HIGHER EDUCATION IN PENNSYLVANIA. 2 vols. Harrisburg, Pa.: Pennsylvania Historical and Museum Commission, 1963. 382 p., 817 p.

Comprehensive history of denominational, secular, private, and state higher education in Pennsylvania, including a unit on women's education.

2509 Sacks, Herbert S., et al. HURDLES: THE ADMISSIONS DILEMMA IN AMERICAN HIGHER EDUCATION. New York: Atheneum Publishers, 1978. 364 p.

Essays on student and family responses to highly selective and less selective colleges and universities, U.S. aspirations for higher education and its effects on youth, women's experiences entering higher education, open admissions, and similar topics.

2510 Safilios-Rothschild, Constantina. WOMEN AND SOCIAL POLICY. Englewood Cliffs, N.J.: Prentice-Hall, 1974. 197 p.

Women's advancement toward equality in all aspects of U.S. life, including schools, colleges, and universities.

2511 Sagan, Edgar L., and Smith, Barbara G. ALTERNATIVE MODELS FOR THE CO-OPERATIVE GOVERNANCE OF TEACHER EDUCATION PROGRAMS. Lincoln: Nebraska Curriculum Development Center, University of Nebraska, 1973. 92 p.

Reviews and criticizes models of governance for the control of teacher education programs.

2512 Sailor, Robert Warren. A PRIMER OF ALUMNI WORK. Ithaca, N.Y.: American Alumni Council, 1944. 216 p.

On alumni office administrators' duties, responsibilities, and opportunities, especially goodwill and fund-raising.

2513 Salazar, J. Leonard, and Martorana, S.V. STATE POSTSECONDARY EDUCATION PLANNING (1202) COMMISSIONS: A FIRST LOOK. Univer-

sity Park: Center for the Study of Higher Education, Pennsylvania State
University, 1978. 101 p.

Analyzes the membership, functions, and practices of 1,202
commissions studying higher education since 1974.

2514 Sammartino, Peter. DEMANAGE HIGHER EDUCATION. East Rutherford,
N.J.: Crispen Co., 1978. 188 p.

Chancellor of Fairleigh Dickinson University, New Jersey, advises administrators to eliminate expensive noneducative activities which bleed tuition fees, and instead to reemphasize
good teaching.

2515 _____. A HISTORY OF HIGHER EDUCATION IN NEW JERSEY. Cranbury, N.J.: A.S. Barnes and Co., 1978. 196 p.

Evolution of New Jersey's sixty colleges and universities, including Princeton and Rutgers. Discusses the development of
community colleges, the role of theological seminaries, curricular developments, and changes in architectural planning.

2516 _____. I DREAMED A COLLEGE. Cranbury, N.J.: A.S. Barnes and
Co., 1977. 172 p.

Founder and former president of Fairleigh Dickinson University
describes financial and administrative problems of its development and gives his philosophy of education.

2517 Sampson, Edward E., and Korn, Harold A., eds. STUDENT ACTIVISM
AND PROTEST: ALTERNATIVES FOR SOCIAL CHANGE. San Francisco:
Jossey-Bass Publishers, 1970. 265 p.

Social, political, and economic causes of 1960s student activism from mainly liberal viewpoints; article on San Francisco
State College student strike.

2518 Sand, Ole, ed. CURRICULUM STUDY IN BASIC NURSING EDUCATION.
New York: G.P. Putnam's Sons, 1955. 225 p.

Five-year study of nursing education at the University of Washington, Seattle; model study on goals, best learning experiences,
curriculum, faculty cooperation, and program appraisal.

2519 Sandeen, Arthur. UNDERGRADUATE EDUCATION: CONFLICT AND
CHANGE. Lexington, Mass.: Lexington Books, 1976. 143 p.

Synthesis of the literature on undergraduate education, including goals, instructional impact on students, and the nature
of undergraduate students. Includes case study of an innovative program.

2520 Sanders, Edward, and Palmer, Hans. THE FINANCIAL BARRIER TO HIGHER EDUCATION IN CALIFORNIA. Claremont, Calif.: Pomona College, 1965. 295 p.

Specific information to aid budget decisions and long-range planning. Compared California's college data with national average.

2521 Sanders, H.C., et al., eds. THE COOPERATIVE EXTENSION SERVICE. Englewood Cliffs, N.J.: Prentice-Hall, 1966. 436 p.

Overview of agricultural education and home economics education extension programs, historically an outreach of land-grant state universities to meet many people's needs.

2522 Sanders, Irwin T., and Ward, Jennifer C. BRIDGES TO UNDERSTANDING: INTERNATIONAL PROGRAMS OF AMERICAN COLLEGES AND UNIVERSITIES. New York: McGraw-Hill Book Co., 1970. 285 p.

Concludes that foundation and government cutoff of funds will require colleges and universities to divide responsibility for area studies (Africa, Asia, others) and to modify other international programs, such as student exchanges and overseas research; examines effects on other campus courses.

2523 Sanders, Tobi Gillian, and Bennett, Joan Frances. MEMBERS OF THE CLASS WILL KEEP DAILY JOURNALS: THE BARNARD COLLEGE JOURNALS OF TOBI GILLIAN SANDERS AND JOAN FRANCES BENNETT, SPRING 1968. New York: Winter House, 1970. 153 p.

Diaries of two sensitive Barnard College women, one northern upper middle class, the other southern black, during the 1968 Columbia University student crisis.

2524 Sandler, Bernice. STATISTICS CONCERNING DOCTORATES AWARDED TO WOMEN. Washington, D.C.: Association of American Colleges, 1972. 12 p.

Data on doctorates awarded to women during 1960-69.

2525 _____. WHAT CONSTITUTES EQUITY FOR WOMEN IN HIGHER EDUCATION? Washington, D.C.: American Association for Higher Education, 1972. 10 p.

The need to end discrimination against prospective women students and faculty and to end discrimination in textbooks.

2526 Sanford, Daniel Sammis. INTER-INSTITUTIONAL AGREEMENTS IN HIGHER EDUCATION. Contributions to Education No. 627. New York: Teachers College, Columbia University, 1934. 112 p.

Analysis of interinstitutional agreements involving 144 colleges and universities of all types. Columbia University, for example, has thirteen cooperative agreements with nearby institutions. Practical questions on administration, student credit hour exchange, financing, planning, and advantages and disadvantages of the cooperative arrangements.

2527 Sanford, Mark. MAKING IT IN GRADUATE SCHOOL. Berkeley, Calif.: Montaigne, 1977. 121 p.

Examines graduate students' attitudes toward the grading system and why some try to skirt requirements and obtain degrees with minimum effort. Recommends changes that would eliminate student incentives to beat the system.

2528 Sanford, Nevitt. WHERE COLLEGES FAIL: A STUDY OF THE STUDENT AS A PERSON. San Francisco: Jossey-Bass Publishers, 1967. 229 p.

Progressive Stanford professor wants to restore the student as the center of college activities. He states the case for individual development as education's primary aim and explores how colleges can use peer culture and other environmental factors to serve this end.

2529 _____, ed. THE AMERICAN COLLEGE: A PSYCHOLOGICAL AND SOCIAL INTERPRETATION OF THE HIGHER LEARNING. New York: John Wiley and Sons, 1962. 1,084 p.

Thirty social scientists analyze the complex relationship between liberal arts colleges and the culture they serve. Several women's education chapters, including "Student Culture at Vassar."

2530 _____. COLLEGE AND CHARACTER: A BRIEFER VERSION OF THE AMERICAN COLLEGE. New York: John Wiley and Sons, 1964. 308 p.

Shorter, tighter, better organized sociological view of Sanford's THE AMERICAN COLLEGE, 1962 (See No. 2529).

2531 Sann, Paul. THE ANGRY DECADE: THE SIXTIES. New York: Crown Publishers, 1979. 324 p.

New York POST editor's illustrated vignettes on how civil rights and Vietnam precipitated student protests, including blacks entering the Universities of Georgia and Mississippi, the Berkeley and Columbia 1968 riots, and others.

2532 Santayana, George. THE LAST PURITAN: A MEMOIR IN THE FORM OF A NOVEL. New York: Charles Scribner's Sons, 1936. 602 p.

Novel about New England character, set partly at Harvard where Spanish-born author taught philosophy and was critical of electives.

2533 Sarah Lawrence College. Undergraduates. SARAH LAWRENCE STUDIES 1940. Bronxville, N.Y.: Moak Printing Co., 1940. 123 p.

> Undergraduate women contributors illustrate Sarah Lawrence's progressive, individual-centered programs on science to social science.

2534 Sarason, Seymour Bernard. THE CREATION OF SETTINGS AND THE FUTURE SOCIETIES. San Francisco: Jossey-Bass Publishers, 1972. 295 p.

> Theoretical study of the setting in which an institution fails or succeeds; chapter on B.F. Skinner's plan for a new technology-based culture.

2535 Sarbin, Theodore Roy, ed. PROCEEDINGS OF THE INSTITUTE ON PLACEMENT SERVICES IN COLLEGES AND UNIVERSITIES. Minneapolis: Center for Continuation Study, University of Minnesota, 1940. 52 p.

> Recruitment, training, role, responsibilities, and opportunities of college and university job placement directors.

2536 Sarton, May. FAITHFUL ARE THE WOUNDS. New York: Rinehart and Co., 1955. 281 p.

> Novel about academic freedom and the tragedy of a politically liberal Harvard professor (author taught at Harvard and Radcliffe).

2537 _____. THE SMALL ROOM. New York: W.W. Norton and Co., 1961. 249 p.

> Novel about academic life at a New England women's college.

2538 Saxton, Alexander Plaisted. GRAND CROSSING. New York: Harper and Brothers, 1943. 410 p.

> Novel about a Harvard student who sees much poverty in the 1930s Depression and transfers to the University of Chicago.

2539 Saylor, John Galen. ANTECEDENT DEVELOPMENTS IN THE MOVEMENT TO PERFORMANCE-BASED PROGRAMS OF TEACHER EDUCATION: AN HISTORICAL SURVEY OF CONCEPTS, MOVEMENTS, AND PRACTICES SIGNIFICANT IN THE DEVELOPMENT OF TEACHER EDUCATION. Lincoln, Nebr.: L and S Center, 1976. 166 p.

> Survey of reports and essays about teacher education during the late 1960s and early 1970s: innovations, increasing federal role, and competency-based programs.

2540 Scanlon, John. HOW TO PLAN A COLLEGE PROGRAM FOR OLDER PEOPLE. New York: Academy for Educational Development, 1978. 113 p.

How to plan, organize, and finance academic programs for middle-aged and older people.

2541 Schaefer, Robert J. THE SCHOOL AS A CENTER OF INQUIRY. New York: Harper and Row, 1967. 77 p.

Teachers College, Columbia University, dean argues that schools should produce knowledge as well as transmit it; suggests ways to rejuvenate teacher education.

2542 Schall, Keith L., ed. STONY THE ROAD: CHAPTERS IN THE HISTORY OF HAMPTON INSTITUTE. Charlottesville: University Press of Virginia, 1977. 183 p.

On Hampton Institute's (Virginia) relations with such political figures as Presidents Garfield and Taft and on administrators, faculty, and distinguished alumni, such as poet and novelist Paul Lawrence Dunbar (1872-1906).

2543 Schein, Edgar H. PROFESSIONAL EDUCATION: SOME NEW DIRECTIONS. New York: McGraw-Hill Book Co., 1972. 163 p.

Universities' problems in producing professional lawyers, engineers, and others during time of rapid change. Recommends that professional schools use part-time faculty, share decision making with faculty and students, and induce constant reform by ongoing self-evaluation.

2544 Scheps, Clarence, and Davidson, E.E. ACCOUNTING FOR COLLEGES AND UNIVERSITIES. 3d ed. Baton Rouge: Louisiana State University Press, 1978. 384 p.

Textbook with accounting problems common to higher education institutions and techniques for solving them.

2545 Schlabach, Theron F. PENSIONS FOR PROFESSORS. Madison: State Historical Society of Wisconsin for the Department of History, University of Wisconsin, 1963. 122 p.

Carnegie Foundation for the Advancement of Teaching (founded 1905) made early provision for retired professors' pensions. Confusion over Andrew Carnegie's intent, controversy between state and private colleges over receiving pension funds, and the founding of the Teachers Insurance and Annuity Association.

2546 Schlachter, Gail Ann. DIRECTORY OF FINANCIAL AIDS FOR WOMEN. Los Angeles: Reference Service Press, 1978. 200 p.

Lists 670 women's scholarships, loans, grants, awards, credit unions, state aid agencies, and financial aid directories.

2547 Schlesinger, Arthur M., ed. HISTORICAL SCHOLARSHIP IN AMERICA, NEEDS AND OPPORTUNITIES: A REPORT BY THE COMMITTEE OF THE AMERICAN HISTORICAL ASSOCIATION ON THE PLANNING OF RESEARCH. New York: Ray Long and Richard R. Smith, 1932. 146 p.

> Trends, areas needing research, and such problems as publications and research methods. Recommends more higher education interdisciplinary studies, training of archivists and museum directors, and improved bibliographical aids.

2548 Schmidt, George P. DOUGLASS COLLEGE: A HISTORY. New Brunswick, N.J.: Rutgers University Press, 1968. 282 p.

> History of Douglass College, now a unit of Rutgers, formerly New Jersey College for Women. Describes student life, 1920s-68.

2549 _____. THE LIBERAL ARTS COLLEGE: A CHAPTER IN AMERICAN CULTURAL HISTORY. New Brunswick, N.J.: Rutgers University Press, 1957. 310 p.

> History of liberal arts colleges during 1636-1950s. Explores the rise of universities and graduate schools, the differing philosophies of John Dewey and Robert M. Hutchins, women's education, and contemporary threats to liberal arts colleges' survival.

2550 Schmitt, Gladys. A SMALL FIRE. New York: Dial Press, 1956. 343 p.

> Novel about the music faculty of a fine arts college; leading character is a voice teacher.

2551 Schmuhl, Robert, ed. THE CLASSROOM AND THE NEWSROOM. Bloomington: Poynter Center, Indiana University, 1979. 140 p.

> Essays on teaching news reporting in journalism schools.

2552 Schneider, Florence Hemley. PATTERNS OF WORKERS' EDUCATION; THE STORY OF BRYN MAWR SUMMER SCHOOL. Washington, D.C.: American Council on Public Affairs, 1941. 158 p.

> Historical account of workers' education within and without trade unions. Describes Bryn Mawr summer school for women factory workers during 1921-41.

2553 Schoenfeld, Clarence A., and Zillman, Donald N. THE AMERICAN UNIVERSITY IN SUMMER. Madison: University of Wisconsin Press, 1967. 225 p.

> Brief history and overview of the summer session in universities; description of summer programs and of student, faculty, and administrative activities.

2554 Scholl, Stephen C., and Inglis, Sandra Cheldelin, eds. TEACHING IN HIGHER EDUCATION: READINGS FOR FACULTY. Columbus: Ohio Board of Regents, 1977. 400 p.

Theory, design, and alternative teaching methods; testing, grading, and evaluation of students and of faculty by students.

2555 Scholz, Nelle Tumlin, et al. HOW TO DECIDE: A GUIDE FOR COLLEGE. Princeton, N.J.: College Board Publications, 1976. 121 p.

Tips to help women set goals and make decisions about their college educations, careers, and personal lives.

2556 Schonborn, Barbara G., and O'Neil, Mary L. SEX EQUALITY IN VOCATIONAL EDUCATION: A CHANCE FOR EDUCATORS TO EXPAND OPPORTUNITIES FOR STUDENTS. San Francisco: Far West Laboratory for Educational Research and Development, 1979. 33 p.

Assesses the problems created by sex discrimination in schools at all levels, including higher education, and the laws and activities that can help to eliminate it.

2557 Schuh, Mary John Francis. THE STATUS OF FRESHMAN ENGLISH IN SELECTED CATHOLIC WOMEN'S COLLEGES. Washington, D.C.: Catholic University of America Press, 1953. 170 p.

Analyzed content of freshman English classes. Found that they met needs of foreign students, yielded six credit hours, and were satisfactory to English department administrators and faculty.

2558 Schultz, Theodore W. THE ECONOMIC VALUE OF EDUCATION. New York: Columbia University Press, 1963. 92 p.

Landmark study found that the increasing amount of schooling through college accounted for one-fifth of the increase in real national income, 1929-59.

2559 Schuster, Jack H., ed. ENCOUNTERING THE UNIONIZED UNIVERSITY. San Francisco: Jossey-Bass Publishers, 1974. 106 p.

Authors (political scientists, negotiators, and academic bargaining specialists) concluded that higher education faculty unionism is likely to grow stronger.

2560 Schwab, Joseph J. COLLEGE CURRICULUM AND STUDENT PROTEST. Chicago: University of Chicago Press, 1969. 303 p.

Analyzes student unrest and recommends reforms that would incorporate extracurricular and community concerns into the curriculum.

2561 _____. SCIENCE, CURRICULUM, AND LIBERAL EDUCATION: SE-LECTED ESSAYS. Chicago: University of Chicago Press, 1979. 394 p.

Essays by University of Chicago emeritus professor of education and natural sciences on the role of science in general education programs.

2562 Schwartz, Alvin. UNIVERSITY: THE STUDENTS, FACULTY, AND CAMPUS LIFE AT ONE UNIVERSITY. New York: Viking Press, 1969. 175 p.

Introduction to campus life using the University of Pennsylvania as a model. Introduces high school students to testing, admissions policies, grading, instructional quality, athletics, sororities and fraternities, costs, research, faculty activities, and problems of blacks on campus.

2563 Schwartz, Mildred A. THE UNITED STATES COLLEGE-EDUCATED POPULATION: 1960. Chicago: National Opinion Research Center, University of Chicago, 1965. 171 p.

Economic, demographic, and personal characteristics of college-educated persons in the 1960 census.

2564 Scientific Manpower Commission. PROFESSIONAL WOMEN AND MINORITIES: A MANPOWER DATA RESOURCE SERVICE. 2d ed. Washington, D.C.: 1978.

Data on women and minorities' higher education enrollments and degrees in the natural and social sciences, engineering, arts, humanities, health fields, education, and other professions. In loose-leaf form for easy updating; twenty-four subject dividers and cross index to data from over two hundred sources.

2565 _____. SCIENCE AND ENGINEERING CAREERS: A BIBLIOGRAPHY. 7th ed. Washington, D.C.: 1974. 48 p.

Outlines training needed and professional employment opportunities for students considering careers as scientists, engineers, and technicians.

2566 Scigliano, Robert G., and Fox, Guy H. TECHNICAL ASSISTANCE IN VIETNAM: THE MICHIGAN STATE UNIVERSITY EXPERIENCE. New York: Praeger Publishers, 1965. 78 p.

History of Michigan State University technical assistance programs to assist Vietnam's police and security services. Impact of the program on cooperating U.S. and Vietnamese agencies. Weaknesses of the project are discussed.

2567 Scimecca, Joseph, and Damiano, Roland. CRISIS AT ST. JOHN'S:

STRIKE AND REVOLUTION ON THE CATHOLIC CAMPUS. New York: Random House, 1967. 213 p.

Two participants and sociologists analyze the 1965-66 efforts to unionize Catholic St. John's University, New York, and the resulting faculty strike. Case study of academic freedom and unionization in Catholic higher education.

2568 Scott, Anne Firor, ed. WOMEN IN AMERICAN LIFE: SELECTED READINGS. Boston: Houghton Mifflin Co., 1970. 214 p.

Several selections on women in teacher education programs and at specific colleges among the fifty articles on U.S. women's struggle for equality.

2569 Scott, Franklin D. THE AMERICAN EXPERIENCE OF SWEDISH STUDENTS: RETROSPECT AND AFTERMATH. Minneapolis: University of Minnesota Press, 1956. 129 p.

Fifty Swedish student exchangees compare their views of U.S. and Swedish university life and education.

2570 Scott, Glenn. A SOUND OF VOICES DYING. New York: E.P. Dutton and Co., 1954. 252 p.

Novel of a young man's first year in a southern college.

2571 Scott, Peter. STRATEGIES FOR POSTSECONDARY EDUCATION. New York: Halsted Press, 1975. 161 p.

British education writer analyzes postsecondary education developments in the United States, Britain, and France. He predicts that private U.S. higher education will grow, especially community colleges, because of their job orientation.

2572 Scott, Robert A. LORDS, SQUIRES, AND YEOMEN: COLLEGIATE MIDDLE MANAGERS AND THEIR ORGANIZATIONS. Washington, D.C.: American Association for Higher Education, 1979. 75 p.

Growth, development, function, status, and role of middle managers in higher education.

2573 Scroggs, Schiller. SYSTEMATIC FACT-FINDING AND RESEARCH IN THE ADMINISTRATION OF HIGHER EDUCATION. Ann Arbor, Mich.: Edwards Brothers, 1938. 133 p.

Checklist of kinds of information needed to administer large higher education institutions; cites the trend toward institutional self-study.

2574 Scurlock, Reagan. GOVERNMENT CONTRACTS AND GRANTS FOR RE-

SEARCH: A GUIDE FOR COLLEGES AND UNIVERSITIES. Washington, D.C.: National Association of College and University Business Officers, 1975. 415 p.

>Describes characteristic procedures of research contracts; analyzes over one hundred clauses in research contracts; gives principles of costing, some specimen contracts, and glossary.

2575 Seabury, Paul, ed. UNIVERSITIES IN THE WESTERN WORLD. New York: Free Press, 1975. 303 p.

>International conference papers on such issues affecting universities in the United States, Italy, Japan, France, West Germany, and other countries as access, governance, and standards.

2576 Sears, Jesse B., and Henderson, Adin D. CUBBERLEY OF STANFORD AND HIS CONTRIBUTION TO AMERICAN EDUCATION. Stanford, Calif.: Stanford University Press, 1957. 302 p.

>Elwood P. Cubberley (1868-1941) was Indiana-born, president of Vincennes (Indiana) University (1891-96), San Diego (California) school superintendent (1896-98), from 1898 professor and then dean (1917-33) of Stanford University School of Education, which he greatly influenced, and book series editor and history of education textbook writer.

2577 Seashore, Carl E. THE JUNIOR COLLEGE MOVEMENT. New York: Henry Holt and Co., 1940. 160 p.

>Overview of the junior college and defense of its democratic, individual student-serving aims.

2578 _____. PIONEERING IN PSYCHOLOGY. Iowa City: University of Iowa Press, 1942. 231 p.

>Combines history of psychology and its relation to education, sciences, and the arts with autobiography of Seashore (1866-1949). At the University of Iowa (1897-1936), he taught psychology, headed the psychology department (1905-36), was graduate school dean (1908-36), and pioneered in psychological testing in music (Seashore Measures of Musical Talent).

2579 Seibel, Dean W. A STUDY OF THE ACADEMIC ABILITY AND PERFORMANCE OF JUNIOR COLLEGE STUDENTS. Princeton, N.J.: Educational Testing Service, 1965. 44 p.

>Follow-up study on performance at two-year and four-year colleges by a national sample of high school seniors. Found that more junior college students had academic difficulty after the first year, and boys had greater difficulty than girls despite the type of college attended.

2580 Seidenbaum, Art. CONFRONTATION ON CAMPUS: STUDENT CHAL-
LENGE IN CALIFORNIA. Pasadena, Calif.: Ward Ritchie Press, 1969.
150 p.

Journalistic account of student unrest at nine California colleges during 1968-69; with photographs.

2581 Seitz, Frederick, et al. SCIENCE, GOVERNMENT, AND THE UNIVER-
SITIES. Seattle: University of Washington Press, 1966. 116 p.

Conference papers on rising government grant support of university science research during 1940-60, government's more
critical review of grants from the mid-1960s, and concern
that scientists were diverting universities from moral issues.

2582 Selden, William K. ACCREDITATION: A STRUGGLE OVER STANDARDS
IN HIGHER EDUCATION. New York: Harper and Brothers, 1960.
138 p.

The executive secretary of the National Commission on Accrediting
presents the rise of general and professional higher education accreditation, the 1950s movement for improved accrediting methods and
policies, and urges self-policing by institutions and professions to
prevent government intervention.

2583 _____. ACCREDITATION AND THE PUBLIC INTEREST. Washington,
D.C.: Council on Postsecondary Education, 1977. 30 p.

Recommends ways public representatives might be chosen to
serve on higher education accrediting bodies. Traces historical and philosophical trends toward a greater public role in
the accrediting process.

2584 Selfert, Mary, ed. GRADUATE PROGRAMS AND FACULTY IN READING.
Newark, Del.: International Reading Association, 1971. 352 p.

Lists, by state, each of over 250 post-A.B. reading programs
in U.S. colleges and universities (Canada listed separately):
program director, program overview, degrees, size of program,
application procedure, costs, financial aid, faculty names,
rank, and specialization.

2585 Seligman, Joel. THE HIGH CITADEL: THE INFLUENCE OF HARVARD
LAW SCHOOL. Boston: Houghton Mifflin Co., 1978. 262 p.

History and criticism of Harvard Law School, its admissions,
curriculum, faculty, and teaching methods--by recent graduate
and disciple of Ralph Nader, who wrote introduction. Proposes separate or integrated "schools of public law" to train
lawyers for government service and to represent the poor and
middle class.

2586 Selitiz, Claire, et al. ATTITUDES AND SOCIAL RELATIONS OF FOR-
EIGN STUDENTS IN THE UNITED STATES. Minneapolis: University of
Minnesota Press, 1963. 434 p.

> Found that the longer foreign students remained here, the more
> likely they were to develop close relations with Americans.

2587 Sellers, James B. HISTORY OF THE UNIVERSITY OF ALABAMA. Vol. I:
1818-1902. University: University of Alabama Press, 1953. 649 p.

> Documented account of the University of Alabama's troubled
> early years, Civil War destruction, Reconstruction dominance
> by carpetbaggers and scalawags, and public opposition when
> science and religion were debated.

2588 Sells, Lucy W., ed. TOWARD AFFIRMATIVE ACTION. San Francisco:
Jossey-Bass Publishers, 1974. 99 p.

> Clarifies goals, issues, and problems of affirmative action for
> women and minorities in higher education; notes problem areas,
> identifies federal policy dangers, and suggests alternative poli-
> cies.

2589 Seltzer, Mildred M., et al., eds. GERONTOLOGY IN HIGHER EDU-
CATION: PERSPECTIVES AND ISSUES. Belmont, Calif.: Wadsworth
Publishing Co., 1978. 261 p.

> Association for Gerontology in Higher Education papers and
> discussion on teaching, administration, research, and community
> relations (on problems of the aging).

2590 Semper, Isadore Joseph. SO YOU'RE GOING TO COLLEGE! AND
OTHER CLARKE COLLEGE TALKS. Dubuque, Iowa: Hardie Printer, 1934.
147 p.

> Eight talks on aims and ideals of Catholic higher education
> for women.

2591 Servin, Manuel P., and Wilson, Iris Higbie. SOUTHERN CALIFORNIA
AND ITS UNIVERSITY: A HISTORY OF U.S.C., 1880-1964. Pasadena,
Calif.: Ward Ritchie Press, 1969. 319 p.

> University of Southern California's 1880 founding by the Metho-
> dist Church, ambitious early plans, and outstanding administra-
> tors such as Rufus Bernhard Von Kleinsmid.

2592 Severinghaus, Aura Edward, et al. PREPARATION FOR MEDICAL EDUCA-
TION IN THE LIBERAL ARTS COLLEGE. New York: McGraw-Hill Book
Co., 1953. 400 p.

> Reports that the best undergraduate preparation for medical edu-
> cation is a sound liberal education.

2593 Sewell, Elizabeth. NOW BLESS THYSELF. Garden City, N.Y.: Doubleday and Co., 1962. 234 p.

Novel of an English woman poet-in-residence at a state university.

2594 Sewell, William H., and Davidsen, Oluf M. SCANDINAVIAN STUDENTS ON AN AMERICAN CAMPUS. Minneapolis: University of Minnesota Press, 1961. 134 p.

Academic and social adjustment of forty Scandinavian students during two years at the University of Wisconsin. They made better grades than the average U.S. student at the same university, liked the informal social life and student-teacher relations, but disliked close supervision of daily assignments and frequent tests.

2595 Sewell, William H., and Hauser, Robert M. EDUCATION, OCCUPATION, AND EARNINGS: ACHIEVEMENT IN THE EARLY CAREER. New York: Academic Press, 1975. 237 p.

Found in ten-year follow-up of 1957 Wisconsin high school graduates that ability more than family background affected educational attainment and that type of college attended had little later effect.

2596 Sexson, John H., and Harbeson, John W. THE NEW AMERICAN COLLEGE. New York: Harper and Brothers, 1946. 312 p.

Describes the four-year junior college (grades eleven-fourteen), a pattern used after 1929 at Pasadena Junior College, where authors worked many years. Reports findings from twenty-three other such colleges and endorses this arrangement as appropriate for community colleges and community service.

2597 Sexton, Patricia. WOMEN IN EDUCATION. Bloomington, Ind.: Phi Delta Kappa Educational Foundation, 1976. 189 p.

Historical-sociological view of women's education in the United States, France, and Britain. Several chapters on women as U.S. higher education students, faculty, and administrators. Appendix A compares men and women recipients of higher education degrees by various fields for 1970-71.

2598 Shaffer, Susan E. GUIDE TO BOOK PUBLISHING COURSES: ACADEMIC AND PROFESSIONAL PROGRAMS. Princeton, N.J.: Peterson's Guides, 1978. 150 p.

Information on more than 200 book publishing courses offered by U.S. colleges, universities, and professional organizations.

2599 Shaffer, Thomas L., and Redmount, Robert S. LAWYERS, LAW STUDENTS AND PEOPLE. Colorado Springs: Shepard's, 1977. 252 p.

Examines U.S. legal education and its moral and emotional effects on students, faculty members, and alumni of three law schools. Argues that law schools fail to help students develop counseling skills and a genuine humanistic concern for clients' welfare.

2600 Shapiro, Sandra, ed. DIRECTORY OF FINANCIAL AID IN HIGHER EDUCATION FOR AFRICANS, AND AMERICANS STUDYING ABOUT AFRICA. Waltham, Mass.: African Studies Association, Brandeis University, 1973. 166 p.

Information on agencies giving financial aid to African students and to U.S. students of African studies: eligibility, fellowships, application requirements, and other data.

2601 Shark, Alan R., et al. STUDENTS AND COLLECTIVE BARGAINING. Washington, D.C.: National Student Education Fund, 1978. 223 p.

A student senate study at City University of New York on student involvement in collective bargaining; the impact of such student participation on educational quality; and reactions of faculty, administrators, and trustees to such student participation.

2602 Sharp, Laure M. EDUCATION AND EMPLOYMENT: THE EARLY CAREERS OF COLLEGE GRADUATES. Baltimore, Md.: Johns Hopkins University Press, 1970. 162 p.

Found that: (1) more women end their education with a B.A. degree than men; (2) more women take graduate courses for academic and intellectual reasons, while most men continue their education for job opportunities; (3) more women than men study part time during their academic career because of financial and family obligations; and (4) women with master's degrees had majored in education and most were teaching on the secondary or college level.

2603 Shaughnessy, Mina P. ERRORS AND EXPECTATIONS: A GUIDE FOR THE TEACHER OF BASIC WRITING. New York: Oxford University Press, 1977. 311 p.

Analyzes types of errors common to university students in remedial writing courses, gives before-and-after samples to show improvement in small classes with ample clerical support. Suggests many strategies, examples, and exercises.

2604 Shaw, Charles B. A LIST OF BOOKS FOR COLLEGE LIBRARIES, 1931-1938. Chicago: American Library Association, 1940. 284 p.

Buying list and bibliography for evaluating college library collections; based on Swarthmore College library purchases and
checked by subject specialists at other U.S. colleges.

2605 Shaw, Wilfred Byron, ed. THE UNIVERSITY OF MICHIGAN, AN EN-
CYCLOPEDIC SURVEY. 4 vols. Ann Arbor: University of Michigan
Press, 1942-58.

Exhaustive history of the University of Michigan.

2606 Shedd, Clarence Prouty. THE CHURCH FOLLOWS ITS STUDENTS. New
Haven, Conn.: Yale University Press, 1938. 327 p.

Historical survey of campus ministries (especially Protestant)
to higher education students, with some details about Catholic
Newman Clubs and Jewish Hillel Foundations. Reviews practices at six universities and cites problems facing religious
workers.

2607 Sheehy, Maurice Stephen [Dom Proface]. COLLEGE MEN: THEIR
MAKING AND UNMAKING. New York: P.J. Kenedy and Sons, 1935.
Reprint. Freeport, N.Y.: Books for Libraries Press, 1967. 314 p.

Fictional conversations between a dean and a series of students
convey students' typical personal and academic problems.

2608 Sheldon, Henry D. HISTORY OF THE UNIVERSITY OF OREGON. Portland, Oreg.: Metropolitan Press, 1940. 288 p.

History (1872-1940) of the University of Oregon, its competition with Oregon State and other institutions, and the eventual
separation of functions to ease competition.

2609 _____. STUDENT LIFE AND CUSTOMS. New York: Appleton-Century-
Crofts, 1901. Reprint. New York: Arno Press, 1969. 366 p.

Social history of U.S. student life and customs, 1636-1900;
considers such aspects as debating societies, fraternities, athletics, student government, and religious organizations. Includes student activities at U.S. secondary schools and European universities.

2610 Shepard, Charles E., and Diehl, Harold S. THE HEALTH OF COLLEGE
STUDENTS. Washington, D.C.: American Council on Education, 1939.
169 p.

Study in 1935-36 of health services and health education as
well as the status of student health in selected U.S. higher
education institutions.

2611 Sherman, Lawrence W., et al. THE QUALITY OF POLICE EDUCATION: A CRITICAL REVIEW WITH RECOMMENDATIONS FOR IMPROVING PROGRAMS IN HIGHER EDUCATION. San Francisco: Jossey-Bass Publishers, 1978. 278 p.

> First nationwide review of higher education for police officers. Among changes recommended for police officer education is for departments to recruit from among the more intellectually able candidates.

2612 Sherman, Robert R., and Kirschner, Joseph, eds. UNDERSTANDING HISTORY OF EDUCATION. Cambridge, Mass.: Schenkman Publishing Co., 1977. 226 p.

> Essays on the role of history in teacher education, the study of the history of education, and related topics.

2613 Sherman, Susan. GIVE ME MYSELF. Cleveland: World Publishing Co., 1961. 231 p.

> Novel about a college girl who spends a summer session nursing a woman professor.

2614 Shields, Thomas Edward. THE EDUCATION OF OUR GIRLS. New York: Benziger Brothers, 1907. 299 p.

> An imaginary conversation among seven people holding opposite views on coeducation. Concluded that women should receive higher education in separate women's institutions and be trained for their prime role as homemakers.

2615 Shinn, Anna Hazel. A STUDY OF SOCIAL LIVING IN CATHOLIC WOMEN'S COLLEGES IN THE UNITED STATES. Washington, D.C.: Catholic University of America Press, 1959. 159 p.

> Examined social activities at Catholic women's colleges and concluded that most colleges emphasized students' personal and social adjustment but that social opportunities in some colleges were too few and too limited.

2616 Shinto, William Mamoru. THE DRAMA OF STUDENT REVOLT. Valley Forge, Pa.: Judson Press, 1970. 94 p.

> Anthology on alienated students, black activists, the silent majority, and others during the 1960s campus unrest.

2617 Shipley, Gertrude Tyson. AN EVALUATION OF GUIDED STUDY AND SMALL-GROUP DISCUSSION IN A NORMAL SCHOOL. Contributions to Education No. 486. New York: Teachers College, Columbia University, 1932. 52 p.

Evaluation of students in study-discussion groups and those
taught conventionally showed similar results. Study-discussion
approach was a useful example of innovative teacher education.

2618 Shipton, Clifford K. SIBLEY'S HARVARD GRADUATES: BIOGRAPHICAL
SKETCHES OF THOSE WHO ATTENDED HARVARD COLLEGE IN THE
CLASSES 1764-1767. Vol. 16. Boston: Massachusetts Historical Society,
1972. 598 p.

Short biographies of Harvard students, 1764-67, edited by former director of American Antiquarian Society.

2619 Shiver, Elizabeth N., ed. HIGHER EDUCATION AND PUBLIC INTER-
NATIONAL SERVICE: PAPERS, ADDRESSES, AND DISCUSSION SUM-
MARY OF A SEMINAR SPONSORED BY THE COMMISSION ON INTER-
NATIONAL EDUCATION OF THE AMERICAN COUNCIL ON EDUCATION
IN COLLABORATION WITH THE DEPARTMENT OF STATE, MARCH, 1967.
Washington, D.C.: American Council on Education, 1967. 128 p.

Contributors include C.W. de Kiewet (role of universities),
Frederick H. Harbison (analysis of educational foreign assistance programs), and Walter Adams and Adrian Jaffe of Michigan State, who propose that government grants replace the contract system.

2620 Shores, Louis, et al., eds. THE LIBRARY-COLLEGE. Philadelphia:
Drexel Institute Press, 1966. 210 p.

Contributors' theme is that a library-type instructional program
involving students, teachers, and librarians could make real
the dictum that the library is the heart of a college.

2621 Shryock, Richard H. THE UNIQUE INFLUENCE OF THE JOHNS HOP-
KINS UNIVERSITY ON AMERICAN MEDICINE. Copenhagen, Denmark:
Ejnar Munksgaard, 1953. 77 p.

Scholarly account of the special role Johns Hopkins University
has played in U.S. medical research and medical education.

2622 Shtogren, John A., ed. ADMINISTRATIVE DEVELOPMENT IN HIGHER
EDUCATION: THE STATE OF THE ART. Richmond, Va.: Higher Education Leadership and Management Society, 1979. 205 p.

Fifteen papers about helping higher education administrators
improve their performance.

2623 Shulman, Irving. GOOD DEEDS MUST BE PUNISHED. New York: Henry
Holt and Co., 1956. 374 p.

Novel of a New York City Italian-American youth at college
on the G.I. Bill involved in fraternity, racial, campus, and
other differences because of his ethnic origins.

2624 Shuster, George Nauman. BROTHER FLO: AN IMAGINATIVE BIOGRA-PHY. New York: Macmillan Co., 1938. 120 p.

Fictional biography of an engaging porter at a Catholic college.

2625 _____. EDUCATION AND MORAL WISDOM. New York: Harper and Brothers, 1960. 146 p.

Essays written during twenty years as Hunter College (New York City) president (1940-60). Shuster's (1894-1977) topics are on academic freedom, administration of a municipal college, and problems of Catholic education (from his view as a Catholic layman).

2626 Sidar, Alexander G., Jr., and Potter, David A. NO-NEED/MERIT AWARDS: A SURVEY BY THE COLLEGE SCHOLARSHIP SERVICE OF THE COLLEGE BOARD. Princeton, N.J.: College Board Publications, 1978. 21 p.

Survey for college administrators on the purpose, cost, funding sources, and extent of use of no-need and merit awards.

2627 Siegel, Max, ed. THE COUNSELING OF COLLEGE STUDENTS: FUNC-TION, PRACTICE, AND TECHNIQUE. New York: Free Press, 1968. 467 p.

For student personnel workers. Chapters range from how to counsel the physically handicapped to the history of college counseling.

2628 Sikes, Melvin P., and Meacham, Paul E., eds. BLACK PROFESSIONALS IN PREDOMINANTLY WHITE INSTITUTIONS OF HIGHER EDUCATION. Austin: Hogg Foundation for Mental Health, University of Texas, 1973. 135 p.

Directory of black professionals working in predominantly white academic institutions; listed by states and indexed by names.

2629 Sikes, Walter W., and Barrett, Laurence. CASE STUDIES ON FACULTY DEVELOPMENT. Washington, D.C.: Council for the Advancement of Small Colleges, 1977. 57 p.

Council-sponsored project in four colleges; designed to improve professional development opportunities of faculty, enhance their collective effectiveness, and increase interaction between faculty members and their administrators.

2630 Sikes, Walter W., et al. RENEWING HIGHER EDUCATION FROM WITH-IN: A GUIDE FOR CAMPUS CHANGE TEAMS. San Francisco: Jossey-Bass Publishers, 1974. 184 p.

To improve the quality of higher education, authors favor using campus change teams who use applied behavioral approach to enrich group processes in committees and other institutional bodies.

2631 Sikkema, Mildred, and Niyekawa-Howard, Agnes M. CROSS-CULTURAL LEARNING AND SELF-GROWTH. New York: International Association of Schools of Social Work, 1977. 121 p.

Describes a graduate program in social work that required students to live and work in a different country. Reports that learning about different cultures improved students' preparation for social work.

2632 Silberman, Harry, ed. EASING THE TRANSITION FROM SCHOOLING TO WORK. San Francisco: Jossey-Bass Publishers, 1976. 123 p.

On the role of community colleges in easing students' transition from schooling to work. Also suggests programs to prepare adults for new careers.

2633 Simonitsch, Roland G. RELIGIOUS INSTRUCTION IN CATHOLIC COLLEGES FOR MEN. Washington, D.C.: Catholic University of America Press, 1952. 327 p.

Found the trend in religion teaching in Catholic higher education was away from theology and toward everyday living. Shortage of adequately trained religion teachers.

2634 Simons, William E. LIBERAL EDUCATION IN THE SERVICE ACADEMIES. New York: Teachers College, Columbia University, 1965. 230 p.

Air Force Academy professor tells of curricular reform at the service academies since 1958 (in response to cold war strategies) and the rapid increase in liberal arts courses.

2635 Simpson, Elizabeth Leonie. HUMANISTIC EDUCATION: AN INTERPRETATION: A REPORT TO THE FORD FOUNDATION. Cambridge, Mass.: Ballinger Publishing Co., 1977. 328 p.

Views U.S. higher education curricular approaches to humanistic education and gives views of such proponents as Weinstein, Brown, and Combs.

2636 Simpson, George Gaylord. CONCESSION TO THE IMPROBABLE. New Haven, Conn.: Yale University Press, 1978. 291 p.

Autobiography of paleontologist Simpson, Harvard emeritus professor (later taught at the University of Arizona) who helped forge a coherent view of evolution which combined Darwin's natural selection with genetics.

2637 Simpson, Lawrence A., ed. A/V MEDIA IN CAREER DEVELOPMENT. Bethlehem, Pa.: College Placement Council, 1976. 100 p.

Use of audiovisual materials in career counseling, how to produce an audiovisual program, and examples of programs developed by college counseling centers. Includes an annotated list of commercial media career programs.

2638 Sims, O. Suthern, Jr., ed. NEW DIRECTIONS IN CAMPUS LAW EN-FORCEMENT. Athens: University Center for Continuing Education, University of Georgia, 1971. 79 p.

Responsibilities of campus police. Recommends that they be upgraded educationally and professionally and that the director report directly to the college president.

2639 Sindler, Allan P. BAKKE, DEFUNIS, AND MINORITY ADMISSIONS: THE QUEST FOR EQUAL OPPORTUNITY. New York: Longman, 1979. 358 p.

Analysis of Bakke, DeFunis, and other reverse discrimination cases illustrates the complexities and moral problem of compensatory preferences given minorities in higher education and professional study.

2640 Sitterly, Charles Fremont. THE BUILDING OF DREW UNIVERSITY. New York: Methodist Book Concern, 1938. 302 p.

Founding and development of Drew University, private nonsectarian university in Madison, New Jersey.

2641 Skinner, B.F. BEYOND FREEDOM AND DIGNITY. New York: Alfred A. Knopf, 1971. 225 p.

Theme of the leading behaviorist at Harvard is that the freedoms we believe we have are illusory, that we are controlled by subtle and complex rewards and punishments of our culture and environment. Skinner advocates controls that shape behavior so as to improve humanity.

2642 _____. THE TECHNOLOGY OF TEACHING. New York: Appleton-Century-Crofts, 1969. 271 p.

Skinner's interpretation of good teaching as influencing and controlling learner's behavior.

2643 Skousen, Fred K., et al. USER NEEDS: AN EMPIRICAL STUDY OF COLLEGE AND UNIVERSITY FINANCIAL REPORTING. Washington, D.C.: National Association of College and University Business Officers, 1975. 139 p.

Specific suggestions on improving college and university financial reports to enable users like state budget officers and others to make better decisions.

2644 Slater, John R. RHEES OF ROCHESTER. New York: Harper and Brothers, 1946. 304 p.

Biography of Rush Rhees, Amherst College graduate; written by a faculty member who taught at the University of Rochester during Rhees's thirty-five year presidency.

2645 Sloan, Douglas. THE SCOTTISH ENLIGHTENMENT AND THE AMERICAN COLLEGE IDEAL. New York: Teachers College Press, 1971. 298 p.

Shows eighteenth-century Scottish university influence on U.S. higher education through sixty-five Presbyterian academies founded during the period; through such Scottish academics who taught in the United States as Francis Alison, John Witherspoon, Samuel Stanhope Smith, and Benjamin Rush; and through case study of the founding and development of the College of New Jersey, later Princeton University.

2646 Sloan Study Consortium. PAYING FOR COLLEGE: FINANCING EDUCATION AT NINE PRIVATE INSTITUTIONS. Hanover, N.H.: University Press of New England, 1974. 137 p.

Study of the financing of undergraduate education at Amherst, Brown, Dartmouth, Harvard, MIT, Mount Holyoke, Princeton, Wellesley, and Wesleyan.

2647 Slosson, Edwin E. GREAT AMERICAN UNIVERSITIES. New York: Macmillan Co., 1910. Reprint. New York: Arno Press, 1977. 525 p.

Describes distinctive features of nine leading private and five leading public universities, with final chapter of comparisons and conclusions.

2648 Smallwood, Frank. FREE AND INDEPENDENT. Brattleboro, Vt.: Stephen Greene Press, 1976. 235 p.

Dartmouth political scientist's autobiographical account of his election and life as a two-year member of Vermont's State Senate and the effect on his teaching about legislative politics.

2649 Smallwood, Mary Lovett. AN HISTORICAL STUDY OF EXAMINATIONS AND GRADING SYSTEMS IN EARLY AMERICAN UNIVERSITIES: A CRITICAL STUDY OF THE ORIGINAL RECORDS OF HARVARD, WILLIAM AND MARY, YALE, MOUNT HOLYOKE AND MICHIGAN FROM THEIR FOUNDING TO 1900. Cambridge, Mass.: Harvard University Press, 1935. 132 p.

History of exams and grading at Yale, William and Mary, Mt. Holyoke, University of Michigan, and Harvard (first recorded exam, 1646).

2650 Smart, John C., and Montgomery, James R., eds. EXAMINING DEPART-MENTAL MANAGEMENT. San Francisco: Jossey-Bass Publishers, 1976. 124 p.

Examines organizational theories of academic departments, career goals of department heads, and their changing roles.

2651 Smelser, Neil J., and Almond, Gabriel, eds. PUBLIC HIGHER EDUCATION IN CALIFORNIA. Los Angeles: University of California Press, 1974. 312 p.

California higher education's institutional structure, science versus humanities conflict, and values; reflects the 500 percent enrollment growth between 1950 and 1970 and the impact of 1960s-70s national social unrest.

2652 Smiley, Marjorie B. INTERGROUP EDUCATION AND THE AMERICAN COLLEGE. New York: Teachers College, Columbia University, 1952. 212 p.

Data on fifty colleges' intergroup education programs. Includes formal classes and other activities to promote understanding of ethnic and racial minorities. Concludes that higher education institutions should become laboratories for improving intergroup relations.

2653 Smith, Alden Wallace. PARTICIPATION IN ORGANIZATIONS: A STUDY OF COLUMBIA COLLEGE ALUMNI. Contributions to Education No. 935. New York: Teachers College, Columbia University, 1948. 69 p.

Concluded that alumni who as students were active in campus government were no more active in civic affairs than were other alumni.

2654 Smith, Alfred G. COGNITIVE STYLES IN LAW SCHOOLS. Austin: University of Texas Press, 1979. 178 p.

Study of the learning patterns of eight hundred students in torts courses at selected U.S. law schools.

2655 Smith, Bardwell L., et al. THE TENURE DEBATE. San Francisco: Jossey-Bass Publishers, 1973. 254 p.

Presents tenure statistics on more than sixty thousand faculty. Assesses connection between academic freedom, faculty unionism, higher education autonomy, and the tenure issue.

2656 Smith, Bruce Lannes. INDONESIAN-AMERICAN COOPERATION IN HIGHER EDUCATION. East Lansing: Institute of Research on Overseas Programs, Michigan State University, 1960. 133 p.

Indonesian-American university relations: roles of top policy-makers, administrators, and professors; campus and overseas coordination; planning and scheduling; and recommendations.

2657 Smith, Bruce L.R., and Karlesky, Joseph J. THE STATE OF ACADEMIC SCIENCE: THE UNIVERSITIES IN THE NATION'S RESEARCH EFFORT. Vol. I: SUMMARY OF MAJOR FINDINGS. New Rochelle, N.Y.: Change Magazine Press, 1977. 250 p.

Examines the effect on higher education science programs of such factors as federal support, student enrollments, student interests, and university finances.

2658 Smith, Cynthia J., ed. ADVANCING EQUALITY OF OPPORTUNITY: A MATTER OF JUSTICE. Washington, D.C.: Institute for the Study of Educational Policy, Howard University, 1978. 205 p.

Conference proceedings on equalizing higher education opportunities for blacks.

2659 Smith, David C. THE FIRST CENTURY: A HISTORY OF THE UNIVERSITY OF MAINE, 1865-1965. Orono: University of Maine at Orono Press, 1979. 295 p.

Illustrated centennial history by the history department chairman, Orono campus.

2660 Smith, David N. WHO RULES THE UNIVERSITIES? AN ESSAY IN CLASS ANALYSIS. New York: Monthly Review Press, 1974. 295 p.

Socialist's view that control of U.S. higher education rests with a distinct ruling class.

2661 Smith, G. Kerry, ed. AGONY AND PROMISE: CURRENT ISSUES IN HIGHER EDUCATION 1969. San Francisco: Jossey-Bass Publishers, 1969. 282 p.

1969 themes are the university and society: urban education, black students, community relations, campus culture, drugs, unrest, research, and future trends.

2662 _____. NEW TEACHING, NEW LEARNING: CURRENT ISSUES IN HIGHER EDUCATION 1971. San Francisco: Jossey-Bass Publishers, 1971. 261 p.

1971 essays range from decision-making structure and open admissions to serving women and disadvantaged students.

2663 _____. STRESS AND CAMPUS RESPONSE: CURRENT ISSUES IN HIGHER EDUCATION, 1968. San Francisco: Jossey-Bass Publishers, 1968. 297 p.

CURRENT ISSUES IN HIGHER EDUCATION series, edited after 1945 by Smith from the American Association for Higher Education annual conference papers, provides a useful year-by-year view of U.S. higher education concerns. The 1968 issue included the place of the university amid revolutionary turmoil, student unrest, and changes in university governance. (Later AAHE conference reports below are in chronological order.)

2664 _____. THE TROUBLED CAMPUS: CURRENT ISSUES IN HIGHER EDUCATION 1970. San Francisco: Jossey-Bass Publishers, 1970. 268 p.

1970 campus unrest is reflected in papers by such higher educators as Buell Gallagher, Harlan Cleveland, and Lyman Glenny.

2665 _____. TWENTY-FIVE YEARS: 1945 to 1970. San Francisco: Jossey-Bass Publishers, 1970. 330 p.

Twenty-five year anthology of AAHE CURRENT ISSUES IN HIGHER EDUCATION conference reports. Included are Charles Frankel's 1961 plea for humanizing liberal arts education, many explorations into the aims of higher education, and contributions by John Kenneth Galbraith, Marshall McLuhan, Paul Goodman, Whitney M. Young, Jr., Talcott Parsons, and Lewis B. Mayhew.

2666 Smith, Goldwin, ed. THE PROFESSOR AND THE PUBLIC: THE ROLE OF THE SCHOLAR IN THE MODERN WORLD. Detroit: Wayne State University Press, 1972. 124 p.

Essays by historians Smith (Wayne State) and J.H. Hexter (Yale) and by the English Elizabethan expert A.L. Rowse on the role of the scholar in the community.

2667 Smith, Harry E. SECULARIZATION AND THE UNIVERSITY. Richmond, Va.: John Knox Press, 1968. 172 p.

University of North Carolina administrator says that secularization of the university has freed it from externally imposed controls, but cautions that such freedom can be perverted.

2668 Smith, Henry Lewis. THIS TROUBLED CENTURY. Chapel Hill: University of North Carolina Press, 1947. 203 p.

Addresses by Smith (1859-1951), physicist who originated the use of x-rays in survery. For thirty years he was president of Davidson College, North Carolina (1901-12), and of Washington and Lee University, Lexington, Virginia (1912-30).

2669 Smith, Huston. THE PURPOSES OF HIGHER EDUCATION. New York: Harper and Brothers, 1955. 218 p.

> Objectives of liberal education based on faculty curriculum study at Washington University, St. Louis. Discusses freedom versus authority, egoism versus altruism, and the individual versus the state.

2670 Smith, James P., and Welch, Finis. LOCAL LABOR MARKETS AND CYCLIC COMPONENTS IN DEMAND FOR COLLEGE TRAINED MANPOWER. Santa Monica, Calif.: Rand, 1979. 31 p.

> To assess the job market, examines earnings of college and high school graduates during 1968-1975.

2671 Smith, John Edwin. VALUE CONVICTIONS AND HIGHER EDUCATION. New Haven, Conn.: Edward W. Hazen Foundation, 1958. 36 p.

> Philosophical consideration of changing values in higher education.

2672 Smith, Leo F., and Lipsett, Laurence. THE TECHNICAL INSTITUTE. New York: McGraw-Hill Book Co., 1956. 319 p.

> Analyzes the work of well-educated and trained technicians, tells how to organize and administer technical education, and gives guidelines for community colleges in enlarging their technical programs.

2673 Smith, Margaret Ruth. STUDENT AID. Contributions to Education No. 704. New York: Teachers College, Columbia University, 1937. 152 p.

> Controlled study of procedures for granting financial aid to students.

2674 Smith, Robert, et al. BY ANY MEANS NECESSARY: REVOLUTIONARY STRUGGLE AT SAN FRANCISCO STATE. San Francisco: Jossey-Bass Publishers, 1970. 370 p.

> Examines the 1968 San Francisco State strikes in a case study of the college under three presidencies, 1966-68, and in the context of fundamental higher education problems.

2675 Smith, Robert Ora. PERSONALITY AND CULTURE FACTORS AFFECTING THE RELIGION OF COLLEGE STUDENTS. Ann Arbor, Mich.: Edwards Brothers, 1948. 194 p.

> Study on religious attitudes of 140 Yale Divinity School students and advice to higher education administrators on better serving students' religious needs.

2676 Smith, Sherman E., et al. ARE SCHOLARSHIPS THE ANSWER? Albuquerque: University of New Mexico Press, 1960. 89 p.

> Statewide New Mexico study, 1952-56, concluded that counseling to raise students' educational aspirations was more important than scholarship aid.

2677 Smith, Shirley W. JAMES BURRILL ANGELL: AN AMERICAN INFLUENCE. Ann Arbor: University of Michigan Press, 1954. 380 p.

> Angell (1829-1916), University of Vermont president (1866-71) and president of the University of Michigan (1871-1909), which he helped make a national intellectual center. Father of James Rowland Angell, Yale University president (1921-37).

2678 Smith, Thomas Vernor. A NON-EXISTENT MAN: AN AUTOBIOGRAPHY. Austin: University of Texas Press, 1962. 280 p.

> Autobiography of Texas-born (1890--) University of Chicago philosophy professor, moderator of the University's radio program "Round Table of the Air," opponent of Robert M. Hutchins' University of Chicago administration, state legislator and U.S. Congressman from Illinois, who later taught at Syracuse University.

2679 Smith, Virginia B., and Bernstein, Alison R. THE IMPERSONAL CAMPUS: OPTIONS FOR REORGANIZING COLLEGES TO INCREASE STUDENT INVOLVEMENT, LEARNING, AND DEVELOPMENT. San Francisco: Jossey-Bass Publishers, 1979. 137 p.

> How large universities can decrease student alienation and increase learning; how small colleges--by sharing facilities and resources--can diversify educational offerings.

2680 Smith, Wilson. PROFESSORS AND PUBLIC ETHICS: STUDIES OF NORTHERN MORAL PHILOSOPHERS BEFORE THE CIVIL WAR. Ithaca, N.Y.: Cornell University Press, 1956. 245 p.

> Essays on pre-Civil War decline in philosophy courses which applied ethical principles to everyday life; concluding essay on the rise of moral theology courses as a parallel to nineteenth-century evangelism.

2681 Snavely, Guy E. CHOOSE AND USE YOUR COLLEGE. New York: Harper and Brothers, 1941. 166 p.

> Association of American College's executive director's introduction to college life for high school students and their parents.

2682 _____. THE CHURCH AND THE FOUR-YEAR COLLEGE: AN APPRAIS-

AL OF THEIR RELATION. New York: Harper and Brothers, 1955. 216 p.

Historical and analytical review of the churches' role in founding many U.S. colleges, the evolution of some church colleges into state institutions, and sources of financial aid to church-related institutions.

2683 Snelling, W. Rodman, and Boruch, Robert F. SCIENCE IN LIBERAL ARTS COLLEGES: A LONGITUDINAL STUDY OF FORTY-NINE SELECTIVE COLLEGES. New York: Columbia University Press, 1972. 285 p.

Background, undergraduate scholastic career, and postgraduate experience of twenty thousand science and math majors. Over half had earned one graduate degree. Ninety percent said they would choose the same undergraduate school. Concluded that many liberal arts colleges continue to provide good science and math education.

2684 Snider, Patricia J., et al. HUMAN RESOURCES PLANNING--A GUIDE TO DATA. Washington, D.C.: Equal Employment Advisory Council, 1977. 298 p.

Lists publications that have information on the number of women and minority-group members available for employment in specific fields. Intended for employers in complying with federal affirmative action and equal-employment laws and regulations.

2685 Snyder, Benson R. THE HIDDEN CURRICULUM. Cambridge: MIT Press, 1973. 214 p.

On campus unrest; says students resented manipulation by subtle forces (the hidden curriculum) emanating from decisions of administrators, professors, and admissions officers.

2686 Soffen, Joseph. FACULTY DEVELOPMENT IN PROFESSIONAL EDUCATION: PROBLEMS OF, AND PROPOSALS FOR RECRUITMENT, PRE-SERVICE, INDUCTION, AND CONTINUING DEVELOPMENT IN SOCIAL WORK EDUCATION. New York: Council on Social Work Education, 1967. 187 p.

Report of a federally financed study of social work education, with recommendations.

2687 Solberg, Winton U. THE UNIVERSITY OF ILLINOIS, 1867-1894: AN INTELLECTUAL AND CULTURAL HISTORY. Urbana: University of Illinois Press, 1968. 494 p.

Shows that succeeding presidents emphasized science, liberal arts, and engineering as much as (and sometimes more than) agriculture. Includes controversies over curriculum, student discipline, student housing, military training, and the elective system.

2688 Solmon, Lewis C. MALE AND FEMALE GRADUATE STUDENTS: THE QUESTION OF EQUAL OPPORTUNITY. New York: Praeger Publishers, 1976. 160 p.

Attempts to define sex discrimination in graduate schools, to determine if it exists, and if so, whether the fault lies with the institution or with earlier conditioning by both sexes. Reviews admissions process, geographic and institutional mobility, and financial aid practices. Concludes that although sex bias exists in Ph.D. programs, a greater proportion of women than men who apply are accepted into graduate school.

2689 Solmon, Lewis C., and Taubman, Paul J., eds. DOES COLLEGE MATTER? SOME EVIDENCE ON THE IMPACTS OF HIGHER EDUCATION. New York: Academic Press, 1973. 415 p.

Papers on the cost-benefit analysis (input-output relationship) in higher education.

2690 Solmon, Lewis C., et al. COLLEGE AS A TRAINING GROUND FOR JOBS. New York: Praeger Publishers, 1977. 204 p.

Follow-up study of 1961 college graduates after almost a decade in the job market. Concluded that the psychological (and probably the economic) benefits of college education are significant.

2691 Songe, Alice H. AMERICAN UNIVERSITIES AND COLLEGES: A DICTIONARY OF NAME CHANGES. Metuchen, N.J.: Scarecrow Press, 1978. 264 p.

Helps trace original names, changes of names, and other identification of colleges and universities.

2692 Sophia Smith Collection. CATALOGS OF THE SOPHIA SMITH COLLECTION, WOMEN'S HISTORY ARCHIVE, SMITH COLLEGE, NORTHAMPTON. MASSACHUSETTS. 7 vols. Boston: G.K. Hall, 1975.

Women's history collection at Smith College which emphasizes U.S. material and includes among its subjects women's education and its leaders.

2693 Sorenson, Herbert. ADULT ABILITIES. Minneapolis: University of Minnesota Press, 1938. 190 p.

Studied adults (mostly teachers and officer workers) taking extension courses in eight universities and compared their mental abilities with those of residential college freshmen. Found that adults were less willing to memorize, made somewhat better grades, and maintained or improved abilities for which they found frequent use. Concluded that adults could learn effectively and needed greater higher educational opportunities.

2694 Sosdian, Carol P. EXTERNAL DEGREES: PROGRAM AND STUDENT CHARACTERISTICS. Washington, D.C.: National Institute of Education, 1978. 54 p.

Studied 244 external degree programs and their students at 134 institutions.

2695 Sosdian, Carol P., and Sharp, Laure M. THE EXTERNAL DEGREE AS A CREDENTIAL: GRADUATES' EXPERIENCES IN EMPLOYMENT AND FURTHER STUDY. Washington, D.C.: National Institute of Education, 1978. 124 p.

Final report of a 1976-77 study to determine the value of external degree programs.

2696 Southern California. University. WAYS AND MEANS OF STRENGTHENING INFORMATION AND COUNSELING SERVICES FOR ADULT LEARNERS. Los Angeles: College of Continuing Education, University of Southern California, 1978. 42 p.

International symposium on guidance and counseling sponsored by the University of Southern California and UNESCO.

2697 Southern Education Reporting Service. A STATISTICAL SUMMARY, STATE BY STATE, OF SCHOOL SEGREGATION-DESEGREGATION IN THE SOUTHERN AND BORDER AREA FROM 1954-THE PRESENT. Nashville: 1967. 44 p.

Regional and state-by-state statistical information on desegregation of southern school systems. Has generalized statistics on public colleges and universities, 1966-67 academic year.

2698 Southern Regional Education Board. THE BLACK COMMUNITY AND THE COMMUNITY COLLEGE: ACTION PROGRAMS FOR EXPANDING OPPORTUNITY. Atlanta: Institute for Higher Educational Opportunity, 1970. 61 p.

Selected community colleges were combining academic and career counseling to help disadvantaged blacks. Found several problems, including a communications gap between black students and high school counselors and between junior colleges and the black community. Also found need for special remedial work and for state coordination between junior college programs and vocational-technical institutions.

2699 _____. THE EMERGING CITY AND HIGHER EDUCATION. Atlanta: 1963. 46 p.

Papers on urban higher adult education, education for civic policy, role of university extension administrators, adult education curriculum, and urban studies programs.

2700 _____. EXPANDING OPPORTUNITIES: CASE STUDIES OF INTERINSTITUTIONAL COOPERATION. Atlanta: 1969. 44 p.

Five case studies of interinstitutional cooperation among mainly white and mainly black southern liberal arts colleges: joint seminars, a shared department, a consortium to eliminate duplication, difficulties, and opportunities.

2701 _____. FACULTY EVALUATION FOR IMPROVED LEARNING. Atlanta: 1977. 64 p.

Reports ways southern colleges and universities judge the performance of their faculty members. Includes recommendations and strategies for evaluating faculty members.

2702 _____. HIGHER EDUCATION: PERSPECTIVES '78. Atlanta: 1979. 47 p.

Papers on financing higher education, public policy and private institutions, the Bakke decision, and other issues.

2703 _____. HIGHER EDUCATION FOR THE FUTURE: REFORM OR MORE OF THE SAME? Atlanta: 1971. 47 p.

Essays support broadening educational opportunities but question ways of doing it. Eli Ginzberg says low tuition subsidizes middle and upper classes. Alexander Astin adds that high selectivity screens out deserving students. Other contributors include Clark Kerr and Georgia Governor Jimmy Carter.

2704 _____. NEW CAREERS AND CURRICULUM CHANGE. Atlanta: 1968. 61 p.

Social, cultural, and economic changes that necessitate curriculum changes in mainly black colleges.

2705 _____. NEW DIRECTIONS IN STATEWIDE HIGHER EDUCATION: PLANNING AND COORDINATION. Atlanta: 1970. 56 p.

On such issues of state higher education as coordinating state planning agencies on graduate education, the relationship of state planning agencies and state legislators, interinstitutional and interstate cooperation, and federal and state aid to private colleges.

2706 _____. PRIORITIES FOR POSTSECONDARY EDUCATION IN THE SOUTH:

A POSITION STATEMENT BY THE SOUTHERN REGIONAL EDUCATION BOARD. Atlanta: 1976. 36 p.

Calls for reassessment of the structure and purpose of all forms of post-high school education in the South. Argues that education must meet the needs of the individual within a changing society. Identifies new priorities for education.

2707 _____. STABILITY AND CHANGE--POSTSECONDARY EDUCATION'S FUTURE. Atlanta: 1978. 48 p.

For southern legislators and educators on issues facing higher education: higher education and employment, collective bargaining, and adjusting to a little or no growth.

2708 _____. SUMMARY OF STATE LEGISLATION AFFECTING HIGHER EDUCATION IN THE SOUTH, 1971. Atlanta: 1971. 43 p.

Summarizes major state legislation affecting higher education in the South.

2709 Southwestern Conference on Higher Education. HIGHER EDUCATION AND SOCIETY: A SYMPOSIUM. Norman: University of Oklahoma Press, 1936. 323 p.

Papers on physical, social, and academic interrelationship of higher education institutions in the Southwest.

2710 Spaeth, Joe L., and Greeley, Andrew M. RECENT ALUMNI AND HIGHER EDUCATION: A SURVEY OF COLLEGE GRADUATES. New York: McGraw-Hill Book Co., 1970. 199 p.

Follow-up seven years later of thousands of 1961 college graduates. Some findings: prime value of college is its liberal arts rather than vocational education (although career training was important to many); if they could do it over, many would take more arts and humanities courses; women graduates read more and had more interest in the arts than men; and alumni were political moderates with slight leftward leanings.

2711 Spafford, Ivol, et al. BUILDING A CURRICULUM FOR GENERAL EDUCATION: A DESCRIPTION OF THE GENERAL COLLEGE PROGRAM. Minneapolis: University of Minnesota Press, 1943. 353 p.

Description and progress report of the two-year Associate of Arts General College (founded 1932) of the University of Minnesota, whose students were advised that their high school record and college entrance exams made doubtful their success in four-year college work.

2712 _____. HOME ECONOMICS IN JUNIOR COLLEGES. Minneapolis: Burgess Publishing Co., 1944. 84 p.

The place, value, and program of home economics in junior colleges.

2713 Spalding, John Lancaster. OPPORTUNITY AND OTHER ESSAYS AND AD-DRESSES. Freeport, N.Y.: Books for Libraries Press, 1900. Reprint. New York: Arno Press, 1968. 228 p.

"Women and the Higher Education" is one of eight addresses by the Roman Catholic bishop of Peoria, Illinois, who comments on the value of higher education for women; its background; and its likely future in women's colleges, coeducational institutions, and particularly in Catholic colleges and universities.

2714 Spaulding, Seth, and Flack, Michael J. THE WORLD'S STUDENTS IN THE UNITES STATES: A REVIEW AND EVALUATION OF RESEARCH ON FOREIGN STUDENTS. New York: Praeger Publishers, 1976. 520 p.

Annotated bibliography of 450 books, articles, reports, policy statements, and other materials on foreign students in U.S. higher education; their admission, English-language training, social life, and the effects of talent migration.

2715 Spear, George E., and Mocker, Donald W., eds. URBAN EDUCATION: A GUIDE TO INFORMATION SOURCES. Urban Studies Information Guide Series, vol. 3. Detroit: Gale Research Co., 1978. 203 p.

Contains a twenty-eight-page bibliography on urban higher education; includes nontraditional programs, degrees, and programs for urban minorities.

2716 Spencer, Anna Carpenter Garlin. WOMAN'S SHARE IN SOCIAL CUL-TURE. New York: M. Kennerley, 1913. Reprint. New York: Arno Press, 1972. 331 p.

Contends that modern societies need educated women's talents to help attain advanced democracy. Describes Oberlin, Ripon, and Antioch Colleges as desirable models for women's higher education.

2717 Spender, Stephen. THE YEAR OF THE YOUNG REBELS. New York: Random House, 1969. 186 p.

Author searches for the meaning of the New Left youth's worldwide campus rebellions and sees it as an expression of their new humanistic concerns.

2718 Splaver, Sarah. NON-TRADITIONAL CAREERS FOR WOMEN. New York: Julian Messner, 1973. 224 p.

Over five hundred hitherto male-dominated professions which

women can enter (law, medicine, dentistry, science, engineering, others), the education needed, and rewards to be expected.

2719 Sprouse, Betsy M., ed. NATIONAL DIRECTORY OF EDUCATIONAL PROGRAMS IN GERONTOLOGY. 2d ed., 1978. Washington, D.C.: Association for Gerontology in Higher Education, 1979. 148 p.

Information on courses, degree programs, financial aid, and research at 120 colleges and universities.

2720 Spurr, Stephen Hopkins. ACADEMIC DEGREE STRUCTURES: INNOVATIVE APPROACHES: PRINCIPLES OF REFORM IN DEGREE STRUCTURES IN THE UNITED STATES. New York: McGraw-Hill Book Co., 1970. 213 p.

Background and development of academic degrees. Critical of master's degree as stockpiling of undergraduate credits and of the Ph.D. as inefficient in time and dropouts. Urges limiting kinds of degrees and uniformity in agreed-on structure of degrees.

2721 Stadtman, Verne A. THE UNIVERSITY OF CALIFORNIA, 1868-1968. New York: McGraw-Hill Book Co., 1970. 594 p.

University of California centennial history with more than half the book on the last thirty years: multiple campus growth, loyalty oaths of the 1950s, expanding faculty research efforts, and the 1964 Berkeley rebellion.

2722 Stalnaker, John M., and Dykman, Ross A. ADMISSION REQUIREMENTS, 1955, OF AMERICAN MEDICAL COLLEGES. Chicago: Association of American Medical Colleges, 1954. 195 p.

Annual (since 1951) handbook for premed students listing entrance requirements and other information on eighty-three U.S. medical schools.

2723 Stanford University. APPROACHING STANFORD. Stanford, Calif.: Stanford University Press, 1970. 141 p.

Handbook for freshman applicants but from a student viewpoint rather than an institutional catalog; embellished with quotations and illustrations.

2724 _____. STANFORD UNIVERSITY: THE FOUNDING GRANT: WITH AMENDMENTS, LEGISLATION, AND COURT DECREES. Stanford, Calif.: Stanford University Press, 1971. 83 p.

Founding documents of Stanford University, including difficulties with board of trustees and the firing of Professor Roth by Jane Lathrop Stanford.

2725 _____. THE UNIVERSITY AND THE FUTURE OF AMERICA. Stanford, Calif.: Stanford University Press, 1941. 274 p.

Symposium papers on wide-ranging topics by such contributors as Robert Millikan and Lewis Mumford.

2726 Stanford University. School of Humanities. ELEMENTARY COURSES IN THE HUMANITIES. Stanford, Calif.: Stanford University Press, 1946. 146 p.

Conference papers on liberal education and discussions on literature, fine arts, languages, philosophy, and general humanities courses.

2727 Stark, Joan S. INSIDE INFORMATION: A HANDBOOK ON BETTER INFORMATION FOR STUDENT CHOICE. Washington, D.C.: American Association for Higher Education, 1978. 348 p.

Ideas from colleges and universities for providing information to students on program and other choices.

2728 _____, ed. PROMOTING CONSUMER PROTECTION FOR STUDENTS. San Francisco: Jossey-Bass Publishers, 1976. 105 p.

Reviews federal efforts to correct abuses of student consumers, action being taken to protect student rights, and implications of the consumers' rights movement for higher education.

2729 Stark, Joan S., et al. THE MANY FACES OF EDUCATIONAL CONSUMERISM. Lexington, Mass.: Lexington Books, 1978. 224 p.

Essays relate consumerism to four-year college students. Traces consumerism's origins, discusses who should protect the education consumer, suggests ways to get more accurate information to students, and how to redress student grievances. Lists seventeen imperatives for improving consumer protection education.

2730 Starrak, James A., and Hughes, Raymond M. THE COMMUNITY COLLEGE IN THE UNITED STATES. Ames: Iowa State College Press, 1954. 114 p.

Sees two-year colleges, predominantly technical and vocational, as the answer to expanding enrollments. Reviews the history of two-year colleges, presents basic standards for organizing them, and includes a plan (on the Iowa model) for developing a state system of community colleges.

2731 _____. THE NEW JUNIOR COLLEGE: THE NEW STEP IN FREE PUBLIC EDUCATION. Ames: Iowa State College Press, 1948. 63 p.

Reasons junior colleges are needed, developments in the junior college movement, and junior colleges as feasible institutions for serving the community.

2732 Staton, Thomas Felix. HOW TO INSTRUCT SUCCESSFULLY: MODERN TEACHING METHODS IN ADULT EDUCATION. New York: McGraw-Hill Book Co., 292 p.

Suggestions applicable to college teaching are on characteristics of learners, teaching methods, and ways to evaluate teaching results.

2733 Stauffer, Thomas M. ASSESSING SPONSORED RESEARCH PROGRAMS. Washington, D.C.: American Council on Education, 1978. 26 p.

Guidelines for college and university presidents and administrators for developing and managing sponsored research programs.

2734 Staupers, Mabel Keaton. NO TIME FOR PREJUDICE: A STORY OF INTEGRATION IN NURSING IN THE UNITED STATES. New York: Macmillan Co., 1961. 206 p.

Tells in historical context reasons separate nursing schools were established for blacks. Gives motives of black nurse pioneers in establishing in 1908 the National Association of Colored Graduate Nurses.

2735 Stearns, Myron M. WHAT KIND OF COLLEGE IS BEST? New York: John Day, 1932. 78 p.

Journalist's introduction to colleges and college life for high school students and their parents.

2736 Stecklein, John E. HOW TO MEASURE FACULTY WORK LOAD. Washington, D.C.: American Council on Education, 1961. 51 p.

Procedures for making a comprehensive analysis of faculty work load.

2737 Stecklein, John E., and Lathrop, Robert L. FACULTY ATTRACTION AND RETENTION: FACTORS AFFECTING FACULTY MOBILITY AT THE UNIVERSITY OF MINNESOTA. Minneapolis: Bureau of Institutional Research, University of Minnesota, 1960. 130 p.

Data from faculty recently appointed to the University of Minnesota, faculty who considered moving to Minnesota but decided against it, Minnesota faculty who accepted jobs elsewhere, and others who rejected job offers in order to remain at Minnesota.

2738 Stegner, Wallace Earle. FIRE AND ICE. New York: Duell, Sloan and Pearce, 1941. 214 p.

Novel about a Depression-poor leftist college youth who flirts with, then rejects communism.

2739 Steiger, JoAnn M. PROBLEMS IN ASSESSING THE IMPACT OF EDUCA-
TION DIVISION PROGRAMS ON GIRLS AND WOMEN. Washington,
D.C.: National Advisory Council on Women's Education Programs, 1978.
14 p.

> Study revealed that the education division of the U.S. Depart-
> ment of Health, Education and Welfare did not know and had
> no way to assess the impact of its program on women.

2740 Stein, Morris Isaac. PERSONALITY MEASURES IN ADMISSION: ANTE-
CEDENT AND PERSONALITY FACTORS AS PREDICTORS OF COLLEGE
SUCCESS. New York: College Entrance Examination Board, 1963. 69 p.

> Reviews four major approaches developed during 1950-60 for
> research into the relationship between college success and such
> factors as personality.

2741 Stein, Morris Isaac, and Heinze, Shirley J. CREATIVITY AND THE IN-
DIVIDUAL. SUMMARIES OF SELECTED LITERATURE IN PSYCHOLOGY
AND PSYCHIATRY. A MCKINSEY FOUNDATION ANNOTATED BIBLIO-
GRAPHY. New York: Free Press of Glencoe, 1960. 428 p.

> Annotated bibliography of over three hundred books and articles
> on the creative processes of engineers, social scientists, bio-
> logical and physical scientists, and others.

2742 Steiner, Bernard C. LIFE OF HENRY BARNARD. Washington, D.C.:
Government Printing Office, 1919. 131 p.

> Barnard (1811-1900), who as assemblyman introduced the bill
> creating the Connecticut state board of common schools (1837),
> was principal of Connecticut state normal school and Connecti-
> cut state superintendent of schools (1850-54); chancellor, Uni-
> versity of Wisconsin (1857-59); president, St. John's College
> (1865-66); first U.S. Commissioner of Education (1867-70);
> and founder and editor (1855-82) of the important AMERICAN
> JOURNAL OF EDUCATION.

2743 Steiner, Gilbert Yale, and Ponleithner, Romayne R., eds. PUBLIC HIGH-
ER EDUCATION IN ILLINOIS: ITS SCOPE AND FUNCTION TO 1975.
Springfield, Ill.: Joint Council on Higher Education, 1961. 198 p.

> On the Illinois master plan for higher education. Factors in-
> fluencing its implementation included state politics, economic
> development, and tradition.

2744 Stephens, Frank F. A HISTORY OF THE UNIVERSITY OF MISSOURI.
Columbia: University of Missouri Press, 1962. 661 p.

> History of the University of Missouri, 1839-1955, by a dean
> emeritus.

2745 Stern, George G. PEOPLE IN CONTEXT: MEASURING PERSON-ENVIRONMENT CONGRUENCE IN EDUCATION AND INDUSTRY. New York: John Wiley and Sons, 1970. 402 p.

Found that colleges differ systematically in the kinds of students they attract and that institutions are perceived quite differently by students who attend them.

2746 Sterne, Emma Gelders. MARY MCLEOD BETHUNE. New York: Alfred A. Knopf, 1957. 268 p.

Biography, for younger readers, of Bethune (1875-1955), black teacher who in 1904 founded Daytona (Florida) Normal and Industrial School for Negro Girls, which later merged to become coeducational Bethune-Cookman College, with Bethune as president.

2747 Stevens, David H. THE CHANGING HUMANITIES: AN APPRAISAL OF OLD VALUES AND NEW USES. New York: Harper and Brothers, 1953. 272 p.

A general look at the humanities in U.S. colleges and universities.

2748 Stevens, George E., and Webster, John B. LAW AND THE STUDENT PRESS. Ames: Iowa State University Press, 1973. 158 p.

Cases and legal decisions (mainly since the early 1960s) involving the student press—high school, college, and underground. Legal tips for those involved with student publications.

2749 Stevens, Walter James. CHIP ON MY SHOULDER. Boston: Meador Publishing Co., 1946. 315 p.

Autobiography of a black Harvard graduate, an opponent of segregation who disagreed with Booker T. Washington's advocacy of segregated industrial education.

2750 Stewart, Clifford T., and Harvey, Thomas R., eds. STRATEGIES FOR SIGNIFICANT SURVIVAL. San Francisco: Jossey-Bass Publishers, 1975. 101 p.

About using new programs, better teaching, organizational development, and institutional self-study to assure that higher education institutions survive.

2751 Stewart, David C., ed. FILM STUDY IN HIGHER EDUCATION: REPORT OF A CONFERENCE SPONSORED BY DARTMOUTH COLLEGE IN ASSOCIATION WITH THE AMERICAN COUNCIL ON EDUCATION. Washington, D.C.: American Council on Education, 1966. 174 p.

About five representative college courses in motion picture appreciation. Three critics attacked the courses from different angles. Included are lists of film distributors, archives, libraries, and film societies.

2752 Stewart, George Rippey. DOCTOR'S ORAL. New York: Random House, 1939. 259 p.

Novel about the day of a candidate's final oral Ph.D. examination; on the results hangs his new junior college teaching job and anticipated marriage.

2753 Stewart, Helen Quien. SOME SOCIAL ASPECTS OF RESIDENCE HALLS FOR COLLEGE WOMEN. New York: Professional and Technical Press, 1942. 188 p.

About the practice of democratic living in supervised women's college dormitories.

2754 Stewart, Robert Bruce, and Lyon, Roy. DEBT FINANCING OF PLANT ADDITIONS FOR STATE COLLEGES AND UNIVERSITIES. West Lafayette, Ind.: Purdue Research Foundation, 1948. 271 p.

Study done for the Central Association of University and College Business Officers using data from about one hundred state institutions. Includes a history of bond issues of higher education institutions.

2755 Stickler, William Hugh, ed. EXPERIMENTAL COLLEGES; THEIR ROLE IN AMERICAN HIGHER EDUCATION. Tallahassee: Florida State University, 1964. 185 p.

Papers on the role of U.S. experimental colleges and on specific experiments at ten colleges and universities.

2756 _____. ORGANIZATION AND ADMINISTRATION OF GENERAL EDUCATION. Dubuque, Iowa: William C. Brown Co., 1951. 431 p.

Reports on various practices and organizations of general education programs at twenty-two colleges and universities.

2757 Stickney, Patricia J., and Resnick, Rosa Perla, eds. WORLD GUIDE TO SOCIAL WORK EDUCATION. New York: International Association of Schools of Social Work, 1974. 297 p.

Directory of basic information on seventy-nine schools of social work and twenty-two national and regional associations of schools of social work in sixty-five countries, including the United States.

2758 Stiles, Lindley J. INTRODUCTION TO COLLEGE: EDUCATION. New York: G.P. Putnam's Sons, 1969. 192 p.

> Aid to students on planning educational choices in college: courses, majors, and careers.

2759 Stilwell, Hart. CAMPUS TOWN. Garden City, N.Y.: Doubleday, Doran and Co., 1950. 273 p.

> Novel about a youth at a southern state college after World War I and his encounters with the Ku Klux Klan and labor unions.

2760 Stimpson, Catharine R., ed. DISCRIMINATION AGAINST WOMEN: CONGRESSIONAL HEARINGS ON EQUAL RIGHTS IN EDUCATION AND EMPLOYMENT. New York: R.R. Bowker Co., 1973. 558 p.

> Edited text of the 1970 congressional hearings on equal rights in employment and education, including higher education. Includes comments and data on sex discrimination, with comparisons of the earning power and education of women today with women in the 1930s and 1950s.

2761 _____. WOMEN AND THE "EQUAL RIGHTS" AMENDMENT: SENATE SUBCOMMITTEE HEARINGS ON THE CONSTITUTIONAL AMENDMENT, 91ST CONGRESS. New York: R.R. Bowker Co., 1972. 538 p.

> Much on women's higher education in several studies included and in some testimony given.

2762 Stock, Phyllis. BETTER THAN RUBIES: A HISTORY OF WOMEN'S EDUCATION. New York: G.P. Putnam's Sons, 1978. 252 p.

> History of women's education in England, France, Germany, Italy, and the United States, with over one hundred pages on twentieth century progress in U.S. higher education for women.

2763 Stoddard, George Dinsmore. FERMENT IN EDUCATION. Urbana: University of Illinois Press, 1948. 224 p.

> Addresses at University of Illinois President Stoddard's inauguration, include talks by Stoddard (social studies is the university's new controversial frontier), Robert M. Hutchins (Americans do not take education seriously), Archibald MacLeish (the teacher is responsible for the future of society), James B. Conant (an educational system must find and develop talent), General Omar Bradley (nation's first defense is in the minds of its people), and others.

2764 _____. KREBIOZEN: THE GREAT CANCER MYSTERY. Boston: Beacon Press, 1955. 282 p.

Former President Stoddard describes the University of Illinois medical center's involvement in the controversial Krebiozen cancer drug which led to his resignation.

2765 _____. ON THE EDUCATION OF WOMEN. New York: Macmillan Co., 1950. 101 p.

Chapters on sex differences in education, women's attitudes toward college, and a curriculum suited to women. Final chapter asks: "Can Women's Education Save Us?"

2766 _____. THE OUTLOOK FOR AMERICAN EDUCATION. Carbondale: Southern Illinois University Press, 1974. 276 p.

Thoughts of experienced university president include internal reforms needed in higher education, nature of the liberal arts, and the education of women.

2767 Stoke, Harold W. VIEWPOINTS FOR THE STUDY OF THE ADMINISTRA- TION OF HIGHER EDUCATION. Eugene: University of Oregon Press, 1966. 40 p.

Theoretical exploration of external influences on university ad- ministration.

2768 Stone, Irving, ed. THERE WAS LIGHT: AUTOBIOGRAPHY OF A UNI- VERSITY, BERKELEY: 1868-1968. Garden City, N.Y.: Doubleday and Co., 1970. 454 p.

Economist John K. Galbraith, chemist Glenn T. Seaborg, car- toonist Rube Goldberg, and educator John W. Gardner are among the thirty-one alumni who tell what attendance at the University of California, Berkeley, meant in their lives and work.

2769 Stone, Isidore F. THE KILLINGS AT KENT STATE: HOW MURDER WENT UNPUNISHED. New York: Vintage Books, 1971. 158 p.

Partisan antinational guard view holds that they should not have been on the Kent State campus, had no self-defense cause to kill students, and that Ohio politicians illegally con- spired to justify the action.

2770 Stone, James Champion. BREAKTHROUGH IN TEACHER EDUCATION. San Francisco: Jossey-Bass Publishers, 1968. 206 p.

Report on forty-three teacher education programs supported by the Ford Foundation; shows trend toward graduate preparation and cooperation among universities and within university depart- ments.

2771 _____. TEACHERS FOR THE DISADVANTAGED. San Francisco: Jossey-Bass Publishers, 1969. 274 p.

> Describes twenty-five programs which prepare teachers of minority students; interviews with professors involved and analysis of effective teaching techniques.

2772 Stone, James Champion, and DeNevi, Donald P., eds. PORTRAITS OF THE AMERICAN UNIVERSITY, 1890-1910. San Francisco: Jossey-Bass Publishers, 1971. 380 p.

> Articles about higher education at the turn of the century when it took on its unique form: graduate schools, science and technology, electives, women and student activism, and strong university presidents. Illustrated with contemporary photos and woodcuts.

2773 Stone, Lawrence, ed. THE UNIVERSITY IN SOCIETY. 2 vols. Princeton, N.J.: Princeton University Press, 1974. 642 p.

> Volume one, articles on Oxford and Cambridge Universities. Volume two, articles on European, Scottish, and U.S. universities: their purposes and nature, student life and concerns, and faculty views of scholarship and research.

2774 Storr, Richard J. THE BEGINNINGS OF GRADUATE EDUCATION IN AMERICA. Chicago: University of Chicago Press, 1953. Reprint. New York: Arno Press, 1969. 195 p.

> Early graduate education before the Civil War, German influence, expansion of higher learning, traditions of graduate education.

2775 _____. HARPER'S UNIVERSITY: THE BEGINNINGS, A HISTORY OF THE UNIVERSITY OF CHICAGO. Chicago: University of Chicago Press, 1966. 411 p.

> From its inception in 1890 to first President William Rainey Harper's death in 1905. Difficulties of creating a new great university in the then culturally barren west and on the bankruptcy of an earlier university; Harper's hiring negotiations for a powerful faculty, his relations with donor John D. Rockefeller and such early professors as John Dewey and Amos Alonzo Stagg.

2776 Straker, Robert Lincoln. HORACE MANN AND OTHERS: CHAPTERS FROM THE HISTORY OF ANTIOCH COLLEGE. Yellow Springs, Ohio: Antioch Press, 1963. 106 p.

> Essays on Antioch College founders Alpheus M. Merrifield and William Mills; presidents Horace Mann, Thomas Hill, and Austin Craig; professors Ada Shepard, Henry C. Badger, and G. Stanley Hall; and trustee Edward Everett Hale.

2777 Strang, Ruth. BEHAVIOR AND BACKGROUND OF STUDENTS IN COL-
LEGE AND SECONDARY SCHOOL. New York: Harper and Brothers,
1937. 515 p.

On student personnel theory and practice; work of college student counselors.

2778 _____. COUNSELING TECHNICS IN COLLEGE AND SECONDARY
SCHOOL. New York: Harper and Brothers, 1949. 302 p.

Student counseling techniques, especially the controversy
between directive and nondirective counseling.

2779 _____. PERSONNEL DEVELOPMENT AND GUIDANCE IN COLLEGE
AND SECONDARY SCHOOLS. New York: Harper and Brothers, 1934.
341 p.

Guidance and counseling of college students.

2780 Stratemeyer, Florence, and Lindsey, Margaret. WORKING WITH STU-
DENT TEACHERS. New York: Teachers College, Columbia University,
1958. 502 p.

On guiding student teachers in their teacher education programs
and through their laboratory and other experiences.

2781 Stratford, William D. SOME RESTRICTIONS AND LIMITATIONS TO THE
FREE INTERSTATE MOVEMENT OF TEACHERS. Contributions to Education
No. 851. New York: Teachers College, Columbia University, 1942.
248 p.

Surveys state certification variations for teachers and differing
standards in their higher education preparation that limit employment mobility in various states.

2782 Stratton, Dorothy C. PROBLEMS OF STUDENTS IN A GRADUATE SCHOOL
OF EDUCATION. Contributions to Education No. 550. New York:
Teachers College, Columbia University, 1933. 167 p.

Teachers College, Columbia University, graduate students' personal problems included finance, part-time work, use of time,
living conditions, and job placement; academic problems included courses, degree completion, and advisement.

2783 Stratton, Julius A. SCIENCE AND THE EDUCATED MAN: SELECTED
SPEECHES OF JULIUS A. STRATTON. Cambridge, Mass.: MIT Press,
1966. 186 p.

Professor and president of Massachusetts Institute of Technology
on kind and degree of science needed in undergraduate education by engineers and physicists, as well as by the non-scientist.

2784 Stribling, Thomas Sigismund. THESE BARS OF FLESH. Garden City, N.Y.: Doubleday, Doran and Co., 1938. 344 p.

Novel about a middle-aged southern politician attending a summer session at a northern university.

2785 Strietelmeier, John. VALPARAISO'S FIRST CENTURY: A CENTENNIAL HISTORY OF VALPARAISO UNIVERSITY. Valparaiso, Ind.: Valparaiso University, 1959. 191 p.

Valparaiso University began as a Methodist Episcopal Church academy, had many finance drives to survive, made strenuous efforts toward accreditation and finally grew progressively stronger under Lutheran leadership into respected university status.

2786 Stroup, Herbert. BUREAUCRACY IN HIGHER EDUCATION. New York: Free Press, 1966. 242 p.

On the inevitability of public university administrative bureaucracy because of having to conform to state regulations.

2787 _____. TOWARD A PHILOSOPHY OF ORGANIZED STUDENT ACTIVITIES. Minneapolis: University of Minnesota Press, 1964. 202 p.

How student activities, given the proper objectives and means of realizing them, can contribute to the college educational process.

2788 Stroup, Thomas B., ed. THE UNIVERSITY IN THE AMERICAN FUTURE. Lexington: University of Kentucky Press, 1966. 111 p.

Kenneth D. Benne on the idea of a university and other speeches on similar themes by Henry Steele Commager and Gunnar Myrdal given at the University of Kentucky's centennial celebration.

2789 Strout, Cushing, and Grossvogel, David I., eds. DIVIDED WE STAND: REFLECTIONS ON THE CRISIS AT CORNELL. Garden City, N.Y.: Doubleday and Co., 1970. 204 p.

Faculty and student essays on Cornell's 1969 campus unrest.

2790 STUDIES IN LUTHERAN HIGHER EDUCATION: THE REPORT OF A COMMITTEE REPRESENTING THE HIGHER EDUCATIONAL INSTITUTIONS OF THE AMERICAN LUTHERAN CONFERENCE. Minneapolis, Minn.: Augsburg Publishing House, 1933. 79 p.

Study of twenty American Lutheran higher education institutions. Analyzes objectives, curriculum, faculty, admissions, testing, and other aspects of Lutheran higher education in our society.

2791 STUDY BASED UPON EXAMINATION OF TAX-SUPPORTED NORMAL SCHOOLS IN THE STATE OF MISSOURI. New York: Carnegie Foundation for the Study of Education, 1920. 475 p.

> Reviews history and purpose of U.S. normal schools. Analyzes Missouri normal schools--their administration, personnel, curricula, and operations. Proposes improvements.

2792 Study Commission on Pharmacy. PHARMACISTS FOR THE FUTURE. Ann Arbor: University of Michigan, 1976. 161 p.

> American Association of Colleges of Pharmacy study discusses pharmacy and the public interest, the pharmacy school curriculum, and the accreditation process for pharmacy schools.

2793 Study Commission on Undergraduate Education and the Education of Teachers. TEACHER EDUCATION IN THE UNITED STATES: THE RESPONSIBILITY GAP: A REPORT. Lincoln: University of Nebraska Press, 1976. 224 p.

> The future of teacher education, with chapters on such topics as licensing and accreditation, information-gathering on teacher education, and recommendations.

2794 STUDY OF THE STATUS OF WOMEN FACULTY AT INDIANA UNIVERSITY, BLOOMINGTON CAMPUS. Bloomington: Indiana University, 1971. 55 p.

> Report on average time men and women were in rank (instructor, assistant, and associate professor) before being recommended by their department for promotion.

2795 Sturtevant, Sarah Martha, and Strang, Ruth. A PERSONNEL STUDY OF DEANS OF WOMEN IN TEACHERS COLLEGES AND NORMAL SCHOOLS. Contributions to Education No. 319. New York: Teachers College, Columbia University, 1928. 95 p.

> History of position of dean of women, their training, relations with staff, social relationships, salaries, teaching duties, committee work, and record keeping. Case studies of deans of women at two teachers colleges.

2796 Sturtevant, Sarah Martha, et al. TRENDS IN STUDENT PERSONNEL WORK AS REPRESENTED IN THE POSITIONS OF DEAN OF WOMEN AND DEAN OF GIRLS IN COLLEGES AND UNIVERSITIES. New York: Teachers College, Columbia University, 1940. Reprint. New York: AMS Press, 1972. 95 p.

> Comprehensive view of deans of women's work. Among findings: 77 percent of public teacher training institutions had deans of women; 76 percent of deans also taught; few deans helped with curriculum planning; over 75 percent supervised extracurricular

activities; and 41 percent had master's degrees.

2797 Sturtevant, Sarah Martha, and Hayes, Harriet, eds. DEANS AT WORK: DISCUSSIONS BY EIGHT WOMEN DEANS ON VARIOUS PHASES OF THEIR WORK. New York: Harper and Brothers, 1930. 295 p.

Professional activities of eight women deans in secondary and teacher training institutions, women's colleges, and universities.

2798 SUBJECT DIRECTORY OF SPECIAL LIBRARIES AND INFORMATION CENTERS. Edited by Margaret L. Young, et al. Vol. 2. Detroit: Gale Research Co., 1977. 149 p.

Descriptions of holdings and special collections of education and information science university libraries; includes audiovisual, picture, publishing, rare book, and recreational libraries. Second of five volumes.

2799 Suchar, Elizabeth W., et al. STUDENT EXPENSES AT POSTSECONDARY INSTITUTIONS 1978-1979. Princeton, N.J.: College Board Publications, 1978. 83 p.

Lists student expenses (tuition, room and board, and commuter costs) at twenty-eight hundred two-year and four-year postsecondary institutions. Includes regional variations.

2800 Suczek, Robert F. THE BEST LAID PLANS: A STUDY OF STUDENT DEVELOPMENT IN AN EXPERIMENTAL COLLEGE PROGRAM. San Francisco: Jossey-Bass Publishers, 1972. 177 p.

Unsuccessful experimental freshman and sophomore program begun in 1965 at the University of California, Berkeley, and research which tried to compare personality development of experimental students with that of regular students. Reasons for the experiment's failure echoed similar attempts at other universities.

2801 Sugg, Redding S., Jr. MOTHERTEACHER: THE FEMINIZATION OF AMERICAN EDUCATION. Charlottesville: University Press of Virginia, 1979. 282 p.

Argues that replacing men with women teachers in the schools has subverted academic authority and intellectualism and promoted self-expression in children.

2802 Sugg, Redding S., Jr., and Jones, George Hilton. THE SOUTHERN REGIONAL EDUCATION BCARD: TEN YEARS OF REGIONAL COOPERATION IN HIGHER EDUCATION. Baton Rouge: Louisiana State University Press, 1960. 179 p.

On origins and development of regional cooperation to benefit higher education in sixteen southern states. Created in 1949 by the Southern Governors' Conference, the Southern Regional Education Board aided education for such professions as medicine, dentistry, veterinary science, and social work by omitting out-of-state fees. Explains operations of the Board and reviews similar efforts in the West and New England.

2803 Sukoff, Albert, and Fink, Ira Stephen. LIVING ON-CAMPUS/LIVING OFF-CAMPUS: CHANGES IN STUDENT HOUSING PATTERNS. Berkeley: University of California, Physical Planning, 1977. 477 p.

Describes forms of student housing on the nine campuses of the University of California and explains changes in student housing patterns during 1965-74.

2804 Sulkin, Sidney. COMPLETE PLANNING FOR COLLEGE. New York: Harper and Row, 1968. 324 p.

On choosing a college and preparing for college entrance. Includes lists of colleges and information sources about testing, financial aid, and other matters.

2805 Summerscales, William. AFFIRMATION AND DISSENT: COLUMBIA'S RESPONSE TO THE CRISIS OF WORLD WAR I. New York: Teachers College Press, 1970. 159 p.

About governance problems at Columbia University during World War I. Includes tensions over academic freedom and focuses on dismissal of professor James McKeen Cattell (1860-1944) for a letter he wrote protesting sending conscientious objectors into combat.

2806 Sunko, Theodore S., and Eulenberg, Milton D. ARITHMETIC: A COLLEGE APPROACH. New York: John Wiley and Sons, 1966. 225 p.

A remedial mathematics textbook for college students and the general public.

2807 Sutherland, Robert L. STUDENTS AND STAFF IN A SOCIAL CONTEXT. Washington, D.C.: American Council on Education, 1953. 34 p.

Urges putting the college extracurricular program under student personnel staff direction. Asserts that extracurricular involvement promotes student growth.

2808 Sutton, Albert Alton. EDUCATION FOR JOURNALISM IN THE UNITED STATES FROM ITS BEGINNING TO 1940. Evanston, Ill.: Northwestern University, 1945. 148 p.

Guide to higher education journalism instruction. Includes

organization, curriculum, degree requirements, placement of graduates, and history, 1869–1940.

2809 Swanson, Clifford J. THE IN-BETWEEN YEARS: LOOKING AT THE COLLEGE EXPERIENCE. Minneapolis, Minn.: Augsburg Publishing House, 1967. 79 p.

Problems of college students are discussed from a Christian viewpoint by a clergyman in a church-related college.

2810 Sweet, Samuel Niles. TEACHERS' INSTITUTES, OR, TEMPORARY NOR-MAL SCHOOLS, THEIR ORIGIN AND PROGRESS. Utica, N.Y.: Hawley, 1848. 139 p.

An early account of teacher education. Tells origins of teachers' institutes, agenda followed, and typical practical hints given teachers.

2811 Swift, Richard N. WORLD AFFAIRS AND THE COLLEGE CURRICULUM. Washington, D.C.: American Council on Education, 1959. 194 p.

Considers specific college courses and programs dealing with world affairs.

2812 Taft, John. MAYDAY AT YALE. Boulder, Colo.: Westview Press, 1976. 224 p.

Case study in student radicalism at Yale in 1970 in the wake of a Black Panther murder and the New Haven Nine trial. Author cites radical irrationality, sympathetic faculty, and administrators' poor judgment as major causes of the chaos.

2813 Talbot, Marion, and Rosenberry, Lois Kimball Mathews. THE HISTORY OF THE AMERICAN ASSOCIATION OF UNIVERSITY WOMEN, 1881-1931. Boston: Houghton Mifflin Co., 1931. 479 p.

Early history by a founder, Marion Talbot, of AAUW, an organization of women college and university graduates, which works to expand opportunities for women's education through research, scholarships, national institutional and international exchanges, and adult education.

2814 Tamara, Martha, et al., eds. WOMEN AND ACHIEVEMENT, SOCIAL AND MOTIVATIONAL ANALYSES. Washington, D.C.: Hemisphere Publishing Corp., 1975. 447 p.

Among essay topics are women as new students, a profile of the woman Ph.D., and higher education sex discrimination.

2815 Tamkus, Daniel. THE MUCH HONORED MAN. Garden City, N.Y.: Doubleday and Co., 1959. 214 p.

Novel in the form of a letter from a physics professor to his prospective son-in-law.

2816 Tannenbaum, Frank, ed. A COMMUNITY OF SCHOLARS: THE UNIVERSITY SEMINARS AT COLUMBIA. New York: Praeger Publishers, 1965. 177 p.

On Columbia University's cross-disciplinary seminars begun in 1945 as an informal monthly dialog among scholars from diverse fields and institutions. Essays by Daniel Bell, Paul Goodman, Margaret Mead, Gilbert Seldes, and others.

2817 Tanner, Leslie B., ed. VOICES FROM WOMEN'S LIBERATION. New York: New American Library, 1970. 443 p.

Articles on women in medical and scientific fields.

2818 Tappan, Henry P. UNIVERSITY EDUCATION. New York: G.P. Putnam, 1851. Reprint. New York: Arno Press, 1969. 120 p.

First president (1852-63) of the University of Michigan called for U.S. universities to follow the German model of university scientific scholarship and freedom of inquiry.

2819 TASK FORCE ON HIGHER EDUCATION: REPORT ON HIGHER EDUCATION. Washington, D.C.: Government Printing Office, 1971. 130 p.

Calls for funding of more such innovations as off-campus education and use of television to break the lock-step college attendance pattern. Also favors increasing autonomy for individual campuses and other changes.

2820 Tate, Gary, and Corbett, Edward P.J., eds. TEACHING FRESHMAN COMPOSITION. New York: Oxford University Press, 1967. 361 p.

Thirty teachers' views on teaching freshman composition.

2821 Tauber, Maurice Falcolm, et al. THE COLUMBIA UNIVERSITY LIBRARIES. New York: Columbia University Press, 1958. 320 p.

In-depth study of Columbia's library system, based on questionnaires and other data from library staff, faculties, and students. Part of an institution-wide self-study.

2822 Taubman, Paul, and Wales, Terence. HIGHER EDUCATION AND EARNINGS: COLLEGE AS AN INVESTMENT AND A SCREENING DEVICE. New York: McGraw-Hill Book Co., 1974. 302 p.

Report on education as a factor in human capital. Among findings: hiring often results from screening devices used rather than education per se, and an undergraduate degree raised earnings thirty-one percent. Authors conclude that there has been an overinvestment in education.

2823 Taylor, Alton L., ed. PROTECTING INDIVIDUAL RIGHTS TO PRIVACY IN HIGHER EDUCATION. San Francisco: Jossey-Bass Publishers, 1977. 82 p.

Advice to administrators, researchers, and data system directors on safeguarding the privacy of students and staff.

2824 Taylor, Calvin W., and Barron, Frank, eds. SCIENTIFIC CREATIVITY: ITS RECOGNITION AND DEVELOPMENT. New York: John Wiley and Sons, 1963. 419 p.

Papers at the first three University of Utah national conferences on creativity.

2825 Taylor, Emily, and Shavlik, Donna. INSTITUTIONAL SELF-EVALUATION: THE TITLE IX REQUIREMENT. Washington, D.C.: American Council on Education, 1976. 43 p.

General procedure to be followed in complying with the sex discrimination regulation, issued by the American Council on Education's Office of Women in Higher Education.

2826 Taylor, Ervin J., ed. FACT BOOK ON THEOLOGICAL EDUCATION, 1971-72. Dayton, Ohio: American Association of Theological Schools, 1972. 86 p.

Facts about theological schools belonging to the association: enrollment trends, distribution of minority students, finance, denominational affiliations, library holdings, and faculty and administrators' numbers and salaries.

2827 Taylor, Harold. HOW TO CHANGE COLLEGES. New York: Holt, Rinehart and Winston, 1971. 180 p.

States that college education reforms are dependent upon the actions of strong administrators.

2828 _____. ON EDUCATION AND FREEDOM. New York: Abelard-Schuman Press, 1953. 320 p.

Sarah Lawrence College president on moral values, the arts, humanities, college president's role, and women's education.

2829 _____. STUDENTS WITHOUT TEACHERS: THE CRISIS IN THE UNIVERSITY. New York: McGraw-Hill Book Co., 1969. 333 p.

Blames university bureaucracy for neglecting students and forcing

them to turn to other students for intellectual and moral leadership. He would return the university to its concept of service,
and return the student to the center of educational effort.

2830 _____. THE WORLD AS TEACHER. Carbondale: Southern Illinois University Press, 1974. 398 p.

Taylor wants teachers professionally prepared to think globally
and to be alert to the ways their country is involved in world
society.

2831 _____, ed. ESSAYS IN TEACHING. New York: Harper and Brothers,
1950. 239 p.

Emphasizes the creative, stimulating, and provocative elements
of the liberal arts curriculum.

2832 Taylor, James Monroe. BEFORE VASSAR OPENED: A CONTRIBUTION
TO THE HISTORY OF THE HIGHER EDUCATION OF WOMEN IN AMERI-
CA. Boston: Houghton Mifflin, 1914. Reprint. New York: Books for
Libraries, 1972. 287 p.

Early history of higher education for women leading to the plan
of Matthew Vassar and the opening of Vassar College in 1865.

2833 Taylor, James Monroe, and Haight, Elizabeth H. VASSAR. New York:
Oxford University Press, 1915. 232 p.

History of Vassar College, Poughkeepsie, New York.

2834 Taylor, Robert Lewis. PROFESSOR FODORSKI. Garden City, N.Y.:
Doubleday, Doran and Co., 1950. 250 p.

Satirical novel about a European refugee engineer at a southern college campus and his interest in football.

2835 Taylor, Robert N., Jr. THIS DAMNED CAMPUS: AS SEEN BY A COL-
LEGE CHAPLAIN. Phillipsburg, N.J.: Pilgrim Press, 1969. 130 p.

College chaplain would reinstate basic religious ethics as answer to the secularization of the culture, depersonalization,
the generation gap, and other manifestations of the 1960s student revolt.

2836 TEACHING METHODS AND FACULTY UTILIZATION: A PRELIMINARY
INQUIRY. White Plains, N.Y.: Nelson Associates, 1961.

Assesses studies of college teaching; has recommendations for
future studies.

2837 Tead, Ordway. CHARACTER BUILDING AND HIGHER EDUCATION. New York: Macmillan Co., 1953. 129 p.

> Urges that higher education teach moral values and the sanctity of life but avoid sectarian divisiveness.

2838 _____. THE CLIMATE OF LEARNING: A CONSTRUCTIVE ATTACK ON COMPLACENCY IN HIGHER EDUCATION. New York: Harper and Row, 1958. 62 p.

> Examination of current attitudes and trends in higher education. Among goals mentioned are emphasizing the higher educational program as central and extraclass activities as peripheral, and preparing students for full participation in a workable world community.

2839 _____. COLLEGE TEACHING AND COLLEGE LEARNING. New Haven, Conn.: Yale University Press, 1949. 56 p.

> On the roles of the college teacher and student, the nature of learning, and the importance of education in helping one become a whole person and preparing one for a life of action.

2840 _____. TRUSTEES, TEACHERS, STUDENTS: THEIR ROLE IN HIGHER EDUCATION. Salt Lake City: University of Utah Press, 1951. 120 p.

> Five papers on administrative methods and educational objectives with special relevance to trustees, teachers, and students.

2841 Templin, Lucinda de Leftwich. SOME DEFECTS AND MERITS IN THE EDUCATION OF WOMEN IN MISSOURI: AN ANALYSIS OF PAST AND PRESENT EDUCATIONAL METHODS AND A PROPOSAL FOR THE FUTURE. Columbia, Mo.: Privately printed, 1927. 256 p.

> Cultural and social history of women's education in Missouri and especially of women in junior colleges. Case studies of particular types of higher education serving women: Stephens College, Lindenwood College, The Principia, Washington University, Northeast Missouri State College, and the University of Missouri.

2842 _____. TWO ILLUSTRIOUS PIONEERS IN THE EDUCATION OF WOMEN IN MISSOURI. St. Charles, Mo.: Lindenwood College, 1926. 32 p.

> Story of George C. Sibley (1782-1863) and Mary Easton Sibley (1800-1878), founders of Lindenwood College for Women in Missouri.

2843 Tenenbaum, Samuel. WILLIAM HEARD KILPATRICK: TRAIL BLAZER IN EDUCATION. New York: Harper and Brothers, 1951. 318 p.

Georgia-born Kilpatrick (1871-1965) taught in public schools and at Mercer University, Georgia, and mainly at Teachers College, Columbia University (1909-38), where he originated the project method, popularized John Dewey's pragmatic philosophy, attracted thousands of students, wrote many books, and helped found Bennington College, of whose trustees he was president (1931-38).

2844 Terry, Marshall, Jr. OLD LIBERTY. New York: Viking Press, 1961. 186 p.

Novel of a Texas youth involved in a fraternity in a small Pennsylvania college.

2845 Terry, Paul W., and Lee, L. Tennent, eds. A STUDY OF STILLMAN INSTITUTE. University: University of Alabama, 1946. 304 p.

Analyzed major aspects of Stillman, a black junior college of the Southern Presbyterian Church, and offered a ten-year plan for improvement.

2846 Tewksbury, Donald G. THE FOUNDING OF AMERICAN COLLEGES AND UNIVERSITIES BEFORE THE CIVIL WAR: WITH PARTICULAR REFERENCE TO THE RELIGIOUS INFLUENCES BEARING UPON THE COLLEGE MOVEMENT. Contributions to Education No. 543. New York: Teachers College, Columbia University, 1932. Reprint. New York: Arno Press, 1969. 254 p.

Documents the important role churches played in founding U.S. colleges, the impact of the moving frontier on higher education, and the tensions between denominational colleges and state institutions as the latter gradually developed before the Civil War.

2847 Thackrey, Russell I. THE FUTURE OF THE STATE UNIVERSITY. Urbana: University of Illinois Press, 1971. 138 p.

History, growth, and contributions of land-grant institutions and other major state universities. Examines the impact on them of social pressures, enrollment decline, and federal involvement.

2848 Thain, Richard J. THE MANAGERS: CAREER ALTERNATIVES FOR THE COLLEGE EDUCATED. Bethlehem, Pa.: College Placement Council, 1978. 114 p.

Guidance details on more than two dozen management careers, including accounting, advertising, banking, industrial relations, marketing, personnel, and small business administration.

2849 Tharp, Louis Hall. UNTIL VICTORY: HORACE MANN AND MARY PEABODY. Boston: Little, Brown and Co., 1953. 367 p.

> Biography of Horace Mann (1796-1859), public education statesman, secretary of Massachusetts State Board of Education (1837-48), and first president of Antioch College (1853-59), which he led to distinction as a nonsectarian coeducational institution. Includes his wife Mary Peabody, who was a subject in Tharp's PEABODY SISTERS OF SALEM.

2850 Thelin, John R. THE CULTIVATION OF IVY: A SAGA OF THE COLLEGE IN AMERICA. Cambridge, Mass.: Schenkman Publishing Co., 1976. 81 p.

> How eight colleges came to be called the "Ivy League," and the development of their education ideals.

2851 Thirteen American Professors. ON GOING TO COLLEGE: A SYMPOSIUM. New York: Oxford University Press, 1938. 298 p.

> Informal essays by distinguished professors on their disciplines; addressed to entering freshmen. Authors include E.K. Rand, J.B. Munn, H.C. Lancaster, Wallace Notestein, R.M. MacIver, A.H. Compton, J.F. Dashiell, Irwin Edman, C.F. Wishart, H.A. Wichelns, Clarence Ward, R.D. Welch and C.B. Tinker.

2852 Thomas, Milton Halsey, ed. BIBLIOGRAPHY OF NICHOLAS MURRAY BUTLER, 1872-1932. New York: Columbia University Press, 1934. 438 p.

> Exhaustive bibliography (oldest entry written at age ten) of writings of Butler (1862-1947), who was professor and president of Columbia University (1885-1945).

2853 Thomas, Russell. THE SEARCH FOR A COMMON LEARNING: GENERAL EDUCATION, 1800-1960. New York: McGraw-Hill Book Co., 1962. 324 p.

> Evolution of general education and the forms in which it is practiced at eighteen representative colleges and universities.

2854 Thompson, Charles. HALFWAY DOWN THE STAIRS. New York: Harper and Brothers, 1957. 277 p.

> Novel's hero later regrets excesses of his Cornell years.

2855 Thompson, Daniel C. PRIVATE BLACK COLLEGES AT THE CROSSROADS. Westport, Conn.: Greenwood Press, 1973. 308 p.

> Sociology professor at southern black college describes problems and future of black colleges, their students, faculty, program, governance, and economic status. Recommendations for survival and growth include mergers, relocation, innovative curricula, and new funding sources.

2856 Thompson, Eleanor Wolf. EDUCATION FOR LADIES: 1830-1860. New York: King's Crown Press, 1947. 170 p.

> The role of women's magazines, 1830-60, in publicizing and urging women's education at all levels, including higher education.

2857 Thompson, Randall. COLLEGE MUSIC: AN INVESTIGATION FOR THE ASSOCIATION OF AMERICAN COLLEGES. New York: Macmillan Co., 1935. 279 p.

> Survey of music education, curriculum, and administration of programs at thirty liberal arts colleges.

2858 Thomson, Frances Coombs, ed. THE NEW YORK TIMES GUIDE TO CONTINUING EDUCATION IN AMERICA. New York: College Entrance Examination Board, 1973. 811 p.

> Lists variety of programs available for older students in 2,281 institutions of higher education; nationwide directory of adult education programs and institutions.

2859 Thorndike, Robert L., and Hagen, Elizabeth P. MEASUREMENT AND EVALUATION IN PSYCHOLOGY AND EDUCATION. 4th ed. New York: John Wiley and Sons, 1977. 693 p.

> Evaluation of tests and measurements used in educational and psychological studies.

2860 Thornton, James W., Jr. THE COMMUNITY JUNIOR COLLEGE. New York: John Wiley and Sons, 1960. 300 p.

> Graduate textbook on the community junior college, its history, organization, types, administration, curriculum, student personnel services, advantages, and problems.

2861 Thornton, James W., Jr., and Brown, James W., eds. NEW MEDIA AND COLLEGE TEACHING. Washington, D.C.: National Education Association, 1968. 184 p.

> Describes and evaluates new media aids in college teaching, including instructional television, films, listening laboratories, programmed instruction, computer-assisted instruction, telephone lectures to small and large groups, simulation systems, and others.

2862 Thorp, Margaret Farrand. NEILSON OF SMITH. New York: Oxford University Press, 1956. 363 p.

> William Allan Neilson (1869-1946), Scottish-born immigrant and Harvard student, English professor at Bryn Mawr (1898-1900), Columbia University (1904-06), and Harvard (1900-04,

1906-17); and longtime president of Smith College, Northampton, Massachusetts (1917-39).

2863 Thorp, Willard, ed. THE LIVES OF EIGHTEEN FROM PRINCETON. Princeton, N.J.: Princeton University Press, 1946. 356 p.

Lives and influence of eighteen Princeton alumni, teachers, and administrators who achieved distinction, including Samuel Kirkland, founder of Hamilton College; John Witherspoon, early Princeton president; Philip Lindsley, president of the University of Nashville; Woodrow Wilson, Princeton president and U.S. President; and F. Scott Fitzgerald, writer.

2864 Thorp, Willard, et al. THE PRINCETON GRADUATE SCHOOL: A HISTORY. Princeton, N.J.: Princeton University Bookstore, 1978. 230 p.

History of graduate education at Princeton from its origin as the College of New Jersey to the present.

2865 Thrasher, Max Bennett. TUSKEGEE, ITS STORY AND ITS WORK. 1900. Reprint. New York: Arno Press, 1977. 215 p.

History of Tuskegee Institute, Alabama, and the work of Booker T. Washington for black education, including higher education.

2866 Threlkeld, Hilda. THE EDUCATIONAL AND VOCATIONAL PLANS OF COLLEGE SENIORS IN RELATION TO THE CURRICULA AND THE GUIDANCE PROGRAM IN FORTY-FIVE PENNSYLVANIA COLLEGES. Contributions to Education No. 639. New York: Teachers College, Columbia University, 1935. 194 p.

Analysis of the educational and vocational plans of 4,246 Pennsylvania college and university seniors.

2867 Thresher, B. Alden. COLLEGE ADMISSIONS AND THE PUBLIC INTEREST. New York: College Entrance Examination Board, 1966. 93 p.

College admissions in theory and practice from the viewpoint of the student, the institution, and the public interest.

2868 Thwing, Charles Franklin. THE AMERICAN AND THE GERMAN UNIVERSITY: ONE HUNDRED YEARS OF HISTORY. New York: Macmillan Co., 1928. 238 p.

German university influence on U.S. higher education, U.S. students in German universities, and German teachers in U.S. universities.

2869 _____. THE AMERICAN COLLEGE AND UNIVERSITY. New York: Macmillan Co., 1935. 244 p.

462

Higher education president writes on college governance, faculty relations, academic freedom, alumni, and other university matters.

2870 _____. A HISTORY OF HIGHER EDUCATION IN AMERICA. New York: D. Appleton and Co., 1906. 501 p.

French, German, English, and Scottish influence on origins, growth, and maturation of Harvard, Yale, and William and Mary. Discussions on finance, women's colleges, and graduate and professional education.

2871 Timpane, Michael, ed. THE FEDERAL INTEREST IN FINANCING SCHOOLING. Cambridge, Mass.: Ballinger Publishing Co., 1979. 295 p.

Papers presented at Rand Corporation's symposium on educational finance and governance.

2872 Tittle, Carol K. STUDENT TEACHING: ATTITUDE AND RESEARCH BASES FOR CHANGE IN SCHOOL AND UNIVERSITY. Metuchen, N.J.: Scarecrow Press, 1974. 225 p.

Student teaching attitudes from the viewpoints of the student teacher, college supervisor, cooperating teacher, and school administrator.

2873 Tobias, Sheila. OVERCOMING MATH ANXIETY. New York: W.W. Norton and Co., 1978. 278 p.

Author believes sex bias is behind the myth that girls and women are less successful than men in understanding mathematics at all school levels, including higher education.

2874 Todd, James M. THE COLLEGE CONUNDRUM. New York: Round Table Press, 1935. 257 p.

Trustee of Beloit College asked the faculty how liberal arts college teaching could be improved.

2875 Tolley, William Pearson. THE ADVENTURE OF LEARNING. Syracuse, N.Y.: Syracuse University Press, 1977. 112 p.

Former Syracuse University chancellor discusses the importance of a liberal education to democracy, the consumer, and the technological sector. Stresses the humanizing value of great books.

2876 Tompkins, Phillip K., and Anderson, Elaine Vanden Bout. COMMUNICATION CRISIS AT KENT STATE: A CASE STUDY. New York: Gordon and Breach Science Publishers, 1971. 153 p.

Based on interviews; author contends that National Guard shooting of students at Kent State University in 1970 resulted from a lack of communication between students, faculty, and administration.

2877 Tonsor, Stephen. TRADITION AND REFORM IN EDUCATION. La Salle, Ill.: Open Court Publishing Co., 1974. 250 p.

Conservative historian's resolution of the 1960s college chaos is to change ways of funding and to restore the value of intellectual growth; particularly applicable to Catholic colleges which have never surrendered their essential values.

2878 Toole, K. Ross. THE TIME HAS COME. New York: William Morrow, 1971. 178 p.

University of Montana conservative history professor is critical of student protesters as irrational and praises the older generation (i.e., establishment) for its accomplishments.

2879 Toombs, William. PRODUCTIVITY AND THE ACADEMY: THE CURRENT CONDITION. University Park: Pennsylvania State University, 1972. 117 p.

Critical of traditional work load and similar quantitative measures of higher education faculty productivity as outmoded. Believes that higher education is a quality-intensive industry and that its faculty should be measured in quality, not quantity, of student output.

2880 Toppe, Christopher, and Brubaker, Paul. AN EVALUATION OF THE SMALL COLLEGE CONSORTIUM, 1977-78. Washington, D.C.: Systems Research, 1979. 266 p.

Study of the effects of the consortium on individual member colleges.

2881 Torrence, Ridgely. THE STORY OF JOHN HOPE. New York: Macmillan Co., 1948. 398 p.

Hope (1868-1936), son of a Scottish immigrant and black mother, attended Brown University (1894) and the University of Chicago (1897-1898), taught at various black colleges in the South, and became president of Atlanta University (1931).

2882 Touraine, Alain. THE ACADEMIC SYSTEM IN AMERICAN SOCIETY. New York: McGraw-Hill Book Co., 1974. 319 p.

French neo-Marxist sociologist sees U.S. higher education as captured by the ruling class, perpetuating class divisions, and as part of the established economic, military, and political order. Student protest of the 1960s was the first step in the overthrow of these shackles.

2883 Towle, Charlotte. THE LEARNER IN EDUCATION FOR THE PROFESSIONS AS SEEN IN EDUCATION FOR SOCIAL WORK. Chicago: University of Chicago Press, 1954. 432 p.

On professional education, its strengths and weaknesses, from the viewpoint of a prominent social work educator.

2884 Townsend, Agatha. COLLEGE FRESHMEN SPEAK OUT. New York: Harper and Brothers, 1956. 136 p.

Study of academic, personal, and social problems of 470 freshmen in twenty-seven colleges.

2885 Townsend, Marion E. THE ADMINISTRATION OF STUDENT PERSONNEL SERVICES IN TEACHER-TRAINING INSTITUTIONS OF THE UNITED STATES. Contributions to Education No. 536. New York: Teachers College, Columbia University, 1932. 115 p.

Evaluation of student personnel services in teacher training institutions and personnel workers' views of methods for improving such services.

2886 Trager, Robert, and Dickerson, Donna L. COLLEGE STUDENT PRESS LAW. Athens: National Council of College Publications Advisors, School of Journalism, Ohio University, 1977. 87 p.

Discusses the legal rights of the college student press. Examines pertinent court cases and decisions.

2887 Train, Arthur Cheney. THE WORLD AND THOMAS KELLY. New York: Charles Scribner's Sons, 1917. 434 p.

Novel whose college hero, although Boston-born, is initially excluded from Harvard clubs of the 1880s because he is poor.

2888 TRAINING AND DEVELOPMENT ORGANIZATIONS DIRECTORY. Edited by Paul Wasserman, and Marlene A. Palmer. Detroit: Gale Research Co., 1978. 614 p.

Describes institutions, including colleges and universities, that provide instruction for those interested in developing on-the-job managerial skills.

2889 Trautman, Ray. A HISTORY OF THE SCHOOL LIBRARY SERVICE, COLUMBIA UNIVERSITY. New York: Columbia University Press, 1954. 85 p.

History of the first U.S. library school, its founding by Melvil

Dewey in 1887 at Columbia, and its brief move in 1889 to Albany.

2890 Traxler, Arthur E., ed. INNOVATION AND EXPERIMENT IN MODERN EDUCATION. Washington, D.C.: American Council on Education, 1965. 159 p.

Papers on creativity, the gifted, linguistics, reading, and new developments in teaching and testing.

2891 _____. THE POSITIVE VALUES IN THE AMERICAN EDUCATIONAL SYSTEM. Washington, D.C.: American Council on Education, 1959. 152 p.

Papers on education at various levels, including higher education. Discussion on values stressed education's role in a free society.

2892 Treffinger, Donald J., et al., eds. HANDBOOK ON TEACHING EDUCATIONAL PSYCHOLOGY. New York: Academic Press, 1977. 384 p.

Survey of practices and problems of teaching educational psychology.

2893 Trent, James W., and Golds, Jenette. CATHOLICS IN COLLEGE: RELIGIOUS COMMITMENT AND THE INTELLECTUAL LIFE. Chicago: University of Chicago Press, 1967. 351 p.

Compares personalities and values of Catholic and non-Catholic students in Catholic and non-Catholic higher education; looks at cooperating clusters of small Catholic colleges.

2894 Trent, James W., and Medsker, Leland L. BEYOND HIGH SCHOOL: A PSYCHOSOCIOLOGICAL STUDY OF 10,000 HIGH SCHOOL GRADUATES. San Francisco: Jossey-Bass Publishers, 1968. 333 p.

Personal, vocational, and educational development and plans of high school graduates; useful for college counselors and administrators.

2895 Trillin, Calvin. AN EDUCATION IN GEORGIA: THE INTEGRATION OF CHARLAYNE HUNTER AND HAMILTON HOLMES. London: Victor Gollancz, 1964. 180 p.

How two remarkable black students defied white student-led rioting against them and became the first blacks at the University of Georgia.

2896 Trinkaus, Charles, ed. A GRADUATE PROGRAM IN AN UNDERGRADUATE COLLEGE: THE SARAH LAWRENCE EXPERIENCE. Middletown, Conn.: Wesleyan University Press, 1956. 119 p.

Critical analysis of the master's degree program begun in 1950 at Sarah Lawrence College emphasizing counseling and an individualized curriculum. Case histories of seven students. Discusses the role of liberal arts colleges in graduate education and deplores research-centered graduate study.

2897 Trites, Donald G., ed. PLANNING THE FUTURE OF THE UNDERGRADU-ATE COLLEGE. San Francisco: Jossey-Bass Publishers, 1975. 110 p.

Specialists examine undergraduate problems and offer suggestions on enrollment, curriculum, needs of women students, and finance.

2898 Trivett, David A. PROPRIETARY SCHOOLS AND POSTSECONDARY EDU-CATION. Washington, D.C.: American Association for Higher Education, 1974. 54 p.

Discusses the nature and problems of postsecondary proprietary schools (i.e., privately owned and operated mainly for profit), their accreditation and sometimes questionable recruiting practices.

2899 Troutt, Roy. SPECIAL DEGREE PROGRAMS FOR ADULTS. EXPLORING NONTRADITIONAL DEGREE PROGRAMS IN HIGHER EDUCATION. Iowa City: American College Testing Program, 1971. 69 p.

Background, kinds, advantages, and problems of U.S. nontraditional college and external degree programs for adults. Author, who pioneered in such a program at the University of Oklahoma, describes the Bachelor of Liberal Studies and Master of Liberal Studies offered there.

2900 Trow, Martin, ed. TEACHERS AND STUDENTS: ASPECTS OF AMERICAN HIGHER EDUCATION. New York: McGraw-Hill Book Co., 1975. 419 p.

Sociologists write on such higher education topics as faculty and student characteristics and attitudes, status of academic women, black students on campus, religious involvement, and scholarly productivity.

2901 Truax, Anne. RESEARCH ON THE STATUS OF FACULTY WOMEN, UNI-VERSITY OF MINNESOTA. Minneapolis: University of Minnesota, 1970. 15 p.

A comparison of ratio of male-female faculty, mean and median salary, and percentage differentials by rank, college, and term at the University of Minnesota.

2902 True, Alfred Charles. A HISTORY OF AGRICULTURAL EDUCATION IN THE UNITED STATES, 1785-1925. Washington, D.C.: Government Printing Office, 1929. Reprint. New York: Arno Press, 1969. 436 p.

History of agriculture education from eighteenth-century societies which promoted agriculture, to the 1862 Morrill Act, and the influence of the resulting land-grant colleges to 1925.

2903 Trueblood, Elton. THE IDEA OF A COLLEGE. New York: Harper and Brothers, 1959. 207 p.

Earlham College (Quaker) philosophy professor advocates Christian-centered liberal arts colleges.

2904 Truman, David B. THE SINGLE SEX COLLEGE--IN TRANSITION? South Hadley, Mass.: Mount Holyoke College, 1970. 10 p.

Says women's colleges help women build leadership qualities, while coeducational colleges put women in competition for and against men, thus forcing women into an identity crisis.

2905 Truman, Margaret. WOMEN OF COURAGE. New York: Bantam Books, 1977. 210 p.

Included among lives of twelve indomitable American women is English-born Elizabeth Blackwell, rejected by nearly a dozen U.S. medical schools before eventually succeeding in becoming the first U.S. woman doctor.

2906 Tryon, Ruth Wilson. THE AAUW, 1881-1949. Washington, D.C.: American Association of University Women, 1950. 52 p.

Origin, growth, research projects, and fellowship programs of the American Association of University Women.

2907 Trytten, Merriam Hartwick. STUDENT DEFERMENT IN SELECTIVE SERVICE. Minneapolis: University of Minnesota Press, 1952. 140 p.

Explains that student deferment from the military draft is in the best interests of effective manpower utilization.

2908 Tucker, Louis Leonard. PURITAN PROTAGONIST: PRESIDENT THOMAS CLAP OF YALE COLLEGE. Chapel Hill: University of North Carolina Press, 1962. 283 p.

Stern clergyman Clap (1703-67), who in 1739 became Yale rector (post renamed president, 1745). He served until 1766, when students protesting his autocratic policies demanded his ouster.

2909 Tuckman, Howard P. PUBLICATION, TEACHING, AND THE ACADEMIC REWARD STRUCTURE. Lexington, Mass.: Lexington Books, 1976. 122 p.

On ways such incentives as tenure, promotion, salary increases, self-satisfaction, and praise of colleagues affect faculty behavior and attitudes toward the profession.

2910 Tuckman, Howard P., and Ford, W. Scott. THE DEMAND FOR HIGHER EDUCATION: A FLORIDA CASE STUDY. Lexington, Mass.: Lexington Books, 1972. 125 p.

> To identify determinants of demand for higher education, authors applied formal economic theory to their findings on how high school seniors and junior college students made decisions about further education.

2911 Tunis, John R. CHOOSING A COLLEGE. New York: Harcourt, Brace and Co., 1940. 249 p.

> For high school students, gives information on college costs, scholarship availability, and the typical budget of an average freshman.

2912 Turabian, Kate L. STUDENT'S GUIDE FOR WRITING COLLEGE PAPERS. 3d ed. Chicago: University of Chicago Press, 1977. 272 p.

> Widely used standard guide; from choosing a topic to final draft of college papers, by editor for twenty-five years of University of Chicago publications and dissertations; equally famous for her A MANUAL FOR WRITERS OF TERM PAPERS, THESES, AND DISSERTATIONS, 1973.

2913 Turner, Cornelius P., ed. A GUIDE TO THE EVALUATION OF EDUCA-TIONAL EXPERIENCES IN THE ARMED SERVICES. Washington, D.C.: American Council on Education, 1968. 527 p.

> Describes all military educational programs with recommenda-tions for college credit by the American Council on Education's Commission on Accreditation of Service Experiences. Also des-cribes the General Educational Development tests and the Col-lege-Level Examination program, two national evaluations of adult educational achievement. Particularly useful for registrars and admissions officers.

2914 Turngren, Annette. CHOOSING THE RIGHT COLLEGE. New York: Har-per and Brothers, 1952. 149 p.

> Reviews financial and educational preparations needed for col-lege, the importance of accreditation, admission procedures, and advantages and disadvantages of various types of colleges.

2915 Turow, Scott. ONE L. New York: G.P. Putnam's Sons, 1977. 300 p.

> Personal experiences of a first-year law student at Harvard Law School; shows the power and role of the professors, in-tense loneliness and self-discipline, and student interactions.

2916 Tussman, Joseph. EXPERIMENT AT BERKELEY. New York: Oxford University Press, 1969. 139 p.

Director writes about experimental two-year college program established 1965 at the University of California, Berkeley, imitating somewhat the Alexander Meiklejohn experiment at the University of Wisconsin, 1928-33 (first year study of Athens, Greece; second year study of modern America; last two years regular program).

2917 Twentieth Century Fund. FUNDS FOR THE FUTURE: REPORT OF THE TWENTIETH CENTURY FUND TASK FORCE ON COLLEGE AND UNIVERSITY ENDOWMENT POLICY. New York: 1975. 215 p.

Policy and management recommendations for higher education endowments.

2918 Tyack, David B. GEORGE TICKNOR AND THE BOSTON BRAHMINS. Cambridge, Mass.: Harvard University Press, 1967. 289 p.

Ticknor (1791-1871), Dartmouth College graduate (B.A., 1807, M.A., 1810), student at the German University of Göttingen (1815-17), and Harvard professor of French and Spanish (1819-35).

2919 Tyler, Leona E. INDIVIDUALITY: HUMAN POSSIBILITIES AND PERSONAL CHOICE IN THE PSYCHOLOGICAL DEVELOPMENT OF MEN AND WOMEN. San Francisco: Jossey-Bass Publishers, 1978. 274 p.

Outlines concepts of development and techniques of evaluation which make individualized assessment practical.

2920 Tyrrell, William G., ed. SOCIAL STUDIES IN THE COLLEGE: PROGRAMS FOR THE FIRST TWO YEARS. Washington, D.C.: National Council for the Social Studies, 1953. 124 p.

Objectives and content of social studies programs analyzed for first two years in eighteen colleges of four types: junior college, four-year liberal arts college, teachers college, and vocational college. Found many traditional subject-centered courses, but some integrated social science programs built around problem-solving themes.

2921 Udolf, Roy. THE COLLEGE INSTRUCTOR'S GUIDE TO TEACHING AND ACADEMIA. Chicago: Nelson-Hall Publishers, 1976. 155 p.

Rewards, penalties, and problems of a college teaching career, and the professional and personal qualities of a successful teacher.

2922 Uhl, Norman P. IDENTIFYING INSTITUTIONAL GOALS: ENCOUR-

AGING CONVERGENCE OF OPINION THROUGH THE DELPHI TECH-NIQUE. Durham, N.C.: National Laboratory for Higher Education, 1971. 86 p.

Tells how to use the Delphi technique with questionnaires to identify institutional goals. Suggests its potential for studying curriculum.

2923 Uhler, John Earle. CANE JUICE: A STORY OF SOUTHERN LOUISIANA. New York: Century Co., 1931. 340 p.

Novel about a Louisiana Cajun youth at the state university to learn how to improve sugar cane growing from which his people earn their livelihood. He is temporarily led astray but returns to complete his education. (Author's resignation was forced as English instructor at Louisiana State University because of objection to his depiction of the university).

2924 Ulam, Adam. THE FALL OF THE AMERICAN UNIVERSITY. La Salle, Ill.: Open Court Publishing Co., 1973. 220 p.

Conservative analysis of 1960s campus crisis. Critical of student activists, liberal administrations, and indecisive faculty. Universities have lost much of their autonomy because of compromise.

2925 Ulich, Robert, ed. EDUCATION AND THE IDEA OF MANKIND. New York: Harcourt, Brace and World, 1964. 279 p.

Contributors Horace M. Kallen, Anne Roe, George N. Shuster, and others discuss how the sciences, behavioral sciences, and aesthetics can contribute to "the idea of mankind" at all school levels, including higher education.

2926 Umble, John Sylvanus. GOSHEN COLLEGE, 1894-1954. Goshen, Ind.: Goshen College Bookstore, 1955. 284 p.

Goshen College history from private shaky beginning in Elkhart, Indiana, to its move to Goshen, under the Mennonites (some of whom opposed education), financial difficulties, origin on the campus of the 1905 Intercollegiate Peace Society, to state accreditation (1941), to 1955 status as a college, theological seminary, and nursing school.

2927 Umstattd, James Greenleaf. INSTRUCTIONAL PROCEDURES AT THE COLLEGE LEVEL: AN ANALYSIS OF TEACHING AT BIARRITZ AMERICAN UNIVERSITY. Austin: University of Texas Press, 1947. 195 p.

Head of the education section and later dean describes college teaching techniques and procedures used for World War II soldiers at the successful Biarritz American University in southern France.

2928   . THE ODYSSEY OF JIM UMSTATTD: EPISODES FROM THE LIFE OF JAMES GREENLEAF UMSTATTD. Austin, Texas: Whitley Co., 1977. 265 p.

> Umstattd's (1896--) student years at the Universities of Missouri and Minnesota, and his teaching at Concord State Teachers College, the University of Minnesota, Wayne State University, and the University of Texas in Austin; also his summer teaching at Marshall College, University of South Dakota, West Virginia University, University of Maine, Harvard and Duke Universities, and the University of Oregon.

2929   . TEACHING PROCEDURES USED IN TWENTY-EIGHT MIDWESTERN AND SOUTH-WESTERN COLLEGES AND UNIVERSITIES. Austin, Texas: University Co-operative Society, 1954. 91 p.

> Information from over one thousand professors indicates homogeneous teaching methods, with informal lecture used the most; more discussion and audiovisual aids; more attention to motivating students; and use of subjective grading, which makes progressive author view formal grading with suspicion.

2930 Umstattd, James Greenleaf, et al. INSTITUTIONAL TEACHER PLACEMENT. Detroit: Wayne University, 1937. 238 p.

> Explores problems of teacher placement including administration, office arrangement, credentials, counseling, high professional standards in placement office, and supply and demand for teachers and school administrators. Lists qualifications for placement directors.

2931 Underwood, Kenneth Wilson, ed. THE CHURCH, THE UNIVERSITY, AND SOCIAL POLICY; THE DANFORTH STUDY OF CAMPUS MINISTRIES. 2 vols. Middletown, Conn.: Wesleyan University Press, 1969.

> The campus minister, his or her self-perception, role within the university and the church, and ways he or she relates campus life to church concerns.

2932 Union for Experimenting Colleges and Universities. INTERVERSITAS MEMBERSHIP DIRECTORY, 1978-1979. Chicago: Northeastern Illinois University, 1979. 58 p.

> Lists institutions and individuals involved in experimental college programs in more than thirty countries, including the United States.

2933 United States. Committee on National Program Priorities in Teacher Education. THE POWER OF COMPETENCY-BASED TEACHER EDUCATION: REPORT. Boston: Allyn and Bacon, 1972. 260 p.

Evolution, philosophical rationale, and five representative case studies of competency-based teacher education programs.

2934 U.S. Bureau of Health Manpower Education. THE FOREIGN MEDICAL GRADUATE: A BIBLIOGRAPHY. Washington, D.C.: Government Printing Office, 1973. 107 p.

Bibliography on foreign medical students' education abroad, foreign medical students coming to the United States, and their training and utilization in U.S. medicine.

2935 U.S. Bureau of the Budget, Executive Office of the President. THE ADMINISTRATION OF GOVERNMENT SUPPORTED RESEARCH AT UNIVERSITIES. Washington, D.C.: Government Printing Office, 1966. 141 p.

Report on the management of federal funding of graduate student research in physical life and behavioral sciences at thirteen universities.

2936 U.S. Cabinet Committee on Opportunity for the Spanish Speaking. SPANISH SURNAMED AMERICAN COLLEGE GRADUATES. Washington, D.C.: Government Printing Office, 1971. 515 p.

Directory of Spanish-surnamed graduates from over 800 colleges and universities (listed alphabetically and by state). Lists majors and graduation dates and shows distribution by disciplines.

2937 U.S. Census Bureau. SCHOOL ENROLLMENT--SOCIAL AND ECONOMIC CHARACTERISTICS OF STUDENTS: OCTOBER 1974. Washington, D.C.: Government Printing Office, 1975. 72 p.

Census report estimates that black college students rose from five percent of all U.S. college students in 1964 to nine percent in 1974, that black female college freshmen have the highest dropout rate of all college freshmen, and that the most dramatic increase in college enrollment in the 1970s was among students aged twenty-five and older.

2938 U.S. Congress. House Committee on Education and Labor. SEX DISCRIMINATION REGULATIONS: HEARINGS JUNE 17-26, 1975, REVIEW OF REGULATIONS TO IMPLEMENT TITLE IX OF PUBLIC LAW 92-318 CONDUCTED PURSUANT TO SEC. 431 OF THE GENERAL EDUCATION PROVISIONS ACT. 94th Cong., 1st sess. Washington, D.C.: Government Printing Office, 1975. 664 p.

Hearings on discrimination against women, mainly in athletics at colleges and universities.

2939 U.S. Congress. Joint Economic Committee. THE ECONOMICS AND FINANCING OF HIGHER EDUCATION IN THE UNITED STATES. 91st

Cong., 1st sess. Washington, D.C.: Government Printing Office, 1969. 683 p.

Papers on economic issues facing higher education in the next decade, particularly for private institutions, and prospects for federal and nonfederal funding.

2940 U.S. Department of Health, Education and Welfare. TOWARD A LONG-RANGE PLAN FOR FEDERAL FINANCIAL SUPPORT FOR HIGHER EDUCA-TION. Washington, D.C.: Office of the Assistant Secretary for Planning and Evaluation, Health, Education and Welfare, 1969. 73 p.

Summarizes national policy issues on financing higher education; discusses alternative means of support; recommends expansion of federal aid and creation of new programs.

2941 U.S. Department of Labor. U.S. MANPOWER IN THE 1970'S: OPPOR-TUNITY AND CHALLENGE. Washington, D.C.: Government Printing Office, 1970. 28 p.

Black college graduates are gaining parity as are black occu-pational gains, but black unemployment at twice the white rate was unchanged, 1960-1970.

2942 U.S. Department of Labor. Bureau of Labor Statistics. OCCUPATIONAL OUTLOOK FOR COLLEGE GRADUATES, 1978-79. Washington, D.C.: Government Printing Office, 1979. 266 p.

Employment outlook estimated through 1985 for over one hun-dred professional fields requiring a college degree: nature of the work, earnings, advancement potential, places of employ-ment, and other information.

2943 U.S. Department of Labor. Wage and Labor Standards Administration, Women's Bureau. TRENDS IN EDUCATIONAL ATTAINMENT OF WOM-EN. Washington, D.C.: 1969. 19 p.

Women earning bachelor's and first professional degrees rose from five thousand in 1900 to 279,000 in 1968. Women earned 20 percent of all master's degrees in 1900 and 40 percent in 1930. Women earning doctoral degrees increased fifteen times between 1900-30 and tripled between 1960-68.

2944 U.S. Department of Labor. Women's Bureau. COLLEGE WOMEN SEVEN YEARS AFTER GRADUATION: RESURVEY OF WOMEN GRADUATES--CLASS OF 1957. Washington, D.C.: Government Printing Office, 1966. 54 p.

Found among 1957 women college graduates, seven years later, rising interest in paid employment and in continuing education.

2945 _____ . FIFTEEN YEARS AFTER COLLEGE: A STUDY OF ALUMNAE OF THE CLASS OF 1945. Washington, D.C.: 1962. 26 p.

Less than one percent of 580 women interviewed fifteen years after college graduation were working; but most wanted future employment and said they would need additional training.

2946 _____ . JOB HORIZONS FOR COLLEGE WOMEN. Washington, D.C.: 1967. 83 p.

Described positions in thirty-two occupations open to college women. Discussed the job market and salaries, accessibility of graduate study, and professional employment of women in recent years.

2947 U.S. Office for Civil Rights. AFFIRMATIVE ACTION AND FACULTY POLICY. Washington, D.C.: Government Printing Office, 1972. 24 p.

U.S. Office for Civil Rights' role in helping colleges and universities establish affirmative action programs.

2948 U.S. Office of Education. LEGAL ASSISTANCE PROGRAM: A SUGGESTED TWO-YEAR POST-HIGH SCHOOL PROGRAM. Washington, D.C.: Government Printing Office, 1979. 69 p.

Plan for establishing two-year college programs in preparing legal assistants. Role of college administrators and program directors, objectives and curriculum, and textbooks and other materials.

2949 _____ . OPPORTUNITIES ABROAD FOR TEACHERS, 1979-80. Washington, D.C.: Government Printing Office, 1978. 28 p.

Annual description of teaching opportunities and seminars available abroad for U.S. teachers under the teacher-exchange program of the U.S. Office of Education and the International Communication Agency.

2950 _____ . TRENDS IN POSTSECONDARY EDUCATION. Washington, D.C.: Government Printing Office, 1970. 261 p.

Papers commissioned by the U.S. Office of Education on proposed universal education through the thirteenth and fourteenth grades. Explores financial requirements, role of junior colleges, and faculty resources needed.

2951 U.S. President's Commission on the Status of Women. REPORT OF THE COMMITTEE ON EDUCATION. Washington, D.C.: Government Printing Office, 1963. 71 p.

Discussion and recommendations about women in elementary,

secondary, and college education, and research on the education of women.

2952 University and College Theatre Association. DIRECTORY OF AMERICAN COLLEGE THEATRE. Edited by Allen S. White. 3d ed. Washington, D.C.: American Theatre Association, 1976. 95 p.

Information on academic theater courses, degrees, enrollments, facilities, and kinds of plays produced at colleges and universities.

2953 University Microfilms International. A DISSERTATION BIBLIOGRAPHY: WOMEN'S STUDIES: WORKING WOMEN. Ann Arbor, Mich.: 1979. 18 p.

Lists 358 nonannotated doctoral dissertations completed during 1976–77, including many on women's education and some on women in higher education. Categories include educational influences on occupational choice, professional and business training of women students, sex discrimination in career training of women, and women as educational administrators.

2954 Urban, George R., ed. HAZARDS OF LEARNING: AN INTERNATIONAL SYMPOSIUM ON THE CRISIS OF THE UNIVERSITY. La Salle, Ill.: Open Court Publishing Co., 1977. 294 p.

Radio Free Europe broadcasts by North American and European specialists on the university crisis of the 1960s and early 1970s, the meaning of higher education, and the university's role in modern societies.

2955 Urban Research Corporation. ON STRIKE . . . SHUT IT DOWN!: A REPORT ON THE FIRST NATIONAL STUDENT STRIKE IN U.S. HISTORY, MAY 1970. Chicago: 1970. 133 p.

Students struck on at least 760 campuses in May 1970 after the Cambodian invasion and the student killings at Kent State and Jackson State, although violence occurred on only 5 percent of the struck campuses. During 1968–70 an average of 23 percent of student strikes led to violence, with police and National Guards involved in fewer than 7 percent and confrontations in only 2 percent.

2956 Usdan, Michael D., et al. EDUCATION AND STATE POLITICS: THE DEVELOPING RELATIONSHIP BETWEEN ELEMENTARY–SECONDARY AND HIGHER EDUCATION. New York: Teachers College, Columbia University, 1969. 190 p.

The interlevel relationships and rivalries of elementary, secondary, and higher education studied in political context in twelve states.

2957 Useem, Elizabeth L., and Useem, Michael, eds. THE EDUCATIONAL ESTABLISHMENT. Englewood Cliffs, N.J.: Prentice-Hall, 1974. 180 p.

Contributors believe that the power structure (rather than faculty, students, or the public) controls higher education, and that economically privileged students get preferential treatment while poor students suffer discrimination.

2958 Vaccaro, Louis C. NOTES FROM A COLLEGE PRESIDENT: ISSUES IN AMERICAN HIGHER EDUCATION. Boston: Beacon Hill Press, 1977. 122 p.

Responsibilities of today's college president on such issues as tenure, governance, decision making, and college and community relations. By president of Colby-Sawyer College.

2959 Vaccaro, Louis C., and Covert, James Thayne, eds. STUDENT FREEDOM IN AMERICAN HIGHER EDUCATION. New York: Teachers College Press, 1969. 165 p.

Essays on 1960s student unrest, student governance, campus sexual revolution, and the church-related college. Authors are deans, a lawyer, a student, and a Jesuit priest.

2960 Valentine, Percy Friars, ed. THE AMERICAN COLLEGE. New York: Philosophical Library, 1949. 575 p.

Contributors from seventeen fields in U.S. higher education tell of their work and careers.

2961 Van de Graaf, John H., et al. ACADEMIC POWER: PATTERNS OF AUTHORITY IN SEVEN NATIONAL SYSTEMS OF HIGHER EDUCATION. New York: Praeger Publishers, 1978. 217 p.

Case studies of authority in national higher education systems of France, Britain, Italy, Japan, Sweden, United States, and West Germany. Identifies ten concepts of academic authority (including professorial, professional, trustee, bureaucratic, and political) and four styles of academic organization; for instance, European, British, American, and Japanese approaches.

2962 Vanderbilt, Kermit. CHARLES ELIOT NORTON: APOSTLE OF CULTURE IN A DEMOCRACY. Cambridge, Mass.: Harvard University Press, 1959. 286 p.

Norton (1827-1908), symbol of the genteel tradition and a leading spokesman for late nineteenth-century idealists, was Harvard's first professor of fine arts (1873-97), and a proponent of social causes who believed that a scholarly elite must educate in the humanistic tradition. Helped found NATION magazine.

2963 Van Doren, Mark. LIBERAL EDUCATION. New York: Henry Holt and Co., 1943. 186 p.

Calls for teaching the great books, as exemplified at St. John's College, Maryland.

2964 Van Dusen, William D., and O'Hearne, John J. A DESIGN FOR A MODEL COLLEGE FINANCIAL AID OFFICE. New York: College Entrance Examination Board, 1973. 61 p.

Recommends standardized definitions, practices, and principles for financial aid officers, a central financial aid office in each institution, a standardized application form for all types of aid, and improved communication among directors of admission, financial aid officers, and students.

2965 Van Male, John. RESOURCES OF PACIFIC NORTHWEST LIBRARIES: A SURVEY OF FACILITIES FOR STUDY AND RESEARCH. Seattle, Wash.: Pacific Northwest Library Association, 1943. 404 p.

Surveyed 108 Pacific Northwest libraries. Found that collections of small denominational and independent colleges were inadequate. Called for more regional cooperation to improve higher education library service.

2966 Van Metre, Thurman W. A HISTORY OF THE GRADUATE SCHOOL OF BUSINESS, COLUMBIA UNIVERSITY. New York: Columbia University Press, 1954. 124 p.

Columbia's School of Business began in 1916 with extension teaching, was looked down on by the academic departments, but won acceptance and a reputation as faculty members helped solve business problems in the world wars and the Depression. It became a graduate school in 1949, with four successful programs.

2967 Vaughan, Marilyn. THE VASSAR INSTITUTE FOR WOMEN IN BUSINESS: A REPORT OF THE PARTICIPANT OBSERVER. Chicago: Center for the Study of Liberal Education for Adults, 1957. 46 p.

Report by participants of a two-week program for business women, the talks given and topics discussed, and a cost analysis for those planning similar programs.

2968 Vaughn, George B., et al. CONSUMERISM COMES TO THE COMMUNITY COLLEGE. Los Angeles: ERIC Clearinghouse for Junior Colleges, University of California, 1976. 35 p.

Contributors argue that community colleges should provide better information and thus more consumer protection for their students. Describes how Monroe Community College in New

York evaluated the adequacy of its information for students and, as a result, developed a new educational prospectus.

2969 Veblen, Thorstein. THE HIGHER LEARNING IN AMERICA; A MEMO-RANDUM ON THE CONDUCT OF UNIVERSITIES BY BUSINESS MEN. New York: B.W. Huebsch, 1918. Reprint. Stanford, Calif.: Academic Reprints, 1954. 286 p.

Scathing classic attack on the conduct of universities by governing boards and officials dominated by moneyed interests to the detriment of an honest search for knowledge and the selection and preparation of moral and ethical leaders.

2970 Venn, Grant, and Marchese, Theodore J., Jr. MAN, EDUCATION, AND WORK: POSTSECONDARY VOCATIONAL AND TECHNICAL EDUCATION. Washington, D.C.: American Council on Education, 1964. 184 p.

Thesis is that all levels of education, particularly higher education and especially the junior college, must quickly assume greater responsibility for preparing youth for vocational and technical education.

2971 Vergara, Allys Dwyer. A CRITICAL STUDY OF A GROUP OF COLLEGE WOMEN'S RESPONSES TO POETRY. Contributions to Education No. 923. New York: Teachers College, Columbia University, 1946. 159 p.

In responses to poetry by seventy-five female college students, found that their comprehension varied according to background, intelligence, and personality.

2972 Vermilye, Dyckman W., ed. THE EXPANDED CAMPUS: CURRENT IS-SUES IN HIGHER EDUCATION 1972. San Francisco: Jossey-Bass Publishers, 1972. 284 p.

Continuing the American Association for Higher Education annual conference series formerly edited by G. Kerry Smith, this 1972 volume (later ones in alphabetical order) stresses philosophical changes in higher education. Topics include equality for women, free universities, unionization, tenure, and the work of the Carnegie Commission on Higher Education.

2973 _____. THE FUTURE IN THE MAKING: CURRENT ISSUES IN HIGHER EDUCATION 1973. San Francisco: Jossey-Bass Publishers, 1973. 208 p.

Essays discuss the changing relationship between higher education and government, education marketing techniques, individualized instruction, curriculum development, technological innovation, and academic standards.

2974 _____. INDIVIDUALIZING THE SYSTEM: CURRENT ISSUES IN HIGHER

EDUCATION 1976. San Francisco: Jossey-Bass Publishers, 1976. 217 p.

Essays on how to provide equal opportunity without sacrificing higher education quality. Discusses the need to individualize and humanize large institutions, progress toward equalizing educational opportunity, and the relation between finances and the issue of quality and equality.

2975 _____. LEARNER-CENTERED REFORM: CURRENT ISSUES IN HIGHER EDUCATION 1975. San Francisco: Jossey-Bass Publishers, 1975. 229 p.

Howard R. Bowen, Ernest L. Boyer, K. Patricia Cross, Harold L. Hodgkinson, and others discuss current efforts to meet student needs by changes in admissions standards, length of formal education, and accreditation. Innovations included are contract learning, colleges for prisoners, and weekend colleges.

2976 _____. LIFELONG LEARNERS: A NEW CLIENTELE FOR HIGHER EDUCATION: CURRENT ISSUES IN HIGHER EDUCATION 1974. San Francisco: Jossey-Bass Publishers, 1974. 177 p.

Discusses current programs to meet the higher educational needs of nontraditional students of all ages.

2977 _____. RELATING WORK AND EDUCATION: CURRENT ISSUES IN HIGHER EDUCATION 1977. San Francisco: Jossey-Bass Publishers, 1977. 282 p.

Contributors Mortimer J. Adler, Ernest L. Boyer, Willard Wirtz, and others on the relationship between work and education and how both affect people's lives.

2978 Vermorcken, Elizabeth Moorhead. THE FORBIDDEN TREE. Indianapolis: Bobbs-Merrill Co., 1933. 277 p.

Novel about the amorous affairs of an English instructor in a midwestern coeducational university.

2979 Veysey, Laurence R. THE EMERGENCE OF THE AMERICAN UNIVERSITY. Chicago: University of Chicago Press, 1965. 505 p.

History of the development of uniquely American universities and their chief advocates, during 1865 to 1910, based mainly on papers of leading university presidents and administrators. Shows how the U.S. university became as characteristic an American institution as was the church three centuries before and yet how the more intellectual universities set themselves off from society, which has viewed them with some suspicion.

2980 Viles, Jonas, et al. THE UNIVERSITY OF MISSOURI: A CENTENNIAL HISTORY, 1839-1939. Columbia: University of Missouri, 1939. 508 p.

Centennial history of the University of Missouri and the activities of its colleges of arts and sciences, agriculture, business and public administration, education, engineering, journalism (first in the United States), law, medicine, and the
graduate school. Also discusses governance for the university's
future.

2981 Visher, Stephen Sargent. SCIENTISTS STARRED, 1903-1943, IN AMERI-
CAN MEN OF SCIENCE: A STUDY OF COLLEGIATE AND DOCTORAL
TRAINING, BIRTHPLACE, DISTRIBUTION, BACKGROUNDS, AND DEVEL-
OPMENTAL INFLUENCES. Baltimore, Md.: Johns Hopkins University
Press, 1947. Reprint. New York: Arno Press, 1975. 556 p.

Study of the backgrounds of distinguished scientists, their higher
education, influential teachers, positions held, family origin,
and recruitment to science.

2982 von Klemperer, Lily, ed. INTERNATIONAL EDUCATION: A DIRECTORY
OF RESOURCE MATERIALS ON COMPARATIVE EDUCATION AND STUDY
IN ANOTHER COUNTRY. Garrett Park, Md.: Garrett Park Press, 1973.
202 p.

Selective annotated bibliography of about thirteen hundred descriptions and comparisons of educational systems at all levels,
including higher education. Also includes publications on
international education exchange.

2983 Wade, George H. FALL ENROLLMENT IN HIGHER EDUCATION, 1973.
Washington, D.C.: Government Printing Office, 1974. 1,053 p.

Enrollment figures by state, institution, type of control, sex,
attendance status, type of program, and level of study.

2984 Wade, Harold, Jr. BLACK MEN OF AMHERST. Amherst, Mass.: Amherst College Press, 1976. 127 p.

Author, Amherst graduate, tells of New England's historic egalitarian acceptance of blacks and of Amherst's success in graduating many middle class blacks who achieved prominence.

2985 Wagner, Geoffrey. THE END OF EDUCATION: THE EXPERIENCE OF
THE CITY UNIVERSITY OF NEW YORK WITH OPEN ENROLLMENT AND
THE THREAT TO HIGHER EDUCATION IN AMERICA. Cranbury, N.J.:
A.S. Barnes and Co., 1977. 251 p.

Critical evaluation of City University of New York's open admissions program. Charges academic liberals' attempts to provide all high school graduates with a college education have
caused lowered academic standards and general decline in higher
education quality.

2986 Waite, Frederick Clayton. WESTERN RESERVE UNIVERSITY, THE HUD-
SON ERA. Cleveland, Ohio: Western Reserve University Press, 1943.
540 p.

> History of Western Reserve University, 1862-82, based on orig-
> inal sources. Discussed New England and Puritan influences,
> the strong interest in theology, and the manual labor system.

2987 Waldo, Dwight, ed. THE RESEARCH FUNCTIONS OF UNIVERSITY BU-
REAUS AND INSTITUTES FOR GOVERNMENT RELATED RESEARCH. Berkeley: University of California, Bureau of Public Administration, 1960.
222 p.

> Papers on the role of university research bureaus in various
> aspects of public and community life related to political science.

2988 Waldstein, Charles. THE STUDY OF ART IN UNIVERSITIES. New York:
Harper and Brothers, 1896. 129 p.

> Favors a wide general education for the artist.

2989 Walford, Alberto J., and Screen, J.E., eds. A GUIDE TO FOREIGN
LANGUAGE COURSES AND DICTIONARIES. Westport, Conn.: Greenwood Press, 1978. 343 p.

> Discusses textbooks, records, audiovisual materials, and dic-
> tionaries for teaching and learning more than twenty-five lan-
> guages.

2990 Walker, Donald E. THE EFFECTIVE ADMINISTRATOR: A PRACTICAL
APPROACH TO PROBLEM SOLVING, DECISION MAKING, AND CAM-
PUS LEADERSHIP. San Francisco: Jossey-Bass Publishers, 1979. 208 p.

> Handbook for academic administrators includes twenty-seven
> axioms for effective administration.

2991 Walker, Marion, and Beach, Mark. MAKING IT IN COLLEGE. New
York: Mason, Charter Publishers, 1977. 227 p.

> Tips to help the minority student choose a college or univer-
> sity, improve academic skills, and adjust personally, socially,
> and academically to college life.

2992 Walker, Robert H. AMERICAN STUDIES IN THE UNITED STATES: A
SURVEY OF COLLEGE PROGRAMS. Baton Rouge: Louisiana State University Press, 1958. 218 p.

> On the development since the 1930s of American studies pro-
> grams. Data from an American Studies Association committee
> from ninety-five institutions found three kinds of programs of-
> fered among twenty-six undergraduate and nine graduate curric-
> ula.

2993 Wallace, Walter L. STUDENT CULTURE: SOCIAL STRUCTURE AND CONTINUITY IN A LIBERAL ARTS COLLEGE. Chicago: Aldine Publishing Co., 1966. 236 p.

> Found that freshman attitude changes toward grades, graduate school, and dating as influenced by faculty, fraternities, and sororities were greatest during their first seven weeks in college.

2994 Wallerstein, Immanuel, and Starr, Paul, eds. THE UNIVERSITY CRISIS READER. 2 vols. New York: Random House, 1971. 558 p., 515 p.

> Documents from a broad ideological spectrum about 1960s campus unrest.

2995 Wallhaus, Robert A., ed. MEASURING AND INCREASING ACADEMIC PRODUCTIVITY. San Francisco: Jossey-Bass Publishers, 1975. 133 p.

> How productivity in higher education can be understood and how to improve measurement and analysis.

2996 Walsh, Chad. CAMPUS GODS ON TRIAL. New York: Macmillan Co., 1953. 138 p.

> On religion and higher education. Indicts materialism, communism, scientism, skepticism, and libertinism.

2997 Walsh, James J. EDUCATION OF THE FOUNDING FATHERS OF THE REPUBLIC: SCHOLASTICISM IN THE COLONIAL COLLEGES, A NEGLECTED CHAPTER IN THE HISTORY OF AMERICAN EDUCATION. Bronx, N.Y.: Fordham University Press, 1935. 377 p.

> Examines the curricula of the seven earliest colonial colleges; concludes that medieval university scholasticism dominated philosophical thinking in colleges well into the nineteenth century.

2998 Walters, Everett, ed. GRADUATE EDUCATION TODAY. Washington, D.C.: American Council on Education, 1965. 246 p.

> Essays by thirteen graduate deans review the past, present, and anticipated future of graduate education.

2999 Waltzer, Herbert. THE JOB OF ACADEMIC DEPARTMENT CHAIRMAN: EXPERIENCE AND RECOMMENDATIONS FROM MIAMI UNIVERSITY. Washington, D.C.: American Council on Education, 1975. 35 p.

> Expectations and realities of the job of academic department chairman.

3000 Walworth, Dorothy. FEAST OF REASON. New York: Farrar and Rinehart, 1941. 320 p.

Novel laid in a progressive women's junior college near New York City.

3001 Warch, Richard. SCHOOL OF THE PROPHETS: YALE COLLEGE, 1701-1740. New Haven, Conn.: Yale University Press, 1973. 339 p.

Analyzes history, curriculum, and the social and religious setting of Yale, 1701-40.

3002 Ward, Jesse L. THE DEVELOPMENT OF FACULTY PERSONNEL ACCOUNTING FORMS FOR AN INSTITUTION OF HIGHER LEARNING. Ann Arbor, Mich.: Edwards Brothers, 1934. 141 p.

Studied faculty personnel forms used at one hundred higher education institutions to select and promote faculty. Identified important criteria and made recommendations applicable to college personnel procedures.

3003 Ward, Mary Jane. THE PROFESSOR'S UMBRELLA. New York: Random House, 1948. 313 p.

Novel about an English instructor in a midwest college who, fired on moral charges, fights back only to find religious prejudice as the cause of his dismissal.

3004 _____. THE TREE HAS ROOTS. New York: E.P. Dutton and Co., 1937. 315 p.

Novel deals with the superintendent of buildings, a handy man, janitors, waitresses, stenographers, and other personnel behind the scenes on a university campus.

3005 Ward, Merle Scott. PHILOSOPHIES OF ADMINISTRATION CURRENT IN THE DEANSHIP OF THE LIBERAL ARTS COLLEGE. Contributions to Education No. 632. New York: Teachers College, Columbia University, 1934. 128 p.

Data from almost three hundred liberal arts deans about their academic training, personal and professional background, and job status; concludes with a profile of the deanship.

3006 Ward, Robert C. MR. PRESIDENT, THE DECISION IS YOURS. DEAL OUT THE DOUGH. Lexington: College of Education, University of Kentucky, 1969. 83 p.

On the value of university departmental planning, finance, and budgeting.

3007 Warnath, Charles Frederick. NEW MYTHS AND OLD REALITIES: COLLEGE COUNSELING IN TRANSITION. San Francisco: Jossey-Bass Publishers, 1971. 172 p.

On the post-World War II emergence of counseling centers
and the late 1960s ambivalence about the role of counseling
and academic counselors.

3008 Warnath, Charles Frederick, et al. NEW DIRECTIONS FOR COLLEGE
COUNSELORS: A HANDBOOK FOR REDESIGNING PROFESSIONAL
ROLES. San Francisco: Jossey-Bass Publishers, 1973. 330 p.

First-hand experiences of college counselors as they attempt
to be more effective on campus. Provides tested alternatives
to traditional counseling and strategies for putting them into
effect. Describes improvements in the. type and quality of
services.

3009 Warren, Constance. A NEW DESIGN FOR WOMEN'S EDUCATION. New
York: Frederick A. Stokes, 1940. 277 p.

Sarah Lawrence College president tells of experiments in individualizing instruction at Sarah Lawrence, Bennington, and
other progressive women's colleges.

3010 Warren, Donald R., ed. HISTORY, EDUCATION, AND PUBLIC POLICY:
RECOVERING THE AMERICAN EDUCATIONAL PAST. Berkeley, Calif.:
McCutchan Publishers, 1979. 318 p.

Chapters on higher education for minorities, adults, and women.

3011 Wasserman, Elga Ruth, and Switzer, E.E. THE RANDOM HOUSE GUIDE
TO GRADUATE STUDY IN THE ARTS AND SCIENCES. New York: Random House, 1967. 361 p.

Information on individual fields of doctoral study. Lists university departments, number of Ph.D. degrees awarded, enrollment, fellowships and other financial aid, graduate school application procedure, testing programs including the graduate
record examination, and study abroad.

3012 Wasserman, Elga Ruth, et al., eds. WOMEN IN ACADEMIA: EVOLVING
POLICIES TOWARD EQUAL OPPORTUNITIES. New York: Praeger Publishers, 1975. 169 p.

American Association for the Advancement of Science conference proceedings on the history, legislation, and policies of
academic institutions regarding discriminatory practices, especially toward women.

3013 Watkin, Lawrence Edward. GEESE IN THE FORUM. New York: Alfred
A. Knopf, 1940. 287 p.

Novel about life in a small southern college in the late 1920s.

3014 Watson, Goodwin, et al. REDIRECTING TEACHER EDUCATION. New York: Teachers College, Columbia University, 1938. 105 p.

Describes desirable characteristics in candidates for admission to the teaching profession. Stresses improvements in teacher preparation.

3015 Wattenbarger, James L., and Bender, Louis W., eds. IMPROVING STATEWIDE PLANNING. San Francisco: Jossey-Bass Publishers, 1974. 93 p.

Proposes structures and functions for statewide leadership in higher education. Stresses factors and problems affecting statewide planning.

3016 Wattenbarger, James L., and Cage, Bob N. MORE MONEY FOR MORE OPPORTUNITY. San Francisco: Jossey-Bass Publishers, 1974. 109 p.

Surveys the theory, history, and resources of financing public community colleges. Summarizes various state formulas used to fund community colleges.

3017 Watts, Anthony Gordon. DIVERSITY AND CHOICE IN HIGHER EDUCATION. Boston: Routledge and Kegan Paul, 1972. 268 p.

Compares British and U.S. data on informing students of choices available to them, the differential effects of higher education, and ways of distributing students among various universities.

3018 Watts, Susan F., ed. THE COLLEGE HANDBOOK, SIXTEENTH EDITION. Princeton, N.J.: College Entrance Examination Board, 1977. 1,385 p.

Information on over two thousand two- and four-year U.S. colleges and universities, including size, location, admissions standards, curriculum, student costs, financial aid, and student life. For students, parents, and guidance counselors.

3019 Wayland, Francis. THOUGHTS ON THE PRESENT COLLEGIATE SYSTEM IN THE UNITED STATES. Boston: Gould, Kendall and Lincoln, 1842. Reprint. New York: Arno Press, 1969. 160 p.

Wayland (1796-1865), president of Brown University (1827-55), recommended such pioneering reforms in higher education as expanding the curriculum and creating alternative programs leading to the B.S. or B. Litt. degree in addition to the B.A.

3020 Weathersby, George B., and Jacobs, Frederic. INSTITUTIONAL GOALS AND STUDENT COSTS. Washington, D.C.: American Association for Higher Education, 1977. 48 p.

Argues that while students pay more of their college costs, they have less voice in college decisions. Suggests that colleges might allow students to pay only for services they desire: classroom instruction, career advising, or academic counseling.

3021 Weaver, Gary R., and Weaver, James H., eds. UNIVERSITY AND RE-VOLUTION. Englewood Cliffs, N.J.: Prentice-Hall, 1969. 180 p.

Essays on aspects of the 1960s university crisis: student activism, role of the university in modern society, generation gap, and black studies.

3022 Wechsler, Harold S. THE QUALIFIED STUDENT: A HISTORY OF SELEC-TIVE COLLEGE ADMISSION IN AMERICA. New York: Wiley-Interscience, 1977. 341 p.

Evolution of college admission policies and practices as exemplified at the Universities of Michigan, Columbia, and Chicago, and of open admissions at the City University of New York, and how these influenced other institutions.

3023 Weeks, Helen Foss. FACTORS INFLUENCING THE CHOICE OF COURSES BY STUDENTS IN CERTAIN LIBERAL-ARTS COLLEGES. Contributions to Education No. 465. New York: Teachers College, Columbia University, 1931. 62 p.

After finding out why a liberal arts student sample took the courses they did (41 percent of courses were taken because they were required, 19 percent were taken because they fitted anticipated job needs), author recommended reducing required courses and substituting student interest electives.

3024 Wegener, Charles. LIBERAL EDUCATION AND THE MODERN UNIVER-SITY. Chicago: University of Chicago Press, 1979. 163 p.

Contends that college libraries and laboratories were small and novel until 1876, when Johns Hopkins opened as the first U.S. graduate university. Afterwards research expanded and enrollments grew as higher education became a route to industrializing and enriching an increasingly democratic society. Wegener wants to restore liberal education's focus on nurturing intelligent individuals.

3025 Weidner, Edward W. THE WORLD ROLE OF UNIVERSITIES. New York: McGraw-Hill Book Co., 1962. 366 p.

Chapters on the role of U.S. universities in technical assistance programs abroad.

3026 Weingarten, Samuel, and Kroeger, Frederick P., eds. ENGLISH IN THE TWO-YEAR COLLEGE. Urbana, Ill.: National Council of Teachers of English, 1965. 112 p.

Recommendations for improving English teachers and teaching in two-year colleges.

3027 Weinstock, Ruth. THE GRAYING OF THE CAMPUS. New York: Educational Facilities Laboratories, 1978. 159 p.

One-third of U.S. higher education institutions have programs for older students. More will do so with an increasingly aging population and a 1979 federal law prohibiting age discrimination in federally aided institutions. Explores myths about aging, presents statistics, and urges administrators and others to integrate aging students on their campuses.

3028 Weisberger, June. FACULTY GRIEVANCE ARBITRATION IN HIGHER EDUCATION: LIVING WITH COLLECTIVE BARGAINING. Ithaca: Institute of Public Employment, New York State School of Industrial and Labor Relations, Cornell University, 1976. 44 p.

Reviews collective bargaining experiences of City University of New York, State University of New York, and Pennsylvania state colleges. Looks at circumstances under which the courts have supported or not supported arbitration decisions.

3029 Weiss, Robert M. THE CONANT CONTROVERSY IN TEACHER EDUCATION. New York: Random House, 1969. 271 p.

Contributors' for-and-against interpretive comments on James Bryant Conant's THE EDUCATION OF AMERICAN TEACHERS, 1963 (see No. 477).

3030 Weld, William Ernest, and Sewny, Kathryn W. HERBERT E. HAWKES, DEAN OF COLUMBIA COLLEGE, 1918-1943. New York: Columbia University Press, 1958. 171 p.

Hawkes was notable for the interdepartmental contemporary civilization course he introduced in 1919 and the general education program he backed.

3031 Weller, George Anthony. NOT TO EAT, NOT FOR LOVE. New York: Harrison Smith and Robert Haas, 1933. 421 p.

Said to be one of the best novels of undergraduate life at the time; set at Harvard during the late 1920s.

3032 Wells, Anna Mary. MISS MARKS AND MISS WOOLLEY. Boston: Houghton Mifflin, 1978. 268 p.

Joint biography of two women educators: Mary Emma Woolley (1863-1947), first woman student at Brown University, taught at Wellesley College (1895-1900), and was president of Mount Holyoke College (1900-37), where her colleague and companion for fifty years, Jeannette Marks, taught literature.

3033 Wells, Harry L. HIGHER EDUCATION IS SERIOUS BUSINESS. New York: Harper and Brothers, 1953. 237 p.

> University vice president on higher education business management, budget, cost control, property management, and financial investment.

3034 Wells, Warren D., ed. THE UNIVERSITY CALENDAR. Washington, D.C.: American Association of Collegiate Registrars and Admissions Officers, 1961. 56 p.

> Historical review of U.S. higher education calendar variations (terms, semesters). Discussion of factors to be considered in college and university calendar planning.

3035 Wertenbaker, Charles. BOOJUM. New York: Boni and Liveright, 1928. 307 p.

> Novel about a bright seventeen-year-old youth, something of a poet, who withdraws from the boisterous aspects of college life.

3036 Wertenbaker, Thomas Jefferson. PRINCETON: 1746-1896. Princeton, N.J.: Princeton University Press, 1946. 424 p.

> Detailed history of the first hundred and fifty years of the College of New Jersey, afterwards Princeton University.

3037 Werts, Charles E. CAREER CHANGES IN COLLEGE. Evanston, Ill.: National Merit Scholarship Corp., 1966.

> Changes in freshman year career plans of male students from 248 heterogeneous colleges who were planning careers as engineers, teachers, physicians, businessmen, lawyers, chemists, accountants, and physicists. Social class and ability analyzed.

3038 Wesley, Edgar Bruce. PROPOSED: THE UNIVERSITY OF THE UNITED STATES. Minneapolis: University of Minnesota Press, 1936. 83 p.

> Movement to establish a national university and its influence upon various institutions. Author sees the University of the United States as still inevitable.

3039 West, Andrew Fleming. SHORT PAPERS ON AMERICAN LIBERAL EDUCATION. New York: Charles Scribner's Sons, 1907. Reprint. New York: Arno Press, 1971. 135 p.

> Eloquent plea for keeping the liberal arts college as central in U.S. higher education, by the dean of Princeton's graduate school.

3040 West, Elmer D. FINANCIAL AID TO THE UNDERGRADUATE: ISSUES AND IMPLICATIONS. Washington, D.C.: American Council on Education, 1963. 153 p.

> On the many issues involved in undergraduate financial aid. Argues that if every child is to have adequate education, we must risk federal control.

3041 Westby, David L. THE CLOUDED VISION: THE STUDENT MOVEMENT IN THE UNITED STATES IN THE 1960S. Lewisburg, Pa.: Bucknell University Press, 1976. 291 p.

> Synthesis and analysis of studies of 1960s student activism. Examines current theories concerning student activism and proposes a new interpretation.

3042 Westerhoff, John H., ed. THE CHURCH'S MINISTRY IN HIGHER EDUCATION: PAPERS AND RESPONSES PRESENTED TO A CONFERENCE AT DUKE DIVINITY SCHOOL, JANUARY 27-28, 1978. New York: United Ministries in Higher Education, 1978. 294 p.

> On the church's role in higher education and such concerns as academic study of religion, the church's role in secular institutions, campus ministries, and ways to involve more women and minorities in theological activities.

3043 Western College Placement Association. DIRECTORY OF EXPERIENTIAL EDUCATION PROGRAMS. San Francisco: 1979. 55 p.

> A guide to on-the-job programs offered by selected industrial corporations, government and non-profit employers, two-year and four-year colleges, and technical institutes.

3044 Western Interstate Commission for Higher Education. SUMMARY OF STATE LEGISLATION AFFECTING HIGHER EDUCATION IN THE WEST: 1970. Boulder, Colo.: 1970. 58 p.

> Annual summary of major state legislation affecting higher education in the West. Succinct state reports are written by professional journalists. Includes a brief regional summary.

3045 Westervelt, Esther M. BARRIERS TO WOMEN'S PARTICIPATION IN POST-SECONDARY EDUCATION: A REVIEW OF RESEARCH AND COMMENTARY AS OF 1973-74. Washington, D.C.: U.S. National Center for Educational Statistics, Government Printing Office, 1975. 74 p.

> On admissions practices, financial aid practices, social constraints, psychological and other barriers to equal higher education opportunities for women.

3046 Westley, William A., and Epstein, Nathan B. THE SILENT MAJORITY: FAMILIES OF EMOTIONALLY HEALTHY COLLEGE STUDENTS. San Francisco: Jossey-Bass Publishers, 1969. 196 p.

> Relationships among ordinary emotionally stable college students and their family backgrounds. Shows how variations in family life affect the emotional health of students.

3047 Weston, Burns H., et al., eds. PEACE AND WORLD ORDER STUDIES: A CURRICULUM GUIDE. New York: Institute for World Order, 1978. 476 p.

> Essays, course outlines, and a bibliography for North American secondary and postsecondary educators on peace education.

3048 Wetherell, June Pat. BUT THAT WAS YESTERDAY. New York: E.P. Dutton and Co., 1943. 278 p.

> Novel which depicts sorority life unfavorably as snobbish.

3049 _____. RUN, SHEEP, RUN. New York: E.P. Dutton and Co., 1947. 287 p.

> Novel about college students graduating during the 1930s depression and their economic insecurity.

3050 Wettach, Robert H., ed. A CENTURY OF LEGAL EDUCATION. Chapel Hill: University of North Carolina Press, 1947. 146 p.

> Essays on the first hundred years of the University of North Carolina Law School. Describes the evolution of legal education from untutored home study to an integral unit of university professional instruction.

3051 Weyer, Frank E. PRESBYTERIAN COLLEGES AND ACADEMIA IN NE-BRASKA. Hastings, Nebr.: Hastings College Bookstore, 1940. 242 p.

> Historical study of educational work by Presbyterians in Nebraska. Deals with Otoe University (1868-72), Bellevue College (1880-1934), Oakdale Seminary (1881-91), Hastings College (1882--), and City Academy (1883-1903).

3052 Wheeler, Joseph L. PROGRESS AND PROBLEMS IN EDUCATION FOR LIBRARIANSHIP. New York: Carnegie Corporation of New York, 1946. 107 p.

> Library school recruitment, organization, faculty, curriculum, graduate programs, and the nature of librarianship.

3053 Whiffen, Marcus, ed. THE ARCHITECT AND THE CITY: PAPERS FROM THE AIA-ACSA TEACHER SEMINAR. Cambridge: MIT Press, 1966. 173 p.

Seminar papers for teachers of architecture call for reform of architecture education.

3054 White, Betty. I LIVED THIS STORY. Garden City, N.Y.: Doubleday, Doran and Co., 1930. 308 p.

Won the Doubleday, Doran and College Humor novel prize about U.S. academic life written by an undergraduate; about a woman's college experiences.

3055 White, Ellis F., and Schilling, Carl. BIBLIOGRAPHY ON ADMINISTRA-TION IN HIGHER EDUCATION. New York: Department of Higher Education, School of Education, New York University, 1968.

Bibliography on higher education administration, faculty, academic affairs, student affairs, business and finance, planning, public relations and fund-raising, research, and other aspects.

3056 White, Herbert S., ed. THE COPYRIGHT DILEMMA. Chicago: American Library Association, 1978. 199 p.

On complying with the 1976 copyright law, with discussions of higher education library photocopying.

3057 White, Lynn, Jr. EDUCATING OUR DAUGHTERS. New York: Harper and Brothers, 1950. 166 p.

Mills College president discusses negative aspects of women's colleges and women in higher education.

3058 White, Virginia P. GRANTS: HOW TO FIND OUT ABOUT THEM AND WHAT TO DO NEXT. New York: Plenum Press, 1975. 354 p.

On federal and private foundation grants to institutions and individuals, how to keep abreast on federal grant opportunities, and how to write grant proposals.

3059 Whitehead, John S. THE SEPARATION OF COLLEGE AND STATE: CO-LUMBIA, DARTMOUTH, HARVARD, AND YALE, 1776-1876. New Haven, Conn.: Yale University Press, 1973. 262 p.

New historical interpretation contends that no real distinction between private and public higher education existed before the Civil War, that the 1819 Dartmouth College case did not imply college distaste for legislative interference, and that the post-Civil War fear of competition from state universities and a proposed national university finally caused such leaders as Eliot of Harvard to call for private institutions to be free of state support and control.

3060 Whitlock, Baird W. DON'T HOLD THEM BACK: A CRITIQUE AND

GUIDE TO NEW HIGH SCHOOL-COLLEGE ARTICULATION MODELS.
Princeton, N.J.: College Board Publications, 1978. 173 p.

> Believing that the last two years of high school and the first
> two years of college overlap course coverage, author, Simon's
> Rock Early College president, 1972-76, advocates advanced
> placement, early admissions, the international baccalaureate,
> cooperative high school-college programs, and early and mid-
> dle colleges.

3061 Whitney, Allen S. HISTORY OF THE PROFESSIONAL TRAINING OF
TEACHERS: AT THE UNIVERSITY OF MICHIGAN FOR THE FIRST HALF-
CENTURY, 1879 TO 1929. Ann Arbor, Mich.: George Wahr Publishing
Co., 1931. 202 p.

> Early professional education of teachers at the University of
> Michigan under professors and presidents James B. Angell,
> William H. Payne, Burks A. Hinsdale, Allen S. Whitney,
> Hutchins, Burton, and Little.

3062 Widmayer, Charles E. HOPKINS OF DARTMOUTH. Hanover, N.H.:
University Press of New England, 1977. 312 p.

> Account of Ernest Martin Hopkins's (1877-1946) presidency of
> Dartmouth College (1916-45), whose reputation he significantly
> enhanced.

3063 Wiener, Philip P. EVOLUTION AND THE FOUNDERS OF PRAGMATISM.
Cambridge, Mass.: Harvard University Press, 1949. 288 p.

> Origins of modern pragmatism among the brilliant members (in-
> cluding Charles Peirce, Chauncey Wright, William James, John
> Fiske, and Oliver Wendell Holmes) of the informal Metaphysi-
> cal Club, Cambridge, Massachusetts.

3064 Wiggins, Samuel P. THE DESEGREGATION ERA IN HIGHER EDUCATION.
Berkeley, Calif.: McCutchan Publishers, 1966. 128 p.

> Interviews with administrators, professors, students, and presi-
> dents of many southern colleges and universities provide inter-
> pretive social history of the evolution of desegregation in higher
> education.

3065 _____. HIGHER EDUCATION IN THE SOUTH. Berkeley, Calif.: Mc-
Cutchan Publishers, 1966. 384 p.

> Higher education in the South, its history and shaping forces.
> Chapters on desegregation, federal role, black colleges, and
> the future.

3066 Wightwick, Irene M. VOCATIONAL INTEREST PATTERNS: A DEVELOP-

MENTAL STUDY OF A GROUP OF COLLEGE WOMEN. New York: Teachers College, Columbia University, 1945. 231 p.

> Compared students' vocational interests while in a small eastern women's college with jobs they held after college and confirmed the permanence of vocational interests.

3067 Wilcox, Thomas W. THE ANATOMY OF COLLEGE ENGLISH. San Francisco: Jossey-Bass Publishers, 1973. 181 p.

> Nationwide study of college English departments: size, structure, staffing, teaching loads, governance, evaluation, tenure, and promotion procedures; freshman English; typical curricula above the freshman level; and the variety of programs for majors and nonmajors.

3068 Wilder, Isabel. LET WINTER GO. New York: Coward-McCann, 1937. 249 p.

> Novel about four people in a New England college town.

3069 Wiley, John. THE EDUCATION OF PETER. New York: Frederick A. Stokes Co., 1924. 313 p.

> Novel set at Yale. Hero's elite family wants him to meet the right people but he opts eventually for intellectuality rather than popularity.

3070 Wilkerson, Marcus M. THOMAS DUCKETT BOYD: THE STORY OF A SOUTHERN EDUCATOR. Baton Rouge: Louisiana State University Press, 1935. 374 p.

> Biography of Boyd (1854-1932) who, like his older brother David French Boyd (1834-99), became president of Louisiana State University (1896) and made major contributions to Louisiana public schools.

3071 Wilkinson, J. Harvie III. FROM BROWN TO BAKKE: THE SUPREME COURT AND SCHOOL INTEGRATION: 1954-1978. New York: Oxford University Press, 1979. 368 p.

> Examines desegregation in public schools and higher education, including the reverse discrimination cases of white Marco DeFunis who sought entry into the University of Washington law school and white Allan Bakke who sought entry into the University of California medical school at Davis.

3072 Will, Roland G. THE UNIVERSITY, COLLEGE, AND NORMAL SCHOOL STUDENTS IN OREGON. Columbus: Ohio State University Press, 1936. 152 p.

Economic and social data on over 85 percent of Oregon's 1929-30 higher education students.

3073 Willey, Malcolm M. DEPRESSION, RECOVERY AND HIGHER EDUCATION: REPORT OF COMMITTEE Y OF THE AMERICAN ASSOCIATION OF UNIVERSITY PROFESSORS. New York: McGraw-Hill Book Co., 1937. Reprint. New York: Arno Press, 1977. 543 p.

Used AAUP members' data to assess personal and institutional impact of the 1929-36 depression on the status of the higher education teaching profession, higher education finances, salaries, attrition, unemployment, enrollments, degrees, students' problems, and the relation of government to higher education.

3074 Williams, Aston R. GENERAL EDUCATION IN HIGHER EDUCATION. New York: Teachers College, Columbia University, 1968. 244 p.

Examines general education at Harvard, MIT, the College of the University of Chicago, and the University College of Michigan State. Also puts into perspective the extensive literature on general education.

3075 Williams, Dorothy, ed. EXPANDING ALUMNI CONTACTS. San Francisco: Jossey-Bass Publishers, 1978.

Investigates the development, purposes, costs, content, and ways to enhance alumni contacts, including newsletters, newspapers, magazines, radio, and television.

3076 Williams, George. SOME OF MY BEST FRIENDS ARE PROFESSORS: A CRITICAL COMMENTARY ON HIGHER EDUCATION. New York: Abelard-Schuman, 1958. 250 p.

Indictment of college professors for selfishness and unconcern about students.

3077 Williams, Robert L. THE ADMINISTRATION OF ACADEMIC AFFAIRS IN HIGHER EDUCATION. Ann Arbor: University of Michigan Press, 1965. 182 p.

Higher education academic administrators' responsibilities; techniques used in solving actual problems.

3078 _____. LEGAL BASES OF BOARDS OF HIGHER EDUCATION IN FIFTY STATES. Chicago: Council of State Governments, 1971. 185 p.

State-by-state laws governing coordinating boards of higher education. Tables on membership, authority, source of appropriations, capital outlay, and legislation regarding budget requests.

3079 Williamson, Edmund Griffith. STUDENTS AND OCCUPATIONS. New York: Henry Holt and Co., 1937. 437 p.

> Career guidance for college men and women in such fields as medicine, engineering, chemistry, agriculture, forestry, home economics, teaching, business, law, journalism, social welfare, ministry, industry, and public service.

3080 _____, ed. TRENDS IN STUDENT PERSONNEL WORK. Minneapolis: University of Minnesota Press, 1949. 417 p.

> Papers on the history of higher education student personnel work, development of testing, conflict over directive and non-directive counseling, faculty role, and other concerns. Papers celebrate twenty-five years of student personnel work and honor Donald G. Paterson (1892–1961), University of Minnesota psychology professor (1917–60), who established its Counseling Bureau.

3081 Williamson, Edmund Griffith, and Biggs, Donald A. STUDENT PERSONNEL WORK: A PROGRAM OF DEVELOPMENTAL RELATIONSHIPS. New York: John Wiley and Sons, 1975. 390 p.

> Topics vary from student activism, disciplinary counseling, research, residence halls, and the reconstruction of student personnel work.

3082 Williamson, Edmund Griffith, and Cowan, John L. THE AMERICAN STUDENT'S FREEDOM OF EXPRESSION: A RESEARCH APPRAISAL. Minneapolis: University of Minnesota Press, 1966. 193 p.

> Views from students, faculty, and administrators at over eight hundred campuses on student freedom to invite campus speakers, organize protests, issue student newspapers, and participate in policymaking.

3083 Williamson, Edmund Griffith, and Foley, J.D. COUNSELING AND DISCIPLINE. New York: McGraw-Hill Book Co., 1949. 387 p.

> On student discipline at the University of Minnesota from historic, philosophical, and psychological viewpoints, with case studies, and in a counseling and rehabilitation framework.

3084 Williamson, Edmund Griffith, and Sarbin, T.R. STUDENT PERSONNEL WORK IN THE UNIVERSITY OF MINNESOTA. Minneapolis: Burgess Publishing Co., 1940. 115 p.

> Theory and practice of student personnel work drawn from University of Minnesota's large student personnel program.

3085 Williamson, Obed Jalmar. PROVISIONS FOR GENERAL THEORY COURSES IN THE PROFESSIONAL EDUCATION OF TEACHERS. New York: Teachers College, Columbia University, 1936. 185 p.

> Origin, development, status, and improvement of education theory courses (i.e., philosophy of teaching) in teacher education.

3086 Willie, Charles V., and Edmonds, Ronald R., eds. BLACK COLLEGES IN AMERICA: CHALLENGE, DEVELOPMENT, SURVIVAL. New York: Teachers College Press, 1978. 292 p.

> Faculty and administrators from black colleges write on the history and special purposes of black colleges where administrative, financial, and teaching problems must accommodate many students' poor backgrounds and inadequate preparation.

3087 Willingham, Calder. END AS A MAN. New York: Vanguard Press, 1947. 350 p.

> Novel about hazing in a southern military academy, similar to the Citadel, which the author attended.

3088 Willingham, Warren W. FREE-ACCESS HIGHER EDUCATION. New York: College Entrance Examination Board, 1970. 240 p.

> Explores the subtle meanings of accessibility to higher education with such demographic data from the fifty states as higher education characteristics, planning, coordination, and populations that colleges do and do not reach. Author favors open access as the only fair way to equalize opportunity in higher education.

3089 Willingham, Warren W., et al. THE SOURCE BOOK FOR HIGHER EDUCATION: A CRITICAL GUIDE TO LITERATURE AND INFORMATION ON ACCESS TO HIGHER EDUCATION. New York: College Entrance Examination Board, 1973. 481 p.

> Annotations of 1,519 entries of books, articles in journals and books, and reports on higher education guidance, finance, admission, curriculum, testing, organization, administration, structure, students, and programs. Also describes major higher education journals, newsletters, proceedings, information centers, and biographical directories.

3090 Wilms, Wellford. PROPRIETARY VERSUS PUBLIC VOCATIONAL TRAINING: A PROFILE OF FIFTY PROPRIETARY AND PUBLIC VOCATIONAL SCHOOLS, AND AN ANALYSIS OF THEIR GRADUATING STUDENTS. Berkeley: Center for Research and Development in Higher Education, University of California, 1977. 117 p.

In comparing grades of fifty proprietary (private-for-profit) and public post-secondary vocational schools, found that their salary expectations were about the same, suggesting that proprietary schools may compensate for their students' less advantaged backgrounds by more intense training and by meeting students' immediate needs.

3091 Wilson, Charles H. A TEACHER IS A PERSON. New York: Henry Holt and Co., 1956. 285 p.

Sketches of teachers and professors the author has known, and a description of the ideal liberal arts college.

3092 Wilson, Howard E. AMERICAN COLLEGE LIFE AS EDUCATION IN WORLD OUTLOOK. Washington, D.C.: American Council on Education, 1956. 195 p.

On the university's responsibility to provide education in world affairs, both in its degree programs and such informal experiences as student activities and overseas travel.

3093 Wilson, Howard E., and Wilson, Florence H. AMERICAN HIGHER EDUCATION AND WORLD AFFAIRS. Washington, D.C.: American Council on Education, 1963. 158 p.

Asks higher education institutions to survey resources and plan activities related to world affairs. Includes an analysis of institutional policy toward world affairs education and a survey of government programs.

3094 Wilson, James W., and Lyons, Edward H. WORK-STUDY COLLEGE PROGRAMS: APPRAISAL AND REPORT OF THE STUDY OF COOPERATIVE EDUCATION. New York: Harper and Brothers, 1961. 240 p.

Studied educational advantages of combining collegiate study and related work experience in business and industry as practiced by over sixty U.S. higher education institutions (an idea conceived in 1906 by Dean Herman Schneider, University of Cincinnati).

3095 Wilson, Kenneth M. ASSESSMENT OF THE GRADUATE STUDY AND CAREER PLANS OF SENIORS AT THREE LIBERAL ARTS COLLEGES FOR WOMEN: A PILOT PROJECT. Poughkeepsie, N.Y.: College Research Center, Vassar College, 1964. 24 p.

Used data from freshmen and seniors at three women's colleges to study the degree aspirations and career plans of women.

3096 _____. OF TIME AND THE DOCTORATE--REPORT OF AN INQUIRY INTO THE DURATION OF DOCTORAL STUDY. Atlanta: Southern Regional Education Board, 1965. 212 p.

In sixteen southern states, studied the time lapse between B.A. and Ph.D. completion (shortest in chemistry and almost thirteen years in English). Found that faculty demands were inconsistent and department administration unpredictable. Called for improving the machinery of graduate education.

3097 _____. SELECTED DATA PERTAINING TO THE HIGHER EDUCATION OF WOMEN. Poughkeepsie, N.Y.: College Research Center, Vassar College, 1967. 15 p.

Women's share of doctoral degrees declined from 18.4 percent in 1944 to 10.8 percent in 1964–65. Sixty percent of women's doctoral degrees earned during 1920–62 were earned between 1950–62. Women's share of higher education positions also declined from 29.8 percent in 1946 to 22.2 percent in 1963. Information presented shows women's share of earned degrees (1895–1965), women's share of higher education positions (1930–1963), productivity of selected undergraduate institutions in turning out women Ph.D. degree candidates, changing roles of women's colleges in producing doctoral degree recipients, and colleges and universities attractive to bright women high school students.

3098 _____, ed. RESEARCH RELATED TO COLLEGE ADMISSIONS. Atlanta: Southern Regional Education Board, 1963. 207 p.

Papers on research for more effective admissions and guidance include assessment of academic potential, admission of transfer students, conditional admissions, and concomitants of increasing selectivity in the admissions process.

3099 Wilson, Logan. THE ACADEMIC MAN: A STUDY IN THE SOCIOLOGY OF A PROFESSION. New York: Oxford University Press, 1942. 248 p.

Landmark sociological analysis of professors and their behavior in mainly large universities. The academic scene is described in terms of conditioning, activity patterns, controls, motivations, tenure, academic freedom, deans and presidents, and professional societies.

3100 _____. AMERICAN ACADEMICS THEN AND NOW. New York: Oxford University Press, 1979. 309 p.

Rising in the interim from sociologist and dean at Tulane to vice president and provost in the Universities of North Carolina and Texas systems, then to president and president-emeritus of the American Council on Education, Wilson recasts and updates his THE ACADEMIC MAN, 1942, in a compact synthesis of the momentous changes during 1940s–1970s in higher education and its professoriate.

3101 _____. SHAPING AMERICAN HIGHER EDUCATION. Washington, D.C.: American Council on Education, 1972. 301 p.

> Speeches and articles by the president of the American Council on Education on topics from national policies for U.S. higher education, to problems of students, faculty, and trustees.

3102 _____, ed. EMERGING PATTERNS IN AMERICAN HIGHER EDUCATION. Washington, D.C.: American Council on Education, 1965. 292 p.

> Essays on changes in the structure of U.S. colleges and universities and in their relationships with one another and with state and federal governments. Major concern is the threat to institutional freedom and autonomy posed by growing interdependence.

3103 Wilson, Logan, et al. STUDIES OF COLLEGE FACULTY: THE PAPERS PRESENTED AT AN INSTITUTE FOR COLLEGE AND UNIVERSITY ADMINISTRATORS AND FACULTY, UNIVERSITY OF CALIFORNIA, BERKELEY, JULY 31- AUGUST 4, 1961. Boulder, Colo.: Western Interstate Commission for Higher Education, 1961. 145 p.

> Lectures by Wilson (academic man revisited), Jonn E. Stecklein (research on faculty recruitment and motivation), Kenneth E. Clark (studies of faculty evaluation), James Doi (proper use of faculty load studies), and others.

3104 Wilson, Louis R. HARRY WOODBURN CHASE. Chapel Hill: University of North Carolina Press, 1960. 55 p.

> Chase (1883-1955) was president of the University of North Carolina (1919-30), University of Illinois (1930-33), and New York University (1933-51).

3105 _____. THE UNIVERSITY OF NORTH CAROLINA, 1900-1930: THE MAKING OF A MODERN UNIVERSITY. Chapel Hill: University of North Carolina Press, 1957. 633 p.

> Transition of the University of North Carolina from a college to a major university. Built around presidents Francis P. Venable, Edward K. Graham, Marvin H. Stacy, and Harry W. Chase.

3106 _____, ed. LIBRARY TRENDS: PAPERS PRESENTED BEFORE THE LIBRARY INSTITUTE AT THE UNIVERSITY OF CHICAGO, AUGUST 3-15, 1936. Chicago: University of Chicago Press, 1937. 388 p.

> Papers put libraries into social context and include Henry M. Wriston on the place of the library in the modern college, Leon Carnovsky on evaluation of public library facilities, and William F. Ogburn on recent social trends.

3107 Wilson, Louis R., and Tauber, Maurice Falcolm. THE UNIVERSITY LIBRARY. New York: Columbia University Press, 1956. 641 p.

Comprehensive coverage of university library finance, buildings, cooperation, administration, and organization.

3108 Wilson, Louis R., et al. THE LIBRARY IN COLLEGE INSTRUCTION: A SYLLABUS ON THE IMPROVEMENT OF COLLEGE INSTRUCTION THROUGH LIBRARY USE. New York: H.W. Wilson Co., 1951. 347 p.

Using the library to improve college instruction; sections on materials for general education at the college level, reading guidance, and the college library as a teaching instrument.

3109 _____. REPORT OF A SURVEY OF THE LIBRARIES OF CORNELL UNIVERSITY. Ithaca, N.Y.: Cornell University, 1948. 202 p.

Wilson, Robert Downs, and Maurice Tauber analyze problems and needs of Cornell University libraries.

3110 Wilson, Louis R., and Milczewski, Marion A., eds. LIBRARIES OF THE SOUTHEAST. Chapel Hill: University of North Carolina Press, 1949. 301 p.

Survey of library service, including service to higher education, in nine southeastern states.

3111 Wilson, Michele S. FINANCIAL AID FOR MINORITY STUDENTS IN BUSINESS. Garrett Park, Md.: Garrett Park Press, 1975. 32 p.

Brief summary of the business field, emphasizing career and educational options for minorities. Describes financial aid for graduate and professional study by national organizations, foundations, professional associations, federal agencies, and individual colleges and universities. Next three entries by same author have similar content for their respective fields.

3112 _____. FINANCIAL AID FOR MINORITY STUDENTS IN EDUCATION. Garrett Park, Md.: Garrett Park Press, 1975. 32 p.

Summary of teaching field, emphasizing career, educational, and financial options for minorities.

3113 _____. FINANCIAL AID FOR MINORITY STUDENTS IN JOURNALISM/COMMUNICATIONS. Garrett Park, Md.: Garrett Park Press, 1975. 32 p.

Brief summary of journalism-communications, emphasizing career, education, and financial aid options for minorities.

3114 _____. FINANCIAL AID FOR MINORITY STUDENTS IN LAW. Garrett Park, Md.: Garrett Park Press, 1975. 32 p.

Brief summary of legal field, emphasizing career, educational, and financial aid options for minorities.

3115 Wilson, Pauline Park. COLLEGE WOMEN WHO EXPRESS FUTILITY. Contributions to Education No. 956. New York: Teachers College, Columbia University, 1950. 166 p.

Study of attitudes of fifty women college graduates toward self, marriage, homemaking, vocational guidance, religious belief, philosophy of life, and other facets revealed a need for more guidance centers in colleges.

3116 Wilson, Robert C., et al. COLLEGE PROFESSORS AND THEIR IMPACT ON STUDENTS. New York: John Wiley and Sons, 1975. 220 p.

Empirical research found that effective teaching is related to how faculty treat students in class and especially outside of class.

3117 Windham, Douglas M. EDUCATION, EQUALITY AND INCOME REDISTRIBUTION: A STUDY OF PUBLIC HIGHER EDUCATION. Lexington, Mass.: D.C. Heath, 1970. 127 p.

Financing of higher education in Florida and its relation to taxation and the redistribution of income.

3118 Wingfield, Clyde J., ed. THE AMERICAN UNIVERSITY: A PUBLIC ADMINISTRATION PERSPECTIVE. Dallas: Southern Methodist University Press, 1970. 101 p.

Papers on university politics and governance. Themes: universities are complex and often immune to management studies, statewide coordination is eroding autonomy, and governance needs rethinking.

3119 Winther, Sophus Keith. BEYOND THE GARDEN GATE. New York: Macmillan Co., 1946. 289 p.

Novel about the indiscretions while in college of the son of a cultured Oregon family.

3120 Wirtz, Willard. THE BOUNDLESS RESOURCE: A PROSPECTUS FOR AN EDUCATION-WORK POLICY. Washington, D.C.: New Republic Book Co., 1975. 205 p.

Advocates a comprehensive U.S. policy to bring education, particularly higher education, and work closer together. Based on two-year study by the National Manpower Institute.

3121 Wisconsin. University. FINAL REPORT ON THE STATUS OF ACADEMIC WOMEN. Madison: 1971. 490 p.

Study of the sixteen University of Wisconsin campuses to determine if women are distributed across the academic levels in
a similar pattern to their male colleagues.

3122 _____ . WOMEN IN COLLEGE AND UNIVERSITY TEACHING. Madison:
1965. 54 p.

Papers on staff needs and women's opportunities in higher education.

3123 Wisconsin Alumni Research Foundation. FIFTY YEARS OF GRADUATE EDU-
CATION AT THE UNIVERSITY OF WISCONSIN. Madison: 1954. 68 p.

Pictorial description of the University of Wisconsin Graduate
School and its research on its fiftieth anniversary. Main
theme is university's scholarly ideals and social responsibilities.

3124 Wise, W. Max. THEY COME FOR THE BEST OF REASONS: COLLEGE
STUDENTS TODAY. Washington, D.C.: American Council on Education,
1958. 68 p.

Studied current changes in fifty-year perspective in college
students' enrollment, age, sex, employment, socioeconomic
background, race, religion, ability, persistence, fields studied,
and graduate study. Recommended reforms in curriculum,
teaching, and other aspects to assure that higher education is
meeting student needs.

3125 Withey, Stephen Bassett, ed. A DEGREE AND WHAT ELSE? CORRE-
LATES AND CONSEQUENCES OF A COLLEGE EDUCATION. New York:
McGraw-Hill Book Co., 1971. 147 p.

Summarizes measurable outcomes of higher education and its
impact on students' values, political beliefs, earning capacity,
and other aspects. Concludes that every year of higher education makes a difference and that the impact is cumulative.

3126 Wittich, John J., ed. CONFERENCE ON COLLEGE AND UNIVERSITY
INTERINSTITUTIONAL COOPERATION. Corning, N.Y.: College Center
of the Finger Lakes, 1962. 87 p.

About organizing, planning projects for, and evaluating interinstitutional cooperation.

3127 Woelfel, Norman. MOLDERS OF THE AMERICAN MIND: A CRITICAL
REVIEW OF THE SOCIAL ATTITUDES OF SEVENTEEN LEADERS IN AMERI-
CAN EDUCATION. New York: Columbia University Press, 1933. 304 p.

Educational philosophies analyzed of professors Herman H.
Horne, Henry C. Morrison, William C. Bagley, Ellwood P.
Cubberley, Thomas H. Briggs, Ross L. Finney, Charles H.

Judd, David Snedden, Edward L. Thorndike, Ernest Horn, Werrett W. Charters, Franklin Bobbitt, John Dewey, George S. Counts, William H. Kilpatrick, Harold Rugg, and Boyd H. Bode.

3128 Woellner, Elizabeth H. REQUIREMENTS FOR CERTIFICATION OF TEACHERS, COUNSELORS, LIBRARIANS, ADMINISTRATORS. Chicago: University of Chicago Press, 1978. 234 p.

Certification requirements for administrators, junior college teachers, librarians, and counselors; issued regularly.

3129 Wolf, Robert Leopold. SPRINGBOARD. New York: Albert and Charles Boni, 1927. 274 p.

Novel of a Cleveland youth at Harvard who falls in love with a Radcliffe girl and goes off to do graduate work in economics.

3130 Wolfe, Thomas Clayton. LOOK HOMEWARD, ANGEL; A STORY OF THE BURIED LIFE. New York: Charles Scribner's Sons, 1929. 626 p.

Novel's hero is Eugene Gant; his college experiences reflect those of author Wolfe's at the University of North Carolina, Chapel Hill, New York University, and Harvard. These experiences are also treated in Wolfe's later novels, OF TIME AND THE RIVER, 1935; and THE WEB AND THE ROCK, 1939.

3131 Wolff, Robert Paul. THE IDEAL OF THE UNIVERSITY. Boston: Beacon Press, 1969. 161 p.

Radical argument for abolishing grades and the Ph.D., removing the university from its certification functions and from political involvement, and returning it to purely intellectual pursuits.

3132 Wolfle, Dael Lee. AMERICA'S RESOURCES OF SPECIALIZED TALENT. New York: Harper and Brothers, 1954. 332 p.

Classic study used extensive data on college graduation trends, occupational distribution of graduates, supply and demand in specialized fields, and characteristics of students entering specific fields. Recommends more effective use of educated specialists.

3133 _____. THE USES OF TALENT. Princeton, N.J.: Princeton University Press, 1971. 204 p.

Says higher education is not so much a job-training experience as a screen for those likely to be good employment risks. Foresees upgrading of educational requirements as employers confront an oversupply of B.A., M.A., and Ph.D. holders.

3134 _____, ed. THE DISCOVERY OF TALENT. Cambridge, Mass.: Harvard University Press, 1969. 316 p.

> Psychologists discuss such topics as diversity of talent, nurturing talent, identifying and conserving talent, and hereditary and environmental influences.

3135 Wolin, Sheldon S., and Schaar, John H. THE BERKELEY REBELLION AND BEYOND: ESSAYS ON POLITICS AND EDUCATION IN THE TECHNOLOGICAL SOCIETY. New York: Vintage Books, 1970. 158 p.

> Interpretations of late 1960s student uprisings emphasize conditions at Berkeley, where authors were located.

3136 Wolters, Raymond. THE NEW NEGRO ON CAMPUS: BLACK COLLEGE REBELLIONS OF THE 1920S. Princeton, N.J.: Princeton University Press, 1975. 370 p.

> Black student strikes in the 1920s at Fisk, Howard, and Lincoln Universities, Tuskegee Institute, and others. Says that the 1920s was a time of rising consciousness among blacks.

3137 Women's University. College of Education. Denton, Texas. THE WOMAN EDUCATOR: DESIGNER OF THE '70S. Denton: 1970. 23 p.

> Describes woman educators of the 1970s and indicates that discriminatory practices and concepts should be abolished.

3138 Wood, Lynn, and Davis, Barbara Gross. DESIGNING AND EVALUATING HIGHER EDUCATION CURRICULA. Washington, D.C.: American Association for Higher Education, 1979. 65 p.

> A practical look at curriculum design and evaluation for administrators and faculty members.

3139 Woodburne, Lloyd S. FACULTY PERSONNEL POLICIES IN HIGHER EDUCATION. New York: Harper and Brothers, 1950. 201 p.

> Practices of forty-six northern U.S. universities and colleges on faculty selection and encouragement, appraisal and promotion, and tenure and dismissal.

3140 _____. PRINCIPLES OF COLLEGE AND UNIVERSITY ADMINISTRATION. Stanford, Calif.: Stanford University Press, 1958. 197 p.

> Introduction to higher education administration; stresses various approaches to problems and structural and organizational aspects.

3141 Woodhouse, Chase Going. BUSINESS OPPORTUNITIES FOR THE HOME ECONOMIST. New York: McGraw-Hill Book Co., 1938. 262 p.

Qualifications and opportunities for college-trained home economists in business-related employment.

3142 _____, ed. AFTER COLLEGE--WHAT? Greensboro: North Carolina
College for Women, 1932. 200 p.

Survey of several thousand women graduates of land-grant institutions revealed that most chose marriage, homemaking, and
teaching; highest earnings went to business executives; married
women in education and home economics earned less than
single women; and children were no handicap to earning.

3143 Woodress, Fred A. PUBLIC RELATIONS FOR COMMUNITY/JUNIOR COL-
LEGES. Danville, Ill.: Interstate Printers and Publishers, 1976. 62 p.

Suggestions for an effective public relations program in a two-
year college.

3144 Woodring, Paul. THE HIGHER LEARNING IN AMERICA: A REASSESS-
MENT. New York: McGraw-Hill Book Co., 1968. 236 p.

Survey of U.S. colleges and universities in 1968.

3145 _____. INVESTMENT IN INNOVATION: AN HISTORICAL APPRAISAL
OF THE FUND FOR THE ADVANCEMENT OF EDUCATION. Boston:
Little, Brown and Co., 1970. 323 p.

History and interpretation of the Fund for the Advancement of
Education. Discusses sensitive educational areas, the status
of U.S. education, and the role of philanthropic organizations.

3146 _____. NEW DIRECTIONS IN TEACHER EDUCATION. New York: Fund
for the Advancement of Education, 1957. 142 p.

On fifth-year professional programs for liberal arts graduates
and programs for older college graduates with some job experience other than teaching.

3147 Woods, Paul J. CAREER OPPORTUNITIES FOR PSYCHOLOGISTS: EX-
PANDING AND EMERGING AREAS. Washington, D.C.: American Psychological Association, 1977. 307 p.

Job opportunities for graduate psychologists in higher education,
human services, industry, business, government, and population
and environmental research.

3148 Woody, Thomas, ed. EDUCATIONAL VIEWS OF BENJAMIN FRANKLIN.
New York: McGraw-Hill Book Co., 1931. 270 p.

Franklin's ideas on education, including the Philadelphia Academy which became the University of Pennsylvania.

3149 Woolery, W. Kirk. BETHANY YEARS. Huntington, W. Va.: Standard Printing and Publishing Co., 1941. 290 p.

> History stressing personalities and social life rather than academic development of Bethany College, West Virginia, founded in 1840 by Disciples of Christ leader Alexander Campbell (born 1788), its president until his death in 1866.

3150 World Studies Data Bank. INTERNATIONAL EDUCATION CONTACTS ON U.S. CAMPUSES: A DIRECTORY. New York: Academy for Educational Development, 1974.

> Lists names, addresses, and telephone numbers of 832 persons responsible for the coordination of international education programs on U.S. campuses.

3151 Worthen, Blaine R., and Roaden, Arliss L. THE RESEARCH ASSISTANT-SHIP: RECOMMENDATIONS FOR COLLEGES AND UNIVERSITIES. Bloomington, Ind.: Phi Delta Kappa, 1975. 116 p.

> Suggests practical ways to strengthen research assistantship training. One recommendation is that the faculty researcher who supervises assistants should receive systematic training.

3152 Wrenn, C. Gilbert. STUDENT PERSONNEL WORK IN COLLEGE. New York: Ronald Press, 1951. 589 p.

> Examples of student personnel procedures, practices, and problems at various higher education institutions. Section by Ruth Strang on group experiences.

3153 Wright, Patricia S., ed. INSTITUTIONAL RESEARCH AND COMMUNICATION IN HIGHER EDUCATION. Berkeley, Calif.: Association for Institutional Research, 1970. 279 p.

> Papers on the responsibility of institutional researchers to communicate with higher education constituencies (including state agencies, administrators, faculty, and students). Topics include long-range planning and management information systems.

3154 Wriston, Henry M. ACADEMIC PROCESSION: REFLECTIONS OF A COLLEGE PRESIDENT. New York: Columbia University Press, 1959. 222 p.

> Wriston (1889–) moved from the presidency of Wisconsin's Lawrence University, Appleton (1925–37), to Brown University (1937–55), where he doubled the endowment, increased the enrollment, and became a major leader in U.S. higher education.

3155 _____. THE NATURE OF A LIBERAL COLLEGE. Appleton, Wis.: Lawrence College Press, 1937. 177 p.

College president's thoughts on liberal education, students, faculty, the library, vocational guidance, discipline, and college structure.

3156 _____. WRISTON SPEAKING. Providence, R.I.: Brown University Press, 1957. 264 p.

Papers by president emeritus of Brown University on such topics as liberal arts, the role of government, and international relations.

3157 Wylie, Francis E. M.I.T. IN PERSPECTIVE: A PICTORIAL HISTORY OF THE MASSACHUSETTS INSTITUTE OF TECHNOLOGY. Boston: Little, Brown and Co., 1976. 220 p.

Author is former public relations director of MIT.

3158 Wylie, Kiskaddon. ALTOGETHER NOW! New York: Farrar and Rinehart, 1932. 342 p.

Novel about a freshman revolted by excesses in an eastern college; written the summer after the author's freshman year.

3159 Wyman, Walker D. THE FROSTING ON THE CAKE: HISTORY OF THE UNIVERSITY OF WISCONSIN-RIVER FALLS FOUNDATION, 1948-1976. River Falls: University of Wisconsin, River Falls Press, 1977. 87 p.

History of the University of Wisconsin, River Falls Foundation, since its creation in 1948.

3160 Wynne, John P. GENERAL EDUCATION IN THEORY AND PRACTICE. New York: Bookman Associates, 1952. 251 p.

Examines philosophy of general education. Comments on extra-curricular activities, the lecture system, and the important role of the teacher in accomplishing the goals of general education.

3161 Yale Daily News, ed. THE INSIDERS' GUIDE TO THE COLLEGES, 1978-79 EDITION. New York: Berkley Publishing Co., 1978. 404 p.

Breezy student-oriented profile of social and academic conditions at 230 U.S. colleges and universities. Supplements standard guides for prospective students who want an inside track.

3162 Yang, C. MEET THE U.S.A.: HANDBOOK FOR FOREIGN STUDENTS IN THE UNITED STATES. New York: Institute of International Education, 1945. 184 p.

For foreign students and teachers, especially Chinese, coming to the United States. Uses author's personal experiences and tells of racial discrimination and other practices inconsistent with U.S. democratic principles.

3163 Yankelovich, Daniel, Inc. THE CHANGING VALUES ON CAMPUS: POLITICAL AND PERSONAL ATTITUDES OF TODAY'S COLLEGE STUDENTS. New York: Washington Square Press, 1972. 246 p.

Attitudes of twelve hundred college students surveyed during 1968-71 on many subjects, including marriage (declining in popularity) to education (growing skepticism). Attitudes are shown in relation to religion, race, socioeconomic status, and other variables.

3164 Yarrington, Roger, ed. EDUCATIONAL OPPORTUNITY FOR ALL: NEW STAFF FOR NEW STUDENTS. Washington, D.C.: American Association of Community and Junior Colleges, 1974. 160 p.

Conference report on the need for pre-service and inservice programs to improve two-year college staff.

3165 _____. INTERNATIONALIZING COMMUNITY COLLEGES. Washington, D.C.: American Association of Community and Junior Colleges, 1979. 103 p.

Papers on the role of international education in community colleges.

3166 _____. USING MASS MEDIA FOR LEARNING. Washington, D.C.: American Association of Community and Junior Colleges, 1979. 89 p.

On faculty involvement and financing patterns in the use of educational television in two-year colleges. Recommends college consortia to pool expertise and resources.

3167 Yeomans, William N. JOBS '77. New York: Berkley Publishing Co., 1977. 294 p.

Vocational guidance for college students on resumes, interviews, and other aspects of getting a job. Lists wide range of jobs and skills and education needed. Special advice for minorities and women.

3168 Young, Betty Irene. THE LIBRARY OF THE WOMAN'S COLLEGE, DUKE UNIVERSITY 1930-1972. Durham, N.C.: Regulator Press, 1978. 140 p.

History of women's education and the Woman's College's library at Duke University.

3169 Young, Douglas Parker. THE LAW AND THE STUDENT IN HIGHER EDU-

CATION. Topeka, Kans.: National Organization on Legal Problems of Education, 1977. 56 p.

Summarizes laws on students in higher education.

3170 _____, ed. HIGHER EDUCATION: THE LAW AND ADMINISTRATIVE RESPONSIBILITIES. Athens: Institute of Higher Education, University of Georgia, 1977. 51 p.

Conference report (1977) on implications of judicial decisions for academic decision making.

3171 _____. HIGHER EDUCATION: THE LAW AND INDIVIDUAL RIGHTS AND RESPONSIBILITIES. Athens: University of Georgia, 1971. 51 p.

Papers on protecting students' civil rights, declining distinction between public and private institutions, and legal questions on faculty contract negotiations.

3172 _____. HIGHER EDUCATION: THE LAW AND INSTITUTIONAL CHALLENGES. Athens: Institute of Higher Education, University of Georgia, 1979. 34 p.

Conference report (1978) on implications of judicial rulings for academic decision making.

3173 _____. THE YEARBOOK OF HIGHER EDUCATION LAW, 1977. Topeka, Kans.: National Organization on Legal Problems of Education, 1978. 173 p.

Describes 1977 higher education court cases involving governance, finance, property, tort liability, employees, and students.

3174 _____. THE YEARBOOK OF HIGHER EDUCATION LAW, 1978. Topeka, Kans.: National Organization on Legal Problems of Education, 1979. 226 p.

Summary and analysis of 1978 state and federal court cases involving higher education.

3175 Young, Douglas Parker, and Gehring, Donald D. THE COLLEGE STUDENT AND THE COURTS. Asheville, N.C.: College Administration Publications, 1973-- . Various pagination.

Quarterly issued briefs on selected court cases involving student and higher education institutional relationships.

3176 Young, Elizabeth Barber. A STUDY OF THE CURRICULA OF SEVEN SELECTED WOMEN'S COLLEGES OF THE SOUTHERN STATES. Contributions to Education No. 511. New York: Teachers College, Columbia University, 1932. 220 p.

Explores chronologically the background, aims, and curricula of seven southern women's colleges. Compares and analyzes their programs, teaching staffs, and size of instructional units. Concludes that, historically, their curricula have resembled those for men but that courses to prepare students for traditional female roles are increasing.

3177 Young, Ella Flagg. ISOLATION IN THE SCHOOL. Chicago: University of Chicago Press, 1900. 57 p.

University of Chicago education professor (later Chicago's superintendent of schools, 1909-15) calls for cooperation among the various educational levels, from kindergarten through university.

3178 Young, James B., and Ewing, James M. THE MISSISSIPPI PUBLIC JUNIOR COLLEGE STORY: THE FIRST FIFTY YEARS, 1922-1972. Jackson: University Press of Mississippi, 1978. 342 p.

Histories of Mississippi public junior colleges, biographies of their leaders, junior college organizations, activities, standards, and laws.

3179 Young, Nancy, and Taylor, Mary Louise, eds. HANDBOOK ON INTERNATIONAL STUDY FOR U.S. NATIONALS: STUDY IN EUROPE. New York: Institute of International Education, 1976. 307 p.

Directory for U.S. undergraduate and graduate students listing Western and Eastern European higher education programs in 170 fields. Includes information on language needs, admissions policy, degrees granted, housing-travel costs, passports and visas, scholarships and fellowships, employment opportunities, and government regulations.

3180 Zallen, Harold, and Zallen, Eugenia M. IDEAS PLUS DOLLARS: RESEARCH METHODOLOGY AND FUNDING. Norman, Okla.: Academic World, 1977. 387 p.

How to obtain research funds from federal agencies, foundations, and industry.

3181 Zapoleon, Marguerite Wykoff. THE COLLEGE GIRL LOOKS AHEAD TO HER CAREER OPPORTUNITIES. New York: Harper and Brothers, 1956. 272 p.

College girls' vocational guide gives characteristics of principal fields open to women college graduates and educational requirements for each.

3182 _____. OCCUPATIONAL PLANNING FOR WOMEN. New York: Harper and Brothers, 1961. 276 p.

Problems of women's education, particularly higher education and continuing education, and suggestions on planning for occupations and professions. For counselors, advisers, parents, and students.

3183 Zauderer, Donald G. URBAN INTERNSHIPS IN HIGHER EDUCATION. Washington, D.C.: American Association for Higher Education, 1973. 37 p.

On improving the structure and design of university-based urban internships (in such fields as education and social work).

3184 Ziegfeld, Ernest Herbert. ART IN THE COLLEGE PROGRAM OF GENERAL EDUCATION. New York: Teachers College, Columbia University, 1953. 239 p.

Surveys historical and contemporary role of art education in college general education programs. Reflects the art education ideas of John Dewey, Susanne Langer, Lewis Mumford, and Herbert Read. Argues that art education should have equal position with sciences in modern education.

3185 Zimmer, Agatho. CHANGING CONCEPTS OF HIGHER EDUCATION IN AMERICA SINCE 1700. Washington, D.C.: Catholic University of America, 1938. 139 p.

While higher education has changed to accommodate technological advances, vocational concerns, and women's educational needs, author says the liberal arts have dominated and ought to dominate for their ethical-moral inculcation. Catholic higher education, while never abandoning liberal arts' moral-ethical values, has included more social sciences.

3186 Zimmermann, Barbara, and Smith, David B. CAREERS IN HEALTH: THE PROFESSIONALS GIVE YOU THE INSIDE PICTURE ABOUT THEIR JOBS. Boston: Beacon Press, 1979. 239 p.

Career information, educational requirements, opportunities, and responsibilities presented through a typical workday of some twenty health care workers, including physician's assistant, clinical pharmacist, laboratory technician, hospital ward clerk, and health educator.

3187 Zinn, Howard. SNCC: THE NEW ABOLITIONISTS. 2d ed. Boston: Beacon Press, 1965. 286 p.

Student Non-Violent Coordinating Committee activities from its founding by sixteen college students during 1960 Greensboro, North Carolina, sit-in demonstrations. On freedom rides, voter registration, and other SNCC activities in Mississippi, Georgia, and Alabama.

3188 Zoglin, Mary Lou. POWER AND POLITICS IN THE COMMUNITY COLLEGE. Palm Springs, Calif.: E.T.C. Publications, 1976. 166 p.

On the power structure in community colleges. How decision making is affected by federal, state, trustee, faculty, and student interests. By the president of the California Community College Trustees, who is also president of the California Community and Junior College Association.

3189 Zook, George F., ed. HIGHER EDUCATION FOR AMERICAN DEMOCRACY: A REPORT OF THE PRESIDENT'S COMMISSION ON HIGHER EDUCATION. 6 vols. Washington, D.C.: Government Printing Office, 1947. Various pagination.

President's Commission on Higher Education (appointed July 1946 by President Truman) predicted that by 1952 higher education faculty should double and by 1960 an additional fifty thousand faculty would be needed to train teachers to serve anticipated increases in school enrollments. The six volumes are on establishing goals; equalizing and expanding educational opportunities; organizing, staffing, and financing higher education; and resource data.

3190 Zook, George F., and Haggerty, Melvin E. PRINCIPLES OF ACCREDITING HIGHER INSTITUTIONS. Chicago: University of Chicago Press, 1936. 202 p.

Discusses North Central Association's new plan for accrediting higher education institutions, how it will be applied, its flexibility, and its goal.

3191 Zorza, Richard. THE RIGHT TO SAY WE: THE ADVENTURES OF A YOUNG ENGLISHMAN AT HARVARD AND IN THE YOUTH MOVEMENT. New York: Praeger Publishers, 1970. 213 p.

On student protest at Harvard in spring 1969; written by a sensitive, radical undergraduate from England.

3192 Zuker, R. Fred, and Hegener, Karen Collier. PETERSON'S GUIDE TO COLLEGE ADMISSIONS: HOW TO PUT THE ODDS ON YOUR SIDE. New York: Monarch Press, 1976. 288 p.

Duke University admissions officer Zuker explains admissions process, test requirements, financial aid available, and special admissions opportunities at fifteen hundred briefly profiled four-year colleges.

3193 Zwerling, Steven L. SECOND BEST: THE CRISIS OF THE COMMUNITY COLLEGE. New York: McGraw-Hill Book Co., 1976. 382 p.

Revisionist author believes that the community college (he

teaches in one) gives the illusion of serving the poor through a second-class two-year Associate of Arts degree. Community colleges' hidden function is to channel lower class potential B.A. candidates into lower paying jobs and protect privileged youths in four-year colleges. He alleges that California discriminates by spending twice as much on four-year colleges as on two-year colleges and that counselors and placement tests are biased against low-income students. Seventy-five percent of entering community college students say they want to get a B.A. degree, but less than twelve percent actually do so. His solution is to eliminate community colleges, have open admissions to four-year colleges, and expand four-year college work-study options.

3194 Zyskind, Harold, and Sternfeld, Robert. THE VOICELESS UNIVERSITY: AN ARGUMENT FOR INTELLECTUAL AUTONOMY. San Francisco: Jossey-Bass Publishers, 1971. 193 p.

Authors see 1960s student protests as wasteful and deflecting the university from its true intellectual function. They urge the silent majority of students, professors, and the public to restore the university to disciplined inquiry.

AUTHOR INDEX

This index includes all authors, editors, compilers, translators, and other contributors to works cited in the text. References are to entry number and alphabetization is letter by letter.

A

Abbott, Frank C. 1-2
Abramson, Joan 3
Academy for Educational Development.
  Management Division 4
Adams, Frank C. 5
Adams, Hazard 6
Adams, Henry 7
Adams, Walter 8-11, 929, 1378
Adler, Mortimer J. 12
Aiken, Henry David 13
Alexander, Louis 14
Alexander, Thomas 15
Alford, Harold J. 16
Allen, Herman R. 17
Allen, John S. 1938
Allmendinger, David F., Jr. 18
Almond, Gabriel 2651
Altbach, Philip G. 1669
Altman, Robert A. 19-20
Altschule, Mark D. 123
Ambrose, Stephen E. 21
American Academy of Arts and
  Sciences 22
American Association for Higher Edu-
  cation and National Education
  Association Task Force 23
American Association of Engineers 24
American College Public Relations
  Association 25

American College Testing Program
  26-27
American Council on Education 28
American Council on Education.
  Committee on Measurement and
  Evaluation 29
American Council on Education.
  Committee on Personnel Methods
  30
American Home Economics Association
  31
American Library Association and the
  Association of College and Ref-
  erence Libraries 32
Amory, Cleveland 33
Anastasi, Anne 34
Andersen, Charles J. 1592
Anderson, Charles H. 35
Anderson, Charles J. 2447
Anderson, Elaine Vanden Bout 2876
Anderson, G. Lester 36-37
Anderson, Richard C. 38
Anderson, Richard E. 39
Andrews, F. Emerson 40-41
Anello, Michael 42
Angell, George W. 43
Angell, James Rowland 44
Angoff, William H. 45
Antione, George H. 2221
Arbeiter, Solomon 793

Author Index

Archer, Jerome W. 46
Argyris, Chris 47
Armstrong, W. Earl 48
Arnstein, George E. 49
Ashby, Eric 50-51
Ashford, Mahlon 52
Ashworth, Kenneth H. 53
Associated Colleges of the St. Lawrence Valley 54
Astin, Alexander W. 55-63, 2235
Astin, Helen S. 64, 1149
Atelsek, Frank J. 65, 994
Augenblick, John 66
Augustine, Grace M. 67
Aussieker, Bill 921
Averill, Lloyd J. 68
Axelrod, Joseph 69
Aydelotte, Frank 70
Ayers, Archie R. 71

B

Babbidge, Homer D. 72
Babbitt, Irving 73
Badger, Henry Glenn 74-75
Baer, Betty L. 76
Bailey, Frederick George 77
Bailey, Robert L. 78
Bailey, Stephen K. 79
Bailyn, Bernard 80
Baird, Leonard L. 81-83
Baker, Carlos Heard 84
Baker, Curtis O. 85-87
Baker, Dorothy Dodds 88
Baker, Liva 89
Bakke, E. Wight 90
Bakke, Mary S. 90
Balderston, Frederick E. 91
Baldridge, J. Victor 92-94, 1483, 2418
Balgley, Frances 1886
Barbash, Jack 95
Barber, Elsie Marion Oakes 96
Barber, Lee O. 922
Barger, Ben 1068
Barish, Norma N. 97
Barlow, William 98
Barnard, John 99
Barnes, B.J. 725
Barr, Stringfellow 100

Barrett, Laurence 2629
Barron, Frank 2824
Barron's Educational Series 101
Barry, Coleman J. 102
Barry, Toni 103
Bartlett, Willard W. 104
Barzun, Jacques 105-6
Baskin, Samuel 107
Bauer, Ronald C. 108
Bayerl, Elizabeth 109
Beach, Arthur G. 110
Beach, Mark 111, 2991
Beals, Ralph A. 112-13
Bean, Donald E. 114
Beatty, Richmond Croom 115
Beaumont, Andre G. 116
Beck, Hubert Park 117
Becker, Carl L. 118
Becker, Gary S. 119
Becker, Howard S. 120-21
Beckett, Frederick E. 122
Beecher, Henry K. 123
Beezer, Robert H. 124
Beggs, David W. III 125
Begin, James P. 126
Belcher, Jane C. 127
Belknap, Robert L. 128
Bell, Daniel 129
Ben-David, Joseph 130
Bender, Louis W. 131, 3015
Benet, Stephen Vincent 132
Benezet, Louis T. 133
Bengelsdorf, Winnie 134
Bennett, A.M. 460
Bennett, Alwina 993
Bennett, Joan Frances 2523
Bennett, John W. 135
Bennett, Margaret Elaine 136
Bennett, Robert L. 137
Bennett, Wendell C. 138
Bennis, Warren G. 139
Benson, Charles S. 140-41
Berdahl, Robert O. 142
Berdie, Ralph F. 143-46
Bereday, George Z.F. 147-48
Berelson, Bernard 149-50
Beresford-Howe, Constance 151
Berg, Ivar 152
Bergen, Dan 153
Bergguist, William H. 154-55

Author Index

Author Index

Author Index

Author Index

Author Index

M

Author Index

Norton, Arthur O. 2172
Norwood, William Frederick 2173
Nosow, Sigmund 2174-75
Notestein, Wallace 2851
Novak, Steven J. 2176
Novalis, Peter N. 1163
Nowlan, James Dunlap 2177
Nye, Russell B. 2178
Nyquist, Ewald B. 2179
Nyre, Glenn F. 2452

O

Oaks, Dallin 2180
O'Banion, Terry 2181-84
O'Connell, Thomas E. 2185
O'Connor, Thomas J. 2186
Odegaard, Charles E. 2187
Offner, Herman Leroy 2188
Ogilvie, William 2189
O'Hara, William T. 2190
O'Hearne, John J. 2191, 2964
Ohio. Board of Regents 2192-93
Ohio. State University. Columbus 2194
Ohio University. Athens. Center for Afro-American Studies 2195
Ohmann, Richard Malin 2196-97
Oinas, Felix J. 2198
Olin, Helen R. 2199
Olson, Keith W. 2200
Oltman, Ruth M. 2201
O'Neil, Mary L. 2556
O'Neil, Robert M. 2202-3
O'Neill, Barbara Powell 2204
O'Neill, Mary Berenice 2205
Orcutt, William Dana 2206
Organization for Economic Co-operation and Development 2207
Orlans, Harold 2208-10
O'Rourke, John T. 2211
Orwig, M.D. 2212
Osgood, Charles G. 2213
Ostheimer, Richard 2214
O'Toole, James 2215
O'Toole, Simon 2216
Ott, Mary Diederich 2217
Otten, C. Michael 2218
Otto, Max C. 2219
Owen, Wyn F. 2221
Ozmon, Howard 2222

P

Pace, Charles Robert 2223-27
Pacific Northwest Conference on Higher Education 2228
Padgett, William 2232
Page, Robert G. 2229
Palinchak, Robert 2230
Palmer, Archie MacInnes 1595, 2231
Palmer, Hans 2520
Palola, Ernest G. 2232
Pangburn, Jessie M. 2233
Pannell, Anne Gary 2234
Panos, Robert J. 61, 2235
Papillon, Cassian Edmund 2236
Paredes, Americo 2237
Parekh, Satish B. 2238-39
Park, Clyde W. 2240
Park, Joe 2241
Parker, Betty June 2245-47
Parker, Clyde A. 2242
Parker, Franklin 2243-47
Parker, Gail Thain 2248
Parker, James Reid 2249
Parker, Orin D. 2250
Parker, Samuel Chester 1435
Parsons, Kermit Carlyle 2251
Parsons, Talcott 2252
Partch, Clarence Elmar 2253
Passell, Peter 2254
Patterson, Franklin Kessel 2255
Patterson, Robert A. 2011
Patterson, Samuel W. 2256
Pattillo, Manning M., Jr. 2257
Patton, Carl V. 2258
Patton, Leslie Karr 2259
Paulsen, Frank Robert 2260
Payne, Charles E. 2261
Peabody, Francis Greenwood 2262
Peabody, Mabel Clarke 2051
Peairs, Richard H. 2263
Peare, Catherine Owens 2264
Pearson, Richard 2265
Peck, Elisabeth S. 2266
Peirce, Adah 2267
Pell, Arthur R. 2268
Peltason, Jack Walter 2269
Pember, Timothy 2270
Penman, Kenneth A. 2272
Penney, James F. 2271

Author Index

R

Radcliffe College Committee on Graduate Education for Women 2346
Rader, Benjamin G. 2347
Rader, Hannelore B. 2348
Radosh, Ronald 1905
Radway, Laurence I. 1853
Raiborn, Mitchell H. 2349
Raines, Max R. 2189, 2350
Rainey, Homer P. 2351
Rainsford, George N. 2352
Ramaley, Judith 2353
Rammelkamp, Charles Henry 2354
Ramsey, Leah W. 1409
Rand, Christopher 2355
Rand, E.K. 2851
Raney, M. Llewellyn 2356
Rapoport, Roger 2357
Rapoza, Rita S. 1093
Rappleye, Willard C. 2358
Rarig, Emory W., Jr. 2359
Rasey, Marie I. 2360
Ratterman, P.H. 2361
Rattigan, Bernard T. 2362
Rauh, Morton A. 2363-64
Raushenbush, Esther 2063, 2365-67
Ray, Anna Chapin 2368
Ray, Robert F. 2369
Reardon, Robert C. 2370
Reck, W. Emerson 2371-73
Redfield, Margaret Park 2374
Redmount, Robert S. 2599
Reece, Ernest J. 2375-77
Reed, Anna Y. 2378
Reed, Germaine M. 2379
Reeves, Floyd W. 2380-90, 2502
Reich, David 235
Reich, Warren T. 2391
Reid, Mary Eliza 2392
Reinert, Paul Clare 2393-94
Renetzky, Alvin 2395
Research Resources Information Center 2396
Resnick, Rosa Perla 2757
Resnick, William C. 2398
Rever, Philip R. 2399-2400
Reynolds, James W. 2401
Rich, Catherine R. 2402-3
Rich, Harvey E. 2404

Richards, Alice L. 1154
Richards, Robert K. 2405
Richardson, Leroy Parker 2406
Richardson, Richard C., Jr. 2045, 2407-8
Richman, Barry M. 2409
Richter, Peyton E. 1580
Rider, Fremont 2410
Rieke, Robert 2411
Riendeau, Albert J. 2412
Riesman, David 1018, 1390, 1670, 2413-15
Rigby, Barry D. 2416
Riker, Harold C. 2417
Riley, Gary L. 2418
Riley, John W., Jr. 2419
Risenhoover, Morris 2420
Ritchie, Andrew Carnduff 2421
Ritchie, Miller Alfred Franklin 2422
Ritterbush, Philip C. 2423
Rives, Stanley G. 278
Rivlin, Alice M. 2424
Rivlin, Harry N. 2425
Roach, Helen P. 2426
Roaden, Arliss L. 3151
Robbins, Gene A. 1678
Robbins, Martin D. 2427
Robbins, Paula I. 2428
Robbins, Rainard B. 2429
Roberts, Dayton Y. 2430-31
Roberts, Michael D. 751
Robertson, D.B. 2432
Robinson, Edgar Eugene 2433-34
Robinson, Lora H. 2435-37
Robson, William A. 2438
Roche, George C. III 2439
Rockart, John Fralick 2440
Rodgers, Walter P. 2441
Rogan, Donald L. 2442
Rogers, Carl R. 2443
Rogers, Dorothy 2444
Rogers, Francis Millet 2445
Roose, Kenneth D. 2447
Root, Edward Merrill 2448
Roper, Elmo 2449
Rose, Arnold M. 2450
Rose, Clare 2451-52
Rosecrance, Francis C. 2453
Rosen, Charles 2454

Skinner, B.F. 2641-42
Skousen, Fred K. 2643
Slater, John R. 2644
Sloan, Douglas 2645
Sloan Study Consortium 2646
Slosson, Edwin E. 2647
Smallwood, Frank 2648
Smallwood, Mary Lovett 2649
Smart, John C. 2650
Smelser, Neil J. 2651
Smiley, Marjorie B. 2652
Smith, Alden Wallace 2653
Smith, Alfred G. 2654
Smith, Barbara G. 2511
Smith, Bardwell L. 2655-65
Smith, Carolyn R. 2312
Smith, David B. 3186
Smith, Goldwin 2666
Smith, Harry E. 2667
Smith, Henry Lewis 2668
Smith, Huston 2669
Smith, James P. 2670
Smith, John Edwin 2671
Smith, Leo F. 2672
Smith, Margaret Ruth 817, 1681-82, 2673
Smith, Robert 2674
Smith, Robert Ora 2675
Smith, Sherman E. 2676
Smith, Shirley W. 2677
Smith, Thomas Vernor 2678
Smith, Virginia B. 2679
Smith, Wilson 1254, 2680
Snavely, Guy E. 2681-82
Snelling, W. Rodman 2683
Snider, Patricia J. 2684
Snow, Jerry J. 2476
Snyder, Benson R. 2685
Snyder, Patricia O. 20, 1982
Soffen, Joseph 2686
Solberg, Winton U. 2687
Solmon, Lewis C. 2688-90
Songe, Alice H. 2691
Sophia Smith Collection 2692
Sorenson, Herbert 2693
Sosdian, Carol P. 2694-95
Southern California. University 2696
Southern Education Reporting Service 2697

Southern Regional Education Board 2698-2708
Southwestern Conference on Higher Education 2709
Spaeth, Joe L. 2710
Spafford, Ivol 2711-12
Spalding, John Lancaster 2713
Spaulding, Seth 2714
Spear, George E. 2715
Speek, Frances Valiant 1784
Spencer, Anna Carpenter Garlin 2716
Spender, Stephen 2717
Splaver, Sarah 2718
Sprouse, Betsy M. 2719
Spurr, Stephen Hopkins 2720
Stadtman, Verne A. 2415, 2721
Stalnaker, John M. 2722
Stanford University 2723-25
Stanford University. School of Humanities 2726
Stark, Joan S. 2727-29
Starr, Paul 2994
Starrak, James A. 2730
Staton, Thomas Felix 2732
Stauffer, Thomas M. 2733
Staupers, Mabel Keaton 2734
Stearns, Myron M. 2735
Stecklein, John E. 2736-37
Stegner, Wallace Earle 2738
Steiger, JoAnn M. 2739
Stein, Morris Isaac 2740-41
Steiner, Bernard C. 2742
Steiner, Gilbert Yale 2743
Stent, Madelon D. 248
Stephens, Clarence W. 5
Stephens, Frank F. 2744
Stern, George G. 2745
Sterne, Emma Gelders 2746
Sternfeld, Robert 3194
Stevens, David H. 2747
Stevens, George E. 2748
Stevens, Walter James 2749
Stewart, Clifford T. 2750
Stewart, David C. 2751
Stewart, George Rippey 2752
Stewart, Helen Quien 2753
Stewart, Robert Bruce 2754
Stickler, William Hugh 699, 2755-56

Author Index

Author Index

Usdan, Michael D. 2956
Useem, Elizabeth L. 2957
Useem, Michael 2957

V

Vaccaro, Louis C. 2958-59
Vairo, Philip D. 2275
Valentine, Percy Friars 2960
Van Aken, Carol G. 1858
Van de Graaf, John H. 2961
Vanderbilt, Kermit 2962
Van Doren, Mark 2963
Van Dusen, William D. 2964
Van Male, John 2965
Van Metre, Thurman W. 2966
Vaughan, Marilyn 2967
Vaughn, George B. 2968
Veblen, Thorstein 2969
Venn, Grant 2970
Vergara, Allys Dwyer 2971
Vermilye, Dyckman W. 2972-77
Vermorcken, Elizabeth Moorhead 2978
Veysey, Laurence R. 2979
Viles, Jonas 2980
Visher, Stephen Sargent 2981
von Klemperer, Lily 2982

W

Wade, George H. 2983
Wade, Harold, Jr. 2984
Wagner, Geoffrey 2985
Wagoner, Jennings L., Jr. 2046
Wagstaff, Lonnie H. 2015
Waite, Frederick Clayton 2986
Waldo, Dwight 2987
Waldstein, Charles 2988
Wales, Terence 2822
Walford, Alberto J. 2989
Walker, Donald E. 2990
Walker, Marion 2991
Walker, Robert H. 2992
Wallace, Walter L. 2993
Wallerstein, Immanuel 2994
Walling, Ruth 765
Walsh, Chad 2996
Walsh, James J. 2997
Walters, Everett 2998

Waltzer, Herbert 2999
Walwada, Mark 2468
Walworth, Dorothy 3000
Warch, Richard 3001
Ward, Clarence 2851
Ward, Jennifer C. 2522
Ward, Jesse L. 3002
Ward, Mary Jane 3003-4
Ward, Merle Scott 3005
Ward, Robert C. 3006
Warnath, Charles Frederick 3007-8
Warren, Constance 3009
Warren, Donald R. 3010
Warren, Jonathan R. 1194
Wasserman, Elga Ruth 3011-12
Watkin, Lawrence Edward 3013
Watson, Fletcher G. 419
Watson, Goodwin 3014
Wattenbarger, James L. 3015-16
Watts, Anthony Gordon 3017
Watts, Susan F. 3018
Wayland, Francis 3019
Weathersby, George B. 3020
Weaver, Gary R. 3021
Weaver, James H. 3021
Weber, Gerald I. 773
Webster, John B. 2748
Wechsler, Harold S. 3022
Weeks, Helen Foss 3023
Wegener, Charles 3024
Weidner, Edward W. 3025
Weingart, John R. 1647
Weingarten, Samuel 3026
Weinstock, Ruth 3027
Weisberger, June 3028
Weisbrod, Burton E. 1094
Weiss, Robert M. 3029
Welch, Finis 2670
Welch, R.D. 2851
Weld, William Ernest 3030 31
Weller, George Anthony 3031
Wells, Agnes O. 86-87
Wells, Anna Mary 3032
Wells, Harry L. 3033
Wells, Warren D. 3034
Wertenbaker, Charles 3035
Wertenbaker, Thomas Jefferson 3036
Werts, Charles E. 3037
Wesley, Edgar Bruce 3038
West, Andrew Fleming 3039

Author Index

TITLE INDEX

This index includes all titles of books cited in the text. References are to entry numbers and alphabetization is letter by letter.

A

Title Index

C

Title Index

Title Index

Title Index

E

Title Index

Title Index

Title Index

Title Index

M

Title Index

Title Index

Title Index

S

Title Index

Title Index

Universities and Research 198
Universities and the Public, The 2318
Universities and Unions in Workers' Education 95
Universities between Two Worlds 2157
Universities Facing the Future 2159
Universities for All 147
Universities in the Urban Crisis 2064
Universities in the Western World 2575
University 2562
University, College, and Normal School Students in Oregon, The 3072
University, The 2462
University, the Citizen, and World Affairs, The 1306
University Administration 717
University Adult Education 2286
University Afield, The 1073
University and Revolution 3021
University and the Future of America, The 2725
University and the State, The 1281
University Authority and the Student 2218
University Calendar, The 3034
University Crisis Reader, The 2994
University Education 2818
University Extension Services 2388
University Faculty, The 2389
University in a Changing World, a Symposium, The 1560
University in Society, The 2773
University in the American Future, The 2788
University in the Forest 545
University in the Web of Politics, A 1074
University in Transition, The 2277
University Is a Place--a Spirit, A 1812
University Libraries, The 2356
University Looks Abroad: Approaches to World Affairs at Six American Universities, The 695
University Looks Abroad: Approaches to World Affairs at Six American

. Universities. A Report from Education and World Affairs, The 1922
University Looks at Its Program, A 688
University of California, 1868-1968, The 2721
University of Chattanooga, The 1011
University of Cincinnati, The 1765
University of Denver Centennial Symposium, The 592
University of Illinois, 1867-1894, The 2687
University of Kansas, The 1038
University of Massachusetts, The 366
University of Massachusetts Dormitory Experiment 2335
University of Michigan, an Encyclopedic Survey, The 2605
University of Michigan, The 620
University of Minnesota, The 1022
University of Missouri, The 2980
University of North Carolina, 1900-1930, The 3105
University of Oklahoma, The 962
University of Pennsylvania Today, The 629
University of Rhode Island, The 748
University of Tulsa, The 1685
University of Utopia 1350
University of Wisconsin, The 547
University on the Heights 813
University Plant Facilities 2390
University President Speaks Out, A 2155
University Problems in the United States 956
University Teaching by Mail 171
University Teaching of the Social Sciences, The 2438
University Training for the National Service 1583
University Women's Opinions on Their Education 1839
Unsilent Generation 295
Until Victory 2849
Unwilling God, The 1838

Title Index

SUBJECT INDEX

This index is alphabetized letter by letter and numbers refer to entries.

A

Abolitionism
    at Illinois College 2354
    at Oberlin College 837
Academic achievement 57, 61, 441, 558, 794
    career changes and 3037
    of Catholic students 1029
    factors affecting 2595
    of Jewish students 652
    prediction of 34
        for minorities 78
        personality in 2740
    reasons for lack of 2307
    relationship to college choice 1274
        to teacher education 1234
        to teaching quality 910
    report on 1415
    tips on 762
    of two-year college students 2579
    See also Dropouts; Intelligence levels
Academic advisers. See Counselors; Personnel services in education
Academic calendar 3034
Academic credit 776, 1200, 1918
    correlation with knowledge gained 1607

from correspondence courses 2133
    by examination 830, 1162, 2179
    exchange of between institutions 2526
    in experimental education 1466–67
    noncredit courses in two-year colleges 1107
    nontraditional programs and 466, 1009, 1508, 2179
    for servicemen 28, 2913
    See also College-Level Examination Program
Academic degrees 1684, 1941, 2720
    benefits of 2269
    in correspondence programs 2133
    statistics 87
        from the University of Chicago 2387
    See also types of degrees (e.g., Masters degrees)
Academic departments 649
    administration of 2650, 2999
    comparative studies of 1785
    conflicts with institutes 1356
    See also College deans; types of departments (English departments)
Academic freedom 53, 247, 516, 642, 729, 1043, 1275, 1278, 1282, 1510, 1744, 1789, 2141, 2339, 2450, 2625, 2869, 3099

Subject Index

Subject Index

in engineering and science 97,
734, 2131
industrialization and 3024
influence of war on 678
following World War II 1747
projections of and trends in
240, 614, 688, 784, 2253,
2295, 2498
methodology for research on
1667
in Michigan 879, 2008
in theological schools 2826
relationship to student aid 2171
in the South 1975
in state universities 2847
statistics on women and minority
2564
in two-year colleges 701, 968
at the University of Chicago 2387
at Yale University 2301
College Entrance Examination Board
212, 893-94, 1155, 1264
assessment of 445
composition test of 979
English exam of 230
College Entrance Examination Board.
Advanced Placement Program
1161
College Entrance Examination Board.
Council on Curriculum (proposed) 1240
College food services 1507
for women 67, 1784, 2083
College graduates
employment of 2128, 2132, 2942
further study by 2132
income of 2670
mobility of 799
statistics 2563
surveys of 374, 889, 2057,
2149, 2226, 2235, 2690,
2710
of Ph.D. holders 2080, 2346
women 64, 863, 869, 960,
1839, 2346
See also Alumni
College-Level Examination Program 449, 1016, 1161,
2913
College libraries 237, 765, 856,

906, 1005, 1572, 1720,
2620, 3024, 3106-7, 3155
administration of 32, 1722, 1833
financial 2309
books for 2604
buildings 1089
central administration's role in
854
in challenging superior students
420
in college instruction 1400,
3108
at Columbia University 2821
computers in 697
contribution to undergraduate education 153
cooperation among 563
in Texas 1573
at Cornell University 3109
cost analysis in 1985
economics of book storage in 727
educational effectiveness of 217
effect of open admissions on 221
explanation of needs of to the
central administration 1719
of the future 2315
guides to 1516, 2798
resources in 630
microfilms in 2410
in the Pacific Northwest 2965
periodicals for 1718
planning of 114
the state in 1076
at Princeton University 1623
problems of 406
professional education and 1615
relationship to the university 1721
for science programs 1293
selection of government documents
for 1942
serials holdings of Texas 1283
in the South 2304, 3110
standards for 1752
at Stephens College 1400
student use of 56, 239
in theological schools 2826
at the University of Chicago
2356
at the University of Michigan
620

1570, 1728, 2015, 2082,
2109, 2144, 2201, 2314,
2439, 2597, 2900-2901,
3121-22, 3137
World War I and 1048
World War II and 1939
at Yale University 2302
See also Academic freedom; Collective bargaining; Student-
faculty relations; Teaching
assistants; Teaching methods
and instructional techniques;
Trade unions
College trustees 93, 273, 278, 320,
717, 741, 1187, 1245,
1855, 2161, 2363-64, 2418,
2840, 3101
of church colleges 1751
legal basis of 719
of Princeton University 1623,
2213
relationship with faculty 1317,
1746
role of 1326
of Stanford University 2724
in two-year colleges 676, 3188
of the University of South
Carolina 1030
women as 2201
Colombia, student rights movement
in 90
Colonialism, effect on higher education 1878
Colorado State University 1091
Columbia College (Illinois) 505
Columbia University 167, 281,
456-58, 894, 1334, 1568,
1842, 1885, 2505, 2852,
2862, 3030
academic senate at 607
admissions policies at 3022
alumni study of 2653
biography of the faculty of 813
cooperation with other institutions
by 2526
fiction about 746
general education at 128-29
history of adult education at 286
honorary degrees from 739
individualized instruction at 1164

interdisciplinary approaches at
2816
opening of to women 952
political and social sciences
faculties of 1317
Robinson's intellectual history
course at 1208
speech education at 2426
state and 3059
student protest movement at 706,
1575, 1653, 2456, 2523,
2531
study of talented graduate fellows
at 958
World War I and 2805
Columbia University. Bureau of
Applied Social Research
1156
Columbia University. Graduate
School of Business 2966
Columbia University. Library 237,
2821
Columbia University. National Manpower Council 560-61
Columbia University. School of
Engineering 802
Columbia University. School of
Library Service 1622,
2377, 2889
Columbia University. Teachers
College 289, 322, 528,
760, 1337, 1406, 1442,
1840, 2495, 2782, 2843
"Teachers for East Africa" program
292
Commencement addresses 1292
Commission on Financing Higher
Education 1264
Commission on Graduate Medical
Education. Advisory Board
for Medical Specialties
2358
Common Fund 738
Communications; communications skills
curriculum for 326
integration with the humanities
1553
student aid for programs in 3113
student evaluation of courses in
650

Subject Index

Subject Index

within the university 1006
See also Democracy
Freedom of speech 381, 3082
Free university movement 2972
French language, study and teaching
of 202
rating of the effectiveness of 396
Fresno State College, administration
of 574, 1746
Friends, Society of. See Guilford
College
Fuess, Claude M. 894
Fulbright scholars 488
Fuller, Buckminster 655
Fund for Adult Education 95
Fund for the Advancement of Education 3145
Fund raising 25, 412, 516, 594,
2481, 2512
for athletic and physical education
programs 234
bibliography on 3055
in Catholic colleges 1028
cooperative 828
fiction about 100, 1829
for two-year colleges 1708

G

Gallatin, Albert 1431
Gambling. See College athletics,
gambling on
Games. See Simulation games
Gannon, Robert I. 919
Garfield, James Abram 2542
General education 186, 262, 636,
755, 1198, 1212, 1252,
1280, 1332, 1366, 1645,
1647, 1767, 1781, 1877,
2040, 2252, 2853, 3074,
3160
accreditation of 2582
at Akron University 1528
the arts in 1817, 3184
in black colleges 593
in Catholic education 2362
at Columbia University 128-29,
286, 398, 414, 3030
comparative study 362
counseling in 143

economic models of 634
employment during 566
evaluation of 643
at Harvard University 1141
history of 1254, 2362
humanities in 1774
libraries in 3108
at Michigan State University 326,
638-39, 1079, 2174, 3156
organization and administration of
2756
personnel services in 238
plans for by college seniors 564
relationship to vocational education
1200
science in 419, 2561
social sciences in 1778
social studies in 1642
student aid in 365, 566
teachers need for a 477
teaching about culture in 1772
in two-year colleges 1341, 1892,
2189
in California 1397
in Florida 1921
in women's colleges 133
at the University of Minnesota
1976, 2711
General Educational Development
tests 2913
evaluation of 646
General Education Board 839
Genetics 965
as an influence on the talented
person 3134
Genovese, Eugene D. 1270
Geography
as a barrier to education 788
changes in the study of 476
George Peabody College for Teachers.
See Vanderbilt University
Georgetown University 668, 919
Georgia, University of 506
blacks at 2531, 2895
graduate education at 2304
German language, correspondence
instruction methods in
teaching 171
Germany
American students in 603, 664,
871, 2868

Subject Index

Subject Index

Subject Index

2005, 2403, 2509, 2703, 2867, 2975
bibliographies on 2714, 3089
from black colleges to graduate schools 116
in Catholic colleges 2236
the commuting student and 399
computers in 303
correlation between data for and future academic success 2057
counseling in 143
criticism of 838, 1462
dental school admissions for blacks 1202
development and training of officers in 2402
direct mail advertising in 1576
discrimination in 2380, 2449, 2639
in economics and agricultural economics programs 2221
evaluation of policies in 924
in evening schools 1288
of foreign students 440, 2124, 2714
of former dropouts 2285
grades as a factor in 191
in graduate and professional schools 1452, 1522, 2124, 2221
guidebooks for 709, 807, 1033, 3193
at Harvard University 1440
the Law School 2585
history of 3022
law of 1112, 1749, 1261, 1294, 2190, 2202
at Lutheran colleges 2790
mathematical models in 501
in medical schools 935, 1112, 1632, 1749, 2229, 2722
blacks 1202
of minorities 78, 157, 450, 539, 990, 2202
in nursing programs 2123
in Ohio 2192
of Pacific-Asian students 1383
in pharmacy education 2292
in private proprietary colleges 2898

psychiatrist's function in 767
racial and ethnic status in 1831
research on 3098
in science programs 1293
sex bias in 2320, 3045
student protest movement and 2685
in teacher education programs 15, 1061
teachers' roles in challenging 1120
testing in 29, 45, 393, 539, 1160
at the University of California (Berkeley) 306
at the University of Pennsylvania 2562
use of school records in 2038
See also Admissions officers; Open admissions; Registrar's office
Reed, Herbert, on art education 3184
Reed College 407
Refugees as scholars 660
Regents. See New York. Board of Regents
Registrar's office, development and training of personnel in 2402
Rehabilitation Act (1973) 492, 2088
Reinhardt, Aurelia Henry 1181
Religion 44, 291, 542, 1157, 1801, 2461, 2835, 2900, 2996, 3042
attitudes toward held by divinity students 2675
in black colleges 1797
in Catholic educational philosophy 653, 2633
and education at Harvard University 1127
and education in Pennsylvania 2273
at Emory University 737
in exploring man's inner dimensions 1057
female graduates' attitudes toward 3115
historic role of colleges in teaching 934
influence of at Vanderbilt University 1973-74

history of 205, 1709, 2188,
2233, 2444, 2810, 3061
multicultural education in 1515
philosophy of education in 3085
professionalism in 1612
relationship to pupil achievement
1234
role of professors in 512
study-decision approach in 2617
summer workshops for 1178, 1436
for teaching the disadvantaged
2771
for teaching the gifted 1211
trends in 1072
at the University of Michigan
3061
See also Normal schools; Teachers
colleges
Teacher-exchange programs 2949
Teachers 106, 1228-29
accreditation and certification of
1241, 1737, 2781, 2793
attitudes and values of 499
bibliography of blacks as 1053
the elderly as 2061
fiction about 256
history of 728, 1626
law and in Pennsylvania 922
mobility of 2781
placement services for 11, 2930
as professionals 860
recruitment of 1003
supply and demand of 695, 1210
survey of retired 1362
women as 553, 1146, 2126,
2151, 2204, 2602, 2801,
2951, 3142
See also College teachers and
teaching; Teacher education
Teachers aides. See Paraprofessionals
Teachers colleges
administration of 2034
comparisons of students in with
liberal arts students 1502
deans of women in 2795-97
personnel services in 2885
See also Normal schools
Teachers Insurance and Annuity Association 2545
Teaching assistants 1018

handbook for 391
use of 604, 610
Teaching machines 1712
in liberal arts colleges 225
Teaching methods and instructional
techniques 106-7, 250,
328, 398, 400, 568, 683,
717, 1018, 1065, 1408,
1439, 1611, 1645, 1845,
1869, 1926, 2890, 2227,
2489, 2552, 2836, 2929
in area studies 785
at the Biarritz American University
2927
bibliographies on 645, 700, 995,
1603, 1874
for terminal education 736
the commuting student and 399
comparative costs of 209
in correspondence courses 171
in continuing education 1676,
2732
cost effectiveness of 343
in dental education 1295
in experimental education 1901
in extension programs 1073
to fit student needs 754
in graduate education 1875
handbook on 1661
in law schools 953, 2585
in liberal arts education 1773
in medical schools 1298
in nontraditional education 1070
in nursing education 2117
for orientation courses 423
for policy studies 497
in political science 485
the preceptorial conference as
519, 711, 2068
in psychiatry 679
psychology of 296
research on 38
in science 1293
for teaching the disadvantaged
2771
technology in 338, 899, 1128,
1135
testing as a 393
trends in 1072
in two-year colleges 189, 1083,
1473

Subject Index

World War II
education of soldiers in 2927
higher education and 1443,
1747, 1939, 2494, 2497
See also Veterans
Wright, Chauncey 3063
Wright, Harry Noble 451
Wriston, Henry M. 3154
Writing. See Composition; Technical
writing
Wyoming, University of 1814

Y

Yale University 167, 275, 317,
537, 543, 601, 1063,
1471, 2243, 2296, 2301-2,
2870, 2908, 3001
economics of library book storage
at 727
examinations and grading system
at 2649
fiction about 132, 1077, 1361,
1412, 1978, 3069
graduate education at 498, 902
library problems of 237
in the pre-Civil War era 18
religious attitudes of divinity
students at 2675
state and 3059
student protest movement at 271,
2176, 2812
women at 1640

FOR REFERENCE
NOT TO BE TAKEN FROM THIS ROOM